Native Bush, Rainbow Springs, Rotorua

The 9th edition of "Charming Bed & Breakfast in New Zealand" is dedicated to the many hosts who continuously provide New Zealand's charming, unique style of Bed & Breakfast hospitality.

For all enquiries please contact Uli or Brian at Travelwise
Ph 0064-3-476 1515. Fax 0064-3-4761514
email: enquiries@travelwise.co.nz
www.bnbnz.com

Charming
BED & BREAKFAST
New Zealand

"Welcome"

year 2007 edition

travelwise publications

Waterfront, Russell, Northland.

Charming

BED & BREAKFAST
New Zealand

Presenting New Zealand's
Charming World of
Bed & Breakfast Hospitality

First published 1998.

ISBN 0-9582094-7-2

Published by Travelwise Ltd.,
PO Box 6226, Dunedin, New Zealand.
Production and design by Travelwise Ltd.

Printed by Printlink, Wellington, New Zealand.

Distributed by Nationwide Distributors, Christchurch.
Front Cover Photo: Photography, **Bill Nichol**.
Support photos by Brian Miller – www.phototrips.info
Furnished by '**McKenzie & Willis**' Dunedin. www.mckenzie-willis.co.nz
Accessories provided by the following Dunedin businesses:
Acquisitions, **Arthur Barnett Department Store** and with
special thanks to Judith and Sandra at '**Elizabeth Russell House**'.

"Experience the real New Zealand – its People"

Welcome to the Charming World *of* Hosted Accommodation in New Zealand.

And what a rich choice it is – from cottages to castles, from budget accommodation to luxurious lodges. You will stay with hosts ranging from those who simply love meeting people to those who have taken hospitality to great entrepreneurial heights. Under the umbrella of Bed & Breakfast you will find: Homestays, Farmstays, Guest Houses, Inns, Lodges, Boutique Accommodation, Countrystays. Bed & Breakfast in New Zealand, where you can get to know the real New Zealand – its people. Stay with teachers, farmers, retired professionals, orchardists, artists, healers and writers. Share the same interests, hobbies or professional background as your hosts. Enjoy unique Bed & Breakfast experiences at a fishing lodge or a high country sheep farm, or at a riding or weaving school, or just find a "home away from home" in town or country. While both hosts and styles of accommodation vary widely, they all reflect the genuine warmth and friendly hospitality that New Zealanders are known for. Wherever you stay, you will be a welcome guest and your stay a pleasant and memorable one. Enjoy the world's finest hospitality.

WHAT TO EXPECT

Bed & Breakfast in New Zealand has a fine reputation for its standard of services. Guests can expect cleanliness, comfortable beds, a good substantial breakfast and warm, generous hospitality. In addition, your hosts can provide you with first-hand in-depth information about their area. They take pleasure in helping you with your pursuits and travel plans. Their invaluable knowledge can enrich your stay immensely.

WHAT IS EXPECTED OF YOU

Your hosts will do everything in their power to make your stay an enjoyable and memorable one. However, it is important to remember that in most cases you are a guest in a private home. So please consider the little things, like arranging to have a house-key if returning late at night, or asking about the tariffs for toll calls prior to using the telephone. Please let your hosts know in time if you will be late. Thoughtfulness on your part will contribute to a satisfying experience for both host and guest.

WHAT TO DO – HINTS

You will avoid any disappointment by booking ahead, especially during the high summer season. It is also advisable to call your hosts one day in advance to confirm your booking and let them know about your expected time of arrival. Some hosts offer a complimentary pick-up service from coach, plane or train if guests don't have their own transport. Please give your hosts one day's notice if you would like to have an evening meal.

Most holiday memories are mere snapshots – images we treasure, but that fade with any passing year. But the people we meet – they become a part of us. They live in us. They travel with us.

PAM BROWN, b 1928

Bed & Breakfast Categories

Bed & Breakfast

Bed & Breakfast is the umbrella term for the variety of hosted accommodations that include a comfortable bed for the night and a substantial breakfast in the morning. The hosts offer warm and generous hospitality throughout your stay.

Homestay

Homestay is the popular Bed & Breakfast accommodation that offers warm and friendly hospitality in a private home. The hosts love meeting people, they enjoy providing their guests with that "home away from home" feeling, knowing that they arrive as strangers but will leave as friends.

Countrystay

Countrystays are often like Homestays. They offer accommodation in a private home. Being in a rural setting, they are associated with all the features and attractions of the countryside. Many Countrystays are close to popular country attractions which offer you the chance to experience rural New Zealand life.

Farmstay

Farmstays are an ideal way to experience real farm life in New Zealand. An opportunity for you to have hands-on contact with the animals and daily life on a farm. A farm tour may be included. Breakfast is usually taken with the family. Many Farmstays offer lunch and evening meals, as restaurants are often not close by.

Bed & Breakfast Categories

Guesthouse/Inn

Guest Houses and Inns are usually larger establishments that cater for more guests, but still offer that personalised style of hospitality. They might have several lounge areas and a breakfast room. Guest Houses do not usually offer an evening meal.

Boutique Accommodation

Within the Bed & Breakfast world Boutique Accommodation has been adopted by those hosts whose unique property features reflect a special ambience – period elegance, grace and charm, romance, art, etc. These features are usually enhanced by the hosts' flair for entertainment and hospitality.

Luxury Accommodation

Luxury Accommodation symbolizes superb facilities, excellent food and an exceptional level of service. Many properties within this category have spectacular settings and offer various additional top class attractions. They represent outstanding accommodation and hospitality.

Self-contained Accommodation

Self-contained accommodation usually includes a separate entrance, own bathroom facilities and an independent lounge area. Kitchen and laundry facilities may be included. It can be a self-contained part of the family home or a separate cottage. Breakfast is either served in the hosts' home, delivered to the doorstep or breakfast provisions provided on the premises.

How to use this guide – "at a glance"

"at a glance"

Easy Contact Panel

Your hosts: who they are, where they are, and how to make quick contact.

Clear Address Details

*Clear address panel displays essential information, including property address, telephone and fax numbers, e-mail and internet address. **NOTE:** When calling from overseas dial New Zealand's international code, 0064, then drop the 0 off the area code (03), for example "Heriot House" 0064-3-477-7228.*

"at a glance"

Tariff Panel

*Each tariff indicates the nightly rate. **Double** indicates the cost for two people sharing one room. **Single** indicates the cost for one person occupying a room. A deposit may be required when booking. Tariffs include breakfast unless otherwise stated. **All prices quoted are in NZ$ – GST inclusive.** Please confirm details with your host.*

YOUR HOSTS: **Kristin and Stuart Campbell Smith** Free Ph: (0800) 232 789 ***Rotorua Central***

EAST WEST-BOUTIQUE B&B AND APARTMENTS
6 Toko Street, Rotorua
Ph (07) 348 5720, Fax (07) 348 5729
Mobile 027-278 5332
email: *eastwesthomestay@xtra.co.nz*
www.eastwesthomestay.co.nz

Tariff : N.Z. Dollars	
Double	$110-150
Single	$75-110
Child	$25

Bedrooms	Qty
Double	8
Twin	5
Single	
Bed Size	**Qty**
Super King	
King	
Queen	6
Double	1
Single	14
Bathrooms	**Qty**
Ensuite	2
Private	3
Guest Share	

Boutique Bed & Breakfast & Self-catering Apartments

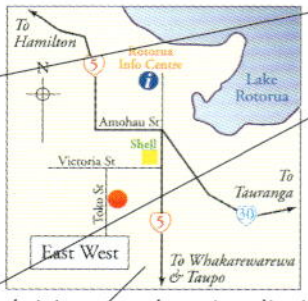

Features & Attractions

- *Central to tourism & leisure*
- *Unique geothermal pool/spa*
- *Geothermal central heating*
- *Quiet, spacious units*
- *Self-catering apartments*
- *Tour bookings*

Your hosts, Stuart, Kristin and Rusty, warmly welcome you to their unique Boutique Bed & Breakfast and Self-catering apartments. Located in Rotorua's thriving central tourism district, their designer home and freshly decorated, fully furnished holiday apartments are minutes from all attractions. You are offered a choice of a spacious studio or one bedroom unit both featuring private ensuite bathrooms, fridge/minibar, tea and coffee facilities, TV/DVD and robes toiletries. Continental breakfast offers fresh fruit, home-made muesli, cereals, yoghurt, conserves, coffee and teas (included in rate). Cooked breakfast available. Also separately located on the property are three sunny, cosy, fully furnished self-catering two and three bedroom apartments, kitchen, laundry facilities, off-street parking, private entrances. Private hot spa, robes/toiletries.

"at a glance"

Category Symbols

These quick-to-spot symbols are designed to make selecting your preferred accommodation easy. Particularly helpful for travellers with a limited knowledge of the English language.

"at a glance"

Category Panel

Your hosts' personal description of their category.

"at a glance"

Features & Attractions

Highlighting the main features and attractions in and around this accommodation and locality.

"at a glance"

Location Map

Your hosts' property is indicated by a red dot. Property name is displayed in white box. Maps may be accompanied by a direction panel outlining easy directions.

"A Personal Warm Welcome"

These words of welcome have been written personally by your hosts. They describe the features of the accommodation and portray their personality and lifestyle.

No Smoking

Abbreviations

SH	–	State Highway
h.p.	–	half price
n/a	–	not applicable
neg	–	negotiable
Qty	–	Quantity
Tce	–	Terrace

Book direct – Reduce costs

By booking direct with your Bed & Breakfast host in New Zealand, you make the personal connection right from the start and avoid many additional costs.

How to use this guide – Guest room details

Bedrooms

Double = Room with bed for two people
Twin = Room with two beds for two people
Single = Room with bed for one person

Bathrooms

Ensuite = Bathroom adjoining bedroom
Private = Separate bathroom for your use only
Guest Share/Family Share =Bathroom shared with other guests or host family

Bedrooms	Qty
Double	
Twin	
Single	
Bed Size	**Qty**
King	
Queen	
Double	
King/Single	
Bathrooms	**Qty**
Ensuite	
Private	
Guest Share	

Bed Size

Super King
180 x 200cm

King
165 x 200cm

Queen
150 x 200cm

Double
135 x 190cm

Single
90 x 190cm

King Single
90 x 200cm

How to use this guide – Category Symbols

- BB Bed & Breakfast
- BA Boutique Accommodation
- C Countrystay
- F Farmstay
- G Guest House / Lodge / Inn
- H Homestay
- LA Luxury Accommodation
- SC Self-contained Accom. & Cottages

How to use this guide – Credit Cards Accepted by Hosts

- Amex – American Express
- Japanese Credit Card
- VISA
- Diners
- Bankcard
- MasterCard
- Maestro
- Eftpos

How to use this guide – Hosts' Associations & Affiliations

- Kiwihost
- Qualmark NZ
- @home NEW ZEALAND.
- Historic Places Trust

@home NEW ZEALAND, **the Association of Farm & Home Hosts** in New Zealand, assures you of a warm welcome in a private home. Guests are treated as friends of the family and given personal care and time by the hosts. Members' homes are inspected on a regular basis.

Dairies and Supermarkets

Dairies, a long-established feature of the New Zealand landscape, are usually open 7 days a week, from early to late. Like the old general country stores, dairies stock a wide variety of goods. You can normally expect to obtain basic foods and commodities, such as bread, milk, newspapers, confectionery and grocery items.

Because of the extended trading hours, and the benefits of convenient locations, prices are normally slightly higher than those at the supermarket. Some dairies, especially in small communities, also offer Post Shop services.

Supermarkets

Nearly all New Zealand towns and cities have supermarkets. Supermarkets provide a wider range of goods for one-stop grocery shopping, and have more competitive prices.

Free parking is normally provided, but only for genuine customers - you may be asked to show your receipt. Some supermarkets now have extended trading hours, and most are open 7 days a week.

The Corner Dairy – so much a part of New Zealand's daily life.

Petrol Stations

Also known as 'Service Stations', provide basic commodities for motor vehicles: fuel, oil, air, water, and general motoring accessories. Although petrol stations do not normally provide repair or maintenance services - these are provided by 'Garages' - those that do may have a sign saying 'Mechanic on duty' or 'Repairs carried out'.

Tourist Radio

Tourist Information FM is a service established to provide information to visitors to New Zealand 24 hours a day, and is available in most tourist areas. For English-language broadcasts, tune to 88.2 FM on your radio. For German-language broadcasts, tune to 100.4 FM, and for Japanese-language broadcasts, tune to 100.8 FM on your radio.

i Visitor Information NETWORK

Visitor Information Network

Visitor Information Centres are identified by the distinctive green italic *i* logo in conjunction with the Visitor Information logo.

Over 80 of them are located throughout New Zealand. They offer a wide range of services. including travel bookings, tours and accommodation.

The staff, who have unparalleled local and national knowledge are trained and committed to providing accurate and appropriate information to visitors.

Emergency Services

If you require the police, ambulance or fire service, dial 111.
There is no charge for making a 111 call from a public phone box.

Posting a Letter

New Zealand's main postal operator is New Zealand Post with a network of 1000 Post Shops and Post Centres covering the whole country, and 5,000 post boxes where you can post letters. Some outlets combine their normal retail activities with providing New Zealand Post services, especially in smaller towns. Look for the red New Zealand Post logo displayed outside shops.

Post Shops

Post Shops offer a wide range of products and services including:

- stamps
- protective packaging
- sending letters and parcels
- sending faxes and telegrams, couriering items overseas or around New Zealand
- stationery, greeting cards, phone cards, gifts (e.g. calendars) and more

Post Shop staff can help you decide which type of packaging will get your parcels delivered as cheaply as possible. A handy Parcel Packaging Guide is also available which contains advice on ways to ensure your parcel arrives safely. Post Shops accept cash, cheque, EFTPOS, MasterCard and VISA for most products and services.

New Zealand Post Shop

If you need help and cannot get to a Post Shop, you can call New Zealand Post freephone 0800 NZPOST (0800 697 678), 8am to 7pm weekdays, or 9am to 1pm Saturdays.

Postal Costs

For Sending letters and packages within New Zealand.

A standard size letter (maximum 129mm x 235mm) costs 45 cents and takes 2-4 days to be delivered. If you want to get it there faster, FastPost costs 90 cents for a standard size letter which is then delivered by the next working day between major towns and cities. (Rural and remote areas may take a little longer.) You can send parcels from $3.40, depending on size and weight. Items can also be couriered from a Post Shop.

POST

For sending letters and packages overseas. You can ask at the local Post Shop about the best way to package and send items overseas. Options include first class air mail, sea post, registered post and courier. By paying an additional $8 and sending your parcel as a customs parcel, New Zealand Post extends cover for loss or damage from NZ$250 to $1,500.

Packages for Japan

For sending packages to Japan, there is a special Kiwi Yu Pack for items up to 5kg, and for delivery within 2-4 working days.

The rural mailbox, a roadside feature throughout New Zealand's countryside.

Money and Banks

Currency

New Zealand has been operating on the decimal currency system with the NZ Dollar as its base since 10 July 1967. Coins in use are: 10c, 20c, 50c, $1 and $2. Bank notes are available in denominations of $5, $10, $20, $50 and $100.

Changing Money

Money exchange facilities exist at all banks and at most New Zealand international airports. New Zealand banks buy and sell all major currencies and offer competitive exchange rates which are updated daily.

Travellers' Cheques

Travellers' cheques can also be cashed at Bureaux de Change and hotels or large stores in resorts and larger cities.

Import or export of foreign currency is not subject to any restrictions.

All banks are listed in the Yellow Pages at the back of the local telephone directory.

Credit cards

Payment by any of the international credit cards, including Visa, Master Card, American Express, Diners Club and JCB (Japanese credit card) is widely accepted. Most shops display the card signs in their windows. If in doubt, please check with a sales person before you commence shopping.

Automatic Teller Machine
24 hour access.

Banks

All trading banks are open for business between the hours of 9:30am and 4:30pm. Monday to Friday inclusive, with the exception of public holidays. Automatic Teller Machines (ATMs), operate on a card and pin number system. Cash can be withdrawn 24 hours a day.

eftpos

eftpos

EFTPOS (Electronic Transfer of Funds at Point of Sale) is a highly used way of cash payments , which is being used all over New Zealand.

You will find operating EFTPOS machines in shops, museums, supermarkets, petrol stations, to name only a few. Instead of a cash payment, the cash amount is transferred directly from the customer's into the selling company's bank account. The transaction takes place at the counter or check out, where customers swipe their EFTPOS card through the machine and type in their pin number. This convenient way of cash payment can be very handy in remote places or after hours. Many stores with EFTPOS facilities also allow you to withdraw cash when making purchases.

Using the Telephone

The phone system in New Zealand is of a high technical standard and performs efficiently. There are two main service providers, **Telecom** and **Clear.** You will find public telephones throughout the entire country. The majority of public telephones in NZ operate the pre-paid phone card system. Telecom **PhoneCards** are available in NZ$5, NZ$10, NZ$20 and NZ$50 denominations. These can be purchased from many outlets including **NZ Post Shops**, supermarkets, dairies, newsagents, **Visitor Information Centres** and petrol stations. You may find it helpful to purchase a **PhoneCard** even if it is only for emergencies. Increasing numbers of credit card operated phones are now being established which accept major international credit cards. Some public telephones are still coin operated, using 10c, 20c, 50c, NZ$1 and NZ$2 coins. When dialling **Freephone** numbers (commencing with 0800) from public phones you will not require any cards or coins.

Typical public phone booths. Coloured for easy recognition, Yellow for Credit card, Green for PhoneCard, and Blue for Coin.

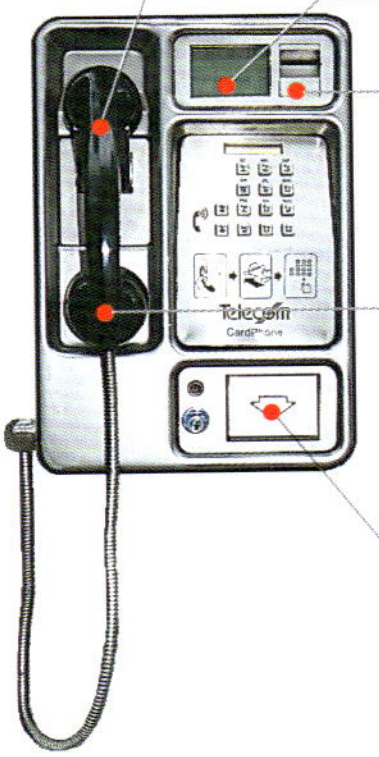

1 Lift handset, do not insert coins.

2 Dial the number you require. The price per minute or part minute will show on screen.

3 Insert coins. Usable coins:10c, 20c, 50c, NZ$1, and NZ$2.

4 Once call is finished replace handset.

5 Unused coins returned, partly used coins not returned.

Telecom PhoneCards available : NZ$5, NZ$10, NZ$20, and NZ$50. They can be easily obtained at many outlets such as Dairies, Post Offices, and Petrol Stations.

Using the PhoneCard

1. Lift handset. 2. Insert Card. 3. Dial number. 4. After call, replace handset. 5. Remove card (Don't forget!)

Coins acepted by Coin Phones:– 10c, 20c, 50c, NZ$1 and NZ$2.

e-Phone Maxi-Save Toll Card

The ***e*-Phone Toll Card** is an easy and convenient way to use almost any touch tone phone at your own expense. It can be used from a private phone, card phone, credit card phone, cellphone, **Your Yost's Phone**, etc.
Using these prepaid phone cards will make you and your host feel less apprehensive when you use their phone. ***e*-Phone Toll Cards** can be purchased in many dairies, super markets and shopping malls.
For detailed information, just call Free Phone 0800-437 4663.

EMERGENCY CALLS......111
Police, Fire, Ambulance

Useful Telephone Numbers

Operator	010
International Operator	0170
National Enquiries	018
International Enquiries	0172
International Access Code	00
Australia dialling code	0061
Germany dialling code	0049
Japan dialling code	008
USA dialling code	001

Driving in New Zealand can be a pleasure, the ever changing scenery is superb.

On the Road

Driving in New Zealand is a pleasure; the scenery is superb, the roads are generally of a high standard and New Zealanders are helpful and courteous.

However, for your safety and that of other motorists, we urge you to take a little time (New Zealand is patient, it will wait for you) and read the following before you begin driving.

The *New Zealand Road Code* is the definitive guide to correct and lawful driving in New Zealand. It is available at a small cost from the Land Transport Safety Authority. Look in the local telephone directory for the nearest office. A useful leaflet, with English, German and Japanese sections, is *Driving Safely in New Zealand*, also available free of charge from the Land Transport Safety Authority.

Driving : Some Basic Points

Keep Left: In New Zealand we drive on the **left**.

Overseas vistors may find this difficult. – We suggest you take time to adjust and plan your journeys accordingly.

Speed Limit: In general, the maximum speed limit on the open road or motorway / freeway, identifiable by this sign, is 100 kilometres per hour.

In cities and towns, it is 50km per hour. There are exceptions, so watch out for signs (positioned on the left of the road) which may indicate a lower specified speed limit.

Road Signs at Intersections:

Stop: Stop completely, then give way to all traffic.

Give way - Drive slowly. Stop if drivers are approaching from left or right, and give way to all traffic, including those opposite if you are turning left.

Seatbelts: The driver and all passengers (adults and children) - including those sitting in rear seats - must use seatbelts or approved child restraints.

The **New Zealand Automobile Association** (*AA*) offers an excellent service nationwide providing maps, guides and touring information. Freephone 0800 500 444 at any time.

Magnificent Contrasts and Colourful Variety

New Zealand's landscapes are as colourful and diverse as its people. No other country can offer such variety of magnificent scenery in such a comparatively small area. In both islands evergreen native bush abounds. In the North Island there are also exotic forests of huge Kauri trees. A wonderland of hot springs, geysers and boiling mud pools is situated near Rotorua in the centre of the North Island. Therapeutic hot springs are located in parts of both islands, and spectacularly beautiful National Parks with their unspoiled scenery and nature will delight the traveller. The South Island offers scenery on the grand scale: mountains, glaciers, lakes and sweeping coastal beaches. Deep-water fiords slice into the south-west coast, with virgin mountain country in the background. One of the most famous fiords - Milford Sound - is accessible by road as well as by the famed Milford Track, the "most beautiful walk in the world". New Zealand has an abundance of aquatic scenery. Take your pick of spectacular waterfalls, raging torrents, broad rivers, lakes big and small, surfing beaches and rocky coast lines.

South Island West Coast - Native bush.

Waitangi Golf Course - *one of the many superb golf courses you will find in New Zealand.*

Most New Zealanders love sport and the outdoors. Their country's natural features support an abundance of outdoor activities: yachting, golf, rugby and mountaineering, to name only a few. All types of winter sports are practised in both islands and wild game and fish provide excellent hunting and fishing.

Tane Mahuta, Waipoua Forest, Northland.

North Island

Houhora Lodge & Homestay

3994 Far North Road, RD 4, Kaitaia
Ph (09) 409 7884, Fax (09) 409 7801, Mobile 021-926 992
email: *houhora.homestay@xtra.co.nz*
www.topstay.co.nz

Tariff : N.Z. Dollars	
Double	$130-160
Single	$100
Child	$25

Bedrooms	Qty
Double	3
Twin	
Single	
Bed Size	**Qty**
Super King	
King	3
Queen	
Double	
Single	6
Bathrooms	**Qty**
Ensuite	2
Private	1
Guest Share	

Your Northern Hideaway
A Fantastic Location

Features & Attractions

- *Geographical isolation*
- *Non commercial*
- *Shell collecting*
- *Dig shellfish for dinner*
- *Spectacular, pristine beaches*
- *Organic garden and eggs*
- *Coastal wilderness hiking*
- *Internet, fax, laundry*

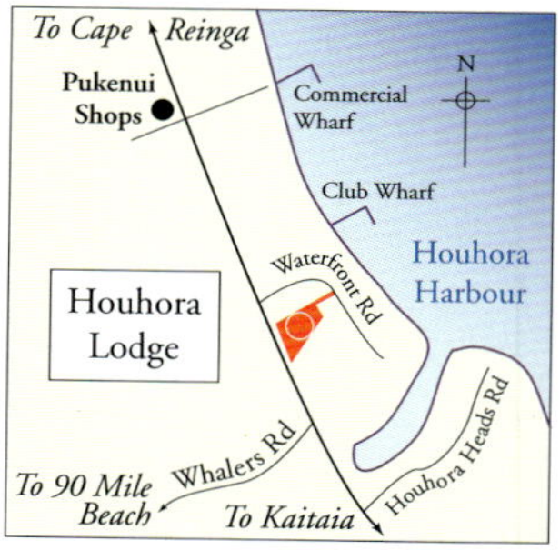

We who live on the slim finger of land at the top of New Zealand welcome you, and look forward to sharing its beauty and secret places with you. This is a small part of New Zealand which is different. Come share our home and the 'good life', home grown vegetables, pure water, fresh air, eggs and fruit and fresh caught fish. This four year old architect designed cedar home is set in 3½ acres. The beautiful airy pavilion opens to the east and west to fine views and amazing sunrises and sunsets with original New Zealand art adorning the walls. We are delighted to provide advice and assistance for your Far North excursions: 4x4 sightseeing, fishing, walks, trips to famous tourist spots and trips to places that few people visit or even know about (by prior arrangement). A complimentary 4x4 trip to view Ninety Mile Beach is offered. Dinner if requested. (All rooms are either double or twin)

Plane Tree Lodge

Pamapuria, RD 2, Kaitaia
Ph (09) 408 0995, Fax (09) 408 0959
Mobile 027-433 8859
email: *reservationsplanetreelodge@xtra.co.nz*
www.plane-tree-lodge.net.nz

Tariff : N.Z. Dollars	
Double	$135-160
Single	$100-125
Cottage	$180-220

Bedrooms	Qty
Double	5
Twin	2
Single	1
Bed Size	**Qty**
Super King	
King	
Queen	5
King Single	2
Single	3
Bathrooms	**Qty**
Ensuite	3
Private	2
Guest Share	

Experience The Difference...
Your Escape to the Cape...

DIRECTIONS: Heading north on SH 1, through the Mangamuka Gorge, continue on SH 1 for 7.5 km. Our sign is on the left. Heading south from Kaitaia on SH 1, go past Pamapuria School. Our home is 300m on the right.

Features & Attractions

- *Cape Reinga and 90 Mile Beach*
- *2 acres of tranquil park-like gardens*
- *Peaceful, rural views from all rooms*
- *Quad bikes over the sand dunes*
- *Fishing, golf, surfing*
- *7mins from Kaitaia*
- *Historic Gum Diggers Park*
- *Spa pool at sunset*

Wake to birdsong and the smell of coffee and bacon and plan your day's activities over a delicious breakfast. A trip to Cape Reinga will allow you to capture the very essence of Northland in its spectacular scenery and diverse culture. On 90 Mile Beach, experience quad-bike riding, fishing or surfing. Visit the Bay of Islands or just relax on one of the many beautiful beaches that abound our doorstep. Each evening return to the peace and tranquillity of the **Lodge**, wash the sand from your hair and enjoy a delicious meal at one of the local restaurants. Alternatively, savour a glass of wine in the spa pool while watching the sun set. At **Plane Tree Lodge** we want to help you create memories which will last a lifetime. The **Lodge** has a guest lounge, 2 double rooms and 1 single, all with ensuite bathroom. Our s/c **Attached Cottage** has 1 double room and 1 twin. The s/c **Private Cottage** has 2 double rooms and 1 twin.

"5-star – you set the bar way up for B&B's" Linda & Andy, USA
"Fabulous place – best B&B so far" Julie & John, Canada

BEACHFRONT

14 Kotare St, PO Box 174, Ahipara,
Ninety Mile Beach
Ph (09) 409 4007, Fax (09) 409 4007
email: *pauljenny@beachfront.net.nz*
www.beachfront.net.nz

Tariff : N.Z. Dollars	
Double	$150-300
Single	$150-300
Child	

Bedrooms	Qty
Double	4
Twin	
Single	
Bed Size	**Qty**
Super King	4
King	
Queen	
Double	
Single	
Bathrooms	**Qty**
Ensuite	4
Private	
Guest Share	

Upmarket Serviced Apartments with stunning views

Features & Attractions

- *Surf views from every pillow*
- *All bedrooms with ensuite*
- *Maximum of two client groups*
- *Privacy & separate entrances*
- *Absolute waters edge*
- *Sky television, DVD & video*
- *Sunset Magic*
- *Full kitchens & BBQs*

DIRECTIONS:
Turn right at Ahipara School toward golf course, take left fork before the fire station. Kotare Street is first on the left - drive at the sea.

Beachfront

Your 5th generation New Zealand hosts Jenny and Paul continue to receive a "buzz" from the reaction of our guests. "Thank you for sharing your bit of heaven. A most wonderful stay in a beautifully appointed suite. Stunning views. We loved every minute". From BC Canada is typical. A warm Kiwi welcome awaits. Both the studio and penthouse are completely private and sleep up to six or seven people. The studio apartment is at the same level as our adjacent home, so gets the best sea level views on Ninety Mile Beach and is seven metres from the high tide mark. From the 100 square metres of luxurious space in the penthouse apartment, the view is even more dramatic. Higher than 90% of clients say "Wow" or as one travel writer described our apartments "World class". Both are serviced daily and fully self-contained. Breakfast available - Dinner by arrangement. The Penthouse is a two bedroom apartment with balconies; Studio Apartment has covered patio with additional bedroom available.

Shipwreck Lodge

70 Foreshore Road, Ahipara, 90 Mile Beach
Ph (09) 409 4929, Fax (09) 409 4928
email: *shipwrecklodge@xtra.co.nz*
www.shipwrecklodge.co.nz

Tariff : N.Z. Dollars	
Double	$200-350
Single	$200-350
Cottage	

Bedrooms	Qty
Double	3
Twin	1
Single	
Bed Size	**Qty**
Super King	1
King	1
Queen	1
King Single	
Single	
Bathrooms	**Qty**
Ensuite	3
Private	
Guest Share	

Absolute Beachfront
Boutique Bed & Breakfast

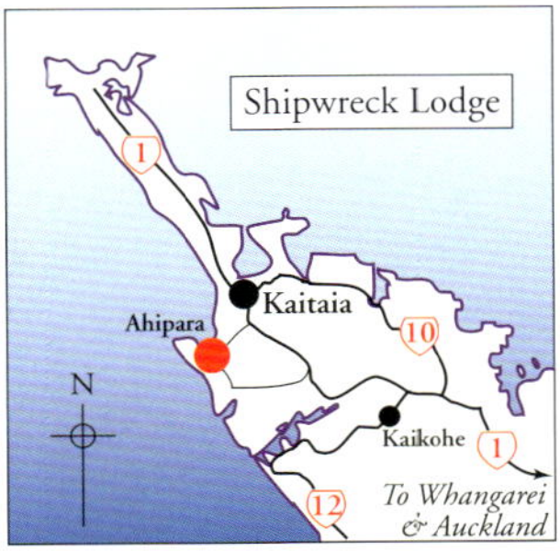

DIRECTIONS:
Take SH 1 north. From Auckland travel through Whangarei, Kawakawa to Kaitaia. As you enter the township of Kaitaia turn left at the town clock.
The road is signposted to Ahipara. Enter Ahipara and turn left just past the school. **Shipwreck Lodge** is 600m on the right.

Features & Attractions

- *Beachfront setting*
- *Spectacular views*
- *Beautifully appointed bedrooms*
- *Private balconies & ensuites*
- *Links golf course*
- *Fishing, swimming, walking*
- *Int. standard golf course close by*
- *Cape Reinga Tours*

Walk in and unwind in our luxurious, contemporary, informal and spacious home. Each of three guest suites opens to a private balcony overlooking 90 Mile Beach and the Tasman Sea. The soothing sound of the waves rolling in is ever present. We have direct beach access for a short stroll or long walk. Watch stunning sunsets from your private balcony with ocean views to the horizon. We offer an informal easy atmosphere and mix "leaving you alone" with "taking care of you". The guest suites are spacious and beautifully appointed in modern furnishings. Each suite has a bi-fold door opening to a private balcony, sitting area, television, fridge and large modern ensuite. Sumptuous continental or cooked breakfasts included.
90 Mile Beach is a treasure to discover! It is a mixture of safe swimming bays, world class surf bays, wild ruggedness, huge desert sand hills, wide open spaces, and stunning coastline. Remote, untouched, vast and very beautiful.

Siesta Guest Lodge & Villa Apartments

Tasman Heights, PO Box 30, Ahipara, Northland
Ph/Fax (09) 409 2011, Mobile 021-260 6732
email: *ninetymile@xtra.co.nz*
www.ahipara.co.nz/siesta

Tariff : N.Z. Dollars	
Double	$150-250
Single	
Child	

Bedrooms	Qty
Double	4
Twin	1
Single	
Bed Size	**Qty**
Super King	
King	1
Queen	3
Double	
King/Single	2
Bathrooms	**Qty**
Ensuite	4
Private	
Guest Share	

Panoramic Views and Privacy
Close to the Beach

Features & Attractions

- *Peace, space & privacy*
- *Safe swimming*
- *Links golf course*
- *Sand-dune wilderness*
- *Cape trip from door*
- *Kauri forest close by*
- *Handy to Bay of Islands*
- *A perfect base to stay awhile*

DIRECTIONS: Take SH north to Kaitaia, turn west to Ahipara. Enter Ahipara and turn left just past school. Drive 1.2 km. Tasman Heights is 1st road up the hill on left, just as you reach the beach car park.

Incredible sunsets, beautiful weather year-round, a multitude of activities for young and old alike, sweeping views of Ninety Mile Beach, a wide choice of accommodation and friendly and knowledgeable hosts. This is why our guests, almost without exception, consider **Siesta Guest Lodge** a place to settle for a few days, weeks, or even months.

All the North's main attractions are within an hour's drive; including the major Kauri Forests, the Bay of Islands and Cape Reinga. If you want to be away from the tourist Mecca, this is the base for you. There are two purpose-built guest suites in the Mediterranean-style main lodge, each with panoramic views of Ninety Mile Beach. In addition, two superior self-contained apartments with dishwasher, bath, satellite TV, CD stereo, video & CD library, etc., etc. large outdoor area. Set in secluded, tropical gardens, **Siesta** is the perfect getaway spot. It is private, romantic, idyllic and popular with honeymooners, tourists and holiday-makers who love beautiful beaches, forests and the outdoors.

YOUR HOSTS: **Susan and Ned Pyne** Ph: (09) 409 4070 ***Ahipara - 90 Mile Beach***

Beach Abode Beachfront Lodge

11 Korora Street, PO Box 134, Ahipara, 90 Mile Beach
Ph (09) 409 4070, Fax (09) 409 4070
email: *ned.susan@xtra.co.nz*
www.beachabode.co.nz

Features & Attractions

- *Remote Beachfront Setting*
- *Expansive Sea views*
- *Sounds of the Sea*
- *Brilliant Sunset*
- *Attentive Self-catering*
- *Impeccably maintained*

$		
	Double	$110-150
	Single	$105-130
	Child	—

Elegant Beachfront Retreat South Pacific Paradise

Bedrooms	Qty
Double	3
Twin	1
Single	
Bed Size	**Qty**
King	
Queen	3
Double	
Single	
Bathrooms	**Qty**
Ensuite	
Private	3
Guest Share	

While on holiday in the Far North, my husband and I were captivated by the majestic 90 Mile Beach. The following year we moved to Ahipara and purchased a private beachfront property with a bush reserve on the northern border. Based on our touristic journey into Ahipara, we realized there was a need for a higher quality accommodation that would appeal to the discerning traveler. Open the front door of our apartments and you feel an immediate sense of welcome. Upon entering the apartment, the Tasman Sea draws you out to the covered deck revealing panoramic sea views and landscaped gardens. Apartments are contemporary, pristine, appointed in a warm tropical ambience. Cotton sheets, beach towels, laundry, fresh coffee, DVD. Scrumptious breakfast and dinner available with a nights notice. We hope you consider a retreat to our remote seaside village. Come by and see us. We are the house facing the sea, next door to the Korora Reserve.

YOUR HOSTS: **Jennifer and Cliff Knight** Ph (09) 406 0344 ***Coopers Beach Northland***

Sails Beachfront Apartment

23 Kupe Road, Coopers Beach, Mangonui
Ph (09) 406 0344, Fax (09) 406 1537
email: *cliff@sails.co.nz*
www.sails.co.nz

Features & Attractions

- *Pohutukawa-fringed beach*
- *Tranquil garden setting*
- *Away from traffic noise*
- *Near Mangonui Historic Village*
- *Close to cafés & restaurants*
- *On Northland Twin-Coast-Route*

$		
	Double	$90-190
	Single	$90-190
	Child	$10

Beachfront in Garden Setting

Bedrooms	Qty
Double	1
Twin	1
Single	
Bed Size	**Qty**
King	
Queen	1
Double	
Single	2
Bathrooms	**Qty**
Ensuite	
Private	1
Guest Share	

Greetings from **Sails** in beautiful Doubtless Bay! Our beachfront apartment is perfect for your seaside holiday and also provides the peace of a sub-tropical garden.
Nearby Mangonui Village and Harbour offers a range of shops and cafés as well as the famous fish shop and licensed bar built over the water.
Sailing, diving and fishing charters are available as well as the famous Cape Reinga-Ninety Mile Beach Trip.
Your hosts are the only other residents on the property, so personal assistance is available to make your stay a happy one.
Sails Apartment is on its own separate level with private access to the car park. The beach has safe swimming, golden sand and, if required, shade under the Pohutukawa trees, which are a special feature of Coopers Beach.

Kerikeri - Bay of Islands

YOUR HOSTS: **Pamela and Ian Adams** Ph (09) 401 7961

DIRECTIONS:From SH10 follow signs to Kerikeri. Take Kerikeri Rd for 1.3km and turn right at Maraenui Dr. **Birchwood** is 20 metres on left.

Birchwood

11 Maraenui Drive, Kerikeri, Bay of Islands
Ph (09) 401 7961, Fax (09) 401 7962
Mobile 027-268 4848
email: *info@birchwoodbedandbreakfast.co.nz*
www.birchwoodbedandbreakfast.co.nz

Features & Attractions

- *New luxurious ensuite rooms*
- *Private deck, gardens, spa pool*
- *Exclusive privacy & relaxation*
- *Walking distance to Kerikeri*
- *On art, craft and wine trails*
- *Central base for Bay of Islands*

Boutique Bed & Breakfast

$	
Double	$150-160
Single	
Child	

Bedrooms	Qty
Double	1
Twin	1
Single	
Bed Size	**Qty**
King	
Queen	1
Double	
King/Single	1
Bathrooms	**Qty**
Ensuite	1
Private	1
Guest Share	

Birchwood offers the luxury of a brand new, beautifully appointed B & B in a relaxed, charming country setting. The ultimate in privacy and comfort is guaranteed with your own entrance, light and spacious ensuite bedroom with plasma screen, plunger coffee and teas, fridge and microwave, quality linen and toiletries. Open the French doors to your private, sunny deck and landscaped garden overlooking the orchards. A tranquil setting to enjoy our popular fresh breakfast, and if you can tear yourself away, a perfect base from which to explore the Bay of Islands. **Birchwood** is in walking distance to Kerikeri village and only 15 minutes drive to sandy beaches. Hosts Pamela and Ian will happily provide local knowledge and process bookings. The rooms are serviced daily and additional facilities include laundry, secure parking, beauty and massage therapy by appointment.

Kerikeri

YOUR HOSTS: **Wendy Hamilton and Tony Waldegrave** Ph (09) 401 7974

DIRECTIONS: From SH10 turn into Kerikeri Rd, proceed through Kerikeri town, past the 'Stone Store' and continue along Landing Rd to Waipapa Landing.

Landing Cottage

184 Landing Road, Kerikeri
Ph (09) 401 7974
Mobile 027- 450 5850
email: *wendy@landingcottage.co.nz*
www.landingcottage.co.nz

Features & Attractions

- *Single party bookings only*
- *Elegantly luxurious*
- *Artist in residence*
- *Minutes from Kerikeri village*
- *Secluded, tranquil setting*
- *Restaurants, shops, vineyards*

Bed & Breakfast Boutique Accommodation

$	
Double	$165-225
Single	$125-155
Group(4)	$300-395

Bedrooms	Qty
Double	3
Twin	
Single	
Bed Size	**Qty**
King	1
Queen	2
Double	
Single	
Bathrooms	**Qty**
Ensuite	
Private	1
Guest Share	

Built 2005, **Landing Cottage** is set amongst secluded native bush and gardens yet only a hundred metres from the picturesque Waipapa Landing Boat Jetty and minutes to Kerikeri village, restaurants, vineyards, golf course, historic sites, and many other attractions. **Single-party-bookings** only guarantees privacy and relaxation in a spacious, luxurious, elegantly decorated suite for up to 4 adults with private entrance, large, private lounge, bathroom, toiletries, 3 bedrooms with quality king or queen beds, luxury linen, TV, DVD, coffee/tea making facilities and garden setting. Enjoy the resident artist's work while having a sumptuous continental or cooked breakfast chosen from the menu. (Home-made, seasonal, local, organic produce and free-range eggs are used when possible). Your hosts, Wendy and Tony, both from a professional background, will be delighted in helping you plan your exploration of the Bay of Islands and the Far North.

Kingfisher Retreat

Kingfisher Drive, RD 1, Kerikeri
Ph (09) 407 8880, Fax (09) 407 8880
email: *kingfisher-retreat@xtra.co.nz*
www.kingfisher-retreat.co.nz

Tariff : N.Z. Dollars	
Double	$120-225
Single	$100-180
Child	

Bedrooms	Qty
Double	3
Twin	
Single	
Bed Size	**Qty**
Super King	
King	2
Queen	1
Double	
Single	
Bathrooms	**Qty**
Ensuite	3
Private	
Guest Share	

**Luxury
Bed & Breakfast**

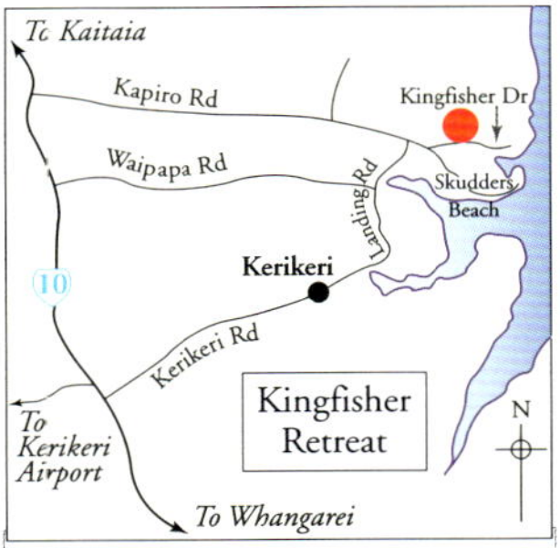

DIRECTIONS: From SH 10 turn into Kerikeri Road, proceed through Kerikeri town, past the Stone Store and continue along Landing Rd. At the Kapiro Road T-junction, turn right for Skudders Beach Road and then left into Kingfisher Drive.

Features & Attractions

- *Historic stone store - 5 min*
- *3 stunning golf courses*
- *Cruise/dolphin/fishing trips*
- *90 Mile Beach/Cape Reinga tours*
- *Waitangi Treaty House - 25 min*
- *Secluded beaches & coves*
- *"Rainbow Warrior" diving*
- *Art, craft & wine trails*

A warm welcome awaits you at **Kingfisher Retreat**. Relax, unwind and sample gracious hospitality and delicious continental or cooked breakfasts. **Kingfisher Retreat** is a newly constructed residence with a Mediterranean influence. For your comfort all rooms are ensuite and equipped with TV, stereo, alarm clocks and coffee/tea making facilities. Our two ground floor rooms each have private entrances, whilst the upper floor room has a balcony with views of the sea. Nestled in Northland's stunning Bay of Islands and enjoying both sea and rural views, **Kingfisher Retreat** is a 5 minute drive from the historic 'Stone Store', nature reserve and the magical Rainbow Falls. In Kerikeri township sample the fine restaurants, wineries and savour its coffee house scene. We would be pleased to arrange excursions – swimming with the dolphins, skydiving or simply cruising the bay; all there waiting to be experienced.

MAGIC COTTAGE

660 Takou Bay Road, Kerikeri, Northland
Ph (09) 407 8065
Mobile 027-545 7633
email: *takouriver@xtra.co.nz*
www.takouriver.com

Tariff : N.Z. Dollars	
Double	$170-220
Extra pp	$40
Child	

Bedrooms	Qty
Double	5
Twin	
Single	
Bed Size	**Qty**
Super King	1
King	2
Queen	2
Double	
Single	
Bathrooms	**Qty**
Ensuite	5
Private	
Guest Share	

BA **Boutique Self-contained Riverside Cottages** SC

Features & Attractions

- *Beautiful riverside retreat*
- *Absolute peace and seclusion*
- *Stunning sup-tropical gardens*
- *Kayaks, fishing & swimming*
- *Alfresco claw-foot baths*
- *Private jetty & boat house*
- *Takou Bay Beach access*
- *Bay of Islands attracions*

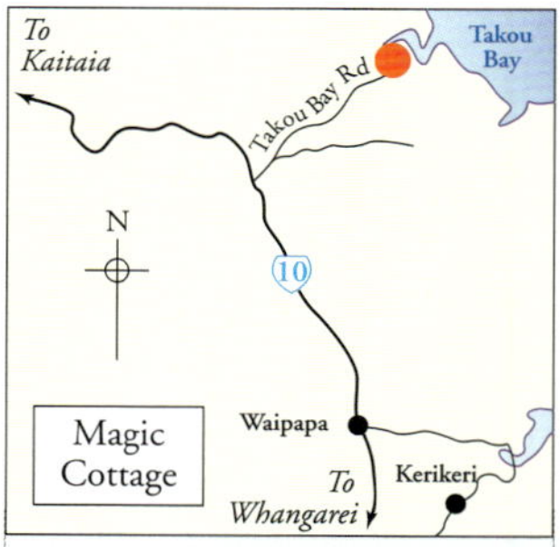

DIRECTIONS:
From SH10, 8 km north of Waipapa, turn right onto Takou Bay Road. Turn left after 1km. Continue for 5.5km. Property is at the very end.

Magic Cottage and **Takou River Lodge** is a beautiful and secluded riverside retreat offering 3 boutique self-catering cottages in 5 acres of sub-tropical gardens. On the banks of the Takou River, **Magic Cottage** offers total privacy; the ultimate romantic retreat featuring an alfresco claw-foot bath and stunning estuary views.

River and **Garden Cottage** guests' enjoy the beautiful Summer House with alfresco claw-foot bath overlooking the gardens. Each cottage provides stylish spacious accommodation featuring timber floors, private sundecks, 2 double bedrooms, 2 ensuite bathrooms, open-plan living, and kitchen.

Centrally located yet away from the hustle and bustle, guests enjoy peace and seclusion, alfresco claw-foot baths, private river frontage, jetty and boathouse, kayaks, sub-tropical gardens, secluded swimming, fishing and access to Takou Bay.

MATARIKI

14 Pa Road, Kerikeri, Bay of Islands
Ph (09) 407 7577, Fax (09) 407 7593
Mobile 027-408 0621
email: *matarikihomestay@xtra.co.nz*
www.bnbnz.com

Features & Attractions

- *Short distance to town*
- *Short walk to historic sites*
- *Handy to golfing & beaches*
- *Large garden with pool*
- *Cafés, crafts & vineyards*
- *Dinners with NZ wines*

Homestay
Boutique Accommodation

$	
Double	$140-160
Single	$100
Child	neg

Matariki is set in a large garden surrounded by sub tropical orchards. Just 3 km from town and an easy 15 minute walk to New Zealand's oldest buildings and church site. We have been home hosting for 17 years and have the experience and knowledge to make sure our guest's stay is informative and enjoyable. Retired sheep farmer and Kerikeri tour operator, David now has a vintage car and guests are offered a short complimentary tour. Alison, ex-nurse, now enjoys serving a three-course meal with New Zealand wines by arrangement. The bedrooms overlook the garden and are spacious and comfortable. Guests are encouraged to use all facilities. Reservations for tours can be booked by hosts. There is a lot to do in this popular area, close to northern beaches and to the top of the country. You can also just relax around the pool with clean air and birds singing. At night, when it's very quiet, a kiwi may be seen...

Bedrooms	Qty
Double	2
Twin	1
Single	
Bed Size	**Qty**
King	1
Queen	1
Double	
Single	2
Bathrooms	**Qty**
Ensuite	1
Private	1
Guest Share	

DIRECTIONS: Take turn to Kerikeri from Highway 10, turn right at roundabout onto Hobson Avenue, continue and turn left into Inlet Road. Pa Road is second on the left. Matariki is no 14.

WAITUI LODGE

Yacht Drive, Opito Bay, RD 1, PO Box 256,
Kerikeri, Bay of Islands
Ph (09) 407 9033, Fax (09) 407 7176
email: *waituilodge@actrix.co.nz*
www.waituilodge.co.nz

Features & Attractions

- *Tea, coffee & TV in rooms*
- *Sea and rural views*
- *Safe swimming beaches*
- *Kiwi habitat*
- *Bush walks*
- *Great fishing*

$	
Double	$140
Single	$110
Child	n/a

A Relaxing Homestay
In A Busy World

Bedrooms	Qty
Double	2
Twin	
Single	
Bed Size	**Qty**
King	
Queen	2
Double	
Single	
Bathrooms	**Qty**
Ensuite	2
Private	
Guest Share	

By day the gardens are alive with native birds. By night hear the call of the morepork and kiwi. **Waitui Lodge** is nestled in a peaceful bush-clad valley, overlooking the Kerikeri Inlet and twelve minutes from Kerikeri shops, restaurants and golf course. We are close to safe swimming beaches, Aroha Island Ecological Centre, bush walks, boat ramps and kayak hire. Catering for a maximum of four guests, our priority is your comfort and relaxation. The spacious rooms have queen beds, luxurious ensuites with heated floors and towel rails. Enjoy our spa and swimming pool, private decks and gardens. Self catering available.

Ours is a stress-free environment – relax and enjoy!

DIRECTIONS: Follow signs to Opito Bay.

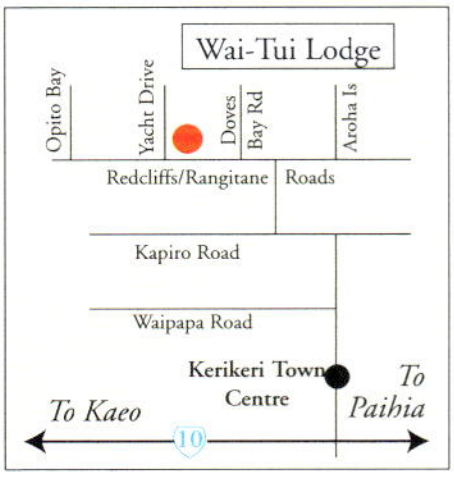

Pau Hana Lodge

1322 State Highway 10, RD 3, Kerikeri
Ph (09) 407 9318, Fax (09) 407 6691
Mobile 021-407 931
email: *pauhanalodge@xtra.co.nz*

Tariff : N.Z. Dollars	
Double	$240-360
Single	$120-150
Child	

Bedrooms	Qty
Double	2
Twin	1
Single	
Bed Size	**Qty**
Super King	1
King	1
Queen	
King/Single	2
Single	
Bathrooms	**Qty**
Ensuite	2
Private	1
Guest Share	

Bed & Breakfast
Luxury Accommodation

Features & Attractions

- *The ultimate place to unwind*
- *Relaxed, friendly atmosphere*
- *Private setting with panoramic views*
- *Double spa baths/massage shower*
- *3 golf courses, incl Kauri Cliffs*
- *Award winning wineries 3 min*
- *Diving, fishing, sailing, kayaking*
- *Craft shops & galleries trail*

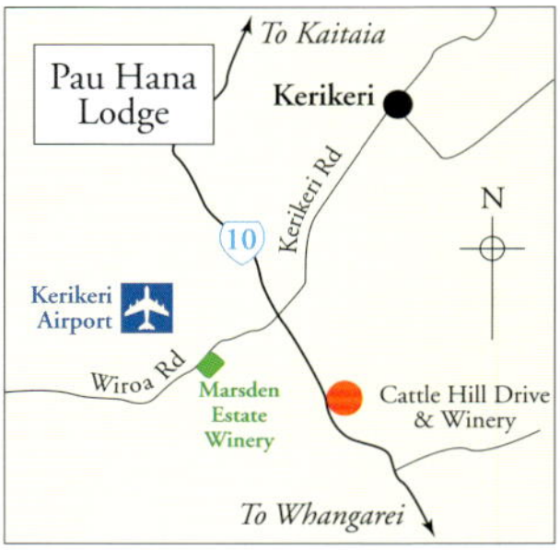

DIRECTIONS:
You will find our sign on SH 10, 300m north of Cottle Hill Winery turn-off.

Welcome to **Pau Hana Lodge** which means 'Finish Work' and that's the way we want our guests to feel.

Our home is set on fifteen acres enjoying panoramic views spanning from Kerikeri to the East Coast. Indulge in your own private bush walk, natural ponds, streams and native birds. Our home offers guests an excellent standard of accommodation, use of laundry facilities, BBQ. Complimentary wine, tea or espresso on arrival, home-baking, comprehensive breakfasts and great selection of books and DVDs.

With wonderful hospitality, warmth and friendship, we are located close to all scenic and recreational activities of the Bay of Islands.

Rainbow Falls Lodge

109 Rainbow Falls Road, RD 2, Kerikeri
Ph (09) 407 4407, Fax (09) 407 4715
Mobile 027-256 3725
email: *ratkinson@xtra.co.nz*
www.rainbowfallslodge.co.nz

Tariff : N.Z. Dollars	
Double	$100-120
Single	$90-105
Child	$30

Bedrooms	Qty
Double	2
Twin	
Single	
Bed Size	**Qty**
Super King	
King	
Queen	2
Double	
Single	
Bathrooms	**Qty**
Ensuite	1
Private	1
Guest Share	

DIRECTIONS: From SH 10 turn right into Kerikeri Rd, drive through Kerikeri town past the Stone Store and across bridge. At roundabout turn left into Waipapa Rd, then left into Rainbow Falls Rd. We are at the end (down Karaka Drive).

Self-contained Bed & Breakfast

Features & Attractions

- *Quiet and peaceful*
- *Sub-tropical gardens*
- *Spa pool*
- *Waterfall and bush walks*
- *In the Bay of Islands*
- *Cafés, craft shops & wineries*
- *Tours & cruises*
- *Historic sites*

Welcome to our new self-contained Bed & Breakfast, located in sub-tropical Kerikeri. Well appointed in a quiet, tranquil setting, we are only a five minute drive from town and handy to Paihia and the Bay of Islands. The spacious self-contained unit has its own deck, where you can relax in the sun, take a relaxing spa while viewing the sub-tropical gardens, or simply just laze around in a nice quiet setting. Privacy and discretion are assured. A short stroll from your door are lovely bush walks to Rainbow Falls and scenic reserves or you could take a short drive to the splendour of Puketi Forest. We are handily based for your Northland experience including beaches, tours and cruises, swimming with dolphins, fishing trips, giant kauri trees and forest walks. Visit the historic Stone Store, Waitangi Treaty House, historic Russell township. Our interests are wildlife conservation, walking, tramping, and gardens. Our pet cat and dog will also welcome you to our home.

Tea Tree Cottage

240 Wharau Road, RD 3, Kerikeri
Ph (09) 407 8060, Fax (09) 407 8060
Mobile 021-150 9032
email: *teatreecottage@xtra.co.nz*
www.teatreecottage.co.nz

Tariff : N.Z. Dollars	
Double	$150-150
Single	$100-100
Child	

Bedrooms	Qty
Double	2
Twin	
Single	
Bed Size	**Qty**
S. King/Single	2
King	
Queen	
Double	
King Single	4
Bathrooms	**Qty**
Ensuite	2
Private	
Guest Share	

Bed & Breakfast
Self-contained Units

VISA MasterCard

Features & Attractions

- *Stunning sea views*
- *Courtyard and BBQ area*
- *Beautifully appointed units*
- *Restaurants, craft shops, vineyards*
- *Kitchen facilities in each unit*
- *Safe swimming beach*
- *Rock fishing, golf courses*
- *Kauri forest & historic sites*

DIRECTIONS:
From SH10 veer right into Hobson Ave at traffic roundabout when you reach Kerikeri town. Turn left into Inlet Road. Go 7.5km to Wharau Road. The Cottage is at number 240.

Tea Tree Cottage is a modern home with two self-contained units. Each unit has tiled floors, a kitchen, ensuite and well appointed bedroom set in native landscaped surrounds. At night it is possible to hear Kiwi in the bush nearby. The main house is a huge open plan living area containing kitchen, dining and living rooms all overlooking the magnificent Bay of Islands. If you prefer, you can relax in the courtyard area especially designed for all-weather comfort. Two minutes down the road you will find a safe beach for swimming or a little rock fishing. We can help arrange your activities in the Bay of Islands: swim with the dolphins, go fishing or cruise the bay. There are several golf courses, craft shops, vineyards and historic sites, or take a leisurely walk through the Kauri forests before returning to Kerikeri to try one of the many fine restaurants or cafés. Our aim is simply to make your stay with us a memorable one.

The Maples Bed & Breakfast

231 B Waipapa Road, R.D. 2, Kerikeri, Northland
Ph (09) 401 7323, Fax (09) 401 7023
Mobile 021-444 712
email: *the.maples@xtra.co.nz*
www.maples.co.nz

Tariff : N.Z. Dollars	
Double	$140-165
Single	$100-140
Child	

Bedrooms	Qty
Double	1
Twin	
Single	1
Bed Size	**Qty**
Super King	
King	1
Queen	
Double	
Single	1
Bathrooms	**Qty**
Ensuite	1
Private	
Guest Share	1

VISA MasterCard

Charming
Bed & Breakfast

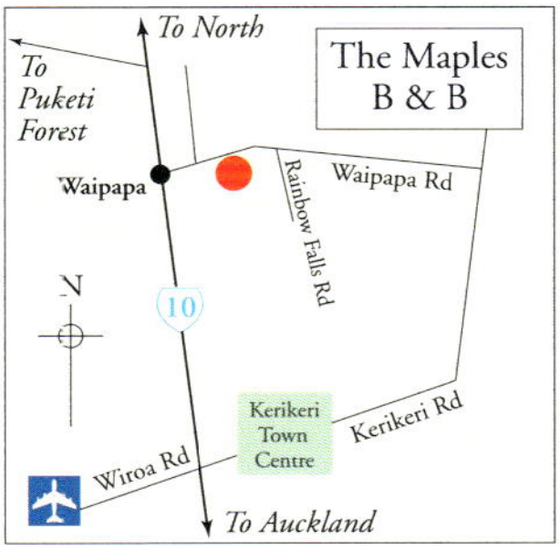

Features & Attractions

- *Special continental breakfast*
- *Quiet, peaceful surrounds*
- *Private entry and courtyard*
- *Laundry, email facilities*
- *Restaurants, cafés, wineries*
- *5 min. to town centre*
- *Beaches, forests, fauna*
- *Smoke-free environment*

Formerly a pottery studio, the **Maples B&B** has been transformed into a home full of character and charm. Our home is surrounded by colourful and fragrant gardens. Our guest room has a luxurious king-size bed, his/hers bathrobes, ensuite, walk-in wardrobe, fridge, Sky TV, library, plunger coffee and a selection of teas. Telephone, laundry, facsimile and internet facilities are available. Your separate entrance through a peaceful courtyard ensures privacy to unwind and relax. Refreshments are served on arrival in the garden. A generous continental breakfast is served with freshly baked bread, healthy cereals and seasonal fruits. Five minutes from Kerikeri township we ensure a relaxed base for you to experience the local vineyards, cafés, restaurants and craft shops. Whether you stay 3, 5 or 7 days, we can assist you with an itinerary that will allow you to explore the breathtaking countryside and beaches of the Bay of Islands and Far North. Come and join Tracey and Andrew along with Rose and Jess, our lovable Jack Russell's. You will be pleased you did.

Crisdon Castle

18 Goffe Drive, Haruru Falls, PO Box 73, Paihia
Ph/Fax (09) 402 6980, Mobile 021-206 7276
email: *info@crisdoncastle.co.nz*
www.crisdoncastle.co.nz

Tariff : N.Z. Dollars	
Double	$120-220
Single	$100-200
Child	neg

Bedrooms	Qty
Double	5
Twin	1
Single	
Bed Size	**Qty**
Super King	
King	1
Queen	4
Double	
Single	2
Bathrooms	**Qty**
Ensuite	3
Private	2
Guest Share	

**Boutique B&B
and Self-contained Units**

- *Uninterrupted 180° views*
- *BBQ and fire area*
- *Tour bookings*
- *Meals available*
- *Private access to all rooms*
- *Internet access available*
- *Guest laundry*
- *Massage and sauna*

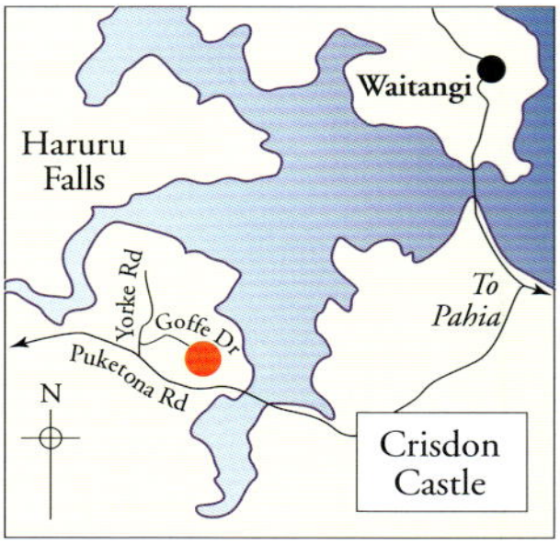

Let us welcome, comfort and indulge you, with one of the best views from your own private oasis, only 3 minutes out of the hustle and bustle of Paihia. Our B&B suites are total luxury, the best linen for your comfort, aromatherapy oils, candles, robes and quality furnishings. The self contained units have everything to make your stay comfortable and breakfast is available on request. All accommodation has TV, DVD, stereo, coffee and tea making facilities, fridge and iron. There is a guest laundry and a DVD library for your use also.

The Royal Suite queen 4-poster bed and sofa bed, lounge area opens to a private deck, there is a luxury en--uite with sunken roman bath/shower.

The Kings Retreat, king sleigh bed with a lounge opening onto a seculded balcony with amazing views. A private hall leads to the ensuite with double shower.

The Knights Nook cozy suite with views from balcony, queen bed and ensuite with a spa bath/shower.

The Queens Quarters, two bedroom self-contained unit, queen bedroom with views over the bay and twin bedroom, the lounge and dine opens to a private courtyard.

The Jesters Court, one bedroom self-contained unit, queen bedroom and ensuite, open plan kitchen/lounge/meals area that opens to your own peaceful garden.

APPLEDORE LODGE

Puketona Road, Paihia
Ph (09) 402 8007, Fax (09) 402 8007
email: *appledorelodge@xtra.co.nz*
www.appledorelodge.co.nz

Tariff : N.Z. Dollars	
Double	$120-180
Studio	$130-170
Cottage	$190-240

Bedrooms	Qty
Double	3
Twin	1
Single	
Bed Size	**Qty**
Super King	
King	2
Queen	1
Double	1
Single	
Bathrooms	**Qty**
Ensuite	4
Private	
Guest Share	

Panoramic River Views From Your Own Deck

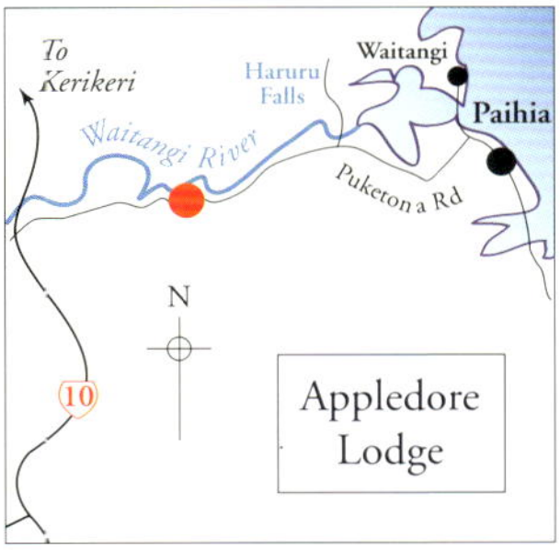

Features & Attractions

- *Spectacular riverside setting*
- *Home made breakfast basket*
- *5 min from Paihia & golf*
- *Trout fishing in our river*
- *Luxuriously appointed accommodation*
- *Internet & email facilities*
- *Outdoor spa pool under the stars*
- *Bush and coastal walking*

Miniature waterfalls and rapids await your arrival as the Waitangi River gently tumbles past your bedroom window. Tranquility and peace is here to rediscover with our spellbinding riverside setting, set in two acres and only twenty-five metres from the riverbank. Victoria Room with Queen Anne style furniture including the draped four-posted bed are served a generous breakfast with homemade bread, muffins, yoghurt and preserves. Luxury Riverside Suite furnished in native rimu, double shower ensuite, ranch slider to grand deck and our self-contained superior and luxuriously appointed Riverside Cottage and Riverside Studio, standing beside the river, take delight in an all home made breakfast basket.

We enjoy classic cars, golf, travel and meeting new guests. With resident ducks, heron, kingfisher and the outdoor spa pool, **Appledore Lodge** offers ingredients that all holidays should contain.

ALLEGRA HOUSE

39 Bayview Road, Paihia, Bay of Islands
Ph (09) 402 7932, Fax (09) 402 7930
email: *allegrahouse@xtra.co.nz*
www.allegra.co.nz

Tariff : N.Z. Dollars	
Double	$140-245
Single	
Child	

Bedrooms	Qty
Double	3
Twin	
Single	
Bed Size	**Qty**
Super King	2
King	1
Queen	
Double	
Single	
Bathrooms	**Qty**
Ensuite	3
Private	
Guest Share	

Bed & Breakfast with Views
Self-contained Apartment

VISA MasterCard

Features & Attractions

- *Spectacular sea views*
- *Central Paihia*
- *Set amongst native bush*
- *Air conditioned rooms*
- *German & French spoken*
- *Peaceful location*
- *Internet access*
- *Spa pool nestled in bush*

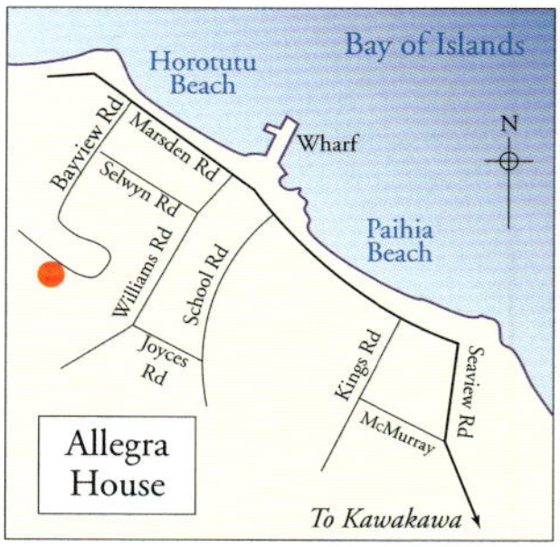

Allegra House, our spacious, modern home is centrally located, just up the hill from Paihia's wharf, shops and restaurants. We have spectacular views from all rooms over the village to Russell and the Bay of Islands. Luxurious accommodation options are: Bed & Breakfast including continental breakfast, ensuite bathroom, your own tea/coffee making facilities, refrigerator, television and balcony; or Self-catering Apartment with super-king bedroom, large tiled bathroom, fully equipped kitchen and spacious lounge opening onto a large balcony. For your comfort each room has its own air conditioning and the whole house is smoke-free. Enjoy our spa pool nestled in the bush and make use of the barbeque, laundry facilities and internet access.
Plenty of good local information is available to help you choose the best options for your time with us. We can book activities such as sailing, dolphin watching and day trips to Cape Reinga.

Bay View Suite

19 Bayview Road, PO Box 574, Paihia
Ph (09) 402 6628, Fax (09) 402 6627
Mobile 027-457 1866
email:*baysales@remax.net.nz*

Tariff : N.Z. Dollars	
Double	$140-170
Single	
Child	

Bedrooms	Qty
Double	1
Twin	
Single	
Bed Size	**Qty**
Super King	
King	
Queen	1
Double	
Single	
Bathrooms	**Qty**
Ensuite	1
Private	
Guest Share	

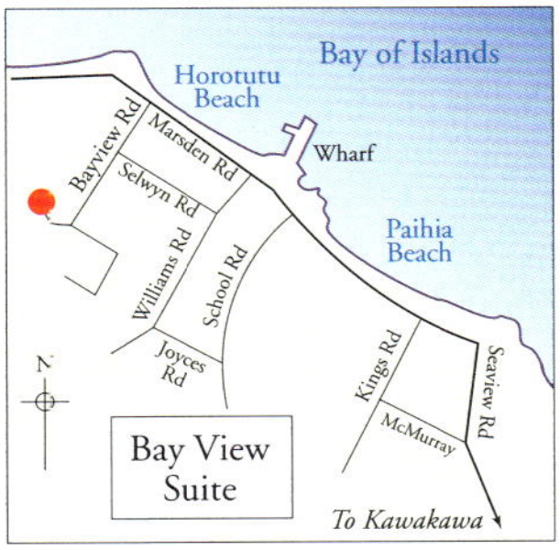

DIRECTIONS:
At 19 Bayview Road
proceed to top of driveway.
Bookings essential.

Self-contained
Central Paihia

Features & Attractions

- *Magic sea & village views*
- *Quality & comfort*
- *Privacy*
- *Warm hospitality*
- *Elevated site*
- *Welcome basket*
- *Spa pool*
- *Quality restaurants*

Elevated setting for privacy and to capture sea view. Enjoy the sea views with twinkling lights at night and ever-changing water views by day. Accommodation is fully self-contained and serviced daily. Extra luxuries include robes, slippers, plunger coffee, iron. From the spa pool you can overlook the bay. The tariff includes a generous continental breakfast, served in your suite so you can enjoy it at your leisure. A five minute walk takes you to all the local attractions, beaches and quality restaurants.

We offer a courtesy pickup and delivery service. A complimentary wine and welcome basket awaits you upon arrival.

Bookings essential. 2 nights minimum stay.

Paihia - Bay of Islands ▶ YOUR HOSTS: Garth and Liz Brinsdon Ph: (09) 402 8003

ABRI APARTMENTS

10 Bayview Rd, Paihia, Bay of Islands
Ph (09) 402 8003, Fax (09) 402 8035
email: *abriaccom@xtra.co.nz*
www.abri-accom.co.nz

Features & Attractions

- *Self-cont. luxury accommodation*
- *Close to all activities/restaurants*
- *Cooking facilities, dishwasher*
- *Panoramic views*
- *Double luxury spa bath*
- *Safe off-street parking*

Self-contained Luxury Apartments

Aptmt.	$150-270
Suite	$130-240
Child	n/a

"Luxury – Privacy – Views"

Take shelter at **Abri** in Paihia, the beautiful centre of the Bay of Islands. **Abri Apartments** are nestled in beautiful gardens with all day sun and private decks that give you panoramic views of Russell and beyond.
Our air conditioned apartments are modern and individually styled using rich native timbers and tasteful furnishings with shower, hairdryer and bathrobes.
The beach, wharf and township are only a minute's walk away giving easy access to all facilities and excursions and to some excellent restaurants.
A warm welcome awaits you and a breakfast basket is complimentary on the first morning of your stay.

Bedrooms	Qty
Double	3
Twin	
Single	
Bed Size	**Qty**
King	
Queen	3
Double	
Single	
Bathrooms	**Qty**
Ensuite	3
Private	
Guest Share	

Paihia - Bay of Islands ▶ YOUR HOST: Jill and Richard Burrows Ph: (09) 402 8696

WINDERMERE

168 Marsden Road, Paihia
Ph (09) 402 8696, Fax (09) 402 5095
Mobile 021- 115 7436
email: *windermere@igrin.co.nz*
www.windermere.co.nz

Features & Attractions

- *Great views & location*
- *Spacious sunny units*
- *Own private entrance*
- *Walk to town or golf course*
- *Spa pool & decks*
- *Sky T.V.*

Bed & Breakfast Self-contained Accom.

Double	$100-175
Single	$100-150
Child	$25

Windermere is a large modern family home set in a bush setting and yet located right on one of the best beaches in the Bay of Islands. Superior accommodation is provided with suites having their own ensuite, kitchen facilities and Sky television. For longer stays one suite has its own laundry, dryer and fully equipped kitchen. The other suite has microwave and refrigerator only. Each suite has its own decks (a barbeque is provided) where you can sit, relax and enjoy the view enhanced by spectacular sunsets. Jill and Richard would welcome your company to enjoy our own little part of paradise. Windermere is the jewel in the Bay of Islands.

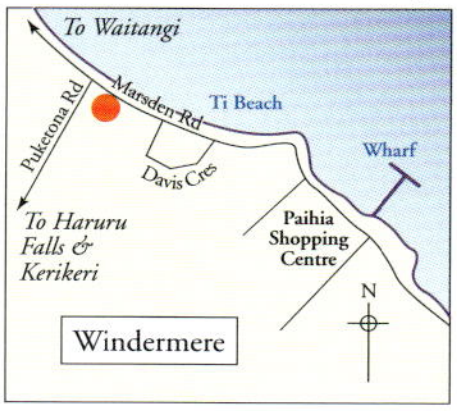

Bedrooms	Qty
Double	2
Twin	
Single	
Bed Size	**Qty**
King	
Queen	2
Double	
Single	2
Bathrooms	**Qty**
Ensuite	2
Private	
Guest Share	

Bay of Islands Beach House

16B Sullivans Road, PO Box 349, Paihia, Bay of Islands
Ph (09) 402 7702, Fax (09) 402 7703
Mobile 027-499 4041
email: *enquiries@boibeachhouse.co.nz*
www.boibeachhouse.co.nz

Tariff : N.Z. Dollars	
Double	$240-295
Single	
Child	

Bedrooms	Qty
Double	3
Twin	
Single	
Bed Size	**Qty**
Super King	1
King	
Queen	1
Double	
Single	2
Bathrooms	**Qty**
Ensuite	1
Private	1
Guest Share	

**Absolute Beachfront
Self-contained Apartments**

Features & Attractions

- *Absolute beachfront, no traffic noise*
- *Easy, short beach walk to town*
- *Golf, fishing, sailing, walking tracks*
- *Golden sands of Sullivans Beach*
- *Gated entry & secure parking*
- *Private all day sun decks*
- *Safe boat anchorage*
- *20 min airport shuttle*

The **Bay of Islands Beach House** is a short beach stroll from Paihia Township where you will find access to many activities and more than 30 restaurants, cafés and bars. The **Penthouse Apartment** is our most luxurious with stunning views, spa bath, kitchenette and large decks. Free DVD rentals every day. The **Beach Apartment** features your own patio, barbeque and path to the safe swimming and golden sands of Sullivans Beach. It has two bedrooms, bathroom, lounge/dining, kitchen, laundry facilities plus an extra (outside) shower. Free DVD rentals every day. Be our guest... bring your boat, enjoy the sun, sea and setting. Watch the boats go by or throw out a line and catch fresh fish for lunch!

THE TOTARAS

6 School Road, Paihia, Bay of Islands
Ph (09) 402 8238, Fax (09) 402 8238
email: *thetotaras@ihug.co.nz*
www.netnz.com/bedandbreakfast.html

Tariff : N.Z. Dollars	
Double	$180-220
Single	$120-165
Child	neg

Bedrooms	Qty
Double	1
Twin	
Single	
Bed Size	**Qty**
Super King	
King	
Queen	1
Double	
Single	1
Bathrooms	**Qty**
Ensuite	1
Private	
Guest Share	

Central Hilltop Bed & Breakfast

Features & Attractions

- *Uninterrupted 180º sea views*
- *Breakfast on sun terrace*
- *Conservatory & in-house library*
- *Adjacent to reserve*
- *Golf course nearby*
- *Insider tips*
- *Pleasant ambience*
- *Photographers dream*

DIRECTIONS:
Coming from Auckland towards central Paihia. Turn left into School Road. Drive approx 400m, Pass No 34, followed by No 6 **The Totaras B&B**.
Use low gear to drive up the hill.

For the sophisticated traveller. Luxury with charm... **The Totaras** is named after a local variety of native trees. It is perched on a hillside overlooking Paihia, its harbour, historic Waitangi, Russell, the islands and endless horizon. Wake up to the sunrise from your spacious well appointed apartment with ensuite and sundeck. Listen to our vivid birdlife. Enjoy the vista of ocean liners and sailing boats - or simply be mesmerized by the stunning view. Within minutes a path will lead you to the village, restaurants, wharf, beaches, bush and coastal tracks. Frank is an internationally known photographer. One of his latest books 'Bay of Islands, A Paradise Found' depicts the beauty of the bay, he and Christine fell in love with many years ago. Christine has a degree in Hotel Management. For breakfast you will be spoiled with delicious Austrian pancakes, fresh fruit and other delights. We welcome you - Auf Ihren Besuch freuen wir uns! (Minimum stay 2 nights).

Chalet Romantica

6 Bedggood Close, Paihia, Bay of Islands
Ph (09) 402 8270, Fax (09) 402 8278
Mobile 027-226 6400
email: *chalet-romantica@xtra.co.nz*
www.chaletromantica.homestead.com/accom1.html

Tariff : N.Z. Dollars	
Double	$125-235
Single	$115-225
Child	$25

Bedrooms	Qty
Double	3
Twin	
Single	
Bed Size	**Qty**
Super King	2
King	
Queen	1
Double	
Single	4
Bathrooms	**Qty**
Ensuite	2
Private	1
Guest Share	

MasterCard VISA

Quality Bed & Breakfast & Self-contained Suites

Features & Attractions

- *Central town location with sea views*
- *Café's & restaurants nearby*
- *Stroll to beach and water activities*
- *Heated pool, spa, mini gym*
- *TV, CD- player, DVD/video, phone in rooms*
- *Laundry facilities, internet and tour desk on site.*
- *42-foot yacht for skippered charters*
- *Francaise and German spoken*

Spoil yourself and experience the magic of **Chalet Romantica**, our own piece of paradise. Nestled on a ridge above Paihia Beach with unsurpassed views of the Bay and township, spectacular by day and night. Each of our rooms has its own balcony with superb sea views, quality furnishings and fittings, crisp linen and extra comfy beds. Having lived here for over 20 years we are proud of our local knowledge, passionate about where we live and love to share it all with you. Spend your days exploring, visit historic Waitangi, Russell or take a tour to 90 Mile Beach. Play a round of golf, walk our picturesque walkways, sail, swim, dive, kayak or just laze at one of the many sandy beaches just a stroll from us. Why not just enjoy your balcony, read and watch the yachts sail past, take a plunge into our heated pool, soak in the hot spa or work out at the gym. What better way to recharge your batteries? Our chalet consists of 1 B&B queen-room and 2 fully self-contained king-size apartment/suites, furnished with light and friendly colours reflecting the sea and scenery. Bookings and 2-day plus stays recommended.

DIRECTIONS:
Please phone for easy directions.

DECKS OF PAIHIA

69 School Road, Paihia
Ph (09) 402 6146, Fax (09) 402 6147
Mobile 021- 263 4726
email: *info@decksofpaihia.com*
www.decksofpaihia.com

Tariff : N.Z. Dollars	
Double	$145-190
Single	–
Child	–

Bedrooms	Qty
Double	3
Twin	
Single	
Bed Size	**Qty**
Super King	3
King	
Queen	
Double	
Single	
Bathrooms	**Qty**
Ensuite	3
Private	
Guest Share	

Luxury Bed & Breakfast

Features & Attractions

- *Quiet, central location*
- *Sun-drenched decks*
- *Lovely sea views*
- *Private ensuites each room*
- *All suites air-conditioned*
- *Spacious guest lounge*
- *Broadband internet access*
- *Tea/coffee making in each room*

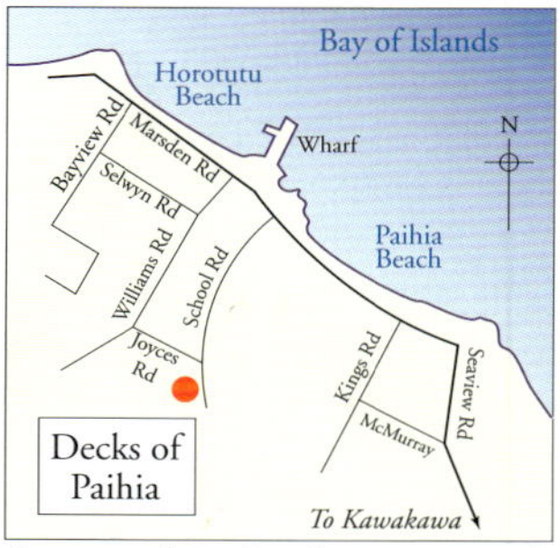

Contemporary designed home, recently opened, October 2005. Three guest suites all with private ensuite bathrooms. All suites offer your own tea/coffee making facilities, TV/DVD, air conditioning, refrigerator, and open onto sheltered decks. Quiet, peaceful, central Paihia location with off-street parking. Very comfortable interiors, stylishly furnished. Guest lounge, located adjacent to suites, offers extended living space in which to relax, with a comprehensive DVD and book library. Private garden area allows the opportunity for a lazy afternoon in the sun. Beautiful sun-drenched upper decks give the option to enjoy your breakfast while taking in the lovely views over Paihia and the Bay of Islands. Philip and Wendy have enjoyed many years in the hospitality industry and are happy to share their home and their extensive knowledge of the Bay of Islands and Northland with you. Philip has strong links to the area – his great grandfather, Patrick McGovern, was the police constable in Russell in the 1880's.

HARBOUR HOUSE VILLA

7 English Bay Road, Opua, Bay of Islands
Ph (09) 402 8087, Fax (09) 402 8688
email: *stay@harbourhousevilla.com*
www.harbourhousevilla.com

Tariff : N.Z. Dollars	
Double	$250-420
Single	$200-280
Child	welcome

Bedrooms	Qty
Double	3
Twin	2
Single	
Bed Size	**Qty**
Super King	1
King	1
Queen	1
Double	
Single	4
Bathrooms	**Qty**
Ensuite	4
Private	
Guest Share	

VISA MasterCard

LA **Luxury Ensuite B&B Rooms**
One & Two Bedroom Suite BA

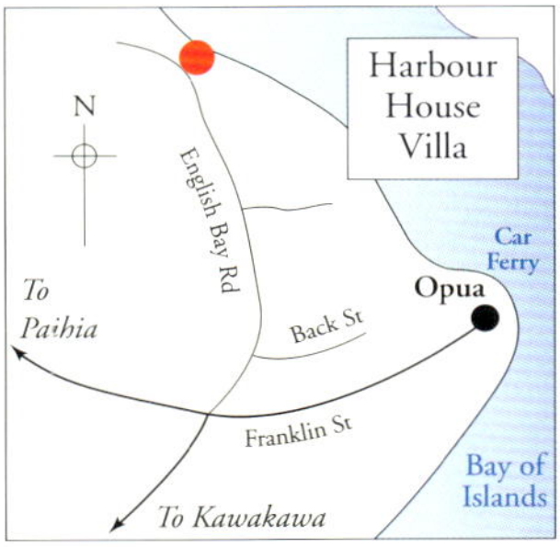

DIRECTIONS: From Auckland, take SH1 past Whangarei to Kawakawa. Take SH11 for 12km towards Opua. At intersection, cross into English Bay Rd. Travel 500m to **Harbour House Villa** on right.

Features & Attractions

- *Sea view from every room*
- *Private and peaceful*
- *Computer / Internet*
- *Japanese spoken*
- *Courtesy transportation*
- *Deep sea fishing*
- *Sailing, cruises & tours*
- *Trip planning & information*

This delightful Villa has the best view of the Bay of Islands extending from the picturesque Opua yacht haven past Paihia, Russell to the Waitangi Treaty grounds, which is connected by the Coastal Walking Path, and to the Kerikeri Inlet at the far end of the Bay's Historic Marine Park. All Villa accommodations are meticulously maintained. Each B&B ensuite room or Suite Guest can choose gourmet Kiwi, Western or Japanese breakfast, which is served on our viewing deck or in the dining room. One and two bedroom suites receive full service and may elect to have breakfast provisions provided in their kitchen. Each suite has its own private deck equipped for outdoor living including BBQ. Pleasing music played on our grand piano complements the panoramic view creating a unique ambience at the Villa. Your hosts, Robert and Masae Serge, are blue water sailors, seasoned travellers and also experienced in providing accommodation for the discerning traveller.

Mako Lodge

18 Pt Veronica Drive, Opua, Bay of Islands
Ph (09) 402 7957, Fax (09) 402 5957
Mobile 021-256 5416
email: *info@makolodge.co.nz*
www.makolodge.co.nz

Tariff : N.Z. Dollars	
Double	$140-180
Single	$130-170
Child	

Bedrooms	Qty
Double	3
Twin	
Single	
Bed Size	**Qty**
Super King	1
King	
Queen	2
Double	
Single	
Bathrooms	**Qty**
Ensuite	3
Private	
Guest Share	

Idyllic Location with Spectacular Views

Features & Attractions

- *Panoramic sea views*
- *Spa-tub overlooking Bay*
- *North facing deck*
- *Sports fishing arranged*
- *Beach towels/umbrellas avail.*
- *Bush and coastal walks*
- *Off-road parking*
- *Generous breakfast*

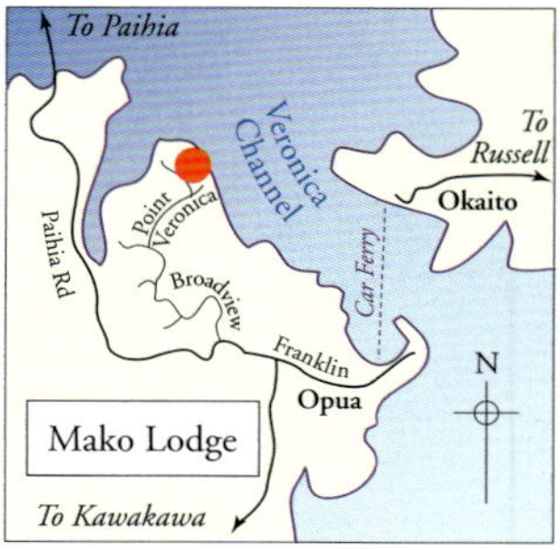

Our Lodge at Point Veronica is in an outstanding, peaceful, coastal location of natural beauty with stunning sea/bush views and sunsets seen from our decks. Only 5 km away is Paihia and Waitangi with its amenities and popular leisure activities for tourists. **Mako Lodge**, completed in 2003, is 5 minutes by car from Opua Marina and the car ferry taking you to Okiato, historic Russell and Long Beach. A 3 minute walk from **Mako Lodge** takes walking enthusiasts to the Coastal Path and bush walks in the area.

Relax in our hot tub overlooking the Bay – you may even spot a pod of dolphins or orcas – or relax in the Bay View garden, which has commanding views over the Bay of Islands looking towards historic Russell.

Mako Lodge is a non smoking environment. All bedrooms have sea views, fridge, mini bar, complimentary tea and coffee making facilities plus TV, VCR and clock radio alarms.

Pt. Veronica Lodge

39 Pt Veronica Drive, Opua, Bay of Islands
Ph (09) 402 5579, Fax (09) 402 5579
Mobile 021-182 0697
email: *stay@ptveronicalodge.co.nz*
www.ptveronicalodge.co.nz

Tariff : N.Z. Dollars	
Double	$150-180
Single	$130-160
Child	

Bedrooms	Qty
Double	2
Twin	
Single	
Bed Size	**Qty**
Super King	
King	
Queen	2
Double	
Single	
Bathrooms	**Qty**
Ensuite	2
Private	
Guest Share	

Peaceful & Enchanting

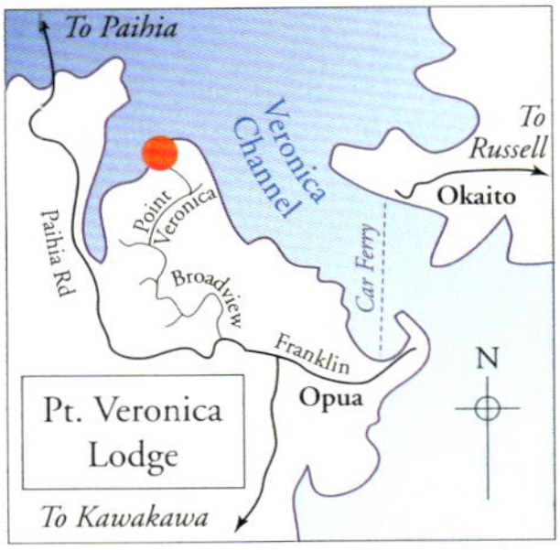

Features & Attractions

- *Overlooking the Bay*
- *Luxury cooked breakfast*
- *North facing decks*
- *6 min. to Paihia/Waitangi*
- *Bush & coastal walks*
- *Internet facilities*
- *Lovely spa on lower deck*
- *Backing onto reserve*

Pt. **Veronica Lodge Homestay** is on a headland in the Bay of Islands. The guest bedrooms look out over an inlet. The lounge and decks have views over the water towards Paihia, Waitangi and Russell. From our garden you can access the coastal walking track and the sea or stay and enjoy the sub-tropical flowers and abundant birdlife.

Built in 2001, our home makes wonderful use of native timbers throughout. All bedrooms are ensuite and have heatpump/air-conditioning, television and radio. Complimentary teas and coffee are available in the kitchen at any time. We hope you will try some of our home baking.

Point Veronica Lodge is ideally located for visiting Opua, Paihia, Waitangi, Russell and Kerikeri. Pick-ups at the door for swimming with the dolphins, Hole-in-the-Rock cruises and scenic flights to Cape Reinga. An ideal centre for summer and winter breaks. Audrey, John and our two lovely dogs invite you to join us in our special place.

WATERVIEW LODGE

14 Franklin Street, Opua, Bay of Islands
Ph (09) 402 7595, Fax (09) 402 7596
Mobile 021-102 3950
email: *info@waterviewlodge.co.nz*
www.waterviewlodge.com

Tariff : N.Z. Dollars	
Double	$150-230
Single	$90-140
Child	$20

Bedrooms	Qty
Double	7
Twin	1
Single	
Bed Size	**Qty**
Super King	2
King/Single	4
Queen	2
Double	2
Single	2
Bathrooms	**Qty**
Ensuite	3
Private	2
Guest Share	

Quality Accommodation
Excellent Service

Features & Attractions

- *Great sea views*
- *Scrumptuous breakfast*
- *Complimentary Internet*
- *Bush and coastal walks*
- *Glow-worm tour*
- *Tourist attractions 5 min.*
- *Restaurant, yacht club, marina in walking distance*

DIRECTIONS:
Drive to Bay of Islands.
Then towards the Opua-Russell car ferry.
Franklin St leads down to the car ferry.
Waterview is on the right,
half way down the hill.

Overlooking the picturesque Port of Opua, **Waterview Lodge** is a quality accommodation establishment. **Waterview Lodge** has 3 private guest suites. The **Harbour** and **River Suites** have private balconies with panoramic sea views of Opua. The **River** and **Garden Suites** have a king and a single bed, the **Harbour Suite** has a king bed only. All suites have quality linen, ensuite, TV, CD, telephone, fridge and tea/coffee making facilities. Computer with internet access is available. Breakfasts are complimentary with the suites and consist of home-made breads and muffins, local fresh fruits, cheeses and yoghurt, a selection of cereals or a cooked breakfast. *Self-contained accommodation* (with well equipped kitchens): The 3 bedroom **Waterview Cottage** is a charming residence capturing sun and sea views. The 2 bedroom **Garden Unit** is situated downstairs next to the **Garden Suite** with a garden outlook and a great outdoor entertaining area.

Your hosts, Antionette and Jess, will offer you the very best in customer service and your stay will be an enjoyable and memorable one. **Waterview Lodge** is a smoke free environment.

YOUR HOSTS: **Shiralee and Dennis Harrison** Ph: (09) 402 7389 ***Opua - Paihia***

ISLAND VIEW LODGE

6 Oromahoe Road, (PO Box 109, Paihia)
Opua, Bay of Islands
Ph/Fax (09) 402 7389, Mobile 021-077 4913
email: *islandviewlodge@hotmail.com*
www.travelwise.co.nz

Features & Attractions

- *Sea views from every room*
- *5 min Paihia Township*
- *Waitangi Golf Course 5 min*
- *Tours & attractions arranged*
- *Walking distance to Opua*
- *Kauri and coastal bush walks*

Self-contained
Bed & Breakfast Accom.

$	
Double	$120-180
Single	$120-150
Child	1/2 price

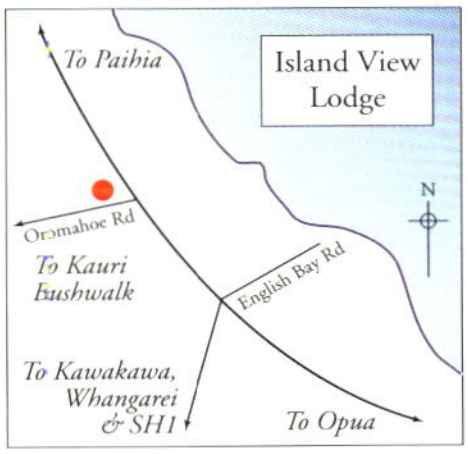

Our large home is on a hilltop overlooking the Bay of Islands and Opua Harbour with fantastic sea and bush views and tropical gardens. We are within walking distance of the Opua wharf, store and marina. Once there, you can take the car ferry to historic Russell, or dine in a restaurant. There is a beautiful coastal walkway and magnificent kauri bush walk close by. Three self-contained studio units with ensuites, kitchenettes and balconies. A large four person self-contained cottage with the same fantastic sea views and tropical gardens. Generous continental breakfast can be provided in your unit. Paihia township and tourist attractions five kilometres away. No shoes in house please. Smoking outside only.

Bedrooms	Qty
Double	4
Twin	2
Single	
Bed Size	**Qty**
King	
Queen	4
Double	
Single	4
Bathrooms	**Qty**
Ensuite	4
Private	
Guest Share	1

YOUR HOSTS: **Peter Johnson** Ph: (09) 403 8410 ***Russell - Bay of Islands***

ANCHORAGE OF RUSSELL

43 Tapeka Road, Russell, Bay of Islands
Ph (09) 403 8410, Fax (09) 403 8410
Mobile 027-497 9318
email: *anchorage.boi@xtra.co.nz*
www.travelwise.co.nz

Features & Attractions

- *Beach front setting*
- *Great breakfasts*
- *Superb local restaurants*
- *Tours/excursions arranged*
- *Complimentary kayaks, bikes*
- *Safe, sandy swimming beach*

Homestay
Bed & Breakfast

$	
Double	$150-195
Single	$120-150
Child	

VISA MasterCard

DIRECTIONS:
Travel through Russell Village, up Flagstaff Hill to Tapeka Point.

Step out of your new suite onto Tapeka Beach – the undiscovered gem of the Bay of Islands. Romantic Russell is a two minute drive offering the ambience of a small picturesque seaside town where enthusiastic explorers will find early European settlement, New Zealand's oldest church, Russell Museum or Flagstaff Hill. There are shops and many restaurants offering a wide range of culinary experiences. Boats depart from here for tours of the Bay, fishing trips and dolphin watching. Back at the Anchorage your suite is complete with tea, coffee, refrigerator, television, stereo and cane furniture. Your hosts Anna and John, who have both spent many years in entertainment, will serve you gourmet breakfast in the dining room or alfresco on the deck. Come and share with them this idyllic seashore haven where you will find comfort, tranquility and peace. Make this your Anchorage where the only sound is the lap of waves.

Bedrooms	Qty
Double	3
Twin	
Single	
Bed Size	**Qty**
King	
Queen	3
Double	
Single	
Bathrooms	**Qty**
Ensuite	3
Private	
Guest Share	

Arcadia Lodge

10 Florance Ave, Russell Village, Bay of Islands
Ph (09) 403 7756, Fax (09) 403 7721
email: *arcadialodge@xtra.co.nz*
www.arcadialodge.co.nz

Tariff : N.Z. Dollars	
Double	$150-295
Single	enquire
Child	

Bedrooms	Qty
Double	6
Twin	1
Single	
Bed Size	**Qty**
Super King	1
King	1
Queen	2
Double	3
Single	
Bathrooms	**Qty**
Ensuite	4
Private	1
Guest Share	1

History, Charm, Good Food and Glorious Views

DIRECTIONS:
By car: On the right side of the road, at the entrance to Russell and round Matauwhi Bay. Watch for the signs. To rear car park, follow into village, go right up Robertson Road and right again onto Brind Road, then down hill again to **Arcadia Lodge** driveway.

Features & Attractions

- *Overlooking Matauwhi Bay*
- *Bayview decks & lounge*
- *All tours/excursions arranged*
- *Healthy café-style breakfast*
- *Close to 2 swimming beaches*
- *Short stroll to village centre*
- *Landmark historic house*

Historic, 100 year old **Arcadia** commands a magnificent position overlooking Russell's best kept secret, tranquil Matauwhi Bay. For many of our guests one of their greatest pleasures is simply to sit and drink in the 180 degree views of water, bush and yachts. Downstairs we have three spacious suites with bay view decks while upstairs are two double rooms with water views and a super-king room. The house is furnished in a casual blend of contemporary and antique furniture on original honey-coloured kauri floorboards with western and Pasifika art helping create a comfortable, relaxing space in which to unwind.

Start your day on the deck with our generous, healthy breakfast: fresh Kerikeri orange juice, Northland fruit, home made muesli, jams and preserves, organic coffee and teas, followed by a delicious café-style cooked special. There's no better set up for a full day out in the bay.

Brisa Cottages

92B Te Wahapu Road, RD 1, Russell, Bay of Islands
Ph (09) 403 7757, Fax (09) 403 7758
email: *brisa@xtra.co.nz*
www.bay-of-islands.net.nz

Tariff : N.Z. Dollars	
Double	$160-220
Single	$160
Child	

Bedrooms	Qty
Double	4
Twin	
Single	
Bed Size	**Qty**
Super King	
King	
Queen	3
King/Single	1
Single	1
Bathrooms	**Qty**
Ensuite	4
Private	
Guest Share	

Boutique Accommodation
Bed & Breakfast

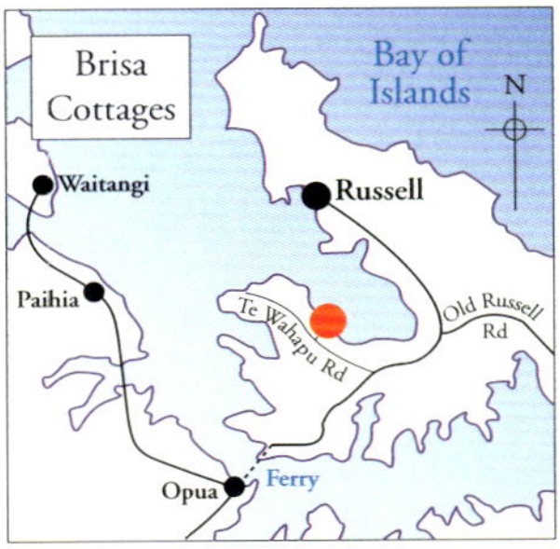

Features & Attractions

- *Delicious full breakfasts*
- *On the water's edge*
- *Peaceful garden setting*
- *Safe off-street parking*
- *Swimming with dolphins*
- *Forest/coastal walks*
- *Kiwi protection zone*
- *Dinner by arrangement*

Brisa Cottages offer a romantic hideaway for two. Enjoy total privacy within a self-contained cottage that has a kitchenette with refrigerator and cooking facilities, a spacious bedroom/lounge area and ensuite bathroom.

Each cottage has its own area of flowers, shrubs and trees, a separate entrance and large deck that overlooks Orongo Bay. The emphasis is on tasteful, comfortable surroundings with all the essential extras such as fresh flowers, home baking, toiletries and bath-robes. Top quality beds and bedding, cotton sheets and soft absorbent towels ensure a feeling of luxury. Our breakfast table is set with white linen, silver and fine china and features fresh coffee, baking, home-grown fruit, our own preserves and eggs from our free range hens.
A dinghy is at hand for fishing or a leisurely paddle from our beach. Historic Russell's museum, restaurants and galleries are just seven minutes away by car.

Russell ▶ YOUR HOSTS: **Vivienne and Bradley Morrison** Ph (09) 403 8109

ARAPOHUE HOUSE B & B

9 Wellington Street, Russell, Bay of Islands
Ph (09) 403 8109, Fax (09) 403 8107
Mobile 027-272 8881
email: *vivmorrison@xtra.co.nz*
www.travelwise.co.nz

Features & Attractions

- *Close to waterfront*
- *Fine dining & cafés*
- *Beautiful beaches*
- *Boat charters*
- *Museum & crafts*
- *Nature walks*

Historic Russell Bed & Breakfast

$	
Double	$185
Single	$165
Child	

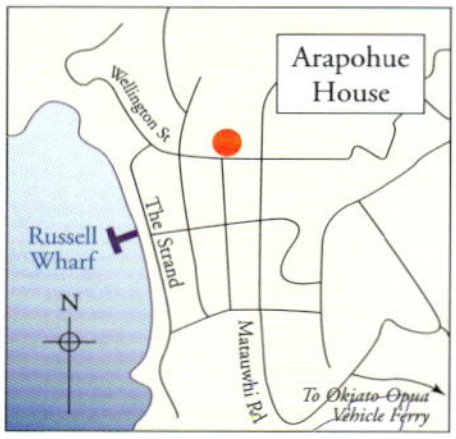

This beautiful re-designed old bungalow has been rebuilt recently with two ensuite bedrooms for guests. Only 200 metres from Russell waterfront, it is an easy leisurely level walk to all the fine restaurants and coffee houses. Historic Russell, with its museum and craft shops, offers a natural history with nature walks and three beautiful beaches. We can organise any trips you wish. Alternatively, you are welcome to spend time in our beautiful garden relaxing with a great book.
All bedrooms have tea and coffee facilities, digital radio clocks, hair dryers, cotton dressing gowns, and colour TVs with Sky TV. A laundry is available.

Bedrooms	Qty
Double	2
Twin	
Single	
Bed Size	**Qty**
King	
Queen	2
Double	
Single	
Bathrooms	**Qty**
Ensuite	2
Private	
Guest Share	

Russell - Bay of Islands ▶ YOUR HOSTS: **Anna and John Boulter** Ph: (09) 403 7882

BELVEDERE LODGE

James Clendon Place, Okiato, RD 1,
Russell (Old Russell), Bay of Islands
Ph/Fax (09) 403 7882
email: *jmboulter@xtra.co.nz*
www.travelwise.co.nz

Features & Attractions

- *Stunning 180° bay views*
- *Excessive tranquility*
- *Russell town 7 min*
- *Swim beach 2 min walk*
- *Beach and bush walks*
- *Initial breakfast supplies*

Self-contained Luxury Waterfront Apartment

$	
Double	$190-250
2nd Ensuite	$80-100
Child	

DIRECTIONS: From the Opua-Okiato ferry, turn left after approx. 400m into Pipiroa Rd, after 50m continue into James Clendon Place. **Belvedere Lodge** is the first residence on the right.

Built in 1997 on the historic site of Britain's first seat of government (***the original Russell***) at Okiato Point. Located above Pipiroa Bay with conservation reserves either side and decks in bush-clad surrounds. With "million dollar" views, bird song and waves lapping gently below, a good night's sleep is the norm.
The ground level apartment is accessed by covered verandah and has full kitchen, newly fitted down to the Kiwi "dish drawer"; dining, lounge and two ensuite bedrooms. Complete with own laundry, BBQ, TV, video and stereo. All in a park-like setting, it is ideal for the longer stay. Bay activities are available in Russell or, via the close-by Okiato-Opua ferry, in Paihia and Waitangi. Not suitable for small children. ***Long stay rates quoted on request.***

Bedrooms	Qty
Double	2
Twin	
Single	
Bed Size	**Qty**
King	
Queen	1
Double	
King Single	1
Bathrooms	**Qty**
Ensuite	2
Private	
Guest Share	

HARDINGS' - AOTEAROA LODGE

Orongo Bay Farm, Aucks Road,
RD 1, Russell, Bay of Islands
Ph/Fax (09) 403 7277, Mobile 021-184 2023
email: *btharding@xtra.co.nz*
www.the-lodge.co.nz

Tariff : N.Z. Dollars	
Double	$185-285
Single	$150-250
Child	

Bedrooms	Qty
Double	4
Twin	2
Single	
Bed Size	**Qty**
Super King	
King	2
Queen	2
King Single	2
Single	
Bathrooms	**Qty**
Ensuite	4
Private	
Guest Share	

Luxury Country Accommodation

DIRECTIONS:
Take the vehicle ferry from Opua to Russell. We are then approximately 4 km on the right hand side.

Features & Attractions

- *Country luxury*
- *The Bay on the doorstep*
- *Hot spa pool & sauna*
- *5 min to Russell village*
- *Warmest hospitality*
- *Space & tranquility*
- *Superb country breakfast*
- *Abundance of activities*

Welcome to **Hardings' – Aotearoa Lodge**, set in seven acres of beautiful rolling countryside overlooking Orongo Bay – yet just minutes from 'Romantic Russell' and all its amenities. We promise warm, friendly hospitality, extremely comfortable accommodation, privacy and delicious breakfasts – using eggs from our own chickens and fresh homegrown produce. Our guest suites are well equipped and we take pride in going 'that extra mile' to make your stay memorable.

The two suites in 'Brook Barn' have their own private lounges and decks, whilst those in the main lodge have an adjoining luxury guest lounge with balcony. Outside we have spacious decks and patio, with a hot spa pool and sauna to help you relax.

All suites have a refrigerator, tea/coffee facilities, soft drinks, hair dryer, toiletries, bath robes and ironing facilites. We will be delighted to help you with planning your activities or excursions during your time in the Bay – be it swimming with dolphins, golf, sailing, fishing or walking. Or you may simply choose to take things easy and soak up the wonderful surroundings.

LA VEDUTA

11 Gould Street, Russell, Bay of Islands
Ph (09) 403 8299, Fax (09) 403 8299
email: *laveduta@xtra.co.nz*
www.laveduta.co.nz

Tariff : N.Z. Dollars	
Double	$180-220
Single	$150-180
Child	$45

Bedrooms	Qty
Double	4
Twin	
Single	
Bed Size	**Qty**
Super King	
King	1
Queen	1
Double	2
Single	1
Bathrooms	**Qty**
Ensuite	3
Private	2
Guest Share	

Quality Boutique Homestay
Bed & Breakfast

Features & Attractions

- *Spectacular views of the Bay*
- *Television room*
- *5 minutes walk to town*
- *Unique stylish bedrooms*
- *Personalised service*
- *Tours & cruises arranged*
- *French & Italian spoken*
- *Excellent restaurants nearby*

DIRECTIONS:
Please phone for easy directions.

Enjoy our mix of traditional European culture in the midst of the beautiful Bay of Islands, historic heartland of New Zealand. **La Veduta** is the perfect "pied-a-terre" for your Northland holiday. We offer our guests a warm welcome, taking care of your smallest needs.
All our bedrooms are individually styled, offering full sea views. You may be served a delicious cooked breakfast on the balcony overlooking the Bay of Russell. Enjoy complimentary afternoon tea. Relax and delight in the sunset over the Bay. **La Veduta** is only a few minutes walk from the township, wharf, sandy beaches and restaurants.

Ounuwhao "Harding House" B & B Homestead

Matauwhi Bay, Russell, Bay of Islands
Ph (09) 403 7310, Fax (09) 403 8310 Mob. 027 414 1310
email: *thenicklins@xtra.co.nz*
www.travelwise.co.nz

Tariff : N.Z. Dollars	
Double	$195-250
Single	$160-200
Child	$45 (u/12)

Bedrooms	Qty
Double	4
Twin	2
Single	
Bed Size	**Qty**
Super King	
King	1
Queen	4
Double	
Single	4
Bathrooms	**Qty**
Ensuite	4
Private	2
Guest Share	

Boutique Accommodation & Self-contained Accommodation

Features & Attractions

- *Detached garden suite*
- *Safe, sandy swimming beaches*
- *Swimming with the dolphins*
- *Hearty, healthy gourmet breakfasts*
- *Historic Russell Village*
- *Sea and island excursions*
- *Coastal and bush walks*
- *Historic homestead*

When visiting Historic Russell take a step back into a bygone era. Spend some time with us in our delightful nostalgic, immaculately restored villa (circa 1894). Enjoy wrap-around verandahs in summer and the large guest lounge with open fire in winter. Each room has traditional wallpapers and paint work with handmade patchwork quilts and fresh flowers to create a lovingly detailed, traditional romantic interior. Breakfast is served in our farmhouse kitchen around the large kauri dining table. It is an all homemade affair, from the fresh baked bread to the yummy daily special and the jam conserves. Our 1930's self-contained cottage is set in park-like grounds for your privacy and enjoyment. With two double bedrooms, large lounge and sunroom and fully self-contained kitchen, it is ideal for people wanting peace and time out. Breakfast is available if required. We look forward to meeting you soon.

EXPERIENCE OUR HISTORIC BED & BREAKFAST,
ENJOY A WORLD OF DIFFERENCE.

DIRECTIONS:
We are on the main road from the vehicular ferry, in Matauwhi Bay 1 km from Russell Village.

Russell ▶ YOUR HOSTS: **Stephen and Emma Jury** Ph (09) 403 7676

The White House

- Te Wharema -

7 Church Street, Russell, Bay of Islands
Ph/Fax (09) 403 7676
email: *info@thewhitehouserussell.com*
www.thewhitehouserussell.com

Features & Attractions

- *Restored & renovated Oct. '05*
- *180m to waterfront*
- *12 midday late check-out*
- *Breakfast buffet incl. until noon*
- *Complimentary port & sherry*
- *Free Broadband Internet access*

Luxury Accommodation Bed & Breakfast

$	
Double	$195-320
Single	$176-288
Child	

DIRECTIONS:
Upon entering Russell, turn right into Church St, past NZ's oldest church, go straight across the next junction. We are about 20m on your right.

The Historic 'White House' Russell
Luxury Bed & Breakfast Accommodation

Come and have a truly unique stay with us in one of Russell's oldest houses (circa 1840). A beautifully restored villa with plenty of character. She features three well appointed rooms with super-king size beds and fresh new ensuites along with guest lounge and full kitchen.
Indulge in absolute luxury ideally situated in the heart of Russell with 12 midday check-out. Enjoy a dip in the spa pool, read a book on the shaded sundeck or wander to the waterfront.

Bedrooms	Qty
Double/Twin	3
Twin	
Single	
Bed Size	**Qty**
Super King	3
Queen	
Double	
Single	
Bathrooms	**Qty**
Ensuite	3
Private	
Guest Share	

Russell - Bay of Islands ▶ YOUR HOSTS: **Sue and Stephen Western** Free Ph (0800) 546 434

Villa Russell

2 Little Queen Street, Russell, Bay of Islands
Ph (09) 403 8845, Fax (09) 4038845
Mobile 027-492 8912
email: *info@kingfishercharters.co.nz*
www.kingfishercharters.co.nz

Features & Attractions

- *Spectacular views of the bay*
- *2 minutes walk to town*
- *Quiet and secluded*
- *Sail the bay with us too*
- *Close to 2 swimming beaches*
- *Delicious breakfast included*

DIRECTIONS: Travel through Russell village into Queen St. Little Queen St is the driveway with white picket fence at bottom of Flagstaff Hill.

Luxury Accommodation with Sailing Option

$	
Double	$165-320
Single	
Child	

Enjoy a welcoming visit to **Villa Russell**, 2 minutes from the beach and Russell's restaurants, yet totally private and secluded. Relax with magnificent views of Russell's bay and wharf from the deck of our beautifully restored 1910 villa, or from our guest cottage with spacious guest rooms, with ensuite, and large verandah, all surrounded by mature native trees and birdsong. Imagine having breakfast al fresco, while seeing nature at its best. A short walk takes you to Long Bay surf beach or historic Flagstaff Hill and native bush. Your suite is complete with tea/coffee facilities, refrigerator, microwave, TV and video, laundry facilities. Off-street parking provided. You may also be greeted by our friendly family dog. Make your stay even more special with a sailing charter on our 11.6m yacht 'Kingfisher' or 15m 'Kama Lua' to further explore the beautiful sights the Bay of Islands has to offer.

Bedrooms	Qty
Double	2
Twin	1
Single	
Bed Size	**Qty**
King	2
Queen	1
Double	
King/Single	2
Bathrooms	**Qty**
Ensuite	3
Private	
Guest Share	

Russell Bay Lodge

71 Wellington Street, Russell
Ph/Fax (09) 403 7376, Mobile 027-417 3310
email: *info@russellbay.co.nz*
www.russellbay.co.nz

Tariff : N.Z. Dollars	
Double	$150-320
Single	
Child	

Bedrooms	Qty
Double	2
Twin	
Single	
Bed Size	**Qty**
Super King	
King	2
Queen	
Double	
Single	
Bathrooms	**Qty**
Ensuite	2
Private	
Guest Share	

Luxury
Self-contained Suites

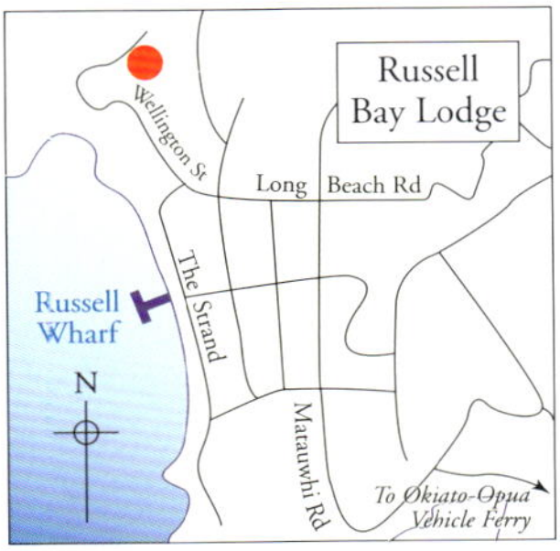

Features & Attractions

- *Stunning sea views*
- *Short walk to village centre*
- *Warm hospitality*
- *Breakfast basket each day*
- *Modern, romantic setting*
- *Luxurious suites*
- *Superb coastal walks*
- *Pristine beaches*

Romantic Russell, luxury accommodation, fabulous bay views... what more could you want! Our newly opened **Russell Bay Lodge** has an idyllic location on the slopes of Flagstaff Hill overlooking Russell Township and its beautiful harbour. It is just a short walk to waterfront cafés, shops and al fresco dining.

The purpose-designed accommodation offers king suites with mini kitchen, TV/DVD/Hifi, and own patio area. Our **Ocean Suite** also has a spa bath, and laundry facilities. We provide a sumptuous breakfast basket each day of your stay. Perfect for a honeymoon, or special holiday treat. If you are planning a wedding in the beautiful Bay of Islands, we would be delighted to help with any or all of your special arrangements.

Select from a wide range of local activities, then later relax on our main balcony soaking up possibly the best sea views in Russell, and reflect on another memorable day in the Bay!

TEN ON ONE COUNTRY/HOMESTAY

5 Ludbrook Road, Pakaraka, Bay of Islands
Ph (09) 405 9460, Fax (09) 405 9461
Mobile 027-227 6001
email: *ten.on.one@ihug.co.nz*
www.tenonone.co.nz

Tariff : N.Z. Dollars	
Double	$115
Single	$80
Child	half price

Bedrooms	Qty
Double	4
Twin	1
Single	
Bed Size	**Qty**
Super King	
King	
Queen	4
Double	1
Single	2
Bathrooms	**Qty**
Ensuite	4
Private	1
Guest Share	

MasterCard VISA

H **Affordable & Relaxing Country - Homestay** C

Features & Attractions

- *Hearty breakfast*
- *Evening meals available*
- *Complimentary tea & coffee*
- *Laundry service/iron avail*
- *Clean towels daily*
- *Courtesy airport & coach pick-up & return*
- *Clean swimming pool*

To all our visitors a warm and friendly greeting, the Bay of Islands awaits you. Our farmlet is situated in central Bay of Islands and is fifteen minutes from most towns and attractions including Paihia, Waitangi, Russell, Kerikeri and the Hokianga region.

Our courtesy coach meets all tours, coaches and air flights. We have exciting attractions to interest you. Would you like to visit Cape Reinga (top of New Zealand), cruise to Cape Brett (Hole in the Rock), see a 2000-year-old Kauri tree (Tane Mahuta), visit famous Waitangi and treaty house, historical Russell Town, glow worm caves, waterfalls, swimming, paragliding, tramping, horse riding, fishing, golf? Hey the list goes on.

Northland can genuinely lay claim to the most compact and diverse scenic orientated wonderland in New Zealand, come and judge for yourself. For your safety our modern home meets all fire and safety regulations. Enjoy our friendly home, feed the animals, collect the eggs, relax around the swimming pool or enjoy a barbeque.

DIRECTIONS:
At intersection of SH 10 and SH 1 travel 80 mtrs north on SH 1. We are first house on left (use Ludbrook Road entrance)

Lupton Lodge

555 Ngunguru Road, Glenbervie, RD 3, Whangarei
Ph (09) 437 2989, Fax (09) 437 2987
email: *info@luptonlodge.co.nz*
www.luptonlodge.co.nz

Tariff : N.Z. Dollars	
Double	$115-185
Single	$99-125
Child	–

Bedrooms	Qty
Double	3
Twin	
Single	
Bed Size	**Qty**
Super King	
King	2
Queen	1
Double	
Single	
Bathrooms	**Qty**
Ensuite	3
Private	
Guest Share	

VISA MasterCard

Contemporary Luxurious Boutique B & B Accommodation

DIRECTIONS:
5.5 km east of the Whangarei Falls turn-off on road between Whangarei and the Tutukaka Coast.

Features & Attractions

- *Tranquil, rural setting*
- *Chef-cooked breakfast/dinner*
- *Large swimming pool*
- *Young, professional hosts*
- *Tutukaka Coast beaches*
- *Poor Knights diving*
- *Whangarei art galleries*
- *1 hour to Bay of Islands*

Welcome to **Lupton Lodge** – a brand new concept in affordable luxury hosted accommodation for modern travellers. The character of an 1896 historic villa, set in picturesque dry-stone walled farmland, has been combined with contemporary uncluttered décor, superior ensuite rooms and extensive guest facilities. Luxurious beds and bathrobes, plunger coffee and DVD players come in all rooms. Indulge in a glass of NZ wine and a game of snooker in the guest lounge before a relaxed restaurant-style dinner on one of the verandas overlooking the pool and sub-tropical gardens. **Lupton Lodge** has been designed with privacy and relaxation in mind. Enjoy the abundance of activities available in the local area, or just sit back and unwind. Gourmet à la carte breakfast, wireless internet, 11am check-out and informed travel advice are complimentary. Only 10 minutes from Whangarei, but a world apart – Glenbervie is 2½ hours from Auckland and ideally located for exploring Northland. Visit Whangarei Falls, the spectacular Tutukaka Coast or the Bay of Islands. Scuba diving, Zion Wildlife Gardens tours, restaurant reservations can be arranged. **Visit our website to book online.**

Glenaldan Lodge Bed & Breakfast

538 Three Mile Bush Road, Kamo, Whangarei
Ph (09) 435 3917, Fax (09) 430 3986
Mobile 027-272 7331
email: *info@glenaldanlodge.co.nz*
www.glenaldanlodge.co.nz

Tariff : N.Z. Dollars	
Double	$150-180
Single	$100-120
Child	

Bedrooms	Qty
Double	3
Twin	
Single	
Bed Size	**Qty**
Super King	
King	
Queen	2
Double	
Single	1
Bathrooms	**Qty**
Ensuite	2
Private	1
Guest Share	

Bed & Breakfast

Features & Attractions

- *Private, peaceful setting*
- *Beautiful gardens*
- *Fruit from the orchard*
- *NZ art on display*
- *Historic stone walls*
- *Local attractions*
- *45 min. Bay of Islands*
- *No stairs for guests*

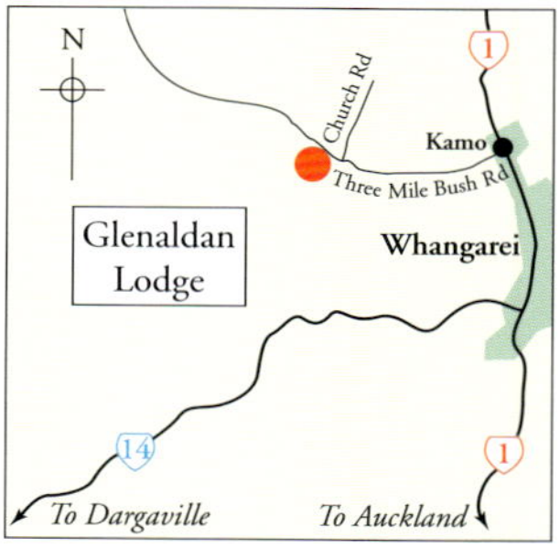

Relax in spacious surroundings. Enjoy the peace and tranquility of our beautiful gardens, where you can also enjoy a game of pétanque or garden chess, all set on four acres. Historical stone walls provide the boundary fences. We provide well appointed rooms, each queen room is well equipped with an LCD television, radio clock, electric blanket and has its own garden entrance. As well, there's a guest lounge and two kitchenettes for your convenience. There is also a large entertainment/theatre room for your enjoyment. Enjoy your breakfast either on the patio outside your room, in either of the guest areas or we can deliver it to your bedside. There are no stairs to worry about at **Glenaldan Lodge.** All guest facilities are easily accessible. Transport can be arranged to any of the nearby restaurants or bars. We are only 45 minutes drive from the Bay of Islands, only minutes from the Lion Park.
In our area you can enjoy bush walks, a game of golf at the local public golf course or just enjoy the sights in Whangarei itself.

Luxury at the Lake Retreat

18 Takahe Street, Tikipunga, Whangarei.
Ph (09) 437 1989, Fax (09) 437 1989
Mobile 027-444 1174
email: *relax@lakeluxuryretreat.co.nz*
www.lakeluxuryretreat.co.nz

Tariff : N.Z. Dollars	
Double	$100-195
Single	
Child	

Bedrooms	Qty
Double	1
Twin	1
Single	
Bed Size	**Qty**
Super King/Twin	1
King	
Queen	1
Double	
Single	
Bathrooms	**Qty**
Ensuite	1
Private	1
Guest Share	

Bed & Breakfast and Self-contained Luxury Retreat

DIRECTIONS:
5km from city centre, north eastwards to Whangarei Falls/Tutukaka.
Please phone for further directions.

Features & Attractions

- *Quiet, unique, secure*
- *Photogenic private lake*
- *Personal gas barbeque*
- *Undercover parking*
- *5min. city town basin*
- *Warm, subtropical climate*
- *Whangarei Falls & Kauris*
- *Safe , sandy beaches*

Sub-tropical Whangarei, for a more personal experience. The perfect base for exploring Northland's natural beauty. One hour to The Bay of Islands. Experience our great bush walks, including the Whangarei Falls and Kauri, beautiful, safe beaches, diving, fishing, choice of 4 golf courses, and award winning restaurants. Our picturesque, private lake, surrounded by beautiful New Zealand native bush, including the silver fern, is just minutes from three supermarkets. **Your Retreat** is self-contained and separate, ideal for the discerning traveller, honeymooners, or for a romantic weekend with that special person in your life. Quiet, spacious accommodation, comfortable bedding, modern quality furniture, cooking facilities, personal gas barbeque and all the comforts of home. Our special self-catering breakfast with 12 noon checkout gives you time to relax and plan the day's activities. **Our Bed & Breakfast** has its own entrance and balcony overlooking the lake, twin beds or super-king, private bathroom, toilet, and TV. A continental breakfast with fresh fruit is included in the tariff, with check out at 10am. For personal and friendly service, come stay with us, you will be glad you did.

PARKHILL

7d Dent Street, Whangarei
Phone (09) 438 8977, Fax (09) 438 8977
Mobile 021-074 1173
email: *parkhilltownbasin@xtra.co.nz*
www.parkhillwhangarei.co.nz

Tariff : N.Z. Dollars	
Double	$120-155
Single	$115
Child	

Bedrooms	Qty
Double	1
Twin	1
Single	

Bed Size	Qty
Super King	
King	1
Queen	
Double	
Single	2

Bathrooms	Qty
Ensuite	2
Private	
Guest Share	

Luxury Bed & Breakfast
Spectacular Harbour Views

Features & Attractions

- *1 min walk to city shopping*
- *2 min Quayside, Town Basin*
- *Quality restaurants nearby*
- *Marina & harbour views*
- *Laundry facilities*
- *Corporate guests welcome*

Discover the comforts and hospitality of our new accommodation, located in the Central Business District. Stroll to the shops and award-winning restaurants. Enjoy spectacular views of the river and the Town Basin. The yachts on their moorings by day and the lights sparkling at night make this a superb location. We have two luxuriously furnished rooms with spacious ensuites (one ensuite with spa bath). All rooms are designated smoke-free. Enjoy the luxury of in-room television, robes and extra toiletries. Exclusive guest facilities include a large lounge with kitchen, which opens onto a deck and garden with stunning views of the harbour. A scrumptious continental breakfast is included in the rates, although a cooked breakfast can be requested. Your experienced hosts, Leo and Lenore Malone, offer a 'home away from home' with kiwi hospitality.

DIRECTIONS:
From north or south follow signage to 'Town Basin & Quayside'.
We are on the corner of Dent St./Rathbone St./Hatea Drive.

YOUR HOSTS: **Braia and Paul Larsen** Ph: (09) 436 5529 ***Whangarei***

CHANNEL VISTA

254 Beach Road, Onerahi, Whangarei, Northland
Ph (09) 436 5529, Fax (09) 436 5529
Mobile 027-448 8507
email: *channelvista@igrin.co.nz*
www.bnbwhangarei.co.nz

Features & Attractions

- *Only 1 hour to Bay of Islands*
- *Many golf courses handy*
- *Restaurants, shopping 5 min*
- *Many interesting walks*
- *Sandy, safe beaches nearby*
- *Top diving, fishing 30 min*

$	
Double	$140-170
Single	$100
Child	

VISA MasterCard eftpos

Harbourside Bed & Breakfast

Bedrooms	Qty
Double	2
Twin	
Single	
Bed Size	**Qty**
King	
Queen	2
Double	
Single	
Bathrooms	**Qty**
Ensuite	2
Private	
Guest Share	

Channel Vista is a modern purpose-built deluxe self-contained Bed & Breakfast situated on the interesting Whangarei Harbour, nine kilometres from central Whangarei and very handy to the Onerahi shopping complex and sports centres (golf, swimming, walks, pools) and only an easy five minute walk along the waterfront to a top restaurant. Bay of Islands, Kerikeri and the West Coast are only one hour away. Poor Knight's Diving and deep sea fishing at Tutukaka is thirty minutes away and lovely Whangarei Heads beaches are so handy. You can see, we are a very handy base for your Northland Holiday. Both self-contained units have lovely decks where you can sit and relax or view the garden or watch superb sunsets.

DIRECTIONS: Follow signs to Onerahi Airport, go past gates to Pah Road, go down Pah Road to roundabout and turn left into Beach Road - No 254.

YOUR HOSTS: **Betty and Snow Campbell** Free Ph 0800 155 896 ***Parua Bay - Whangarei***

TARAUNUI FARMSTAYS

388 Taraunui Rd, RD 1, Onerahi, Parua Bay, Whangarei
Ph (09) 436 5896, Fax (09) 436 5895
email: *b.campbell@xtra.co.nz*
www.taraunuifarmstays.co.nz

Features & Attractions

- *See the sheepdogs working*
- *Kayak the estuary*
- *Many lovely walks*
- *Surf & swimming beaches*
- *Fishing/diving charters*
- *Golf course nearby*

Bed & Breakfast/Farmstay Self-contained Accommodation

$	
Double	$100
Single	$80
Child	$20

Enjoy peace and privacy at **Taraunui**, which lies at the head of the Pataua Estuary, just twenty minutes from Whangarei. See the sheepdogs working, explore the beautiful estuary by kayak or dinghy, enjoy the many walks set amidst the spectacular scenery of the Whangarei Heads area, or just relax by the pool.

Fishing, surfing, boating, diving and golf are popular activities, with many beaches, boat ramps, golf course, art galleries and cafés nearby. Fishing trips arranged on request. The self-contained, wheelchair friendly unit sleeps four and has a well-equipped kitchen, television, super king or single beds and wet area bathroom. Continental breakfast is available and children and well-behaved pets are welcome. Our background is farming and teaching and our interests include outdoor activities, boating, tennis, reading and music.

We look forward to welcoming you to our piece of paradise.

Bedrooms	Qty
Double	1
Twin	
Single	
Bed Size	**Qty**
King	
Queen	
Double	1
Single	2
Bathrooms	**Qty**
Ensuite	1
Private	
Guest Share	

ARCHES ON TREE TOP LODGE

396-398 Owhiwa Rd, Parua Bay, Whangarei
Ph (09) 436 1103
Mobile 027-449 2475
email: *chillout@treetoplodge.co.nz*
www.treetoplodge.co.nz

Tariff : N.Z. Dollars	
Double	$120-160
Single	$100-120
Child/Extra	$30

Bedrooms	Qty
Double	3
Twin	1
Single	
Bed Size	**Qty**
Super King	3
King	
Queen	
Double	
Single	3-9
Bathrooms	**Qty**
Ensuite	1
Private	
Guest Share	1

Delightful Country Retreat
Interactive Farm Experience

Features & Attractions

- *Separate guest dwelling*
- *Peace and privacy assured*
- *Romantic hideaway or...*
- *Spacious family retreat*
- *Free laundry facilities*
- *Evening meals as required*
- *Internet access at office*
- *Inspections welcome*

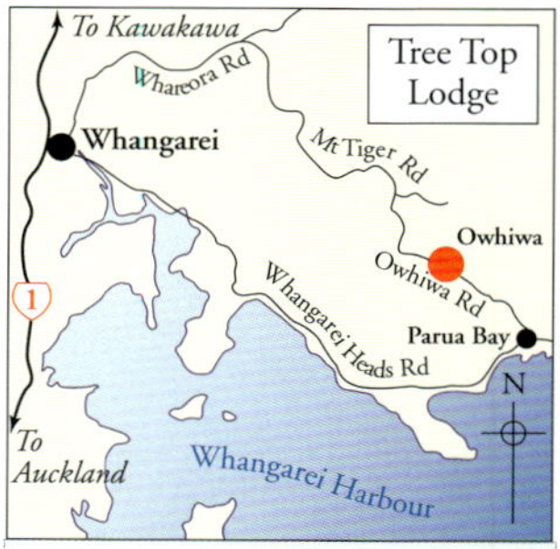

Directions: Follow Whangarei Heads Rd 1.5km past the Parua Bay Tavern, turn left onto Owhiwa Rd. 4 km on the right hand side, **Arches on Tree Top Lodge** awaits you.

Situated on Ridgeland Farm Estate's South Suffolk Sheep Stud, on the scenic route, Whangarei Heads to Tutukaka; this comfortable accommodation provides a welcome stop between Auckland and the Bay of Islands, and a delightful home-base for your Northern explorations. All upper rooms open to covered deck and stunning views over 100 acres – pasturelands and native forest reserves to the dramatic outcrops of Mt Manaia and the sea. Cafés, restaurant, tavern, boat ramp and mini market 6 min. away, 4 golf courses 9 – 30 min. Diving, fishing, tramping and beaches Whangarei Heads and Tutukaka.

Once you have settled in, choose a DVD from our collection – don one of our cosy bathrobes and enjoy your complimentary wine on the deck. At bedtime snuggle into your soft feather pillows, securely enjoying all the comforts of home. Your pantry tempts with fresh breakfast provisions – plus ample stock of teas, coffees and miscellaneous goodies. Lower floor ensuite – wheel chair friendly. 300 metres from owner's residence.

PARUA HOUSE

Parua Bay, Whangarei Heads Road, RD 4, Whangarei
Ph (09) 436 5855
Mobile 021-186 5002
email: *paruahomestay@clear.net.nz*
www.paruahomestay.homestead.com

@ home NEW ZEALAND

Tariff : N.Z. Dollars	
Double	$150
Single	$90
Child	half price

Bedrooms	Qty
Double	2
Twin	1
Single	1
Bed Size	**Qty**
Super King	
King	
Queen	2
Double	
Single	3
Bathrooms	**Qty**
Ensuite	2
Private	1
Guest Share	

MasterCard VISA

Farmstay - Boutique Accommodation

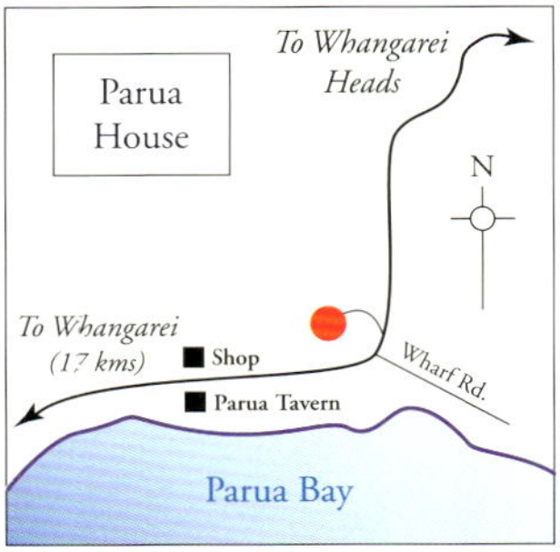

Features & Attractions

- *Outstanding panoramic views*
- *Peaceful setting*
- *Homegrown fruit & produce*
- *Golf course nearby*
- *Superb swimming beaches*
- *Spa pool*
- *Featured on TV: "Ansett NZ-Time of Your Life" & "Corban's Taste NZ"*

Parua House is a classical colonial house built in 1883, comfortably restored and occupying an elevated site with panoramic views of Parua Bay and Whangarei harbour. The property covers 29 hectares of farmland with lush valleys leading into steep slopes of native bush. Two protected reserves on the property are rich in a variety of native trees (including kauri) and native birds abound. Guests are welcome to explore the farm, milk the Jersey house cow, track through the bush beside the Kohinui stream, explore the olive grove, sub-tropical and orchard or just relax in the spa pool or on the verandah overlooking the marina. A safe swimming beach adjoins the farm with a short walk to a fishing jetty. Two marinas and an excellent golf course are nearby. We have travelled extensively and especially welcome overseas guests. Our interests are wide including travel, photography, patchwork-quilting and horticulture. The house is attractively appointed with antique furniture and a rare collection of spinning wheels. We enjoy good food, wine and conversation. Fresh home-grown produce is used where possible along with home-baked bread and freshly squeezed orange juice. Vegetarian food is provided if requested. A warm welcome awaits you.

Tide Song

Beasley Rd,Taiharuru Estuary, Whangarei, Northland
Ph (09) 436 1959
Mobile 027 636 5888
email: *stay@tidesong.co.nz*
www.tidesong.co.nz

Features & Attractions

- *Quiet privacy*
- *Spectacular walks*
- *Bush bath*
- *Bush setting - Fishing*
- *Choice of ocean beaches*
- *Safe estuary for boating*

Bed & Breakfast Homestay
Self-contained Accom. optional

$	
Double	$110
Single	$75
Child	½

From Whangarei drive east for twenty-five minutes to our eight acres on the Taiharuru Estuary. With a bush and seaside setting, there is a small jetty, and a variety of small craft to use on the estuary. Spots for fishing and shellfish are close. There is a variety of wonderful walks, with Pacific views and peaks, available to differing levels of fitness. A choice of ocean and surf beaches ten to twenty minutes away. We have a farming and teaching background and there's a small flock of sheep. We are interested in sailing, cycling, conservation, gardening, home-cooking and music. We enjoy having company and looking after guests. Our accommodation is a separate upstairs two bedroom flat with ensuite, kitchen and television. Also a downstairs bedroom with ensuite and TV. We can provide extra home-cooked meals if you wish; or cafés & restaurant are ten minutes away. Looking forward to showing you Northland hospitality.

Members of Northland Sustainable Tourism Charter means that at Tidesong we are involved in caring for the environment.

Bedrooms	Qty
Double	3
Twin	
Single	
Bed Size	**Qty**
King	
Queen	3
Double	
Single	1
Bathrooms	**Qty**
Ensuite	1
Private	1
Guest Share	

Appin Cottage

"Appin" 2432 Whangarei Heads Road,
McKenzie Bay, RD 4 Whangarei
Ph (09) 434 0819 Mobile 021-023 43114
email: *dougiechowns@orcon.net.nz*
www.aotea.co.nz/NZ_Art/Chowns

Features & Attractions

- *Peaceful setting*
- *Superb mountain seascapes*
- *Fine art & Celtic music*
- *Safe, private swimming*
- *Hot bread with breakfast*
- *Featured NZ Geographic*

VISA MasterCard

$	
Double	$130
Single	
Child	n/a

Self-contained Cottage with Continental Breakfast

Bedrooms	Qty
Double	1
Twin	
Single	
Bed Size	**Qty**
King	
Queen	
Double	1
Single	
Bathrooms	**Qty**
Ensuite	
Private	1
Guest Share	

Near Whangarei, below craggy peaks of Mt Manaia, this self-contained cottage is in the subtropical garden of McKenzie Homestead, settled 1857 by Nova Scotians from St Anns, Cape Breton. Between palms, our old homestead fronts a secluded white, sandy beach and 200 metres of our pohutukawa-fringed shoreline. The cottage is fully furnished and almost new – you will sleep in comfort to the sound of the sea. Mt Manaia and other magnificent ranges offer many accessed walkways: Smugglers Bay, Peach Cove, Bream Head, Mt Aubrey and Ocean Beach. Sprats, shellfish, snapper or marlin, boats, canoes and music are part of our lifestyle and well known to visitors from the Western Isles of Scotland and Cape Breton. Gaelic and Spanish spoken. Previously resident in UK, Portugal, Spain and the Caribbean before 34 years in McKenzie Bay we live as crofters in the South Pacific. We welcome you to enjoy the sea for breakfast and share our paradise.

DIRECTIONS:
From State Highway 1 follow signs to Whangarei Heads. 31 km from Town Basin yachts **Appin** McKenzie Bay is on right beyond mountain and Taurikura.

Bayfields Farmstay

Pataua South Road, RD 1, Onerahi, Whangarei
Ph (09) 436 5653, Fax (09) 436 5653
Mobile 025-242 4504
email: *bayfields@xtra.co.nz*

Features & Attractions

- *Private unit in garden*
- *Pines Golf Club 5 min*
- *Fishing, diving charters*
- *Bush & coastal walkways*
- *Whangarei 20 min away*
- *Safe swim beaches 5 min*

$	
Double	$100
Single	$80
Child	

Dairy Farmstay Self-contained Cottage

Bedrooms	Qty
Double	1
Twin	
Single	
Bed Size	**Qty**
King	
Queen	1
Double	
Single	
Bathrooms	**Qty**
Ensuite	
Private	1
Guest Share	

We only have one unit so can guarantee you privacy and personal service. A generous continental style breakfast basket with home baking can be delivered to your unit when you arrive, so eat breakfast at your leisure. Sleep in or rise early, it is your choice. Email and laundry facilities. Complimentary tea and coffee. Russell is interested in fishing and we can arrange trips with local charter boats for fishing and diving. Angela loves patchwork so can take you to the local club meetings and the best shops in Whangarei for supplies.
Our home is a working dairy farm of 400 acres, milking 300 cows. You can try milking and other farm activities, or just relax with a book on your deck overlooking the farm. The separate bedroom has a queen size bed and a double sofa bed in the lounge. Evening meals by arrangement.
Non smokers please.

Whangarei ▶ YOUR HOSTS: Diane and Mike James Ph (09) 434 6399

JUNIPER HOUSE

49 Proctor Road, Maungatapere
Whangarei RD9
Ph (09) 434 6399, Fax (09) 434 6399
Mobile 027-422 4498
email: *diane.james@xtra.co.nz*

Features & Attractions

- *Art, craft, cafés*
- *Golf courses handy*
- *Fishing, sailing, charters*
- *Rural tranquility*
- *Guests tea & coffee facility*
- *Home-cooking*

Bed & Breakfast Homestay

Double	$120-135
Single	$60-70
Child	

Juniper House is a comfortable welcoming home, surrounded by a young avocado orchard. Relax in the extensive grounds, enjoy a game of tennis or swim in our saltwater pool. For the snooker enthusiast we have a full size billiard table, or simply relax and enjoy the peace and quiet. We are an easy fifteen-minute drive from the museum and the kiwi house, golf courses, cafés, galleries and the Whangarei yacht basin. We offer a full breakfast, dinner and drinks by arrangement. Our interests include sailing, fishing, classic cars and decorative art. You may like to join us for happy hour and a BBQ on Friday or Saturday, or for a traditional Christmas, when the house is dressed in its best! We have an orchard cat.

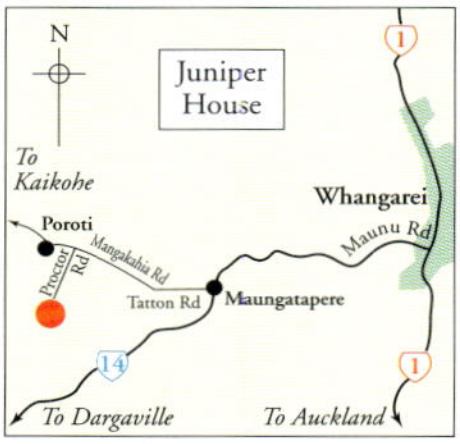

Bedrooms	Qty
Double	2
Twin	1
Single	
Bed Size	**Qty**
King	
Queen	1
Double	1
Single	2
Bathrooms	**Qty**
Ensuite	1
Private	
Guest Share	1

Otaika - Whangarei ▶ YOUR HOSTS: Minnie and George Whitehead Ph: (09) 434 7554

OWAITOKAMOTU

727 Otaika Valley Road, Maungatapere, Whangarei
(*Postal:* PO Box 6067, Otaika, Whangarei)
Ph (09) 434 7554, Mobile 025-806 954
email: *minniegeorge@xtra.co.nz*

Features & Attractions

- *Golf course, Kiwi House*
- *Museum & homestead*
- *Featured Whangarei garden*
- *Beaches, diving, fishing*
- *1 hour Bay of Islands*
- *1 hour Matakohe Museum*

Bed & Breakfast Homestay

Double	$85-100
Single	$65
Child	neg

Come and enjoy the tranquility of **Owaitokamotu**, 'Place of Water', with magnificent rocks in all shapes and sizes. Pristine native bush awaits your rambling walks. **Owaitokamotu** is set in ten acres with easy contoured and newly created gardens, featuring ponds, bridges, archways, windmill and 1850's style shanty. Our newly built home is wheelchair-friendly. All bedrooms have private access from exterior and television, tea & coffee facilities and home-baked cookies. A wide verandah offers relaxation. Join us for a three course evening meal ($25 pp). Restaurants are nearby. Our interests are travel, wood carving and creating our garden. We are smoke-free indoors. Laundry facilities are available. A very warm welcome awaits you.

Bedrooms	Qty
Double	2
Twin	1
Single	
Bed Size	**Qty**
King	
Queen	2
Double	
King Single	2
Bathrooms	**Qty**
Ensuite	
Private	1
Guest Share	1

Kauri House Lodge

Bowen Street, PO Box 382, Dargaville
Ph (09) 439 8082, Fax (09) 439 8082
Mobile 027-454 7769
email: *kaurihouse@xtra.co.nz*

Tariff : N.Z. Dollars	
Double	$200-275
Single	$200
Child	

Bedrooms	Qty
Double	2
Twin	1
Single	
Bed Size	**Qty**
Super King	1
King	1
Queen	
Double	
King/Single	1
Bathrooms	**Qty**
Ensuite	3
Private	
Guest Share	

Luxury Historic Bed & Breakfast

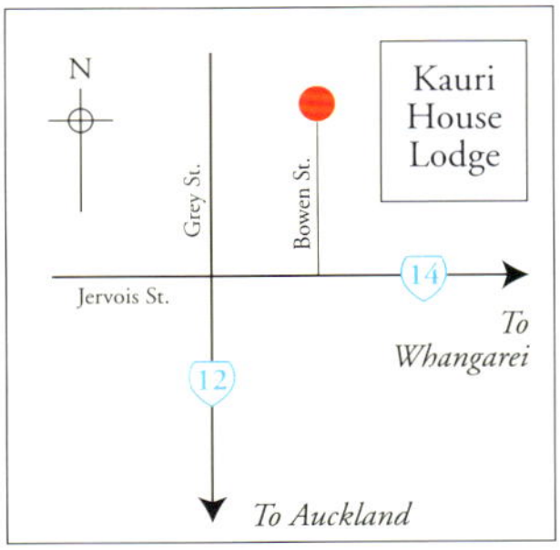

Features & Attractions

- *Kauri villa over 5000 sq ft*
- *Farm bush walk included*
- *Hearty breakfast*
- *Summer swimming pool*
- *Peaceful & tranquil location*
- *Beach, lakes & bush walks*
- *Historic homestead*
- *Close to Waipoua Forest*

Original features of this 1880s style villa include the detailed verandah balustrading, stained glass, pressed ceilings, sash windows and native Kauri panelling. Completed in 1910 by a leading bushman as a spacious family residence, **Kauri House** now offers three private ensuite guest rooms and three lounge rooms – a billiard room, library and television lounge – furnished with antiques. Only three kilometres from the township of Dargaville, with many nice restaurants. **Kauri House** is set in three hectares of garden with abundant native birdlife including fantails, wood pigeons and seasonal tui. A swimming pool provides relaxation and exercise in summer only. Nearby is Doug's forty hectare farm on which he runs steers and donkeys. This land includes sixteen hectares of protected native bush.

"Perfect accommodation, good host, these things make holidays worthwhile" *Frank & Annie, Holland*
"Fantastic house and timber furniture, best we've seen" *Gary & Trish, Australia*

Tangowahine - Dargaville ▶ YOUR HOSTS: Pauline and Hugh Rose Ph: (09) 439 1570

Tangowahine Farmstay

1078 Tangowahine Valley Rd, RD 2, Dargaville
Ph (09) 439 1570, Fax (09) 439 5253
Mobile 027-439 1570
email: *holiday@tangowahine.co.nz*
www.tangowahine.co.nz

Features & Attractions

- *Native forest/farm tours*
- *Giant kauri snails*
- *Bird lovers' paradise*
- *Centrally located in Northland*
- *Hot spa in bush*
- *Dinner by arrangement*

$	
Double	$120-180
Single	$100-120
Child	

VISA · SC · **Self-Contained Farmstay Bed & Breakfast** · F

Bedrooms	Qty
Double	3
Twin	
Single	1
Bed Size	**Qty**
Super King	1
Queen	3
King Single	2
Single	1
Bathrooms	**Qty**
Ensuite	2
Private	1
Guest Share	1

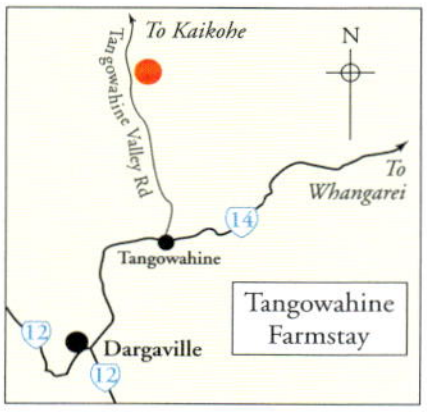

Relax in a haven of tranquility – a new, purpose-built facility on a 250 acre farm central to Dargaville, Kaikohe and Whangarei. The ideal base for a Northland holiday, it's close to Kaiiwi Lakes, Trounson Kauri Park, Baylys Beach;ideally located for day trips to the Bay of Islands, Waipoua Forest and the Matakohe Museum. Experience bushwalks, waterfalls, streams and abundant birdlife at **Tangowahine** – literally 'place to take a woman'. Pamper yourself in the self-contained **Taraire Cottage** and enjoy a hot soak in total privacy in our wood-fired bush spa. Relax in the **Tutamoe Suite** with views to Mt Tutamoe and the private lakeside garden spa.

DIRECTIONS: Take SH 14 west from Whangarei (40 km) or east from Dargaville (10 km). At Tangowahine turn north into Tangowahine Valley Road. **Tangowahine Farm** is on the right, 10 km from the turn-off. Look for the bright red letterbox.

Te Kopuru-Northland ▶ YOUR HOSTS: Annette Scarfe Ph (09) 439 5946

Lilac Villa

847B Pouto Rd, Te Kopuru, Poutu Peninsula, Northland
Ph (09) 439 5946, Fax (09) 439 5946
Mobile 027-678 3190
email: *lilacvilla@ihug.co.nz*
www.luxurycountrystay.co.nz

Features & Attractions

- *Picnics on request*
- *Spring- or rainwater*
- *Massage/facials available*
- *Organic or local grown produce*
- *Feather or goosedown quilts*
- *Easy drive forests or museums*

VISA · MasterCard · BB · **Countrystay** · C

$	
Double	$115-125
Single	$90
Child	

Lilac Villa is nestled under the hill at Te Kopuru with a view of the Northern Wairoa River. Built in 1879 it has a 'Historic Places' grade 2 listing. It has been restored and now invites you to relax for a few days. Trips to see kiwi, giant weta, local farms, colonial museums and golf can be arranged. Breakfast includes home-made breads, jams and eggs from our own chickens. Meals on request, using organic or locally grown produce where possible. Goosedown / feather duvets are provided for your comfort (alternatives available). While you are here, book a facial with **'Sensé'** products or a massage. Annette and animals look forward to welcoming you.

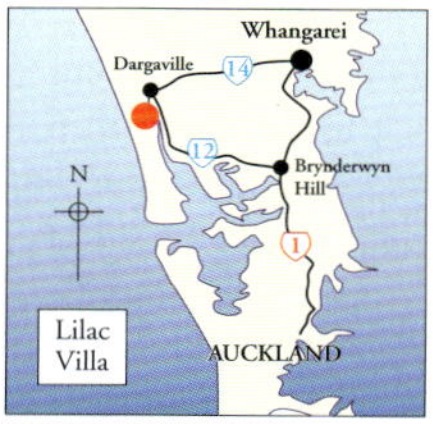

DIRECTIONS: Main road through Dargaville past 'Caltex' station, over Kaihu River bridge, 1st right after bridge, follow signs to Te Kopuru. Lilac Villa is visible after Aratapu Tavern.

Bedrooms	Qty
Double	1
Double/Twin	1
Twin King	1
Bed Size	**Qty**
King/Twin	1
Queen	
Double	1
Single Twin	2
Bathrooms	**Qty**
Ensuite	
Private	1
Guest Share	1

Zany's Haven B & B

298/11 Cove Road, RD2, Waipu, Northland
Ph (09) 432 1517
Mobile 027-658 5217
email: *corralieb@yahoo.com*
www.zanyhaven.co.nz/www.zanyhaven.com

Features & Attractions

- *Peaceful and quiet*
- *Panoramic views*
- *Restaurants/ shops 3km*
- *Walking distance to beach, river*
- *On Twin Coast Discovery Route*
- *Close to horsetrekking, golf, caving*

$	
Double	$150
Single	$120
Child	

Coastal and Scenic Ensuite Accommodation

Bedrooms	Qty
Double	2
Twin	1
Single	
Bed Size	**Qty**
King	1
Queen	
Double	1
Single	2
Bathrooms	**Qty**
Ensuite	3
Private	
Guest Share	

Our new Bed & Breakfast is situated on a quiet and peaceful hill overlooking beautiful Bream Bay beaches in northern New Zealand, thirty minutes south of Whangarei. Only two hours north of Auckland. On the 'Twin Coast Discovery Route' off SH1. We are located halfway between Waipu Centre and Waipu Cove with fabulous views of Bream Bay, the Waipu River Estuary, Whangarei Heads and Hen and Chicken Islands.

Within easy reach of beaches, walks and tourist amenities such as golf, kayaking, horse-trekking – good for re-charging the batteries and recovering from jet-lag.

We offer two double/twin ensuite rooms and one self-contained flat. Not suitable for children.

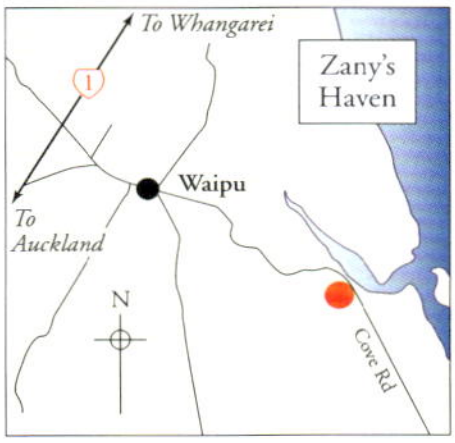

Flower Haven

53 St Ann Road, Waipu Cove, Northland 0582
Ph (09) 432 0421, Mobile 027-432 0050
email: *beds@flowerhaven.com*
www.flowerhaven.com

Features & Attractions

- *Panoramic ocean view*
- *Garden retreat*
- *Surf patrol in summer*
- *Extensive beach walks*
- *Walk to bird sanctuary*
- *Golf courses & fishing*

$	
Double	$116-136
Single	–
Child	–

Bed & Breakfast Self-contained Accom.

Bedrooms	Qty
Double	2
Twin	
Single	
Bed Size	**Qty**
King	
Queen	
Double	2
Single	
Bathrooms	**Qty**
Ensuite	
Private	1
Guest Share	

At **Flower Haven** we enjoy an elevated position, views of Bream Bay and sleeping to the sound of the surf. We are retired, with interests in genealogy, meeting people and gardening and developing the grounds as a garden retreat. Our accommodation is a self-contained downstairs two bedroom apartment with separate access, fridge/freezer, stove, microwave, washing machine, TV, radio and tiled bathroom. Linen, duvets, blankets and bath towels are provided. We are a 5 min. walk to restaurant, shop, rocks and sandy surf beach and are near many places of interest; bird sanctuaries, museums, golf courses, horse-riding treks, fishing trips, limestone caves, walking tracks, oil refinery visitors centre. Auckland is 90, Whangarei 35 min. away. Visit our website for more details.

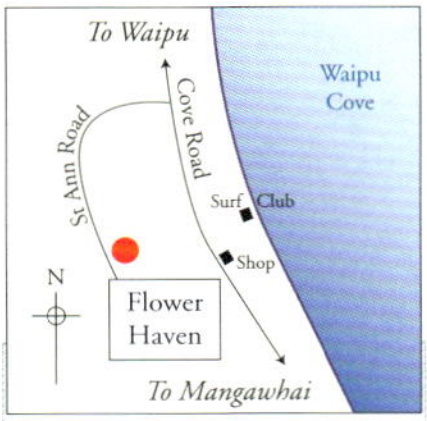

DIRECTIONS: 8 km south of Waipu on Cove Road, right into St Ann Road, **Flower Haven** is the last house on left.

Mangawhai Lodge

"A ROOM WITH A VIEW"

4 Heather Street, Mangawhai Heads, Northland
Ph (09) 431 5311, Fax (09) 431 5312
email: *mlodge@xtra.co.nz*
www.seaviewlodge.co.nz

Tariff : N.Z. Dollars	
Double	$155-175
Single	$135-155
Child	

Bedrooms	Qty
Double	4
Twin	
Single	
Bed Size	**Qty**
Super King	
King	3
Queen	1
Double	
King Single	3/6
Bathrooms	**Qty**
Ensuite	3
Private	1
Guest Share	

Boutique Bed & Breakfast Inn

Features & Attractions

- *Beaches & walkways*
- *Fishing & water activities*
- *Ideal for couples & groups*
- *Arts, crafts & wine trails*
- *Adjacent to championship golf course*
- *2 hours to international airport*
- *Off-street parking*
- *Walk to shops & cafés*

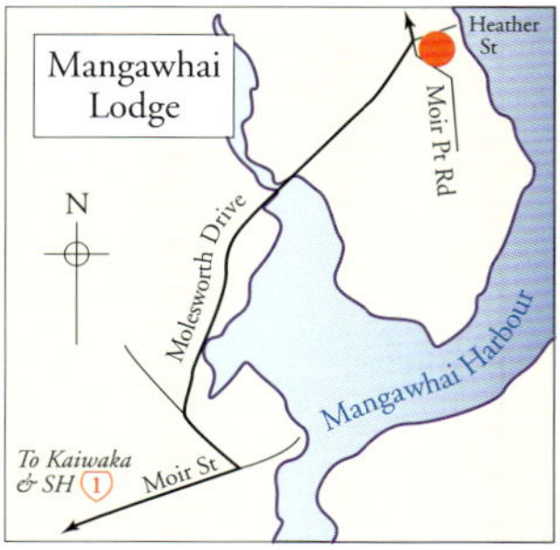

Indulge, escape to the tranquility and magic of **Mangawhai Lodge**. Midway between Auckland Airport and the Bay of Islands, **Mangawhai Lodge** offers the perfect beach retreat for rest and relaxation or base to discover the treasures of Northland. Spectacular sea and island views of the Hauraki Gulf, Bream Bay, and white sandy beaches of Mangawhai make **Mangawhai Lodge** the ultimate "room with a view". The self-contained apartment and three stylish guest rooms open onto wrap-around verandahs. Spend your days on the championship golf course, explore beaches and walkways, curl up reading or watch the boats sail by. A licensed café and championship golf course are adjacent, harbour access 400m. Sleep to the sound of the sea, awake to sumptuous cooked and continental breakfast. Having travelled extensively, we look forward to ensuring your stay is enjoyable and relaxing.

Bookings and two-day stay recommended.

ZENFORD LODGE

1034 Cove Rd, Langs Beach, RD 2, Waipu
Ph (09) 432 0757, Fax (09) 432 0757
Mobile 021-400 383
email: *enquiries@zenfordlodge.co.nz*
www.zenfordlodge.co.nz

Tariff : N.Z. Dollars	
Double	$140-240
Single	$120-190
Child	enquire

Bedrooms	Qty
Double	4
Twin	1
Single	
Bed Size	**Qty**
Super King	1
King	2
Queen	1
Double	
King/Single	1
Bathrooms	**Qty**
Ensuite	3
Private	1
Guest Share	

VISA MasterCard eftpos

Bed & Breakfast Tranquility
Rural, Sea and Native Bush Views

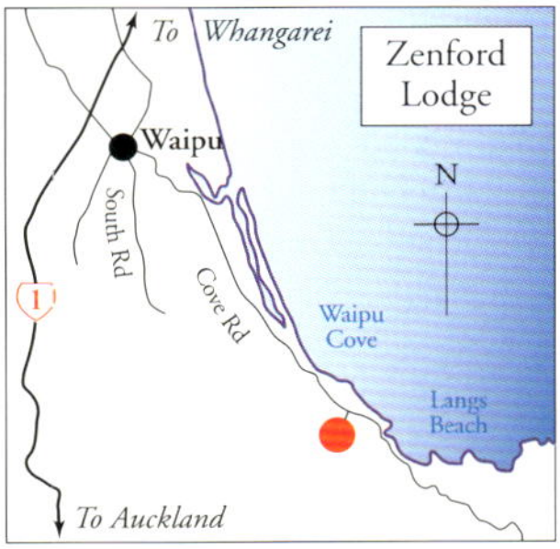

DIRECTIONS: Please phone or email for bookings and directions.

Features & Attractions

- *Warm, friendly Kiwi hospitality*
- *Multicultural décor*
- *Rural, sea and bush views*
- *Croquet and activities lawn*
- *Private native bush walk*
- *Restaurants and local arts*
- *Golf, beach, bush & water activities*
- *Midway Auckland & Bay of Islands*

Centrally located between Auckland and the Bay of Islands, **Zenford Lodge** enjoys ten acres of gardens, native bush and rural countryside with views over Bream Bay. Also centrally located between Waipu Historic Village and Mangawhai Heads, the immediate area offers two wonderful beaches, two golf courses, a variety of cafés and restaurants, art galleries, bird sanctuaries, bush walks, horse treks, water activities and much more! Your choice of accommodation offers four rooms decorated to reflect New Zealand's multicultural flavours and providing tea and coffee making facilities, complimentary snacks and refreshments, fridge, TV, hair dryer and toiletries with fine linen and bedding. All rooms have access to balconies or courtyards. Enjoy venturing out to the beaches and attractions, and after enjoying a delicious meal at one of the local restaurants, each evening returning to the serenity of **Zenford Lodge** to relax to the sound of the surf, waterfall and bird life. We look forward to meeting and sharing our home and experiences with you over a coffee or glass of wine, and helping to make your stay enjoyable and memorable.

Pahi - Paparoa

YOUR HOST: **Jenny and Hector MacKinnon** Ph: (09) 431 6689

PALM HOUSE

Pahi Road, RD 1, Paparoa
Ph (09) 431 6689, Mobile 027-688 8296
email: *palmhouse@paradise.net.nz*

VISA MasterCard

Features & Attractions

- *Close to Matakohe Museum*
- *Home cooked dinners*
- *Complimentary kayak*
- *Golf course nearby*
- *In house & s/c garden cottage*
- *Excellent restaurant nearby*

BB **On the River Bed & Breakfast** SC

$	
Double	$110
Single	$75
Child	$50

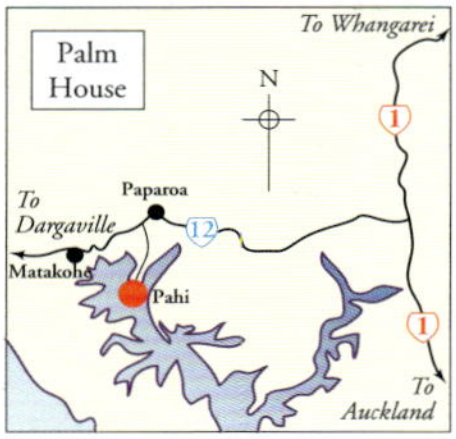

Hector and Jenny are renowned for their relaxed, friendly hospitality; delicious meals of fine local produce, accompanied by fine New Zealand wines.
Enjoy staying at peaceful Pahi. Stroll along the tideline or stand on the wharf and watch the fish jump. Just two hours from Auckland, thirteen kilometres from the famous Matakohe Museum and en route to the spectacular Kauri Forest.
Signposted on the main Highway 12, travel seven kilometres down Pahi Road and reach **Palm House.**

Bedrooms	Qty
Double	2
Twin	
Single	1
Bed Size	**Qty**
King	
Queen	2
Double	
King Single	2
Bathrooms	**Qty**
Ensuite	1
Private	
Guest Share	1

Matakohe

YOUR HOSTS: **Linda and Guy Bucchi** Ph: (09) 431 7552

PETITE PROVENCE

703c Tinopai Road, RD 1, Matakohe
Ph (09) 431 7552, Fax (09) 431 7552
email: *petite-provence@clear.net.nz*
www.petiteprovence.co.nz

@ home NEW ZEALAND

Features & Attractions

- *2 hrs from Auckland*
- *Dinner by arrangement*
- *Complimentary tea/coffee*
- *Matakohe Kauri Museum 9km*
- *Swimming, fishing - Tinopai 13km*
- *Excellent local cafés*

C **Quality Countrystay Bed & Breakfast** BB

$	
Double	$130
Single	$90
Child	

DIRECTIONS:

From Matakohe Kauri Museum drive 2 km south, turn into Tinopai Road, drive approx 7 km. 703c is on your left just before Hukatere Reserve, look for sign on roadside. Welcome to Petite Provence.

Bienvenue to **Petite Provence,** set amongst rolling farmland with neighbouring native bush and distant water views. We are 2 hours north of Auckland on the route to Waipoua Forest and 9 km south of Matakohe Kauri Museum. All rooms open onto covered decks. Guy is French, Linda is a New Zealander. Our family home in the south of France was also a homestay. Mediterranean/vegetarian/local cuisine (home-grown vegetables and local seafood when possible). Loopy is our outside dog. Advance bookings preferred.

Bedrooms	Qty
Double	2
Twin	1
Single	
Bed Size	**Qty**
King	
Queen	2
Double	
Single	2
Bathrooms	**Qty**
Ensuite	2
Private	1
Guest Share	

Ambiente

61 Golf Road, PO Box 735, Warkworth
Ph (09) 422 2529, Fax (09) 422 2529
Mobile 021-714250
email: *info@ambientematakana.co.nz*
www.ambientematakana.co.nz

Tariff : N.Z. Dollars	
Double	$195-245
Single	$165-185
Child	

Bedrooms	Qty
Double	2
Twin	
Single	
Bed Size	**Qty**
Super King	
King	
Queen	2
Double	
Single	
Bathrooms	**Qty**
Ensuite	1
Private	1
Guest Share	

Luxurious Boutique Accommodation

DIRECTIONS:
From Auckland, take State Highway 1 (SH 1) north to Warkworth. Turn right at 2nd set of traffic lights. Take left fork into Matakana Rd. Travel about 2km, turn right into Golf Rd with Golf Course on corner. **Ambiente** is on the left at No.61.

Features & Attractions

- *Boating nearby / parking available*
- *500m to 18-hole golf course*
- *Restaurants/cafés 3 min. drive*
- *Close to wineries & vineyards*
- *Close to unique shops/galleries*
- *Surfing at Omaha 10 min. drive*
- *Sandspit Ferry 15 min. drive*
- *Goat Island 20 min. drive*

Located adjacent to Warkworth 18 hole Golf Club, **Ambiente** is set in over 3ha of native bush. Guests are accommodated in a luxurious self-contained apartment or a separate self-contained bed-sit suite with private bathroom. Guests' areas feature quality funishings including silk cushions, silk bathrobes and slippers for guest use. A generous continental breakfast is provided, and apartment guests have self-catering facilities as an option. The bed-sit suite has coffee/tea making facilities. In a sunny, bush-clad situation with views down into the Matakana valley and nearby chestnut farm. **Ambiente** is situated in Matakana Coast Wine Country, providing easy access to the many vineyards, restaurants, cafés and galleries nearby.

Matakana - Warkworth ▶ YOUR HOSTS: Noreen and Norm Harvey Ph: (09) 422 7903

CASA D'ORO - MATAKANA

Whitmore Estate, 4/449 Whitmore Rd,
Matakana, RD 6, Warkworth
Ph (09) 422 7903, Fax (09) 422 7904 Mobile 021-971 562
email: *harville@clear.net.nz*
www.casadoro.co.nz

Features & Attractions

- *Separate guest entry*
- *Peaceful & secluded*
- *Tea/coffee facilities*
- *Television in guest suite*
- *Amazing views*
- *Wineries & cafés*

Boutique Accommodation
Luxury Bed & Breakfast

Double	$195
Single	$175
Child	

Bedrooms	Qty
Double	1
Twin	
Single	
Bed Size	**Qty**
King	
Queen	1
Double	
Single	
Bathrooms	**Qty**
Ensuite	1
Private	
Guest Share	

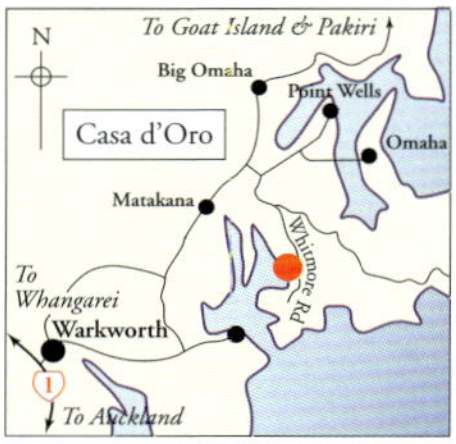

Just an hour north of Auckland. 5 minutes from Matakana Village and popular Saturday morning markets. 12 minutes to quaint riverside Warkworth. Escape, enjoy the seclusion and privacy of this little piece of paradise. Views across the waters of the Sandspit/Matakana River estuary, sunsets words cannot describe.
Set in 3 acres **Casa d'Oro Matakana** provides relaxing gracious accommodation in an exclusive guest suite. Private entrance, front terrace, parking at the door. Just minutes away, the delights of Matakana Coast Wine Country; wineries, cafes, restaurants,pottery, arts and crafts, Kawau Island/historic Mansion House. We look forward to making your stay a relaxing, enjoyable and memorable one.

Warkworth ▶ YOUR HOSTS: Shona and Julian Huxtable Ph (09) 422 2579

THE CEDAR HOUSE

Cowan Bay Road, RD 3 Warkworth
Ph (09) 422 2579
Mobile 021-238 3850
email: *thecedarhouse@xtra.co.nz*

Features & Attractions

- *40 min. from Auckland*
- *Warm, friendly hospitality*
- *Dinner available on request*
- *Luxuriously appointed*
- *Peaceful location*
- *Art, craft & wine trails*

Luxury Homestay
Panaromic Views

Double	$130-160
Single	
Child	

Bedrooms	Qty
Double	2
Twin	
Single	
Bed Size	**Qty**
King	
Queen	2
Double	
Single	
Bathrooms	**Qty**
Ensuite	2
Private	
Guest Share	

Set in 7 acres of rolling pasture and surrounded by native Bush. **The Cedar House** commands magnificent views and the panorama takes in Kawau, Little and Great Barrier Islands and The Coromandel. Relax beside the pool with a drink and a book or take a stroll around the landscaped gardens. For the more energetic, play with our pet collie Frank before enjoying a sumptious breakfast. We also offer a 3-course dinner, enhanced by the use of home-grown produce and a glass of wine.
Situated just 40 minutes from Auckland via SH1 between Puhoi and Warkworth. Nearby is the vineyard area of Matakana and the golf courses at Warkworth and Omaha. Kawau Island and the marine reserve at Goat Island are great places to visit. So come and enjoy a warm and friendly welcome.

DIRECTIONS: 8km south of Warkworth, 6km north of Puhoi. Cowan Bay Road is situated on the east side of SH1. The Cedar House is 600m along on the right.

Alegria Beautyfarm

180 Monarch Downs Way, RD 2, Warkworth
Ph (09) 422 7211, Fax (09) 422 7833
email: *alegriabeautyfarm@xtra.co.nz*
www.beautyfarm.co.nz

Tariff : N.Z. Dollars	
Double	$145-180
Single	on request
Child	12 yr. +

Bedrooms	Qty
Double	2
Twin	
Single	
Bed Size	**Qty**
Super King/Twin	1
Super King	1
King - Single	2
Queen	
Single	
Bathrooms	**Qty**
Ensuite	1
Private	1
Guest Share	

Boutique Accommodation
Beautyfarm & Pampering Place

Advance booking essential.

Features & Attractions

- *Professional face & body treatments*
- *Mouthwatering breakfast*
- *Swimming Pool*
- *Magnificent view, peaceful*
- *Wheat-free home baking*
- *Wineries, markets, art & craft close by*
- *Golf course, beaches, regional parks*
- *Diving, snorkeling at Goat Island*

A perfect Mediterranean setting provides spectacular views across the vineyards to Kawau Island and Warkworth with magnificent sunrises and sunsets. "Where the wine grapes flourish, so do good times". Claudia, Alex and Julia(14) welcome you at **Alegria Beautyfarm**, which is the ideal place to experience the good living of the Matakana Coast Wine Country and offers rare tranquillity to unwind and relax. Two tastefully appointed rooms, each with its own charm and amenities like tea/coffee making facilities, television, hair dryer and underfloor heating in the large European-style bathrooms. The ensuite room has a private entrance and patio. The other room, with private bathroom, is in the main house. In the morning your appetite will be teased with the aroma of fresh coffee brewing. Enjoy home-baked German bread, the famous home-made muesli and a mouth-watering variety of sweet and savoury delicacies from around the world. Claudia is a German-trained beauty therapist and loves to pamper you in her cosy **Beautyfarm**. Indulge in unique face and body treatments using the best ingredients. All your senses are getting spoiled, leaving you with glowing skin, more energy and calmness. German, French and Japanese spoken.

Belvedere Homestay

38 Kanuka Road, RD 2, Sandspit, Warkworth
Ph (09) 425 7201, Mobile 027-284 4771
email: *belvederehomestay@xtra.co.nz*
www.belvederehomestay.co.nz

Tariff : N.Z. Dollars	
Double	$130-145
Single	$100
Child	$45 pp

Bedrooms	Qty
Double	2
Twin	1
Single	
Bed Size	**Qty**
Super King	
King	
Queen	2
Double	
Single	2
Bathrooms	**Qty**
Ensuite	1
Private	2
Guest Share	

Quality Homestay
Bed & Breakfast

Features & Attractions

- *Panoramic sea views*
- *Air conditioned home*
- *Dinner an occasion*
- *Warm, friendly hospitality*
- *Home produce for breakfast*
- *Glassed spa pool & games room*
- *"Goat Island" marine reserve*
- *Beaches, wineries, pottery*

Warkworth Sandspit is the perfect stop going to and from the Bay of Islands. **Belvedere Homestay** is sited on top of the hill with 360° views overlooking the spit where the ferries leave for Kawau Island and Governor Grey's restored mansion. The view is awesome which you will enjoy while relaxing on our spacious decks and terraces. Stroll around our property with sunken barbeque, rose garden, orchards, lawns, native birds and bush and two lily ponds and enjoy a friendly game of pétanque (boule) or pool. Laundry facilities available. Fishing off the beach or boat, golf, tennis, swimming etc are all within seven kilometres. Our house is for your comfort and enjoyment and as Roger Hall (NZ/ English stage and televison playwright) wrote about **Belvedere Homestay**: "It is no wonder people come for one day and stay a week." Margaret's flair with cooking is a great way to relax after an adventurous day, with pre-dinner drinks and two course meal and wine ($45pp). Come and enjoy a friendly, relaxing stay with Margaret and Ron. – Good, safe parking available.

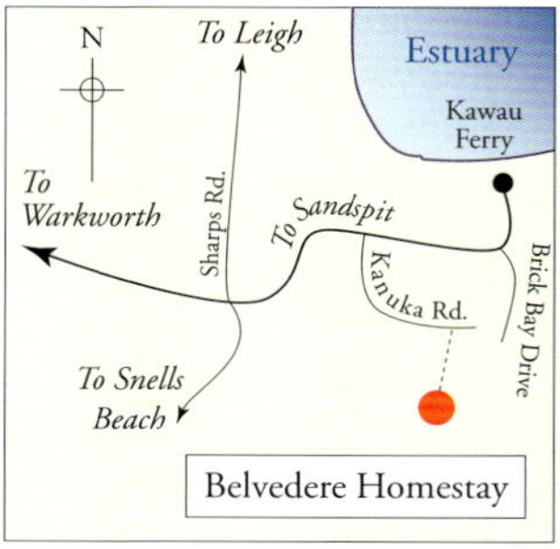

Ribbonwood B&B - Warkworth

7 Thompson Road, PO Box 444, Warkworth
Ph (09) 422 2685, Fax (09) 422 2684
email: *berris@ribbonwoodwarkworth.co.nz*
www.ribbonwoodwarkworth.co.nz

Tariff : N.Z. Dollars	
Double	$120-160
Extra pp	$30-60
Child	

Bedrooms	Qty
Double	1
Twin	1
Single	
Bed Size	**Qty**
Super King	
King	
Queen	1
Double	
Single	2
Bathrooms	**Qty**
Ensuite	
Private	1
Guest Share	

Upmarket B&B Apartment
Great Location

Features & Attractions

- *True NZ hospitality*
- *Delicious dinner & little extras*
- *Self-cater facilities*
- *3 mins to village cafés*
- *Private entrance & patio*
- *Lounge, dining, kitchen*
- *Bath, walk-in shower*
- *Country, forest, sea views*

Your own quality apartment in the heart of Warkworth – Matakana Wine Country! Here you have space, peace and privacy with every comfort. A generous living area with kitchen, dining, DVD, TV, internet facilities and NZ reference library. A large luxury bathroom with bath and walk-in shower. A deliciously comfortable queen bedroom. A twin room and sofabed are also available for extra guests. All in a delightful country setting with an expansive view to the Mahurangi Harbour. Enjoy the personal touch. A generous continental breakfast with homemade delights on your private patio; a cooked breakfast, hors d'oeuvre platter, delicious evening meal from 'The Spice Kitchen'. Local wineries and cafés are also begging to be sampled with the famous Matakana Farmers Market, golf, beaches, arts, crafts and walking all close by. We're easy to find, on the edge of historic Warkworth Village, 45 minutes north of Auckland, 2½ hours south of the Bay of Islands. We look forward to welcoming you to **Ribbon Wood**!

SHOAL WATER BED & BREAKFAST

1 Kanuka Road, Sandspit, Warkworth
Ph (09) 425 0566, Fax (09) 425 0567
Mobile 021-126 0081
email: *shoalwater@xtra.co.nz*
www.shoalwater.co.nz

Tariff : N.Z. Dollars	
Double	$150-180
Single	$140-170
Child	$50

Bedrooms	Qty
Double	2
Twin	
Single	
Bed Size	**Qty**
Super King	
King	
Queen	2
Double	
Single	
Bathrooms	**Qty**
Ensuite	2
Private	
Guest Share	

LA

Luxury Self-contained Bed & Breakfast

SC

Features & Attractions

- *45 min north of Auckland*
- *Golf courses, beaches, regional parks*
- *Stunning water views from each studio*
- *Luxuriously appointed accommodation*
- *Peaceful private setting*
- *Art, craft & wine trails*
- *Separate studios & entrances*
- *Goat Island & Kawau Island*

Situated on the waterfront with breathtaking views over the moored boats and tidal flows of Sandspit estuary. The different lights of day and sunset give a forever changing vista, with the surrounding trees home to our New Zealand native birds. We have two new luxurious studios with magical water views, their own entrance to give maximum privacy, freshly cut flowers and candles to add a touch of romance. Each studio has a large tiled ensuite, lounge chairs, dining table, tea/coffee, refrigerator, microwave, stereo, television, video etc, all the comforts of home to ensure you have a memorable stay. Visit the boutique vineyards, restaurants, cafés, potteries, art galleries, beaches, golf courses, regional parks, short walk to Kawau Island ferry or just relax, enjoy the forever changing water views and listen to sounds of native birds in a truly tranquil setting, a world away from the bustle of Auckland and yet only a mere forty-five minute drive.

DIRECTIONS:
Entrance is down the right of way to 9A Kanuka Road and is well sign posted. Booking in advance is recommended.

Kawau Island Experience

North Cove, Kawau Island
Ph (09) 422 8831, Fax (09) 422 8832
Mobile 021-951 038
email: *mail@sailingholiday.co.nz*
www.sailingholiday.co.nz

Tariff : N.Z. Dollars	
Double	$175
Single	$150
Child	

Bedrooms	Qty
Double	2
Twin	
Single	
Bed Size	**Qty**
Super King	
King	
Queen	2
Double	
Single	
Bathrooms	**Qty**
Ensuite	2
Private	
Guest Share	

Island Retreat
Gourmet Meals

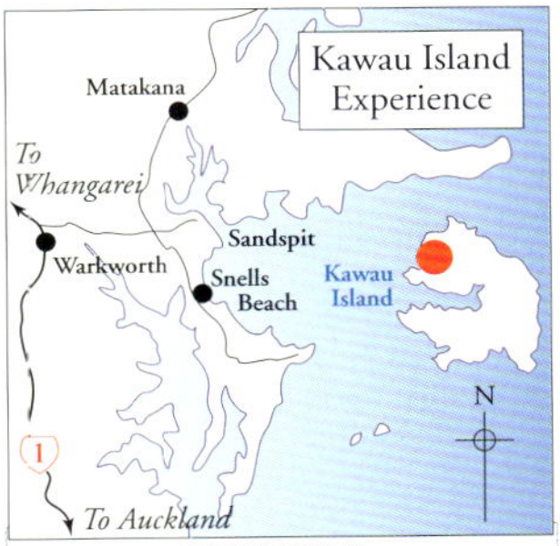

DIRECTIONS:
Approaching Warkworth from Auckland, follow directions to Sandspit. Contact Kawau Kat ferry service. Phone 09 425 8006 prior to arrange either a ferry crossing or water taxi out to Kawau Island.

Features & Attractions

- *Only 1½ hrs. from Auckland*
- *Tranquil, peaceful location*
- *Kayaks and dinghy*
- *Superb alfresco dining*
- *Bush and coastal walks*
- *Relaxed, friendly hosts*
- *Underfloor heating in ensuites*
- *Sailing option on 42' yacht*

Experience peace and tranquility only 1 hour's drive from Auckland city. **Kawau Lodge** is set in picturesque North Cove on Kawau Island. From the minute you step off the ferry or water taxi onto our private, all-tide jetty, you will be captured by the quietness of your surroundings, only interrupted by the songs of the native birds. From your tastefully appointed queen room, complete with its own coffee/tea making facilities, television and luxurious ensuite, you will enjoy magical bush and sea views. A delicious breakfast with a choice of continental or gourmet, served with fresh fruit, yoghurt, cereal and specialty muffins, can be served in your room either outside on your deck or upstairs in the dining alcove. Enjoy a fabulous hosted evening dinner, made from a fine selection of carefully prepared local produce. Our salads and vegetables are often picked fresh from our garden. Local wine list available. Great for honeymooners or that special weekend away.

Warkworth Country House

18 Wilson Road, RD 1, Warkworth, Auckland
Ph (09) 422 2485, Fax (09) 422 2485
email: *paulalan@xtra.co.nz*

Tariff : N.Z. Dollars	
Double	$120-140
Single	$95
Child	–

Bedrooms	Qty
Double	1
Twin	1
Single	
Bed Size	**Qty**
Super King	
King	
Queen	1
Double	
Single	2
Bathrooms	**Qty**
Ensuite	2
Private	
Guest Share	

Quality Countrystay
Bed & Breakfast

Features & Attractions

- *Private entrances and patios*
- *Tea & coffee making facilities*
- *Television in each room*
- *45 min north of Auckland*
- *Generous breakfasts*
- *Near regional parks and reserves*
- *Peaceful country environment*
- *Each room with ensuite*

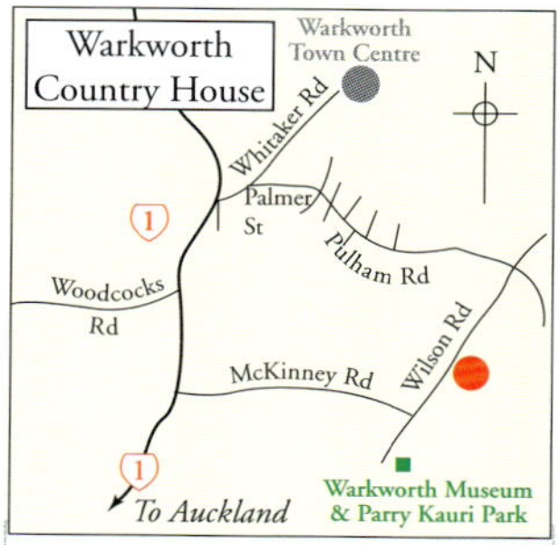

DIRECTIONS: Approaching Warkworth from Auckland turn right into McKinney Rd signposted Warkworth Museum/Parry Kauri Park, then turn left into Wilson Road.

Warkworth Country House, set in two acres of gardens and native bush, offers you peace, tranquility and tasteful accommodation. Each ensuite room has a private entrance and patio, tea and coffee making facilities, radio/ alarm, television, hairdryer, electric blankets and toiletries. A generous breakfast is served in the country-style dining room or alfresco if preferred. A two minute walk takes you to the historic Warkworth Museum ad Perry Kauri Park with its bush walk amongst ancient kauri trees. The township of Warkworth, with craft and antique shops, cafés, restaurants and riverside walk, is just a three minute drive away. We are close to beaches, horse riding, kayaking, a golf course, potteries, vineyards, regional parks and the ferry to Kauwau Island. With sheep and cows as neighbours we assure you of a relaxing stay. We look forward to welcoming you to our country home. A discount is offered for 'room only' accommodation or a stay of 3+ nights.

Our Farm-Park

450 Krippner Rd, Puhoi,
postal: RD 3, Kaukapakapa, Auckland 0873
Ph/Fax (09) 422 0626, Mobile 021-215 5165
email: *ofp@friends.co.nz*
www.friends.com

Tariff : N.Z. Dollars	
Double	$125-195
Single	$115-150
Child - no charge	

Bedrooms	Qty
Double	1
Twin	1
Single	
Bed Size	**Qty**
Super King	
King	
Queen	1
Double	
Single	2
Bathrooms	**Qty**
Ensuite	
Private	1
Guest Share	

Organic Farmstay ...the gentle way

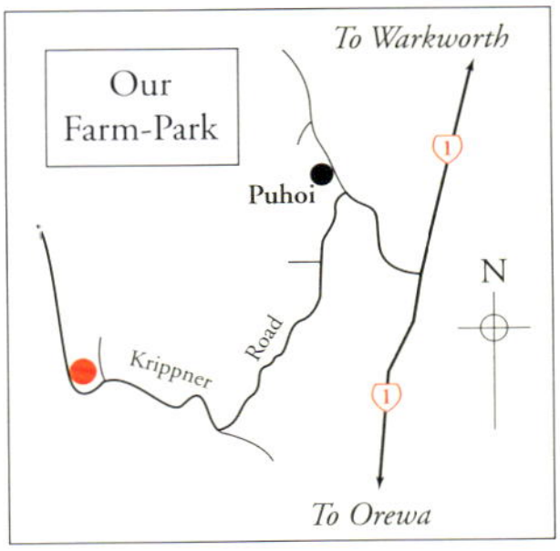

Features & Attractions

- *Children welcome*
- *International cuisine*
- *Gentle treatment of animals*
- *"Conversation English" courses*
- *Activities provided for children*
- *Educational courses*
- *Organic & GE free food*
- *Nobody smokes here*

Farmstay, the gentle, organic way. Your family are the only guests when you are here. We farm with kindness sheep, Belted Galloway cows with calves at foot, horses, ducks, poultry running free, providing milk, butter, yoghurt, ice-cream, cheeses.
International cuisine - taste-filled organic meals included in tariff. Includes fruit and vegetables we grow and fresh baking. Come relax (no charge for your welcomed children), sleep off 'jet-lag'. Our beds are very comfortable. Panoramic views, fresh air, clean water. Share experiences, ideas and knowledge over dinner. Walk through our 'Farm' fields and the 'Park' - trees, streams, bird life, flora and fauna, private and secluded places. Gardeners will love it here. Use our library, email, business facilities... more information at www.ustay2.com.

The Sheep & Shag

6A Roberts Road, Gulf Harbour, Whangaparaoa
Ph (09) 428 5256
Mobile 021-645 485
email: *info@sheepandshag.co.nz*
www.sheepandshag.co.nz

Features & Attractions

- *Panoramic views*
- *20m solar-heated pool*
- *Purpose-built in 2001*
- *Private entrances & patio*
- *Golf, swimming, boating*
- *Tiritiri bird sanctuary*

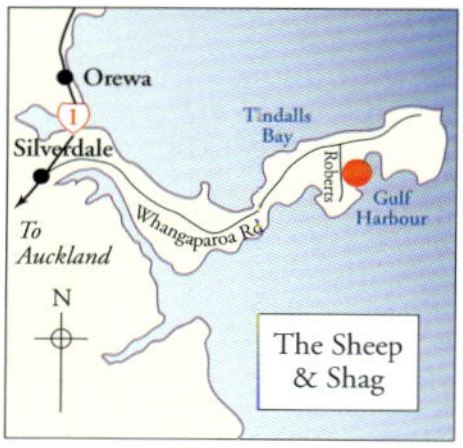

Superior Bed & Breakfast
Self-contained Apartment

$	
Double	$108-165
Single	$100-135
Child	neg

Relax around the pool in our sunny, modern facilities on a lifestyle block on the beautiful Hibiscus Coast. Viable alternative to staying in downtown Auckland and close to shops, restaurants, beaches and golf courses, including the Gulf Harbour Country Club – venue for the NZ Open.

Guest lounge available for your convenience. Laundry, SKY TV, DVD, and assistance with transportation and onward arrangements will help make your stay a memorable experience. Plenty of parking for your boat, if required. Our single-level home was purpose-built in 2001 with a guest accommodation wing for your enjoyment.

Bedrooms	Qty
Double	3
Twin	
Single	
Bed Size	**Qty**
King	
Queen	3
Double	
Single	2
Bathrooms	**Qty**
Ensuite	3
Private	
Guest Share	

PUAWAI BAY

31 Glenelg Road, Red Beach, Orewa
Ph (09) 426 1165
Mobile 027-245 3954
email: *info@puawaibay.co.nz*
www.puawaibay.co.nz

Tariff : N.Z. Dollars	
Double	$150-300
Single	$100-250
Child	n/a

Bedrooms	Qty
Double	6
Twin	
Single	
Bed Size	**Qty**
Super King	3
King	
Queen	3
Double	
Single	
Bathrooms	**Qty**
Ensuite	3
Private	3
Guest Share	

VISA MasterCard

BB **Red Beach - Orewa** SC

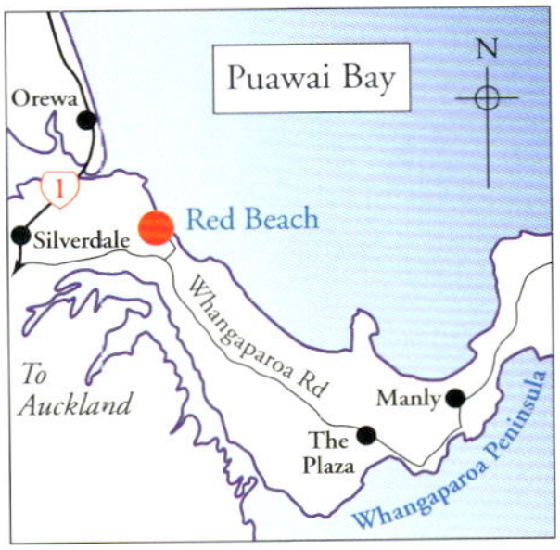

Features & Attractions

- *Stunning sea views*
- *Listen to the waves*
- *Airy, spacious apartments*
- *Self-service style breakfast*
- *Cliff-edge pool with gym & sauna*
- *25 min. north of Auckland*
- *Close to Hauraki Gulf & wineries*
- *Private boutique vineyard*

Enjoy panoramic views from this spacious cliff-edge location or kick back in our own picturesque vineyard. Beautifully appointed and very secluded, the choices are: a one bedroom luxury apartment with spa bath and sauna, a spacious two bedroom apartment with two bathrooms and a standard one-bedroom apartment. All apartments have stunning sea views. The property has a beautiful cliff-edge swimming pool, a sauna and a gym.

Very close to vineyards (including our own), Tiri Tiri Bird Sanctuary, Goat Island Marine Reserve and more than a dozen fabulous beaches. Only twenty five minutes from Auckland, **Puawai Bay** is an ideal first or last night stay in New Zealand. Or stay for a few days and enjoy our beaches, our wine and our amazing local attractions. Continental self-service breakfast is included. Dinner and picnic baskets are available on request.

BAYVIEW BED & BREAKFAST

1Beach Road Manly Village, Whangaparaoa Peninsula,
Hibiscus Coast, North Auckland
Ph/Fax (09) 428 0990, Mobile 027-280 8346
email: *bayviewmanly@xtra.co.nz*
www.bayview-manly.co.nz

Tariff : N.Z. Dollars	
Double	$125-159
Single	$115-149
Child	n/a

Bedrooms	Qty
Double	3
Twin	1
Single	
Bed Size	**Qty**
Super King	
King/Twin	1
Queen	2
Double	
Single	
Bathrooms	**Qty**
Ensuite	2
Private	1
Guest Share	

Quality Bed & Breakfast
***with* Spectacular Sea Views**

Features & Attractions

- *30min. North of Auckland*
- *Bay of Islands 2½ hours*
- *Central Plateau 3hrs*
- *Dolpin/whale watching arranged*
- *Super guest lounge with patio*
- *Tea/coffee & television in room*
- *Special full breakfast*
- *Discount for stays over 3 nights*

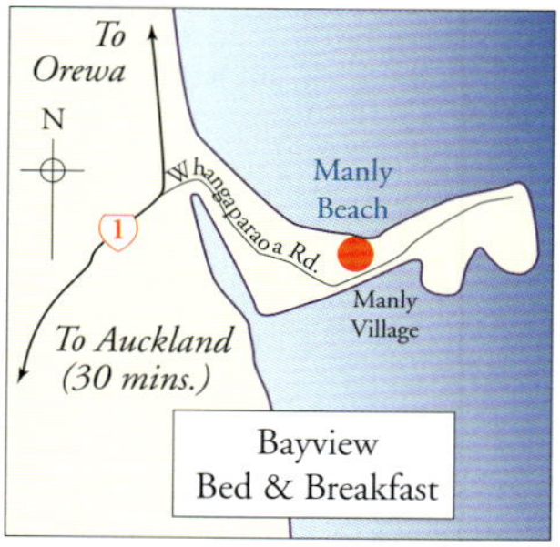

Bayview is an exceptional Bed & Breakfast experience on the beautiful Hibiscus Coast. Just north of Auckland, the perfect location between the Central Plateau, Rotorua and the Bay of Islands. A place to stay for more than a day. Our sunny home above big Manly Beach is adjacent to Manly Palms Village, with five excellent restaurants, shops. Whangaparaoa Peninsula has twelve uncrowded beaches, three golf courses, fishing, bush walks, ferry to world renowned bird sanctuary Tiri Tiri Matangi and more. Wineries and hot pools nearby. Arrive to a welcome drink on the patio then settle into your comfortable ensuite room with balcony and spectacular sea views, then a one minute walk to the restaurant of your choice. Stroll along the beach walk before the "Bayview Breakfast" – usually served alfresco, overlooking the bay. Enjoy Lavazza Coffee, fresh fruit platters, home baking and a choice of cooked dishes. Originally from the UK we are well travelled and are happy to assist with onward bookings and travel information.

Guest comment: *"Just perfect"*

PEONE PLACE

35 Surf Road, Stanmore Bay, Whangaparaoa
Ph (09) 424 1455, Fax (09) 424 1455
Mobile 027-353 7745
email: *info@peone.co.nz*
www.peone.co.nz

Tariff : N.Z. Dollars	
Double	$100-150
Single	$80
Child	neg

Bedrooms	Qty
Double/Twin	3
Twin	1
Single	
Bed Size	**Qty**
Super King	2
King	
Queen	1
Double	
Single	3
Bathrooms	**Qty**
Ensuite	
Private	1
Guest Share	1

VISA MasterCard eftpos

Bed & Breakfast Homestay & Self-contained Apartment

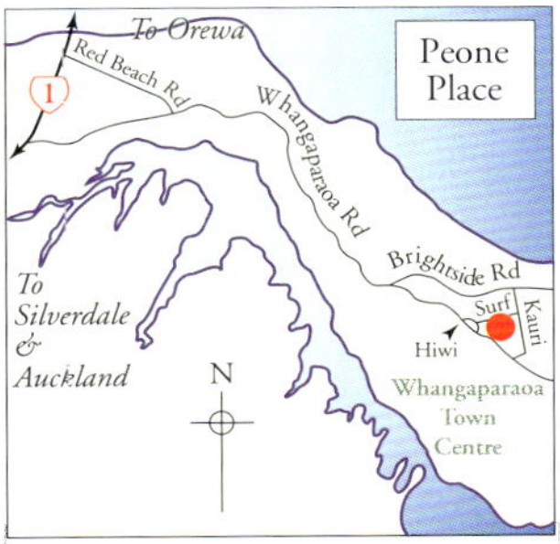

DIRECTIONS:
Travelling on Northern Motorway from City, exit at Silverdale, right at traffic lights into Whangaparaoa Road. After 5km, just past 'Placemakers' turn left into Hiwi Cresc. (this runs into Surf Rd). We are number 35

Features & Attractions

- *½ hr Nth Auckland City*
- *5 min. walk to safe beach*
- *Ample off-street parking*
- *Internet access*
- *Extended stay/group rates*
- *Children welcome*
- *Dinners by arrangement*
- *5 minutes to restaurants*

Welcome to **Peone Place**, your "home away from home", with extensive sea views and a private garden, 7km from the northern motorway and only 1 hr from Auckland Airport. Choose a self-contained, spacious tourist flat with its own entrance or quiet super-king/twin single accommodation upstairs with tea/coffee making facilities and a deck into the garden. Wake to bird song and the aroma of freshly baked bread. Enjoy generous breakfasts while soaking up the sun on the deck or in our dining room which looks northward to the Hauraki Gulf. Whangaparaoa, "Gateway to Northland", has much to offer with many safe beaches and regional parks to explore, an indoor snow slope, a Leisure Centre with heated pools, 3 golf courses, Thermal Hot Pools, and ferry trips to outer islands including Tiritiri Matangi Bird Sanctuary. The shopping complex, markets, factory shops, cinema and a good selection of restaurants are within 5 min. of **Peone Place.**

Waters Edge Manly

83 Laurence Street, Manly
Whangaparaoa, Auckland
Ph (09) 428 0102, Fax (09) 428 2103
Mobile 027-492 1926
email: *watersedge@paradise.net.nz*

Tariff : N.Z. Dollars	
Double	$150-200
Single	
Child	

Bedrooms	Qty
Double	2
Twin	1
Single	
Bed Size	**Qty**
Super King	1
King	
Queen	1
Double	
Single	4
Bathrooms	**Qty**
Ensuite	1
Private	1
Guest Share	1

Luxury Beachfront Accommodation

Features & Attractions

- *Absolute watersedge*
- *Spacious & comfortable*
- *Private entrance*
- *Golf courses incl international*
- *Fishing and boating available*
- *Excellent dining nearby*

DIRECTIONS:
Take northern motorway out of Auckland, take Silverdale turn-off. At the top of Silverdale Hill turn right at lights, follow Whangaparaoa Rd to Plaza Town Centre - 10 min. Through 3 sets of lights take 2nd road on left- Ladies Mile - to the end. We are on corner Ladies Mile/ Lawrence St.

We invite you and your friends to share our magical location right on the shores of one of North Auckland's most beautiful beaches.

Enjoy a continental or cooked breakfast on the deck to the soothing sounds of lapping waves while you contemplate a lazy day on the beach (towels provided). Or we can arrange a Tee time for you and your party at one of three golf courses nearby, including, the internationally acclaimed Gulf Harbour Course. Boating/fishing excursions on the Hauraki Gulf can also be organised. Comfort is assured.

Our spacious, sunny rooms have their own tea/coffee facilities (with home baking), microwave, fridge, TV and video. Laundry, facsimile and internet facilities are also available. Relaxing, rejuvenating, we look forward to your company at **Waters Edge** very soon.

The Palms on Tindalls

75 Deluen Avenue, Tindalls Bay, Whangaparaoa
Ph (09) 424 1930, Fax (09) 424 1930
Mobile 027-293 4929
email: *davies@palmsretreat.co.nz*
www.palmsretreat.co.nz

Tariff : N.Z. Dollars	
Double	$150-280
Single	$150-280
extended stay neg	

Bedrooms	Qty
Double	2
Twin	
Single	
Bed Size	**Qty**
Super King	
King	
Queen	1
Double	1
Single	
Bathrooms	**Qty**
Ensuite	
Private	1
Guest Share	

Beachfront Luxury Retreat

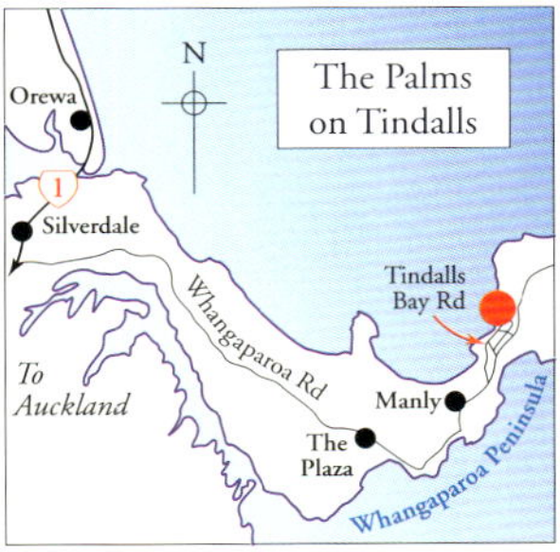

Features & Attractions

- *Romantic ambience*
- *Beachfront & tranquil*
- *Close Hauraki Gulf & Islands*
- *30 min north of Auckland City*
- *Superb scenery & parklands*
- *5 min restaurants & cafés*
- *Handy boat ramp & golf course*
- *Self service breakfast available*

Enjoy and delight in the magic of this private, **beachfront**, luxury, cabana-style villa. **The Palms on Tindalls** beach, is one of the twelve fabulous beaches on the incredible **Whangaparaoa Peninsula**. The area is popular for water sports and many other recreational activities. It is handy to amazing regional parks, geothermal hot pools, Gulf Harbour marina and golf course, Snowplanet, shopping centres and top quality restaurants. Your fully equipped kitchen, Italian tiled bathroom, full laundry, together with spacious lounge and cosy gas fire will ensure a romantic and restful ambience. All rooms have French doors opening to the tropical garden and views over the bay. The two separated and beautifully appointed bedrooms, together with the gentle sounds of the sea will complete for you another day in paradise.

WAIARI

85 Whangaparaoa Rd, Hadley Park,
Red Beach, Auckland
Ph (09) 427 5914, Mobile 0274-850 170
email: *waiari@xtra.co.nz*
www.waiari.co.nz

Waiari Bed and Breakfast

Tariff : N.Z. Dollars	
Double	$120
Single	$100
Child	n/a

Bedrooms	Qty
Double	3
Twin	
Single	
Bed Size	**Qty**
Super King	
King	
Queen	2
Double	1
Single	
Bathrooms	**Qty**
Ensuite	3
Private	
Guest Share	

Bed & Breakfast
Homestay

Features & Attractions

- *20 min north of Harbour Bridge*
- *World class golf courses*
- *Waiwera thermal pools*
- *Close to Orewa Beach*
- *Quiet, rural hideaway*
- *Stopover for Tiri Tiri Matangi Bird Sanctuary*
- *The perfect place to relax*

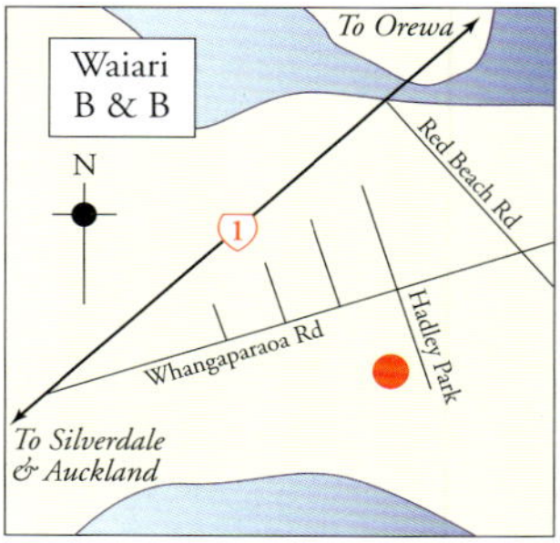

Waiari is a quality purpose-built guest house, set on two acres of gardens and lifestyle block running down to the Weiti River, which is a tidal estuary. Enjoy the ever-changing moods of the river with the seclusion and rural lifestyle that **Waiari** offers, yet be only minutes away from everything that the coast and surrounding areas has available including world-famous golf courses, marina, regional parks and fabulous beaches. An ideal stopover for a visit to the thermal pools at Waiwera, the vineyards and potteries at Matakana, historic Puhoi and fabulous Tiri Tiri Matangi Bird Sanctuary. We are only 20 minutes north of the bridge. The ideal stop-over for inbound and outbound visitors. We have three guest bedrooms. All have their own private facilities and patios. One double room with views over the estuary and two queen size with views over the gardens and surrounding farmlands. The perfect place to relax with a pre-dinner drink and watch the fabulous sunsets. Awaken to the dawn chorus of the Tuis throughout the valley.

WHITEHILLS

224 Whitehills Road, Wainui, RD 1, Kaukapakapa
Ph (09) 420 5666, Fax (09) 420 5666
Mobile 027-448 9503
email: *d-mevans@xtra.co.nz*
www.bnbauckland.co.nz

Tariff : N.Z. Dollars	
Double	$115-130
Single	$75
Child	neg

Bedrooms	Qty
Double	1
Twin	2
Single	
Bed Size	**Qty**
Super King	
King	
Queen	1
Double	
Single	5
Bathrooms	**Qty**
Ensuite	2
Private	
Guest Share	

MasterCard VISA

Bed & Breakfast and Self-contained Accommodation

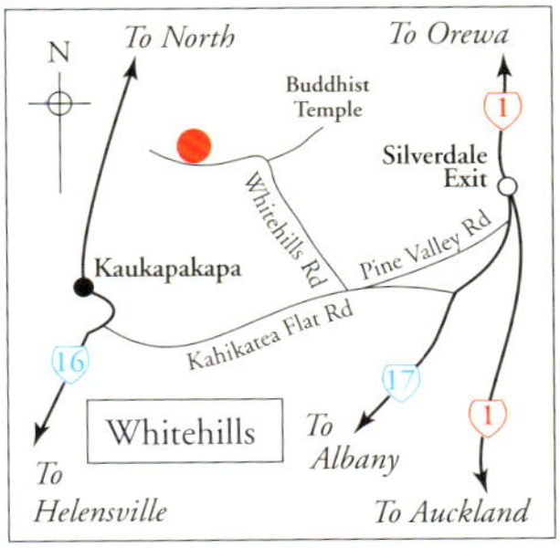

Features & Attractions

- *Genuine hospitality*
- *Tea, coffee & TV in rooms*
- *Native bush & bird life*
- *Peaceful surroundings*
- *Orewa 15 minutes*
- *Continental breakfast*
- *Golf courses close by*
- *Laundry facilities available*

Relax and unwind at **Whitehills** which is situated 30 minutes north of the Auckland Harbour Bridge and seven minutes from the Silverdale Motorway exit. It is convenient for shops, beaches and golf courses. If you have just arrived in New Zealand or are travelling north to the Bay of Islands, **Whitehills** would be a perfect "stopover" for you.

Enjoy quality Bed & Breakfast accommodation in the main house with a choice of twin or double room in guest wing. The comfortable separate self-contained accommodation has its own entrance and deck and breakfast provisions can be provided.

You are most welcome to wander around our garden, take a walk in the six acres of native bush or simply relax on the covered verandah. An evening meal is available by prior arrangement at $30 per person.

We offer genuine hospitality and look forward to meeting you.

KAIPARA HOUSE B&B

Cnr State Highway 16 & Parkhurst Road, Helensville
Ph (09) 420 7462, Fax (09) 420 7458
Mobile 027-661 103 or 027-814 617
email: *kaiparah@ihug.co.nz*
www.travelwise.co.nz

Tariff : N.Z. Dollars	
Double	$120
Single	$65
Child	

Bedrooms	Qty
Double	2
Twin	2
Single	2
Bed Size	**Qty**
Super King	
King	
Queen	3
Double	
Single	4
Bathrooms	**Qty**
Ensuite	3
Private	
Guest Share	1

SC **Bed & Breakfast and Self-contained Accommodation** BB

Features & Attractions

- *Restored 1894 villa*
- *Surrounded by gardens*
- *3 min Helensville & Parakai*
- *Adventures & sightseeing*
- *Quality studio summerhouses*
- *Ozone spa*
- *All amenities on request*
- *Fabulous hospitality*

DIRECTIONS:
Situated at the corner of State Highway16 and Parkhurst Rd (roundabout). 3 minutes from Helensville, 3 minutes from Parakai.

Our 112 year old villa, set in nearly an acre of seasonal gardens, has been lovingly restored and adorned with yesteryear's furniture and today's lovely rich colours which enhance the enchanting architecture of older homes. We offer you an Edwardian or Victorian room with morning sun and comfort through our home, with an open fire in winter. We also have two self-contained Studio Summerhouse units, facing north and east with your own open flame gas fireplace. With queen beds, ensuite and kitchenette you can have either a rural view or look over our picturesque garden with its gazebo and large ozone chlorine-free spa. Quality linen and furnishings.
Rate: $110.00 per night. Breakfast extra on request. We are in our 40's, young at heart, have a scotty dog and three cats and have enjoyed travel throughout New Zealand and abroad. Being on the Northland Tourist Route we can advise you on local activities and attractions – we have them all!

YOUR HOSTS: **Kay and Kerry Hamilton** Free Ph: 0800 501 850 ***Kumeu - Auckland***

CALICO LODGE

250 Matua Road, RD 1, Kumeu
Ph (09) 412 8167
Mobile 025-286 6064
email: *bed@calicolodge.co.nz*
www.calicolodge.co.nz

Tariff : N.Z. Dollars	
Double	$130-185
Single	$100-150
Child	

Bedrooms	Qty
Double	2
Twin	2
Single	
Bed Size	**Qty**
Super King	1
King	
Queen	2
Double	
King Single	1
Bathrooms	**Qty**
Ensuite	2
Private	1
Guest Share	

Arrive as Guests – Depart as Friends

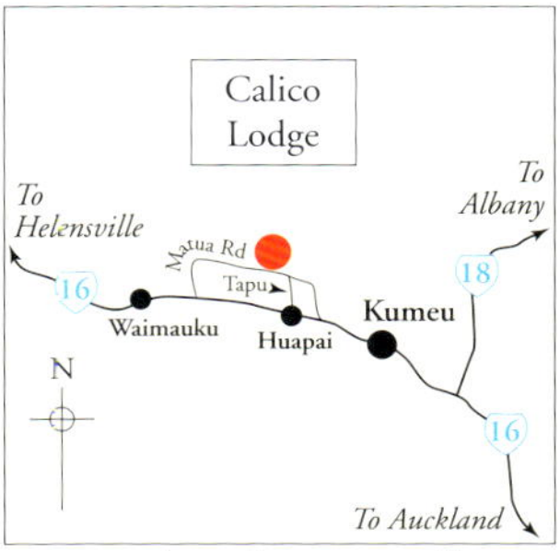

Features & Attractions

- *Friendly Kiwi hospitality*
- *Separate guest wing*
- *Guest lounge, tea/coffee*
- *Peaceful, tranquil garden*

- *Tame coloured sheep*
- *Wineries & cafés*
- *Golf courses nearby*
- *Muriwai gannet colony*

Kerry and Kay, Zippy our little dog, three cats and tame sheep welcome you to **Calico Lodge**. Set amidst the wineries of Matua, Westbrook, Nobilos, Coopers, Soljans, and many more, 25 minutes northwest of Auckland, our modern home on four acres has beautiful trees and tranquil gardens. Nearby are many wedding venues – Gracehill, Markovina and Rivermill. Muriwai's black sand surf beach, golf course and renowned gannet colony are only 20 minutes away.

Hand-made teddy bears and patchwork quilting (for sale) adorn the bedrooms in separate guest wing with private entrance. Heated towel rails, heaters, hairdryers, robes, fresh flowers and amenities complete the bathrooms – ensuite, private or guest share. A guest lounge with television, refrigerator, tea and coffee making facilities opens onto a private deck, where peace and beautiful bush views complete the picture. Two minutes from SH 16 and Kumeu village we love to share our little piece of paradise.

PANORAMA HEIGHTS

42 Kitewaho Road, Swanson, Waitakere City
Ph (09) 832 4777, Fax (09) 833 7773
Mobile 025-272 8811
email: *nzbnb4u@clear.net.nz*
www.panoramaheights.co.nz

Tariff : N.Z. Dollars	
Double	$145
Single	$105
Child	

Bedrooms	Qty
Double	2
Twin	1
Single	
Bed Size	**Qty**
Super King	
King	
Queen	2
Double	
Single	2
Bathrooms	**Qty**
Ensuite	3
Private	
Guest Share	

Bed & Breakfast
With a Little Indulgence

Features & Attractions

- *Dinner on request*
- *30 min. to Auckland City*
- *Kumeu Wineries 16km*
- *Non-smoking environment*
- *45 min to airport*
- *Train to the city*
- *Shopping centres 10 min.*
- *Two scenic golf courses*

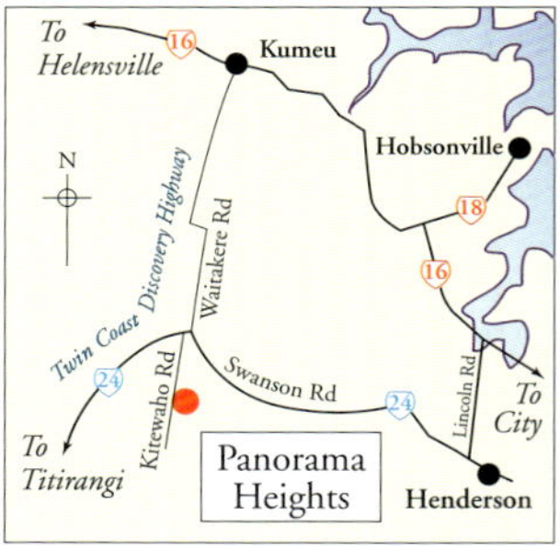

Paul and Allison invite you to visit and enjoy their private, peaceful location high in the Waitakere Ranges' Native Rainforest – Gateway to the Wild West Coast of Auckland. (The environment that inspired the "Silver Gilt flora", award-winning 100% Pure NZ garden at the 2006 Chelsea Flower Show).

Panorama Heights is a unique base to explore; west coast beaches of Karekare, Piha, Bethells and Muriwai; 250km of walking/hiking trails in 17,000 hectares of surrounding Regional Park or just perfect for taking it easy in this wonderful setting. Your hosts, who reside next-door, encourage you to relax and be pampered with all the comforts of home. Having travelled extensively we appreciate the importance of excellent accommodation at a reasonable price and we offer you this in our guest home with breathtaking views across native bush/kauri trees to Auckland City and Rangitoto Island beyond. Unwind on the deck or in the spacious lounge.
A delicious 'Panorama' breakfast is served in the dining room at your leisure. You'll love it here.
Directions to bring you 'stress-free' to our place are available.

Okura River Cottage

12 Deborah Place, Okura, Albany, RD 2, Auckland
Ph (09) 473 6298
Mobile 027-542 6699
email: *okuracottage@xtra.co.nz*
www.okuracottage.co.nz

Tariff : N.Z. Dollars	
Double	$150-195
Single	
Child	

Bedrooms	Qty
Double	2
Twin	
Single	
Bed Size	**Qty**
Super King	
King	
Queen	1
Double	1
Single	
Bathrooms	**Qty**
Ensuite	1
Private	1
Guest Share	

**Boutique Self-contained
River Tranquility**

DIRECTIONS: Please phone for easy directions. No smoking inside.

Features & Attractions

- *On river's edge*
- *Tranquil location*
- *20 min from Auckland*
- *Marine Reserve*
- *Genuine Kiwi hospitality*
- *Wonderful bird life*
- *Minutes to shops & beaches*
- *Bush & coastal walks*

Okura River Cottage is nestled alongside Auckland's prettiest river and marine reserve. The charm and tranquility of Okura is one of Auckland's hidden secrets, which we want to share with you. The view from the cottage is stunning. Imagine waking up to sun streaming on calm water and bush clad hills. You may be tempted to start your day strolling along wonderful bush and coastal walks – literally at your doorstep. Unspoilt swimming beaches are also only minutes away whilst you can be in downtown Auckland within half an hour. Our self-contained top quality detached cottage has all the comforts you would expect. Spacious bedroom with adjacent ensuite, separate cozy lounge and of course a kitchenette. We offer by arrangement, in addition to a hearty breakfast, picnic lunches or evening meals. All scrumptious home cooked food. **Okura River Cottage** is ideal for either a first or last stop to the airport or base for a holiday in or away from Auckland.

St Clair Bed & Breakfast

30 St Clair Place, Browns Bay, Auckland
Ph (09) 475 5230, Fax (09) 475 5303
Mobile 027-620 7704
email: *st_clair@xtra.co.nz*

Features & Attractions

- *Friendly Kiwi hospitality*
- *Exclusive cul-de-sac*
- *Beautiful views*
- *Full English breakfast*
- *Guests lounge*
- *Beaches, cafés, restaurants*

Luxury Bed & Breakfast
Beautiful Sea Views

Double	$130
Single	$80
Child	

Welcome to my modern New-England style purpose-built Bed & Breakfast. Enjoy the antiques, bric-a-brac and memorabilia or maybe relax on the spacious deck with magic views of Coromandel, Rakino Island and the Noises. Minutes drive to Browns Bay shops and glorious beach with full view of Rangitoto Island, North Harbour Stadium for shows and sporting events, Albany Mega Centre for great shopping and convenient access to North and South Motorway. Queen bed, ensuite, kitchenette, TV or king bed, private spa/bathroom, TV, private balcony for both bedrooms. Off-street parking. Well behaved family dog.

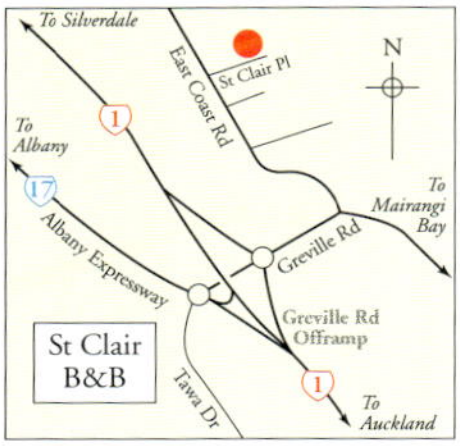

DIRECTIONS: When on East Coast Rd, look for No 826a. This is the 'Northcross Community Church', which is well sign-posted. St Clair Pl is directly opposite the church. Drive to bottom of small cul-de-sac. We are 2nd to last house on left.

Bedrooms	Qty
Double	2
Twin	
Single	
Bed Size	**Qty**
King	1
Queen	1
Double	
Single	
Bathrooms	**Qty**
Ensuite	1
Private	1
Guest Share	

Warblers Retreat

8/361 Paremoremo Road, Albany, Auckland
Ph (09) 413 6553, Fax (09) 413 6554
Mobile 027-259 2624
email: *pru_young@hotmail.com*

Tariff : N.Z. Dollars	
Double	$150
Single	$110
Child	$35

Bedrooms	Qty
Double	1
Twin	
Single	
Bed Size	**Qty**
Super King	
King	
Queen	1
Double	
King/Single	1
Bathrooms	**Qty**
Ensuite	
Private	1
Guest Share	

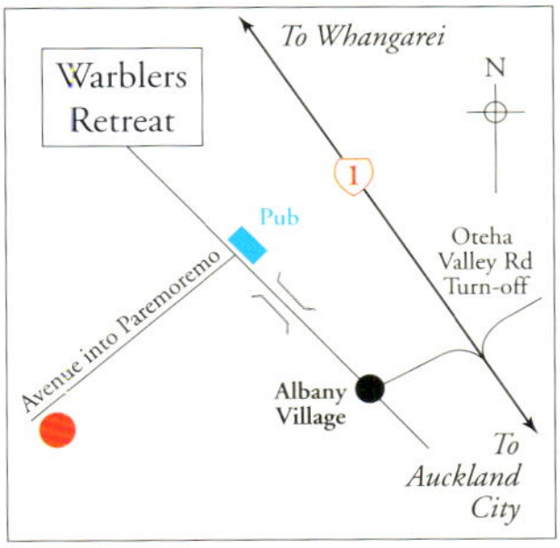

Peace & Tranquility
Self-contained Bed & Breakfast

Features & Attractions

- *Tranquil bush setting*
- *Bush walks on property*
- *Park at the door*
- *West Coast beaches*
- *Albany Mega Centre 6 min*
- *Free range hens and eggs*
- *Close to all major highways*
- *Local vineyards*

Welcome to paradise. Just twenty minutes north of Auckland City and two hours from Whangarei. A quiet getaway of native bush and birdlife. Set on five acres, our self-contained accommodation offers serene ambience and tranquility.

Your accommodation includes a romantic upstairs bedroom and downstairs guest lounge with fold-down sofa sleeper which can accommodate one or two small children or one other adult. Sky television, refrigerator, tea/coffee making facilities, facsimile and internet are all available. Beautiful tiled bathroom (no bath). Breakfast hamper delivered to your door.

With our three beautiful, happy dogs we invite you to share our hospitality. An ideal base from which to visit the vineyards of West Auckland, wild West Coast beaches and numerous great local restaurants.

Auckland Number One House

1 Princes Street, Northcote Point, Auckland Northshore 0627
C064
Ph (09) 480 7659, Fax (09) 480 7657
Mobile 021-143 8645
email: *briankh@xtra.co.nz*
www.nz-homestay.co.nz

Tariff : N.Z. Dollars	
Double	$185-200
Single	$120
Child	$20

Bedrooms	Qty
Double	3
Twin	
Single	
Bed Size	**Qty**
Super King	
King	
Queen	2
Double	1
Single	
Bathrooms	**Qty**
Ensuite	2
Private	1
Guest Share	

Bed & Breakfast Plus
Self-Contained Apartment

Features & Attractions

- *200° spectacular harbour view*
- *Delightful, warm, picturesque villa*
- *On water's edge*
- *Shuttle right to the door*
- *Excellent restaurants close*
- *Rental cars arranged*
- *Romantic jacuzzi, looking at city lights*

DIRECTIONS:
Over Harbour Bridge to North Shore. first left is Stafford. Up the hill and left to Queen, left at Northcote Tavern into King, right into Princes then under bridge as far as possible. We are next to Stokes Park Reserve.

Their guest book says *"NZ's best B&B"*, *"Far and away the friendliest place in NZ"*. They welcome tired travellers with a meet service at the airport and your flag at the door. **No 1 House** is only 8 minutes from the city centre by ferry – and a world away. The view of harbour and city from nearly every room is stunning – wait till you see the magical city lights at night! **No 1 House** even has its own swimming beach. Did we mention Jay's superb full cooked breakfasts? World famous in Auckland! **No 1 House** features a new family friendly self-contained apartment, an enchanting Hobbit House in the garden, and a 12m sailing catamaran to take you on the water. This couple sail yachts, ride motorbikes, bush walk, travel regularly and drink champagne – even have been known to jump off the Skytower! They will share as much or as little time with you as you wish, and help you plan your holiday. Book two nights minimum and really enjoy Auckland.
Certified Kiwi Hosts with NZ Tourism Board.

Aorangi Gardens

29B Aorangi Place, Birkenhead, Auckland
Ph (09) 480 1973, Mobile 027-284 1704
Email: *aorangi-gardens@xtra.co.nz*
www.aorangi-gardens.co.nz

@ home NEW ZEALAND

Tariff : N.Z. Dollars	
Double	$135-150
Single	$90-110
Child	neg

Bedrooms	Qty
Double	1
Twin	
Single	
Bed Size	**Qty**
Super King	
King	1
Queen	
Double	1
Single	
Bathrooms	**Qty**
Ensuite	1
Private	
Guest Share	

Self-contained Bed & Breakfast

Features & Attractions

- *Tranquil & central – CBD 10 min*
- *Harbour Bridge & Motorway 5 min*
- *To city via ferry on beautiful harbour*
- *Large semi-tropical garden setting*
- *Bush walk to beach 20 min*
- *Stroll to cafés & shops*
- *Spacious lounge & bedroom*
- *Free internet connection*

At the end of our tree lined drive you will find our lovely home in a semi-tropical garden setting overlooking acres of native bush. Imagine being in such an idyllic tranquil setting yet so close to all the attractions that a vibrant city like Auckland has to offer. Spend your days enjoying the garden and bush walk or exploring the wonderful North Shore beaches. Stroll up the road to Le Roys Bush Reserve and be amazed as you walk through established native bush to emerge at Little Shoal Bay adjacent to the Harbour Bridge. There are an interesting variety of cafés and restaurants only a ten minute walk away. Your spacious ground floor suite is self contained with a studio kitchen, bedroom area with ensuite and lounge/dining. The kitchen is well stocked with a variety of teas and coffees. Home baking and a bottle of New Zealand wine are complimentary. Your choice from our comprehensive breakfast menu can be served in the garden or in your room overlooking the garden. The lounge/dining area has a comfortable double sofa bed, Sky satellite TV. Private entrance. Off street parking. – ***Aorangi Gardens*** *is lower left in main photo.*

DIRECTIONS:
Please phone for easy directions.
Advance booking recommended.

DEVONPORT CLIFFTOP APARTMENT

31 Stanley Point Road, Devonport, Auckland
Ph (09) 446 1130
Mobile 021-550 814
email: *clifftop@ihug.co.nz*
www.devonportclifftop.co.nz

Tariff : N.Z. Dollars	
Double	$165-230
Single	$165
Child	–

Bedrooms	Qty
Double	1
Twin	
Single	
Bed Size	**Qty**
Super King	
King	
Queen	1
Double	1
Single	
Bathrooms	**Qty**
Ensuite	1
Private	
Guest Share	

LA **Luxury Bed & Breakfast**
Self-contained SC

Features & Attractions

- *Stunning harbour views*
- *Shoreline access*
- *Private & peaceful*
- *Dining in sunny courtyard*
- *Separate entrance & parking*
- *Tennis, bikes, kayak*
- *Breakfast provisions/home baking*
- *Kitchen & laundry*

DIRECTIONS:
Turn right at Mt Victoria roundabout, after 400m turn into fourth road on right, Calliope Road, which becomes Stanley Point Road. We are on left, first house down long shared driveway.

Clifftop Apartment is situated on the ground floor of our large modern home in Stanley Point, Devonport. The Apartment has its own entrance, outdoor eating area with BBQ and car park. You will enjoy stunning views of Auckland Harbour while reclining in the window seat in the sunny lounge. Wander through the native garden, take a seat on the cliff edge and watch the action in the harbour and Devonport Naval Base. Continue down the steps and swim or kayak from the private jetty. A peaceful place to relax after a busy day sightseeing.

Clifftop Apartment is perfect for longer stays with a fully equipped kitchen, queen bedroom, bathroom and laundry facilites - extra sleeping on double bed settee in the lounge. We are 2 km from historic, picturesque Devonport with its many cafes, antique shops and art galleries. Auckland CBD is a 10 minutes ferry ride from Devonport village. When you are weary with shopping and sightseeing visit two of Aucklands best beaches, Cheltenham and Narrow Neck, which are 5 mins drive away. Long term rates available.

EASTVIEW

2 Parkside Road, Hobsonville, Auckland
Ph (09) 416 9254, Fax (09) 416 9254
email: *eastview@xtra.co.nz*
www.eastview.co.nz

Tariff : N.Z. Dollars	
Double	$105-135
Single	$85-100
Child	$30

Bedrooms	Qty
Double	2
Twin	1
Single	
Bed Size	**Qty**
Super King	
King	
Queen	2
Double	
Single	2
Bathrooms	**Qty**
Ensuite	
Private	2
Guest Share	

DIRECTIONS:
From city/south take SH16. Turn right T-intersection onto Hobsonville Rd. SH18. 6th street on right Westpark Drive, 2nd left Parkside Road. **From north** take SH18 Greenhithe/Upper Harbour highway into Hobsonville Rd.

Bed & Breakfast/ Homestay With Panoramic Views

Features & Attractions

- *Stunning daytime views*
- *Amazing views by night*
- *Quiet & restful location*
- *Off-street parking*
- *Welcoming hosts*
- *Friendly cat & small dog*
- *15 min. to Auckland City*
- *Divine breakfasts*

Eastview, so *Easy-to-Find* from the airport and travel routes north and south, is located ideally for exploring Auckland. Favoured with panoramic water to city views it's just the place to unwind at the end of a long journey or a day of sightseeing. **Eastview** provides two sunny, spacious accommodation options. Relax in the comfort of the **Marina Suite**, bathed in all-day sun and opening onto a colourful garden. This area has two bedrooms, one queen, one twin, a private bathroom and a comfortable lounge with studio kitchen. **Rosie's Retreat** offers a queen-size bedroom with private bathroom. An inviting, sunny lounge is available for your use and a log fire for winter evenings.
Be pampered with many additional comforts, tea/ coffee making facilities, fresh fruit, flowers, electric blankets, fluffy towels, bathrobes, delicious home-baking, complimentary port. In the evenings dine at delightful, reasonably priced restaurants close by. Stroll around the nearby Marina or catch a ferry to the city. Discover superb beaches, rainforest-clad hills, gannet colonies, golf courses, thermal pools or harbour excursions. Handy to Kumeu wineries – popular wedding venues.

The Big Blue House

103 Garnet Road, Westmere, Auckland
Ph (09) 360 6384, Mobile 021-884 662
email: *info@thebigbluehouse.co.nz*
www.thebigbluehouse.co.nz

Features & Attractions

- *Close to city centre*
- *Panoramic views*
- *Swimming pool & spa*
- *Spacious comfortable rooms*
- *Near Ponsonby cafés & restaurants*
- *Adjacent to zoo & parks*

BB **Be 'at home' in comfort** H

$	
Double	$130-180
Single	$80-160
Child	$10-20

Kate and Lynne warmly invite you to share their unique Homestay B&B close to central city and harbour. Be greeted by our friendly cat and dog. Enjoy the sense of retreat in our spacious rooms – luxury of king-size beds, robes and heated towels. Relax in spa, play in pool or watch cable television. Coffee and tea making facilities, refrigerators, desks and internet connections. Generous breakfasts.

Take an easy stroll to cafés, restaurants, Auckland Zoo or Western Springs Park. Shop at nearby Ponsonby or hop on the bus to city centre (15 minutes). We have a range of rooms to suit your needs. The very large 'Seaview Room' with ensuite, king bed (extra single) suits couples or families. The 'Mountview Room', large with king bed and shared bathroom (own basin and facilities) provides a very comfortable option. The 'Hideaway Room' offers a cosy retreat for the single traveller.

-"Make yourself at home!"

Bedrooms	Qty
Double	2
Twin	
Single	1
Bed Size	**Qty**
King	2
Queen	
King/Single	1
Single	1
Bathrooms	**Qty**
Ensuite	1
Private	
Family Share	2

Hastings Hall

99 Western Springs Road, Western Springs, Auckland
Ph (09) 845 8550, Fax (09) 845 8554
Mobile 021-300 006
email: *unique@hastingshall.co.nz*
www.hastingshall.co.nz

Tariff : N.Z. Dollars	
Double	$145-375
Single	$115-325
Child	

Bedrooms	Qty
Double	8
Twin	2
Single	
Bed Size	**Qty**
Super King	
King	2
Queen	6
Double	2
Single	
Bathrooms	**Qty**
Ensuite	6
Private	1
Guest Share	3

Unique Heritage Bed & Breakfast

Features & Attractions

- *Beautifully landscaped early New Zealand mansion*
- *Walk to parks, zoo, golf*
- *Easy access to city centre*
- *Fax, phone, email, library*
- *Beautifully appointed suites*
- *Pool, spa & guest function room*
- *Conference – seminar facility*

This magnificently restored 1878 colonial mansion, set in beautifully landscaped extensive grounds, is just five minutes by motorway from Auckland City. Within walking distance is Kingsland with its cafés and ethnic restaurants, Auckland Zoo, and the beautiful Western Springs Park, Chamberlains Golf Course, the Transport Museum and Western Springs Stadium. Hastings Hall is ideal for the tourist, businessman or as a retreat. Enjoy gourmet breakfasts in the conservatory, formal dining room, gazebo (above the pool and spa pool) or in your suite with own verandah. Seven of the nine themed guest suites have marble ensuites, one for disabled guests. Choose from the Grand Hastings Suite with private lounge to the Moulin Rouge loft suite in the Lodge. Enjoy extensive tropically landscaped grounds, formal lounge and large pool lounge with library, home theatre, computer and email and fax facilities. All rooms are furnished with antiques and early New Zealand furniture from the period, fine linen and fluffy towels. Come and experience a bygone era with today's refinements.

Great Ponsonby Bed & Breakfast

30 Ponsonby Terrace, Ponsonby, Auckland
Ph (09) 376 5989, Fax (09) 376 5527
email: *info@greatpons.co.nz*
www.greatpons.co.nz

Tariff : N.Z. Dollars	
Double	$180-350
Single	
Child	

Bedrooms	Qty
Double	5
Twin	6
Single	
Bed Size	**Qty**
Super King	6
King	
Queen	5
Double	
Single	
Bathrooms	**Qty**
Ensuite	11
Private	
Guest Share	

A Small Hotel

Features & Attractions

- *Place to have fun*
- *Free fast internet available*
- *Non smoking inside*
- *Eco friendly*
- *Breakfasts a speciality*
- *Winter rates*
- *Cotton sheets*
- *Hospitality & service*

Ponsonby is the liveliest area of Auckland, full of restaurants, cafés, boutiques and ceramic shops. The Great Ponsonby, a large, restored villa, is tucked away in a quiet street. No traffic noises. Centrally located, close to major attractions, walk or bus to harbour and downtown. Off-street parking. Bus every ten minutes. The white exterior is deceptive. Inside is a bold profusion of colour with art from the Pacific Islands and New Zealand. Queen rooms, roomier courtyard studios, palm garden suites. All rooms have colourful, understated modern design. Private bathroom with heated mirror and towel rail, hairdryer. Tea and coffee making facilities, Sky television, DDI phones, internet access. Studios have a refrigerator, king or twin beds, leather couch, CD player, video player. Bath in suites. Leisurely breakfasts served from our extensive menu. Jason Cochrane, editor of Frommer's travel magazine, November 2002 said "*my top choice is Great Ponsonby B&B*". English travel guide "Footprint" says "*one of the best B&Bs in the city*". The Great Ponsonby topped accommodation chosen by NY Times 26/1/03. Resident cat and dog.

We can take pets under some conditions, so please telephone to make a booking.

MOANAVISTA

60 Hamilton Road, Herne Bay-Ponsonby, Auckland
Ph (09) 376 5028, Fax (09) 376 5025
Mobile 021-376 150
email: *info@moanavista.co.nz*
www.moanavista.co.nz

Tariff : N.Z. Dollars	
Double	$180-240
Single	$140-180
Child	

Bedrooms	Qty
Double	3
Twin	
Single	
Bed Size	**Qty**
Super King	
King	
Queen	3
Double	
Single	
Bathrooms	**Qty**
Ensuite	2
Private	1
Guest Share	

Luxury Accommodation
Bed & Breakfast

Features & Attractions

- *Close to city, Ponsonby restaurants*
- *Quiet and peaceful*
- *Wireless high-speed internet*
- *Sea views, beach nearby*
- *Modernised Victorian villa*
- *Continental breakfast*
- *LCD TV/DVD in all rooms*
- *Grand piano, open fire*

Stylish Boutique Accommodation

Moanavista, a stylish and comfortable boutique guest house, is situated in the quiet leafy suburb of Ponsonby, close to award winning restaurants, cafés, shops, beaches and city. Buses to Downtown Auckland are five minutes walk away. With the grace and elegance of the 1890s this modernised Victorian villa has two furnished rooms upstairs with superb sea views, verandahs and ensuite/private bathrooms. On the ground floor the Pacific Suite has an ensuite bathroom and French doors to the garden. All rooms have heated towel rails, soaps, shampoos, hair dryer and dressing robes. Enjoy a continental breakfast with fresh fruits, cereals, bakery before checking your emails on our complimentary high speed computer. Your hosts Tim and Matthew are well travelled (Tim is a gardener and Matthew a flight attendant with Air New Zealand) and enjoy sharing their knowledge on Auckland and beyond. You are welcome to join them for a complimentary cocktail. The atmosphere at **Moanavista** is casual and relaxed - a home away from home! Long term rates available. Supershuttle from the airport will bring you to our door at NZ$20 or NZ$25 /2 people.

Ponsonby - Auckland

YOUR HOSTS: Reg and Chrissy Price — Ph (09) 376 0250

Ponsonby Studio Loft

9 Picton Street, Ponsonby, Auckland
Ph (09) 376 0250
Mobile 021-336 640
email: *info@ponsonbystudioloft.co.nz*
www.ponsonbystudioloft.co.nz

Features & Attractions

- *4 houses from Ponsonby Road*
- *Quiet tree-lined street*
- *Shops, cafés, bars close by*
- *Central city bus every 10 min.*
- *Sky TV*
- *Separate shower/separate toilet*

Separate Self-contained Studio Luxury Bed & Breakfast

Double	$210
Single	$180
Child	$30

We are so close to the cute, historic cafés and shops of Ponsonby, yet nestled away in a tree-lined street of early 1900's wooden villas. The modern studio is completely separate and self-contained. Its elevated position and balcony provides a city outlook, yet retains a cozy and private feeling. King bed with fine linen.

Ponsonby Studio Loft is very central. Up the street, the Link Bus leaves every ten minutes for central city, shopping in quaint Parnell, upmarket Newmarket, ethnic Karangahape Road, funky High Street, ferries to the gulf, Viaduct waterfront bars and restaurants and connections to wider Auckland. We offer a breakfast with local fresh fruit and cereals etc, but also encourage our guests to try out the many great cafés as part of the Ponsonby experience. Please inquire about our special bed-only and winter pricing. Free broadband internet connection in room.

Bedrooms	Qty
Double	1
Twin	
Single	
Bed Size	**Qty**
King	1
Queen	
Double	1
Single	
Bathrooms	**Qty**
Ensuite	1
Private	
Guest Share	

Parnell - Auckland

YOUR HOST: Jane Barclay — Ph: (09) 309 0290

Chalet Chevron - A Great Little Hotel

14 Brighton Road, Parnell, Auckland
Ph (09) 309 0290, Fax (09) 373 5754
email: *info@chaletchevron.com*
www.chaletchevron.com

Features & Attractions

- *Historic hotel*
- *Unbeatable location*
- *Charming surroundings*
- *Stunning views*
- *Stroll to restaurants*
- *1.5kms from city centre*

Historic Parnell A Great Little Hotel

Double	from $180
Single	from$105
Child	$40

Chalet Chevron has a rich history of providing comfortable lodging in charming surroundings to travellers for generations. This great little hotel offers personal service, comfort, informality, a sense of fun and a warm welcome in one of Auckland's premier locations - 12 guest rooms with ensuite bathrooms at prices that won't blow the budget. To stroll down Parnell Road is to indulge your senses. It is abuzz with an amazing selection of restaurants, cafés and bars - traditional, quirky or hip. From some of the best fish and chips you will ever taste to goumet burgers and gastronomic delights. It is all here, as is New Zealand's highest concentration of Art Galleries side by side with the best fashion designers, fine New Zealand and imported products and specialty shops - all just 1.5kms from the city centre.

Bedrooms	Qty
Double	5
Twin	3
Single	4
Bed Size	**Qty**
King	
Queen	2
Double	4
Single	12
Bathrooms	**Qty**
Ensuite	12
Private	
Guest Share	

Sunderland House

1A Cox Street, Herne Bay, Auckland
Ph (09) 376 6336
Mobile 025-249 9025
email: *sunderlandhouse@ihug.co.nz*

Tariff : N.Z. Dollars	
Double	$185-215
Single	$165
Child	

Bedrooms	Qty
Double	2
Twin	
Single	1
Bed Size	**Qty**
Super King	
King	2
Queen	1
Double	
Single	
Bathrooms	**Qty**
Ensuite	3
Private	
Guest Share	

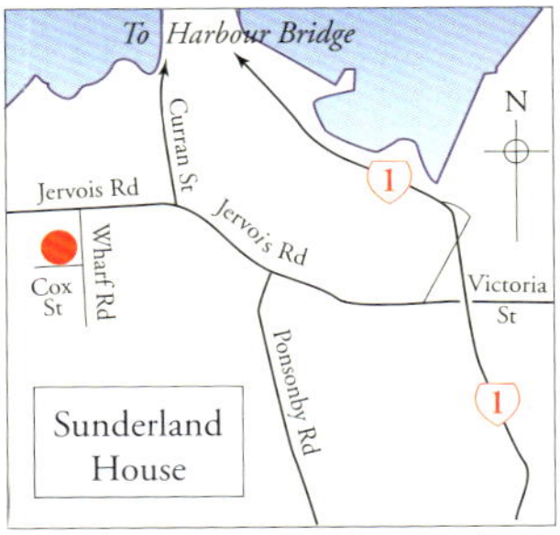

Luxury Boutique Accommodation

Features & Attractions

- *Elegant sumptous villa*
- *Great service & hospitality*
- *Walk to cafés & restaurants*
- *Walk to Ponsonby shopping*
- *Breakfast a specialty*
- *Close to central city*
- *Rooms all ensuite*
- *Beautiful library*

Television personality and interior designer Donald and his wife Kathy invite you to share their elegant and sumptuous replica Victorian villa. Built to compliment its historic area but with stunning modern facilities, your privacy and comfort is paramount in the beautiful ensuite rooms. The principle suite features a balcony with sky tower views and a magnificent claw-foot bath set luxuriously in the bedroom. The second suite has Mt Eden views and a spa bath designed for two. The top floor is exclusively for guest use and includes tea and coffee making facilities. Indulge yourself at breakfast with fresh fruit, home-made muffins, cereals and great espresso coffee in the French farmhouse kitchen and unwind in the evening with complimentary port in the library. Restaurants and cafés are a short stroll, trendy Ponsonby shopping is within easy walking distance and the city centre is 3km (bus every 20 min.).
PS: A springer spaniel called Ben lives on the property.

ASCOT PARNELL

St Stephens Avenue, Parnell, Auckland 1
Ph (09) 309 9012, Fax (09) 309 3729
email: *info@ascotparnell.com*
www.AscotParnell.com

Tariff : N.Z. Dollars	
Double	$195-365
Single	$195-325
Child	$50

Bedrooms	Qty
Double	
Twin	3
Single	
Bed Size	**Qty**
Super King	1
King	
Queen	2
Double	
Single	
Bathrooms	**Qty**
Ensuite	3
Private	
Guest Share	

Bed & Breakfast in a charming atmosphere

DIRECTIONS: From airport take road No. 20 motorway to Auckland city, exit at Queenstown Rd, follow Auckland centre. Follow Manukau Rd (Road No 12) to Parnell. Turn right at the Cathedral of the Holy Trinity into St. Stephens Ave. The **Ascot Parnell** is 300m down on your left.

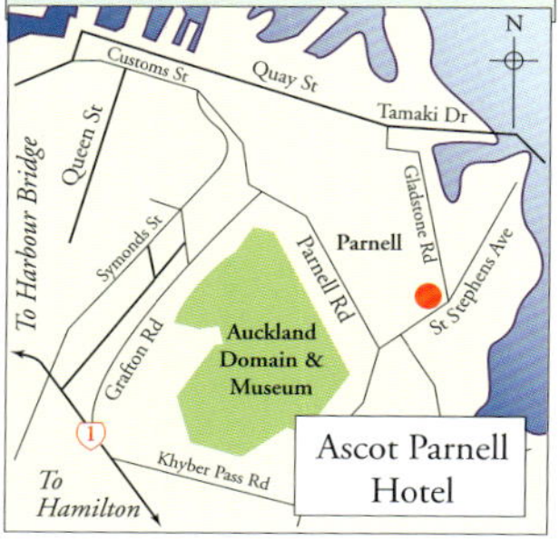

Features & Attractions

- *Walk to all city attractions*
- *City-centre at 1 mile (1.5 km)*
- *Airport bus stops at the door*
- *Free internet access*
- *Helpful and friendly hosts*
- *Garden setting, gourmet food*
- *Free cookies, teas, coffee, juice*
- *Free parking inside building*

A tranquil, convenient, central location, a moment's stroll from Parnell Village cafés, restaurants and city centre attractions. Built amidst the sub-tropical gardens of this historic neighbourhood, Ascot Parnell provides bright and airy guest suites with luxury bathrooms, spectacular views of Auckland's harbour and city skyline. Free car parking inside building. Guest suites are tastefully furnished and have comfortable queen or super-king beds with fine quality linen. Each room has a luxury bathroom, with shower and/or full bath-tub, underfloor heating, hair dryer, television, climate control, internet connection and telephone. The spacious lounge opens up to a large sunny balcony with spectacular panoramic harbour views. A desk with Mac-PC offers free internet access. On cool nights cuddle up around the open fireplace with a hot drink or a glass of wine. Breakfast is a sumptuous affair with such choices as fresh organic fruit, yoghurt, Belgian pancakes, French toast, crépes, gourmet omelettes etc, and is served in the morning room or alfresco on the balcony. We cater for special diets. Complimentary fresh coffee, teas and cookies are available throughout the day. Reservations essential.

St Georges Bay Lodge

43 St Georges Bay Road, Parnell, Auckland
Ph (09) 303 1050, Fax (09) 303 1055
Mobile 021-214 1473
email: *carol@stgeorge.co.nz*
www.stgeorge.co.nz

Features & Attractions

- *Hop on/off regular city link bus*
- *Stunning garden & park walks*
- *Adjacent to NZ's top restaurants*
- *PC & free internet access*
- *Sky TV in TV lounge*
- *Complimentary NZ port*

$	
Double	$215-255
Single	$195-215
Child	

Luxury Boutique Bed & Breakfast

Bedrooms	Qty
Double	3
Twin	1
Single	
Bed Size	**Qty**
Super King	1
Queen	
Double	
King/Single	4
Bathrooms	**Qty**
Ensuite	4
Private	
Guest Share	1

Prestigious inner city location, handy to world class yacht and tennis clubs, public and private gardens, renowned parks and reserves, museum, domain, winter and rose gardens, designer boutiques and speciality stores, great cafés, restaurants and nightclub life. There is no better place for your stay in Auckland City! **St Georges Bay Lodge** is an elegant Victorian villa with the charm of colonial New Zealand, and the comfort of modern amenities. The Lodge features luxurious bedding with woollen underlays, library and private guest lounge, elegant ensuites and bathrooms, native timber furniture, and modern conservatory with arched windows, flowing to a sunny balcony, with central city and harbour views. Enjoy complimentary New Zealand port and a fine choice of sumptuous full healthy continental and cooked breakfasts. Take pleasure from the night-time views of the twinkling city and sparkling harbour in our slice of paradise.

Akarana's Nautical Nook - Sailing

23B Watene Crescent, Okahu Bay, Orakei, Auckland
Ph (09) 521 2544
email: *nauticalnook@bigfoot.com*
www.nauticalnook.com

@home NEW ZEALAND

The view from our balcony

Features & Attractions

- *Complimentary sailing!*
- *Great place to unwind*
- *Swimming beach 100m*
- *Perfect central location*
- *Pay cash 10% discount*
- *Early 'am' check-in available*

$	
Double	$110-150
Single	$90-110

Homestay Bed & Breakfast Harbour Yacht Sailing

Bedrooms	Qty
Double	3
Twin	
Single	
Bed Size	**Qty**
King/Twin	1
Queen	2
Double	
Single	
Bathrooms	**Qty**
Ensuite	1
Private	2
Guest Share	

Friendly, relaxed, beachside hospitality overlooking park/harbour, 4.8km from Downtown. 100m from Okahu Bay, fringed by Pohutukawa trees, for swimming and picnics. Gourmet cooked breakfast, served at Captains Table or Promenade Deck. Stroll along picturesque promenade to Kelly Tarlton's Underwater World, Mission Bay beach, cafés and bars. Bus at door to Downtown, ferry terminal, museums and Vector Stadium. Unwind for 2-3 day stopover – our home is your home (take our handsome Irish Setter Shamus for a walk). Enjoy the thrill of complimentary sailing on the sparkling harbour on our 34ft yacht. We have a wealth of local knowledge and international travel experience and can assist with sightseeing and travel planning. Take taxi or shuttle to our door. **Welcome!** Excellent website.

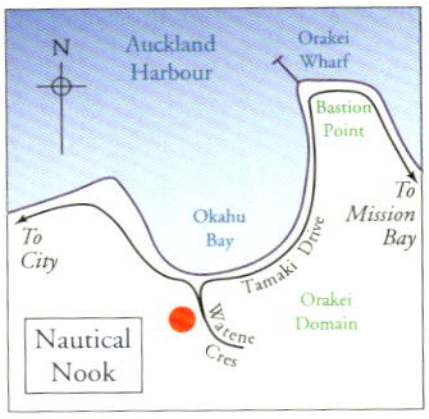

 YOUR HOSTS: **Susan and John Sweetman** Free Ph 0800 155 463

Braemar on Parliament Street

7 Parliament Street, Central Auckland
Ph (09) 377 5463, Fax (09) 377 3056
Mobile 021-640 688
email: *braemar@aucklandbedandbreakfast.com*
www.aucklandbedandbreakfast.com

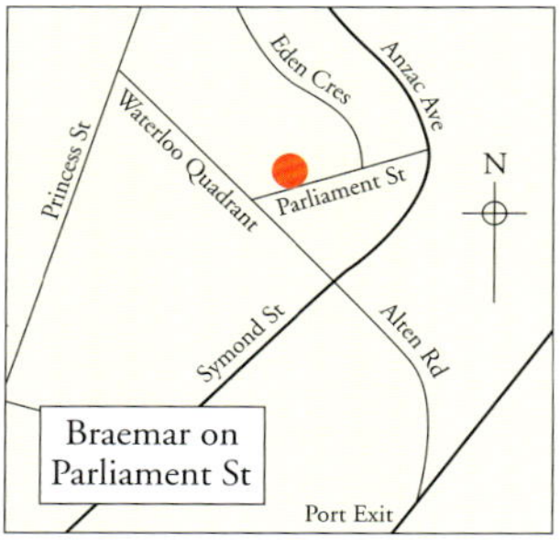

DIRECTIONS:
Take the PORT exit from the motorway. At the traffic lights take the free left turn up Alten Rd. Turn right at lights into Anzac Ave. Parliament St. is the 1st street on the left. We are the 4th building on the right, opposite the high court and next to Middle Courtville.

Tariff : N.Z. Dollars	
Double	$180-295
Single	
Child	

Bedrooms	Qty
Double	4
Twin	
Single	
Bed Size	**Qty**
Super King	
King	
Queen	2
Double	2
Single	
Bathrooms	**Qty**
Ensuite	1
Private	1
Guest Share	1

Elegant Inner City Haven

Features & Attractions

- *In downtown Auckland*
- *Walk to city attractions*
- *Non smoking indoors*
- *Heritage building*
- *Projector Television*
- *Pet poodles*

Braemar on Parliament Street is an elegant heritage-listed home in the Auckland Central Business District. We offer a comfortable high-quality environment. Being in the heart of Auckland means that our Bed & Breakfast is a short walk from all the city amenities. Close to all public transport and the inner city's beautiful parks.
If nightlife is what you are after, you can saunter to theatres, cinemas, cafés, restaurants and bars, or if you crave the quiet life, we can provide that too.
All of our bedrooms feature posturepaedic beds, goose-down duvets and fluffy pillows. All of our bathrooms feature walk-in showers and large claw-foot baths. Toiletries are complimentary.
Savour a full cooked breakfast in our Rose Dining-Room with fine linen, silver cutlery and bone china. Relax in the guest lounge and watch wide screen TV from our projector and enjoy our collection of Kiwi movies.

Laurel Cottage

83 Ranfurly Road, Epsom, Auckland
Ph (09) 630 4384, Fax (09) 630 4384
Mobile 027-498 6909
email: *enquiry@laurelcottage.co.nz*
www.laurelcottage.co.nz

Tariff : N.Z. Dollars	
Double	$170-190
Single	$140-150
Child	

Bedrooms	Qty
Double	1
Twin	
Single	
Bed Size	**Qty**
Super King	
King	
Queen	1
Double	
Single	
Bathrooms	**Qty**
Ensuite	1
Private	
Guest Share	

Boutique, Quality, Self-contained Bed & Breakfast Accommodation

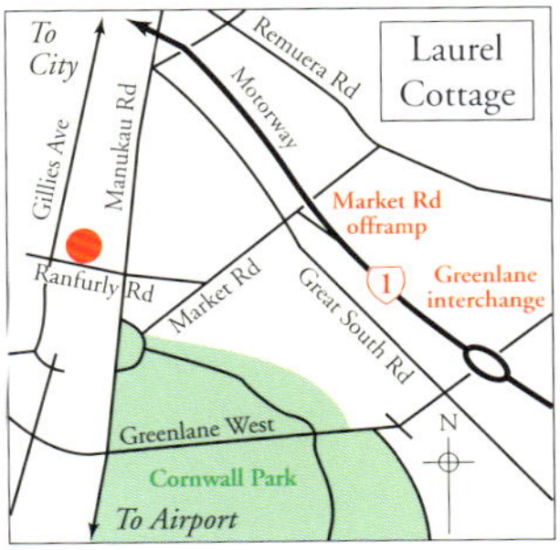

Features & Attractions

- *Perfect central location*
- *Basic grocery provisions*
- *Laundry available*
- *Antiques, arts & crafts*
- *Near tourist attractions*
- *Near beaches, tennis, golf*
- *Help with bookings*
- *Privacy & sunny courtyard*

Welcome to **Laurel Cottage**, a tastefully renovated early 1900s cottage, situated in a lovely and very central suburb. The cottage has luxurious furnishings and bed linen, stereo, television, fully equipped kitchen, and much more to make your stay with us comfortable. We are twenty minutes from the airport and a few minutes by car to the city and harbour, an ideal base for the many attractions Auckland has to offer. Laurel Cottage is within easy strolling distance of many cafés and restaurants, NZ Expo Centre, Alexandra Park Raceway, Greenlane, Brightside and Mercy Hospitals. Bus stops are also nearby. For those who enjoy a walk in the park, we are a few minutes walk from beautiful Cornwall Park or Eden Gardens. Close by is the popular shopping and entertainment centre of Newmarket. At the end of your busy day relax in our private, sun-filled courtyard. Whether you are here for leisure or business, we feel sure you will enjoy our warm hospitality and peaceful surroundings.

Amerissit

20 Buttle Street, Remuera, Auckland
Ph (09) 522 9297, Fax (09) 522 9298
Mobile 027-284 4883
email: *barbara@amerissit.co.nz*
www.amerissit.co.nz

Tariff : N.Z. Dollars	
Double	$185-250
Single	$150-225
Child	neg

Bedrooms	Qty
Double	3
Twin	
Single	
Bed Size	**Qty**
Super King	
King	2
Queen	1
Double	
Single	
Bathrooms	**Qty**
Ensuite	3
Private	
Guest Share	

Luxury Accommodation

Features & Attractions

- *Private and peaceful*
- *Elegant, modern décor*
- *Art galleries/museums*
- *High-tech guest rooms*
- *Minutes to central city*
- *and Viaduct Harbour*
- *Stroll to cafés & restaurants*
- *Local bush & beach walks*

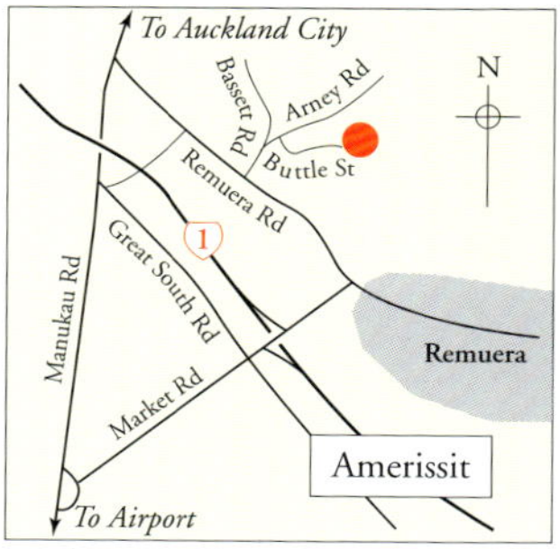

Amerissit is architecturally designed and close to Newmarket. Located among prestigious streets in a quiet cul-de-sac, the emphasis is on privacy, peace and tranquillity. By car it's only a few minutes to the city's popular tourist attractions, the restaurants, bars, cafés, shopping, art galleries, museums of Viaduct Harbour, Parnell and Newmarket. All motorway access is within easy reach. **Amerissit's** minimalist-style suites are designed with the executives and the discerning traveller in mind. Latest technology includes slimline TVs, Sky, DVDs, CDs, and tuner at the touch of a button, in-wall or ceiling speakers, direct-dial phone and high-speed internet access. All rooms are non-smoking with ensuite, balcony/patio and offer total privacy, the finest bed linen and facilities. Suites maximise the views of Remuera, Mt Hobson and surrounding trees and gardens. Breakfast is a sumptuous affair with a choice of continental or gourmet, served in your room, dining room or on the balcony. **Amerissit** is the perfect choice for the working week, that indulgent weekend and as a base to explore Auckland.

OMAHU LODGE

33 Omahu Road, Remuera, Auckland
Ph (09) 524 5648, Fax (09) 524 5108
Mobile 021-954 333
email: *info@omahulodge.co.nz*
www.omahulodge.co.nz

Tariff : N.Z. Dollars	
Double	$175-250
Single	$160-200
Child	

Bedrooms	Qty
Double	4
Twin	
Single	
Bed Size	**Qty**
Super King	
King	1
Queen	2
Double	1
Single	
Bathrooms	**Qty**
Ensuite	4
Private	1
Guest Share	

A Boutique Resort

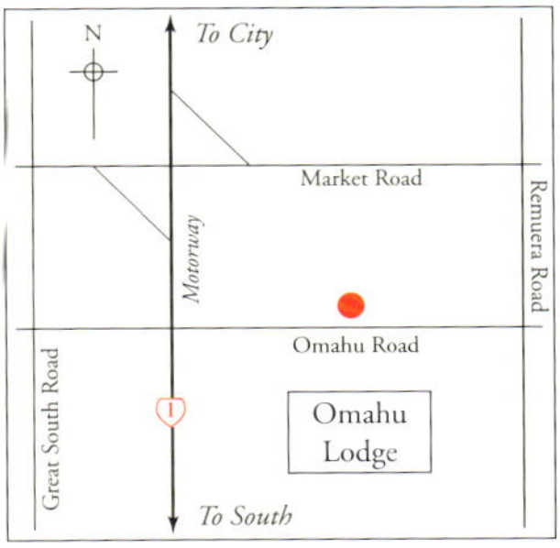

Features & Attractions

- *Spacious, private setting*
- *Solar-heated pool*
- *Spa, sauna, central heating*
- *Large plasma/DVD room*
- *Minutes to central city*
- *Walk to restaurants/cafés*
- *Parnell, Newmarket 5 min*
- *Mt Hobson/Cornwall Park 5 min*

Omahu Lodge offers luxury Bed & Breakfast accommodation with total privacy in a peaceful residential setting. The Lodge is very spacious with beautifully appointed bedrooms all with ensuites, fine bed linen, heated towels, bathrobes, slippers, hair dryers, ironing and tea/coffee facilities. Rooms have views of Cornwall Park, Mt Hobson, Mt St John and the eastern suburbs. Relax in the large lounge amongst the antiques or in the separate entertainment room with a large plasma television, DVD and CD player or enjoy the solar heated pool, sauna or spa. **Omahu Lodge** is a boutique resort. The city centre and Auckland's renowned harbour are just 10 minutes away by car. Remuera, Parnell and Newmarket's exclusive shopping, restaurants and antique shops are only minutes away. Walks in Cornwall Park, Mt Hobson and Mt St John add to the peaceful ambience of the suburban setting. A full sumptuous breakfast is served in the conservatory overlooking the pool, on the patio beside the pool or room service is available. Dinner is available by arrangement.

WOODLANDS

18 Waiatarua Road, Remuera, Auckland
Ph (09) 524 6990, Fax (09) 524 6993
email: *jude.harwood@xtra.co.nz*
www.travelwise.co.nz

Tariff : N.Z. Dollars	
Double	$135-155
Single	$105
Child	n/a

Bedrooms	Qty
Double	2
Twin	1
Single	
Bed Size	**Qty**
Super King	
King	1
Queen	
Double	1
Single	2
Bathrooms	**Qty**
Ensuite	1
Private	1
Guest Share	

Bed & Breakfast in Native Woods

Features & Attractions

- *Secluded, peaceful woodland setting*
- *On bus route*
- *Divine breakfasts*
- *Handy to Auckland airport*
- *Solar heated swimming pool*
- *Close to Ericcson stadium*
- *Day trips - 1/2 day trips organised*

Our three bedrooms overlook the solar heated swimming pool and lush native greenery. The ensuite king-sized room is large with French windows opening out to a private conservatory, for your use only, and a private entrance to the pool. The 'Pool Room' with a private bathroom, steps out directly to the pool – have a swim before breakfast. The smaller 'Deck Room' opens to the pool area, suitable for two friends, as it is a twin room. Each room has a coloured TV, tea/coffee making facilities, pool towels, heated towel rails, and hairdryers. A guest refrigerator is provided. The rooms are very quiet and secluded. Safe off-street car parking provided. Breakfasts are very special – we use fresh seasonal fruit, then a cooked breakfast of your choice, home-made jams and preserves, herbal teas/teas or percolated coffee, cereals, freshly squeezed juices, muesli.

Visitors book comments 2006: "A magic stay – such a stunning place and superb hosts", "Wow, what a wonderful start to our Honeymoon – you spoilt us", "Gorgeous breakfast, great, divine hosts", "PERFECT, first class, I mean 11/10!!", "Tres Bon – Magnifique!!"

Join us for a glass of New Zealand wine by the pool. Arrive as a guest and leave as a friend.

ELLERSLIE BED & BREAKFAST INN

6 Walpole Street, Ellerslie, Auckland
Ph (09) 589 1997, Fax (09) 589 1994
Mobile 021-258 2632
email: *info@ellersliebbi.co.nz*
www.ellersliebbi.co.nz

Tariff : N.Z. Dollars	
Double	$140-160
Single	$100-130
Child	n/a

Bedrooms	Qty
Double	2
Twin	1
Single	
Bed Size	**Qty**
Super King	
King	
Queen	2
Double	
Single	2
Bathrooms	**Qty**
Ensuite	3
Private	
Guest Share	

Bed & Breakfast
Boutique Accommodation

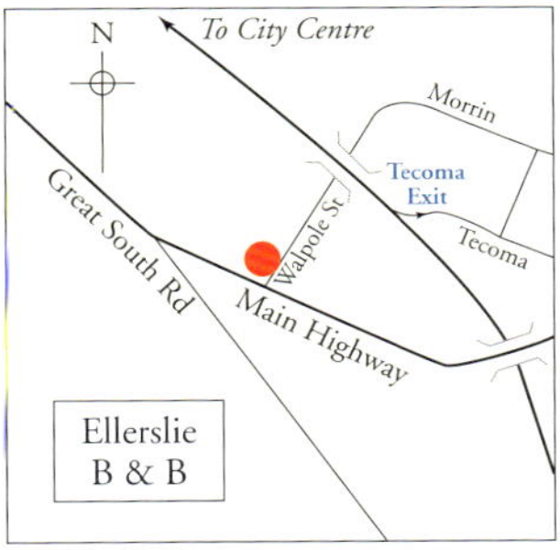

Features & Attractions

- *'Warm Hospitality'*
- *Central to motorway system*
- *Stroll to café's and shops*
- *Dinner by arrangement*
- *Close to Ellerslie Race Course*
- *Convention centre*
- *Bus stops 100m from door*
- *Mt Smart Stadium*

We invite you to join us in our gorgeous new, modern brick home, nestled in a quiet part of Ellerslie/Greenlane, yet situated midway between the airport and Auckland City. Our cosy guest-only lounge boasts an area set up with Sky digital TV, and coffee/tea making facilities. The guest PC on wireless offers free internet access, however if it's privacy you're looking for, then curl up in your comfy queen bed in your cosy ensuite bedroom, tucked between pure cotton sheets and your down duvet and catch a movie or a sport (whoever wins the toss!) on your private 'in-room' LCD TV. Brian, a chef in his own right, loves to offer our guests a special cooked breakfast with plenty of variety and a delight to the eye as well as the palate. You will enjoy! We can help with travel arrangements, if required. We have a cat. **Ideally suited for the tourist or the corporate traveller, we will do our best to accommodate your schedule.**

MARTINI HOUSE

183 Whitford Road, PO Box 38406, Howick, Auckland
Ph (09) 534 8585
Mobile 027-496 1987
email: *martinico@xtra.co.nz*

Tariff : N.Z. Dollars	
Double	$155-185
Single	$110-140
Child	

Bedrooms	Qty
Double	3
Twin	
Single	
Bed Size	**Qty**
Super King	
King	1
Queen	2
Double	
Single	
Bathrooms	**Qty**
Ensuite	1
Private	
Guest Share	1

BB **Luxury Bed & Breakfast** LA

VISA MasterCard

DIRECTIONS:
Please phone for directions.

Features & Attractions

- *Airport & city 25 min.*
- *Cafés & restaurants nearby*
- *Car ferry to Waiheke Island*
- *Ferry to Auckland City*
- *Pacific Coast Highway link*
- *Local walks & golf courses*
- *Relaxing ambience*
- *Healthy, hearty breakfast*

Martini House is an architecturally designed home offering visitor accommodation with a touch of luxury.

If you are looking for a staging post for your New Zealand tour after landing in Auckland, we are located 25 minutes from the airport, 25 minutes from Auckland central, and most significantly we are also very conveniently positioned at the gateway to the Seabird Coast which leads into Coromandel. When you stay with us, you will relax and revitalise. You can unwind either outdoors, or inside with our magazine library and home theatre. We will set you up for the day with our generous breakfast and share our local knowledge to assist you to enjoy your visit.

Facilities include a guest lounge with plasma screen home theatre and private garden area, in-ground swimming pool (unheated) and off-street parking.

Local features include historic Howick village, art gallery and artist studios, Botany shopping complex, Manukau City Centre 15 minutes drive and safe swimming beaches. There are 25+ restaurants, cafés and brasseries nearby with courtesy transfers available.

Cockle Bay Homestay B&B

81 Pah Road, Cockle Bay, Howick, Auckland
Ph (09) 535 0120 Fax (09) 535 0120
Mobile 027-242 2646
email: *cocklebay@bnbnz.co.nz*
www.bnbnz.co.nz

Tariff : N.Z. Dollars	
Double	$170
Single	$145
Child	

Bedrooms	Qty
Double	2
Twin	
Single	
Bed Size	**Qty**
Super King	
King	1
Queen	1
Double	
Single	
Bathrooms	**Qty**
Ensuite	1
Private	1
Guest Share	

Luxury Accommodation
Spectacular Sea Views

Features & Attractions

- *Ferries to city, Waiheke Is*
- *Shuttle to / from airport*
- *Quiet & peaceful location*
- *Historical Village Museum*
- *Gateway to Pacific Coast Highway*
- *Walk to beach & historic restaurant*
- *Auckland airport / city 25 minutes*
- *Golf courses (four) within easy reach*

DIRECTIONS: Please phone for directions.

Welcome to our modern, comfortable home above Cockle Bay Beach, a quiet location with superb sea views. Make a booking with us, at the same time book your rental car from our website and receive instant online confirmation for both. **Special rates for two nights or more**. The ferry runs daily to Downtown Auckland (35 min.) a wonderful way to see the harbour with no parking hassles. City bus at our gate. Howick Village for shopping, cafés and restaurants is 3km away.

The Taylor Suite with queen-size bed is one large room with ensuite, 2 comfortable chairs, coffee table and private balcony. **The Evan Room** with king-size bed, private bathroom, bathrobes, deck with chairs and table close by for your use. Both guest rooms are well appointed with TV, ceiling fans, tea and fresh coffee facilities and hairdryers. A fridge is conveniently situated in the hallway for the use of both rooms.

We enjoy planning your days with us. Come and enjoy our warm Kiwi hospitality, and wonderful breakfast discussions. We do not take children under 12 years.

BROOKWOOD LODGE

33 Bell Road, Beachlands, Auckland
Ph (09) 536 6975, Fax (09) 536 6976
Mobile 027-479 6453
email: *info@brookwoodlodge.co.nz*
www.brookwoodlodge.co.nz

Tariff : N.Z. Dollars	
Double	$120-150
Single	$90
Child	

Bedrooms	Qty
Double	3
Twin	
Single	
Bed Size	**Qty**
Super King	
King	1
Queen	
Double	2
Single	2
Bathrooms	**Qty**
Ensuite	1
Private	
Guest Share	1

Bed & Breakfast
Semi-rural Homestay

Features & Attractions

- *Warm, relaxed hospitality*
- *Tranquil semi-rural setting*
- *Ferry to Auckland City*
- *Swimming pool*
- *Close to 2 golf courses*
- *Dinner by arrangement*
- *Internet & email facilities*
- *Your comfort our priority*

DIRECTIONS:
Please phone or email for easy directions.

Brian, Heather and our friendly cocker spaniel, invite you to relax and unwind at **Brookwood Lodge**, our charming 100 year old villa, set in four acres of cottage gardens, sweeping lawns and paddocks. Two double bedrooms, the **Tulip Room** with its pretty antique brass bed and the **Rose Room**, are within our main house and share a guest bathroom. The **Lavender Suite**, our beautiful garden suite, offers total privacy with its own entrance and ensuite bathroom. All rooms are well-appointed and comfortable with TV, electric blankets, bathrobes, hairdryer, tea and coffee making facilities and personal toiletries. Indulge in a sumptuous breakfast in our dining room or in summer on the patio overlooking our swimming pool. Enjoy the tranquillity of our small sea-side village, yet only 30 minutes from the centre of Auckland City via our regular ferry service. Waiheke Island, famous for its vineyards, olive groves, restaurants and beautiful beaches, is also only a few minutes away by ferry. Explore the surrounding countryside with its beautiful regional park walks, boutique wineries, safe swimming beaches and excellent restaurants. We look forward to making your stay with us a happy and memorable one.

TOTARA LODGE

327 Redoubt Road, Manukau, Auckland
Ph (09) 263 7777, Fax (09) 263 7777
Mobile 027-488 5535
email: *totara-lodge@xtra.co.nz*
www.nzaccommodation.co.nz

Tariff : N.Z. Dollars	
Double	$100-230
Single	$75-110
Child	

Bedrooms	Qty
Double	2
Twin	1
Single	1
Bed Size	**Qty**
Super King	
King	
Queen	2
King/Single	2
Single	1
Bathrooms	**Qty**
Ensuite	2
Private	1
Guest Share	1

Luxury Bed & Breakfast

Features & Attractions

- *15 minutes to Airport*
- *Peace and quiet, bush walks*
- *Wireless broadband available*
- *Auckland City 20 min*
- *5 acres of gardens around the Lodge*
- *400 acres of Totara Park and Botanical Gardens adjacent*
- *Complimentary laundry*

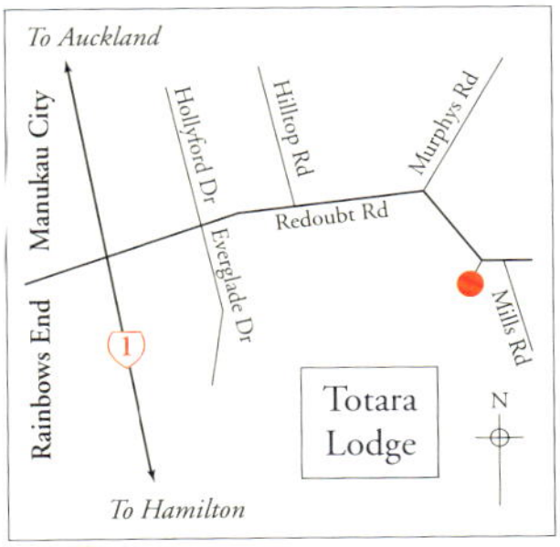

Sited adjoining Totara Park, the Lodge is set in five acres of gardens with established trees and a pond. Extensive views, overlooking the 400 acres of Park Reserve with native bush and farmland to the harbour beyond, enhance the peace and quiet of this secluded location, yet Manukau City is only five minutes drive away, Auckland City twenty minutes away. Built in 1988, **Totara Lodge** features French and old English interior style. Guests have tea and coffee facilities, refrigerator, television, hair dryer and bathrobes. Breakfast is served in the dining room or alfresco on the deck looking out on to the pastoral scene beyond the harbour. Lunch and dinner with complimentary wine are also available at an extra charge. Staying at Totara Lodge is like staying in an oasis, no traffic noise, just peace and quiet. You will think you are miles away from the hustle and bustle, yet shops and restaurants are minutes away.

Hillpark Homestay

16 Collie Street, Hillpark, Manurewa, Auckland
Ph (09) 267 6847, Fax (09) 267 8718
Mobile 021-207 2559
email: *stay@hillpark.co.nz*
www.hillpark.co.nz

Tariff : N.Z. Dollars	
Double	$100
Single	$60
Child	$20

Bedrooms	Qty
Double	1
Twin	2
Single	
Bed Size	**Qty**
Super King	
King	
Queen	
Double	1
Single	4
Bathrooms	**Qty**
Ensuite	1
Private	
Guest Share	1

Bed & Breakfast Homestay

Features & Attractions

- *Friendly, helpful hosts*
- *Near to airport –15 min.*
- *Ellerslie Flower Show*
- *Regional botanic garden*
- *Pacific events centre*
- *Tipapa events centre*
- *Close to motorway Nth/Sth*
- *Dinners available $20 pp*

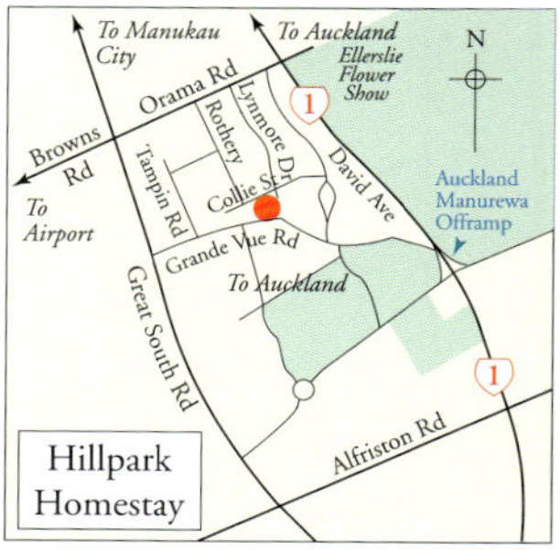

Welcome to our sunny, spacious home in Hill Park, a quiet, pleasant suburb of Manurewa, where our friendly Tonkinese cat will greet you. The beds are comfortable, with electric blankets and wool underlays. Katrine is an occasional primary school relief teacher. Graham has retired from working for the Red Cross. We are 15 min. from Auckland International Airport, 20 min. from Auckland city centre, on the route south and the Pacific Coast Highway. Nearby are restaurants, regional botanic garden – site of the Ellerslie Flower Show, Pacific Events Centre, Tipapa Events Centre, Nathan Homestead, Manukau City Shopping Centre, Rainbows End Adventure Park, the Manukau Superclinic and Surgery Centre and attractive bush walks. Our interests include teaching, classical music, painting, gardening, photography, Christian activities, reading and travel. We offer warm, relaxed hospitality and like conversation and sharing experiences with guests. Come and enjoy home-made bread and dinner with fresh garden vegetables in season from Graham's garden. Visit our web site for more information.

Airport Bed & Breakfast

1 Westney Road, Mangere, Auckland
Ph (09) 275 0533, Fax (09) 275 0968
Mobile 027-270 5810
email: *airportbnb@xtra.co.nz*
www.airportbnb.co.nz

Features & Attractions

- *5 min Auckland Airport*
- *Internet access & Wi-Fi*
- *Car, cycle, luggage storage*
- *Sky television lounge*
- *Central heating*
- *Buffet breakfast*

Guest House Bed & Breakfast

Double	$90-120
Single	$75-105
Child	

A warm Kiwi welcome awaits you at **Airport Bed & Breakfast**. Just five minutes from Auckland Airport, a courtesy transfer is available from 6.30am to 8.45pm. Dial 28 on airport freephone.

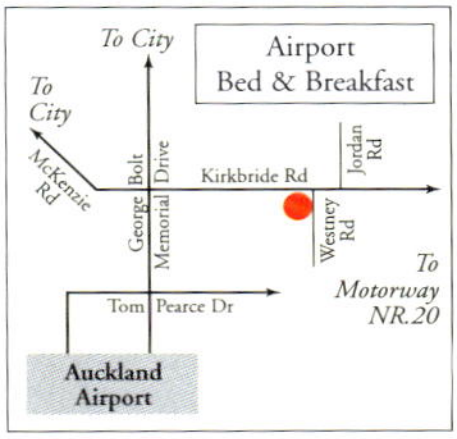

Airport Bed & Breakfast is comfortable, clean and cost effective accommodation – so convenient to Auckland International and Domestic Airports. Restaurants, takeaways, dairy, liquor store and city bus stop are all within an easy stroll. See our lovely city by bus/ferry on the $10 day pass. Rental cars, sightseeing and New Zealand-wide tours can be arranged.

Complimentary tea and coffee. Internet access Wi-Fi zone, car, cycle and luggage storage is available.

Bedrooms	Qty
Double	8
Twin	2
Single	
Bed Size	**Qty**
King	1
Queen	2
Double	5
Single	9
Bathrooms	**Qty**
Ensuite	4
Private	
Guest Share	3

YOUR HOSTS: Linda and Frank Weterman Ph (09) 291 9359 **Karaka - Auckland**

De Kalmte

79 Bungard Rd, Karaka, Auckland
Ph (09) 291 9359, Mobile 027-301 4930
email: *info@dekalmte.co.nz*
www.dekalmte.co.nz

Features & Attractions

- *Internet & email access*
- *Spa pool*
- *Dutch spoken*
- *Golf clubs available*
- *30min. Auckland Airport*
- *40min. Auckland City*

Double	$110-130
Single	$80-100
Child	$25

Self-contained Country Bed & Breakfast

Bedrooms	Qty
Double	1
Twin	
Single	
Bed Size	**Qty**
King	
Queen	1
Double	
Single	
Bathrooms	**Qty**
Ensuite	
Private	1
Guest Share	

Enjoy the surroundings of our small hobby farm whilst relaxing in our self-contained one bedroom country cottage called 'Allistragh'. **De Kalmte** is located in Karaka, southwest of Auckland. Join us and experience a snapshot of rural life on our 4.5 acre property. We are an easy drive from Auckland Airport and the Auckland Central Motorway. Our guests have a choice of wonderful restaurants throughout Karaka and the surrounding Franklin area or by arrangement may choose to enjoy lunch or dinner cooked by our family chef, Frank. Whether your stay is for business, to rest and relax, or you are ready to explore the many features of the local area, we can offer you a comfortable and hospitable environment.

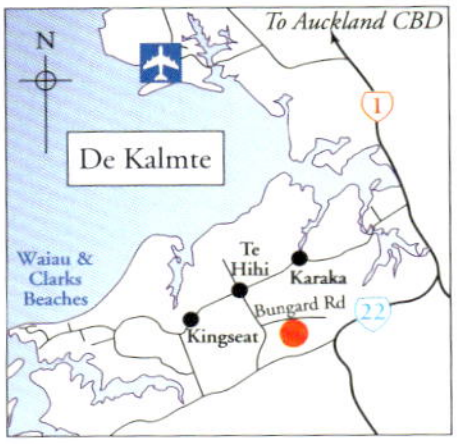

Karaka Point Vineyard and Lodge

35c Wallace Dr, Waiau Pa, Franklin South of Auckland
Ph (09) 232 0025, Fax (09) 232 0525
Mobile 027-477 7155
email: *info@karakapointvineyard.co.nz*
www.karakapointvineyard.co.nz

Tariff : N.Z. Dollars	
Double	$250
Single	$200
Child	$50

Bedrooms	Qty
Double	3
Twin	
Single	
Bed Size	**Qty**
Super King	
King	
Queen	3
Double	
Single	
Bathrooms	**Qty**
Ensuite	1
Private	
Guest Share	1

BA **Vineyard Luxury Lodge** LA

- *Wine, vineyards & gardens*
- *Close to golf courses*
- *Local arts and crafts*
- *Award winning restaurants*

- *Private and luxurious*
- *Heated indoor pool*
- *Venue for weddings etc*
- *Sky, digital, DVD & music*

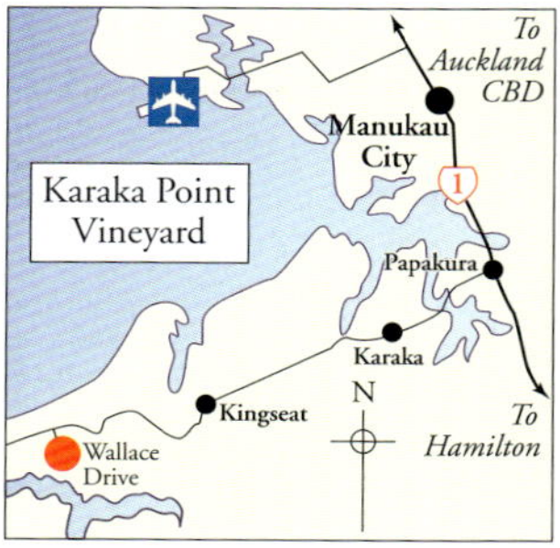

Karaka Point Vineyard and Lodge is located on the Karaka Point Peninsula, southwest of Auckland, New Zealand. Set in beautiful estate gardens the Vineyard and Lodge provide an experience for wine and garden lovers alike, enjoy a visit to 'The Cellar Door' or relax for the weekend soaking up the tranquil surroundings in luxury from your private suite. Our guests will enjoy a French country inspired master suite with antiques, sumptuous linen and designer ensuite, leading to their private French antique style living area for dining, relaxing by the fire with a good movie, or lounging back with a glass of wine. Enjoy breakfast served in the conservatory, perhaps followed by a morning swim in the heated indoor pool. Picnics, lunches and dinners at the **Lodge** are available by prior arrangement or visit one of the many fine restaurants in the Franklin area. In the evening enjoy drinks at sunset in one of the many idyllic spots you will find in the majestic quarter-century-old gardens. KPV is also the perfect place for special events.

Four Oaks

Taraire Dr., Drury Hills Rd, PO Box 141,
Drury, Auckland 2247
Ph (09) 294 8196, Fax (09) 294 8112
Mobile 021-921 281
email: *stay@fouroaks.co.nz*
www.fouroaks.co.nz

Tariff : N.Z. Dollars	
Double	$175-250
Single	$100-120
Child	

Bedrooms	Qty
Double	3
Twin	1
Single	
Bed Size	**Qty**
Super King	
King	2
Queen	1
Double	
King/Single	2
Bathrooms	**Qty**
Ensuite	2
Private	2
Guest Share	

Boutique Accommodation
Bed & Breakfast

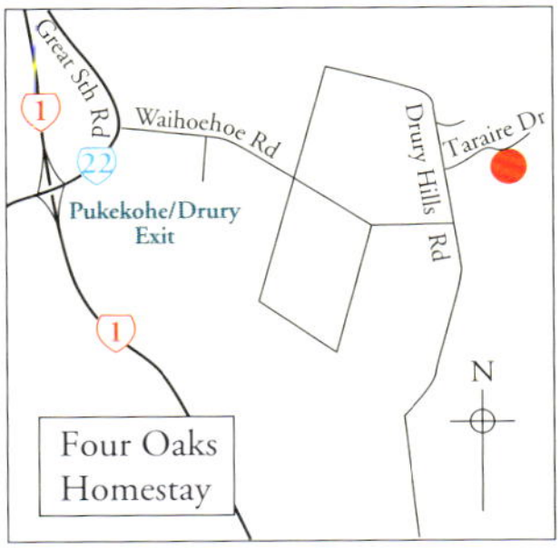

Features & Attractions

- *20 min. to Auckland Airport*
- *30 min. to Auckland City*
- *Stunning views, peace and quiet*
- *Native bush and bird life*
- *Saltwater pool*
- *Tennis court and gym*
- *Close to golf courses*
- *Airport pick-up/drop-off*

Judy and Phil welcome you to their magnificent home, set in ten acres of pasture and native bush, nestled in the hills above Drury. The property offers expansive views of Auckland, yet is only 20 minutes from Auckland Airport and 30 minutes from the city.

There is plenty of room to relax and unwind in pleasant surroundings. Facilities offered include saltwater pool, tennis court, fully equipped gym, Sky Digital TV and internet access. The property has extensive gardens with quiet areas to stroll amongst the native bush or just sit and listen to the native birdsongs.

Choose from our breakfast menu plus tea and coffee making facilities offered with home baking. We offer complimentary Auckland Airport pick-up or drop-off.

For those with a passion for flying like Phil (PPL), Ardmore Aerodrome is 10 minutes away and you can be at the Auckland Gliding Club in 3 minutes.

Four Oaks is your ideal place to start and finish your holiday in style.

Drury - Auckland ▶ YOUR HOSTS: Carolyn and Ron Booker Ph (09) 294 9030

The Drury Homestead

349, Drury Hills Rd, RD1, Drury
Ph (09) 294 9030, Fax (09) 294 9035
Mobile 021-158 5061

Features & Attractions

- *Quiet country setting*
- *Near local restaurants*
- *Large verandahs, great sunsets*
- *20 mins. from airport*
- *Native bush and stream*
- *Character-filled colonial home*

Country Paradise Bed & Breakfast

Double	$120
Single	$70
Child	neg

DIRECTIONS:
From State Highway 1 (SH1) exit at the Pukekohe/Drury off ramp and follow the map below to 349 Drury Hills Rd.

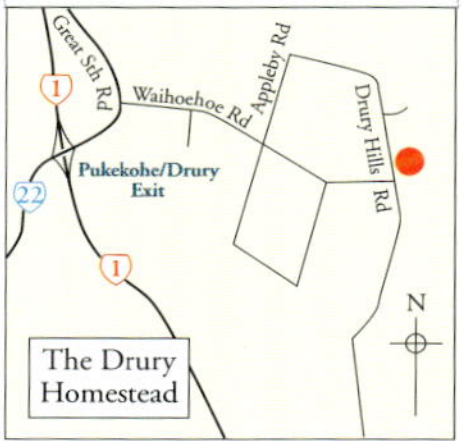

The Drury Homestead is our wonderfully restored early colonial home, set amidst paddocks and bordered by native bush and stream. Choose from four character-filled bedrooms, lovingly refurbished with an emphasis on comfort and style. The **Lily Room** is a queen-sized studio with kitchen, ensuite and its own entrance on the ground floor. Upstairs the **River Room**, queen-size with ensuite, overlooks our stream whilst **Dunedin**, also queen-size with ensuite, has views over the country side. **Cape Reinga** has twin king/single beds and a private bathroom. We provide a warm and friendly introduction to your New Zealand experience, 20 minutes from the airport, 5 minutes off SH1 and 35 minutes from Auckland City. Children welcome. Family cat and dogs.

Bedrooms	Qty
Double	3
Twin	1
Single	
Bed Size	**Qty**
King	
Queen	3
Double	
King/Single	2
Bathrooms	**Qty**
Ensuite	3
Private	1
Guest Share	

Drury ▶ YOUR HOSTS: Susan and Pat Baker Ph: (09) 294 8748

Tuhimata Park

697B Runciman Road, Runciman, RD 2, Drury
Ph (09) 294 8748, Fax (09) 294 8749
email: *tuhimata@iprolink.co.nz*

Features & Attractions

- *20 minutes from airport*
- *Close to main route south*
- *Quiet country setting*
- *30 minutes from City centre*
- *Games room, indoor garden*
- *Relaxed friendly hospitality*

Homestay Bed & Breakfast

Double	$90-120
Single	$60-80
Child	neg

Our spacious, comfortable and relaxing home is an ideal place to start or finish a New Zealand holiday. Set in expansive lawns and giant oak trees with comfortable bedrooms, wide verandahs overlooking rolling green farmland, an indoor garden and barbeque in a large conservatory, tennis court, swimming pool, spa pool and games room. Laundry facilities available. Pat and Susan have travelled extensively and were involved for many years in farming, national politics and education and enjoy nothing more than conversing with guests over a hot or cold drink in their welcoming open-style home.

Proud members of @home NEW ZEALAND – a guarantee of quality accommodation.

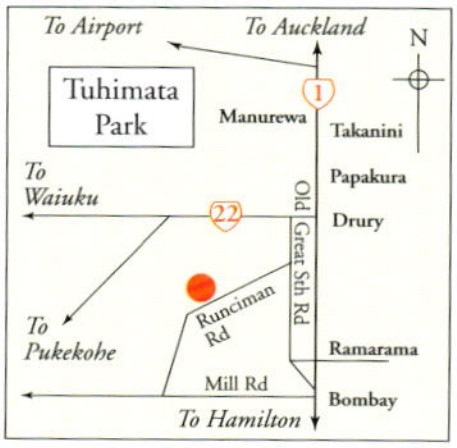

Bedrooms	Qty
Double	2
Twin	1
Single	
Bed Size	**Qty**
King	
Queen	2
Double	
Single	2
Bathrooms	**Qty**
Ensuite	2
Private	
Guest Share	1

YOUR HOSTS: **Sue and Archie McPherson** Ph (09) 236 0044 ◀ ***Ramarama - Bombay***

THISTLEDOWN LODGE

1810 Great South Road, Ramarama, Auckland
Ph (09) 236 0044
Mobile 027-473 6313
email: *inquiries@thistledownlodge.co.nz*
www.thistledownlodge.co.nz

Features & Attractions

- *25 min. from airport*
- *Easy to find, secure parking*
- *Friendly farm animals*
- *Heated pool, spa, sauna*
- *Spacious bedrooms*
- *Country hospitality*

$	
Double	$110-130
Single	$80
Child	neg

Quality Bed & Breakfast

Bedrooms	Qty
Double	3
Twin	1
Single	
Bed Size	**Qty**
King	1
Queen	2
Double	
King/Single	3
Bathrooms	**Qty**
Ensuite	2
Private	1
Guest Share	

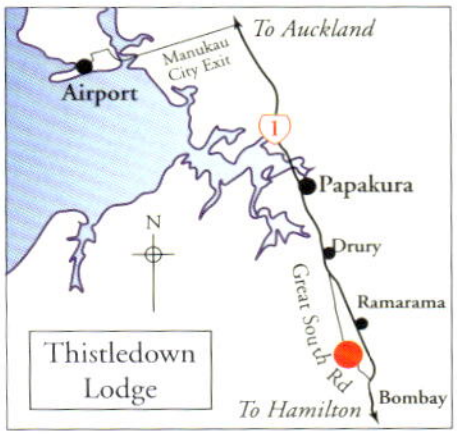

Enjoy warm country hospitality in a peaceful setting just minutes from the southern motorway. Find out why guests remember Archie's breakfasts and keep returning for more! It's the perfect start or end to your holiday.

The English colonial style home has spacious second floor bedrooms with welcoming extras.

Relax in the heated swimming pool, spa (jacuzzi) or infra-red sauna. Or feed Big Ears and her Suffolk Sheep mates or Eric the friendly Highland Steer. Meals and family groups by arrangement.

Thistledown Lodge is on the old main highway, midway between the Ramarama and Bombay motorway exits.

YOUR HOSTS: **Anthea and David Adams** Ph: (09) 235 9812 ◀ ***Waiuku - Franklin***

NGODEVWA GARDEN BED & BREAKFAST

8 Whiriwhiri Road, RD 2, Waiuku
Ph (09) 235 9812, Fax (09) 235 9812
Mobile 021-397 259
email: *daadams@ps.gen.nz*

Features & Attractions

- *Peaceful & relaxing*
- *Delightful planters garden*
- *Charming 90-year-old house*
- *Rural setting near coast*
- *Arabian horse stud*
- *45 min from Airport*

Bed & Breakfast Countrystay

$	
Double	$125
Single	$90
Child	n/a

Welcome to **Ngodevwa** (Tibetan for 'Flowers of the Angels'). Set in two hectares of tree studded colourful garden and pasture, **Ngodevwa** offers peace and tranquility with intimate areas for relaxation. Let the magic of the garden relax and rejuvenate you. Guests have queen bed accommodation, private bathroom and a sunny sitting room overlooking the garden. Full cooked or continental breakfast is served in the conservatory overlooking pond and fountain in courtyard. We have arabian horses to befriend, two siamese cats to cuddle, our golden retriever, and a rare 1932 convertible Sunbeam car. Local attractions include the beautiful Awhitu Peninsula with its surf and harbour beaches and the Glenbrook Vintage Railway.

DIRECTIONS: Going south turn off Sthn Motorway at Drury direct to Waiuku, or north turn off at Bombay, through Pukekohe to Waiuku. At town centre turn left. 3 km to Ngodevwa on RH corner of Whiriwhiri Rd

Bedrooms	Qty
Double	1
Twin	
Single	
Bed Size	**Qty**
King	
Queen	1
Double	
Single	
Bathrooms	**Qty**
Ensuite	
Private	1
Guest Share	

Brookfield Lodge

2114 State Highway 1, RD, Bombay,
Auckland South
Ph (09) 236 0775
Mobile 027-292 1422
email: *brookfieldleen@xtra.co.nz*

Photo: Cheryl Fuller

Tariff : N.Z. Dollars	
Double	$120-130
Single	$100
Child	neg

Bedrooms	Qty
Double	2
Twin	1
Single	
Bed Size	**Qty**
Super King	
King	
Queen	2
Double	
Single	2
Bathrooms	**Qty**
Ensuite	1
Private	2
Guest Share	

Luxury Bed & Breakfast
Homestay

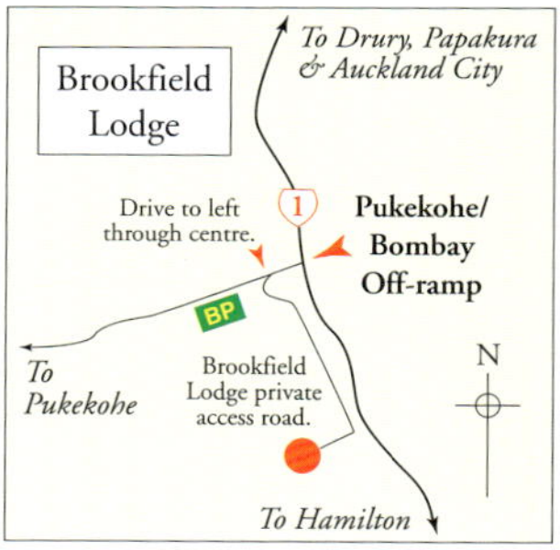

Features & Attractions

- *Main route south easy access*
- *25 minutes from airport*
- *Beautiful Auckland show garden*
- *Sub-tropical areas*
- *Relaxed, friendly hospitality*
- *Surrounded by sunny patios*
- *30 minutes from Auckland*
- *Small flock of sheep*

Easily accessed on the Main South Highway. Only 25 minutes from the airport. A perfect and memorable place to start and finish your holiday. **Brookfield Lodge** is set in 5 acres with lovely established trees, lawns and gardens, and with a small flock of sheep. This is one of Aucklands frequently visited gardens. Our spacious and attractive home is comfortable, relaxing and surrounded by sunny patios. One ensuite queen bedroom opens onto a deck in a sub-tropical garden. Pretend you are in Fiji.

Ensuring your comfort and pleasure will be our priority. Fresh flowers, bathrobes, hair driers, complimentary tea, good coffee and home-baking will add to your enjoyment. Guests consider our breakfasts to be special and delicious. Two or three course dinners are available by arrangement. Alternatively there are many nearby restaurants.

We have retired from farming and working with thoroughbred horses and enjoy travelling and meeting with other travellers.

Hunua Gorge Country House

482 Hunua Road, PO Box 27, Papakura, Auckland
Ph (09) 299 7926, Fax (09) 299 7926
Mobile 021-669 922
email: *hunuagorge@xtra.co.nz*

Tariff : N.Z. Dollars	
Double	$125-150
Single	$90
Child	

Bedrooms	Qty
Double	3
Twin	1
Single	1
Bed Size	**Qty**
Super King	
King	1
Queen	1
Double	1
Single	3
Bathrooms	**Qty**
Ensuite	1
Private	1
Guest Share	1

Countrystay Bed & Breakfast

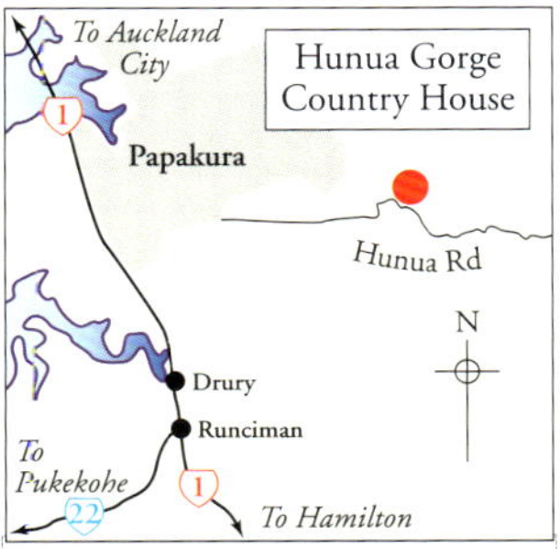

DIRECTIONS: SH1 off-ramp at Papakura proceed east along Beach Rd, thru 2 sets of lights onto Settlement Rd. Hunua Rd is on right corner of Edmond Hilary School, proceed 5 km thru housing and light industrial, into Hunua Gorge. We are on left, opp. Winstones Aggregates entrance with a steep gravel drive.

Features & Attractions

- *Stunning views*
- *Sunsets*
- *Dinners a speciality*
- *Farm animals*
- *Native plants and birds in garden*
- *Parking, laundry, internet*
- *Wineries, beaches, golf close by*
- *Fishing, scenic flights, shops close by*

Welcome to the character-filled **Hunua Gorge**, just off the beaten track, where nature abounds, yet half an hour to Auckland City, Auckland and Ardmore Airports. We are half an hour to either coast and on route to Coromandel.

Come and discover the wonders of Auckland, something for everyone on offer.

We have a choice of superior rooms and delicious breakfasts and dinners. We live in the food basket of Auckland. Vegetarians are catered for gladly, alternatively enjoy our wonderful seafood or famous lamb and beef. Prior notice is appreciated. Weather permitting dine alfresco under the southern stars.

We are 3 personable generations on 50 acres of a magic country. ***Welcome!***

Clevedon - Auckland

YOUR HOSTS: Iman and Mariette Sprenger Ph: (09) 292 8886

Highridge Farm B&B

144 Highridge Road, Clevedon
Ph (09) 292 8886, Fax (09) 292 8886
email: *highridgefarm@clear.net.nz*
Mobile 021-445 548
http://home.clear.net.nz/pages/msprenger/index.htm

Features & Attractions

- *Peaceful country setting*
- *Close to town & attractions*
- *See web via www.bnbnz.com*
- *Wine trails, walks*
- *35 min to airport*
- *Splendid sea views*

Countrystay Self-contained Bed & Breakfast

Double	$120
Single	$90
Child	

We are of Dutch and Swiss origin and speak Dutch and French. Our farm is a 57 acre beef and sheep raising farm near the township of Clevedon, the polo capital of New Zealand. We offer comfortable accommodation to the discerning traveller. The setting is beautiful, very private and quiet. Views of the Pacific Ocean, the Clevedon Valley and our farm can be enjoyed from every room. The accommodation includes spacious guest lounge, fully equipped kitchenette, large private patio, barbeque and ample parking. Meals and transport by prior arrangement. Located close to Clevedon Village, beaches, vineyards, Te Papa Equestrian Centre, Karaka Horse Complex, golf courses, Auckland Kennel Club grounds, Pukekohe Park Raceway. Auckland City is 45 km away and Auckland Airport is a thirty five minute drive. We look forward to welcoming you to our home and will happily assist you with any travel arrangements.

DIRECTIONS: Please ring for exact directions. Bookings are essential.

Bedrooms	Qty
Double or Twin	1
Twin	
Single	1
Bed Size	**Qty**
Super King	1
Queen	
Double	
Single	
Bathrooms	**Qty**
Ensuite	1
Private	
Guest Share	

Auckland Brookby Clevedon

YOUR HOSTS: Pat and Trevor Simpson Ph: (09) 530 8576

DIRECTIONS; From Auckland take Manurewa turn-off. From Hamilton take Takanini turn-off.

Top of the Hill Country Homestay

183 Fitzpatrick Road, Brookby,
RD 1, Manurewa, Auckland
Ph/Fax (09) 530 8576, Mobile 027-280 0536
email: *topofthehill@xtra.co.nz*
www.visions.co.nz/topofthehill.

Features & Attractions

- *Discounted 3-day stays*
- *Fantastic views, every room*
- *Genuine Kiwi hospitality*
- *Airport/city 25 min.*
- *Great country breakfast*
- *Native bush & bird life*

Luxury Countrystay

Double	$120-140
Single	$80-90
Child	n/a

Pat and Trevor love sharing their spacious home – purpose-built by Trevor and lifted high up on secluded bush-clad hills – and their life style only millions dream about. Spectacular 360 degree views of landscape, dotted with sheep and cows, to the sparkling waters of Auckland's harbour – all viewed from the comfort of the large guest lounge. Our guest wing has ensuite bedrooms with TV, tea-coffee making facilities and kitchenette with laundry. Enjoy a scenic ferry trip to Auckland's city centre (30 min). Nearby attractions are Manukau's Super Centre, Auckland's Botanical Gardens, golf, polo, village fairs, or a drive on the stunning 'Scenic Pacific Coast Highway' to the beautiful Coromandel.

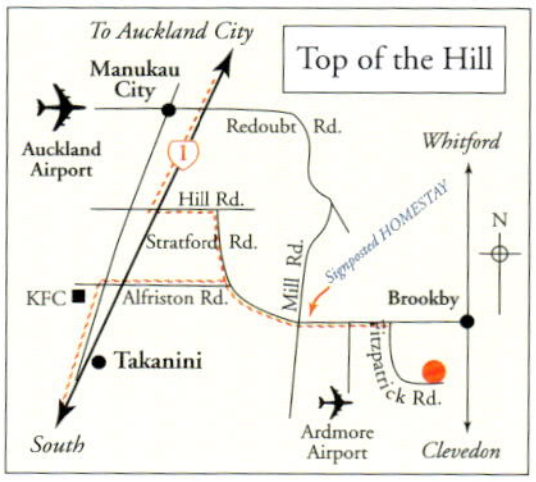

Bedrooms	Qty
Double	2
Twin	1
Single	
Bed Size	**Qty**
Super King	1
King	1
Double	
King/Single	2
Bathrooms	**Qty**
Ensuite	3
Private	
Guest Share	

TIKAPA MOANA LODGE

30 Pukekereru Lane, RD 3, Waharau, Kaiaua
Ph (09) 232 2550, Fax (09) 232 2577
Mobile 027-2964082
email: *tikapalodge@seabirdcoast.co.nz*
www.tikapamoanalodge.co.nz

Tariff : N.Z. Dollars	
Double	$120-150
Single	$90-120
Extra pp	$30

Bedrooms	Qty
Double	1
Twin	
Single	1
Bed Size	**Qty**
Super King	
Queen	1
Double	
King/Single	
Single	1
Bathrooms	**Qty**
Ensuite	
Private	1
Family Share	

VISA

Tranquil Seaside Orchard Retreat on Seabird Coast

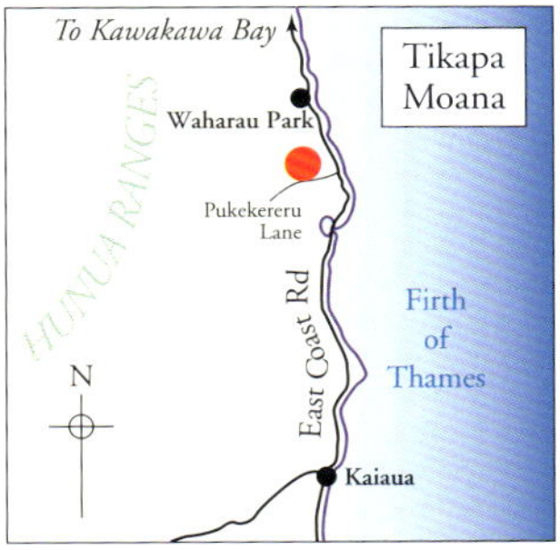

Features & Attractions

- *Miranda Hot Springs*
- *Safe swimming beaches*
- *On-site bodywork therapist*
- *Safe kayaking and fishing*

- *Migratory bird sanctuary*
- *3 regional coastal parks*
- *Organic subtropical fruit*
- *Rural seaside tranquility*

Set in a 4 acre organic subtropical orchard and garden on the western shore of the Firth of Thames, opposite the Coromandel Peninsula. A sunny homestay apartment in eco-friendly rammed earth house (sleeps 3). **Also available:** 3 bedroom holiday house for larger groups. Receive therapeutic massage or Watsu (aquatic body therapy), swim in the local Miranda Hot Mineral Pools. Experience sea kayaking, guided ecological walks, Waharau and Tapapakanga coastal parks, tramping in extensive Hunua Ranges trail network, lovely safe beaches, excellent snapper and kahawai fishing. See 1000s of migratory birds around the Miranda Shorebird Centre and world heritage coastal wetland and Chenier Plain. Dine at the famous Kaiaua Fish n' Chips shop and restaurant. Iconic country pub. Unique dragon pottery. Close to antique trail and 2 golf courses. Situated on the Seabird Coast, 50 min. drive south of Auckland Airport along the scenic and tranquil Pacific Coast Highway to the Coromandel Peninsula and all points south. Breakfast ($15) on request. Dinner by prior arrangement. French and Spanish spoken.

Mangatarata - Thames ▶ YOUR HOSTS: Ian and Linda Weight Ph: (07) 867 3305

WESTWIND HOMESTAY

228 North Road, Mangatarata, RD 6, Thames
Ph (07) 867 3305, Fax (07) 867 3356
Mobile 021-803 293
email: *beds@westwindhomestay.co.nz*
www.westwindhomestay.co.nz

@ home NEW ZEALAND

Features & Attractions

- *Enchanting bushwalk*
- *Mouth-watering breakfasts*
- *Woodturning workshop*
- *Friendly farm animals*
- *Alfresco dining*
- *Star filled skies*

H **Country Homestay We aim for Excellence** C

Escape the city to absolute country quiet overlooking native bush and feel exhilarated by the breathtaking views towards Coromandel. Expect to be pampered and rejuvenated from the moment you arrive. Feel the stresses melt away. Enjoy fabulous fresh New Zealand food and wine, coffee to die for and choose Ian's fluffy pancakes for breakfast. Stretch out on the king-sized bed and cuddle up with the softest feather duvets for the best night's sleep ever. Be amazed by the Miranda seabirds or unwind with a game of golf. Gateway to deserted white sandy Coromandel Beaches and Rotorua's Thermal wonderland. Only one hour south of Auckland International Airport. Take time out, have heaps of fun. Your haven at **Westwind** will not disappoint.

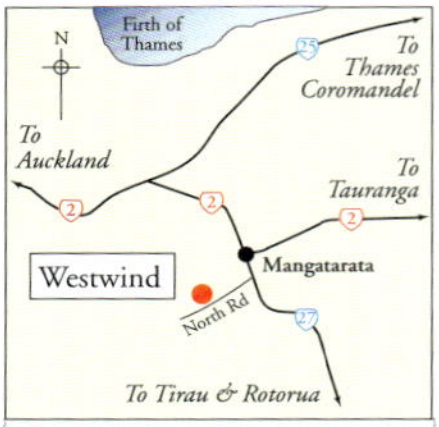

DIRECTIONS: From north: Take exit 477, travel 35km south/east on SH 2. Take RH fork at Coromandel intersection, continue for 5km on SH 2. At Tirau/ Tauranga turn-off go straight ahead 100m on SH 27. Turn right into North Road.

$	
Double	$120
Single	$85
Child	

Bedrooms	Qty
Double	1
Twin	1
Single	
Bed Size	**Qty**
King	1
Queen	
Double	
Single	2
Bathrooms	**Qty**
Ensuite	1
Private	
Guest Share	1

Kopu - Thames ▶ YOUR HOST: Rosemary Burks Ph: (07) 868 8929

WHARFEDALE FARMSTAY

Kopu, RD 1, Thames, Coromandel Peninsula
Ph (07) 868 8929, Fax (07) 868 8926
email: *wharfedale@xtra.co.nz*

Features & Attractions

- *Personal attention*
- *Healthy hearty breakfast*
- *Period English furniture*
- *Safe private swimming*
- *Quiet tranquil setting*
- *1¼ hrs Auckland Airport*

C **Country Homestay Self-contained Accomm.** SC

For fifteen years our guests have enjoyed the beauty of **Wharfedale** which has featured in Air NZ "Airwaves" and Japan's "My Country" magazines. We invite you to share our idyllic lifestyle set in nine acres of parklike paddocks and gardens surrounded by native bush. Delight in private river swimming and abundant bird life. We enjoy wholefood and organically grown produce. There are cooking facilities in the studio apartment. We have no children or indoor animals. Cool shade in summer, and cosy log fires and electric blankets in winter. Close to Thames Golf Club and restaurants. We look forward to meeting you. Unsuitable for children.

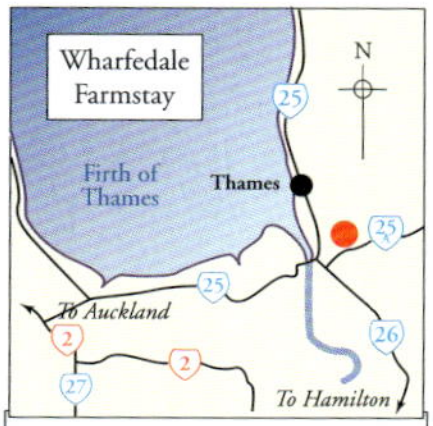

DIRECTIONS: 3 miles south of Thames to Kopu, turn left onto SH 25A to Tairua, approx 2 miles on right.

$	
Double	$135
Single	$95
Child	n/a

Bedrooms	Qty
Double	1
Twin	1
Single	
Bed Size	**Qty**
King	
Queen	
Double	1
Single	2
Bathrooms	**Qty**
Ensuite	2
Private	
Guest Share	

The Heights Bed & Breakfast

300 Grafton Rd, Thames, Coromandel Peninsula
Ph (07) 868 9925, Fax (07) 868 9925
Mobile 021-150 9642
email: *info@theheights.co.nz*
www.theheights.co.nz

Tariff : N.Z. Dollars	
Double	$175-225
Single	
Child	

Bedrooms	Qty
Double	2
Twin	
Single	
Bed Size	**Qty**
Super King	1
King	1
Queen	
Double	
Single	
Bathrooms	**Qty**
Ensuite	2
Private	
Guest Share	

The Views Go On Forever...

Features & Attractions

- *Beaches, fishing, sea*
- *Hot Water Beach*
- *Hiking, eco-tours, birds*
- *Ancient kauri groves*
- *Arts, crafts, dining*
- *Historic gold rush towns*
- *Scenic railroads*
- *Explore the Coromandel*

Sweeping views of sea, mountains and historic Thames are all yours from **The Heights**.
The short climb to Te Moana Room gives you the best views in the house, while garden view Te Koru Room has a cosy fireplace. Both let you relax in spacious luxury with a private deck or patio, private entrance, ensuite, king or super-king bed, fine linens, tea making, fridge, SKY TV/DVD, internet and guest lounge. A warm welcome from our friendly cats and special touches like home-made cookies, turndown service and full breakfast in our romantic garden help make a memorable stay.
Discover the best of Coromandel Peninsula – the spectacular coastal drive, ancient kauri groves, great hiking, historic towns, crafts, fine dining, plus every imaginable way to enjoy the sea. Then end the day in our garden spa. Only 1.5 hours from Auckland, **The Heights** is ideal for your first or last night in New Zealand or as a home base for exploring the Coromandel.

DIRECTIONS: From SH25 in Thames, at BP turn onto Bank St. which becomes Parawai. Left at Grafton Rd. **The Heights** is on the right, across from Millington Pl.

COTSWOLD COTTAGE

46 Maramarahi Road, Totara, Thames
Ph (07) 868 6306, Fax (07) 868 6202
Mobile 021-525 139
email: *jr.jd@xtra.co.nz*
www.cotswoldcottage.co.nz

Features & Attractions

- *Picturesque view*
- *Quiet and comfortable*
- *5 min from Thames*
- *Gateway to Coromandel Penins.*
- *Cooked breakfast included*
- *Private entrance & ensuites*

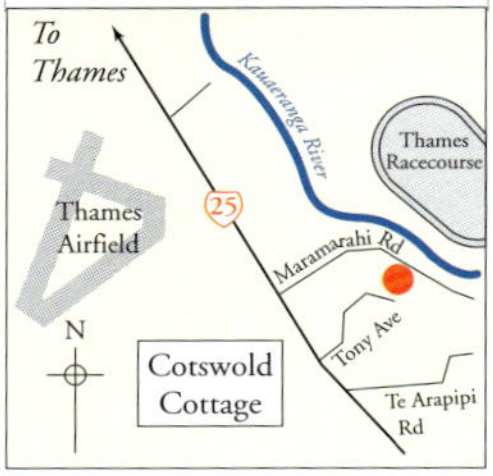

Homestay Bed & Breakfast

Double	$120-140
Single	$75
Child	$15

Just one hour drive from Auckland and five minutes from Thames, **Cotswold Cottage** is the perfect place to stopover before seeing the Coromandel Peninsula. Shifted from Epsom in 1990, our gracious old villa was re-sited at Totara overlooking Thames and the Kauaeranga River/ Valley. Initially a restaurant, the guest wing was added in 1995. Now, three sunny well appointed rooms with private ensuites, offer guests stunning views and a private entrance to come and go as they please. The lounge, conservatory and terrace offer a choice of places to read, write or simply relax. Tea and coffee making facilities. We offer dinner by arrangement.

Bedrooms	Qty
Double	2
Twin	1
Single	
Bed Size	**Qty**
King/Single	2
Queen	
Double	2
Single	
Bathrooms	**Qty**
Ensuite	3
Private	
Guest Share	

Thames - Coromandel ▶ YOUR HOSTS: **Shona and Bruz MacGregor** Ph (07) 868 9730

TOTARA VALLEY BARNS

65 Totara Valley Rd, RD 1, Thames
Ph/Fax (07) 868 9730, Mobile 027-310 3644
email: *info@totarabarns.co.nz*
www.totarabarns.co.nz

Features & Attractions

- *True Kiwi hospitality*
- *Base to explore the Coromandel*
- *Delicious evening meals*
- *Quiet and comfortable*
- *Safe off-road parking*
- *Large established garden*

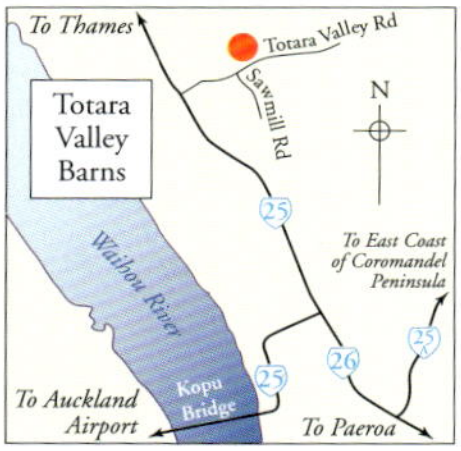

Barnstay Bed & Breakfast

Double	$120
Single	$100
Child	

Unique, recently converted quality accommodation in a tranquil, rural setting with separate guest lounge. Ninety minutes south of Auckland, **Totara Valley Barns** is perfect as a base or a relaxing, indulgent get-away. In easy reach of Coromandel Town, Hot Water Beach and Cathedral Cove.
Quiet, with safe off-road parking, a generous continental breakfast and a beautiful garden to unwind in at day's end. Delicious evening meal with local produce on request.
Try us, Shona and Bruz, local hosts that assure you of true Kiwi hospitality.

Bedrooms	Qty
Double	2
Twin	
Single	
Bed Size	**Qty**
King	
Queen	2
Double	
Single	
Bathrooms	**Qty**
Ensuite	2
Private	
Guest Share	

Kauaeranga Country Bed & Breakfast

33 Pakaraka Lane,
446 Kauaeranga Valley Rd, RD 2, Thames
Ph/Fax (07) 868 6895, Mobile 027-426 1157
email: *kauaeranga.country@xtra.co.nz*
www.thames-info.co.nz/KauaerangaCountry

Tariff : N.Z. Dollars	
Double	$120-140
Single	$90
Child	neg

Bedrooms	Qty
Double	1
Twin	1
Single	
Bed Size	**Qty**
Super King	
King	
Queen	1
Double	
Single	2
Bathrooms	**Qty**
Ensuite	
Private	1
Guest Share	

Self-contained Accommodation
Countrystay

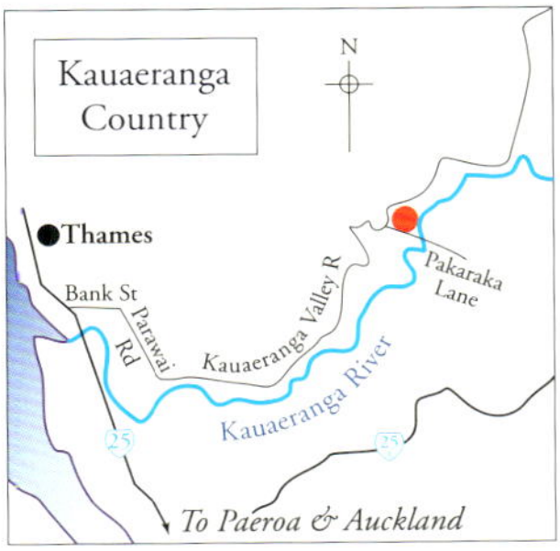

DIRECTIONS: Thames 6.2 km from the Thames Toyota Plant. Pakaraka Lane is No 446 Kauaeranga Valley Road, we are first left down the lane.

Features & Attractions

- *Peaceful rural hideaway*
- *Booked exclusively to you*
- *Safe private swimming*
- *Laundry facilities*
- *Kayaks for river fun*
- *Forest Park Visitors Centre*
- *Fish for elusive Rainbow Trout*
- *Gateway to forest park walks*

At **Kauaeranga Country** a warm welcome and comfortable bed await. Fluffy duvets and electric blankets for winter warmth and crisp cotton sheets for summer. To add to your comfort, your kitchen is complete with refrigerator, microwave, tea and coffee facilities. Guests can enjoy the privacy of their own apartment, while relaxing and enjoying the scenery close enough to touch. A large comfortable lounge area with books on New Zealand and local history overlooks the rambling bush garden.

The beautiful Kauaeranga River is literally on the doorstep with its 100% pure New Zealand water, great for swimming or kayaking. The valley offers hiking both easy and strenuous and we will happily recommend the walk to suit you.

Our ten acre property is home to our horses, a passion we share. We also enjoy travelling and meeting people from other parts of the world. With only one party of guests at a time, we can ensure your stay with us is the very best it can be.

Thames - Coromandel

YOUR HOSTS: **Paula and Bill Olsen** Ph: (07) 868 2866

Te Puru Coast Bed & Breakfast

2a Tatahi Street, Te Puru, Thames Coast, Coromandel
Ph (07) 868 2866, Fax (07) 868 2866
Mobile 027-656 6058
email: *tepurucoastbnb@xtra.co.nz*
www.tepurucoastbnb.co.nz

Features & Attractions

- *Self-contained unit*
- *Lovely beach & bush walks*
- *Swimming*
- *Historical visits*
- *Laundry facilities*
- *Off-street parking*

$	
Double	$125
Single	$75
Twin	$105

Bed & Breakfast
Plus Self-contained Unit

Bedrooms	Qty
Double	3
Twin	1
Single	1
Bed Size	**Qty**
King	
Queen	1
Double	2
Single	2
Bathrooms	**Qty**
Ensuite	1
Private	1
Guest Share	

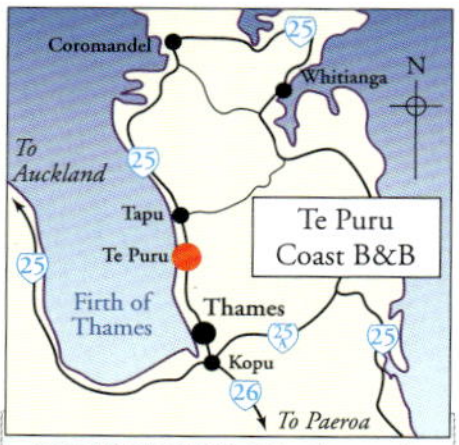

DIRECTIONS: 12 min north of Thames. Turn left off main road at Te Puru into Aputa Avenue, turn right into Tatahi Street. We are the second house on the right. Look for our sign.

Welcome to the beautiful Thames Coast. Our modern home is just twelve minutes from Thames and eighty metres off the main coast road with off-street parking. Your guest lounge has TV and tea/coffee facilities. Enjoy crisp, cool linen in summer and fluffy, warm duvets and electric blankets in winter. You may choose continental or cooked breakfast. Evening meals are on request ($35.00 pp) with complimentary wine or beer. Our large deck is your's to enjoy or take a short two minutes stroll to the beach. Our lovely, separate self-contained unit (do your own cooking) has double bedroom, laundry, kitchen/dining/lounge, BBQ area and double sofa bed in lounge. Tarriff is $125.00 for two people. Extra person $25.00.

Coromandel Town

YOUR HOST: **Gwen Whitmore** Free Ph 0800 473 364

The Green House Bed & Breakfast

505 Tiki Road, Coromandel Town
Ph (07) 866 7303
email: *paradise@Kaeppelis.co.nz*
www.greenhousebandb.co.nz

Features & Attractions

- *Beautiful views*
- *Relaxed and friendly*
- *Generous hospitality*
- *Short walk to town*
- *Excellent eating places*
- *Many attractions, walks etc.*

$	
Double	$140-155
Single	$95-120
Child	n/a

Quality Bed & Breakfast

Bedrooms	Qty
Double	2
Twin	
Single	
Bed Size	**Qty**
King	1
Queen	1
Double	
Single	
Bathrooms	**Qty**
Ensuite	2
Private	
Guest Share	

The Green House is a modern home with beautiful views from the dedicated guest lounge, the **Seascape** (king bed) and **Upper Deck** (queen bed) rooms. The lounge has many facilities including television, videos, CDs and games and tea/coffee facilities available at all times. There is a refrigerator for guests' use. Rooms have robes, slippers, hair dryer, toiletries etc.

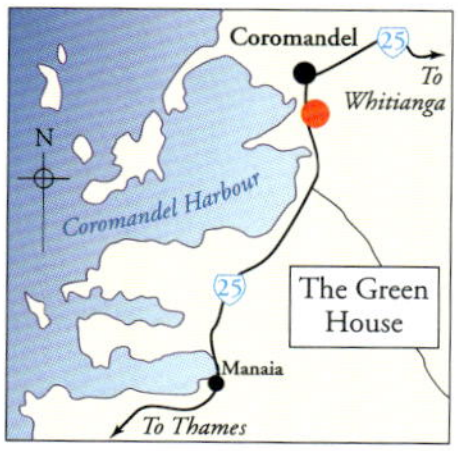

The local attractions are many and varied, for example great day trips to Hot Water Beach and Cathedral Cove, or The Coastal Walkway.

Other nearby attractions are easily organised. The coastal road from Thames to Coromandel offers some of New Zealand's most beautiful scenery. Coromandel Town is quaint, friendly and relaxed, with excellent restaurants. A small, friendly dog is on site.

Driving Creek Villas

21A Colville Road, Coromandel Town
Ph (07) 866 7755, Fax (07) 866 7753
Mobile 021-116 6393
email: *reservations@drivingcreekvillas.com*
www.drivingcreekvillas.com

Tariff : N.Z. Dollars	
Double	$245-295
Single	$225
Child	$25

Bedrooms	Qty
Double	2
Twin	2
Single	
Bed Size	**Qty**
Super King	
King/Twin	
Queen	2
Double	
Single	4
Bathrooms	**Qty**
Ensuite	2
Private	
Guest Share	

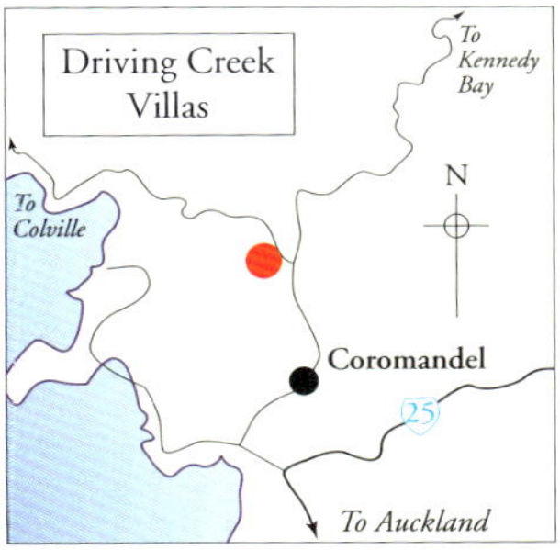

Boutique Self-contained Cottages

Features & Attractions

- *5 min walk to Driving Creek Railways*
- *5 min drive to the beach*
- *Fantastic fishing, native bush walks*
- *Private bush setting*
- *Handy to fine restaurants*
- *Private Japanese hot tub*
- *Fully self-contained*
- *Wireless broadband*

Set in beautiful, private bush surrounds, our spacious, fully self-contained boutique villas offer the perfect place to unwind – beside the meandering stream where gold was first discovered in New Zealand over 150 years ago.

Purpose-built to a high standard, **Driving Creek Villas** combine colourful pacific themes with modern colonial styling, providing a unique Coromandel accommodation experience.

Enjoy a breakfast in your own private sunny north facing garden and listen out for the captivating birdsong of Tui, Bellbird and Fantail, or chill out under the stars in your own Japanese hot tub.

On the fringe of Coromandel Town, the popular Driving Creek Railway is only a short stroll away. There you can view some of New Zealand's finest ceramic art and enjoy the bush railway.

KAEPPELI'S BED & BREAKFAST

40 Gray Avenue, Kuaotunu, RD 2, Whitianga
Ph (07) 866 2445, Mobile 027-656 3442
email: *paradise@kaeppelis.co.nz*
www.kaeppelis.co.nz

Features & Attractions

- *Ausgezeichnetes Essen*
- *Unbeatable sea views*
- *Alfresco dining*
- *Unschlagbare Meersicht*
- *Exquisite meals*
- *Quiet, peaceful setting*

Panoramic Coastal Paradise

Double	$120-180
Single	$85-120
Child	neg

Country living in style and comfort, with exquisite meals, glorious views, privacy, character and simplicity. Robert is an excellent Swiss chef using top quality local produce and the wood fired oven. Jill's Swiss bread makes a pleasant change from toast. Meals served in our panoramic gazebo or guests dining room. A unique peaceful place off the main road where you can relax and enjoy the beauty and tranquility of Kuaotunu. Short walk to the beach. There's a choice of clean, safe, white sandy beaches, bush walks, fishing, tennis, kayaking, swimming, Matarangi's championship golf course and horse trekking nearby. Our daughter and pets make children welcome. Ideal for exploring the Coromandel Peninsula.

AND OUR VIEW?? SIMPLY THE BEST!

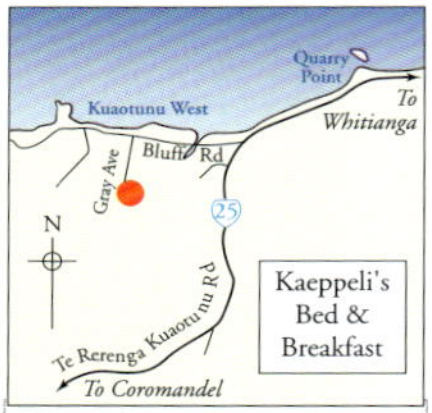

DIRECTIONS: In Kuaotunu west turn off SH 25 into Bluff Road, across bridge, first left into Gray Avenue, end of Gray Avenue up hill on gravel driveway.

Bedrooms	Qty
Double	2
Twin	2
Single	
Bed Size	**Qty**
King	2
Queen	
Double	
Single	4
Bathrooms	**Qty**
Ensuite	4
Private	
Guest Share	

YOUR HOSTS: **Lorraine and Bill Muir** Ph: (07) 866 4396 **_Whitianga_**

Kuaotunu Bay Lodge

State Highway 25, Kuaotunu, RD 2, Whitianga
Ph (07) 866 4396, Fax (07) 866 4396
Mobile 027-601 3665
email: *muir@kuaotunubay.co.nz*
www.kuaotunubay.co.nz

Tariff : N.Z. Dollars	
Double	$160-225
Single	$160
Child	n/a

Bedrooms	Qty
Double	3
Twin	1
Single	
Bed Size	**Qty**
Super King	
King	
Queen	3
Double	
King/Single	2
Bathrooms	**Qty**
Ensuite	3
Private	1
Guest Share	

Boutique Accommodation & Self Service Accommodation

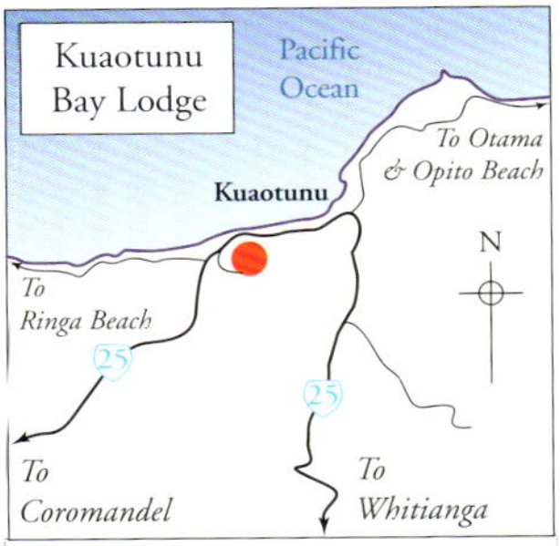

DIRECTIONS: 18 km north of Whitianga on SH 25.
Please phone for bookings and easy directions.

Features & Attractions

- *Affordable luxury*
- *Panoramic views*
- *Purpose-built*
- *Overlooking safe beach*
- *Golf nearby*
- *Central to all activities*
- *Decks own entrance*
- *2.5 hrs Auckland airport*

Welcome to our elegant beach house, set in four hectares of bush and pasture, offering panoramic views of the Peninsula and Mercury Island.
Savour a generous breakfast watching the waves. The safe, sandy beach is just a short walk through the garden. Central to all activities a two or three day stay allows time to explore the whole peninsula. Bush/beach walks, kayaking, horse riding all within easy reach.
A choice of fine dining in Whitianga or at the local Golf Club. Having enjoyed this property since 1972 we offer our guests affordable luxury and a true 'Kiwi' experience. A tastefully decorated self-service unit is also available.

Leighton Lodge

17 Stewart Place, Opito Bay, RD 2, Whitianga
Ph (07) 866 0756, Fax (07) 866 5867
Mobile 025-230 0656
email: *leightonlodge@xtra.co.nz*
www.leightonlodge.co.nz

Tariff : N.Z. Dollars	
Double	$110-150
Single	$90-110
Child	$30

Bedrooms	Qty
Double	2
Twin	
Single	
Bed Size	**Qty**
Super King	
King	
Queen	2
Double	1
Single	
Bathrooms	**Qty**
Ensuite	1
Private	1
Guest Share	

Bed & Breakfast
Self-contained Haven

Features & Attractions

- *Views of Mercury Islands*
- *Safe swimming & boating*
- *Excellent diving*
- *Peace & tranquility*
- *Special dinners*
- *Great local fishing*
- *Local gourmet seafood*
- *Watch the dolphins*

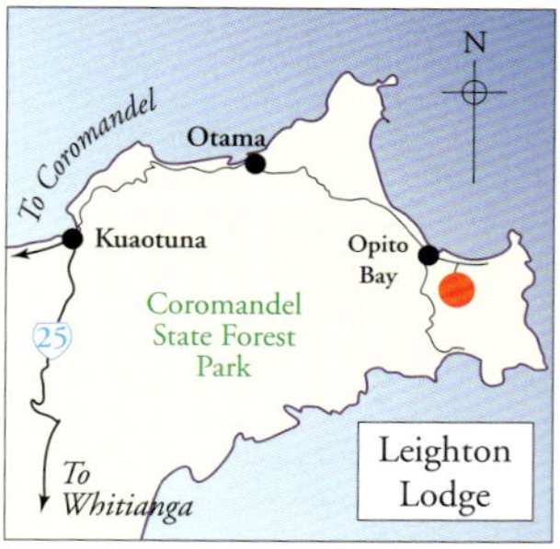

Maire and Wally welcome you to share the tranquil and peaceful environment of their Coromandel Peninsula paradise. Our spacious deck commands panoramic views of the Great Mercury Islands. You are just two minutes walk from the stunning white sands of Opito Bay beach. Enjoy a scenic walk to the historic Maori Pa site or a beach ramble (our dog will lead the way). Excellent diving, safe swimming, or fishing and boating are available. There are two golf courses in the area. Alternatively you may like to sit under a pohutukawa tree or laze in our hammock with a good book. Sometimes you can swim with the dolphins that regularly visit.

We offer either our **Pacific Room** – a large double bedroom with ensuite or the privacy of our self-contained apartment which includes a bedroom kitchen/living area and bathroom. Sample the excellent local seafood. Delicious home cooked dinners can be prepared by prior arrangement. We are a non-smoking family.

YOUR HOSTS: **Maria and Guy Clark** Ph: (07) 866 4987 **Whitianga**

At Parkland Place

14 Parkland Place, PO Box 59, Whitianga
Ph (07) 866 4987, Fax (07) 866 4946
Mobile (021) 404 923
email: *parklandplace@wave.co.nz*
www.atparklandplace.co.nz

Features & Attractions

- *European hospitality*
- *Luxurious, romantic*
- *Sunny outdoor area*
- *Spa pool and barbecue*
- *Dinner by arrangement*
- *Quiet and peaceful*

$	
Double	$135-200
Single	$100-150
Child	Neg

Boutique Accommodation
Luxurious Bed & Breakfast

Bedrooms	Qty
Double	5
Twin	1
Single	
Bed Size	**Qty**
Super King	4
Queen	1
Double	
King Single	2
Bathrooms	**Qty**
Ensuite	5
Private	
Guest Share	

Enjoy European hospitality in Whitianga's most luxurious boutique hotel style Bed & Breakfast. Maria, a ship's chef from Poland and her New Zealand husband Guy, a Master Mariner, will make your stay a memorable experience with hospitality that has become renowned around the world. Large luxuriously appointed rooms with television, radio, writing desk and comfortable beds. Take your time over a magnificent breakfast and let Maria surprise you with a superb dinner or barbecue. Relax in the large guest lounge, watching Sky television, reading a book or listening to music. Enjoy the sunny outdoors relaxing in the spa pool or take a quiet stroll along the reserve to popular Brophy's Beach. Being situated next to farmland and reserves ensures absolute peace and quiet. You will never regret your stay! Privacy and discretion is assured.

DIRECTIONS: Take SH 25 to Whitianga. Drive through township along Buffalo Beach Road for 4 km. Turn left into Centennial Drive, then first left into Parkland Place.

YOUR HOSTS: **Johanna and Paul Blackman** Ph: (07) 866 0279 **Whitianga**

Centennial Heights Bed & Breakfast

141 Centennial Drive, Whitianga
Phone (07) 866 0279, Fax (07) 866 0276
Mobile 027-237 9086
email: *blackmanmathis@xtra.co.nz*
www.centennialheights.unitrental.com

Features & Attractions

- *Spectacular sea views*
- *Friendly border collie*
- *Comfortable luxury*
- *Quiet peaceful enviroment*
- *Tennis court nearby*
- *Swimming beach*

$	
Double	$130
Single	$75
Child	

Luxury Boutique Accommodation
with Spectacular Sea Views

Bedrooms	Qty
Double	2
Twin	1
Single	1
Bed Size	**Qty**
King	
Queen	2
King/Single	1
Single	1
Bathrooms	**Qty**
Ensuite	3
Private	1
Guest Share	

Centennial Heights Bed & Breakfast sits atop Centennial Drive, overlooking the sparkling waters of the Whitianga Harbour. Paul, Johanna and Mollie (our lovable border collie) offer warm and friendly hospitality in elegant surroundings. Buffalo and Simpsons Beaches are within easy reach and the township is a five minute drive. Over pre-dinner drinks we can assist you with information on the best of the area's attractions including fishing, kayaking, tramping, scuba diving and snorkelling, boat cruises, dining out, etc. We offer a delicious, wholesome cooked and continental breakfast which can be enjoyed along with the spectacular sea views. We look forward to welcoming you and making your stay a pleasant and memorable experience. We welcome overseas guests. Johanna is fluent in German and French.

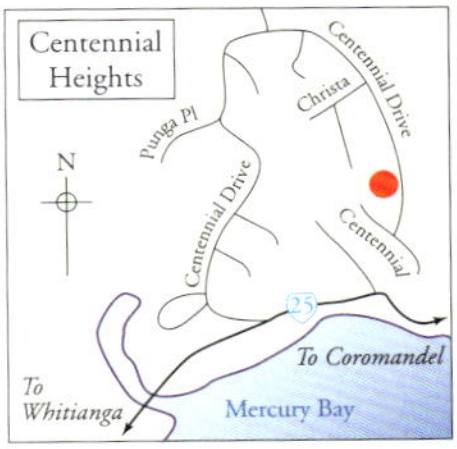

Cosy Cat Cottage

41 South Highway, (town end), Whitianga, Mercury Bay
Coromandel Peninsula
Ph (07) 866 4488, Fax (07) 866 4488
email: *cosycat@xtra.co.nz*
www.cosycat.co.nz

Features & Attractions

- *Picturesque cottage*
- *Amusing catty decor*
- *A-la-carte breakfast*
- *Separate self-contained cottage*
- *Comfortable guest lounge*
- *Helpful, friendly service*

Bed & Breakfast Self-contained Cottage

VISA MasterCard

Double	$90-110
Single	$65-75
Child	

DIRECTIONS:
1 km south of the town centre

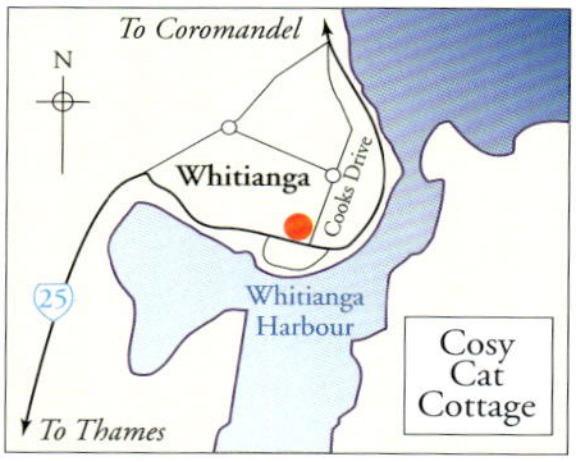

Welcome to our picturesque cottage and enjoy the amusing catty décor and unique feline ambience! Cosy queen/double/twin/single bedrooms with ensuite/private bathrooms are available all year. Delicious a-la-carte breakfasts are complimentary and teas or coffees can be served when required. An easy drive may take you to Hot Water Beach, Cathedral Cove and other fascinating places. Friendly and helpful service is assured and you will probably like to meet Sylvie the Tonkinese cat and perhaps visit the "cat hotel" in the garden. A self-contained cottage is also available with two queen bedrooms, bathrooms and kitchen.

Bedrooms	Qty
Double	2
Twin	1
Single	1
Bed Size	**Qty**
King	
Queen	2
Double	
Single	2
Bathrooms	**Qty**
Ensuite	2
Private	1
Guest Share	

Ferry Landing Lodge

1169 Purangi Rd, Ferry Landing, RD 1, Whitianga
Ph (07) 866 0445, Fax (07) 866 0792
Mobile 027-250 3388
email: *info@ferrylandinglodge.co.nz*
www.ferrylandinglodge.co.nz

Features & Attractions

- *Your tariff includes*
- *Guided walk to Maori Pa*
- *Fresh home-baking*
- *Kayak to explore the bay*
- *Beach chairs, bikes*
- *Golf course nearby*

Coastal Retreat in Unbeatable Location

Double	$150-220
Single	$130-200
Child	$30-60

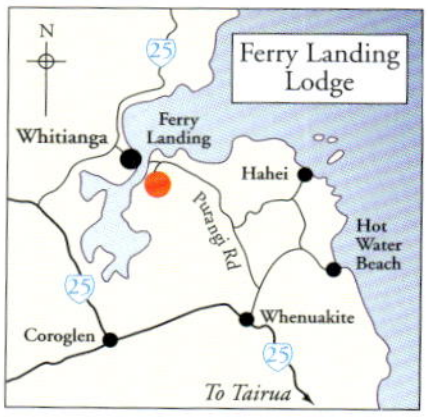

"Our goal was to find accommodation close to Cooks Beach, Hahei and Whitianga! Well, we found it! The perfect location, superb hospitality, and the ferry 'cross the harbour' – a delight, watch fish jumping under the sickle moon whilst waiting for the ferryman – simply unforgettable..." "Wonderful fresh breakfasts with Pam's home-made fruit preserves, jams and breads. Fresh produce from the garden, mmm!" "Beautiful gardens, comfortable, spacious accommodation, relaxed conversations with friendly, helpful hosts and Rob's tour/history lesson made this our favourite B&B." Designed with privacy in mind, semi-contained suites provide the perfect retreat for exploring beautiful Mercury Bay. Close to Cathedral Cove and Hotwater Beach. Ferry access to Whitianga.

Bedrooms	Qty
Double	4
Twin	
Single	
Bed Size	**Qty**
King	2
Queen	2
Double	
Single	2
Bathrooms	**Qty**
Ensuite	
Private	2
Guest Share	

Flaxhaven Lodge

995 Purangi Road, Flaxmill Bay, RD1, Whitianga
Ph (07) 866 2676, Fax (07) 866 2396
Mobile 021-286 1088
email: *johnlee@wave.co.nz*
www.flaxhavenlodge.co.nz

@ home NEW ZEALAND

Tariff : N.Z. Dollars	
Double	$190-230
Single	$170-210
Child	

Bedrooms	Qty
Double	3
Twin	
Single	
Bed Size	**Qty**
Super King	1
King	
Queen	2
Double	
King/Single	2
Bathrooms	**Qty**
Ensuite	
Private	2
Guest Share	

VISA MasterCard

LA **Luxury Coastal Accommodation** SC

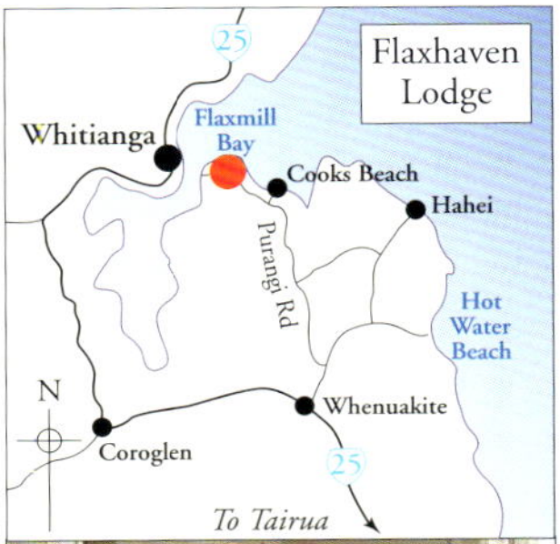

Features & Attractions

- *Centrally located*
- *4 safe sandy beaches all within a short stroll*
- *Close to cafes restaurants*
- *Historic bush walks*
- *Boating kayaking fishing*
- *Purpose-built 2005*
- *Internet wi-fi*

Flaxhaven Lodge is nestled alongside picturesque Flaxmill Bay, set in 1.5 acres of gardens surrounded by countryside and native bush. Flaxmill Bay and Eggcentric Café are a 2 minute walk. In 3 minutes on the quaint passenger ferry to Whitianga town you can experience numerous cafés and retail opportunities. Famous Cathedral Cove and Hot Water Beach are a 10 minute drive. Luxury accommodation is designed for guests' relaxation, privacy and comfort, with quality linens and fittings, TVs, fridges, tea and coffee making facilities, tiled bathrooms, laundry, private entrances and patios. A separate cottage has a queen-size bedroom with ensuite, livingroom and kitchenette with microwave. A private wing of the house has 2 bedrooms, bathroom and separate toilet. This wing would be used exclusively by one couple, a family or two couples travelling together. Enjoy special breakfasts in the sunny kitchen or alfresco on the patio. We will welcome you with warmth, help you unwind with refreshments and share with you our home and the beautiful Coromandel coastline.

Cooks Beach YOUR HOSTS: **Christine and Paul Hopkins** Ph: (07) 866 5786

The Mussel Bed

892 Purangi Road, Cooks Beach, RD 1, Whitianga
Ph (07) 866 5786, Fax (07) 866 5706
Mobile 027-234 8747
email: *welcome@musselbed.co.nz*
www.musselbed.co.nz

Features & Attractions

- *Capt Cooks 1769 Discovery*
- *White, sandy beaches*
- *Bush & coastal walks*
- *Hot Water Beach 10min.*
- *Passenger Ferry Whitianga 5min.*
- *Famous 'Eggsentric Café' nearby*

Bed & Breakfast
Luxury Accommodation

Double	$175-250
Single	$150-225
Child	$50

We have the best of both worlds at The Mussel Bed, nestled amidst native bush, gardens and streams, yet only 5 minutes walk to historical Cooks Beach. A perfect base to explore nearby Cathedral Cove and Hot Water Beach! Kayak the stream from our jetty and enjoy the natural bird habitat, exploring caves and walking on gorgeous Lonely Bay! Finish your day unwinding by the fire, with a wine from our local vineyard, in the company of fellow travellers!
Our guest wing has 3 luxurious suites, tiled ensuites and french doors opening onto private decks with all those special touches our guests love! We bring breakfast to you to enjoy in the garden, room or deck – try our delicious homemade muesli and bread, yoghurt drizzled with honey, fruit compote and maybe muffins to take on your picnic. We look forward to making your stay on the beautiful Coromandel a special one!

Bedrooms	Qty
Double	5
Twin	
Single	
Bed Size	**Qty**
King	1
Queen	4
King Singles	2
Single	2
Bathrooms	**Qty**
Ensuite	3
Private	1
Guest Share	

Whitianga YOUR HOSTS: **Gaye Butcher and Fred Brinsden** Ph: (07) 866 0166

Halcyon Heights Country Retreat

365 Mill Creek Road, RD 1, Whitianga
Ph (07) 866 0166, Fax (07) 866 0166
Mobile 021-172 0561
email: *p.park@xtra.co.nz*
www.halcyonheights.co.nz

Features & Attractions

- *Tranquil setting*
- *15 acre farmlet*
- *Bird aviaries & gardens*
- *Beaches & restaurants 10 min*
- *Comfortable, relaxed atmosphere*
- *Dinner by arrangement*

Country Retreat
Bed & Breakfast

Double	$120
Single	
Child	

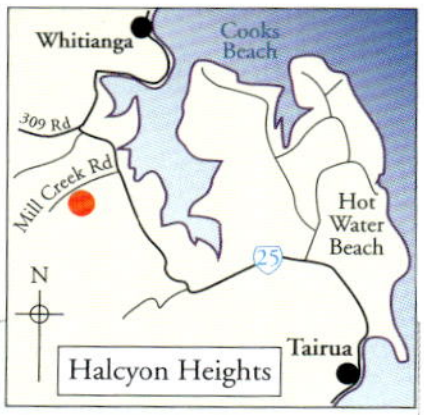

DIRECTIONS:
Just 3.6 km along Mill Creek Road off State Highway 25.
Just south of Whitianga.

Halcyon Heights is set in a peaceful valley with a bush backdrop. We offer a warm welcome with nothing but peace and tranquility, set on fifteen acres. Enjoy breakfast outside on the deck, while listening to the many native birds. Later, enjoy a walk through our park-like gardens and view our bird aviaries, housing over forty species of birds and parrots. Amble along our stream walkway when you visit our friendly donkeys and farm animals.
On the way back to the house, eat the fruit from a variety of vines and trees. Plan on spending more than one night while using **Halcyon Heights** as a base for exploring the Coromandel Peninsula.

Bedrooms	Qty
Double	1
Twin	2
Single	
Bed Size	**Qty**
King/Twin	1
Queen	2
Double	
Single	4
Bathrooms	**Qty**
Ensuite	2
Private	1
Guest Share	

YOUR HOSTS: **Barry and Heather Scott** Ph (07) 866 3119 **Cooks Beach - Whitianga**

Mercury Orchard Bed & Breakfast

141 Purangi Road, RD 1, Whitianga
Ph (07) 866 3119, Fax (07) 866 3115
email: *relax@mercuryorchard.co.nz*
www.mercuryorchard.co.nz

Features & Attractions

- *Outdoor bath, swimming pool*
- *Private deck with BBQ*
- *Tranquil garden setting*
- *Golf course nearby*
- *Hot Water Beach and Cathedral Cove 8min.*

$	
Double	$130-160
Single	$120-140
Child	$20

Peaceful Garden Cottages

Bedrooms	Qty
Double	3
Twin	
Single	1
Bed Size	**Qty**
King	1
Queen	2
Double	
Single	2
Bathrooms	**Qty**
Ensuite	3
Private	
Guest Share	

Fig Tree Cottage and **Paua Bach** are nestled amongst five acres of peaceful country gardens and orchard. Self-contained country-style luxury with French doors opening out into the orchard, crisp cotton bed linen, bathrobes, fresh fruit, flowers and candles. Special to **Paua Bach** – an old fashioned outdoor bath. (To be taken with a glass of wine and bubbles). Watch the variety of our birdlife while enjoying a full breakfast brought out to your private deck. Freshly squeezed orange juice, in season fruit, home-made muesli, our own free-range eggs. Quiet and relaxing. Perfect for that special anniversary or as a restful stay while visiting nearby attractions. Meet our friendly sheep, kunekune pigs, donkey, cat and dog. Beautiful Cathedral Cove and Hot Water Beach are seven to eight minutes drive. Restaurants are close. Alternatively, barbeque your evening meal Kiwi style. We normally have fresh produce available from our garden.

DIRECTIONS:
14 km north of Tairua turn into Hot Water Beach Rd. – 1.5 km left into Purangi Rd. – 1.5 km on left is **Mercury Orchard**.

YOUR HOSTS: **Kay and Peter Harrison** Ph (07) 866 3281 **Hahei - Whitianga**

Hahei Horizon

20 Grierson Close, Hahei, RD 1, Whitianga
Ph (07) 866 3281, Mobile 021-160 7213
email: *pkharrison@xtra.co.nz*
www.haheihorizon.co.nz

Features & Attractions

- *Cathedral Cove close by*
- *Cafés & restaurants*
- *Kayak, dive, boat trips*
- *Sparkling, safe beach*
- *Golf & tennis nearby*
- *Hot Water Beach 5 min.*

$	
Double	$130-220
Single	on request
Child	

Dare to Dream Quality Accommodation

Bedrooms	Qty
Double	3
Twin	
Single	
Bed Size	**Qty**
King	2
Queen	1
Double	
Single	2
Bathrooms	**Qty**
Ensuite	3
Private	
Guest Share	

Peter and Kay invite you to share their little piece of this special part of New Zealand. **Hahei Horizon**, our home on the hill, is ideally suited for Bed & Breakfast. Every room has a stunning view of the coast and the native surrounding. With down to earth Kiwi hospitality, relaxation is hard to avoid. Enjoy a cooked or a continental breakfast on the deck. At the end of the day join us for refreshments before dining at one of Hahei's 3 fine restaurants. The large rooms, prepared with quality linen and electric blankets, have ensuites, tea/coffee facilities and a fridge. Internet connection is available. Rest and relaxation or fun and exhilaration! Walk or cruise to Cathedral Cove, snorkle or dive in the Marine Reserve, kayak or swim at our beautiful beach, play golf or tennis or soak in a hot self-dug thermal pool. We can arrange it all – except the weather.

DIRECTIONS:
From SH25 follow signs to Hahei. Grierson Close is 4th left along main Beach Rd between speed bumps. **Hahei Horizon** is at end of street, up the private driveway on right.

Hahei Haven B&B

8 Robyn Crescent, Hahei, RD 1, Whitianga
Ph (07) 866 3136, Fax (07) 866 3137
Mobile 027-622 1700
email: *info@hahei-haven.co.nz*
www.hahei-haven.co.nz

Tariff : N.Z. Dollars	
Double	$120-160
Single	$120
Child	

Bedrooms	Qty
Double	2
Twin	
Single	
Bed Size	**Qty**
Super King/Twin	1
King	
Queen	
Double	1
Single	
Bathrooms	**Qty**
Ensuite	2
Private	
Guest Share	

Quality Bed & Breakfast

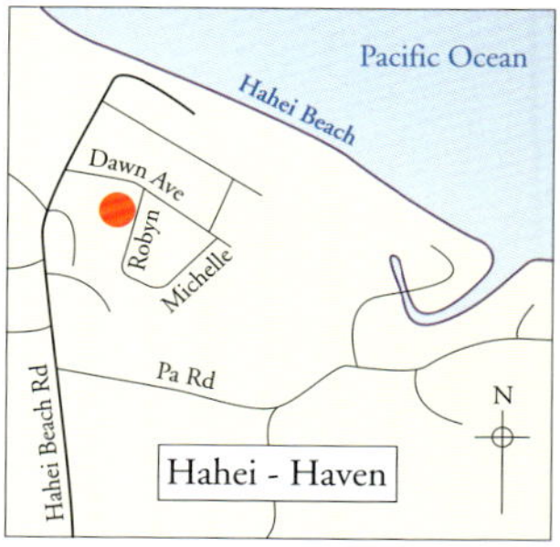

Features & Attractions

- *Cathedral Cove*
- *White sandy beach walks*
- *Snorkelling, diving*
- *Maori pa site*
- *Kayak and boat trips*
- *Horse riding*
- *Golf & tennis nearby*
- *Thermal bathing*

Hahei Haven, newly purpose-built for Bed & Breakfast, is superbly located in the heart of Hahei. Only a few minutes walk to the beach and cafés. We offer upstairs guest rooms with their own ensuites, television. Refrigerator, tea and coffee facilities. Cooked breakfast is served in our dining room. We offer great views of the ancient Maori pa and a glimpse of the sea. Walk to Cathedral Cove, bathe in the thermal water at Hot Water Beach, or stroll on Hahei Beach and enjoy a touch of paradise.

We are happy to organise activities such as a scenic cruise to Cathedral Cove, stunning sea caves and nearby islands. Relax in our secluded garden or sit by our large outdoor fireplace after a day's activities before going to the café for dinner. We look forward to welcoming you along with our 12-year-old blind labrador.

Hot Water Beach Bed & Breakfast

48 Pye Place, Hot Water Beach, Coromandel Peninsula
Ph (07) 866 3991, Fax (07) 866 3291
Mobile 027 479 9620
email: *TKnight@xtra.co.nz*
www.hotwaterbedandbreakfast.co.nz

Tariff : N.Z. Dollars	
Double	$180-220
Single	$160-180
Child	

Bedrooms	Qty
Double	2
Twin	
Single	
Bed Size	**Qty**
Super King	
King	
Queen	2
Double	
Single	
Bathrooms	**Qty**
Ensuite	2
Private	
Guest Share	

Quality Homestay Bed & Breakfast

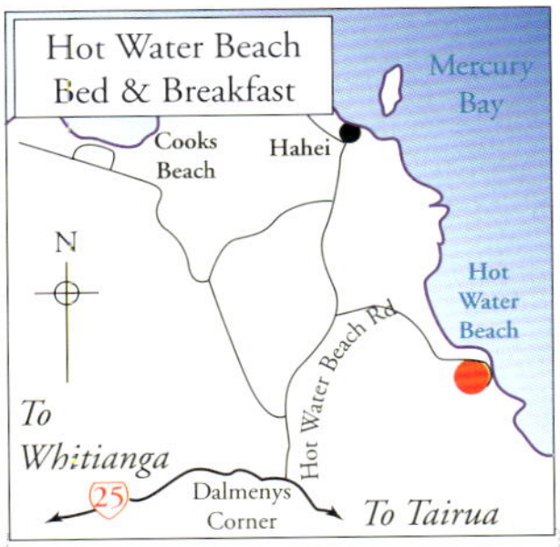

DIRECTIONS:
Follow Hot Water Beach Road from SH 25.
Travel past Beach Shop and carpark.
We are 50m on right uphill.

Features & Attractions

- *Wide sea/beach views*
- *Hot springs on beach*
- *Surf beach walks*
- *Golf package*
- *Spa pool, billiard table*
- *Spectacular night skies*
- *Sun-drenched decks*
- *Restaurants 5 min drive*

Escape now to this premier Bed and Breakfast on the Coromandel Peninsula, situated approximately two hours drive from Auckland, Hamilton and Tauranga.

Our modern home, which is only a stone's throw from the beach, has been specifically designed for the comfort of our guests.

On the beach you can swim, surf or observe the native bird life. You can use our spades to dig your own natural hot spring pool close to low tide. This can be a truly romantic experience if done in the evening with a bottle of wine under the spectacular night skies. Enjoy a generous breakfast on our extensive sun-drenched decks. Relax with a fresh coffee or cool drink and view the dolphins which often come to play in the bay.

Nearby activities include Cathedral Cove, bush walks, kayaking, horse treks, diving, fishing and a unique fruit winery. Ask us about our special golf package, clubs included. We have one cat and a sociable Boxer. – Proud to be members of @home New Zealand.

Tairua YOUR HOSTS: **Linda and Wayne Jury** Ph (07) 864 7040

HARBOUR VIEW LODGE

179 Main Road, Tairua, Coromandel Peninsula
Ph (07) 864 7040 , Fax (07) 864 7042
Mobile 021-357 437
email: *info@harbourviewlodge.co.nz*
www.harbourviewlodge.co.nz

Features & Attractions

- *Expansive harbour views*
- *Swimming, boating, diving*
- *Tramping & bush walks*
- *Restaurants/shops 5 min. walk*
- *Cathedral Cove & Hot Water Beach – 20 minutes drive north*

Bed & Breakfast Homestay

Double	$165-185
Single	$130-150
Child	

Harbour View Lodge is situated on the foothills of **Tairua** on the east coast of the beautiful Coromandel Peninsula, 2 hours drive from Auckland, Hamilton and Tauranga. Our Bed & Breakfast has been purpose-built with three ensuite guest rooms on ground level. Tastefully decorated and furnished with quality linens, toiletries, hairdryer and electric blankets on all beds for your comfort. Tea/coffee facilities in rooms. A comfortable guest lounge with TV, video and fridge opens onto the courtyard with swimming pool. Enjoy a sumptuous breakfast buffet upstairs in the dining area while watching the everchanging views across Tairua Harbour to Paku Mountain. Let us help you arrange your day's activities over breakfast. Dig your own spa at Hot Water Beach or have a picnic lunch at Cathedral Cove. Off-street parking, laundry facilities, fast internet access. Make us your base on the Coromandel Peninsula and stay a few days to explore.

On the Main Road, SH 25, 1 km south of Tairua Village.

Bedrooms	Qty
Double	2
Twin	1
Single	
Bed Size	**Qty**
King	1
Queen	2
Double	
King/Single	1
Bathrooms	**Qty**
Ensuite	3
Private	
Guest Share	

Colonial Homestay

202 Paku Drive, Tairua, Coromandel Peninsula
Ph (07) 864 7743, Fax (07) 864 7743
Mobile 027-290 9555
email: *colonialhomestay@paradise.net.nz*
www.colonialhomestay.co.nz

Tariff : N.Z. Dollars	
Double	$170-180
Single	$100-150
Child	

Bedrooms	Qty
Double	2
Twin	
Single	
Bed Size	**Qty**
Super King	
King	
Queen	2
Double	
Single	1
Bathrooms	**Qty**
Ensuite	1
Private	1
Guest Share	

Homestay
Bed & Breakfast

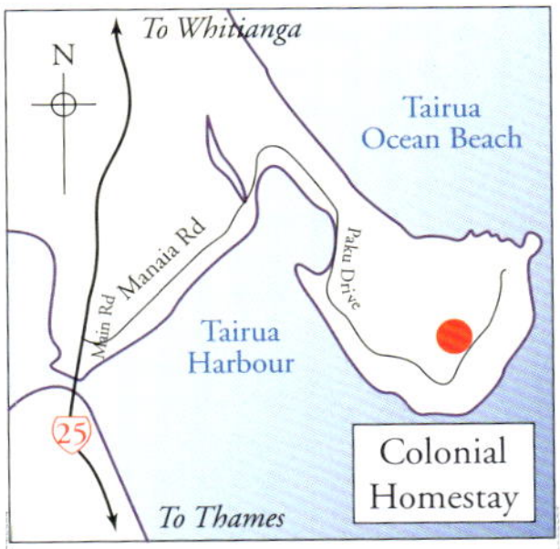

DIRECTIONS: Follow SH 25 to Tairua, after one-way bridge turn 1st right onto Manaia Road, then right onto Paku Drive up to the top of hill.

Features & Attractions

- *Warm & friendly hospitality*
- *Relaxed & peaceful setting*
- *Stunning views*
- *Bush walks*
- *Golf course nearby*
- *Laundry facilities*
- *Internet access*
- *Elevator to all floors*

Jenny and Bob welcome you to **Colonial Homestay** where you can make our home "your home" in a quiet and restful location. Our home is situated high on Paku Mountain with panoramic views of the ocean and offshore islands. With our extensive knowledge of the area, we can assist with sightseeing, activities and travel plans, helping you to experience the wonderful Coromandel. Why not try one of the many walks around Mount Paku including the summit where fabulous views of the ranges, harbour, coast and islands can be enjoyed? We are only a short drive to marvellous beaches including Sailor's Grave, Hot Water Beach and Cathedral Cove. There is a good choice of restaurants for evening meals. Enjoy a magnificent breakfast overlooking the views. Refreshments can be served on the surrounding decks on your arrival or at the end of the day. Stay a few nights or a few weeks; we look forward to your company.

Copsefield Bed & Breakfast

1055 SH 25, RD 1, Whangamata
Ph (07) 865 9555, Fax (07) 865 9510
Mobile 021-895 566
email: *copsefield@xtra.co.nz*
www.copsefield.co.nz

Tariff : N.Z. Dollars	
Double	$180
Single	$130
Child	–

Bedrooms	Qty
Double	2
Twin	1
Single	
Bed Size	**Qty**
Super King	
King	
Queen	2
Double	
Single	2
Bathrooms	**Qty**
Ensuite	3
Private	
Guest Share	

Countrystay Bed & Breakfast and Self-contained Cottage

Features & Attractions

- *Stunning country scenery*
- *Canoes & mountain bikes available*
- *Peace and tranquillity*
- *Six hole pitch'n putt*
- *Hot tub*
- *3 acres of garden*
- *River, views*
- *Close to beaches*

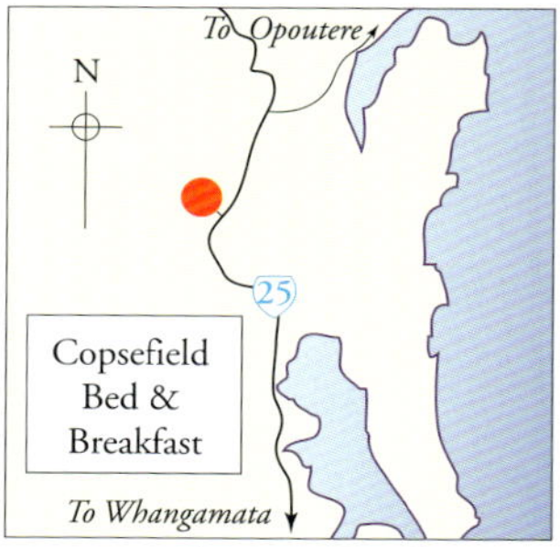

Copsefield is situated at the southern end of the stunning Coromandel Peninsula and is set in 3 acres of garden, orchard and native bush. We offer you peace, tranquillity and tasteful accommodation. Our home is close to exquisite native fauna and flora, magnificent beaches, and walks. It has been designed for your comfort. Each bedroom has its own ensuite and adjoining verandah.

Relax in the private lounge with complimentary tea or coffee. We serve a glass of New Zealand wine before your evening meal. The nearest restaurant is some four minutes drive away. A full breakfast is served either in the dining room or outside.

We have bikes and canoes for your use and beaches are close by. Our stream swimming hole is a fantastic experience.

Come and enjoy our piece of paradise. Lynn and Wayne offer a warm welcome and personal attention.

YOUR HOSTS: **Linda and Peter Bigge** Ph (07) 865 6128 ◀ ***Whangamata***

KOTUKU

422 Otahu Road, Whangamata, Coromandel
Ph (07) 865 6128, Fax (07) 865 6128
Mobile 027-358 1227
email: *lindapeter@slingshot.co.nz*
www.kotukuhomestay.co.nz

Features & Attractions

- *New home, solar heating*
- *Close to estuary and surf beach*
- *Campervan facility*
- *Outdoor spa*
- *Bikes, kayaks*
- *Internet access*

$	
Double	$120
Single	$100
Child	

Homestay Bed & Breakfast
Self-contained Studio Unit

Bedrooms	Qty
Double	3
Twin	
Single	
Bed Size	**Qty**
King	
Queen	3
Double	
Single	
Bathrooms	**Qty**
Ensuite	3
Private	
Guest Share	

We offer you comfortable accommodation in a purpose-built home. Rosie, our friendly Huntaway cross and Elizabeth, the cat, will give you a warm welcome too. Relax in the spacious lounge or private patio. Enjoy the Coromandel sunset from our deluxe outdoor spa.

Kotuku is situated at the quieter end of Whangamata, just a two minute stroll to the lovely Otahu Estuary and Reserve; ideal for swimming, kayaking or just walk along the reserve to the beach and observe the fascinating shore birds.

Our **Studio Unit** (with queen, large single bed and a cot) at the rear of the house, is fully self-contained and suitable for a family with young children. They will love playing in the safe estuary!

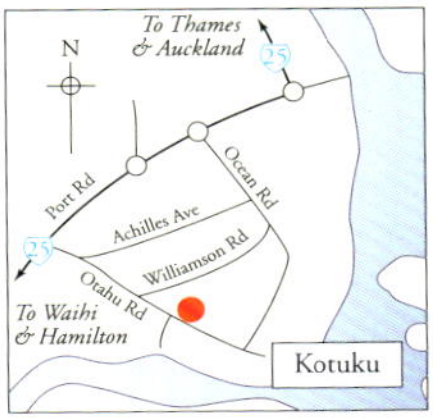

YOUR HOSTS: **Shirley and John Killick** Ph (07) 865 7440 ◀ ***Whangamata***

PATIKI BAY VIEW

102 Bruce Wallace Place, Whangamata
Ph (07) 865 7440, Mobile 027-497 2389
email: *jkgilli@value.net.nz*
www.patikibay.co.nz

Features & Attractions

- *Quiet and peaceful*
- *Views over Patiki Bay*
- *Cafés nearby*
- *Phone or email for directions*
- *Surf beach in Whangamata*
- *Gateway to Corom. Peninsula*

$	
Double	$140
Single	$120
Child	n/a

Self-contained Accommodation
or Bed & Breakfast

Bedrooms	Qty
Double	1
Twin	
Single	
Bed Size	**Qty**
King	
Queen	1
Double	
Single	
Bathrooms	**Qty**
Ensuite	1
Private	
Guest Share	

Patiki Bay View Apartment is situated in a quiet street with views over a peaceful garden and across Patiki Bay. The sunny, north-facing unit is fully self-contained with fridge, oven, hob top, microwave, dishwasher, queen bed, leather lounge suite and TV. It is a special apartment for couples. The beautiful Whangamata surf beach and harbour are a short walk away. The town centre has wonderful shops and cafés for lunches and evening meals. Whangamata is the gateway to the Coromandel Peninsula with fantastic bush walks, arts and crafts, Hot Water Beach and Cathedral Cove. The clean, white sands and blue water of the beaches are a special feature of the area. Boat trips and fishing are available. – Your hosts, John and Shirley, have been artists and potters for many years. They have a good local knowledge of the area, and can direct guests to all the special places to visit.

Trout & Chicken @ Drift House

9137 State Highway 2, RD 2, Waihi
Ph (07) 8636964, Fax (07) 8636966
Mobile 027-206 4080
email: *troutandchicken@paradise.net.nz*
www.troutandchicken.co.nz

Features & Attractions

- *On an organic orchard*
- *Peaceful, rural setting*
- *Excellent quality*
- *Full-sized double rooms*
- *Purpose-built/rural views*
- *Waitete stream on boundary*

Boutique Accommodation or Self-contained

Double	$120-180
Single	$90-110
Studio	$60pp

We strongly recommend a minimum of two nights in this award winning town to give you time to soak up the history, see the goldmine, walk on the beach, play golf, see the art, the gardens, taste the coffee. Breakfast in our dining room or the deck, enjoy the *'oh so comfortable beds'*. In winter, a weekend in front of the open fire in a family-size lounge with a blueberry muffin. Our organic blueberries are a favourite as are eggs from our hens. Feed the trout, fish the Ohinemuri River, take a spectacular walk in the Karangahake Gorge or on the coast, guided or on your own. Restaurants, cafés, shops close by.
We look forward to welcoming you to our home.

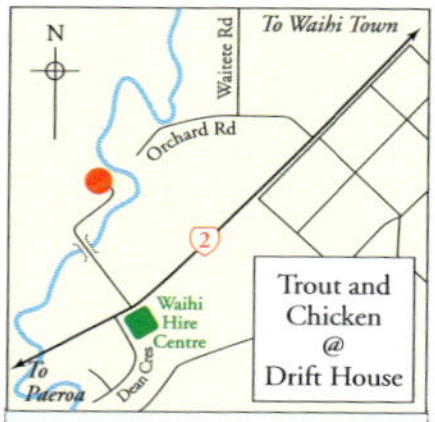

DIRECTIONS: Less than 2km west of Waihi Town on SH2

Bedrooms	Qty
Double	2
Twin	1
Single	
Bed Size	**Qty**
King	
Queen	2
King/Single	2
Single	2
Bathrooms	**Qty**
Ensuite	2
Private	1
Guest Share	

Waihi Beach Lodge

170 Seaforth Road, Waihi Beach, Coromandel
Ph (07) 863 5818, Fax (07) 863 5815
Mobile 021-657 888
email: *waihi.beach.lodge@xtra.co.nz*
www.waihibeachlodge.co.nz

Tariff : N.Z. Dollars	
Double	$220-265
Single	$195-235
Child	n/a

Bedrooms	Qty
Double	4
Twin	
Single	
Bed Size	**Qty**
Super King	
King	3
Queen	1
Double	
Single	
Bathrooms	**Qty**
Ensuite	3
Private	1
Guest Share	

Luxury Coastal Accommodation

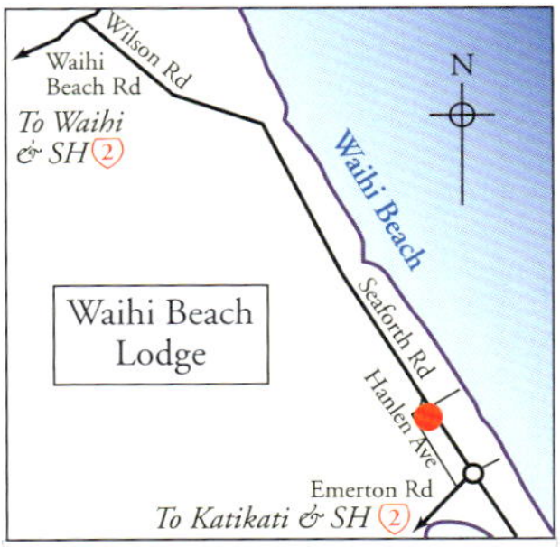

DIRECTIONS:
From North: Turn off SH2 to Waihi Beach, turn right at roundabout, 1½ km on right after shopping village. Cnr Seaforth Rd and Hanlen Ave with main entrance off Hanlen Ave.
From South: Turn off SH2 to Waihi Beach, turn left at roundabout, 400 m on left. Proceed as above.

Features & Attractions

- *Stunning sea and rural views*
- *Short stroll to beach*
- *Full gourmet breakfasts*
- *Quality linen and décor*
- *Close to K'gorge walks*
- *5 local cafés*
- *Pre-dinner drinks*
- *Less than 2hrs – Auckland*

Waihi Beach is a friendly seaside resort and one of the safest surf beaches in New Zealand. Your restful escape from a bustling lifestyle or your gateway to the Coromandel. Surrounded by natural beauty **Waihi Beach** offers a whole range of leisure opportunities from beach and gorge walks to golf and fishing. Or if you prefer, relax and experience the many sea views available from the **Lodge** with a book from our library. We have 3 king bedrooms with ensuites and a modern studio apartment with a queen-size bed. 3 rooms have private entrances. All rooms are furnished with quality beds, cotton linen, bath robes, toiletries, hair dryers, televisions, DVD players and fridges. Pre-dinner drinks are offered each evening. Waihi Beach has great cafés for dining or we would be happy to provide a 3-course meal by prior arrangement. Scrumptuous full breakfasts are served in the dining room or alfresco on one of the many decks.

Te Kauwhata ▶ YOUR HOSTS: Trish and Ian Budd Ph: (07) 826 3031

HERB GARDEN BED & BREAKFAST

114A Plantation Road, Te Kauwhata
Ph (07) 826 3031, Fax (07) 826 3035
Mobile 021-251 4170
email: *info@herbhaven.co.nz*
http://www.herbhaven.co.nz

Features & Attractions

- *Renowned herb garden*
- *Private spa*
- *Superb meals on request*
- *Wineries, golf clubs*
- *Heritage attractions*
- *Peace & tranquility*

Romantic Herb Garden B&B With Rural Views

$	
Double	$150-190
Single	
Child	

A 'well kept secret', 1km from State Highway 1, nestled in the heartland of the Waikato. Experience the charms of a romantic setting amidst a country lifestyle. Savour the 'famous' lavender scones on arrival and relax in the **Rose**, **Lily**, or **Lavender Rooms**. Enjoy the tranquility while meandering through a 'herb haven', or soak in a private spa on one of the large verandahs which overlook rural New Zealand and the lingering sunsets. Scrumptious meals are available with a selection of fine wines. The boutique villa is separate to owners, with large lounge and dining room for your privacy and comfort. A gift shop features specialty gourmet food and gifts. Only 40 minutes to Auckland or Hamilton International Airports.

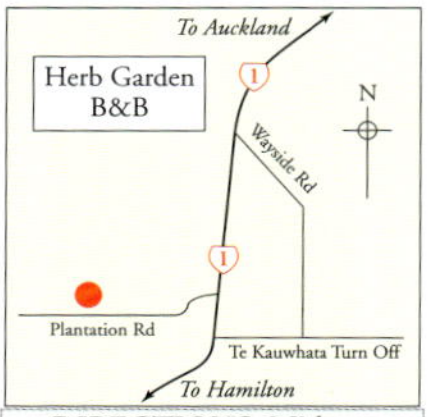

DIRECTIONS: Midway Auckland – Hamilton. 1km off SH 1. On the right hand side down Plantation Road.

Bedrooms	Qty
Double	3
Twin	
Single	
Bed Size	**Qty**
King	1
Queen	2
Double	
Single	
Bathrooms	**Qty**
Ensuite	1
Private	
Guest Share	1

Huntly ▶ YOUR HOSTS: Wendy and Grahame Hinkley Ph (07) 828 7771

LAKEVIEW HOMESTEAD BED & BREAKFAST

503 Rotowaro Rd, RD1 Huntly 3771
Ph (07) 828 7771, Fax (07) 828 7772
Mobile 021-738 592
email: *hinkleys@ihug.co.nz*
www.nwt.org.nz/members/lakeview

@home NEW ZEALAND

Features & Attractions

- *Central location*
- *Enjoyable breakfasts*
- *Hamilton city 35 min.*
- *Hot springs near by*
- *Auckland Airport 60 min*
- *Wendy spreekt ook Nederlands*

$	
Double	$120-140
Single	$95-105
Extra pp	$30

B & B Countrystay and Self-contained Cottage

Bedrooms	Qty
Double	2
Twin	
Single	
Bed Size	**Qty**
King	
Queen	1
Double	1
Single	
Bathrooms	**Qty**
Ensuite	1
Private	1
Guest Share	

Enjoy beautiful views of lakes, hills and peaceful farmland. Our 1920s character farm homestead in cream and red colours is on the crest of a hill. Friendly hospitality, comfortable beds and a good night's sleep in spacious accommodation on one level awaits you. A great place for welcome time-out or stop-over after arrival or before departure from NZ. **The Homestead** has a comfortable double bedroom with private bathroom. The self-contained one bedroom cottage offers privacy, comfort, stress-free surroundings and a modern bathroom with walk-in shower. Can sleep four. Both have generous parking and easy access entrances. We are just 5 minutes from Huntly and are centrally located to many tourist attractions, including walkways, hot springs, golf courses and beaches.

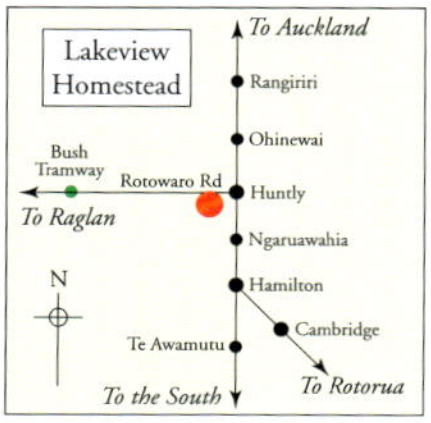

DIRECTIONS: Leave SH 1 at traffic lights by Huntly KFC, cross river and continue straight ahead into Rotowaro Rd. 503 is on the left.

Herons Ridge Farmstay & Sport Horse Stud

1131 Lake Waikare Scenic Dr,
RD 1, Te Kauwhata, Waikato
Ph (07) 826 4646, Fax (07) 826 4646
email: *herons.ridge@xtra.co.nz*
www.huntly.net.nz/herons.html

Features & Attractions

- *Rural tranquility*
- *Horse riding*
- *Wineries*
- *River & country walks*
- *Four golf courses*
- *Hot pools nearby*

$	
Double	$100-140
Single	$60-80
Child	

Farm Stay & Horse Stud & Quality Garden Studio

Bedrooms	Qty
Double	3
Twin	1
Single	1
Bed Size	**Qty**
King	1
Queen	2
Double	1
Single	1
Bathrooms	**Qty**
Ensuite	2
Private	1
Guest Share	

Welcome to **Herons Ridge**, your home in the Waikato. One hour from Auckland and Hamilton, quality in-house suites and superb Garden Studio, overlooking both pool and garden, a perfect setting. Close to the shores of Lake Waikare and three of New Zealand's international wetlands. A selection of fine local wines can be served with a scrumptious homecooked dinner. Whilst respecting your privacy we are delighted to share our home with you. Seniors Card New Zealand is welcome here.

DIRECTIONS: From State Highway 1 travel through Te Kauwhata village, travel 6 km east along Waerenga Road turn right at Waikare Rd, **Herons Ridge** is 1 km on right

YOUR HOSTS: **Sharon and David Payne** Ph: (07) 828 8781 **Huntly**

Parnassus Farm & Garden

191 Te Ohaki Road, Huntly
Ph/Fax (07) 828 8781, Mobile 021-458 525
email: *parnassus@xtra.co.nz*
www.parnassus.co.nz

Features & Attractions

- *Only minutes off SH1*
- *Auckland under 1 hour*
- *Bush and farm walks*
- *Working farm*
- *Glorious gardens*
- *Families welcome*

Bed & Breakfast Farmstay on "Real Working Farm"

$	
Double	$120-140
Single	$70-100
Child	neg

Experience farm life or simply relax on a working farm, 1hr south of Auckland and only 4km off SH 1. All our bedrooms are beautifully appointed with private facilities, we also have a small self-contained private unit. We have extensive gardens which supply produce and preserves for the 'Farm to Fork' dining experience that we are renown for and showcase a diverse range of trees and shrubs, fruits and vegetables.

We are very centrally located for day trips to the thermal wonderlands of Rotorua and Taupo and to either east or west coast beaches. Farm, bush and wetland walks are easily accessible and there is a beautiful 18 hole golf course just a few kilometres along the road.

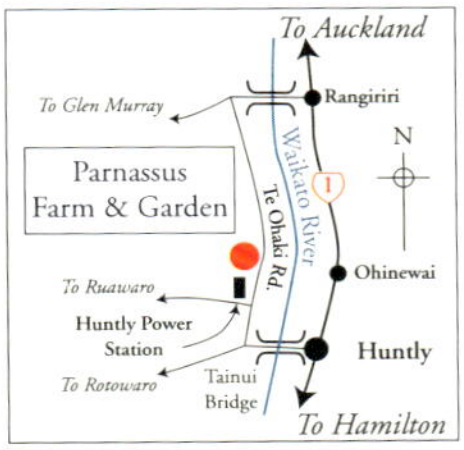

DIRECTIONS: Leave SH 1 at traffic lights by Huntly KFC. Cross river, turn right into Harris Street 2 km, right into Te Ohaki Road, 1.9 km on left

Bedrooms	Qty
Double	2
Twin	1
Single	
Bed Size	**Qty**
Queen	
Double	2
King Single	2
Single	2
Bathrooms	**Qty**
Ensuite	
Private	3
Guest Share	

Hamilton YOUR HOSTS: **Clyde and Gloria Morriss** Ph: (07) 829 5765

MATANGI OAKS

634 Marychurch Road, Matangi, RD 4, Hamilton
Ph (07) 829 5765, Fax (07) 829 5765
Mobile 027-242 7429
email: *matangi.oaks@xtra.co.nz*
www.matangioaks.co.nz

Tariff : N.Z. Dollars	
Double	$185
Single	$120
Child	

Bedrooms	Qty
Double	2
Twin/Double	1
Single	
Bed Size	**Qty**
Super King	1
King	
Queen	1
Double	1
Single	
Bathrooms	**Qty**
Ensuite	1
Private	1
Guest Share	

Countrystay - Bed & Breakfast

VISA MasterCard

Features & Attractions

- *Midway Hamilton & Cambridge*
- *Stud tours available*
- *Maungatautari Sanctuary*
- *Hamilton Gardens*
- *10 min. to Mystery Creek*
- *Peaceful and relaxing*
- *Waikato River Cruises*
- *Dinner by arrangement*

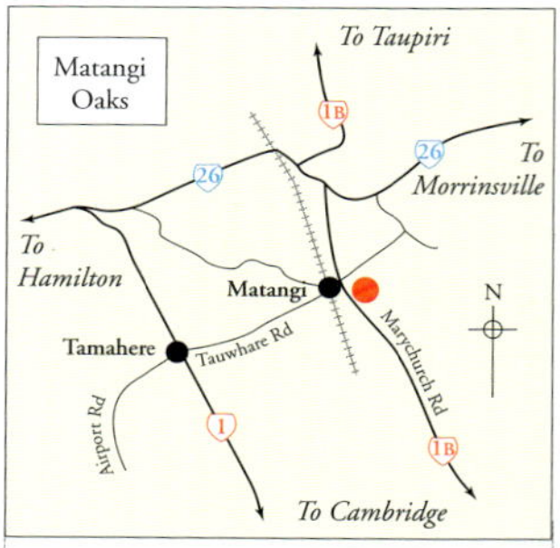

DIRECTIONS: From SH 1 at Tamahere turn onto Tauwhare Road to Matangi. Cross railway line, turn 1st right, SH 1B. We are 500m on left. From Taupiri travel 33km along SH 1B towards Cambridge.

Matangi Oaks is situated midway between Hamilton and Cambridge on State Highway 1B in a delightful rural setting. Our American Colonial Home, built in 1997, offers peace and tranquillity while being only 12 minutes from the city. An ideal stopover for visits to the National Agricultural Field Days at Mystery Creek or for taking a tour of some of the famous thoroughbred horse studs in the district. Only 10 minutes from Hamilton Airport. For the golfing enthusiasts there are 12 golf courses within half an hour's drive. An hour's drive and you can be in Rotorua, Tauranga, Mt Maunganui and Waitomo Caves and only 1½ hrs to Lake Taupo and Auckland Airport. Cooked and continental breakfasts are provided and tea and coffee making facilities are available. Three-course evening meals are available with your hosts with great locally-grown vegetables. Pre-dinner drinks and dinner wines are all included at a cost of $50 pp. A separate guest lounge is available or visitors are welcome to join their hosts in the evening. Extra bedroom available upstairs for one party. Laundry facilities available.

LAS PALMAS B&B HOMESTAY

16A Acacia Crescent, Hamilton South
Ph (07) 843 3769, Fax (07) 843 3242
Mobile 025-275 5200
email: *las_palmas2002@hotmail.com*

Tariff : N.Z. Dollars	
Double	$90
Single	
Child	

Bedrooms	Qty
Double	2
Twin/Double	
Single	
Bed Size	**Qty**
Super King	1
King	
Queen	1
Double	
Single	
Bathrooms	**Qty**
Ensuite	1
Private	1
Guest Share	

Bed & Breakfast Homestay
Superior Self-catering

DIRECTIONS:
Please phone for easy directions.
Same day bookings are fine with us if we have a vacancy

Features & Attractions

- *Peaceful private setting*
- *Delicious full breakfasts*
- *Luxury self-contained unit*
- *Swimming pool & spa*
- *Dinner by arrangement*
- *10 min Mystery Creek*
- *5 hole golf course*
- *Family pets welcome*

Caroline and Malcolm guarantee you a warm welcome. **Las Palmas** is set on five acres of parklike gardens with a five hole 'golf course', swimming and spa pools, pétanque and garden walks. We offer either a luxury self-catering unit with a kitchenette, refrigerator, microwave and laundry facilities; or a queen size bedroom in the house with private bathroom. Both rooms have fresh flowers, fruit, bathrobes and luxury towels. Full or continental breakfast is offered which usually includes fresh fruit from the garden and home preserves. Dinner can be provided by arrangement. A complimentary beverage is offered on arrival. We are only eight minutes from central Hamilton with its celebrated public gardens, river walks, a plethora of cafés and restaurants and just ten minutes from Mystery Creek and the airport. **Las Palmas** is the ideal base from which to visit Rotorua, Taupo, Tauranga, Waitomo Caves, Raglan and the West Coast surf beaches. Rates are negotiable for longer stays. Airport transfers are available. We and the family dog Quincee and cat Hudson will endeavour to make your stay enjoyable.

Sunnyholme Countrystay

816 Whatawhata Road, RD5, Hamilton
Ph (07) 847 6141 Fax (07) 847 6140
Mobile 021-0228 8833
email: *sunnyholmestay@hotmail.com*

Tariff : N.Z. Dollars	
Double	$130-150
Single	$110
Child	$55

Bedrooms	Qty
Double	1-2
Twin	1
Single	
Bed Size	**Qty**
Super King	
King	
Queen	1-2
Double	
Single	2
Bathrooms	**Qty**
Ensuite	1
Private	
Guest Share	1

Quality Rural Accommodation Minutes from the City

Features & Attractions

- *Warm, friendly welcome*
- *Versatile accommodation*
- *Restaurants/cafés nearby*
- *Magnificant rural views*
- *Families welcome*
- *Handy to tourist attractions*
- *Quality continental breakfast*
- *Spa bath & outdoor spa*

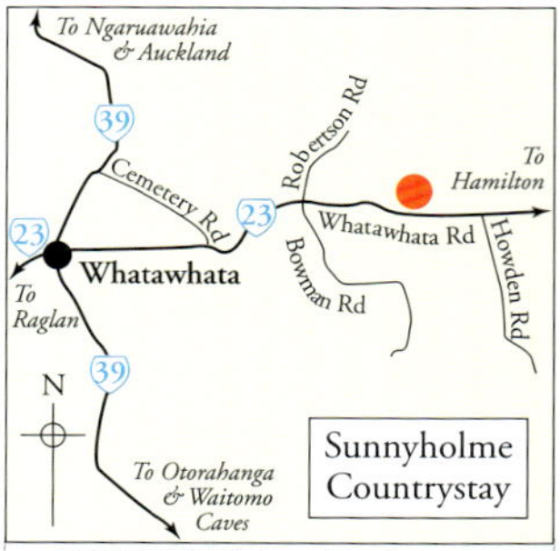

DIRECTIONS: From Hamilton, turn right into shared driveway just before 65km bend. First tree-lined driveway on the right between stone pillars.

Sunnyholme Countrystay offers an ideal choice of accommodation for national and international travellers and business people to central Waikato. Our large 2year old country home with sweeping rural and city views is situated only 10 minutes from Hamilton's CBD. We are on the main road to world-renowned Raglan surf beach, and within an hour from the wonders of Waitomo Caves. Auckland, Rotorua, Tauranga and the Coromandel Peninsula are an easy 90 minute drive. Thoughtful styling offers comfortable sleeping for 1-6 persons. The spacious **Merlot Room** features ensuite, dressing room and private deck; the **Lavender Room** is suitable for those requiring separate sleeping arrangements and/or business people, who wish to utilise

the computer and have access to the internet. The **Sage Room** is furnished as a cosy guest sitting room with sky TV. However, for larger groups this becomes an additional double room. All rooms are equipped with hairdryers, robes, complimentary toiletries, and tea & coffee making facilities. Dinner is available on request at $55 per person (advanced booking essential). A welcoming complimentary drink awaits your arrival. **@home applied for.**

Lakeviews Bed & Breakfast

68 Lake Crescent, Hamilton
Ph (07) 8383854
Mobile 027-630 0003
email: *Ron.Pam.Ball@xtra.co.nz*

Features & Attractions

- *Spacious, quiet garden setting*
- *Own access, off-street parking*
- *Airport, 'Fieldays' venue 20min.*
- *Waikato Hospital & city close*
- *2 hrs. Rotorua, Auckland*
- *Adjacent to lake walkways*

$	
Double	$120-150
Single	$120-150
Child	

Self-contained Bed & Breakfast

Bedrooms	Qty
Double	1
Twin	
Single	
Bed Size	**Qty**
King	
Queen	1
Double	
Single	
Bathrooms	**Qty**
Ensuite	
Private	1
Guest Share	

At **Lakeviews Bed & Breakfast** we offer you our self-contained spacious unit in a quiet garden setting. Only ten minutes from central city and close to Waikato Hospital, you will have off-street parking, your private entrance and self-catering facilities with breakfast ingredients provided. You can relax on the sunny deck whilst enjoying lovely lake views. Alternatively you may wish to make the most of **Lakeviews**' location and go for a pleasant walk as it is positioned right on the lake walkway. Hamilton Airport and 'Fieldays' venue Mystery Creek are only 20 minutes away.
Hamilton is an excellent base for day trips to Rotorua, Waitomo Caves, Taupo and surf beaches.

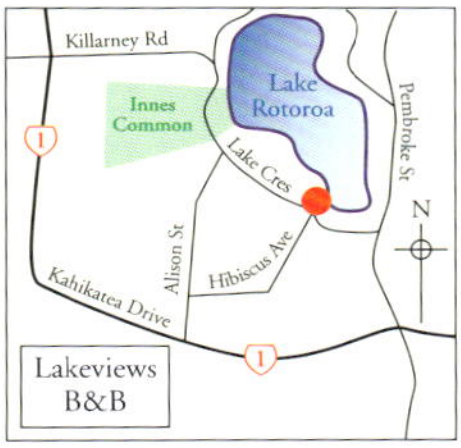

Saxon Lodge 'The Organic Place'

Rural No 266, Peacockes Road, RD 2, Hamilton
Ph (07) 843 3497, Fax (07) 843 3473
email: *saxonlodge@ihug.co.nz*
http://homepages.ihug.co.nz/~saxonlodge

Features & Attractions

- *Dawn chorus*
- *Stylish one storey home*
- *Great gardens & orchard*
- *Comfortable beds*
- *Campervan facilities*
- *Handy to city & airport*

$	
Double	$150
Single	$130
Child	$50

Organic Homestay

Bedrooms	Qty
Double	
Twin	2
Single	
Bed Size	**Qty**
King	4
Queen	
Double	
Single	
Bathrooms	**Qty**
Ensuite	
Private	1
Guest Share	

Saxon Lodge, 'The Organic Place', is set on two acres just south of Hamilton. You wake up to the 'dawn chorus' – the birds greeting you and the morning. After a morning cup of herbal tea you can collect fresh eggs from our hens (the girls) and pick in season fruit for your breakfast. Our dog Possum (a Pembroke corgi) and our cat Tara will help! You may have to chase the wild ducks, rabbits and pukekos (a native bird) out of your way! The house, designed by a local architect, is a stylish New Zealand single storey home with high raked timber ceilings and brick veneer. We love it and would like you to enjoy it too.

VISA MasterCard

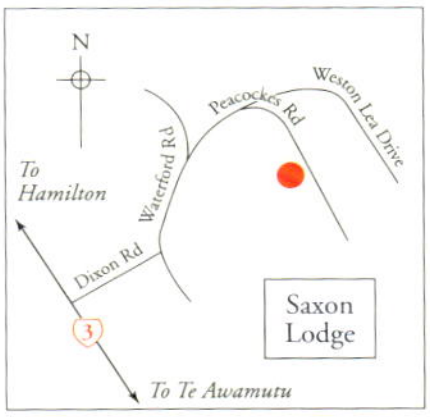

KUA MAKONA

142 Reid Road, Ngahinepouri, RD 2, Ohaupo, Waikato
Ph (07) 825 2852, Fax (07) 825 2852
Mobile: 027-496 0064
e-mail: *themarcrofts@nettel.net.nz*

Tariff : N.Z. Dollars	
Double	$135-155
Single	$100
Child	$50

Bedrooms	Qty
Double	2
Twin	1
Single	
Bed Size	**Qty**
Super King	
King	
Queen	2
Double	
Single	2
Bathrooms	**Qty**
Ensuite	1
Private	
Guest Share	1

H **Countrystay Deer Farm** C

VISA MasterCard

Features & Attractions

- *Deer Farm*
- *Swimming pool & spa pool*
- *Formal garden*
- *Quiet and relaxing*
- *Auckland & Rotorua 1½ hour*
- *Waitomo Caves 40 minutes*
- *Otorohanga Kiwi House and Aviary 20 minutes*

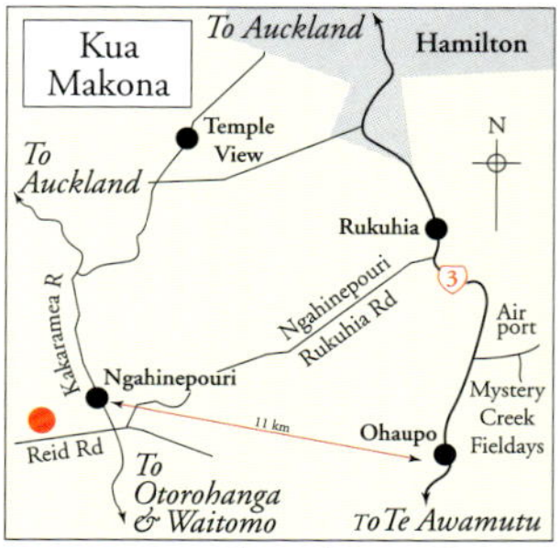

Relax in a quiet rural setting with homestyle welcome and atmosphere. Centrally situated for tourist attractions, 1½ hours from Auckland Airport and Rotorua, Waitomo Caves 40 minutes, Tongariro National Park two hours, Otorohanga Kiwi House & Aviary 20 minutes and National Field days site and Hamilton Airport 15 minutes. We run a deer finishing unit. The surrounding district has traditional dairy and beef farms as well as a diverse range of horticulture: asparagus, nashis, apples, flowers and vegetables.

There is a superb country golf course just down the road and an award winning vineyard close by. Transfers from Hamilton or airport can be arranged. Relax by a cosy fire in the formal lounge in the winter or cool off beside the pool in the summer. There is also an outdoor spa pool and croquet. French doors open out into the garden from all the bedrooms, which are furnished in country style complete with fresh flowers, hairdryers, robes and complimentary toiletries. There's also a cot should you require one. Fax, internet and laundry facilities available. Cooked or continental breakfast is included and dinner by request $45 per person. We have one Burmese cat.

Tapanui Country Home

1714 Oparure Road, RD 5, Te Kuiti
Ph (07) 877 8549, Fax (07) 877 8541
Mobile 027-494 9873
email: *info@tapanui.co.nz*
www.tapanui.co.nz

Tariff : N.Z. Dollars	
Double	$180-195
Cottage	$200
Child	n/a

Bedrooms	Qty
Double	4
Twin	
Single	
Bed Size	**Qty**
Super King	3
King	
Queen	1
Double	
Single	
Bathrooms	**Qty**
Ensuite	1
Private	2
Guest Share	

Elegant Country Retreat
Homestead and Cottage

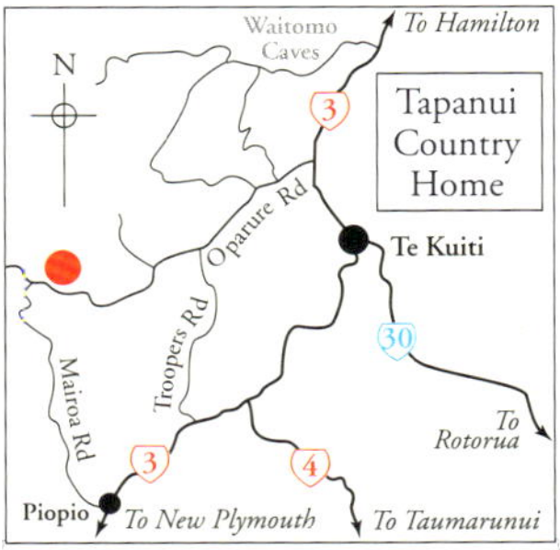

DIRECTIONS: From Te Kuiti, take SH 3 north for 3km. Turn left into Oparure Rd and continue for 17 km. **Tapanui Country Home** is on the right, through limestone entrance.

Features & Attractions

- *Near renowned Waitomo Caves*
- *Delicious meals with NZ wine*
- *Comfortable SuperKingTwin beds*
- *Adults only*
- *NZ farming hospitality*
- *Peace and tranquillity*
- *Friendly farm animals*
- *Kiwi House, golf courses*

Elegant country retreat located near the renowned Waitomo attractions. **Tapanui** is a 770-hectare sheep and beef farm with over 4,000 sheep and 650 cattle roaming the hillsides. The purpose-built homestead offers two spacious guestrooms, the **Romney** in the main house with a private bathroom, and the **Huntaway** with ensuite in the guest wing. Experience NewZealand farming hospitality and delicious home-cooked meals with NZ wine, while recharging from Waitomo activities. Meet the friendly farm animals and resident cat while enjoying peace and tranquility. Relax and revitalize with quality super-king/twin beds, cotton waffle bathrobes, toiletries, hairdryers, heated towel rails, spacious ensuite and private bathroom. An attractively decorated two bedroom self-contained **Cottage** is close by for guests that require a little independence. Recently refurbished in a style similar to the homestead, the **Cottage** contains 1 super-king/twin and 1 queen bedroom with bath/shower and 2 toilets – minimum 2 nights stay. Guests welcome after 4pm.

Waitomo - Otorohanga

YOUR HOSTS: **Georgina and John Owen** Ph (07) 873 6685

REDWOOD LODGE

222 Puketawai Road, RD 6, Otorohanga
Ph (07) 873 6685, Fax (07) 873 6694
Mobile 021- 411 905
email: *welcome@redwood-lodge.co.nz*
www.redwood-lodge.co.nz

Features & Attractions

- *Explore Waitomo Caves*
- *Great bush treks*
- *Glow-worm walks*
- *Blackwater rafting*
- *Excellent fly-fishing*
- *Kiwi House native birds*

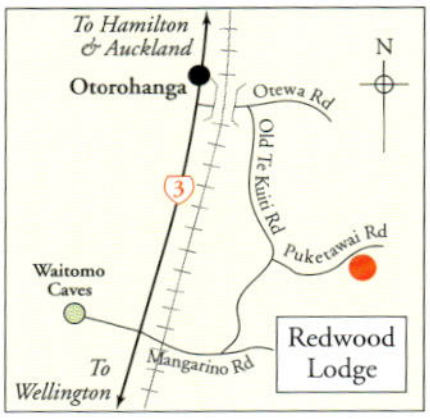

Deluxe Homestay Bed & Breakfast

Double	$120-160
Single	$100-120
Child	neg

Only ten minutes from Waitomo Caves, **Redwood Lodge** offers travellers a tranquil escape from the hustle and bustle of town, whilst being conveniently situated for explorations of Otorohanga (Kiwiana capital of NZ) and Te Kuiti (world sheep shearing capital). John and Georgina Owen welcome you into their comfortable and well-appointed home, offering a choice of four large heated/air-conditioned ensuite bedrooms. Rooms are comfortable and spacious with tea/coffee making facilities and ranch sliders opening onto the garden. Following a restful night's sleep, guests can enjoy a choice of continental or delicious full English breakfast. There is a guest lounge with sky TV and pool table; guests can relax outside on the patio or take a relaxing dip in our sparkling pool.

Bedrooms	Qty
Double	4
Twin	
Single	
Bed Size	**Qty**
King	1
Queen	3
Double	
Single	3
Bathrooms	**Qty**
Ensuite	4
Private	
Guest Share	

Waitomo Caves

YOUR HOSTS: **Helen Fortescue and John Anderson** Ph: (07) 878 7815

ABSEIL BREAKFAST INN

709 Waitomo Caves Road, Waitomo Caves
Ph (07) 878 7815
email: *abseilinn@xtra.co.nz*
www.abseilinn.co.nz

Features & Attractions

- *Romantic themed rooms*
- *Canopied queen beds*
- *Spectacular rural views*
- *Private guest lounge*
- *At Waitomo Caves*
- *Near N Z's best bush walk*

Rural Splendour Romantic Accommodation

Double	$120-160
Single	$120
Child	

Romance, relaxation, recreation, comfort and tranquility all await you at the **Abseil Inn**. The **Abseil** is purpose-built, contemporary, boutique accommodation. Neither a traditional Bed & Breakfast, nor an impersonal hotel, the **Abseil** with four individually themed ensuite rooms is designed for comfort and romance. From the 'Farm Room', with spectacular views out over the Waitomo Valley, to the 'Bush Room', with its magnificent canopy (a favourite for honeymooners), to the 'Swamp Room' with its bath built for two and a range of bath oils and candles, each room has unique appeal. Take time to enjoy our cooked breakfasts of local produce, or just to enjoy bread, cheese and a bottle of premium New Zealand wine on the deck gazing at the surrounding hills, bush, forests and fields. To gain the view does mean that the driveway is steep. Like everything else at the **Abseil** it must be approached with enthusiasm.

Bedrooms	Qty
Double	3
Twin	1
Single	
Bed Size	**Qty**
King	
Queen	3
Double	1
Single	1
Bathrooms	**Qty**
Ensuite	4
Private	
Guest Share	

Glenelg

6 Curnow Place, Cambridge
Ph (07) 823 0084, Fax (07) 823 4279
email: *glenelgbnb@ihug.co.nz*

Features & Attractions

- *Ensuite accommodation*
- *Warm hospitality*
- *Quiet, peaceful setting*
- *Hamilton Airport 15 min*
- *Spa and air bath*
- *5 min to Lake Karapiro*

$	
Double	$100
Single	$65
Child	$25

Quiet Rural Outlook
B&B, Homestay

Bedrooms	Qty
Double	3
Twin	1
Single	
Bed Size	**Qty**
King	
Queen	3
Double	
Single	3
Bathrooms	**Qty**
Ensuite	3
Private	1
Guest Share	

Cambridge, 15 km from Hamilton and 1 hour from Rotorua, is famous for its picturesque old English atmosphere and known as the "Town of Trees". If you are looking for a "Home away from Home", restful and away from the hustle, bustle and traffic noise, **Glenelg** is the place for you to be. We have a new, modern home in a quiet, peaceful setting with 200 roses in our garden. Breakfast is either cooked or continental with a menu to choose from – evening meals by prior arrangement. Guest laundry and off-street parking is available. We are in comfortable driving distance from the main tourist attractions: Mystery Creek Events Centre 10 min, Rotorua 1 hour, Waitomo Caves 45 min, Auckland or Taupo 2 hours.

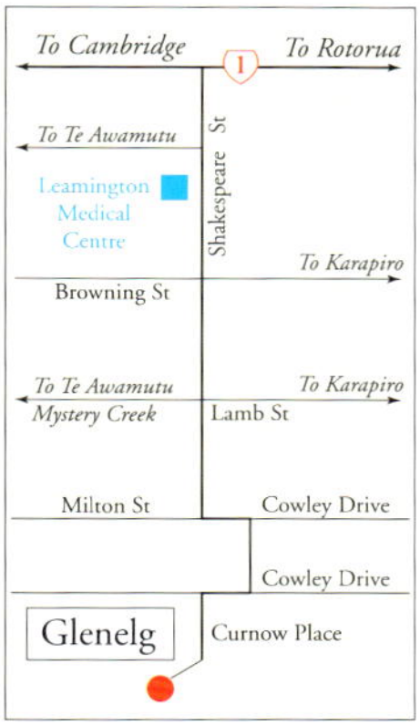

Riversong Bed & Breakfast Countrystay

213 Horahora Road, RD 1, Tirau, South Waikato
Ph (07) 883 1477, Fax (07) 883 1477
Mobile 027-642 3239
email: *riversong.bb@xtra.co.nz*

Features & Attractions

- *Relaxed rural setting*
- *Antiques, arts & crafts*
- *Water sports & golf*
- *Mystery Creek - Field days 30 min*
- *Central to Waikato, Rotorua, BOP*
- *Hobbiton tours close by*

$	
Double	$90-125
Single	$70
Child	neg

Bed & Breakfast Countrystay
Self-Contained Accommodation

Bedrooms	Qty
Double	2
Twin	2
Single	
Bed Size	**Qty**
King	1
Queen	
Double	1
Single	4
Bathrooms	**Qty**
Ensuite	1
Private	1
Guest Share	1

You are assured a warm welcome at **Riversong** situated in the heart of the beautiful South Waikato with Lake Karapiro views. We are an ideal base for touring the central North Island, only 45 mins from Rotorua, Tauranga 50 mins, Hamilton Airport 30 mins. Our new, fully equipped two bedroom unit (one queen and one twin) will ensure your comfort and privacy. Tariff $125 per night two persons, $15 each extra person. The main house has three bedrooms, one double with ensuite, one twin and one double, both with private bathrooms. Breakfast is full cooked or continental. Dinner by prior arrangement. Tea and coffee facilities in all rooms. Guest comment: Joan & David, UK have stayed several years and say *"We are their home down-under!"*

DIRECTIONS: Heading south turn right off SH 1. 500m south of Route 29 (Tauranga) **Riversong** is 2.13 km on left opposite lake. Right hand driveway.

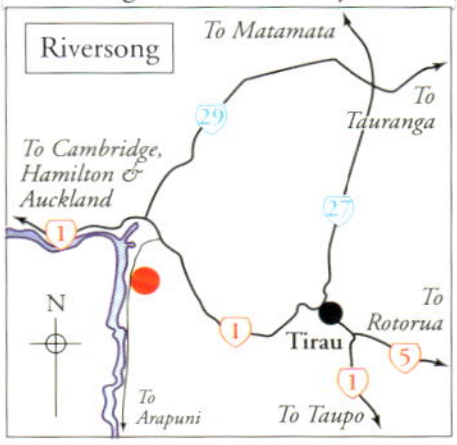

Katikati YOUR HOSTS: **Barbara and Phil McKernon** Ph: (07) 549 1882

PANORAMA COUNTRY LODGE

901 Pacific Coast Highway (SH 2), RD 1, Katikati
Ph (07) 549 1882, Fax (07) 549 1882
Mobile 021-165 5875
email: *mckernon@xtra.co.nz*
www.panoramalodge.co.nz

Tariff : N.Z. Dollars	
Double	$140-180
Single	$100-120
Child	neg

Bedrooms	Qty
Double	2
Twin	1
Single	
Bed Size	**Qty**
Super King	
King	1
Queen	1
Double	
Single	2
Bathrooms	**Qty**
Ensuite	1
Private	1
Guest Share	

Quality Bed & Breakfast with Magnificent Sea Views

Features & Attractions

- *Secluded peaceful & rural retreat*
- *Homecooked gourmet breakfasts*
- *Landscaped gardens, swimming pool*
- *Awesome sun & moon risings*
- *Relaxed hospitality*
- *Room service*
- *5 min to Waihi Beach*
- *Internet access*

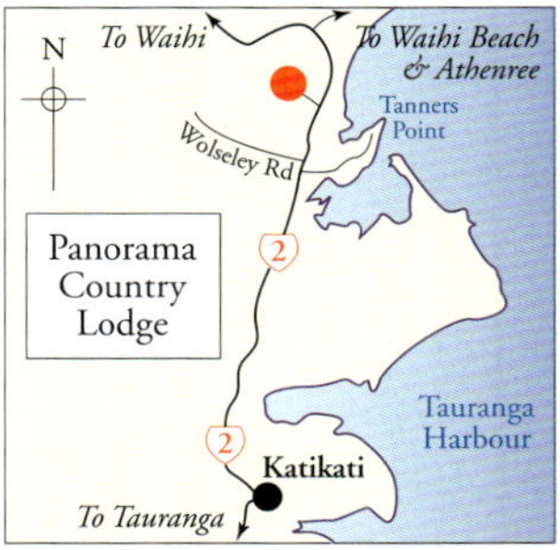

Panorama Country Lodge is perfectly located between beautiful Waihi Beach and the mural town of Katikati. Nestling in the foothills of the Kaimai Mountain Ranges it commands outstanding views of the Pacific Ocean and outlying islands. Only minutes from wineries, cafés and restaurants, a good base for exploring the western Bay of Plenty and the Coromandel Peninsula which offer many attractions and activities (beaches, golf courses, museums, bush walks, fishing and boating etc). The spacious private guest suites are situated in the northern wing with french doors to the swimming pool and terrace, quality furnishings, television DVD and CD player, radio, fresh coffee and tea making facilities, slippers, robes, hair dryers and wonderful sea views! Let yourself be pampered a little, enjoy generous gourmet breakfasts, relax and soak up the wonderful surroundings or roam the grounds Kiwifruit and Avocado orchards and say *Hi* to our boys (the Alpacas). We love it here – so will you!

Cotswold Lodge Countrystay

183 Ongare Point Road, RD 1, Katikati
Ph (07) 549 2110, Fax (07) 549 2109
email: *cotswold@ihug.co.nz*
www.cotswold.co.nz

Tariff : N.Z. Dollars	
Double	$130-150
Single	$100
Child	
Bedrooms	**Qty**
Double	2
Twin	1
Single	
Bed Size	**Qty**
Super King	
King	
Queen	2
Double	1
Single	1
Bathrooms	**Qty**
Ensuite	3
Private	
Guest Share	

Country Bed & Breakfast - with a little Luxury

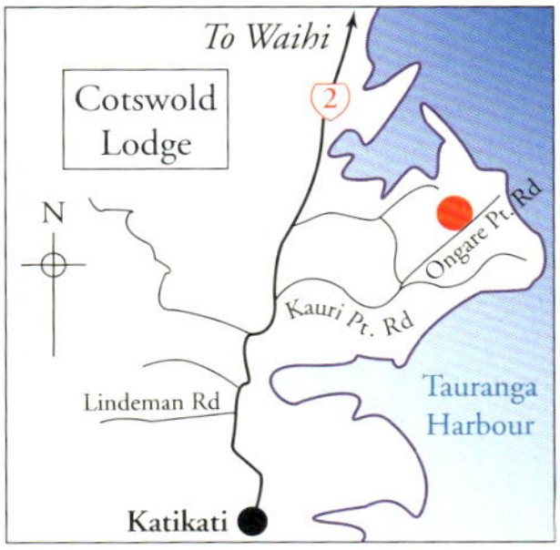

Features & Attractions

- *Stunning country scenery*
- *Peace & tranquility*
- *Hot spa for relaxation*
- *Abundant birdlife*
- *Scenic walks from lodge*
- *Laundry available*
- *Romance package available*
- *Tours can be arranged*

Cotswold Lodge Countrystay is just north of Katikati "Mural Town" and only two hours drive from Auckland Airport. We offer warm kiwi hospitality, a little luxury, and a relaxed peaceful environment in our rural colonial style home. Gourmet breakfasts. Evening meals by prior arrangement. All rooms have ensuite bathrooms with bathrobes, toiletries, hair dryers etc. Guest refrigerator, tea and coffee facilities available. Cotswold Lodge is a great base to explore the Bay of Plenty, Coromandel Peninsula or Rotorua. Wander through the garden, kiwifruit or avocado orchard or down to Ongare Point. Our dog will show the way. Sit on the deck with a drink and enjoy the view to the Kaimai Ranges or relax in the spa and listen to the birds. Nearby: restaurants, wineries, galleries, beaches, golf, walking tracks etc.

Burr-wood Countrystay

449 Lund Rd, RD 2, Katikati
Ph (07) 549 2060, Fax (07) 549 2061
email: *nzjewellery@clear.net.nz*

Tariff : N.Z. Dollars	
Double	$100
Single	$60
Child	neg

Bedrooms	Qty
Double	1
Twin	1
Single	
Bed Size	**Qty**
Super King	
King	
Queen	1
Double	
Single	2
Bathrooms	**Qty**
Ensuite	
Private	1
Guest Share	

Peaceful and Private Country Homestay

Features & Attractions

- *Stunning coastal views*
- *Friendly hospitality*
- *One party only*
- *Native timber jewellery*
- *Beautiful garden, secluded & quiet*
- *Dinner by arrangement*
- *Complimentary pre-dinner drinks*
- *Tourist attractions & golf nearby*

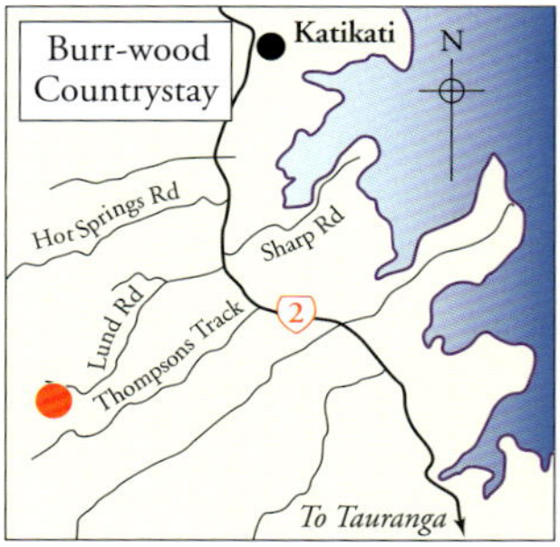

Welcome! **Burr-wood** is set in a 2½ acre well known garden and surrounded by native bush. Positioned in an elevated situation, we overlook a panorama of land, sea, harbour and islands. Relax and enjoy cooked or continental breakfast including home-made bread and jams, on our verandah or indoors. Enjoy complimentary pre-dinner drinks. A delicious dinner is available by arrangement. Home produce is used where possible. We are five minutes from State Highway 2 and within easy reach of Bay of Plenty attractions, including our 'Mural Town'. Bush walks about two minutes.

You are welcome to view our unique jewellery which we make from New Zealand native timbers in our studio at home. And of course you are welcome to wander through our tranquil garden. As we only have one party at a time, your relaxation is assured. We offer home-baking, tea/coffee on arrival. Laundry available.

Look forward to seeing you.

Middle Gable

51 Grammer Road, RD 1, Katikati 3063
Ph (07) 549 1837, Fax (07) 549 1837
Mobile 021-632 842
email: *kskelton@xtra.co.nz*

Features & Attractions

- *Secluded and quiet*
- *Guest sitting room*
- *Open air art*
- *Old fashioned rose gardens*
- *One party only*
- *Complimentary tea & coffee*

$	
Double	$100
Single	$70
Child	

Countrystay
Bed & Breakfast

Bedrooms	Qty
Double	2
Twin	
Single	
Bed Size	**Qty**
King	
Queen	1
Double	1
Single	
Bathrooms	**Qty**
Ensuite	
Private	
Guest Share	1

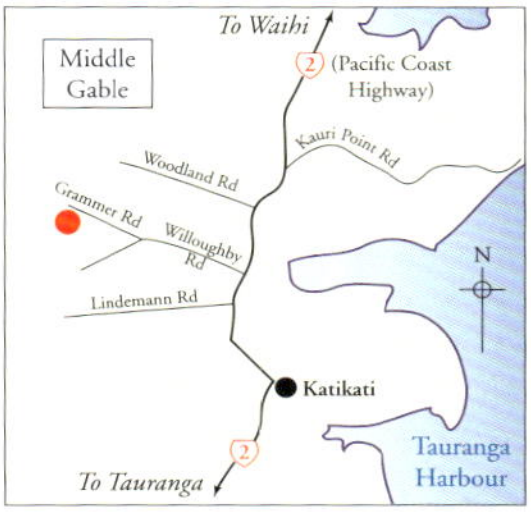

Welcome to **Middle Gable**, our garden of old fashioned roses and avocado orchard nestled in the foothills of the Kaimai Ranges. Wide views of Tauranga Harbour and surrounding farmland, just 4½ kilometres from Katikati noted for its murals and "Haiku" walkway along the Uretara River. Restaurants, cafés, wineries, four golf courses, ocean and harbour beaches and hot pools all close by. Tauranga City and airport only about thirty minutes away.

DIRECTIONS: Turn off SH 2, 2 km north of Katikati onto Willoughby Rd, 1.8 km take the right fork into Grammer Rd. We are first house on the left, 510m up Grammer Road

Tauranga YOUR HOSTS: **David and Anna Barons** Ph: (07) 548 0229

Sagewood Lodge

14D Sagewood Road, Pahoia, RD 6, Tauranga
Ph (07) 548 0229, Fax (07) 548 2029
Mobile 027-609 4932
email: *sagewood@ihug.co.nz*
www.sagewoodlodge.com

Tariff : N.Z. Dollars	
Double	$220
Single	$200
Child	

Bedrooms	Qty
Double	3
Twin	1
Single	
Bed Size	**Qty**
Super King	3
King	
Queen	
Double	
Single	2
Bathrooms	**Qty**
Ensuite	4
Private	
Guest Share	

LA **Luxury Country Accommodation** C

Features & Attractions

- *Tennis court*
- *Olive grove*
- *Wineries nearby*
- *French doors open to garden*
- *Swimming and spa pool*
- *2 golf courses 10 min away*
- *Laundry facilities*
- *Generous breakfast*

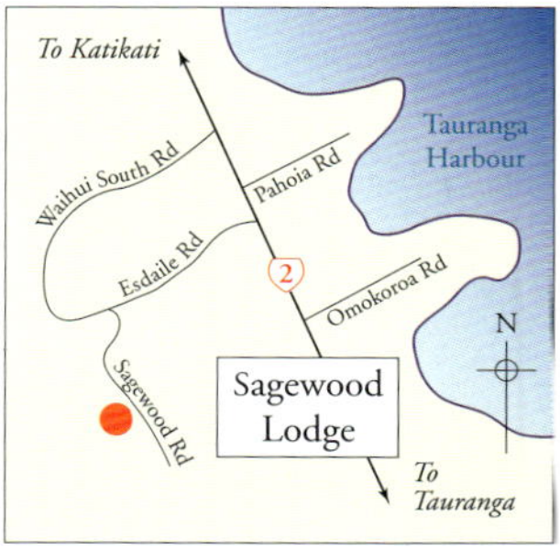

DIRECTIONS:
Please phone for easy directions

Sagewood Lodge is a fine luxurious Queensland-style home midway between Tauranga and Kati-Kati. It is set in 65 acres, including an olive grove and has breathtaking views over Mayar and Matakana Islands. Extensive gardens include a swimming and spa pool and tennis court. Ensuite bedrooms all have tea making, fridge, robes etc.

Hearty breakfasts may be taken on the terrace or in the dining room. Gourmet suppers with fine wines by arrangement.

BOATSHED MOTEL APARTMENTS

31 Maranui Street, Mt Maunganui, Tauranga
Ph (07) 572 1044, Fax (07) 572 2092
Mobile 027-493 7325
email: *info@boatshed-accommodation.co.nz*
www.boatshed-accommodation.co.nz

Tariff : N.Z. Dollars	
Double	$100-220
Single	$90-140
Child	neg

Bedrooms	Qty
Double	8
Twin	10
Single	8
Bed Size	**Qty**
Super King	8
King	
Queen	
Double	
Single	30
Bathrooms	**Qty**
Ensuite	6
Private	6
Family Share	2

VISA MasterCard eftpos bankcard

Self-contained Accommodation and Homestay

Please telephone for bookings and easy directions.

Features & Attractions

- *Groups and corporates a speciality*
- *Jet boating, stock cars*
- *Fishing and diving*
- *Golf and driving range*
- *Kiwifruit country tour*
- *Mini farm, feed animals*
- *Vintage car display*
- *Hot salt water pools*

Boatshed Apartments are new, architect designed with brilliant interior colours with 3-piece wicker lounge suite, large bifold doors opening onto large balconies, full kitchen, dishwasher, refrigerator, deep freeze, Sky television, gas hobs. Super king beds, rollaway beds available. These units are serviced daily. Three apartments have some sea views. Two units can sleep up to seven or eight people. The Penthouse Suite (sleeps four) on the third floor has panoramic sea and city views. All units have their own barbeque. There is also a separate private spa. We are situated one minute's walk to white sandy safe beach, one minute's walk to fish shop and pizza restaurant, 2 km to golf course, 1 km to Bay Fare Shopping Mall and BayWave Hot Pools. We are approximately 6 km to Mt Maunganui shopping centre. Walk around the Mount and then take a swim in the hot salt water pools. Also approximately 8 km to Tauranga Shopping Centre. We offer the discerning traveller a place to unwind and rediscover the simple pleasures in life with good old Kiwi hospitality. Corporate rates continental breakfast available. Mini putt, island trips, kitesurfing, adventure park, animal park, ten pin bowls, visit winery, kiwifruit guided tour, Vintage Cars Auto Barn. Groups and corporates a speciality.

Cornthwaite Cottage

33A Churchill Road, Judea, Tauranga
Ph (07) 578 7025, Fax (07) 578 7065
Mobile 027-499 4281
email: *pioneercottage@xtra.co.nz*

Tariff : N.Z. Dollars	
Double	$200-250
Single	$180-220
Child	

Bedrooms	Qty
Double	2
Twin	
Single	
Bed Size	**Qty**
Super King	
King	
Queen	1
Double	1
Single	
Bathrooms	**Qty**
Ensuite	
Private	1
Guest Share	

LA

Pioneer House
Superior Self-contained Cottage

SC

Features & Attractions

- *Stunning, cosy, unique*
- *Hidden in a valley*
- *2 min. to downtown*
- *Bath in the bush*
- *Half acre of cottage gardens*
- *Bush walks nearby*
- *Off-street parking*
- *Laundry available*

Relive history and stay in the romance of the late 19th century. Step back in time to the 1900's in our exclusive gold miner's cottage. It was transported from the Waihi Goldmine and has been lovingly recreated with attention to the smallest detail.

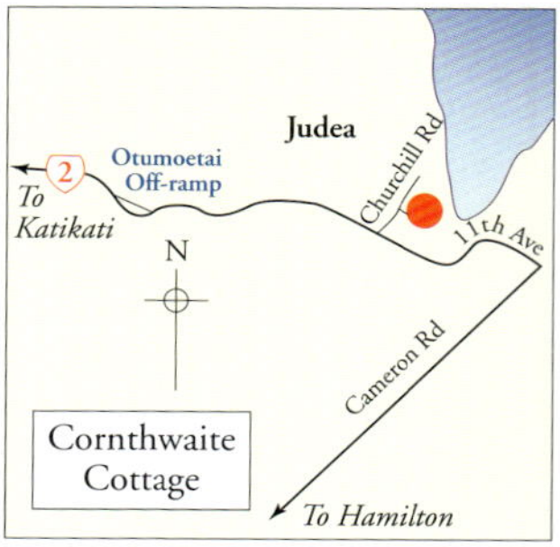

Cornthwaite Cottage is named after the orginal family who built it. 90% of the cottage and fittings are original, with replicas where necessary. No expense has been spared.Fully furnished with late Victorian furniture, working coal range, copper pot, open fire, 6-foot claw bath, antiques from the gold mining era and outside claw bath (hot water on tap). There are no modern conveniences displayed. Breakfast is delivered to the door – fresh fruit and baked bread, fresh eggs from our own chickens (we do have cooking facilities hidden behind kauri doors). Internet available.

Dinner is by arrangement – our forté is coal range roast pork. We are only 40 minutes from Rotorua and one hour from Whakatane.

Tau Tau Lodge

1133 Pyes Pa Road, Greerton, Tauranga
Ph (07) 543 1600, Fax (07) 543 1601
email: *tautaulodge@ihug.co.nz*
www.tautaulodge.co.nz

Tariff : N.Z. Dollars	
Double	$150-190
Single	$120
Child	neg

Bedrooms	Qty
Double	4
Twin	
Single	
Bed Size	**Qty**
Super King	
King	
Queen	3
Double	1
Single	
Bathrooms	**Qty**
Ensuite	3
Private	
Guest Share	1

Superior Bed & Breakfast with Stunning Bay of Plenty Views

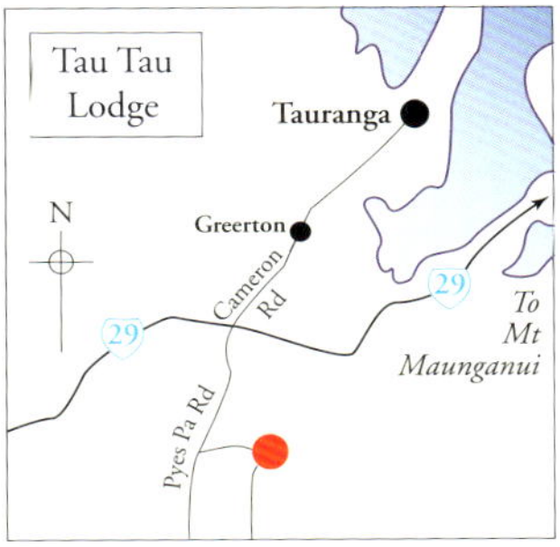

Features & Attractions

- *Tauranga 15 minutes*
- *Peace, privacy & tranquillity*
- *Rotorua 35 minutes*
- *Email, fax & laundry*
- *Close to golf courses & fishing*
- *Close to bush walks & hot pools*
- *Quilting, needlework and giftware shop on premises*

Tau Tau Lodge is located on the direct road from Tauranga to Rotorua. Situated on 2 acres of beautiful gardens and lawns, commanding stunning views over Tauranga, Mt Maunganui, Kaimai Ranges and the Coromandel and offering total peace, privacy and tranquillity. We offer 4 superior bedroom suites, 3 with their own private bathroom. Lovely views, completely private guest lounge with balcony, library, TV and antique furniture. Chocolates, fresh flowers and hairdryer in each bedroom. Tea and coffee facilities in each room. Pre dinner drinks and hors d'oeuvres are also offered on arrival. Included in the tariff is a full farmhouse-style breakfast or gourmet continental and croissants which can be served either alfresco on the front patio or in the dining room. A 2-3 course evening meal is available by prior arrangement. A very select wine list is also available. Whakatane 1 hour travel and Whitianga 4 hours travel, Matamata 45 min. travel from **Tau Tau Lodge**.

Villa Collini

36 Kaiate Falls Road, RD 5, Welcome Bay, Tauranga
Ph (07) 544 8322, Fax (07) 544 8322
Mobile 021-047 8394
email: *margrit@naturetours-nz.com*
www.villacollini.co.nz

Features & Attractions

- *Very quiet hilltop location*
- *Gourmet cuisine*
- *Close to Kaiate waterfalls*
- *Tauranga/beach 15 min*
- *NZ Tour operator*
- *German spoken*

Quality Bed & Breakfast with Panoramic Views

Double	$110-160
Single	$80-110
Child	neg

"Paradise means different things to different people, but for us **Villa Collini** is as close as it gets" (guest comment). Enjoy spectacular panoramic views of Mt. Maunganui and the sea in a quiet relaxing atmosphere, get spoiled with a warm welcome and great hospitality, gourmet Mediterranean dinners ($40pp), comfortable beds, spa under the stars and generous continental breakfast with homemade breads, croissants, cereals, cheese, sliced cold meat, Italian coffee etc. Relax in our parklike garden or walk the endless beaches of Papamoa. Our location is an ideal base for Rotorua, Tauranga or White Island. We both have travelled the world and nationwide so there is a lot to talk about. "Come as a stranger and leave as a friend"

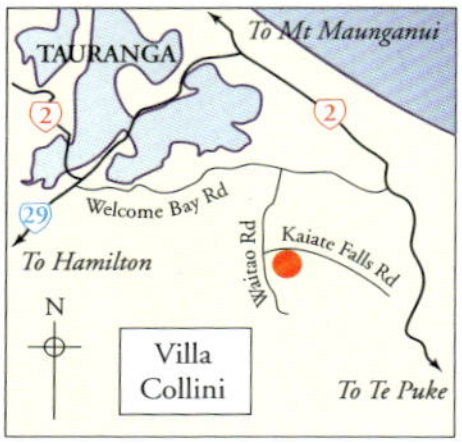

Bedrooms	Qty
Double	2
Twin	
Single	
Bed Size	**Qty**
Super King/Twin	1
Queen	1
Double	
Single	
Bathrooms	**Qty**
Ensuite	1
Private	
Guest Share	1

Sandtoft

83 Simpson Road, Papamoa Beach, Tauranga
Ph (07) 542 3459, Fax (07) 542 3459
email: *sandtoft@xtra.co.nz*
email: *sandtoft@excite.com*

Features & Attractions

- *Short walk to ocean beach*
- *Off street parking*
- *Close to restaurants & shops*
- *Complimentary tea, coffee etc*
- *Handy to laundromat*
- *Dinner by arrangement*

Beachstay Bed & Breakfast

Double	$100
Single	$70
Child	neg

Sandtoft is a comfortable home, just two minutes walk from the beautiful Pacific Ocean. Enjoy a stroll along the sandy beach, sunbathe, swim, surfcast. Sample our local restaurants. We offer two spacious bedrooms with double/queen and single beds. These rooms each have their own wash basin, coffee table, and comfy chairs, plus a north facing balcony. Also available is a smaller double/single bedroom at a lower rate. Bath, shower, toilet facilities are each separate. A guest refrigerator, television, tea/coffee are at your disposal. Continental only and/or cooked breakfast is offered. We are a semi-retired couple who enjoy travelling and meeting people. To meet you would be a pleasure.

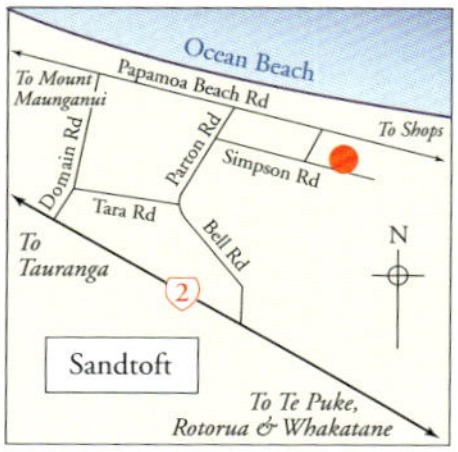

Bedrooms	Qty
Double	3
Twin	2
Single	1
Bed Size	**Qty**
King/Single	2
Queen/Double	3
Double	
Single	3
Bathrooms	**Qty**
Ensuite	
Private	
Guest Share	1

ALRAES

1 Santa Cruz Drive, Palm Springs, Papamoa Beach
Ph/Fax (07) 542 3818
Mobile 027-119 0071
email: *relax@alraes.co.nz*
www.alraes.co.nz

Tariff : N.Z. Dollars	
Double	$95-140
Single	
Child	

Bedrooms	Qty
Double	2
Twin	1
Single	
Bed Size	**Qty**
Super King	1
King	
Queen	1
Double	
Single	2
Bathrooms	**Qty**
Ensuite	
Private	
Guest Share	

Homestay
Bed & Breakfast

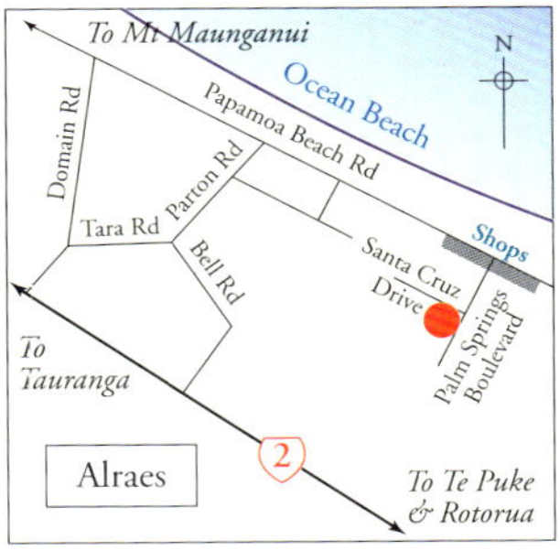

Features & Attractions

- *2003 award-winning show home*
- *Laundry/email/fax*
- *Pétanque court, outdoor checkers*
- *Handy shops, restaurant, medical centre*
- *Full/continental breakfast*
- *Complimentary tea/coffee*
- *Ideal holiday base*
- *Golf, swimming, beach*

A warm welcome awaits you in a 'home-away-from-home'. This luxuriously appointed home offers everything for your comfort. A relaxing, comfortable guest lounge leads into a conservatory, which looks out over the lovely outdoor area. Sit under the gazebo with a relaxing drink or play pétanque or outsize draughts in the quiet garden. We offer a room with king bed and ensuite. An additional room with queen bed is available. This award-winning home is well located and an ideal base for exploring the beautiful Bay of Plenty. Mount Maunganui is 20 min. drive away with its popular scenic walk around the "The Mount". Tauranga, well known for its lovely water coastline, is great for shopping. A Mecca for yachtsmen, boating, deep sea fishing charters and swimming with the dolphins. A short coastline drive to Whakatane for the flight/boat trip to White Island. Te Puke and golf courses are a short drive. Rotorua, the Thermal City, is 45 min. drive. We look forward to meeting you. Arrive as a stranger, leave as a friend.

POHUTUKAWA BEACH B&B & COTTAGE

693 State Highway 2, (RD 4, Whakatane), Pikowai/Matata
Ph (07) 322 2182, Fax (07) 322 2186
email: *joe@prinztours.co.nz*
www.prinztours.co.nz

@ home NEW ZEALAND

Tariff : N.Z. Dollars	
Double	$110
Single	$90
Child	

Bedrooms	Qty
Double	3
Twin	1
Single	
Bed Size	**Qty**
Super King	
King	1
Queen	2
Double	1
King Single	2
Bathrooms	**Qty**
Ensuite	2
Private	1
Guest Share	

VISA MasterCard

F **Coastal Country Stay and Cottage** SC

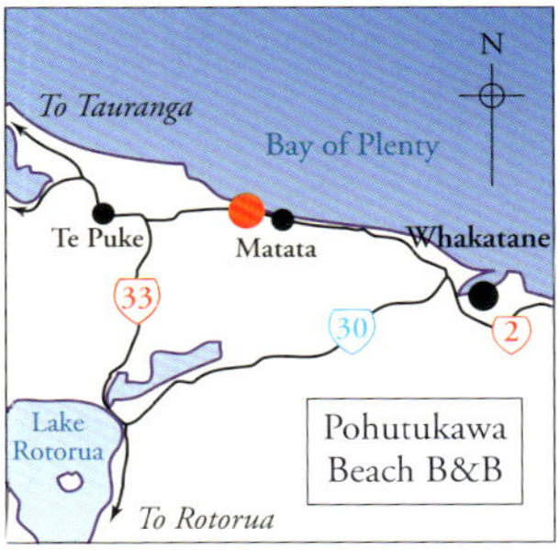

DIRECTIONS:
Directly on State Highway 2.
8 km west of Matata, 34 km east of Te Puke.

Features & Attractions

- *Cottage SC from $150*
- *Cottage B&B from $180*
- *Sauna, organic farm*
- *Guided tours*
- *100 metres to the beach*
- *Outdoor swimming pool*
- *Dinner on request*
- *German spoken*

Pohutukawa Beach Bed & Breakfast and Cottage are set in a picturesque location on the Pacific Coast Highway offering outstanding ocean views. Glance up from the breakfast table and see active volcano White Island. Sometimes dolphins and even whales pass by.

The Farmhouse is the base of our tour company "Prinz Tours". We are specialists for guided tours and offer day tours in the area and personalised itineraries for New Zealand-wide holidays. We encourage visitors to stay several days. There is so much to see and do in the Bay of Plenty region. Or simply relax in our garden, by the pool, at the beach or have a "talk" to our many farm animals. Dinners with ingredients from our organic farm on request. We also speak German and are looking forward to meeting you.

FOTHERGILLS ON MIMIHA

84 Mimiha Road (RD 4, Whakatane) Pikowai/Matata
Ph (07) 322 2224, Fax (07) 322 2224
Mobile 021-131 5171
email: *beverlyf@xtra.co.nz*
www.fothergills.co.nz

Tariff : N.Z. Dollars	
Double	$110-150
Single	$90-120
Child	$20

Bedrooms	Qty
Double	2
Twin	1
Single	1
Bed Size	**Qty**
Super King	
King Single	1
Queen	2
Double	
Single	2
Bathrooms	**Qty**
Ensuite	1
Private	1
Guest Share	

Bed & Breakfast/Homestay and Self Contained Cottage

Features & Attractions

- *Warm and friendly hosts*
- *Close to beach and SH2*
- *Gorgeous garden surrounds*
- *Covered parking alongside*
- *Kitchen facilities*
- *BBQ available*
- *Fabulous spa pool*
- *Pentanque/Boulles*

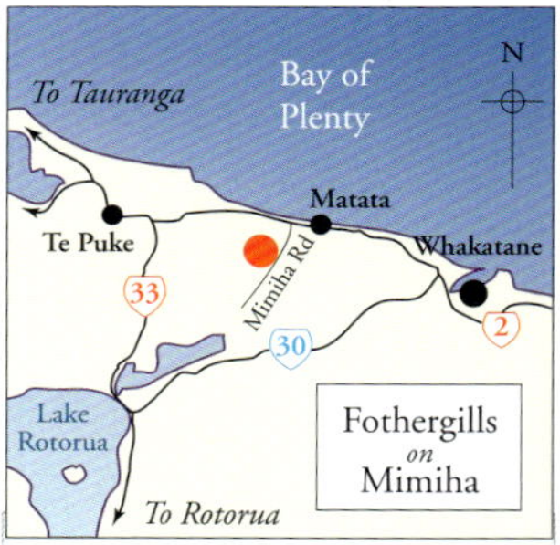

DIRECTIONS: Approximately halfway between Te Puke and Whakatane (25min each way) Mimiha Rd turns off Pacific Coast Highway 5 km north of Matata.

Hilton and Bev offer you an upstairs two-bedroom Bed & Breakfast unit or a self-service cottage on their property in a beautiful location on a quiet country road. The very comfortable self-contained B&B unit is separated from the main house by a covered carport. Breakfast is hosted in our house with emphasis on food organically grown in our vast garden and freshly prepared to produce tasty, healthy foods and includes our special preserves. **Mimiha Cottage** is built beside the Mimiha stream. This fully equipped two-bedroom cottage is wheelchair accessible and tastefully furnished. One queen room with an ensuite bathroom, and bunks in the other room. The beds are new and comfortable. Outside is a paved courtyard with shade covers. Our friendly fox terrier, Mo, will show you the way when you walk up the hill then follow the winding stream round the garden, inspect the new pond or take a spa. Come and enjoy this slice of heaven!

Whakatane Homestay - Leaburn Farm

237 Thornton Road, RD 4, Whakatane
Ph (07) 308 7487, Fax (07) 308 7966
email: *kath.law@theredbarn.co.nz*
www.whakatanehomestay.co.nz

Tariff : N.Z. Dollars	
Double	$85-95
Single	$55-65
Child	

Bedrooms	Qty
Double	1
Twin	1
Single	
Bed Size	**Qty**
Super King	
King	
Queen	1
Double	
Single	2
Bathrooms	**Qty**
Ensuite	
Private	
Guest Share	1

Homestay 'On a Farm'

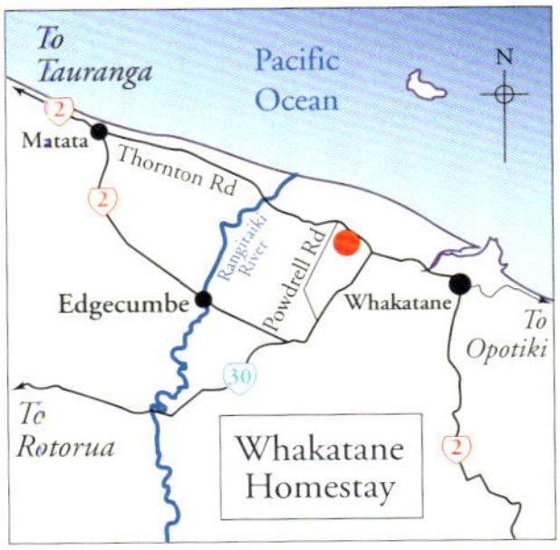

Features & Attractions

- *Relaxed, friendly hosts*
- *Craft shop and café*
- *Handy to town & Golf links*
- *Hosts have wide interests*
- *Local knowledge – help given*
- *Dinner by arrangement*
- *On Pacific Coast Highway*
- *Rural surroundings -two dairy farms*

Looking for peace and quiet or explore this sunshine coast? If stimulating conversation is something you enjoy, or a browse in our extensive library, you are welcome at our place. Other guests' comments over the 23 years we have been home-hosting, include: "We especially enjoyed talking with you and creating a new friendship" – Ron and Dorothy,Pa.USA. "Yummy home-cooked meals and fantastic hosts" – Steve, Australia. "Wish we could have stayed longer" – David and Margaret, Dorset, UK.

As 'young oldies' we enjoy company and are proud to show off our lifestyle, talk farming, travel. We are handy to the golf course, 7kms to thriving Whakatane township. Our special interests are travel, genealogy, Lions Club, bowls and crafts. We have a craftshop/café on the property. Our guest room is adjacent to a bathroom, separate shower and toilet and is shared only with other guests, if the twin room is occupied. Be as busy as you like or enjoy the restful country atmosphere, so close to town.

BEIGHTONS

124 East Bank Road, Thornton, Whakatane
Ph (07) 304 8789, Fax (07) 304 8784
Mobile 027- 447 3061
email: *lyell@xtra.co.nz*
www.beightons.co.nz

Tariff : N.Z. Dollars	
Double	$130-160
Single	$100
Child	

Bedrooms	Qty
Double	2
Twin	
Single	
Bed Size	**Qty**
Super King	
King	1
Queen	1
Double	
Single	
Bathrooms	**Qty**
Ensuite	2
Private	
Guest Share	

Quality Riverside Rural Accommodation

Features & Attractions

- *Whakatane 10 min.*
- *Whale & dolphin tours*
- *Deep-sea fishing*
- *Internet facilities*
- *Rotorua 60min.*
- *White Island tours*
- *Rafting & Jetboating*
- *Laundry facilities*

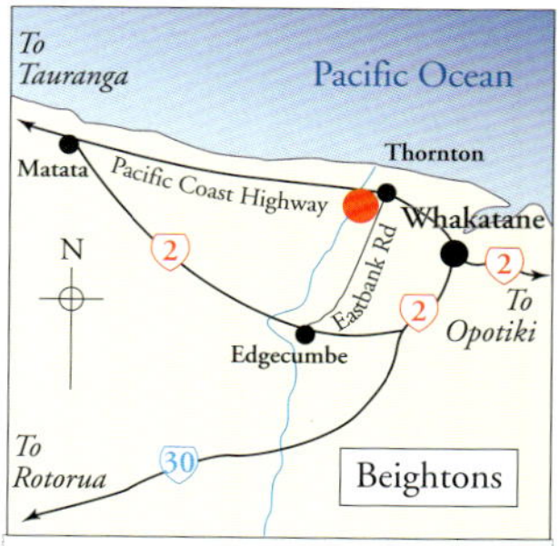

DIRECTIONS:
1 km off the Pacific Coast Highway,
or 7 km from Edgecumbe

Set in acres of park-like grounds alongside the Rangitaiki River, our very comfortable architecturally designed English-style home, in a very peaceful yet convenient location, is waiting to welcome you. As semi-retired international hoteliers, we have prepared **Beightons** for the most discerning guests. Downstairs, with separate entry, is a very spacious ensuite guest room with private patio, kingsize bed and lounge area. Upstairs, the ensuite guest room with a queen-size bed overlooks native trees and amazing bird life. Additional rooms are available if sold in conjunction with these rooms. Both ensuite guest rooms have airconditioning, security safe, TV/DVD, radio, CD, fridge, tea/coffee, electric blankets, robes, toiletries, hairdryer and to welcome you, wine and refreshments on arrival. Monty, our friendly golden retriever, will be delighted to escort you around our grounds, or to kayaks or bicycles, if you would like to explore our private jetty, river, or nearby Thornton Beach. Picnic lunches and dinners are available by prior arrangement.

OCEANSPRAY HOMESTAY

283A Pohutukawa Avenue, Ohope, Bay of Plenty
Ph (07) 312 4112, Fax (07) 312 4192
Mobile 027-286 6824
email: *frances@oceanspray.co.nz*
www.oceanspray.co.nz

Tariff : N.Z. Dollars	
Double	$120-150
Single	$80-100
Child	neg

Bedrooms	Qty
Double	3
Twin	2
Single	
Bed Size	**Qty**
Super King	
King	
Queen	3
Double	
Single	4
Bathrooms	**Qty**
Ensuite	1
Private	2
Guest Share	

Quality Beachfront Homestay & Self-contained Cottage

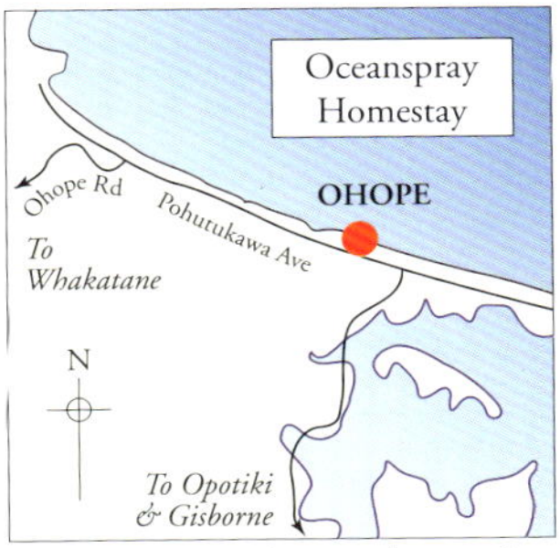

Features & Attractions

- *Absolute beachfront*
- *Separate downstairs unit*
- *Self-contained cottage*
- *Views to White Island*
- *Deep-sea fishing nearby*
- *Safe swimming beach*
- *Swimming with dolphins*
- *Two golf links nearby*

We warmly welcome you to **Oceanspray Homestay** – a beachfront property 100m from the Pacific Ocean surf. Panoramic views from the upstairs decks extend to the East Cape and to White Island, an active volcano 50km offshore. **Oceanspray Homestay** has three attractively furnished bedrooms, lounge/kitchen, two bathrooms (one is ensuite) and is a downstairs, private, self-contained unit within our home.

We also offer a cosy, well furnished, two bedroom, self-contained cottage adjacent to our house. We offer an excellent standard of accommodation, use of laundry facilities, barbeque, beach gear. Complimentary wine and delicious home-baking on your arrival. Comprehensive breakfast provisions are supplied into your unit and renewed daily or when required. A great selection of books, videos, toys – children well catered for, makes this an ideal family holiday retreat. John enjoys kayaking and longline fishing, Frances enjoys entertaining and cooking.

Hamurana - Rotorua YOUR HOST: **Christine King and David Perry** Ph (07) 332 2618

Panorama Country Homestay

144 Fryer Rd, Hamurana, RD 2 Rotorua
Ph/Fax (07) 332 2618, Mobile 021-610949
email: *panoramahomestay@xtra.co.nz*
www.panoramahomestay.co.nz

Tariff : N.Z. Dollars	
Double	$170-240
Single	$110-150
Child	$30-50

Bedrooms	Qty
Double	2
Twin	1
Single	
Bed Size	**Qty**
Super King	1
King	1
Queen	1
Double	
Single	2
Bathrooms	**Qty**
Ensuite	2
Private	1
Guest Share	

Peaceful Luxury Homestay

Features & Attractions

- *Private and peaceful retreat*
- *Spacious ensuite rooms*
- *Magnificent lake views*
- *Heated massage spa pool*
- *Championship sized tennis court*
- *15 min. from Rotorua*
- *Close to all major attractions*
- *Internet access / SKY TV*

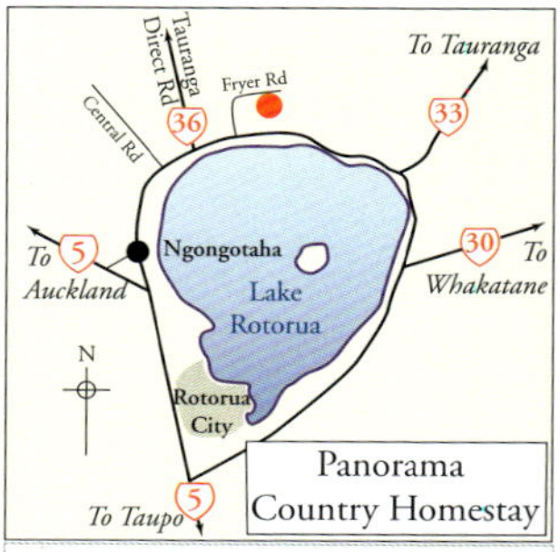

DIRECTIONS: Take SH 5 to roundabout. Travel north around lake through Ngongotaha towards Hamurana. Turn left into Fryer Rd and travel 1.5km to **Panorama** driveway on your right (No 144).

Aptly named, **Panorama** is your ideal base to stay near Rotorua's many attractions. Take in the magnificent views overlooking Lake Rotorua and legendary Mokoia Island, Mt. Tarawera and surrounding country-side. Feel the peace and tranquility as you relax under the stars in the outdoor heated massage spa pool, then curl up in front of the log fire in winter. You may prefer an energetic game of tennis or take in fantastic walks before you stretch out on the extra large beds in **Panorama's** peaceful surrounds for a perfect nights' sleep. The large house is centrally heated and wheelchair accessible. The 3 spacious luxury bedrooms have private bathrooms/ensuites containing toiletries, heated towel rails, hairdryers, shaving points and heaters. The large, comfortable inner-spring beds are warmed with electric blankets, woollen underlays, and feather quilts in winter. Only 15 min. from Rotorua, smoke free and away from sulphur smells.

Lakeside Bed & Breakfast

155G Okere Road, Okere Falls, RD 4,
Lake Rotoiti, Rotorua
Ph/Fax (07) 362 4288, Mobile 027-452 1483
email: *stay@lakesidebnb.co.nz*
www.lakesidebnb.co.nz

Tariff : N.Z. Dollars	
Double	$150-160
Single	$120
Child	$10-22

Bedrooms	Qty
Double	3
Twin	
Single	
Bed Size	**Qty**
Super King	1
King	
Queen	2
Double	
King Single	2
Bathrooms	**Qty**
Ensuite	2
Private	1
Guest Share	

Bed & Breakfast Homestay

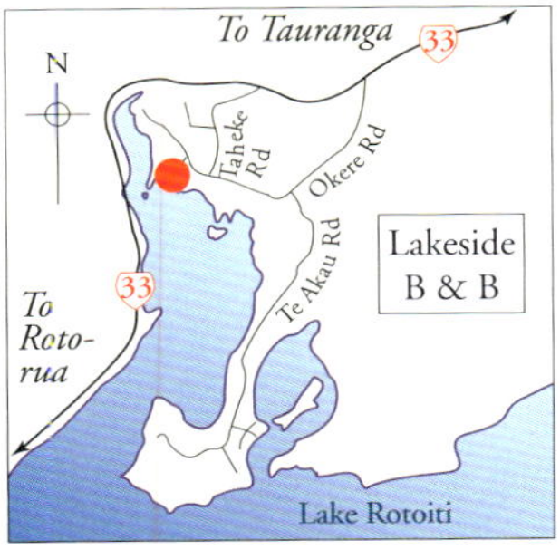

DIRECTIONS:
From Rotorua follow SH 33. 2 km past the green "Welcome to Okere Falls" sign turn right into Taheke Road, then right Okere Road. 155G on left.
From Tauranga: turn left Okere Road or Taheke Road. Proceed to 155G

Features & Attractions

- *Spacious and comfortable*
- *Friendly hospitality*
- *Scenic walks, glow worms*
- *Rowing and sailing*
- *No sulphur fumes*
- *Free laundry facilities*
- *Café nearby*
- *Handy location*

If you enjoy comfort, food, beautiful views and warm hospitality, then come and share our lovely home beside Lake Rotoiti. The bedrooms are spacious and have very comfortable beds with cotton bed linen, TV, refrigerator, hair dryer and tea/coffee making facilities.

We are just 1 kilometre off the Taupo-Rotorua-Tauranga-Coromandel Highway and within easy driving distance of all attractions. You can stroll by the lake, or walk to the Okere Falls, where you may see white-water rafting. A dinghy and kayaks are complimentary. A highlight for many guests is an evening stroll to see glow worms and the night sky.

Light meals can be provided for weary travellers. Alternatively dinner is available with 24 hours notice. After a delicious breakfast we are happy to help you plan your day's activities.

Te Ngae Lodge

54 State Highway 33, RD 4, Rotorua
Ph (07) 345 4153, Fax (07) 345 4153
Mobile 025-620 9312
email: *enquire@tengae.co.nz*
www.tengae.co.nz

Tariff : N.Z. Dollars	
Double	$100-200
Single	$80-115
Child	

Bedrooms	Qty
Double	3
Twin	1
Single	
Bed Size	**Qty**
Super King	
King	
Queen	3
Double	
Single	2
Bathrooms	**Qty**
Ensuite	1
Private	2
Guest Share	

BB **Country Homestay** BA

American Express MasterCard VISA

Features & Attractions

- *Quiet country setting*
- *Two acres of attractive gardens*
- *Views of Lake Rotorua sunsets*
- *Elegant antique dining room*
- *Dinners with New Zealand wines*
- *Home grown vegetables*
- *Bush walks & fishing trips arranged*
- *Handy to geothermal attractions*

DIRECTIONS:
Coming from Rotorua on SH 30, which becomes SH 33, we are 300m past the turn-off to Whakatane. **Te Ngae Lodge** driveway is on the right.

Te Ngae Lodge – for the discerning guest wanting to enjoy hospitality with superior accommodation in a tranquil garden setting. Wake to bird song in the morning.

Mokoia Suite looks to Mokoia Island and Lake Rotorua, furnished with antique and modern pieces.

The Garden Room outlooks to mature trees and opens to an attractive deck.

The Library Room has a view of garden and trees.

All comfortable queen size beds, while the Mokoia Suite has a second bedroom with twin beds.

Enjoy pre-dinner drinks with your hosts, our special dinners, or a more casual meal alfresco. We are twelve minutes drive from Rotorua City and handy to all geothermal attractions.

Finish the day in the spa pool. Relax and enjoy.

KOTARE LODGE

1000J Hamurana Road, Hamurana, Rotorua
Ph (07) 332 2679, Fax (07) 332 2678
Mobile 025-236 8468
email: *pollards@kotarelodge.co.nz*
www.kotarelodge.co.nz

Tariff : N.Z. Dollars	
Double	$175-195
Single	$165-175
Child	neg

Bedrooms	Qty
Double	2
Twin	
Single	
Bed Size	**Qty**
Super King Twin	1
King	
Queen	1
Double	
Single	3
Bathrooms	**Qty**
Ensuite	1
Private	1
Guest Share	

Lakefront Luxury Homestay

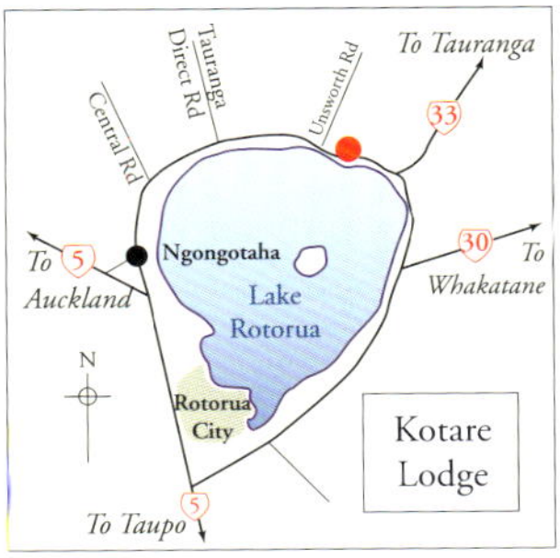

DIRECTIONS: **Kotare Lodge** is located on the northern shores of Lake Rotorua. Please ring/fax for simple directions.

Features & Attractions

- *Absolute lake front*
- *Secluded tranquil beauty*
- *Delicious breakfasts*
- *Sulphur free location*
- *Glorious views & sunsets*
- *Luxurious private suites*
- *Restaurants 10 min away*
- *Free e-mail*

Welcome to the perfect retreat. Designed with your comfort in mind, **Kotare Lodge**, set in beautiful parklike grounds, is situated on the shores of Lake Rotorua. The views across to the city and surrounding hills are magnificent.

The **Rimu Suite** has a queen bedroom, private bathroom and garden lounge. The **Garden Suite**, separate from main house, has a super king/twin bedroom, ensuite bathroom. The lounge, with fridge and TV, can sleep another two people. Your private suite has glorious views of the lake, heated towels, robes, toiletries, hairdryers, fresh flowers and tea/coffee making facilities.
Easy, level access to patios, decks, lawn and lakefront. There is also a spacious guest lounge which offers audio/visual entertainment. Relax with us at **Kotare Lodge**, enjoy a memorable stay of peaceful nights, luxury, wonderful breakfasts and warm, friendly hospitality.

Rotorua ▶ YOUR HOSTS: Deborah Young and Roy Inglis Ph (07) 345 5911

Rotokawa Lodge

1135c Te Ngae Road, RD4, Rotorua
Ph (07) 345 5911, Fax (07) 345 5910
Mobile 027-447 6533
email: *rotokawalodge@xtra.co.nz*
www.rotokawa-lodge.co.nz

Features & Attractions

- *Relaxed country hospitality*
- *Secluded but central to city*
- *Shuttle service to airport*
- *Japanese spa bathhouse*
- *Golf courses 10 min. away*
- *Great restaurants close by*

Bed & Breakfast
Peaceful and Relaxing

$	
Double	$160-175
Single	$160-175
Child	

Bedrooms	Qty
Double	5
Twin	
Single	
Bed Size	**Qty**
Super King	3
Queen	2
Double	
Single	
Bathrooms	**Qty**
Ensuite	3
Private	
Guest Share	2

Take time out and unwind. Enjoy Kiwi hospitality in our Cedarwood Lodge nestled on the shores of Lake Rotorua overlooking Mokoia Island. Just on the outskirts of Rotorua City but central to Rotorua's famous tourist attractions, ie: Hells Gate, Fairy Springs, trout fishing etc. We offer sunny, spacious super king or queen-size ensuite rooms, supplied with refrigerator, tea/coffee facilities, or a super king or queen-size room with shared bathroom. Our 'Japanese Spa Bathhouse' is a must. Laundry and dryer accessibility, Digital Sky TV, your own guest lounge area and library. Our hearty breakfasts are either continental or cooked, served in our dining room or if you wish on the verandas that surround the lodge.

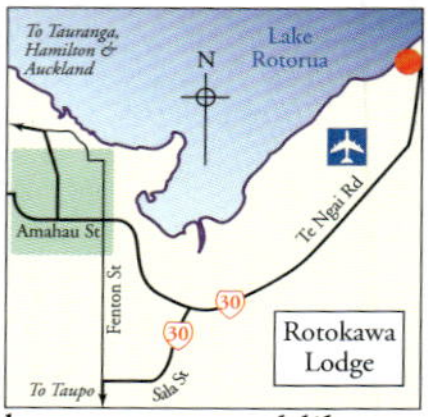

Come and take delight in our lovely rural, spacious surroundings and let us pamper you. Our cat, Benny, looks forward to showing you all the sunny, cosy spots for a catnap!!

Rotorua ▶ YOUR HOSTS: Leonie and Paul Kibblewhite Ph: (07) 345 6303

Aroden

2 Hilton Road, Lynmore, Rotorua
Ph (07) 345 6303, Fax (07) 345 6353
Mobile 027-696 4211
email: *aroden@xtra.co.nz*

Features & Attractions

- *Central – 4km to city*
- *Luxuriant garden, patio*
- *Two lounge areas*
- *Leonie parle francais*
- *Memorable breakfast*
- *Central heating, open fire*

Delightful Homestay
Bed & Breakfast

"Taupo" Paul's guide dog.

$	
Double	$120-130
Single	$90
Child	neg

Bedrooms	Qty
Double	2
Twin	
Single	
Bed Size	**Qty**
King	
Queen	2
Double	
Single	
Bathrooms	**Qty**
Ensuite	1
Private	1
Guest Share	

Discover real character, warmth and comfort nestled in a secluded garden, en route to the lakes and just five minutes from the city centre. Relax in a choice of sunny, private and attractive spaces both indoors and out, take a tour of the native tree collection and stroll to the magnificent Redwood Grove nearby (glow-worms at night!). Enjoy well-appointed rooms, comfortable beds with quality linen, modern tiled bathrooms with excellent showers, full bath in one room.

Leonie, who has a teaching background, and Paul, scientist, are fifth generation Kiwis, who delight in their country – share in their enthusiasm and knowledge over complimentary refreshments, tea coffee etc. or a wine (New Zealand of course!).....and meet the charming 'Taupo', Paul's guide dog. Breakfast is indeed special, fresh fruit and juice, cereals, home baking, a tempting choice of cooked course – this couple enjoys food! Smoke-free inside. Laundry.

DIRECTIONS: Route 30 east 2.5 km (towards airport). Turn right at roundabout onto Tarawera/Blue Lake Road, 3rd street left Lynmore Avenue, 2nd right Hilton Road, opposite corner store. No 2 is on left.

Maple House

154A Tarawera Road, Lynmore, Rotorua
Ph (07) 345 8434, Fax (07) 345 8434
email: *j.nicol@actrix.co.nz*
www.maplehouse.co.nz

Tariff : N.Z. Dollars	
Double	$130
Single	$90
Child	$25

Bedrooms	Qty
Double	1
Twin	1
Single	
Bed Size	**Qty**
Super King	
King	
Queen	1
Double	
Single	2
Bathrooms	**Qty**
Ensuite	
Private	1
Guest Share	

Homestay
Bed & Breakfast

DIRECTIONS:
Route 30 East 2.5km (towards airport). Turn right at roundabout onto Tarawera Road. Maple House is 154A, just past Hilton Road.

Features & Attractions

- *Close to major attractions*
- *New warm comfortable home*
- *Quiet nights*
- *Delicious breakfast menu*
- *Scenic forest walks*
- *Spacious bathroom*
- *Single party bookings*
- *Free laundry facilities*

You've found it! Walk in, relax and experience genuine New Zealand hospitality in a warm, quiet, well appointed home. Choose from a comfortable queen or twin bedroom with spacious private bathroom and separate toilet. After a busy day you will enjoy the tranquillity of the sunny lounge, share refreshments on the garden patio or curl up beside a cosy fire in Winter. Across the road is Whakarewarewa Forest with scenic trails, magnificent redwoods, tree ferns and glow worms. Just five minutes to airport, town centre, restaurants, golf courses, or the luxury of thermal spa facilities. Use your hosts' wide local knowledge of scenic, thermal, adventure and cultural activities to help you plan a memorable visit. We have travelled and worked extensively overseas. Joan loves gardening, walking, museum guiding, entertaining, theatre. Barry, avid reader and rugby follower, enjoys company and a red wine! Once you've shared the wonders of Rotorua, you'll want to return again and again bringing your friends!

"Your beautiful home and exceptional hospitality made Rotorua a memorable stay!" – GUEST COMMENT.

APPLEDALE COTTAGE

26 Springfield Road, Rotorua
Ph (07) 348 6630, Fax (07) 348 6065
Mobile 021-202 9653 or 027-605 9949
email: *appledalecottage@clear.net.nz*

VISA MasterCard

Features & Attractions

- *Charming yesteryear décor*
- *Warm, friendly hosts*
- *Swimming pool*
- *Sumptuous cooked breakfast*
- *Gourmet dinners if required*
- *Restaurant/ golf courses close by*

BA **Boutique Bed & Breakfast and Self-contained Cottage** SC

$		
Double	$120-160
Single	$90
Child	neg

Appledale Cottage offers something with a difference for you.
Appledale Cottage is an English summer house, which is nestled amongst trees and cottage gardens.
We have Boutique Bed & Breakfast rooms and in addition our fully self-contained cottage with old-world, charming yesteryear furniture and romantic atmosphere for you.
What we have to offer to you is your hosts, Bruce and Justine, who are well travelled and enjoy meeting new people. Your comfort and experience whilst in Rotorua is our top priority. We offer complimentarty nibbles and drinks upon arrival and serve a sumptuous, fully cooked breakfast, prepared by a gourmet cook.
We also offer gourmet dinners by arrangement. We are happy to assist with bookings and information for your tourist attractions and sightseeing arrangements.

Bedrooms	Qty
Double	3
Twin	
Single	
Bed Size	**Qty**
King	
Queen	2
Double	1
Single	2
Bathrooms	**Qty**
Ensuite	
Private	2
Guest Share	

ROBERTSON HOUSE

70 Pererika Street, Rotorua
Ph (07) 343 7559
email: *info@robertsonhouse.co.nz*
www.robertsonhouse.co.nz

Features & Attractions

- *Old world charm*
- *Perfect central location*
- *Beautiful cottage garden*
- *Warm & friendly hosts*
- *All activities easily arranged*
- *Quiet & relaxing*

H **Charming Bed & Breakfast Homestay** BB

VISA MasterCard

$		
Double	$110-170
Single	$80-120
Child	

Our historic home, only 2 minutes drive from the city centre, was built by one of Rotorua's forefathers in 1905. Under the auspices of the Historic Places Trust it has been carefully renovated, retaining its colonial charm.

Relax in its warm, comfortable atmosphere, or take time out on the veranda and enjoy our old English cottage garden resplendent with colour and fragrance, citrus trees and grape vines.
Our friendly hosts are happy to assist with information and bookings for Rotorua's many Maori cultural, and sightseeing attractions.
Robertson House – a historic colonial villa, carefully restored, is warm and inviting with a peaceful cottage garden.

Bedrooms	Qty
Double	4
Twin	1
Single	
Bed Size	
Super King	1
Queen	2
Double	2
King/Single	4
Bathrooms	**Qty**
Ensuite	3
Private	
Guest Share	1

Innes Cottage

18A Wylie Street, Rotorua
Ph (07) 349 1839, Fax (07) 349 1890
Mobile 027-498 2100
email: *chris@clican.com*
www.innescottage.co.nz

Features & Attractions

- *Very central location*
- *Quiet tree-lined street*
- *Fishing & golf 5 min*
- *Close to thermal attractions*
- *City centre just 5 min*
- *Friendly welcome, lots of fun*

$	
Double	$100-130
Single	$85-100
Child	neg

Bed & Breakfast Homestay

Bedrooms	Qty
Double	2
Twin	1
Single	
Bed Size	**Qty**
King	
Queen	2
Double	
Single	2
Bathrooms	**Qty**
Ensuite	1
Private	1
Guest Share	1

Enjoy the tranquil surroundings of our centrally situated home in a quiet tree-lined street, within easy walking distance to the city. Our spacious guest rooms overlook a sunny garden. An easy walk will bring you to the 'Te Puia' thermal area, with the famous Pohutu Geyser, and other major attractions are only a short distance away. We have travelled extensively and have a wealth of knowledge and many valuable contacts. Chris does private tours around the region and throughout New Zealand and can help with any arrangements you require to make your stay more memorable. We serve a generous continental breakfast, giving you a great start to the day. We assure you warm hospitality and a memorable fun-filled stay.

Moana Rose Lakeside Bed & Breakfast

23 Haumoana Street, Koutu, Rotorua
Ph (07) 349 2980, Fax (07) 349 2997
Mobile 027-273 2008
email: *moanarose@bktours.co.nz*
www.bktours.co.nz

Features & Attractions

- *Within minutes of:*
- *Sporting venues*
- *All major attractions*
- *Excellent Cafés*
- *Shopping/city centre*
- *Trout fishing*

$	
Double	$140
Single	$90
Child	$35

Lakeside Homestay Bed & Breakfast

Welcome to the peace and tranquility of our garden lakeside home. Enjoy our company or relax in the guests' sitting room with tea/coffee making facilities, fridge and Sky TV. As we are small and intimate, we only cater for single party bookings. From the breakfast table admire the view, then wander down to the lake edge and watch the birdlife with Lizzie, our cat, in hot pursuit.
Relaxing in our garden courtyard spa is a wonderful way to complete your day. Pauline's interests are art and crafts, and Bruce is a licenced tour operator and will gladly assist with your sightseeing or travel arrangemets. For your convenience, high speed internet and wireless services are available.

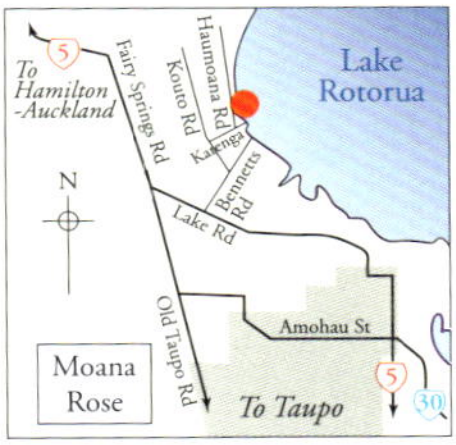

DIRECTIONS: From Lake Road turn into Bennetts Road, left into Koutu Road, right into Karenga Street, left into Haumoana Street.

Bedrooms	Qty
Double	1
Twin	1
Single	
Bed Size	**Qty**
King	
Queen	1
Double	
Single	2
Bathrooms	**Qty**
Ensuite	
Private	1
Guest Share	

EAST WEST-BOUTIQUE B&B AND APARTMENTS

6 Toko Street, Rotorua
Ph (07) 348 5720, Fax (07) 348 5729
Mobile 027-278 5332
email: *eastwesthomestay@xtra.co.nz*
www.eastwesthomestay.co.nz

@ home NEW ZEALAND

Tariff : N.Z. Dollars	
Double	$110-150
Single	$75-110
Child	$25

Bedrooms	Qty
Double	8
Twin	5
Single	
Bed Size	**Qty**
Super King	
King	
Queen	6
Double	1
Single	14
Bathrooms	**Qty**
Ensuite	2
Private	3
Guest Share	

BA **Boutique Bed & Breakfast & Self-catering Apartments** SC

eftpos VISA MasterCard

Features & Attractions

- *Central to tourism & leisure*
- *Unique geothermal pool/spa*
- *Geothermal central heating*
- *Quiet, spacious units*
- *Self-catering apartments*
- *Tour bookings*

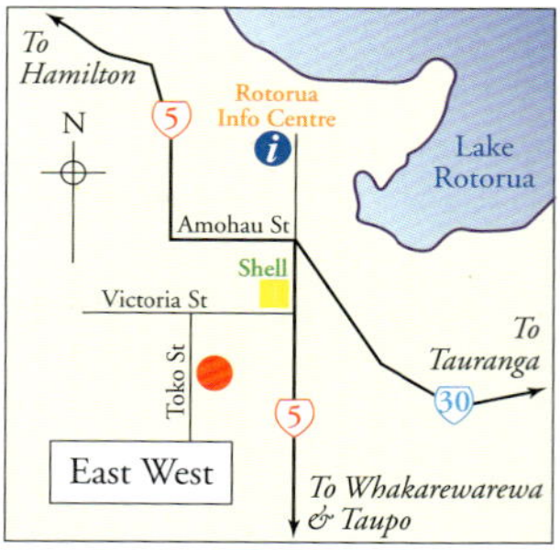

Your hosts, Stuart, Kristin and Rusty, warmly welcome you to their unique Boutique Bed & Breakfast and Self-catering apartments. Located in Rotorua's thriving central tourism district, their designer home and freshly decorated, fully furnished holiday apartments are minutes from all attractions. You are offered a choice of a spacious studio or one bedroom unit both featuring private ensuite bathrooms, fridge/minibar, tea and coffee facilities, TV/DVD and robes toiletries. Continental breakfast offers fresh fruit, home-made muesli, cereals, yoghurt, conserves, coffee and teas (included in rate). Cooked breakfast available. Also separately located on the property are three sunny, cosy, fully furnished self-catering two and three bedroom apartments, kitchen, laundry facilities, off-street parking, private entrances. Private hot spa, robes/toiletries. Breakfast charges extra.

Koura Lodge Rotorua

209 Kawaha Point Road, PO Box 1600, Rotorua
Ph (07) 348 5868, Fax (07) 348 5869
email: *stay@kouralodge.co.nz*
www.kouralodge.co.nz

Tariff : N.Z. Dollars	
Double	$245-495
Single	–
Extra pp	–

Bedrooms	Qty
Double	8
Twin	3
Single	–
Bed Size	**Qty**
Super King	–
King	6
Queen	3
Double	–
King Single	5
Bathrooms	**Qty**
Ensuite	All
Private	–
Guest Share	–

Unique Lake Edge Retreat

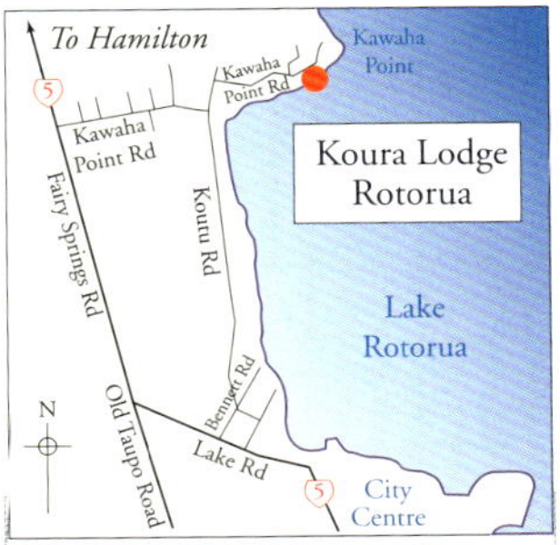

DIRECTIONS: From north, take SH 5 towards Rotorua City. Turn left into Kawaha Point Road, left into Koutu and right again. Travel to Lodge at end. From city, take SH 5 north. Turn right into Kawaha Point Road. Then as above.

Features & Attractions

- *Championship tennis court*
- *European style breakfasts*
- *5 minutes from City centre*
- *Finnish sauna*
- *Fishing & hot pool trips*
- *On-site canoes, windsurfer*
- *Helicopter & Floatplane trips*
- *Open-air spa pool*

Koura Lodge is situated on the tip of Kawaha Point, nestled in sub-tropical gardens, only five minutes drive from the City Centre, yet secluded from traffic noise and sulphur fumes.

The Lodge offers a range of double accommodation as well as family suites and a penthouse apartment, all with private ensuites, veranda seating and spectacular lake views. Other on-site facilities and activities include lake-edge sauna/spa complex, Astro-grass tennis court, canoes, fishing, helicopter and floatplane excursions.

Koura Lodge is minutes from three well-known golf courses, mountain bike trails and dozens of restaurants.

AFFORDABLE WESTMINSTER LODGE

58A Mountain Road, Rotorua
Ph (07) 348 4273, Fax (07) 348 4205
email: *westminster@slingshot.co.nz*
www.westminsterlodge.co.nz

Tariff : N.Z. Dollars	
Double	$100-140
Single	$70-90
Child	$20-25

Bedrooms	Qty
Double	4
Twin	5
Single	5
Bed Size	**Qty**
Super King	
King	
Queen	4
Double	2
Single	6
Bathrooms	**Qty**
Ensuite	3
Private	2
Guest Share	

Quality & Affordable Bed & Breakfast

Features & Attractions

- *Only 5 min to city centre*
- *Close to all major attractions*
- *Laundry facilities*
- *Telephone, fax and email*
- *Maori concert & hangi*
- *Spa pool*
- *Friendly animals*
- *Very generous breakfast*

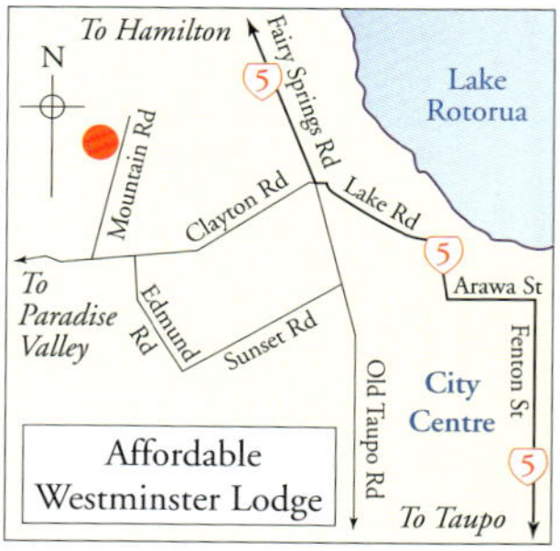

Westminster Lodge is an English tudor home, nestled on the slopes of Mount Ngongotaha overlooking the city of Rotorua. So country, yet only five minutes to the city centre. Panoramic views in the day and fairyland at night. We offer superior Bed & Breakfast accommodation in semi self-contained units or lodge rooms at affordable prices. Enjoy our delicious continental breakfast with fresh fruit salad, yoghurt and cereal, hot apple muffins (baked daily) and a freshly laid egg or a scrumptuous fully cooked breakfast at a small extra cost. Experience all the comforts of home in a warm and friendly atmosphere, ensuring your stay in our family home will always be remembered. Breathe in the fresh mountain air and, at the end of your busy day, relax in our spa pool overlooking the city.

We have small dexter cows originating from Ireland, sheep, chickens, and Mrs Pig. All the animals are friendly and can be hand fed.

TIROHANGA-NUI

21 Grand Vue Road, Kawaha Point, Rotorua
Ph (07) 349 4810, Fax (07) 349 4811
Mobile 021-170 3477
email: *a_thompson@clear.net.nz*
www.bigview.co.nz

Tariff : N.Z. Dollars	
Double	$130-150
Single	$90
Child	$30

Bedrooms	Qty
Double	2
Twin	
Single	
Bed Size	**Qty**
Super King	
King	
Queen	2
Double	
Single	
Bathrooms	**Qty**
Ensuite	1
Private	1
Guest Share	

Homestay - Bed & Breakfast
Self-contained Accommodation

Features & Attractions

- *Spa & swimming pool*
- *5 min from City Centre*
- *Panoramic views*
- *'Made to measure tours'*
- *Cooked - continental breakfast*
- *Dinner by arrangement*
- *Central heating*
- *Sailing trips arranged*

Your hosts, Angela and Tony, invite you to share in the experience, the peace and serenity of Tirohanga-nui with its magnificent panoramic lake and city views, only five minutes from the city and local attractions. Accommodation is offered either self-contained with own entrance and private deck area or in the upstairs bedroom with private bathroom. Angela and Tony have visited all areas of New Zealand and extended their adventures in over twenty countries around the globe. Their wealth of knowledge of the Rotorua area would benefit any visitors keen to learn more about this beautiful country. They can also arrange 'Made to Measure' tours in their four wheel drive vehicle or assist guests with their daily travel plans. Tony, a keen recreational and competitive sailor, is always happy to arrange sailing trips. Rotorua is the 'Adventure Capital' of New Zealand where you can experience Maori culture, geothermal activity, beautiful lakes and bush walks. Please allow yourself enough time to discover this beautiful area.

BURTONSINPARADISE

311 Endean Rd, RD 2, Paradise Valley, Rotorua
Ph (07) 350 3351, Fax (07) 350 3351
Mobile 027-620 2620
email: *burtonsinparadise@wave.co.nz*
www.burtonsatparadise.co.nz

Features & Attractions

- *Welcoming hosts*
- *Bush walks*
- *Farm interaction*
- *Dinner by arrangement*
- *Cottage & homestead accommodation*
- *Tranquil, picturesque surroundings*

Self-contained Accommodation
Country Homestay

Double	$130-160
Single	$80-110
Child	neg

Your hosts, Andrew and Linda, welcome you to enjoy the peace and tranquility of their 50 acres farm overlooking Paradise Valley, with views of Rotorua in the distance. We run a Dorper sheep stud, and also farm cattle and run horses. We have available for your use a queen bedroom with ensuite and a double bedroom with shared bathroom. We also have a self-contained bed-sit with queen-sized bed, ensuite and a kitchen. We live right on the edge of thousands of acres of native bush which offers interesting walks to suit all abilities. Glow worms are able to be viewed by night and we also offer small game hunting if the conditions are right. We are animal friendly and our dogs and cat will welcome you to visit us just 11 kilometres from Rotorua.

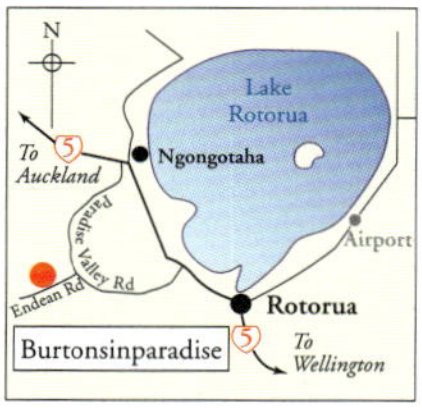

DIRECTIONS: From SH5 north into Paradise Valley Rd, continue past 'Rhodo Hill Nursery' to Endean Rd on right. Follow road for 3km – house at top of road on left. From Rotorua take Clayton Rd into Paradise Valley Rd, 300m past Paradise Valley Springs.

Bedrooms	Qty
Double	3
Twin	
Single	
Bed Size	**Qty**
King	
Queen	2
Double	1
Single	
Bathrooms	**Qty**
Ensuite	1
Private	1
Guest Share	

DEER PINE LODGE

255 Jackson Road, PO Box 22,
Ngongotaha, Rotorua
Ph (07) 332 3458, Fax (07) 332 3458
Mobile 027-312 0338
email: *deerpine@clear.net.nz*

Tariff : N.Z. Dollars	
Double	$60-100
Single	$75-80
Child	neg

Bedrooms	Qty
Double	4
Twin	1
Single	
Bed Size	**Qty**
Super King	
King	3
Queen	1
Double	
Single	2
Bathrooms	**Qty**
Ensuite	5
Private	
Guest Share	

Farmstay Bed & Breakfast
Self-contained Accommodation

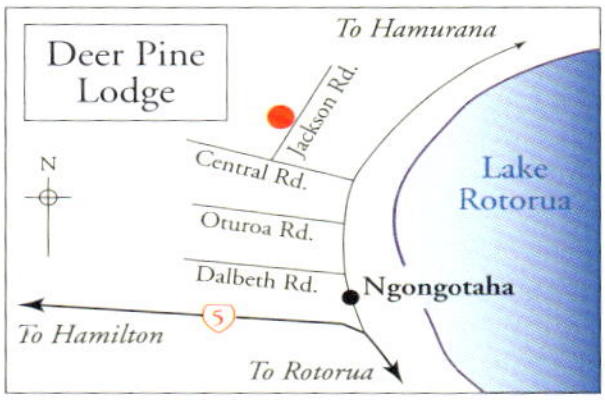

DIRECTIONS:
Please phone or write for brochure and easy directions.

Features & Attractions

- *Quiet, peaceful surroundings*
- *Beach 30 minutes away*
- *Architecturally designed units*
- *Beautiful views of lake*
- *Tourist attractions nearby*
- *Telephone & Email facilities*
- *Horse riding close by*
- *No sulphur smells*

Welcome to **Deer Pine Lodge**. Come and relax in peaceful, quiet countryside surroundings with lovely views of Lake Rotorua and wake up to the singing of the birds. During your stay you are most welcome to have a look at the stags and sheep and take photographs. Our property is surrounded with trees, planted by New Zealand Forest Research. We have a cat and a Boxer (Jake), who is very gentle. The nearby city of Rotorua is fast becoming New Zealand's most popular tourist destination. Our bed/breakfast units/rooms are private with ensuite, television, radio, refrigerator, microwave, heaters, electric blankets on all beds and tea/coffee making facilities. There are heaters and hair dryers in bathrooms. Our two-bedroom fully self-contained units, designed by prominent Rotorua architect Gerald Stock, each have a private balcony, carport, sundeck, ensuite, spacious lounge, kitchen, also laundry facilities, television, radio, heaters etc (cot/highchair available). Smoke detectors fitted in all bedrooms and lounges, fire extinguishers installed in all kitchens. We hold the NZ Certificate in Food Hygiene, which ensures high standards of food preparation and service.

An evening meal with pre-dinner drinks is available by prior arrangement. Hosts John and Betty, originally from Scotland, have travelled extensively overseas and have many years experience in hosting. We look forward to your stay with us.

Ariki Lodge

2 Manuariki Ave, Ngongotaha, PO Box 578, Rotorua
Ph (07) 357 5532, Fax (07) 357 5562
email: *rgforgie@xtra.co.nz*
www.arikilodge.co.nz

@ home NEW ZEALAND

Tariff : N.Z. Dollars	
Double	$140-230
Single	$120-210
Child	neg

Bedrooms	Qty
Double	3
Twin	
Single	
Bed Size	**Qty**
Super King	1
King	
Queen	2
Double	
Single	
Bathrooms	**Qty**
Ensuite	3
Private	
Guest Share	

Bed & Breakfast
Luxury Accommodation

Features & Attractions

- *Lake edge*
- *Close to major attractions*
- *Trout fishing*
- *Quiet and relaxing*
- *Warm and friendly hosts*
- *Generous breakfasts*
- *Quality bedding and furnishings*
- *Your comfort is our business*

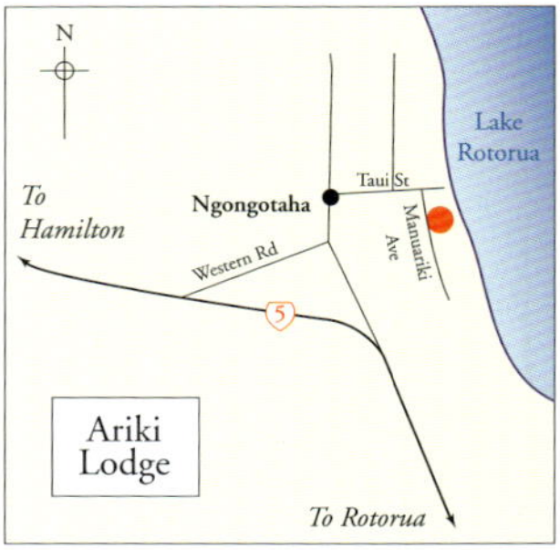

Set on the edge of Lake Rotorua, **Ariki Lodge** offers luxury accommodation in a tranquil garden setting, where you can relax in comfort and style. Enjoy our friendly hospitality, or should you prefer total privacy, that's fine with us. Situated close to the Ngongotaha trout fishing stream and a short stroll along the beach to the Waiteti Stream and famous fly fishing spots. The bedrooms are beautifully appointed with quality linen, fresh flowers, toiletries and hair-dryers. The suite has an Italian-tiled bathroom with spa bath, private sitting room with refrigerator, tea and coffee making facilities. **Ariki Lodge** is spacious and comfortable. Two rooms can be converted to twin. We can help you arrange your time to experience Rotorua's many sights and attractions including fishing, Maori cultural performances, thermal areas, lake cruises, scenic flights, golf, bush walks, Maori arts and crafts. Only ten minutes drive to the centre of Rotorua and many

DIRECTIONS: Drive to Ngongotaha. At shops turn right into Taui Street, through "Give Way" sign towards Lake and right into Manuariki Avenue.

BAYADERE LODGE

38 Hall Road, PO Box 288, Ngongotaha
Ph (07) 357 5965, Fax (07) 357 5965
Mobile 027-292 8520
email: *c.clark@clear.net.nz*
www.bayaderelodge.com

Tariff : N.Z. Dollars	
Double	$170-190
Single	$150-170
Child	neg

Bedrooms	Qty
Double	2
Twin	1
Single	
Bed Size	**Qty**
Super King	2
King	1
Queen	
Double	
King Single	2
Bathrooms	**Qty**
Ensuite	3
Private	
Guest Share	

Boutique B & B Accommodation

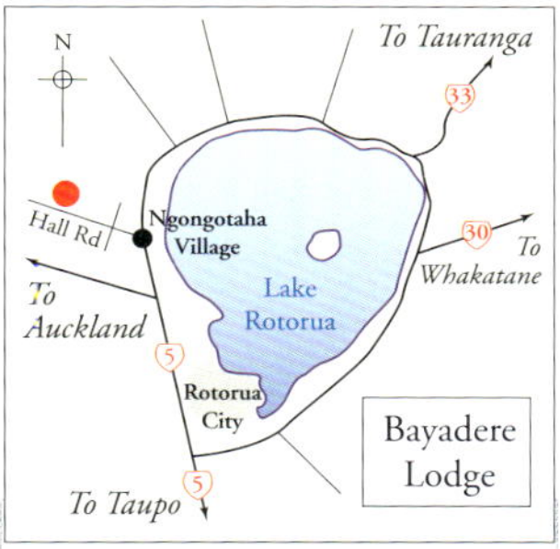

DIRECTIONS: From SH 5 take SH 36 into the centre of Ngongotaha village, approximately 1 km. Turn left into Hall Rd. Travel up the hill 400 metres. We are on the right.

Features & Attractions

- *Lake and rural views*
- *Quiet & relaxing setting*
- *Wireless Internet*
- *Guest lounge*
- *Delightful breakfasts*
- *Dinner by arrangement*
- *Close to tourist attractions*
- *Trout streams nearby*

Bayadere Lodge offers you superior accommodation in a modern, spacious home. Just 8 km from Rotorua, but far enough away to be sulphur free. It has splendid views of the lake and surrounding countryside. Walking distance to famous trout fishing streams. Quiet nights in the bedroom of your choice with superior beds, robes and other extras. Your own ensuite with hairdryer, quality toiletries and linen. You will be amazed at our wonderful garden, which is colourful and peaceful. So sit on the deck and enjoy. Each morning you will arise to our delightful breakfast with a cooked dish of the day, local and tropical fruits, home-baking, tea or coffee. The guest lounge has a cosy fire for cool winter evenings and Sky TV. Take the opportunity to use our local knowledge as we help you plan your days visiting the local attractions. We offer a discount for multiple nights. Secure parking. Wireless connection facility for notebooks. Warm hospitality.

Clover Downs Estate

175 Jackson Road, Ngongotaha, Rotorua
Ph (07) 332 2366, Fax (07) 332 2367
Mobile 021-712 866
email: *reservations@cloverdowns.co.nz*
www.accommodationinrotorua.co.nz

Bedrooms	Qty
Double	4
Twin	
Single	
Bed Size	**Qty**
Super King	3
King	1
Queen	
Double	
Single	
Bathrooms	**Qty**
Ensuite	4
Private	
Guest Share	

C **Fine Country Bed & Breakfast Retreat** LA

Tariff : N.Z. Dollars	
Double	$225-335
Single	$205-310
Child	neg

Features & Attractions

- *Secluded, peaceful rural retreat*
- *Spacious home-like comfort*
- *Telephone & email facilities*
- *Laundry facilities available*
- *Tourist attractions nearby*
- *Trout fishing trips available*
- *Close to horse-riding*
- *Deer & ostrich farm tour*

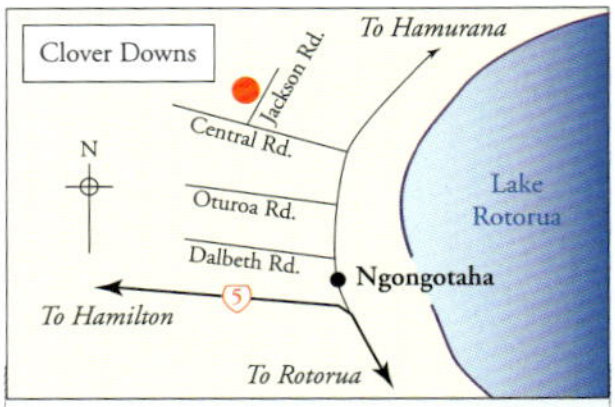

DIRECTIONS:
Take SH 5 to roundabout. Travel north around lake, through Ngongotaha on Hamurana Road. Take 3rd left into Central Road, then turn right into Jackson Road. Travel 1.75 km to **Clover Downs** on left.

"A Unique Place to Stay"

So country yet so close to town... just fifteen minutes drive north of the city centre. For the discerning traveller, we offer a place to unwind and rediscover the simple pleasures in life whilst having the best facilities available. Experience the tranquillity and style of our character home, situated on a secluded six acre deer and ostrich farm with magnificent rural and Lake Rotorua views. We offer fine country accommodation with a choice of four beautifully appointed king-size suites, each equipped with tea and coffee making facilities, refrigerator, telephone, television and video. Enjoy the privacy of an ensuite bathroom in each bedroom complete with toiletries, hair dryer and bathrobes. After a sumptuous breakfast take a farm tour with Lloyd and the dogs, maybe try a game of pétanque or just relax and enjoy the rural vistas from your own private deck. Major tourist attractions, trout fishing, golf and horse riding are all nearby.

Country Villa

351 Dalbeth Road, RD 2, Rotorua
Ph (07) 357 5893, Fax (07) 357 5893
email: *countryvilla@xtra.co.nz*
www.countryvilla.biz

Tariff : N.Z. Dollars	
Double	$175-245
Single	$175-225
Child	neg

Bedrooms	Qty
Double	4
Twin	1
Single	1
Bed Size	**Qty**
Super King	
King	
Queen	4
Double	
Single	5
Bathrooms	**Qty**
Ensuite	4
Private	1
Guest Share	

Romantic Country Home B&B and Self-contained Loft

Features & Attractions

- *Quiet location – close to town*
- *Large gardens*
- *Close to golf course*
- *Choice of excellent restaurants*
- *Maori culture*
- *Tourist attractions 5-20 min.*
- *Forest walks*
- *White-water rafting*

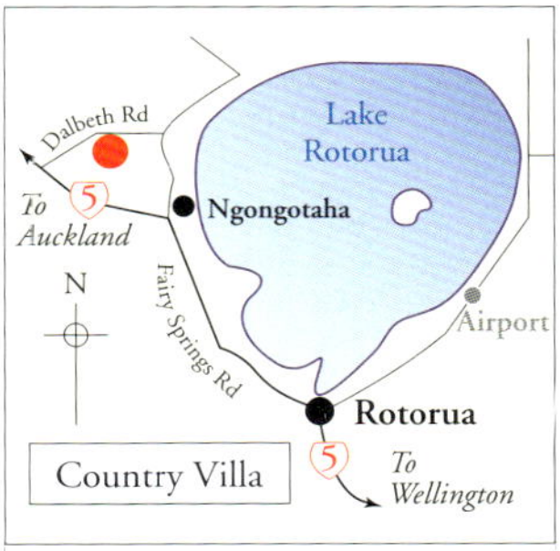

DIRECTIONS: From SH 5, turn left past the Lakeview Golf Course into Dalbeth Rd. From Rotorua, through Ngongotaha, over railway crossing, first road left.

Away from sulphur fumes and traffic noise, **Country Villa** is an elegant restored villa in an idyllic and peaceful setting on the outskirts of Rotorua. Surrounded by large gardens with many native birds, views over green fields towards Lake Rotorua and in the distance Mount Tarawera – just how you expected New Zealand to be! **Country Villa** was originally built in Auckland in 1906 and transported in 3 parts to Rotorua, 90 years later. The turret is a lovely sitting area and part of the two bedroom suite upstairs. All rooms have ensuite or private bathroom. Enjoy a stroll through the garden or curl up with a good book in front of the log fire in the guest lounge. Breakfast is served in the conservatory with beautiful stained glass windows. New is the self-contained loft with private entrance. Continental breakfast provisions supplied for guests staying in loft. Make Rotorua your 'base' for exploring Central North Island. Taupo and Tauranga 1 hours drive.

Ashpit Place

815 Ashpit Road, Rerewhakaaitu, Rotorua
Ph (07) 366 6709, Fax (07) 366 6710
Mobile 021-117 0317
email: *samarshall@clear.net.nz*
www.ashpitplace.co.nz

Features & Attractions

- *Farm, lake & mountain views*
- *Fire heating ducted through home*
- *Continental or cooked breakfast*
- *Double spa bath in ensuite*
- *Dinner by arrangement*
- *Plenty of parking spaces*

C

**Peaceful Rural Retreat
Bed & Breakfast**

BB

$		
	Double	$180
	Single	$160
	Child	neg

Welcome to our spacious modern home overlooking Lake Rerewhakaaitu to the south and Mt Tarawera to the North. Escape to the tranquillity and quiet of the country with good clean air and water. We are central to Thermal attractions, hot pools, Rotorua and Taupo. Our home is located on a run-off block to our Dairy farm. We offer you a warm comfortable stay, with spa bath in ensuite, TV/DVD, tea coffee making facilities, electric blanket, continental or cooked breakfast, dinner by arrangement. You are welcome to watch your favourite movies in your own suite or in our theatre room.
Our lake is great for swimming, fishing, water-skiing, jet skiing, kayaking etc. Our interests include Moto-X, trail bike riding, Jet Ski touring, farming, gardening.

Bedrooms	Qty
Double	1
Twin	
Single	
Bed Size	**Qty**
King	
Queen	1
Double	
Single	
Bathrooms	**Qty**
Ensuite	1
Private	
Guest Share	

DIRECTIONS:
From Rotorua take H/W 5 south, turn left at Rainbow Mountain (H/W 38) take 3rd left to Rerewhakaaitu, travel to T intersection, turn left, then take next left travel to No 815 just before seal ends. (30mins drive from Rotorua)

www.phototrips.info

Ngongotaha Lakeside Lodge

41 Operiana Street, Ngongotaha, Rotorua
Ph (07) 357 4020, Fax (07) 357 4020
Mobile 021-266 1341
email: *lake.edge@xtra.co.nz*
www.rotorualakesidelodge.co.nz

Tariff : N.Z. Dollars	
Double	$150-210
Single	$130-190
Child	neg

Bedrooms	Qty
Double	2
Twin	1
Single	
Bed Size	**Qty**
Super King	
King	1
Queen	1
Double	
Single	2
Bathrooms	**Qty**
Ensuite	3
Private	
Guest Share	

Lakeside Quality Bed & Breakfast

DIRECTIONS:
Drive through Ngongotaha Village, cross over railway line, then 1st right into Wikaraka Street, left into Okana Cres, left again into Operiana St. We are on the right.

Features & Attractions

- *Absolute lake edge*
- *Separate guest floor*
- *Special breakfasts*
- *Activities arranged*
- *Fly fishing in lake and stream*
- *Fishing gear provided*
- *Licenses sold*
- *Bird watching: telescope*

"Where the magic begins"

Come, stay a while and feel the peace and tranquility of your Lakeside 'home-away-from-home'.
Relax in the guest conservatory or garden with a fresh coffee or wine. Unwind as you soak up the atmosphere and enjoy the many moods of Lake Rotorua. Your ensuite bedroom is all you could wish for; superior beds guarantee a restful night's sleep and a special breakfast sets you up for another exciting day. Feed the ducks, paddle the canoe, experience the thrill of fly fishing at the lake edge and have your catch pan-fried for breakfast or smoked at '**Trout Time**' with pre-dinner drinks. Sit with a book, daydream, sip a wine...**Ngongotaha Lakeside Lodge**...your perfect Bed & Breakfast choice.
Ideal as a base for central island touring and for the longer stay, with multiple night discounts. Quiet, restful, great food and facilities, with warm hospitality at affordable prices. Close to all major tourist attractions, but far enough away to be '**Sulphur Free**'. Free use of fly fishing gear; licenses sold; BBQ and canoe; off-street parking.

Ngakuru - Rotorua YOUR HOSTS: **Susan and John Shaw** Ph: (07) 333 2829

LAKEHILL COUNTRY RETREAT

1149 Whirinaki Valley Road, RD 1, Ngakuru, Rotorua
Ph (07) 333 2829 Fax (07) 333 2029
Mobile 027-450 7995
email: *lakehill@xtra.co.nz*
www.lakehill.co.nz

@ home NEW ZEALAND

Tariff : N.Z. Dollars	
Double	$140-160
Single	$100
Child	neg

Bedrooms	Qty
Double	2
Twin	1
Single	
Bed Size	**Qty**
Super King	
King	
Queen	2
Double	
Single	3
Bathrooms	**Qty**
Ensuite	1
Private	1
Guest Share	

C **Luxury Countrystay Accommodation** LA

Features & Attractions

- *Warm country hospitality*
- *Great food*
- *Pet dog & cat to pamper*
- *Hearty breakfasts*
- *Golf course*
- *Birdwatching on lake*
- *Local thermal attractions*
- *Tennis court & swimming pool*

DIRECTIONS:
From Rotorua, take SH 5 south to SH 30. Turn right and travel 13 km. Turn left onto Whirinaki Valley Road, travel 11.5 km to **Lakehill Country Retreat**, south of Ngakuru Village.

Susan and John invite you to experience the best of country hospitality in a tranquil rural setting. Lakehill Country Retreat is ideally situated between Rotorua and Taupo making an ideal base for central North Island sightseeing. Max, our very gentle black labrador, will also be waiting to welcome you.

Start the day with a hearty country style breakfast before heading off to visit the many attractions of the region. You are also welcome to join us for a delicious evening meal (by prior arrangement) featuring fresh New Zealand produce. Lamb dishes are a speciality. The homestead interior features New Zealand native timbers, creating a warm and inviting atmosphere. Both bedrooms are light and airy and have their own bathroom facilities. A third bedroom is available if required.

Enjoy the landscaped grounds with extensive trees, lawns and gardens, a four hole par three golf course, grass tennis court and swimming pool. Or if you prefer, you can just relax with a book in a comfortable chair in the lounge or garden.

Te Ana Farmstay

Poutakataka Road, Ngakuru RD 1, Rotorua
Ph (07) 333 2720, Fax (07) 333 2720
Mobile 021-828 151
email: *teanafarmstay@xtra.co.nz*
www.teanafarmstay.co.nz

Tariff : N.Z. Dollars	
Double	$100-150
Single	$90
Child	neg

Bedrooms	Qty
Double	2
Twin	2
Single	
Bed Size	**Qty**
Super King	
King	
Queen	2
Double	
Single	4
Bathrooms	**Qty**
Ensuite	2
Private	
Family Share	1

Farmstay
Bed & Breakfast

Features & Attractions

- *Sheep and cattle*
- *Proximity to Rotorua/Taupo*
- *Cottage & homestead accommodation*
- *4-wheel drive farm tour*
- *Spacious country garden*
- *Mountain/lake views*
- *Local thermals*
- *Canoe & Lake*

"Rural New Zealand at its Best"

Te Ana, in the Oberer family since 1936, offers peace and tranquillity in a spacious, rural garden setting, affording magnificent views of lake, volcanically formed hills and lush farmland. A wonderful opportunity for the keen photographer. Cosily wrapped in the warmth of a down-filled duvet atop a woollen underlay awake to the sounds of the dawn chorus heralding another adventure-packed day Downunder. Enjoy a leisurely stroll on the farm or in the garden, before joining your hosts for an extremely generous country breakfast, as healthy or indulgent as you desire. Soak in the wonderful views of hills and lake over a last coffee before heading off to Waiotapu or Waimungu Thermal Reserves, Waikite Thermal Mineral Swimming Pool, or another of the many Rotorua/Taupo attractions.

A Farm Tour, by arrangement, introduces guests to sheep and cattle, with small plantations of pinus radiata dotting the landscape. A three course dinner is available – by prior arrangement only. Families welcomed by Sam, our loyal Jack Russell.

Kinara Country Homestay

159 Palmer Mill Road, RD 1, Wairakei, Taupo
Ph (07) 378 8837, Fax (07) 378 8837
Mobile 027- 478 5606
email: *info@kinara.co.nz*
www.kinara.co.nz

Tariff : N.Z. Dollars	
Double	$160-185
Single	$160-185
Child	neg

Bedrooms	Qty
Double	2
Twin	1
Single	

Bed Size	Qty
Super King	
King	
Queen	2
Double	
Single	2

Bathrooms	Qty
Ensuite	2
Private	1
Guest Share	

Country Homestay
Bed & Breakfast

Features & Attractions

- *Mountain & lake views*
- *Quiet, comfortable home*
- *Safe off-street parking*
- *Huka Falls, Aratiaia Rapids*
- *Close to tourist sites*
- *Highland cattle*
- *12 min. to Lake Taupo*
- *Relaxed country setting*

*"Welcome to **Kinara Country Homestay**!"*

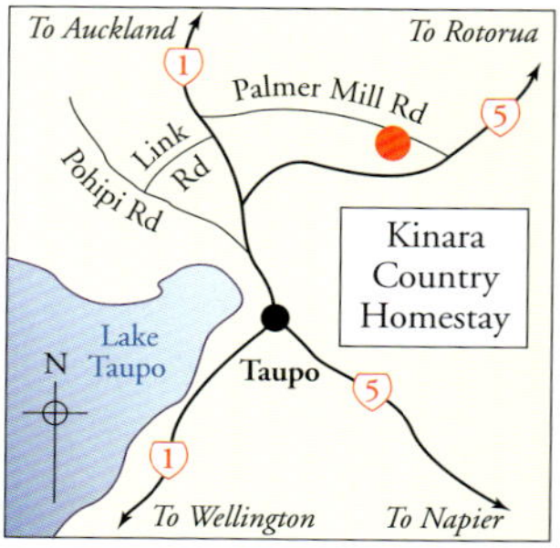

We have a new, large, comfortable, modern home with a touch of the Mediterranean, out in the countryside. Relax in our beautiful, tranquil garden and natural surroundings and enjoy what **Kinara** has to offer you. Have a relaxing sleep in our comfortable, warm and cozy beds. Awaken to birdsong and the smell of breakfast cooking and freshly brewed coffee.

Would you like to be close to a lot of Taupo's tourist attractions, such as Huka Falls, Aratiatia Rapids and Wairakei Geothermal Park? If so, then come and join us, as these amenities are only five minutes away from our home.

We look forward to seeing you at **Kinara** and welcoming you as a friend.

DIRECTIONS:
Palmer Mill Road links both SH1 & 5, approx. 5km from the Wairakei intersection.
Just look for the big orange sign on Palmer Mill Road and phone us,
follow the driveway round and look for the terracotta roof.

South Claragh and Bird Cottage

Ph (07) 372 8848, Fax (07) 372 8047
email: *welcome@countryaccommodation.co.nz*
www.countryaccommodation.co.nz

Features & Attractions

- *Tranquil mature gardens*
- *Comfortable relaxed atmosphere*
- *Fine country cooking*
- *Friendly donkeys, black sheep*
- *On routes to/from Waitomo to Rotorua, Tongariro*

$	
Double	$110-160
Single	$25-90
Child	$15-45

Countrystay and Self-contained Cottage

Bedrooms	Qty
Double	2
Twin	1
Single	1
Bed Size	**Qty**
King	
Queen	1
Double	1
Single	3
Bathrooms	**Qty**
Ensuite	
Private	2
Guest Share	

Turn into our leafy driveway and relax...

Both **Bird Cottage** and our comfortable, centrally heated **Farmhouse** are set in rambling gardens. Summer means picnics under the walnut tree, snoozing in a hammock, drinks on our wisteria-shaded terrace. In autumn wake to misty, russet mornings. Snuggle up by the fire in winter or share good conversation over dinner. Enjoy the wonderful spring garden. Home-grown produce and excellent cooking make dining recommended. Great fishing, trekking and golf within 20 min. Accommodation options: 1. The Farmhouse – spacious guestroom with private deck and garden access. Farmhouse tariff includes delicious breakfasts. 2. Bird Cottage – through a stand of trees, ferns and redwoods, private, with french doors to verandahs from both bedroom and living room. Self-contained and cosy, perfect for 2, but will sleep 4. Linen and firewood provided. No meals included in Cottage tariff but available by arrangement. Details and pictures on website.

DIRECTIONS: Easy to find from whichever direction you come. Contact us by phone/email/fax or check our website for map.

Brackenhurst

801 Oruanui Road, RD 1, Taupo
Ph (07) 377 6451, Fax (07) 377 6451
Mobile 027-445 6217
email: *rgbg@xtra.co.nz*

Features & Attractions

- *Dinner by arrangement*
- *Peace and tranquility*
- *14 acres of picturesque farmland*
- *Separate cottage*
- *Friendly highland cattle*
- *Tourist attractions nearby*

$	
Double	$100-150
Single	$60
Child	$30

Homestay Self-contained Accomm.

Bedrooms	Qty
Double	3
Twin	
Single	1
Bed Size	**Qty**
King	
Queen	2
Double	1
Single	4
Bathrooms	**Qty**
Ensuite	2
Private	1
Guest Share	

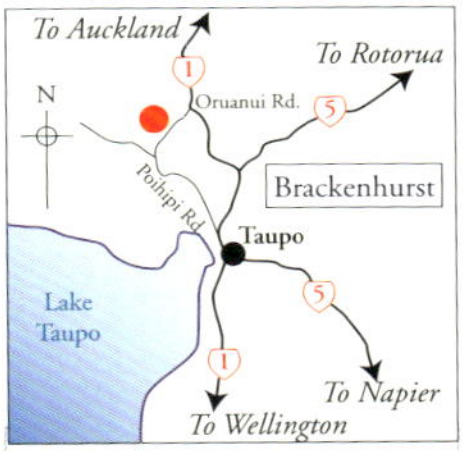

DIRECTIONS: Turn off SH 1 approx. 9km north of Wairakei- "Challenge" fertilizer-bins on Oruanui Road corner - 500m on right. Please phone first.

Brackenhurst is a warm, comfortable, modern Lockwood design home, enjoying beautiful views over 14 acres of peaceful countryside. We offer a warm welcome, wonderful food, peace and tranquility. Whilst enjoying your breakfast you may see twenty different kinds of birds and enjoy the sounds of tuis and bellbirds. A private guest wing in the house or a separate annex offer the ultimate in 'away-from-home' comforts. Breakfast to suit, either continental style or a full English. Come and enjoy **Brackenhurst** and share in our warm hospitality (dinner $40 pp). We are in reach of the famous Huka Falls, five golf courses, geothermal activity, trout fishing (river or lake), ski-fields, Rotorua and Waitomo.

Bellbird Ridge Alpaca Farm

68 Tangye Road, RD 1, Taupo
Ph (07) 377 1996, Fax (07) 377 1992
Mobile 027-668 7754
email: *lharrison@xtra.co.nz*
www.bellbirdridge.co.nz

Tariff : N.Z. Dollars	
Double	$130-140
Single	$100-120
Child	$30

Bedrooms	Qty
Double	2
Twin	1
Single	1
Bed Size	**Qty**
Super King	
King	
Queen	2
Double	
Single	3
Bathrooms	**Qty**
Ensuite	1
Private	1
Guest Share	

Farmstay & Self-contained Accommodation

Features & Attractions

- *Quality accommodation*
- *Secluded garden setting*
- *Deck overlooking pond*
- *Beautiful large garden*
- *10 acre farm*
- *Friendly alpacas & sheep*
- *Tourist attractions nearby*
- *13 km north of Taupo*

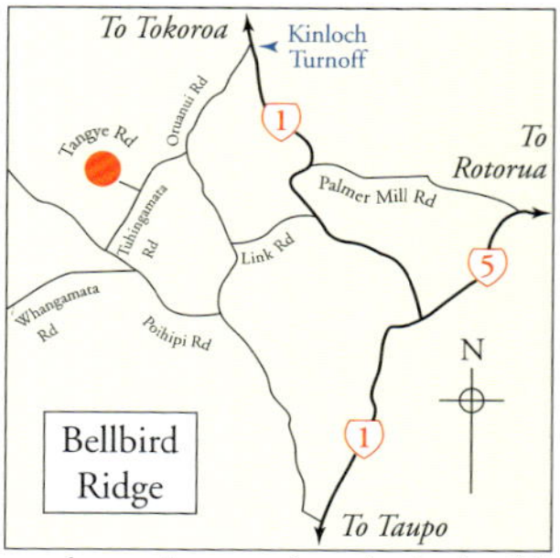

Our farm is only 15 minutes from LakeTaupo and Kinloch, 45 minutes from Rotorua and is the perfect location to base your holiday in the central North Island. Take a break from your travels, unwind in our charming and secluded self-contained cottage and enjoy our beautiful garden and friendly alpacas and coloured sheep. Taupo has many activities from the most relaxing to the most extreme and New Zealand's famous thermal areas are nearby. The cottage has one bedroom with ensuite together with lounge/dining/kitchen area and deck overlooking the garden and pond. Quality fittings include a queen bed with feather duvet, gas heating, full cooking facilities and we include generous provisions of home-baked bread, juice, cereals, bacon and our own eggs for a hearty breakfast. We also offer Bed & Breakfast in a private wing of our home, where you would be our only guests. We have double, twin and single rooms available with your own bathroom. A generous cooked breakfast is included.

MINARAPA

620 Oruanui Road, RD 1, PO Box 1310, Taupo
Ph (07) 378 1931
Mobile 027-272 2367
email: *info@minarapa.co.nz*
www.minarapa.co.nz

@ home NEW ZEALAND

Tariff : N.Z. Dollars	
Double	$120-145
Single	$95-110
Child	POA

Bedrooms	Qty
Double	2
Twin	2
Single	
Bed Size	**Qty**
Super King	
King/Twin	1
Queen	2
Double	
Single	2
Bathrooms	**Qty**
Ensuite	2
Private	1
Guest Share	

VISA MasterCard

Countrystay
Bed & Breakfast

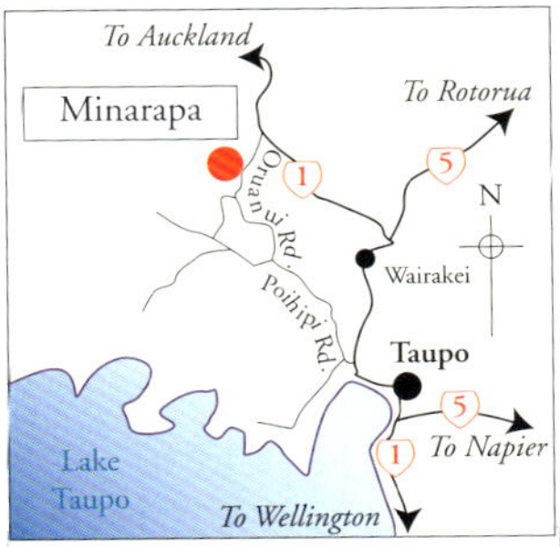

DIRECTIONS:
Please phone for easy directions.

Features & Attractions

- *Tree-lined drive*
- *Park-like grounds*
- *Tennis and billiards*
- *Peace, privacy and space*
- *Tourist attractions nearby*
- *Dinner by arrangement*
- *German spoken*
- *Lifestyle farming*

Wind your way along a wonderful tree-lined drive into rural tranquillity. **Minarapa**, our eleven acre country retreat, is twelve minutes from Taupo, forty-five minutes from Rotorua and within easy reach of major tourist activities and attractions, including Huka Falls, Wairakei Terraces and Waitomo Caves, Orakei Korako and other thermal areas. **Minarapa** offers space and character a plenty. Downstairs, relax in the large guest lounge with full-sized billiard table, television and refrigerator. Upstairs retire to one of the guestrooms – light, spacious, appointed with a view to your comfort and decorated in individual style. Two have ensuite bathroom, balcony and television and all have tea/coffee facilities. They overlook park-like grounds where you may play tennis, wander among colourful tree-sheltered gardens and across the pond and stream to visit our friendly farm animals, or simply sit and enjoy the birdsong.

In addition to continental or cooked breakfast, an evening meal with wine is available on request. We enjoy travel, gardening, walking and golf. Barbara spricht fliessend deutsch.

KINLOCH LODGE

3 Yasmin Lane, Kinloch, Taupo
Ph (07) 378 6332, Fax (07) 378 6332
Mobile 027-481 6345
email: *relax@kinlochlodgetaupo.co.nz*
www.kinlochlodgetaupo.co.nz

Tariff : N.Z. Dollars	
Double	$145-165
Single	$100-120
Child	POA

Bedrooms	Qty
Double	3
Twin	
Single	
Bed Size	**Qty**
Super King	1
King	1
Queen	1
Double	
Single	2
Bathrooms	**Qty**
Ensuite	3
Private	
Guest Share	

Quality Homestay Bed & Breakfast

Features & Attractions

- *Only 15 minutes to Taupo*
- *Experienced & friendly hosts*
- *Comfortable beds*
- *Adjoins local golf course*
- *Close to lake edge beach & Marina*
- *Professional fishing guides available*
- *Comprehensive tourism assistance*
- *Local café & restaurant*

DIRECTIONS:
Take the Te Kuiti/Kinloch turn-off north of Taupo on SH 1 (Poihipi Road). Turn left into Whangamata Rd and follow the signs to Kinloch. On entering Kinloch, take the first turning left after the roundabout (Kenrigg Road), then next left to Yasmin Lane.

Nestled near the Western shores of Lake Taupo in this world-renowned trout fishing, volcanic, golfing and adventure region, **Kinloch Lodge** offers high standard accommodation in the picturesque, tranquil village of **Kinloch**. Relaxing and comfortable, the Lodge provides guests with en-suite bathrooms, a private lounge/library with tea and coffee making facilities, Sky Television, CD and email. Relax with a glass of wine on the deck overlooking the delightful garden. Step through the gate onto the golf course. Boat or fly fish with our recommended local professional guides. Stroll to the lake and marina or take a relaxing lake tour. A short drive from the hustle of Taupo, **Kinloch Lodge** is ideally located to explore our many exciting and unique area attractions, with easy access to other nearby regions. Our extensive local knowledge enables us to provide helpful advice in planning your activities to ensure you maximise your visit. A two-day stay is highly recommended. Our scrumptious breakfasts are legendary. An evening meal and wine are available by arrangement, or enjoy our local restaurant by the lake. As totally committed "Home Hosts", we invite you to experience our warm hospitality, and look forward to welcoming you to our home. We assure you of a memorable stay.

Twynham at Kinloch

84 Marina Terrace, Kinloch, Lake Taupo
Ph (07) 378 2862, Fax (07) 378 2868
Mobile 027-285 6001
email: *twynham.bnb@xtra.co.nz*
www.twynham.co.nz

Features & Attractions

- *Five minutes stroll to Lake*
- *Short 15 min drive to Taupo*
- *Coffee, cake and relaxation*
- *Compl. kayak/fishing tackle*
- *Hearty breakfasts & dinners*
- *Email and fax facilities*

$		
	Double	$145-175
	Single	$110
	Child	POA

Country Village Accommodation

Bedrooms	Qty
Double	2
Twin	1
Single	
Bed Size	**Qty**
Super King	1
King	1
Queen	1
Single	2
Bathrooms	**Qty**
Ensuite	2
Private	1
Guest Share	

Nestled within large private gardens in the picturesque lakeside village of Kinloch - **Twynham** is a haven for fresh air, good coffee and relaxation and unequaled as a base for exploring the delights of the Taupo region, plus the more strenuous delights of golf (adjacent), fishing (five minutes), water sports, snow skiing, bush and mountain walks. Hearty breakfasts, wholesome dinners and warm welcomes assure guests of an enjoyable stay. Guest accommodation is a private wing with bedrooms, bathrooms and elegant lounge. Laundry service available. Elizabeth has a wide knowledge of the volcanic and geothermal history of the region. Paul is a New Zealand Kennel Club Judge and golf, music, dog sports and travel are family interests. We are owned by two friendly dogs. Pets are welcome.

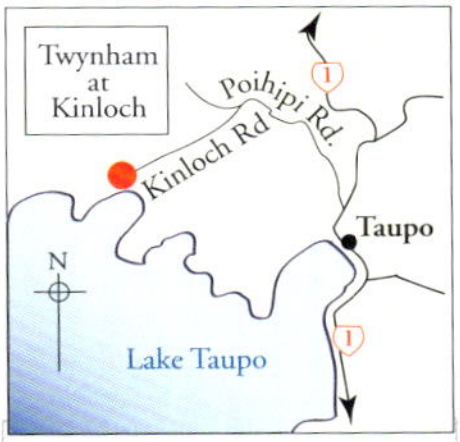

DIRECTIONS: Driving north out of Taupo on SH 1 take the Te Kuiti/Kinloch turn-off on left (Poihipi Road). Follow Kinloch signs to village.

HAZELDENE LODGE

119 Acacia Heights Drive, Acacia Bay, Taupo
Ph (07) 377 0560, Fax (07) 377 0561
Mobile 021-066 5512
email: *hazeldene@xtra.co.nz*
www.hazeldenelodge.co.nz

Tariff : N.Z. Dollars	
Double	$195-275
Single	$185-265
Child	POA

Bedrooms	Qty
Double	4
Twin	
Single	
Bed Size	**Qty**
Super King/Twin	1
King	
Queen	3
Double	
Single	
Bathrooms	**Qty**
Ensuite	4
Private	
Guest Share	

Luxury Accommodation

Features & Attractions

- *Quiet and relaxing*
- *Stunning views*
- *Warm, friendly hospitality*
- *Tree-lined drive*
- *Ample parking*
- *Generous breakfasts*
- *Fishing and golf nearby*
- *Close to all major attractions*

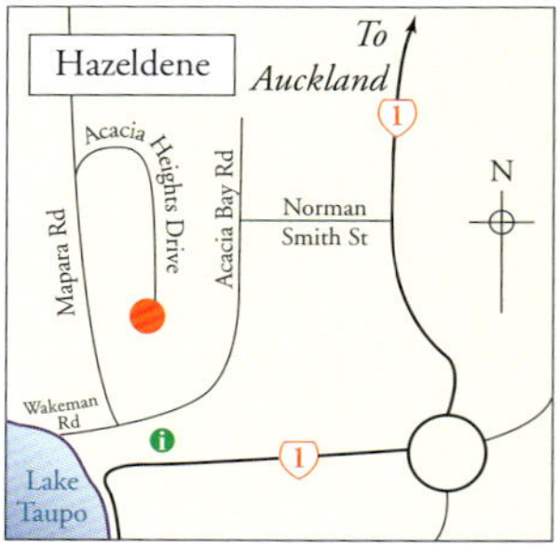

We warmly invite you to stay with us at Hazeldene Lodge, which is architecturally designed. Set in two acres of landscaped gardens planted with native shrubs/bushes and English plants. We have stunning views of Mount Tauhara and Lake Taupo. You can easily access the nearby attractions of Taupo, Huka Falls, international golf courses, geothermal activity, and excellent restaurants just seven kilometres away.

We ran a successful bed and breakfast in Devon, England for three years before coming to New Zealand and we are offering the same high standard "home from home" accommodation. All bedrooms have been tastefully furnished and fitted out with luxuries, such as television, electric blankets, hair dryers, iron and ironing board, tea and coffee making facilities. All bedrooms have spectacular views during the day and by night the twinkling lights of Taupo are gorgeous. We assure you a very relaxing time and comfortable stay. Please telephone, fax or email for bookings, or visit our website.

Highland Cottage

50 Highland Drive, Acacia Bay, RD 1, Taupo
Ph (07) 377 1117, Fax (07) 377 1124
Mobile 021-956 020
email: *highland.cottage@hotmail.com*

Tariff : N.Z. Dollars	
Double	$150
Single	$90
Child	$30

Bedrooms	Qty
Double	1
Twin	
Single	
Bed Size	**Qty**
Super King	
King	
Queen	1
Double	
Single	
Bathrooms	**Qty**
Ensuite	1
Private	
Guest Share	

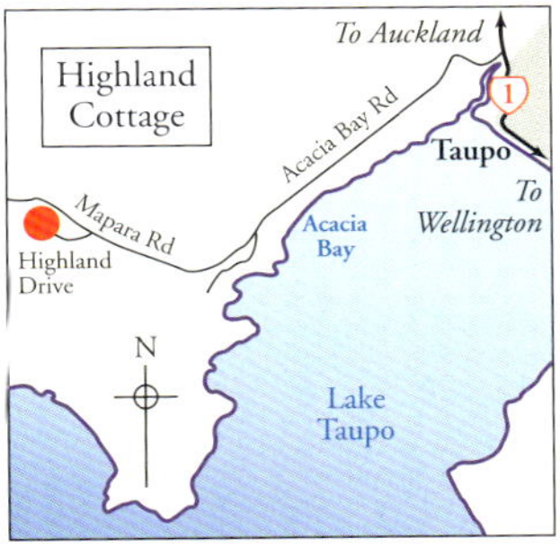

Quiet Country Get-Away
Self-contained Bed & Breakfast

Features & Attractions

- *Fully self-contained*
- *Rural garden setting*
- *5min. to excellent restaurant*
- *5min. walk to licensed art café*
- *Secure parking at door*
- *Laundry & cooking facilities*
- *Sunny outdoor deck*
- *Walk to lake – 20min.*

Highland Cottage is situated on peaceful, private five acres overlooking the Tukairangi Valley. Lake Taupo is accessible in 15 minutes by foot, for a swim or a fish. Also within a 5 minute drive are tennis courts, restaurant/bar and shop. Vineyard, golf course and boat ramps are all close by.

The Cottage includes 1 queen-size bedroom with ensuite, a fold-out double bed, a self-contained kitchen with full cooking facilities, dining area and lounge with TV and cosy fire.

Enjoy your self-help breakfast 'al-fresco'-style on your own sunny deck. It includes free-range eggs and bacon, or provisions for continental breakfast as required.

Alternatively take a short wander down the quiet road to the café for a coffee and view some local art.

Fishing trips (by arrangement), thermal attractions, beaches, ski fields (1 hour away) and mountain bike riding all easily accessible.

Paeroa Lakeside Homestay

21 Te Kopua Street, Acacia Bay, Taupo
Ph (07) 378 8449, Fax (07) 378 8449
Mobile 027-481 8829
email: *bibbys@taupohomestay.com*
www.taupohomestay.com

Tariff : N.Z. Dollars	
Double	$250-350
Single	$250-300
Child	POA

Bedrooms	Qty
Double	3
Twin	
Single	
Bed Size	**Qty**
Super King	1
King	1
Queen	1
Double	
Single	2
Bathrooms	**Qty**
Ensuite	3
Private	
Guest Share	

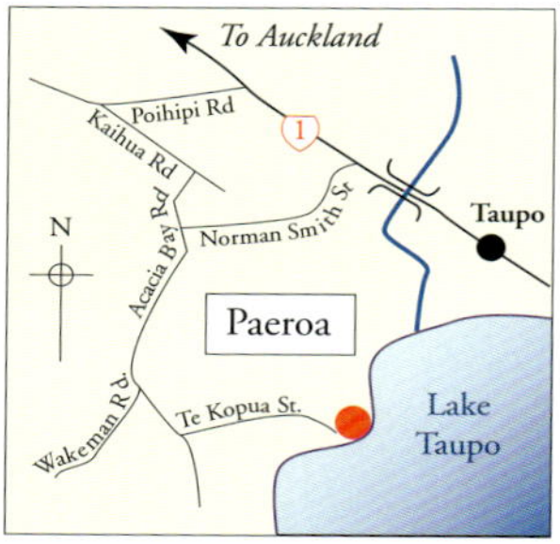

Absolute Lakefront Luxury Accommodation

Features & Attractions

- *Comfortable beds*
- *Private beach & jetty*
- *Generous breakfasts*
- *Quiet and relaxing*
- *Uninterrupted panoramic views*
- *Boat fishing, sightseeing trips*
- *Close to all major attractions*
- *Hot pool and golf nearby*

Paeroa Lakeside Homestay set on the lake edge with private beach, native bush and gardens, in sheltered Acacia Bay, with panoramic views of Lake Taupo and beyond. A warm, welcoming environment waits – comfort, private facilities, spacious lounge areas and outdoor living. Guest areas and beds are warm, comfortable and tastefully decorated. Television and tea/coffee facilities in rooms, email and laundry service available.
Retired sheep farmers, we enjoy living in our peaceful, private home beside the beach next to a bushwalk, just minutes from the town centre.
Three golf courses, thermal areas, restaurants, boating, fishing and all major attractions, and within easy driving distance from mountains, National Park, extensive thermal areas and wineries. Amongst our interests are travel, golf, gardening, fishing, hospitality, having travelled and fished extensively overseas. Guided fishing and sightseeing experiences available from John's new 30 foot cruiser. The catch can be smoked or may be cooked for breakfast. A welcome tea or coffee on arrival. We assure you of a memorable stay. Please email, fax or phone for bookings.

Te Moenga Lodge

60 Te Moenga Park, Acacia Bay, Taupo
Ph (07) 378 0437, Fax (07) 378 0438
Mobile 027-452 1459
email: *temoenga@xtra.co.nz*
www.temoenga.com

Tariff : N.Z. Dollars	
Double	$150-295
Single	$120-220
Child	POA

Bedrooms	Qty
Double	4
Twin	
Single	
Bed Size	**Qty**
Super King	
King	2
Queen	2
Double	
Single	
Bathrooms	**Qty**
Ensuite	4
Private	
Guest Share	

VISA MasterCard

Chalet Accommodation and Bed & Breakfast

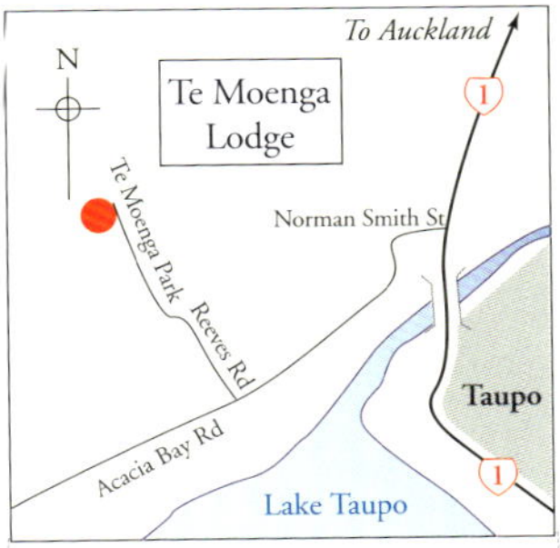

DIRECTIONS: Follow directions to Acacia Bay. Take 1st street on right, Reeves Rd and continue on to **Te Moenga** Park to end.

Features & Attractions

- *Magnificent panoramic views*
- *Luxury private chalets*
- *Studio suites with garden views*
- *Trout fishing arranged*
- *TV, tea and coffee in suites*
- *Secure off-street parking*
- *Small group options*
- *Perfect garden wedding site*

Te Moenga Lodge, supremely located overlooking Lake Taupo, presents guests with a unique opportunity to enjoy the NZ lifestyle within close proximity to all the scenic, recreational and sporting attractions of the Taupo Region. Each private chalet has outstanding views and can accommodate up to four people. The accommodation is luxurious with king- twin beds, separate lounges, ensuites and chalets with spa baths. Our two units have double beds, ensuites and garden views. Breakfasts with a difference can be enjoyed either in the hosts' kitchen or in the privacy of your own accommodation. Our extensive home includes decks to enjoy a late afternoon platter and wine or cosy up with a port in the lounge by the fire. We also cater for small groups or wedding parties. Our grounds are spacious and allow for safe off-street parking. We can happily arrange any travel arrangements or excursions and look forward to making your stay at **Te Moenga Lodge** rank amongst the most memorable of your visit to Taupo, New Zealand.

Fourwinds Bed & Breakfast

57 Woodward Street, Taupo
Ph (07) 376 5350, Fax (07) 376 5360
Mobile 027-476 5350
email: *bnb@fourwindsbedandbreakfast.co.nz*
www.fourwindsbedandbreakfast.co.nz

Tariff : N.Z. Dollars	
Double	$125
Single	$95
Child	neg

Bedrooms	Qty
Double	1
Twin	1
Single	
Bed Size	**Qty**
Super King	
King	
Queen	
Double	1
Single	2
Bathrooms	**Qty**
Ensuite	
Private	
Guest Share	1

Homestay
Bed & Breakfast

Features & Attractions

- *Panoramic views*
- *Quiet relaxed atmosphere*
- *Warm friendly hospitality*
- *Close to all attractions*
- *Short walk to shops & restaurants*
- *Transfer airport/coach depots*
- *Email & laundry facilities*
- *Home away from home*

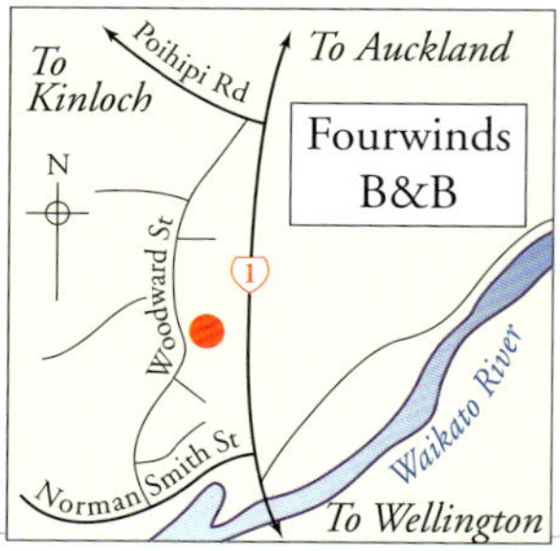

DIRECTIONS:
From north (SH 1) take Acacia Bay turn-off then left twice. From south (SH 1)cross Waikato River, left Norman Smith St, right Woodward St.

A warm welcome and a refreshing cup of tea await your arrival. **Fourwinds**, a charming home, is close to all Taupo's main attractions and town, with panoramic views over the town, lake and mountains. Guests are accommodated in a double or twin room with shared bathroom (shower and bath) and a separate toilet. A generous cooked or continental breakfast is served in the dining room overlooking the view.

Taupo's central position makes an ideal base for day trips to Rotorua, Hawkes Bay, Tongariro National Park and Waitomo with guests returning each night to the same warm welcome and comfortable bed. At day's end watch the magnificent sunsets over the mountains and find the Southern Cross in the night sky.

Magnifique

52 Woodward Street, Taupo
Ph (07) 378 4915, Mobile 021-388 498
email: *rex&gay@magnifique.co.nz*
www.magnifique.co.nz

@ home NEW ZEALAND

Tariff : N.Z. Dollars	
Double	$125-145
Single	$80-100
Child	

Bedrooms	Qty
Double	2
Twin	1
Single	
Bed Size	**Qty**
Super King	
King	
Queen	2
Double	
Single	2
Bathrooms	**Qty**
Ensuite	
Private	2
Guest Share	

VISA MasterCard

Quality Homestay Bed & Breakfast

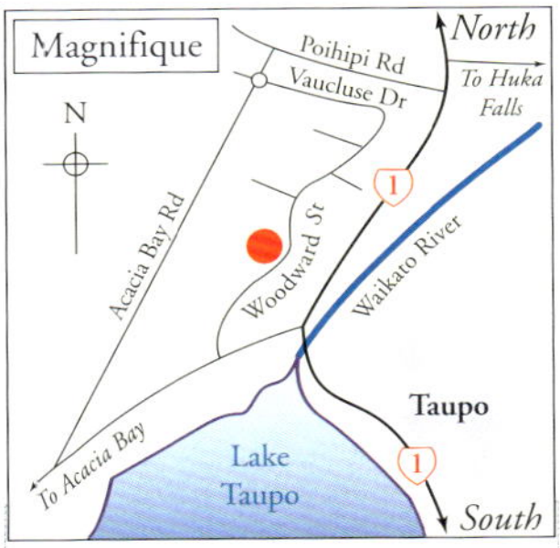

DIRECTIONS: From north (SH 1) turn off to Acacia Bay, then 1st left twice. From south (SH 1) - just over bridge, take 1st left, then 1st right.

Features & Attractions

- *Magnificent sweeping views*
- *Dinner by arrangement*
- *Overlooking Boat Harbour*
- *Short walk to town*
- *Golf, fishing, skiing*
- *Guest laundry*

Welcome to **Magnifique** with stunning views of beautiful Lake Taupo, framed by the snow-clad Central Plateau and mountain ranges. Only seven minutes walk to Taupo's superb shops and restaurants. The accommodation includes an upstairs double bedroom with television, tea making facility and private bathroom, or downstairs self-contained double unit with living and kitchen facilities, television and bathroom. Being central, Taupo is ideal for day trips to Rotorua, Hawke's Bay art deco and wineries, Tongariro National Park or Waitomo Caves. More and more of our guests are choosing this option and returning to the same comfortable bed and welcome. Allow us to assist you with plans that will maximise your Taupo experience. Rex is always looking for an excuse to take the boat on the lake. Our focus in life is "people", having many friends in New Zealand and beyond with capacity for many more. Enjoy a relaxed stay in our lovely home and special attention to details.

Above the Lake at Windsor Charters

46 Rokino Road, Taupo
Ph (07) 378 8738
Mobile 027-272 9856
email: *windsor-charters@xtra.co.nz*
www.troutfishingtaupo.com

@home NEW ZEALAND

Tariff : N.Z. Dollars	
Double	$150-180
Single	$130-150
Child	POA

Bedrooms	Qty
Double	3
Twin	1
Single	
Bed Size	**Qty**
Super King	1
King	
Queen	2
Double	
Single	2
Bathrooms	**Qty**
Ensuite	1
Private	1
Guest Share	

Boutique Bed & Breakfast
Lake Fishing/Cruising with Hosts

VISA MasterCard

Features & Attractions

- *Chartered fishing with host*
- *Close to all major attractions*
- *Golf 5 minutes*
- *Activities advice*
- *Breathtaking lake views*
- *Kiwi-style breakfast*
- *Stroll to lake swimming*
- *Quality accommodation*

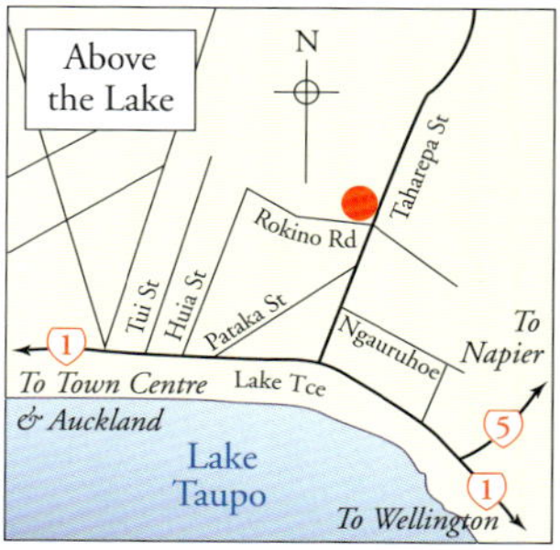

At **Windsor Charters** you will be pampered and well taken care of. On arrival enjoy a wine or coffee with your hosts, Angela, Bruce and golden retriever Koda. Relax and take in the magical lake and mountain views. In the morning wake to a generous Kiwi-style cooked breakfast. Accommodation is first class and tastefully decorated. The ground floor suite features a queen-size bedroom and twin room, guest lounge opening to private sunny courtyard. Ideal for friends travelling together. On the upper floor the **Lake View Suite** is a romantic private haven. Queen bed, panoramic water views, sitting room, spa bath. Suites have tea/coffee facilities, fridge, heating, electric blankets TV, iron and toiletries in the bathrooms. The pristine lake and award winning restaurant are just a stroll away. We are close to golf courses and all tourist attractions. Boat fishing or lake sightseeing with your hosts aboard MSA registered **Fish 'N'Fun** is optional and could be the highlight of your vacation.

The Pillars

7 Deborah Rise, Bonshaw Park, RD 3, Taupo
Ph (07) 378 1512, Fax (07) 378 1511
email: *info@pillars.co.nz*
www.pillarstaupo.co.nz

Tariff : N.Z. Dollars	
Double	$275-475
Single	
Child	13 yrs.+

Bedrooms	Qty
Double	4
Twin	
Single	
Bed Size	**Qty**
Super King/Twin	1
King/Twin	1
Californian King/Twin	4
Single	
Bathrooms	**Qty**
Ensuite	4
Private	
Guest Share	

Luxury Homestay Retreat

Features & Attractions

- *Offers privacy and tranquility*
- *5 acre park-like rural grounds*
- *Lake and mountain views*
- *Tennis court & swimming pool*
- *World famous trout fishing*
- *Golf courses nearby*
- *Ski fields only 1 hour away*
- *Hot pools nearby*

DIRECTIONS: 5.7 km from the lake edge up SH 5 towards Napier. Turn into Caroline Drive. Deborah Rise is the first on your left.

Welcome to Taupo's exclusive Homestay Retreat offering privacy and tranquility amidst five acres of park-like rural grounds with views of lake and mountains. At Lake Taupo, – New Zealand's largest lake, covering 616 square kilometres – you will be amazed about how much there is to do in both summer and winter. **The Pillars**, built in Mediterranean style, is set in landscaped gardens, featuring a pond, gazebo, swimming pool and tennis court (racquets and balls provided). All rooms have underfloor heating, complimentary toiletries and quality furnishings, including television, radio-clock, refrigerator with bottled water, selection of teas and coffee, fresh fruit and a complimentary bottle of wine. Fresh flowers, home-cooked biscuits, bathrobes and hair dryers will add to the enjoyment of your stay with us. The room and winter rates includes a continental breakfast. With prior notice we will provide a three-course evening meal with aperitifs, nibbles and a night cap for $65 per person. If you wish to visit Taupo's many bars and restaurants, we will provide complimentary transport. Brochure available on request.

Fairviews

8 Fairview Terrace, Taupo
Ph (07) 377 0773
email: *fairviews@reap.org.nz*
www.reap.org.nz/~fairviews

Tariff : N.Z. Dollars	
Double	$125-145
Single	$95-125
Child	n/a

Bedrooms	Qty
Double	1
Twin	1
Single	

Bed Size	Qty
Super King	
King	
Queen	1
Double	
Single	2

Bathrooms	Qty
Ensuite	1
Private	1
Guest Share	

Homestay
Boutique Accommodation

Features & Attractions

- *Email/laundry (small charge)*
- *Generous breakfasts*
- *Tea/coffee facilities*
- *Private entrance/patio*
- *Extensive local knowledge*
- *Unrivalled hospitality*
- *Off-street parking*
- *Airport pick-up*

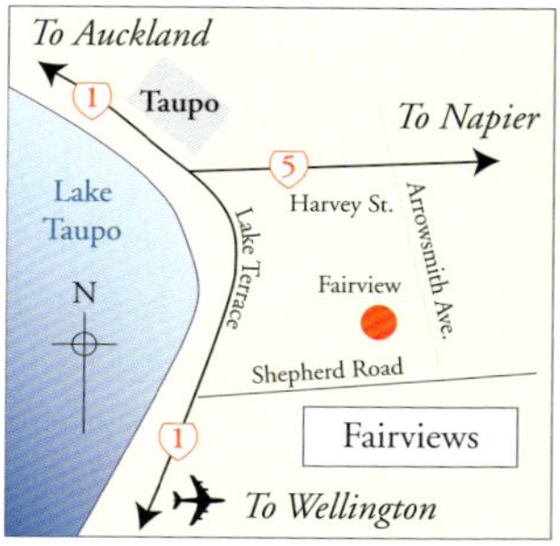

DIRECTIONS: Approaching from State Highway 1, turn onto State Highway 5. Take first turning on the right then second turning on the right. **Fairviews** is on the left.

Brenda and Mike welcome you to **Fairviews** and invite you to stay in our comfortable, modern home situated in a quiet, safe neighbourhood. Whether you desire privacy or company, we will host you in a friendly, relaxed atmosphere. **Fairviews** provides an excellent standard of accommodation and, as we are seasoned travellers, we know the importance of superior service. We take pride in going the extra mile for our visitors. **Fairviews Homestay** recently featured in the "Readers Recommend" Column of the LA Times.
Our interests include travel, cycling, computers, theatre, antiques/ collectibles, gardening and tramping. **Fairviews** is situated 4.5 km from town, five minutes from the lake, botanical gardens and Taupo Hot Springs. Discover the stunning beauty of Taupo – relax and enjoy your time at **Fairviews**.

Ambleside Bed & Breakfast

5 Te Hepera Street, Taupo
Ph/Fax (07) 378 1888, Mobile 027-483 6888
email: *scandic@xtra.co.nz*
www.ambleside.co.nz

Tariff : N.Z. Dollars	
Double	$150-175
Single	$150
Child	n/a

Bedrooms	Qty
Double	2
Twin	
Single	
Bed Size	**Qty**
Super King	
King	
Queen	2
Double	
Single	
Bathrooms	**Qty**
Ensuite	1
Private	1
Guest Share	

Boutique Accommodation
Bed & Breakfast

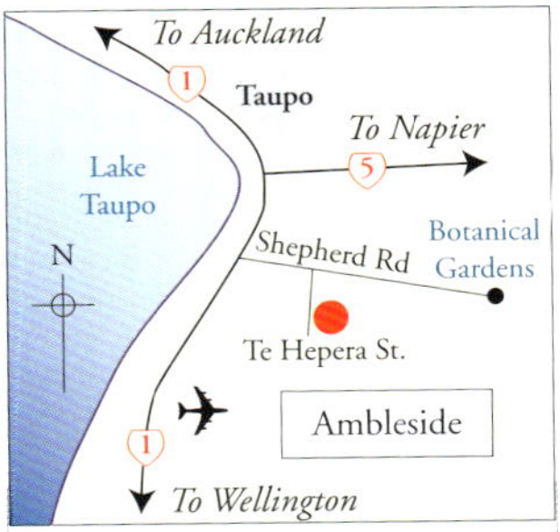

DIRECTIONS:
Travelling south on SH1 take 2nd left turn after Napier SH 5 turnoff, onto Shepherd Road, then 1st right into Te Hepera Street.

Features & Attractions

- *Quality accommodation in private and tranquil setting*
- *Panoramic lake, mountain & town views*
- *Delicious cuisine & warm hospitality*
- *Private thermal pool*
- *Fishing, sightseeing on lake*
- *Close to local attractions*
- *Ample off-street parking*

Magnificent views, private geothermal plunge pool, delicious cuisine, five-star friendliness - just some of the pleasant surprises that await you when you stay at Ambleside. Built for the sun and views, our home is situated in a quiet cul-de-sac, a stroll away from the lake and restaurants. Upstairs is exclusive to you. Two queen bedrooms offer stunning views. Both have Sky television, refrigerators (complimentary refreshments) and tea/coffee facilities, and both suites are air conditioned. One bedroom adjoins a well equipped guest lounge, and these open onto a sunny balcony. Capture one of life's better experiences when you relax in our geothermal plunge pool set in the fern garden. Robes are provided. You are welcome to use our internet facilities at no extra expense. As one guest put it "It's all about human warmth and wit". Enjoy sharing travel stories and life's adventures with us whilst you enjoy a gourmet breakfast. Take the opportunity to use our knowledge to plan your day, and experience the magic of Taupo.

Finial House

51 Ngauruhoe Street, Taupo
Ph (07) 377 4347, Fax (07) 377 4348
Mobile 027-685 8255
email: *n.j.fleming@xtra.co.nz*
www.finial-homestay.co.nz

Features & Attractions

- *Fabulous 180° views*
- *Delicious quality breakfast*
- *Spa pool with views*
- *Spacious, quiet & comfortable*
- *Central heating*
- *Off-street parking*

Homestay Bed & Breakfast

Double	$120-150
Single	$90-125
Child	neg

We are just as keen to hear of your home, family and lifestyle, as we are to tell you of the wonders of the Taupo Region and ourselves, perhaps with some background music and the 'pop' of the wine bottle. Relax in the evening while watching the activities on the lake that covers the entire view from our spacious lounge and decks.

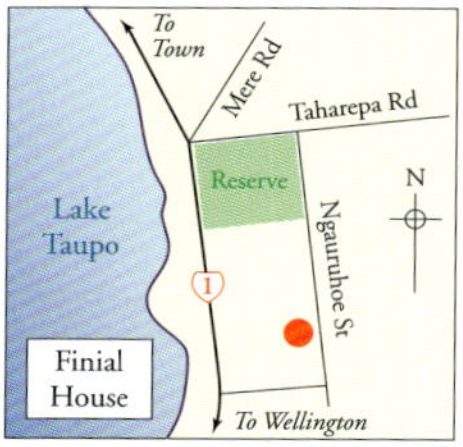

In the morning, waken to the smell of fresh home-baked bread and grilled bacon. Watch the morning moods of the lake while you enjoy a choice of fruit and cereal and await your healthy cooked breakfast as you contemplate your next destination.

Bedrooms	Qty
Double	2
Twin	1
Single	
Bed Size	**Qty**
King Single	2
Queen	2
Double	
Single	
Bathrooms	**Qty**
Ensuite	2
Private	
Family Share	1

Moselle

3 Te Hepera St, Taupo
Ph/Fax (07) 377 2922
Mobile 021-254 4511
e-mail: *ragevelvin@xtra.co.nz*

Features & Attractions

- *Handy to the lake*
- *Superb lake views*
- *Quiet cul de sac*
- *Full laundry facilities*
- *Off-street parking*
- *Guests' private entrance*

Self-contained Luxury Accommodation

Double	$150-200
Single	$150
Child	

This property offers quality furnishings in a French theme. Brand new super king bed and top quality linen. New, modern ensuite and full laundry facilities. Full kitchen facilities and fresh breakfast food supplied daily to your requirements. Specialty foods are no problem. A DVS system and night store heater have been installed for warmth, comfort, and to prevent allergies. A five minute drive to the Taupo township and walking distance to the lake. Private parking outside this accommodation. All this for $150.00 per night off-peak and $200.00 per night peak time.

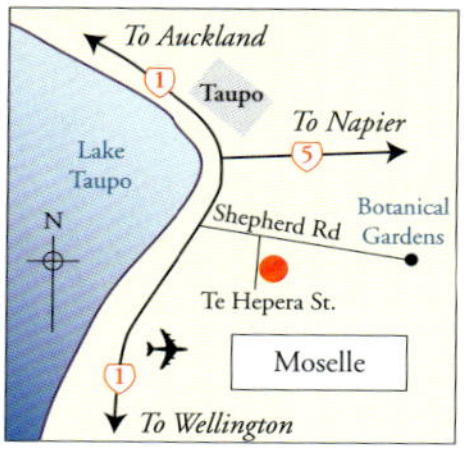

DIRECTIONS: Travelling south on SH 1 take the second left turn after the Napier SH 5 turn-off, onto Shepherd Road, then first right into Te Hepera Street.

Bedrooms	Qty
Double	1
Twin	
Single	
Bed Size	**Qty**
Super King	1
Queen	
Double	
King/Single	2
Bathrooms	**Qty**
Ensuite	1
Private	
Guest Share	

PATAKA HOUSE

8 Pataka Road, Taupo
Ph (07) 378 5481, Fax (07) 378 5461
email: *pataka-homestay@xtra.co.nz*
www.patakahouse.co.nz

Features & Attractions

- *Quality hospitality in spacious home*
- *Private garden room with ensuite*
- *Central to Taupo's many attractions*
- *Quiet neighbourhood*
- *Large colourful garden*
- *Outdoor swimming pool*

$	
Double	$110-130
Single	$75
Child	$30

Homestay and Garden Cottage

DIRECTIONS: We are 100 metres off the Lake Taupo lakefront drive. Please phone or fax for bookings or directions.

Bedrooms	Qty
Double	2
Twin	2
Single	
Bed Size	**Qty**
King	
Queen	2
Double	
Single	4
Bathrooms	**Qty**
Ensuite	1
Private	1
Guest Share	1

Pataka House is highly recommended for its hospitality. We assure guests that their stay lives up to New Zealand's reputation as being a home away from home. We are easily located, one turn off the lakefront and up a tree-lined driveway. Our garden room is privately situated, has an appealing décor and is extremely popular to young and old alike. Stay for one night or stay for more as Lake Taupo will truly be the highlight of your holiday.

We have a private spacious parking area. We can plan your fishing trips and, if required, help to plan your day's activities. Enjoy a relaxed stay at Pataka House and experience the magic of Taupo.

AMANZIKULU

57 Mahuta Road, Five Mile Bay, RD 2, Taupo
Ph/Fax (07) 377 0859
Mobile 027-200 1813
email: *john.norli@xtra.co.nz*
www.amanzikulu.co.nz

Features & Attractions

- *Home of ex New Zealand cricket captain*
- *Great fishing base*
- *Handy to many attractions*
- *Wine & dine with us*
- *Cricket memorabilia*

$	
Double	$140
Single	$110
Child	neg

Cricketer's Homestay B&B or Self-contained

Bedrooms	Qty
Double	1
Twin	1
Single	
Bed Size	**Qty**
King	
Queen	1
Double	
Single	2
Bathrooms	**Qty**
Ensuite	2
Private	
Guest Share	

Amanzikulu – Zulu for 'big water'

Amanzikulu is a peaceful Homestay in a relaxed atmosphere. Designed to make you feel at home yet offers you privacy and facilities for your independence. Stroll across to the lake edge with its good swimming beach, or visit John's study, full of international memorabilia, collected over the years of his participation in Cricket. Then enjoy our hospitality in a relaxed atmosphere, along with our 2 well behaved border collies. Accommodation is warm and comfortable, (electric blankets etc) two lounges, a shady cool verandah. Dine with us by arrangement or sample Taupo's excellent choice of restaurants – the nearest one is 3 minutes by car. Easy drive to all of Taupo's attractions. We welcome you to our home.

DIRECTIONS: Five Mile Bay. 8 km south of Taupo SH 1. Phone for easy directions.

Lake Edge Lodge

60 Mahuta Road, Five Mile Bay, RD 2, Taupo
Ph (07) 378 0563, Fax (07) 378 0564
Mobile 021-780 563
email: *jean@lakeedgelodge.co.nz*
www.lakeedgelodge.co.nz

Tariff : N.Z. Dollars	
Double	$180-300
Single	$180
Child	neg

Bedrooms	Qty
Double	3
Twin	1
Single	
Bed Size	**Qty**
Super King	
King	1
Queen	2
Single	2
Bathrooms	**Qty**
Ensuite	3
Private	
Guest Share	
Family Share	

Homestay & Self-contained Lakefront Accommodation

Features & Attractions

- *Absolute lake edge luxury*
- *10 min south of Taupo*
- *Two lake front studio rooms*
- *Spacious garden apartment*
- *Double spa baths*
- *Email & laundry facilities*
- *Barbeque, Kayaks, rowing boat*
- *Breakfast hamper available*

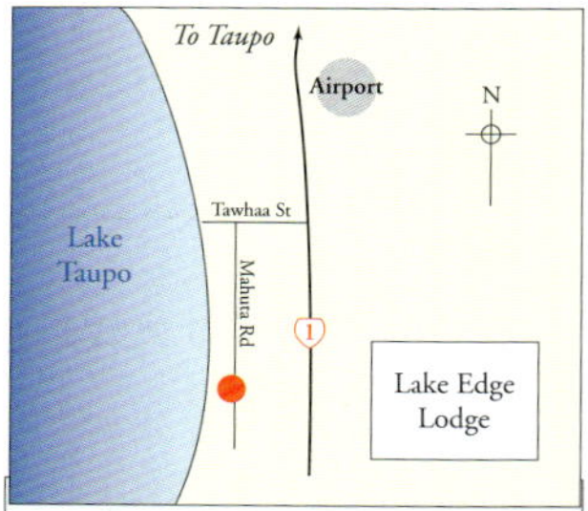

DIRECTIONS:
Five Mile Bay is clearly signposted
8 km south of Taupo

Relax and unwind from your journey with afternoon tea served on the balcony overlooking beautiful Lake Taupo. Lake Edge Lodge offers absolute lake edge, luxury, self-contained accommodation consisting of two studio rooms and a two bedroom apartment. Our Tui and Kowhai Rooms open onto sunny garden settings with a backdrop of panoramic lake and mountain views. Kitchenette, king/queen beds, television, comfortable seating, ensuites with heating. Our light and spacious Boat Shed incorporates modern design and furnishings with a private patio garden setting. Sleeps four comfortably, open plan kitchen/dining/lounge, full cooking facilities with dishwasher, washing machine, television and video, CD player, air conditioning, bathroom with heating. The choice for breakfast is yours – enjoy a generous continental breakfast hamper in the privacy of your own room, alfresco in the garden, on the beachfront or simply do your own thing. Tea/coffee, bath robes, toiletries, heated towel rails and hair dryers are provided.

Tui Lodge

196 Taupahi Road, Turangi
Ph (07) 386 0840, Fax (07) 386 0843
Mobile 027-441 1625
email: *tui-lodge@xtra.co.nz*
www.tui-lodge.co.nz

Tariff : N.Z. Dollars	
Double	$240
Single	$150
Child	

Bedrooms	Qty
Double	4
Twin	
Single	
Bed Size	**Qty**
Super King	4
King	
Queen	
Double	
King/Single	8
Bathrooms	**Qty**
Ensuite	4
Private	
Guest Share	

Luxury Bed & Breakfast

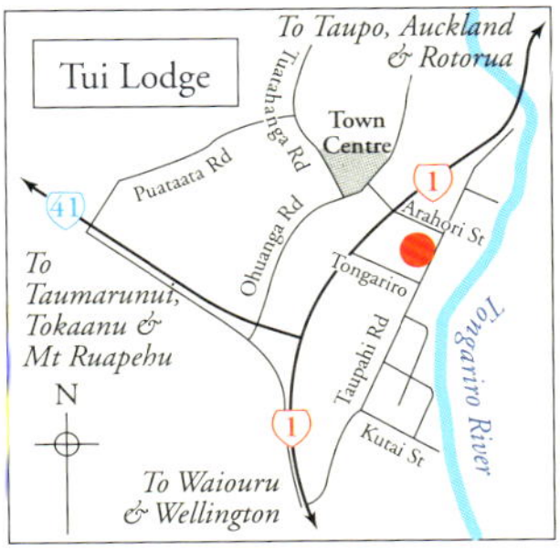

Features & Attractions

- *Personalised Maori culture tours*
- *Fly fishing*
- *Tongariro crossing and short walks*
- *Tongariro trout centre 5min. away*
- *Whakapapa ski fields*
- *Tokannu thermal area 5 min.*
- *Rafting 4x4 & horse trekking*
- *Train trip (spiral)*

Tui Lodge is located near the Tongariro River, renowned for fly fishing for Brown and Rainbow Trout. All year round fishing with the Back Country Rivers offering seasonal fishing.

Tui Lodge, purposely built as a Bed & Breakfast and opened in 2005, is a blend of classic and contemporary design. Peaceful luxury accommodation. Offering four ensuited guest bedrooms, large guest lounge, open fire, underfloor heating with views of Mt Pihanga and the Kaimanawa Ranges.

Close vicinity to wonderful bush and river walks. Apart from the skiing on the mountains, there are many beautiful short walks and several day tramps around the mountain.

Very good restaurants within walking distance. A haven for artists. Trout fishing guide Ian is a member of the professional guides association and a talented artist.

Turangi ▶ YOUR HOST: **Jenny Barnett** Ph: (07) 386 0114

Pukatea Homestay

29 Rangimoana Avenue, Motuoapa, RD 2, Turangi
Ph (07) 386 0114, Fax (07) 386 0345
Mobile 027-227 3319
email: *spocky@xtra.co.nz*

Features & Attractions

- *Native garden setting*
- *Friendly & relaxed atmosphere*
- *Dinner by arrangement*
- *Fantastic lake view*
- *45 min to ski fields*
- *Adventure activities area*

Homestay Bed & Breakfast

$	
Double	$110-130
Single	$80-100
Child	

Bedrooms	Qty
Double	2
Twin	
Single	
Bed Size	**Qty**
King	1
Queen	1
Double	
Single	
Bathrooms	**Qty**
Ensuite	1
Private	
Family Share	1

Pukatea offers quality accommodation in a peaceful, native garden setting with magnificent views over Lake Taupo. A warm and friendly welcome awaits you from your host Jenny, border collie Jess and our cat Mr Spock.
Relax in the sun and enjoy expansive views from the lounge and the deck, or take advantage of the many activities available in the region – Tongariro National Park is on our doorstep. We are just ten minutes north of Turangi and thirty minutes south from Taupo.
Delicious breakfasts are included. Dinner, with complimentary wine, is available upon request. Vegetarians are catered for but advance notice is always appreciated.

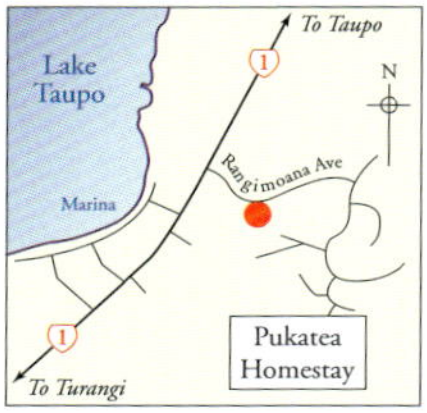

Turangi ▶ YOUR HOSTS: **Chris and Peter Stewart** Free Ph: 0800 FOUNDERS

Founders at Turangi

253 Taupahi Road, Turangi
Ph (07) 386 8539, Fax (07) 386 8534
Mobile 025-854 000
email: *founders@ihug.co.nz*
www.founders.co.nz

Features & Attractions

- *Fly fishing guides available*
- *Rafting, kayaking, skiing*
- *Golf, horse treks, 4x4 bikes*
- *Tongariro Nat. Park tramping*
- *Lake Taupo water sports*
- *Thermal pools, historic sites*

Bed & Breakfast Homestay

$	
Double	$170
Single	$120
Child	

Bedrooms	Qty
Double	4
Twin	
Single	
Bed Size	**Qty**
S.King/Twin	1
Queen	3
Double	
Single	
Bathrooms	**Qty**
Ensuite	4
Private	
Guest Share	

Peter and Chris Stewart offer you a warm welcome to their home in Turangi, a small town at the southern end of Lake Taupo, where you can 'get away from it all'. **Founders at Turangi** is new and purpose built to ensure you a comfortable, relaxed base from which to visit the volcanoes of Tongariro National Park or flyfish nearby rivers. We are close to Lake Taupo, where you can sit in a quiet bay and enjoy the beauty, swim, sail, water ski or cruise. Breakfast in our sunny dining room is a good start to each morning as you set out to explore the unique magic that is the North Island's Central Plateau. Stroll to dinner at good local restaurants each evening.

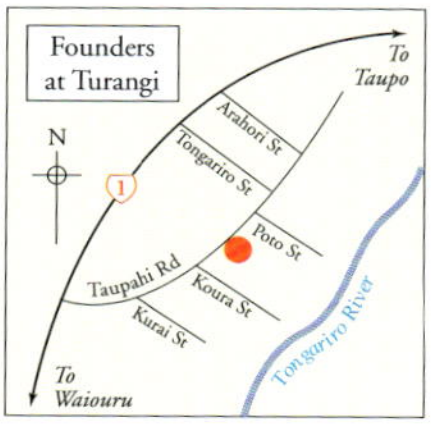

Southern Comfort Homestay

35 Taupahi Road, PO Box 312, Turangi
Ph (07) 386 7172, Fax (07) 386 7172
Mobile 027-251 2715
email: *homestaytaupo@xtra.co.nz*
www.homestaytaupo.co.nz

Tariff : N.Z. Dollars	
Double	$110-130
Single	$90
Child	n/a

Bedrooms	Qty
Double	2
Twin	
Single	
Bed Size	**Qty**
Super King	
King	1
Queen	1
Double	
Single	
Bathrooms	**Qty**
Ensuite	2
Private	
Guest Share	

VISA MasterCard

Homestay
Boutique Accommodation

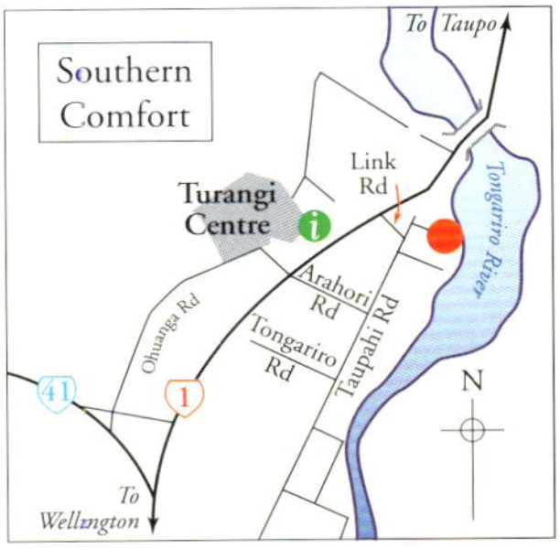

DIRECTIONS:
From SH1 turn into Link Road, then left into Taupahi Road. No 35 is on right. **Southern Comfort** is at end of the driveway on right.

Features & Attractions

- *Quiet peaceful setting*
- *Ensuite bathrooms*
- *Dinners a speciality*
- *Swimming pool*
- *Backs onto Tongariro River*
- *Just two minutes off SH 1*

Southern Comfort Homestay welcomes you to Turangi, trout fishing and adventure paradise. Conveniently situated equal distance between Auckland and Wellington, only one minute from the Tongariro River. A good place to break your journey through the North Island. Let me offer you an oasis to rest, relax and make yourself at home. Working locally in the tourism sector, I am able to advise you on the area's exciting outdoor adventures – skiing, whitewater rafting, golfing, trout fishing, birdwatching or tramp the fabulous 'Tongariro Crossing'. The choice is yours. With a background in corporate catering, providing a special three course evening meal (with New Zealand wine) is my specialty. Together with my feline friends, Sid and Wylie, I look forward to welcoming you.

The Birches

13 Koura Street, Turangi
Ph (07) 386 5140, Fax (07) 386 5149
Mobile 021-149 6594
email: *tineke.peter@xtra.co.nz*

Features & Attractions

- *Tongariro River 2 min. stroll*
- *Fly-fishing, rafting*
- *Quiet, peaceful setting*
- *Skiing, golf, tramping*
- *Thermal pools*
- *Special breakfasts*

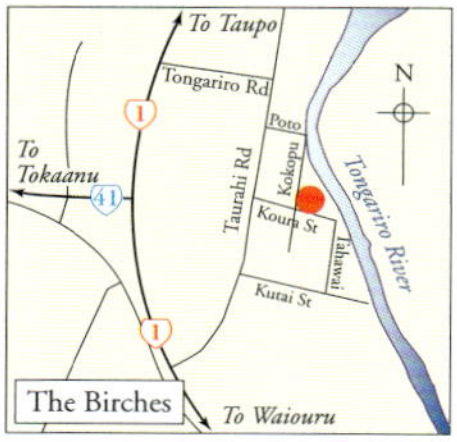

Bed & Breakfast
Homestay

$	
Double	$150
Single	$120
Child	

Close to the world-renowned Tongariro River we welcome you to our attractive residence, set in park-like surroundings on a quiet street. This unique location is ideally situated for many outdoor pursuits such as fly fishing, skiing, tramping, golf and rafting.

We offer superior and spacious ensuite accommodation with TV and coffee/tea making facilities in a separate part of the house. Your Dutch/Canadian hosts have considerable international experience through living in Canada, the Netherlands, France, Belgium and Singapore and can speak Dutch and French.

Dinner by prior arrangement.

Bedrooms	Qty
Double	1
Twin	
Single	
Bed Size	**Qty**
King	
Queen	1
Double	
Single	
Bathrooms	**Qty**
Ensuite	1
Private	
Guest Share	

www.phototrips.info

Omori Lake House

31 Omori Rd, Omori, (PO Box 334) Turangi
Ph (07) 386 0420, Fax (07) 386 0420
Mobile 021-667 092
email: *stay@omorilakehouse.co.nz*
www.omorilakehouse.co.nz

Features & Attractions

- *New specialist-built luxury lodge*
- *Kiwi hospitality at its best*
- *Kiwi cuisine with dining options*
- *Panoramic views*
- *Volcanic landscape*
- *World-class trout fishing*

$	
Double	$120-150
Single	
Child	

Boutique Lodge
Opening February '07

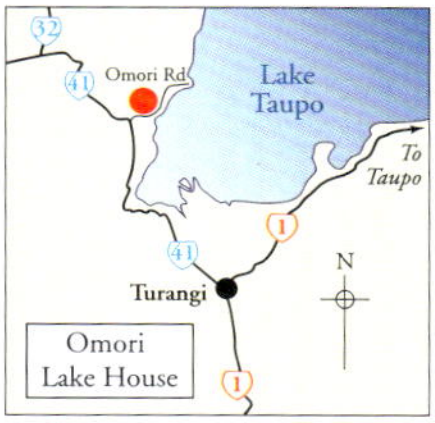

Bedrooms	Qty
Double	2
Twin	
Single	
Bed Size	**Qty**
Super King	2
Queen	
Double	
Single	
Bathrooms	**Qty**
Ensuite	2
Private	
Guest Share	

We invite you to experience Kiwi hospitality at its best. We offer brand-new Boutique Accommodation, set high above Omori with stunning views looking across to Taupo. There are two luxury guest rooms with king-size beds, ensuites, tea/coffee facilities and private deck.
One room suits disabled with wide access, handrails and wet-floor shower, while the other has its own bath.
Raewyn loves to cook and eating well is part of the experience. Enjoy barbeques in summer or sit at the large rimu table for Kiwi cuisine with Kiwi classics on the menu.
Omori, on the south-west of lake Taupo, is close to a variety of activities including world-renowned fly fishing, bush walks, thermal hot pools and ski slopes.

Willsplace

145 Omori Road, RD 1, Omori, Turangi
Ph (07) 386 7339, Fax (07) 386 7339
Mobile 027-228 8960
email: *willsplace@wave.co.nz*
www.willsplace.co.nz

Features & Attractions

- *Private suite*
- *Bush & lakeside walks*
- *Children welcome*
- *Fabulous lake views*
- *Good fishing & boating*
- *Close to National Park*

$	
Double	$125
Single	$90
Child	neg

Lakeside
Bed & Breakfast

Bedrooms	Qty
Double	2
Twin	
Single	
Bed Size	**Qty**
King	
Queen	2
Double	
Single	3
Bathrooms	**Qty**
Ensuite	
Private	1
Guest Share	

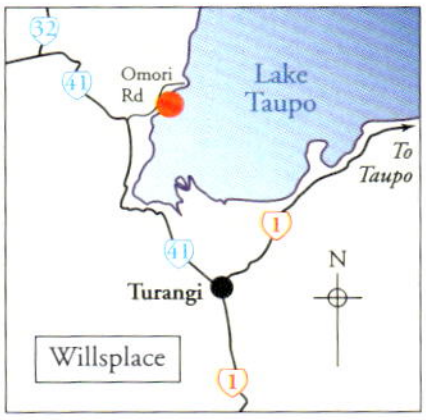

DIRECTIONS: From Turangi take SH 41. After 14 km turn right into Omori Road. Drive 2.5 km towards lake, small uphill climb, 2nd house on right.

Our home overlooks the lake in the beautiful southwest corner of Lake Taupo. Just off the beaten track, yet only 10-15 min. to Tokaanu hot thermal pools, Tongariro River and Turangi town. Forty min. to Tongariro National Park and ski fields. We offer you a superior, comfortable, spacious two bedroom suite with your own entry. Separate living area with tea-making facilities, refrigerator, microwave, TV, books and games to enjoy. A full-sized bathroom with bath and shower. Laundry available. Start the day with a substantial breakfast. After your day's activities sample Turangi's restaurants, or with prior arrangement, come home to a delicious home-cooked meal. Omori is a special place that we would love to share with you.

Anaura Bay - Eastland ▶ YOUR HOSTS: Judy and David Newell Ph: (021) 633 372

RANGIMARIE BEACHSTAY

930 Anaura Road, Anaura Bay, East Coast
Fax (06) 868 9340, Mobile 021-633 372
email: *anaurastay@xtra.co.nz*
www.anaura-stay.co.nz

Features & Attractions

- *Beach front accommodation*
- *Gisborne Airport pick-ups*
- *Special dietary needs catered for*
- *Sensational views*
- *Bush walks*
- *Peaceful retreat*

Beachstay Bed & Breakfast
Self-contained cottage

Double	$90-160
Single	$70-140
Child	neg

Rangimarie covers 1.5 acres, sweeping down to a white, sandy beach and is bordered on one side by a native bush reserve. All suites have private decks with sensational views of the Bay and sunrises. Guests enjoy relaxing in time-out spots such as the secluded bush sleeping platform, the outdoor bath, or swing seat with an elevated view of the surrounds. Hosting has become a focal point in our lives. We enjoy the wonderful guests we share our 'piece or paradise' with and look forward to the frequent return visits. There are no restaurants on the Bay – we are happy to prepare lunches and dinners by prior arrangement or guests are welcome to use the outdoor cooking facilities. Sky and DVD/video players in all suites. **Rangimarie Cottage** has a large, tiled bathroom with twin showers and claw foot bath, great for winter stays, and is available for self-contained rental.

Bedrooms	Qty
Double	1
Twin	2
Single	
Bed Size	**Qty**
Super King	1
Queen	1
Double	1
Single	
Bathrooms	**Qty**
Ensuite	1
Private	2
Guest Share	

Gisborne ▶ YOUR HOSTS: Chris and Jenny Meban Free Ph: 0800 686 218

TE HAU STATION FARMSTAY

332 Te Hau Road, RD 4, Te Karaka, Whatatutu
Ph (06) 862 1822, Fax (06) 862 1997,
Mobile 021-251 4186
email: *tehaustn@xtra.co.nz,*
www.tehau.co.nz

Features & Attractions

- *5700 acres*
- *All meals available*
- *Lots of pets*
- *100 year old homestead*
- *Spa and swimming pool*
- *Children and pets welcome*

Farmstay
Bed & Breakfast

Double	$110
Single	$70
Child	half price

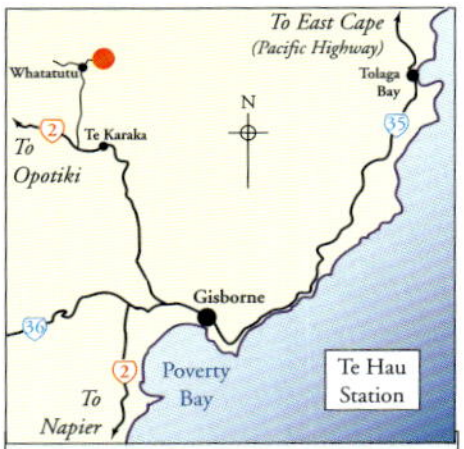

DIRECTIONS:
Please phone for simple directions.

Our 100 year old Colonial Farmhouse, on a large hill country station, is an easy forty minute drive from Gisborne, off SH 2 North. Enjoy hands-on farm experiences, learning about life on a sheep and cattle station. Watch the shepherds riding horses and expertly handling stock with their sheep dogs. Walking, clay-bird shooting and hunting are other options or choose to relax and enjoy the many facilities we have to offer. Our two young sons take pleasure in showing guests their many pets. Delicious country meals available.

Winner of Eastland Tourism 2000 Award for "Hosted Accommodation"

Bedrooms	Qty
Double	2
Twin	1
Single	
Bed Size	**Qty**
King	1
Double	2
Single	2
Bathrooms	**Qty**
Ensuite	1
Private	
Guest Share	
Family Share	1

Best Beach View

8 Tuahine Cres, Wainui, Gisborne
Ph (06) 868 9757
Mobile 021-022 60053
email: *bestbeachview@xtra.co.nz*

Tariff : N.Z. Dollars	
Double	$115
Single	$60
Child	

Bedrooms	Qty
Double	2
Twin	
Single	
Bed Size	**Qty**
Super King	
King	
Queen	2
Double	
Single	
Bathrooms	**Qty**
Ensuite	2
Private	
Guest Share	

Bed & Breakfast
Homestay

Features & Attractions

- *Good parking*
- *Quiet location*
- *Stunning sea views*
- *One of NZ's nicest beaches*
- *8 minute walk to restaurant*
- *One of NZ's best golf courses*
- *Tennis courts, horse trekking*
- *Wineries*

Annabel Reynolds, your host, welcomes you to a peaceful, comfortable and memorable stay from an elevated section, with breathtaking and panoramic views of Wainui Beach. Unwind with a swim or a walk on the beach which is right on your doorstep. Gisborne is quickly being discovered as a jewel on the East Coast. The city is beautiful with different species of palm trees lining the streets and a great selection of cuisine from excellent cafés and restaurants on the water and in the CBD.

The city has its own charm and is very beautiful with beaches and rivers running through it and surrounding it. There are wineries to visit and Eastwood Hill Arboretum is internationally recognised as having the greatest selection of oak trees in Australasia.
Gisborne is a tremendous experience and staying at Wainui Beach at Annabel's **Best Beach View B&B** will remain a special memory.

Cottage By The Sea

66 Lower Turangi Road, RD 43, Waitara, New Plymouth
Ph (06) 754 4548 or (06) 754 7915
email: *cottagebythesea@clear.net.nz*
www.cottagebythesea.co.nz

Tariff : N.Z. Dollars	
Double	$145-175
Single	$135-165
Child	neg

Bedrooms	Qty
Double	2
Twin	
Single	
Bed Size	**Qty**
Super King	
King/Single	1
Queen	1
Double	2
Single	
Bathrooms	**Qty**
Ensuite	2
Private	
Guest Share	

Spectacular Sea Views
Quiet Garden Setting

Features & Attractions

- *Total privacy, beach access*
- *Picturesque & peaceful*
- *Modern & spacious*
- *Art, crafts, museums*
- *20 min. north of New Plymouth*
- *Near golf courses, cafés*
- *Tramping, garden trails*
- *Breakfast optional extra*

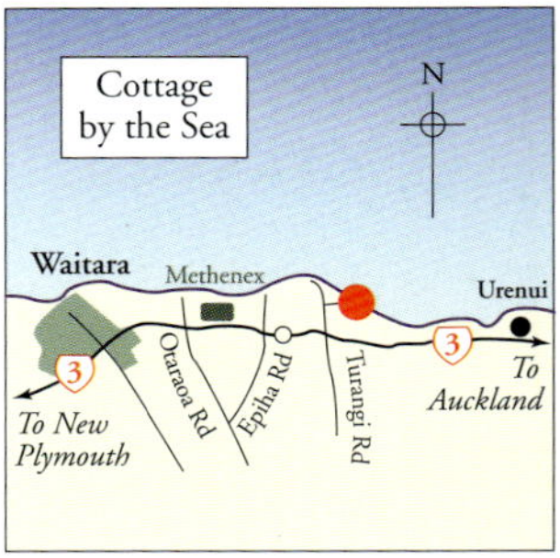

DIRECTIONS: Nearest Town: New Plymouth - about 25km north, just a 20min drive. 1/2 km off State Highway 3 between Waitara and Urenui

Sounds of the sea and a chorus of birds surround these modern cottages. Treat yourself to the magnetism that brings guests back again and again. Our property is set amongst ten acres of landscaped gardens, avocado trees and a hidden, tranquil sunken garden for you to discover. Beach access is down 100 handcrafted steps, through bush, to a black sand beach strewn with driftwood. It's a safe swimming beach and also perfect for surf-casting, tide pool exploration or long walks. Each cottage, set in its own private area, has one bedroom, bathroom with shower, lounge with a double futon sofa/bed, dining area and full-kitchen. **Seacliff Villa** has a king-size bed, breakfast bar looking out to sea, and DVD/CD player with movies. **Cottage by the Sea** has a queen-size bed, CD stereo and video player with movies. A cot is also available on request. There is one-step access to both cottages. Breakfast is an optional extra. We offer discounts for stays of six or more days. Extra adult tariff is $25 per person – no charge for infants. Regrettably the property is not suitable for children. Two new studio units will open in January 2007.

Hideaway Cottage

231 Henwood Road, Bell Block, New Plymouth
Ph (06) 755 1360, Fax (06) 755 1361
Mobile 027-212 7099
email: *donrobyn@xtra.co.nz*
www.hideawaycottage.co.nz

Tariff : N.Z. Dollars	
Double	$275
Single	$250
Child	

Bedrooms	Qty
Double	1
Twin	
Single	
Bed Size	**Qty**
Super King	
King	
Queen	1
Double	
Single	
Bathrooms	**Qty**
Ensuite	1
Private	
Guest Share	

MasterCard VISA

BA **Boutique Accommodation**
Luxury Bed & Breakfast SC

DIRECTIONS:
Please telephone for easy directions.

Features & Attractions

- *Peaceful and secluded*
- *Sumptous breakfast*
- *Free airport pickup*
- *BBQ available*
- *Just 3 min. from SH3*
- *5 golf courses within 10min.*
- *10 min. to city or surf*
- *20 min. to Mt Taranaki*

If privacy, tranquility and centrality are high on your list of holiday accommodation requirements, follow the tree-lined path to **Hideaway Cottage**. Just ten minutes north of New Plymouth, but a world away from the bustling city, the cottage is tucked away in an established Bell Block country garden overlooking a native forest valley. **Hideaway Cottage** is both very private and exceptionally comfortable and well appointed (complete with DVD movies available and 29-inch TV). Hosts Don and Robyn Johnson offer a free airport pick-up and spoil guests with a complimentary bottle of wine each night to be enjoyed beside the solar-heated pool, or as the season dictates, tucked up in front of a roaring log fire or soaking in the outdoor spa pool. A 'Honeymooners Paradise'.
A sumptuous breakfast, often featuring the produce from the property's extensive avocado orchard, is delivered to your doorstep – fuel for a day of sightseeing, fishing, golfing, tramping or simply savouring the hideaway atmosphere.

93 By the Sea

93 Buller Street, New Plymouth
Ph (06) 758 6555, Mobile 025-230 3887
email: *pat@93bythesea.co.nz*
www.93bythesea.co.nz

Tariff : N.Z. Dollars	
Double	$130-160
Single	$100-130
Child	

Bedrooms	Qty
Double	2
Twin	1
Single	
Bed Size	**Qty**
Super King	1
King	
Queen	1
Twin/Single	1
Single	
Bathrooms	**Qty**
Ensuite	1
Private	1
Guest Share	

Boutique Bed & Breakfast

Features & Attractions

- *Central yet peaceful*
- *Off-street parking*
- *Ensuite or private spa bathroom*
- *Private guest entrance*
- *On the Coastal Walkway*
- *National Park nearby*
- *Dinner by prior arrangement*
- *Laundry facilities available*

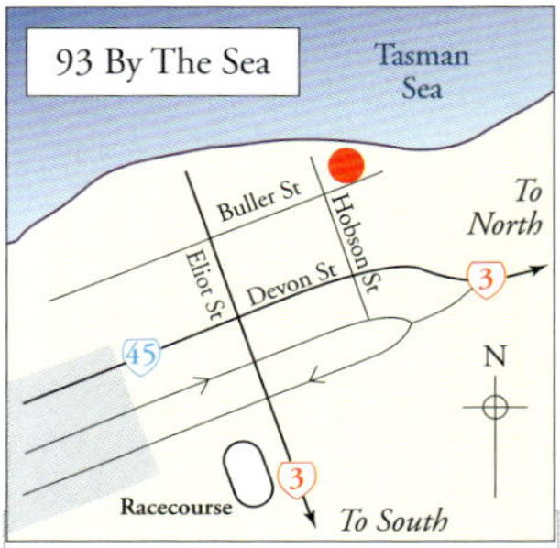

DIRECTIONS:
Please phone for easy directions.

We are ideally centrally situated near the award-winning 7 kilometre Coastal Walkway, leading from the mountain-fed river mouth to sea-port, past a golf course, beaches, cliffs, city centre, amenities and parks. **93 By the Sea** is a supremely comfortable, revitalised 1930's bungalow within easy walking distance to shops, restaurants, riverways, beaches and gardens. Choose either the **Gingkho Room** with a spacious lounge, private bathroom with spa bath, or the **Rimu Room**, totally cosy with ensuite, sea outlook and gas fire. Neither will disappoint. Enjoy my especially prepared sumptuous breakfasts in the north-facing dining area (in or outside) that treats you to lovely views of Bruce's garden and surf and swimming beaches bordering the everchanging Tasman Sea. This is also a relaxingly wonderful spot to enjoy that evening moment Let us spoil you! Cheers, Pat.

"The sound of waves upon the shore,
The smell of roses by the door,
A spa to ease the muscles sore,
Who could ask for anything more?"
Dale Cameron, Auckland

Glen Almond House

18C Glen Almond Street, New Plymouth
Ph (06) 758 2920, Mobile 021-054 1555
email: *sleep@glenalmondhouse.co.nz*
www.glenalmondhouse.co.nz

Tariff : N.Z. Dollars	
Double	$100-150
Single	$90-125
Child	neg

Bedrooms	Qty
Double	2
Twin	1
Single	
Bed Size	**Qty**
Super King	
King	2
Queen	
Double	
Single	2
Bathrooms	**Qty**
Ensuite	
Private	2
Guest Share	1

Boutique Bed & Breakfast

DIRECTIONS:
From city follow SH 45 towards Oakura, along Devon Street West (1 km), turn left at Belt Road, up the hill, 50m turn right, Glen Almond St, driveway on right 100m.

Features & Attractions

- *Secluded location*
- *Balcony with sea views*
- *Aromatherapy massage*
- *Private drawing room*
- *Character house with original features*
- *10 min walk to coastal walkway*
- *Fast internet facilities*
- *Warm & friendly atmosphere*

Indulge yourself in total comfort and pleasure at **Glen Almond House**! Located minutes from the city, tucked down a private driveway with a peaceful, sunny enclosed garden and courtyard for your enjoyment. Enjoy stunning sea and city views from this fully restored historic home. Share in the elegance of a bygone era. For your comfort the residence is centrally heated and offers two generous size double bedrooms with king-size beds and a twin bedded room, all furnished with high quality linen, with two private and one shared bathrooms. The **Balcony Room** overlooks the city and coastline, enjoys all day sun, enjoy a quiet drink on the private verandah.

The **Glyndwr Room** is on the ground floor for ease of access. We are a Kiwi/Welsh couple who are well seasoned travellers and who know what is needed to make your stay memorable. We offer you our convivial company, delicious home-made breads and muffins, a choice of hearty, healthy breakfasts and more...! Anne is a London trained beauty therapist specialising in aromatherapy massage. So for total body and mind relaxation you can be pampered with a massage of your choice. Ideal after a hard day of sightseeing!

Avocado Abodes

14 Arthur Rd, RD 3 Bell Block, New Plymouth
Ph (06) 755 4123, Fax (06) 755 2296
Mobile 027-277 4520
email: *avocado.abodes@xtra.co.nz*
www.avocadoabodes.co.nz

Features & Attractions

- *Peaceful, relaxing environment*
- *Free airport transfers*
- *Under 10min. city/attractions*
- *Five golf courses 10min. away*
- *Separate, modern & spacious*
- *Set amongst avocado farm*

Modern, Boutique Self-contained Accommodation

$	
Double	$130-150
Single	$120-140
Child	

Avocado Abodes is lodging with a difference - so close to the city, but away from the hustle and bustle, set amongst a working avocado farm. Enjoy a new, completely separate, modern unit with two ensuited bedrooms, full kitchen, dining and lounge with laundry facilities. Being just minutes from five golf courses it's ideal as your Taranaki base. A haven to return to after the Rhodo festival or the province's many tourist attractions. Just the place for a romantic night or two retreat, away from it all with that someone special... You choose, it's your slice of luxury in Taranaki just waiting for you. Continental breakfast provided, cooked meals or provisions by arrangement. Discounts for long stays, group or corporate bookings.

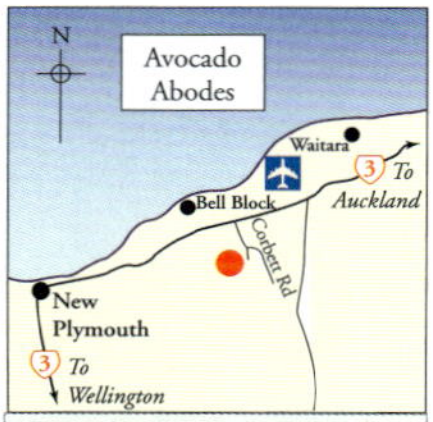

DIRECTIONS: On SH3 from airport to New Plymouth, take 1st left, Corbett Rd - 1.3km on right is Arthur Rd before railway crossing. **Avocado Abodes** is up long Row at the very end on right.

Bedrooms	Qty
Double	1
Twin	1
Single	
Bed Size	**Qty**
King	1
Queen	
Double	
King/Twin	2
Bathrooms	**Qty**
Ensuite	2
Private	
Guest Share	

New Plymouth ▶ YOUR HOSTS: **Rosemary and John Lucas** Ph (06) 755 2273

Villa Heights Bed & Breakfast

333 Upland Road, RD 2, New Plymouth, Taranaki
Ph (06) 755 2273, Mobile 027-416 4131
email: *hosts@villaheights.co.nz*
www.villaheights.co.nz

Features & Attractions

- *15 minutes to city*
- *Off-street parking*
- *Full cooked breakfast*
- *Spacious rooms with views*
- *Dinner by arrangement*
- *Internet access*

Quiet and Peaceful Setting Gracious Victorian Villa

$	
Double	$120-150
Single	$110
Child	

John and Rosemary warmly welcome you to their newly restored Victorian villa, set in lovely gardens with views of Mt. Egmont and the sea.

Spacious, quality, smoke-free accommodation with private entrance. Guest lounge with tea and coffee facilities and fresh home-baking. Full breakfast. Open fires in winter. Off-street parking. Evening meal by arrangement with complimentary wine. Special rates for more than one night. Free pick-up from airport and bus terminal.

We are just fifteen minutes away from New Plymouth City, beaches, golf courses, beautiful gardens, restaurants and the lovely coastal walkway. Egmont National Park is just a thirty minute drive away.

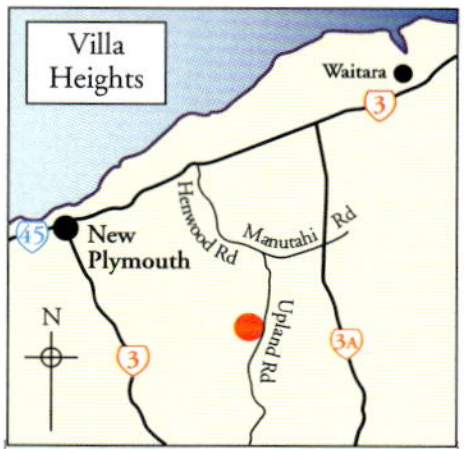

DIRECTIONS: For easy directions please phone 06-755 2273.

Bedrooms	Qty
Double	2
Twin	1
Single	
Bed Size	**Qty**
King	
Queen	2
Double	
Single	2
Bathrooms	**Qty**
Ensuite	2
Private	
Family Share	1

HATHAWAY HOUSE

3500 Mountain Road, RD 24, Stratford
Ph (06) 765 4189 , Fax (06) 765 0437
Mobile 027-450 1723
email: *hathawayhouse@xtra.co.nz*

Features & Attractions

- *Superior accommodation*
- *Close to shops & skifield*
- *Peaceful country setting*
- *Excellent meals available*
- *Historic 1890's homestead*
- *Warm, friendly welcome*

$	
Double	$110-160
Single	$100-140
Child	

Country Homestay

Bedrooms	Qty
Double	3
Twin	
Single	
Bed Size	**Qty**
King	
Queen	4
Double	1
Single	
Bathrooms	**Qty**
Ensuite	2
Private	1
Guest Share	

Hathaway House in Stratford is one of Taranaki's landmark historic houses which was built as a "Gentleman's Residence"in the 1890's and offers superior accommodation for the discerning corporate or touring visitor. Two large queen sized bedrooms with ensuites are available with television and quality lounge furniture for visitors who seek privacy and comfort. A third bedroom with shared bathroom facilities is also available – all guests are very welcome to use the house lounge and enjoy conversation with Bert and his staff and experience the unique ambience of a Kiwi Bed & Breakfast. **Hathaway House** is situated on five picturesque hectares with a lake in the foreground and the mighty mountain in the background. Only a short distance from Stratford, gorgeous parks and native busy walkways, or an easy drive to New Plymouth and the Mt Taranaki skifield. The house is ideally situated for the sightseeing visitor or the business traveller.

DIRECTIONS: Western side of SH 3, approx 800m north of Stratford town boundary. 200m north of Stallard Farm. Look for our sign opposite 'Sheepskin Shop' sign.

TE POPO GARDENS

636 Stanley Road, RD 24, Stratford, Taranaki
Ph (06) 762 8775, Fax (06) 762 8775
email: *tepopo@clear.net.nz*
www.tepopo.co.nz

Features & Attractions

- *Private suites in guest wing*
- *Fine food and wines*
- *Taranaki, a gardeners' paradise*
- *Beautiful environment*
- *Famous for its birds*
- *Wonderful wood fires*

DIRECTIONS:
Please phone for easy directions or download from our website for easy access from SH 3 or SH 43.

$	
Double	$150-190
Single	$120-140
Child	

Country Garden Retreat Bed & Breakfast

Bedrooms	Qty
Double	2
Twin	2
Single	
Bed Size	**Qty**
Super King	1
King	2
Queen	1
Single	2
Bathrooms	**Qty**
Ensuite	4
Private	
Guest Share	

This natural environment is a special place – secluded, quiet and idyllic. **Te Popo Gardens** is a 'Garden of National Significance' – a large rural woodland garden and park merging imperceptibly into old growth forest that clothes the 20m deep ravines encircling the property. The Homestead's guest wing has 4 spacious suites, each with ensuite, wood-fire, sound system, TV, superior beds/linen and private access to the garden. Enjoy fine food and wine – special breakfast, in the sunny conservatory, and dinner (by arrangement). Self-catering available. We offer you warm hospitality and every comfort to enjoy your stay. Wonderful dogs. Explore Mt Taranaki and surrounding activities including great golf courses and gardens. Easily accessible from the 'Forgotten World Highway' (SH43) – to/from Taupo.

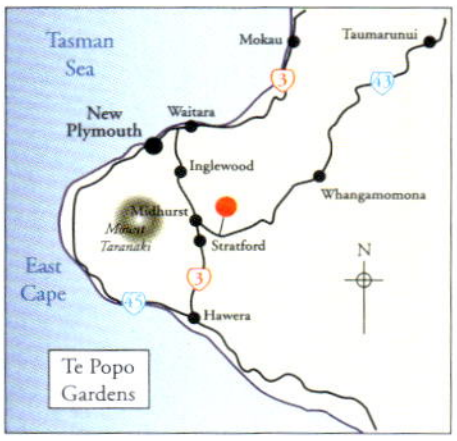

FERNLEAF

58 Tunanui Road, RD 1, Owhango, Taumarunui
Ph (07) 895 4847, Fax (07) 895 4837
Mobile 027-285 1441
email: *fernleaf.farm@xtra.co.nz*
www.travelwise.co.nz

Tariff : N.Z. Dollars	
Double	$110
Single	$85
Child	neg

Bedrooms	Qty
Double	3
Twin	
Single	1
Bed Size	**Qty**
Super King	
King	
Queen	2
Double	1
Single	2
Bathrooms	**Qty**
Ensuite	
Private	2
Guest Share	1

Bed & Breakfast
Farmstay

Features & Attractions

- *Beautiful country setting*
- *Ruapehu skifields*
- *Midway Auckland/Wellington*
- *Pet lambs in season*
- *Dinner by arrangement*
- *Enjoy our friendly pets*
- *Log fire in winter*
- *Stroll across the farm*

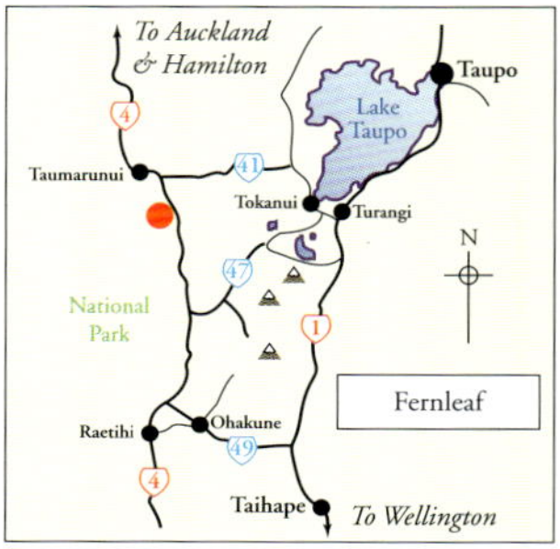

Relax in the tranquil Tunanui Valley midway between Auckland and Wellington. Just 500m from SH 4, close for convenience, far enough away for peace and quiet.

We are the third generation to farm **Fernleaf** and our Romney flock has been recorded for eighty years. The views from various vantage points are awesome, taking in the mountains Ruapehu, Ngaruahoe, Tongariro and in the far distance Taranaki.

Enjoy our generous country hospitality, wonderful breakfasts, our beautiful dalmatian and friendly cats. Dinner by arrangement.

Forest Lodge Cottages/Motel

13 Omaki Road, P O Box 101, Owhango
Ph (07) 895 4773
email: *forest.lodge@xtra.co.nz*
www.forest-lodge.co.nz

Features & Attractions

- *Quiet country village*
- *Tongariro/Whanganui NPs*
- *Breakfast optional*
- *Scenic walks/trout fishing*
- *Ruapehu ski fields/LOTR-tours*
- *Midway Auckland-Wellington*

$	
Double	$65-120
Single	$50-80
Child	neg

Bed & Breakfast
Self-contained Accommodation

Bedrooms	Qty
Double	4
Twin	2
Single	
Bed Size	**Qty**
King	
Queen	2
Double	2
Single	4
Bathrooms	**Qty**
Ensuite	1
Private	2
Guest Share	2

Nestled in a quiet country village, away from the main road and surrounded by native bush and bird life, the accommodation is modern, warm and comfortable. You'll find electric blankets, double duvets and heating in all rooms. Large decking, dining and lounge with all day sun.
Beautiful bush walks, tramps, trips to the 'Forgotten Highway', guided 'Lord of the Rings' tours in Tongariro National Park. 25 min. Mt Ruapehu, Tongariro National Park, skiing, Tongariro Crossing 45 min. Whanganui National Park, 1-5 day canoe trips, jet boating. Home of 42nd Traverse, mountain biking. World-class trout fishing in 30 local rivers and lakes. Swimming, rafting, horse-riding. Mountain bike hire, quad bikes, fishing gear, skiis. BBQ. Guides available.
Drop-off and pick up – hotel, dairy, café. Half way Auckland – Wellington.

Mountain Heights Lodge

State Highway 4, PO Box 43,
Tongariro National Park Village
Ph (07) 892 2833, Fax (07) 892 2850
email: *mountainheights@xtra.co.nz*
www.mountainheights.co.nz

Features & Attractions

- *Private guest wing*
- *Tongariro Crossing*
- *Hot spa*
- *15 minutes to ski fields*
- *Spacious, self contained accomm*
- *Delicious breakfasts*

$	
Double	$100-150
Single	$80-100
Child	neg

Bed & Breakfast
Self-contained Accomm.

Bedrooms	Qty
Double	3
Twin	3
Single	
Bed Size	**Qty**
King	
Queen	2
Double	3
Single	4
Bathrooms	**Qty**
Ensuite	4
Private	
Guest Share	2

Mountain Heights is situated on the edge of Tongariro National Park, a World Heritage Area. An ideal place from which to explore the mountains and volcanoes of the Central Plateau. Activities abound for all abilities, including the world renowned **Tongariro Crossing**, classed as the best one-day walk in New Zealand. Excellent mountain bike rides, horse trekking, canoeing the Whanganui River and scenic flights across the volcanoes.
For the less strenuous, enjoy the comfort of our centrally heated lodge. Soak in the hot spa or relax in front of the log fire with a good book or a game of chess. After a good night's sleep enjoy a delicious breakfast with freshly baked bread.

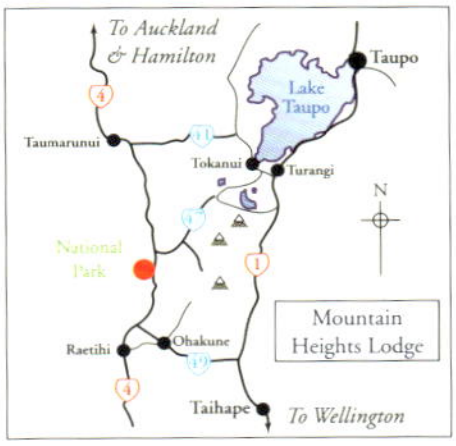

Spiral Gardens

Raurimu Road, RD 1, Owhango, Raurimu
Ph (07) 892 2997, Fax (07) 892 2653
Mobile 027-475 3482
email: *spiralgardens@xtra.co.nz*

Tariff : N.Z. Dollars	
Double	$110-130
Single	$95-110
Child	$20-30

Bedrooms	Qty
Double	4
Twin	
Single	
Bed Size	**Qty**
Super King	
King	
Queen	3
Double	4
Single	
Bathrooms	**Qty**
Ensuite	2
Private	1
Guest Share	

Homestay - Bed & Breakfast & Self-contained Cabin

Features & Attractions

- *Location, Location, Location*
- *Skiing, golf, tramping*
- *Discover hidden treasures*
- *Dinner by arrangement*
- *Central to activities/attractions*
- *Fishing, hunting, biking*
- *Families welcome*
- *Vegetarians catered for*

Our home overlooks the Piopiotea Stream and a magnificent stand of native bush. We are five minutes north of National Park Village, gateway to the Tongariro and Whanganui National Parks. The Whakapapa ski area is a 25 minute drive. Transport to the world renowned Tongariro Crossing day walk is available at National Park Village. We can organise any of the adventure activities on offer in the Central Plateau area, horse treks, river rafting, guided hunting and fishing tours. Our luxury suites feature a queen bed, ensuite or private bathroom, a double bed settee, casual chairs and table, writing bureau and refrigerator.

We have central heating throughout in winter. Coffee and tea making facilities are on hand for guest use in our family kitchen and we encourage you to use the lounge and decks in casual relaxation. The cabin is small and cosy with a pot belly fire, stereo, television, private deck and carport and self-catering.

Tarata Fishaway

Mokai Road, Mokai Valley, RD 3, Taihape
Ph (06) 388 0354, Fax (06) 388 0954
Mobile 027-279 7037
email: *fishaway@xtra.co.nz*
www.tarata.co.nz

Tariff : N.Z. Dollars	
Double	$120-180
Single	$60-90
Child	half price

Bedrooms	Qty
Double	6
Twin	4
Single	
Bed Size	**Qty**
King	4
Queen	5
Double	1
King Single	4
Bathrooms	**Qty**
Ensuite	4
Private	1
Guest Share	1
Spa Bath	1

DIRECTIONS: Central North Island – Turn off SH 1, 6 km south of Taihape, at the Gravity Canyon Bungy and Ohotu signs. Follow signs for 14 km to the Bungy Bridge. We are 6 km past here on Mokai Road.

F

Fishingstay-Farmstay- B&B
River Retreat-Honeymoon Suite

LA

Features & Attractions

- *Trout fishing and scenic rafting*
- *Visit LOTR, Middle Earth*
- *6km past Bungy & Flying Fox*
- *'Mini' Golf (with a difference)*
- *Swimming & spa pool*
- *Bush walks & spotlight safaris*
- *Camp outs*
- *Clay-bird shooting*

We are very lucky to have a piece of New Zealand's natural beauty. **Tarata** is nestled in bush in the remote Mokai Valley where the picturesque Rangitikei River meets the rugged Ruahine Ranges. With the wilderness and unique trout fishing right at our doorstep, it is the perfect environment to bring up our three children. Stephen offers guided fishing and rafting trips for all ages. Raft down the gentle crystal clear waters of the magnificent Rangitikei River, visit Middle Earth and a secret waterfall, stunning scenery you will never forget. Our spacious home with guest bedrooms and our large garden allow guests private space to relax and unwind. Whether it is by the pool on a hot summer's day with a book, soaking in the spa pool after a day on the river or enjoying a cosy winter's night in front of our open fire with a glass of wine. Come on a farm tour meeting our many friendly farm pets and experience our 'nightlife' on our free spotlight safari. Stay in our homestead or in **Tarata's** fully self-contained 'River Retreats' where you can enjoy a spa bath with 'million dollar views' of the river and relax on the large decking amidst native birds and trees. Peace, privacy and tranquillity at its best! We will even deliver a candle light dinner to your door. Approved pets welcome. We think **Tarata** is truly a magic place and we would love sharing it with you.

Mangaweka ▶ YOUR HOSTS: Virginia and Neil Travers Ph (06) 382 5726

Mt Huia

906 Ruahine Road, Mangaweka
Ph (06) 382 5726, Fax (06) 382 5776
email: *info@mthuia.co.nz*
www.mthuia.co.nz

Features & Attractions

- *Midway Rotorua – Wellington*
- *9 km from SH1*
- *Peaceful and scenic*
- *Large country garden*
- *3-course dinner*
- *Many local attractions*

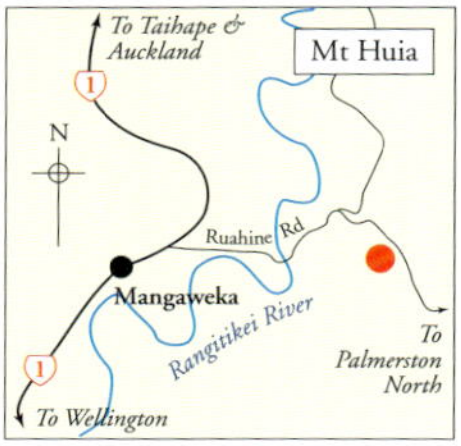

Sheep and Cattle Farm
Dinner, Bed & Breakfast

$	
Double	$240
Single	$150
Child	n/a

A 10 minute drive from SH1 takes you to an area of unique scenery around this authentic sheep and cattle hill country farm. Enjoy refreshments on the sunny verandah or spacious deck, overlooking the attractive garden and stands of native bush.

If time allows, Neil can take you on a 4-wheel drive tour of the farm, or you may prefer to follow the marked farm walk for some fresh air and exercise. Renowned golf courses, gardens, hiking trails and adventure activities all close by. Personal attention is guaranteed in a friendly, relaxed environment, where even Jessie, the dog, will be pleased to see you! Meals are of a high standard using plenty of farm and fresh produce. Prior booking essential.

Bedrooms	Qty
Double	1
Twin	
Single	
Bed Size	**Qty**
King	
Queen	
Double	1
Single	
Bathrooms	**Qty**
Ensuite	1
Private	
Guest Share	

Mahia Peninsula ▶ YOUR HOSTS: Louise Schick Ph: (06) 837 5898

Reomoana

629 Mahanga Road, RD 8, Nuhaka, Hawke's Bay
Ph (06) 837 5898, Fax (06) 837 5990
email: *reomoana@paradise.net.nz*
www.reomoana.co.nz

Features & Attractions

- *Panoramic ocean view*
- *Morere Hot Springs*
- *Mahia Scenic Reserve*
- *Safe, white sandy beaches*
- *Fishing charters arranged*
- *Sunset Point Restaurant 6 km*

DIRECTIONS:
Please phone for easy directions

Coastal Bed & Breakfast
Self-contained Unit

$	
Double	$120
Single	$60
Child	$20

Welcome to **Reomoana** – the voice of the sea. Pacific Oceanfront farm at beautiful Mahanga Beach on the Mahia Peninsula, the spacious, rustic home with Hungarian and New Zealand creativity makes this a home of character, with cathedral ceilings and hand-carved furniture. Breathtaking views to the Pacific Ocean. Come and relax and bring your paints - the area is a painter's paradise. Enjoy the miles of white sandy beaches. Go swimming, surfing, fishing or discover the unique rocky reefs of Mahia. Lake Waikaremoana in the Urewera National Park can be enjoyed as a day trip – or visit Mahia's Scenic Reserve. 'Sunset Point Restaurant' is 6 km away or else dinner may be served by prior arrangement. **Reomoana** is one hour south of Gisborne or 2¼ hours north of Napier. **Cottage** is available in avocado orchard – ideal for families – self-contained.

Bedrooms	Qty
Double	2
Twin	
Single	1
Bed Size	**Qty**
King	
Queen	2
Double	
Single	1
Bathrooms	**Qty**
Ensuite	1
Private	1
Guest Share	

YOUR HOSTS: **Robert McGregor** Ph: (06) 835 7434 **Napier**

A Room With A View

9 Milton Terrace, Napier
Ph (06) 835 7434, Fax (06) 835 1912
email: *roomwithview@xtra.co.nz*

Features & Attractions

- *Spectacular view*
- *Central location*
- *Fourth generation property*
- *Internet available*
- *Art deco expertise*
- *My home is your home*

$	
Double	$100
Single	$70
Child	n/a

Homestay Bed & Breakfast

Bedrooms	Qty
Double	1
Twin	
Single	
Bed Size	**Qty**
King	
Queen	1
Double	
Single	
Bathrooms	**Qty**
Ensuite	
Private	1
Guest Share	

Having home-hosted for ten years with my late wife, I'm continuing to enjoy conversation and laughter with guests from the world over. My two-storeyed home on the sunny side of the Napier Hill is set in a large 100-year-old garden. Breakfast can be served in the dining room or in the generous guest room where you can enjoy the 180° view over Hawke Bay and parts of Napier to the distant Ruahine Mountains. It's only a fifteen minute walk to our world-famous Art Deco city centre or the historic port area, at both of which there are many excellent restaurants. I'm interested in travel, gardening, the arts and especially local history, as I am Executive Director of the Art Deco Trust. Other amenities include television, tea making facilities in your room, separate bath and shower, free laundry facilities, free pick-up service and off-street parking.

DIRECTIONS: From Marine Parade take Tennyson Street, Milton Road, veer left into Milton Terrace. More detailed instructions via email.

YOUR HOSTS: **Janet Tinney and Wayne Huntley** Ph: (06) 842 1116 **Napier**

Broughton House

383 Kennedy Road, Napier
Ph (06) 842 1116, Mobile 027-491 1169
email: *broughtonhouse@xtra.co.nz*
www.broughtonhouse.co.nz

Features & Attractions

- *Superb hospitality*
- *Swimming pool*
- *Off-street parking*
- *5 min from Napier's art deco city*
- *Private guest wing with separate entrance*
- *Handy to beaches & wineries*

$	
Double	$120
Single	$80
Child	neg

Quality Bed & Breakfast Accommodation

Bedrooms	Qty
Double	2
Twin	
Single	
Bed Size	**Qty**
King	
Queen	1
Double	1
Single	
Bathrooms	**Qty**
Ensuite	2
Private	
Guest Share	

Janet and Wayne of **Broughton House** welcome you to relax in their peaceful, friendly home. Our private guest wing is beautifully furnished with country-style décor and offers all the extra touches that you would expect to find in quality accommodation. Our two guest rooms each have an ensuite bathroom, tea and coffee making facilities, television, bath robes, hair dryer and complimentary toiletries and confectionery, along with freshly picked flowers and magazines to browse through at your leisure.

We offer both continental and cooked breakfast, including when available, home-baked muffins and fresh produce from our garden. After a day's sightseeing in the beautiful Hawke's Bay you can relax with a glass of wine by the pool or take a stroll around our cottage garden. We pride ourselves on our superior hospitality and attention to detail, which makes **Broughton House** so special.

Napier YOUR HOSTS: **Rayma and Phillip Jenkins** Free Ph: 0800 426 233

Cobden Garden Homestay

1 Cobden Crescent, Bluff Hill, Napier
Ph (06) 834 2090, Fax (06) 834 1977
Mobile 025-540 062,
email: *info@cobden.co.nz*
www.cobden.co.nz

Features & Attractions

- *Quiet, private surroundings*
- *Extensive views*
- *Guest computer provided*
- *10 minute walk to city centre*
- *Guest laundry facilities*
- *Off-road parking & easy access*

Boutique Homestay Bed & Breakfast

Double	$150-190
Single	$130-170
Child	$50

We invite you to stay in our quiet, sunny colonial villa on Bluff Hill. Relax in a spacious room with ensuite. Feel pampered in king or twin single beds with fine cotton linen, duvets, electric blankets, plump pillows and robes. Enjoy lounge seating, TV, heater, fan, tea/coffee making facilities and complimentary refreshments in your room. Unwind with a walk around our ½ acre garden or take in the view from our verandah, guest lounge or upstairs sunroom. Prior to indulging your taste-buds at a local restaurant join us on the verandah or in the lounge for complimentary tasting of local wine and produce. Choose your breakfast from our menu of local foods and home-made delights. We make every effort to make your stay extra special and memorable. When booking, please advise of any special dietary requirements. Two unobtrusive cats in residence.

Bedrooms	Qty
Double	3
Twin	
Single	
Bed Size	**Qty**
Super King	2
King	1
Double	
Single	5
Bathrooms	**Qty**
Ensuite	3
Private	
Guest Share	

Napier YOUR HOSTS: **Christine Grouden and Graham Storer** Free Ph: 0800 624 766

Maison Béarnaise Bed & Breakfast

25 France Road, Bluff Hill, Napier
Ph (06) 835 4693, Fax (06) 835 4694
email: *chrisgraham@xtra.co.nz*

Features & Attractions

- *Single level*
- *Colourful patio garden*
- *Gannet colony experience*
- *Walk to art deco city centre*
- *Wineries - restaurants & tastings*
- *Golf, walks, trout fishing nearby*

Quality Homestay Bed & Breakfast

Double	$155
Single	$110
Child	

A warm invitation to share our charming oasis of ever changing gardens - for as long as you need - our door is open 365 days a year. Christine, Napier born, happily assists with local and national sightseeing suggestions. Both large guest rooms are privately appointed with ensuite bathrooms, have comfortable queen beds, electric blankets, hairdryers, tea/coffee making facilities and DVD television. Email access is available in the light and airy guest lounge, or you may prefer to curl up with a book, newspaper or magazine. The sunny private courtyard provides the opportunity to relax and savour the delicious breakfast choices including homemade and local produce. Napier city centre is a ten minute walk away and the historic suburb of Ahuriri, with many fine eateries, is two minutes drive away. Off-street parking, courtesy transfers and laundry service available. Welcome, unwind we want you to feel at home.

DIRECTIONS: North on Marine Parade. Left Coote Road. Right Thompson Road. Left France Road (first driveway on left).

Bedrooms	Qty
Double	2
Twin	
Single	
Bed Size	**Qty**
King	
Queen	2
Double	
Single	
Bathrooms	**Qty**
Ensuite	2
Private	
Guest Share	

Kerry Lodge

7 Forward Street, Greenmeadows, Napier
Ph (06) 844 9630, Fax (06) 844 1450
Mobile 025-932 874
email: *kerrylodge@xtra.co.nz*
www.kerrylodge.co.nz

Tariff : N.Z. Dollars	
Double	$120-180
Single	$90
Child	$45

Bedrooms	Qty
Double/Twin	3
Twin	
Single	
Bed Size	**Qty**
Super King/Twin	2
King	1
Queen	1
Double	
Single	
Bathrooms	**Qty**
Ensuite	1
Private	1
Guest Share	

Bed & Breakfast
Homestay

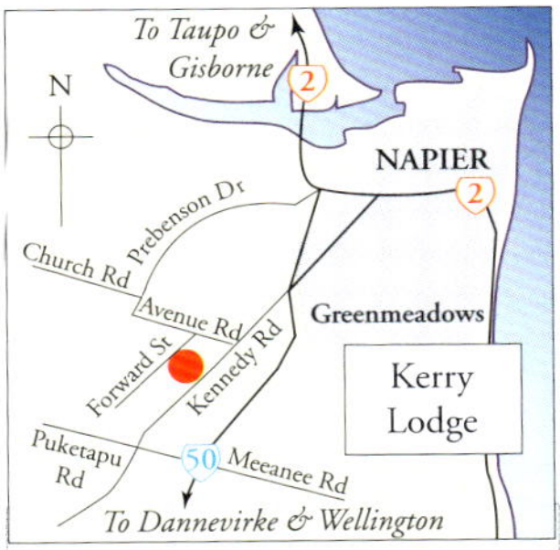

DIRECTIONS: From Napier, travel along Kennedy Road & Gloucester Street until Greenmeadows, turn right into Avenue Rd, then left into Forward Street

Features & Attractions

- *Spacious rooms*
- *Quiet location*
- *Off-street parking*
- *Wheel chair accessible*
- *Tranquil, spacious gardens*
- *Caring, informative hosts*
- *Close to wineries, restaurants*
- *Laundry available*

Within walking distance to restaurants, shops and wineries. Set in spacious, tranquil gardens, we invite our guests to share the warmth and comfort of our home. From the large comfy beds, the 24 hour complimentary refreshments, television, relaxing spa , refreshing swimming pool and patio area, to the scrumptious breakfast, which includes locally grown produce and home-made conserves, your satisfaction is our pleasure. Let us help plan your time in Napier over a coffee and share with you some of our natural treasures. We're happy to drive you to your evenings restaurant, make reservations and help make your time in Napier memorable.

The **Garden Cottage**: Our new 2-bedroom, self-contained cottage, with fully equipped kitchen, dishwasher, laundry and large spa bath, offers an alternative accommodation style for minimum 2 night stays. A continental breakfast is included.

 YOUR HOSTS: **Catherine and Evert van Florenstein** Ph: (06) 835 0202

Seaview Lodge

5 Seaview Terrace, Napier
Ph (06) 835 0202, Fax (06) 835 0202
Mobile 021-180 2101
email: *cvulodge@xtra.co.nz*
www.aseaviewlodge.co.nz

Features & Attractions

- *Overlooking Pacific Ocean*
- *3 min walk to city centre*
- *Across from heated pools*
- *Quiet, elevated location*
- *Off-street parking*
- *Quality bed linen*

Quality, Central City Bed & Breakfast

Double	$130-160
Single	$100-120
Child	n/a

Seaview Lodge is a lovingly renovated, spacious late Victorian home. This inner city, beachside Bed & Breakfast offers a warm welcome and spectacular views over the city and ocean. Enjoy your continental breakfast of fresh croissants and fruit salad on the lower verandah while watching the waves break on the shore. At the end of the day relax in the comfortable guest lounge or on the large upstairs balcony and enjoy a glass of local wine while watching the sun set.
A spacious single and a double room share the large guest lounge with TV and tea/coffee making facilities. The other double/twin room has its own lounge area including TV. All rooms are stylishly furnished and show attention to detail.

Bedrooms	Qty
Double	1
Twin	1
Single	1
Bed Size	**Qty**
SuperKing/Twin	1
King	1
Queen	
King/Single	1
Bathrooms	**Qty**
Ensuite	1
Private	2
Guest Share	

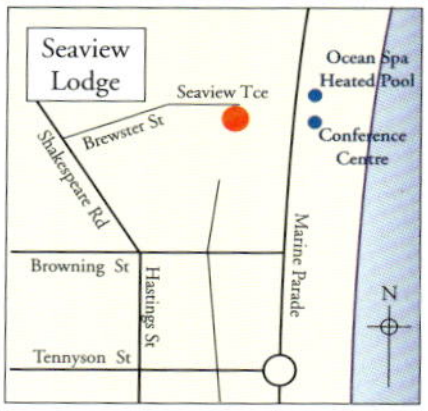

 YOUR HOSTS: **Kay and Stewart Spence** Free Ph: 0800 117 890

Spence Homestay

17 Cobden Road, Napier
Ph (06) 835 9454, Fax (06) 835 9454
email: *ksspence@actrix.gen.nz*

Features & Attractions

- *Guest suite and garden patio*
- *Art deco walk and museum*
- *Visit gannet colony*
- *Close to Napier City Centre*
- *Wineries tasting and lunch*
- *Visit excellent gardens*

Quality Homestay Bed & Breakfast

Double	$140
Single	$95-100
Child	

Welcome to our comfortable, quality, new home, with a touch of the Mediterranean, situated on Napier's Bluff Hill. Quiet area, 10-15 minute walk from the Art Deco city centre. Guest suite opening onto patio and attractive walled garden with petanque court. Lounge includes double bed settee, TV, tea-making, refrigerator, microwave. The bedroom has a queen and a single bed, for those requiring a twin room and a well appointed ensuite bathroom. From the breakfast area upstairs take in the panoramic views.
Napier, Hawke's Bay is a great place to be and we hope it will be for you. We have hosted for over ten years and enjoy overseas travel. Able to meet public transport.

Bedrooms	Qty
Double	1
Twin	
Single	
Bed Size	**Qty**
King	
Queen	1
Double	
Single	1
Bathrooms	**Qty**
Ensuite	1
Private	
Guest Share	

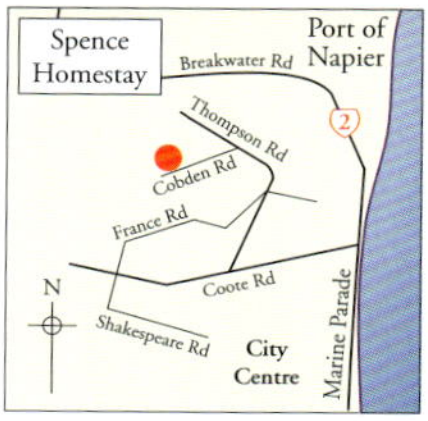

DIRECTIONS: Port end Marine Parade, Coote Road, right into Thompson Rd, left into Cobden Rd, opposite water tower.

The Green House On The Hill

18B Milton Oaks, Milton Road, Napier
Ph (06) 835 4475, Fax (06) 835 4475
Mobile 021-187 3827
email: *ruth@the-green-house.co.nz*
www.the-green-house.co.nz

Features & Attractions

- *Friendly, relaxed atmosphere*
- *Central, yet peaceful location*
- *Art Deco Napier 5 min. away*
- *Free email access*
- *Laundry facilities*
- *Off-street parking*

$	
Double	$110-130
Single	$80-90
Child	neg

Vegetarian Bed & Breakfast

Bedrooms	Qty
Double	3
Twin	
Single	
Bed Size	**Qty**
King	
Queen	3
Double	
Single	1
Bathrooms	**Qty**
Ensuite	1
Private	
Guest Share	1

Our home is situated on a hillside in quiet woodland only 5 minutes walk from the heart of 'Art Deco' Napier. We offer a friendly and peaceful base for your visit to Hawkes Bay. All rooms have TV, radio, bathrobes, toiletries, hairdryer, magazines, tea/coffee and snacks. I make my own bread and preserves and use local,organic produce as much as possible. I am always happy to cater for special diets, just ask! We are originally from the south west of England, have lived in New Zealand for 13 years and are happy to share our knowledge of this scenic and interesting area. There are many things to do and see in Hawkes Bay. Highlights are: Art Deco walk; gannet colony visit; wine tours; farmers market; national aquarium; great scenery…and lots more.

A stay of at least 2 nights is recommended.

Touch Th' Tide

7 Charles Street, Westshore, Napier
Ph/Fax (06) 835 7280
Mobile 027-222 9321
email: *suggy@xtra.co.nz*

Features & Attractions

- *Absolute beachfront, safe*
- *Off-street parking*
- *Email/laundry facilities*
- *Walk to village/restaurants*
- *Shuttle from airport/bus*
- *Central to tourist amenities*

$	
Double	$140
Single	$95
Child	

Absolute Beachfront Bed & Breakfast

Bedrooms	Qty
Double	2
Twin	
Single	
Bed Size	**Qty**
King	
Queen	2
Double	
Single	2
Bathrooms	**Qty**
Ensuite	
Private	
Guest Share	1

Welcome to our home, a quiet and gracious place with fine Kiwi hospitality and quality comfort. Watch the waves, the yachts, the distant port, people fishing or meandering along the reserve. Swim, then after a relaxed 'top of the morning' breakfast on the terrace soaking in the view, your hosts can help plan your day. Take a stroll along the walkways, visit the historic village of Ahuriri, which has excellent cafés and watersport facilities. Drive ten minutes to the world renowned Art Deco city, its Ocean Spa and beautiful shops. Visit the Gannet Colony, the wineries, or play golf. We are a well travelled, recently retired pharmacist and registered nurse who have lived locally for many years. We share our home with you. It includes lounge, dining room, and kitchen (for tea making). We endeavour to repay some of the wonderful hospitality we have experienced ourselves. We welcome you.

VILLA VISTA

22A France Road, Bluff Hill, Napier
Ph (06) 835 8770, Fax (06) 835 8770
Mobile 027-435 7179
email: *accommodation@villavista.net*
www.villavista.net

Tariff : N.Z. Dollars	
Double	$145-160
Single	$110-125
Child	

Bedrooms	Qty
Double	5
Twin	
Single	
Bed Size	**Qty**
Super King	
King	
Queen	4
Double	
Single	3
Bathrooms	**Qty**
Ensuite	4
Private	
Guest Share	

Bed & Breakfast and Self-contained Apartment

Features & Attractions

- *Pacific Ocean views*
- *Spacious & private bedrooms*
- *Delicious continental/cooked breakfast*
- *3 minutes drive to CBD*
- *Off-street parking*
- *Art Deco attractions*
- *Winery tours*
- *Families welcomed*

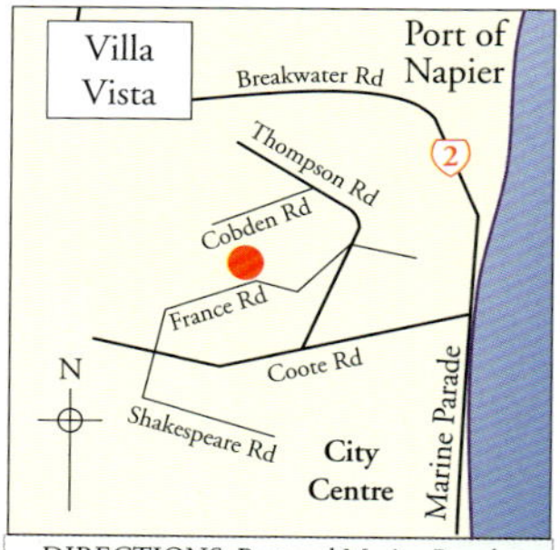

DIRECTIONS: Port end Marine Parade, Coote Road, right into Thompson Road, left into France Road, house on your right.

Villa Vista is a beautiful turn-of-the century Edwardian villa with fantastic uninterrupted views of Cape Kidnappers, Te Mata Peak and the Pacific Ocean, located 10 min. walk and 3 min. drive from the CBD. We offer 3 large, private rooms, situated on the top floor.

One double room has a balcony. Every room has delightful views, en-suite, TV, coffee/tea making facilities, air conditioning, hair dryer and bathrobes. Continental and cooked Kiwi breakfast is served in the spacious dining room. A variety of home-made delicacies will set you up for a busy or relaxing day in all that Hawke's Bay has to offer, such as wineries, Art Deco tours, gannet colonies.

Villa Vista also offers a self-contained 2 bedroom apartment with full kitchen facilities, laundry and outdoor living, where the views can also be admired. Ideally suited for families. Special discounts for stays longer than 5 nights.

~ Welcome to Napier, Hawke's Bay.

Mission Vista

359 Church Road, Greenmeadows, Napier
Ph (06) 844 5727, Fax (06) 844 5727
Mobile 027-452 0725
email: *mission.vista@xtra.co.nz*
www.missionvista.co.nz

Tariff : N.Z. Dollars	
Double	$120-150
Single	$80-100
Child	neg

Bedrooms	Qty
Double	3
Twin	1
Single	
Bed Size	**Qty**
Super King/Twin	1
King	
Queen	2
Double	1
Single	2
Bathrooms	**Qty**
Ensuite	1
Private	1
Guest Share	1

Homestay
Self-contained Apartment

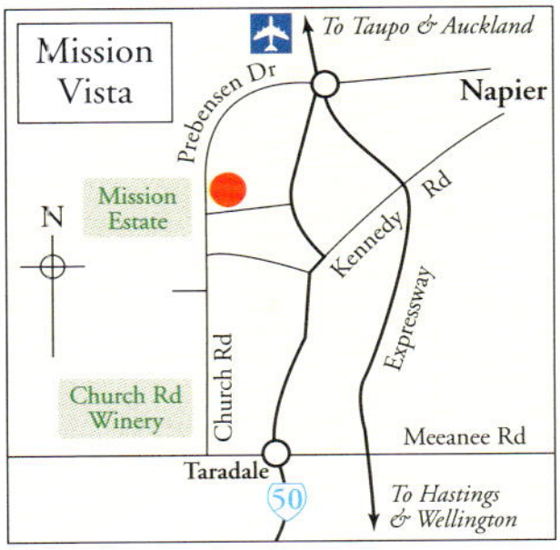

Features & Attractions

- *Personalized trips organised*
- *Halfway Napier/Hastings*
- *Cafés & restaurants nearby*
- *4 golf courses within 30 min.*
- *Pottery Ceramic Design Studio workshop on site*
- *Art deco attractions*
- *36 wineries within 30 min.*

We have a luxurious self-contained apartment, also spacious queen and twin accommodation with adjoining lounge and bathroom. All have tea and coffee making facilities. Enjoy a continental or fully cooked breakfast. Ideally situated for a Hawke's Bay getaway holiday, we are 5 min. from the airport, and 10 min. from Napier/Hastings. If needed, we will pick you up from any public transport. Fine and casual dining is available within walking distance. In close proximity are shops, golf course, garden centres and the Mission and Church Road Wineries. As we are both experienced tour guides and 4th generation Napierites, we are more than happy to organise specialized tours and to share our knowledge and love of the Bay. Our Pottery Ceramic Design Studio workshop is on site. Drop in for a chat whilst we are working, we are happy to direct you to all the things to do for a relaxed or busy holiday and help make it a great time for you to remember.

"279" Church Road

279 Church Road, Taradale, Napier
Ph (06) 844 7814, Fax (06) 844 7814
Mobile 021- 447 814
email: *sandy.279@homestaynapier.co.nz*
www.homestaynapier.co.nz

Features & Attractions

- *Quality accommodation*
- *Superb hospitality*
- *Dinner by arrangement*
- *Adjacent to wineries & restaurants*
- *Golf courses & Art Deco nearby*
- *Internet, fax, laundry available*

Quality Homestay Bed & Breakfast

Double	$120
Single	$90
Child	

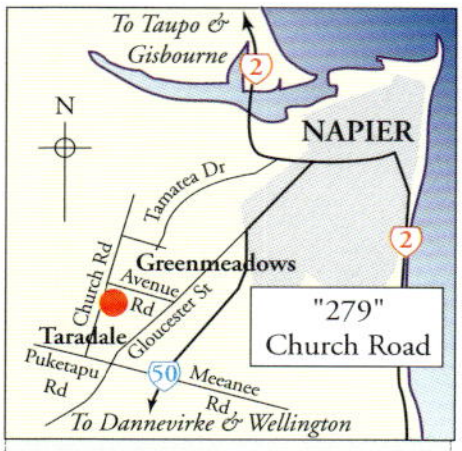

DIRECTIONS:
From Greenmeadows shops take Avenue Road to Church Road. Turn left.

"279", an elegant spacious home set in ¾ acre of gardens and trees, offers New Zealand and overseas visitors a peaceful haven to unwind from travelling or exploring the region's wineries, architecture etc. Bedrooms are located upstairs, while living areas, including lounge and games room, are downstairs. Breakfast, continental or full, is served at a time to suit you and nearby restaurants offer a variety of cuisine for evening dining.

As your host, I delight in offering relaxed and friendly hospitality, and strive to make your stay a memorable experience – my visitors book is a testament to this. I look forward to welcoming you to "279" and helping to make your stay in Hawke's Bay the highlight of your travels.

Bedrooms	Qty
Double	1
Twin	1
Single	
Bed Size	**Qty**
King	
Queen	1
Double/Twin	1
Single	
Bathrooms	**Qty**
Ensuite	
Private	
Guest Share	1

Ashcroft Garden Homestay

51 Jervois Road, Taradale, Napier
Ph (06) 844 9446, Fax (06) 844 4221
Mobile 027-441 5740
email: *croft@paradise.net.nz*
www.geocities.com/ashcroft_homestay

Tariff : N.Z. Dollars	
Double	$90-120
Single	$65
Child	neg

Bedrooms	Qty
Double	3
Twin	
Single	
Bed Size	**Qty**
Super King	1
King	1
Queen	1
Double	
Single	2
Bathrooms	**Qty**
Ensuite	2
Private	
Family Share	1

Homestay
Bed & Breakfast

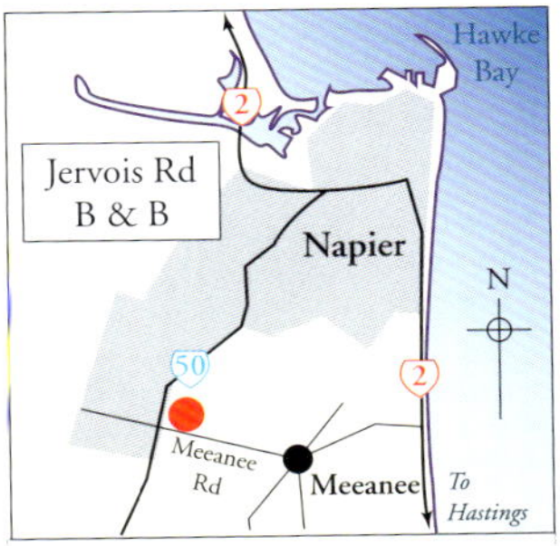

DIRECTIONS:
From motorway turn into Meeanee Road, then first left into Jervois Road.

Features & Attractions

- *Delightful semi rural setting*
- *Halfway Napier - Hastings*
- *Restaurants, golf courses nearby*
- *Minutes from wineries & shops*
- *Friendly atmosphere*
- *Large swimming pool*
- *Two cats - Sugar & Spice*
- *Peaceful garden setting*

Our home is in a semi-rural setting. We offer our guests warm hospitality combined with relaxed and comfortable accommodation. Breakfasts at our home are prepared in a relaxed, informal atmosphere and feature fresh, local organic fruits, cereals or full cooked breakfast, if required. Our large family room, which opens onto its own patio and garden, has a king bed, two single king beds plus ensuite and coffee making facilities. The pool room with super king bed, ensuite and coffee making facilities, offers privacy and relaxation in the garden by the pool or under the trees. Sally's passion for gardening, combined with her experience in garden centres, has led to the creation of a garden retreat which features a wide variety of tropical, succulent and other plants. We have two delightful, friendly cats, Sugar and Spice, who may greet you.

Botany Way Homestay & Cottage

145 Meeanee Road, Taradale, Napier
Ph (06) 844 8408, Fax (06) 844 8408
Mobile 027-298 8837
email: *hosts@botanyway.co.nz*
www.botanyway.co.nz

Features & Attractions

- *Private guest wing*
- *Secluded, sunny courtyards*
- *Large lawns & garden area*
- *Separate entrances*
- *Home-made treats*
- *Gas barbeque available*

$	
Double	$100-160
Single	$90-100
Child	neg

Homestay, Bed & Breakfast & Cottage

Bedrooms	Qty
Double	6
Twin	
Single	
Bed Size	**Qty**
Super King	4
Queen	
Double	2
Single	
Bathrooms	**Qty**
Ensuite	1
Private	1
Guest Share	1

Welcome – come and share 'The Good Life' on our one acre lifestyle property, (remember Tom & Barbara). Let us extend genuine friendship and generous Kiwi hospitality. Relax and unwind in our spacious guest lounge before retiring to watch colour TV from luxurious Super King beds in comfortable, private guest rooms. Enjoy an invigorating mains pressure shower or a 2 person spa in the ensuite bathroom. Breakfast on fresh fruits, cereals and home preserves or try our fabulous free-range egg treats. We grow various organic fruits and vegetables in nutrient rich compost from our worm farm. Our new, 2 bedroomed cottage offers tasteful, fully self-contained congeniality for two or three couples or family groups. Travel experiences have taught us the requirements that discerning tourists seek and our goals are to satisfy these needs. We are central to all tourist attractions and we guarantee that you will enjoy your stay.

DIRECTIONS: 250 metres towards the sea from the Expressway / Meeanee Rd intersection.

Taradale - Napier ▶ YOUR HOSTS: **Marie and Colin Dudley** Ph: (06) 844 6580

Dudley's Bed & Breakfast/Homestay

12 Weathers Place, Taradale, Napier
Ph (06) 844 6580, Fax (06) 844 6580
Mobile 027-280 6610
email: *candmdudley@xtra.co.nz*

Features & Attractions

- *Quality accommodation*
- *Warm friendly hospitality*
- *Off-street parking*
- *Laundry & email facilities*
- *Dinner by arrangement*
- *Restaurants, wineries nearby*

Homestay Bed & Breakfast

$	
Double	$105-115
Single	$75-80
Child	

Bedrooms	Qty
Double/Twin	1
Twin	
Single	
Bed Size	**Qty**
Super King/Twin	1
Queen	
Double	
Single	
Bathrooms	**Qty**
Ensuite	
Private	1
Guest Share	

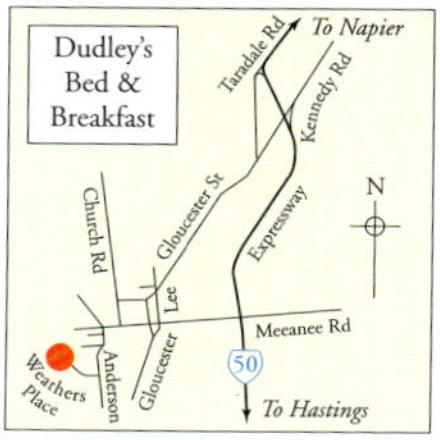

For business or pleasure enjoy a relaxing stay in our comfortable well appointed home, situated in a quiet cul-de-sac with attractive private gardens. We offer a bright, sunny super king/twin bedroom with tea and coffee making facilities. Private bathroom with shower and luxury spa bath. Separate guest toilet. Guest's television/reading room or join us in the lounge for coffee and chat or watch Sky television. Continental or gourmet breakfast is provided. Dinner available by prior arrangement. In-ground swimming pool, barbeque area, email facilities. A substantial, popular suburban shopping centre with many good restaurants is only a 7 minute stroll. Wineries, golf courses Pettigrew/Green Arena close by, courtesy car if required for arrival and departure. Sightseeing and tours to numerous wineries can be arranged.

YOUR HOSTS: **Kate and Roger Ladson** Ph (06) 844 9396 ***Waiohiki - Napier***

OMARUNUI HOMESTAY

69 Omarunui Road, Waiohiki, Napier
Ph (06) 844 9396, Fax (06) 844 9396
Mobile 021-071 0159
email: *ladsons@slingshot.co.nz*

Features & Attractions

- *Quiet, peaceful location*
- *Private entrance & patio*
- *Laundry, email available*
- *Wineries & golf courses nearby*
- *Centrally heated in winter*
- *Tea, coffee making facilities*

$	
Double	$150
Single	$130
Child	

Quality Bed & Breakfast With Panoramic Views

Bedrooms	Qty
Double/Twin	1
Twin	
Single	
Bed Size	**Qty**
Super King/Twin	1
Queen	
Double	
Single	
Bathrooms	**Qty**
Ensuite	1
Private	
Guest Share	

Our traditional New Zealand homestead, which we share with our two friendly cats, Sooty and Tiddles, stands in an acre of secluded gardens overlooking vineyards, the Tutaekuri River and, in the distance, the Kaweka range of mountains. We are centrally located between the lovely Art Deco city of Napier and Hastings, with Taradale shops and restaurants only 5 minutes away.

We love meeting new people and enjoy travel, golf, good food and good company. We invite you to start your day with a delicious cooked or continental breakfast before exploring the many attractions of Hawke's Bay. Come home to relax before joining us on the deck in the evening sun for a glass of wine.

A visit to one of the many fine restaurants in the area will complete your day in this lovely part of New Zealand.

YOUR HOSTS: **Diana and Barry Thompson** Ph: (06) 844 8623 ***Taradale - Napier***

WHINFIELD

615 Puketapu Road, RD 3, Taradale, Napier
Ph (06) 844 8623, Fax (06) 844 8623
email: *whinfield@xtra.co.nz*

Features & Attractions

- *Art, craft & wine trails*
- *Art deco attractions*
- *Gannet safari & fishing*
- *2 self-contained ensuite rooms*
- *Peaceful lifestyle*
- *Outdoor chess board*

$	
Double	$130
Single	$85
Child	

Countrystay Bed & Breakfast

Bedrooms	Qty
Double	1
Twin	2
Single	1
Bed Size	**Qty**
Super King	1
King Single	1
Queen	
Single	4
Bathrooms	**Qty**
Ensuite	2
Private	
Guest Share	2

Whinfield is a comfortable country home with spectacular river views. Our new accommodation is in a separate cottage in the garden and offers two ensuite bedrooms opening onto a large sunny verandah. Enjoy breakfast on the terrace of the main house and then have a game of chess on the outdoor board or stroll down to the river to swim or fish. There are excellent shops and restaurants just 5 minutes away in Taradale, an excellent golf course, or the art deco attractions of Napier just 20 minutes away. We are retired farmers grazing a few cattle and our many visitors enjoy the peace and quiet of the countryside while being within easy reach of the attractions of Hawkes Bay.

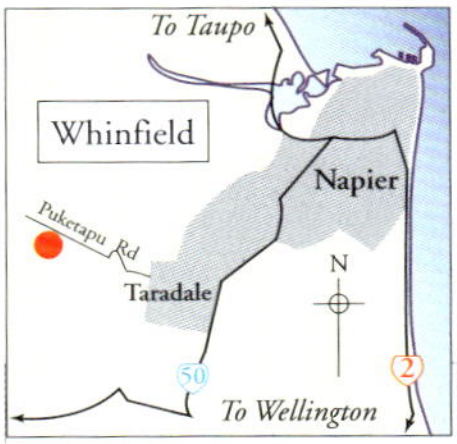

DIRECTIONS: Take Puketapu Rd at roundabout in Taradale - Whinfield is 6.15 km on left.

Waiwhenua Farmstay

808 River Road, RD 9, Hastings
Ph (06) 874 2435, Fax (06) 874 2465
Mobile 027-479 4094
email: *info@waiwhenua.co.nz*
www.waiwhenua.co.nz

Tariff : N.Z. Dollars	
Double	$120-150
Single	$60-100
Child	$50

Bedrooms	Qty
Double	2
Twin	2
Single	
Bed Size	**Qty**
Super King	
King	
Queen	1
Double	1
Single	3
Bathrooms	**Qty**
Ensuite	
Private	1
Family Share	1

F **Unique Farmstay** SC

VISA MasterCard bankcard

Features & Attractions

- *Extensive sheep, beef & deer farm*
- *Families & children welcome*
- *Historic homestead & cottage*
- *Relaxing swimming pool*
- *Trout fishing onsite*
- *Informative farm tours*
- *Fresh farm-style meals*
- *Bush and farm walks*

DIRECTIONS: Turn off SH 50 between Napier and Hastings into Taihape Rd at Omahu/Fernhill. Travel 35 km to River Rd on right. Travel along River Rd for 8 km **Waiwhenua #808.** Drive100m from mail box on right. **Annie's Cottage #746** on right.

To avoid disappointment, please book ahead.

The perfect place to experience a genuine farmstay and friendly rural hospitality at our 120 year old historic homestead. Come and join us on our extensive 440 ha sheep, beef and deer farm. Enjoy guided tours and farm activities, fish in our trout-filled river, or just relax with a book on our cool verandahs or in our garden. Our home and family offer guests a friendly environment, catering for individuals or families interested in the outdoor life. (Two night stay recommended.) Enjoy specialty farm-cooked meals of homegrown beef, lamb or venison, complimented with fresh garden vegetables and fruit. Enrich your stay by including other outdoor activities at our backdoor; hunting, fishing, bush and farm walks, garden tours, jet boating and extensive mountain hikes, plus many attractions in the greater sunny Hawkes Bay area.

SC "**Annie's Cottage**" - For those seeking total privacy and a longer stay at Waiwhenua. Our recently renovated, fully self-contained, cosy, three bedroom rural retreat awaits visitors.
Sleeps six people at $150-$200 per night.

Merriwee Homestay

29 Gordon Road, Te Awanga, Hawke's Bay
Ph (06) 875 0111, Fax (06) 875 0111
Mobile 021-214 5023
email: *merriwee@xtra.co.nz*
www.merriwee.co.nz

Tariff : N.Z. Dollars	
Double	$180-250
Single	$180
Child	$50

Bedrooms	Qty
Double	4
Twin	1
Single	
Bed Size	**Qty**
Super King	
King	1
Queen	3
Double	
King Single	2
Bathrooms	**Qty**
Ensuite	2
Private	1
Guest Share	

Quality Homestay Accommodation

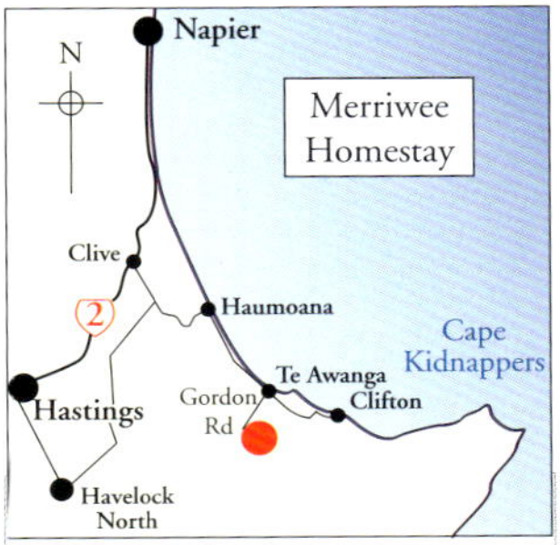

Advance booking recommended.
Please phone for easy directions

Features & Attractions

- *5mins to Cape Kidnappers golf course*
- *15 min to Napier/Hastings/Havelock*
- *Large grounds with sea views*
- *5 min to beach and wineries*
- *Near Gannet Colony*
- *Art and wine trails*
- *Swimming pool*
- *Golf course nearby*

Merriwee offers guests peace, comfort and relaxation. It was built in 1908, and is set in an apricot orchard, just a stroll from Te Awanga Beach. The secluded ten acre property lies on the stretch of coastline between Napier and Hastings, a short distance from the famous Cape Kidnappers Gannet Colony. The homestead is elevated and spacious, with quality décor and furnishings, open fires and french doors leading to verandahs and gardens. There is a large guest sitting room. The main accommodation area is self-contained, with private entrance, sitting room, open fire and kitchen. The large grounds include a swimming pool, pétanque court and sea views. Mags, the terrier and cat Floyd will greet you. There are many local attractions and wineries nearby. Merriwee is fifteen minutes from Napier, Hastings and Havelock North.

The Loft Homestay

10 Woodford Heights, Havelock North
Ph (06) 877 5938
Mobile 021-474 729
www.hawkesbayhomestay.co.nz

Features & Attractions

- *Refreshments on arrival*
- *Fax, e-mail,*
- *Tea making & TV in Queen Room*
- *Non smoking*
- *Superb views*
- *Great breakfasts*

Premium Homestay Bed & Breakfast

$	
Double	$110-135
Single	$100-120
Child	

We offer you warm hospitality and private Bed & Breakfast accommodation in our non-smoking home with views. Our architectural home has many unique features. Your comfortable room/s on the ground floor are in the guest wing of the house. Queen room has television, with adjoining bathroom and spa bath. There is a double room available, being let only to the same party as the bathroom would be shared with four guests. Reading/TV/computer room adjoining You may use the spacious deck or intimate courtyard to socialise and enjoy your refreshments. A sumptuous breakfast is served in the dining area with a wonderful view, or on the deck in good weather. Two minutes by car from our picturesque village, good restaurants and boutique shopping. Hastings and Napier cities, both with excellent shopping, beaches, some of Hawke's Bay top wineries, Te Mata Peak and the gannet colony at Cape Kidnappers are all close by.

Bedrooms	Qty
Double	2
Twin	
Single	
Bed Size	**Qty**
King	
Queen	1
Double	1
Single	
Bathrooms	**Qty**
Ensuite	1
Private	
Guest Share	

OPTIONS

92 Simla Avenue, Havelock North, Hawke's Bay
Ph (06) 877 0257, Fax (06) 877 0257
Mobile 027-653 7270
email: *gr.duff@xtra.co.nz*

Tariff : N.Z. Dollars	
Double	$125
Single	$100
Child	neg

Bedrooms	Qty
Double	2
Twin	1
Single	
Bed Size	**Qty**
Super King	
King	1
Queen	1
Double	
Single	2
Bathrooms	**Qty**
Ensuite	1
Private	1
Guest Share	

Bed & Breakfast
Homestay

DIRECTIONS:
OPTIONS is easy to find.
Please ring for directions.
Advance booking recommended

Features & Attractions

- *Wine, gannets & Art Deco - all within 30minutes*
- *Near Te Mata Peak – views*
- *Internet with wireless connection*
- *Swimming pool & spa*
- *Laundry facilities*
- *Mini petanque court*
- *Private patios*

OPTIONS is halfway between the centre of Havelock North village and Te Mata Peak which at 399 metres is the best place to start sightseeing in Hawkes Bay. The wineries, Cape Kidnappers with the gannets, and Napier with its Art Deco buildings are all within thirty minutes of **OPTIONS**.

OPTIONS offers friendly hospitality and guests are accommodated within our home in either a large double bedroom with king-size bed and ensuite, or a suite with a double room with queen-size bed, a twin room, a private bathroom and separate lounge. The internet is available to guests and all rooms have wireless connection.

In its elevated position, **OPTIONS** has lovely views and with the private patios there is a choice of sun or shade. The pool, heated to extend the summer season, and spa offer respite after a day's sightseeing. During winter the fire is welcoming.

A delicious breakfast of your choice is served inside or outside depending on the weather. In the village there is a range of restaurants available. Sharing an evening meal with us, at an additional cost, is a great way to learn about our area.

ABBOTSFORD OAKS

85 Abbotsford Road, PO Box 37, Waipawa, Hawke's Bay
Ph (06) 857 8960, Fax (06) 857 8961
Mobile 025-296 1160
email: *nicolette@abbotsfordoaks.co.nz*
www.abbotsfordoaks.co.nz

Tariff : N.Z. Dollars	
Double	$170-325
Single	$140-290
Child	

Bedrooms	Qty
Double	4
Twin	
Single	
Bed Size	**Qty**
Super King	
King	1
Queen	3
Double	
Single	
Bathrooms	**Qty**
Ensuite	1
Private	3
Guest Share	

Boutique Accommodation
Bed & Breakfast

VISA MasterCard

Features & Attractions

- *Luxurious spacious rooms*
- *Park-like grounds*
- *Golf & fishing close by*
- *Email & fax facilities*
- *Friendly hospitality*
- *Ample parking*
- *Dutch spoken*
- *Dinner available*

DIRECTIONS:
Please phone for easy directions.
Advanced booking recommended.

Nicolette and Chris warmly welcome you to **Abbotsford Oaks.** Nestled in picturesque central Hawke's Bay and surrounded by 3.5 acres of gardens, **Abbotsford Oaks** offers a relaxing and special venue for those wanting a break from their busy lifestyle. It is an ideal base to explore the many attractions Hawke's Bay has to offer. Beaches, wineries and art deco/spanish mission architecture are only thirty minutes away. Golf courses and trout fishing are close by.

Our property was purpose built as a children's home in the 1920s and has been renovated to provide quality Boutique Bed & Breakfast accommodation. It has spacious rooms most with their own sitting/sun room and private bathroom, with wonderful views of the grounds and countryside. Breakfast, either cooked or continental, can be served in the dining room, the garden or your private lounge. Dinner is available by arrangement. Visit our web site for more details.

YOUR HOSTS: **Diana and Jeromy Greer** Free Ph 0800 857 5117 **Waipawa**

THE BROW

190 Argyll East Road, RD 3, Waipawa, Hawkes Bay
Ph (06) 857 5117, Fax (06) 857 5117
Mobile 027-249 6175
e-mail: *thebrow@xtra.co.nz*

Features & Attractions

- *Winery and farm tours can be arranged*
- *Separate private cottage*
- *Trout fishing*
- *Peace & tranquility*
- *Delicious home-cooked meals*

$	
Double	$180
Single	$90
Child	

Countrystay & Homestay
Dinner & Breakfast included

Bedrooms	Qty
Double	2
Twin	
Single	
Bed Size	**Qty**
King	
Queen	2
Double	
Single	
Bathrooms	**Qty**
Ensuite	
Guest Share	1
Family share	1

DIRECTIONS: From Hastings Waipawa, right at BP station into Ruataniwha Street, onto Tikokino Rd. After approx. 11km right into Argyll East Rd. Travel 2km, go over bridge, sign on our gate on right.

Our farm, **The Brow**, is a well known Hawkes Bay property. We are handy to a great variety of the wonderful tourist attractions that Hawkes Bay has to offer. We have a private, small semi self-contained cottage with tea and coffee making facilities.

Our large menagerie of farm animals include Dugald and Rosie, the cairn terriers, Annie and Abbie the labradors, cats, hens, and pet lambs in the spring. Enjoy real farm experiences as well as trout fishing in our local river, and we can organise winery tours with our local operators. Take time to unwind in our special and peaceful part of the world and finish the day off with a delicious home-cooked evening meal, using only the freshest of Hawkes Bay produce and our home-grown beef and lamb. Please book ahead to avoid disappointment. Tariff includes an evening meal and a cooked breakfast.

YOUR HOSTS: **Annabelle and David Hamilton** Ph: (06) 857 8093 **Waipukurau**

MYNTHURST FARMSTAY

912 Lindsay Road, RD 3, Waipukurau
Ph: (06) 857 8093, Fax:(06) 857 8093
Mobile 027-232 2458
email: *mynthurst@xtra.co.nz*

Features & Attractions

- *Excellent working farm*
- *Trout fishing*
- *Children welcome*
- *Swimming pool - trampoline*
- *Dinner by arrangement*
- *Farm tours complimentary*

Genuine Farmstay
Excellent Accomodation

$	
Double	$175
Single	$95
Child	$35

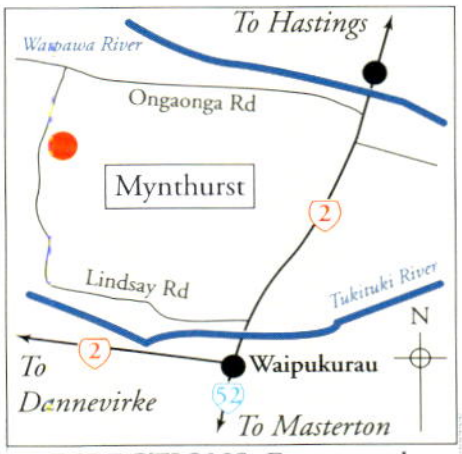

DIRECTIONS: From north, turn right into Onagonga Road. Travel 6 km, turn left into Lindsay Road. **Mynthurst** 3 km on left. From south left into Lindsay Rd. **Mynthurst** 9 km on right.

Mynthurst is a genuine working sheep and cattle farm covering 1350 acres. Guests from New Zealand and around the world have been welcomed and entertained for over twenty years. The homestead is large, warm and comfortable, in idyllic surroundings, with unspoilt views of the Ruahine Ranges. Feel free to observe the farm activities. Farm tour complimentary. Relax beside the pool, trampoline, tennis. Trout fishing available in local streams. Three golf courses nearby. Visit local vineyards. Enjoy the many attractions of Hawke's Bay. Dinner available on request, we use only the finest locally grown produce. Children of all ages welcome. If you are looking for a short break in the heart of beautiful Hawke's Bay, you'll find Mynthurst the perfect retreat. Booking avoids disappointment.

Bedrooms	Qty
Double	2
Twin	1
Single	1
Bed Size	**Qty**
Super King/Twin	1
Queen	
Double + Cot	1/1
Single	3
Bathrooms	**Qty**
Ensuite	1
Private	1
Guest Share	

Dannevirke - Tararua YOUR HOSTS: **Lyn and Michael Charlton** Free Ph: 0800 4 COTTAGE

GARDENSTONE FARMSTAY AND B&B COTTAGE

Otope Road, RD 5, Dannevirke
Ph (06) 374 8259
Mobile 021-930 022
email: *gardenstone@paradise.net.nz*
www.gardenstone.co.nz

Features & Attractions

- *Working dairy farm*
- *Cretan Labyrinth*
- *Large rural garden*
- *1 km bush walk*
- *3 friendly donkeys*
- *Swimming pool*

Farmstay
Bed & Breakfast Cottage

Double	$110-135
Single	$90-100
Extra adult $35	

Bedrooms	Qty
Double	2
Twin	
Single	1
Bed Size	**Qty**
King	
Queen	1
Double	
King Single	1
Bathrooms	**Qty**
Ensuite	1
Private	1
Guest Share	

"Enchanting gardens, fantastic cottage, great bath and generous hosts"

Gardenstone is a 3 times Regional Tourism Supreme Award Winner, situated 5 minutes from Dannevirke. It features 19th century restored cottage with popular outdoor bath (indoor shower!). Full farmhouse breakfast supplied, served at the homestead or with our midday checkout you can enjoy it for brunch! A log fire welcomes you in winter. Books, videos, games, petánque and croquet. Fully self-contained with TV, video, iron, hairdryer, electric blankets, plenty of pillows and extra duvet. By arrangement you can hire a mountain bike, indulge in a relaxing massage, luxury bath pack, lunches, teas or a delicious 3-course meal.
Our homestead room has its own entrance and ensuite. We are happy to help with information and bookings. Experience the real New Zealand by taking time out in Tararua Country.

Dannevirke YOUR HOSTS: **Phyllis and David** Ph (06) 374 7079

RUAHINE VIEW

185 Tipapakuku Road, Dannevirke
Ph (06) 374 7079
Mobile 021-292 9887
email: *ryanholt@clear.net.nz*
www.ruahineview.co.nz

Features & Attractions

- *Stunning views of the ranges*
- *Evening meal by arrangement*
- *Offers intimacy & privacy*
- *Gateway to the outdoors*
- *Rural tranquility*
- *Laundry facilities*

Homestay
Bed & Breakfast

Double	$110-135
Single	$90-100
Child	neg

Bedrooms	Qty
Double	2
Twin	
Single	
Bed Size	**Qty**
King	1
Queen	1
King/Single	2
Single	
Bathrooms	**Qty**
Ensuite	
Private	1
Guest Share	

Ruahine View offers you a friendly, warm welcome; with the opportunity to surround yourself with panoramic views of both the Ruahine and the Tararua Ranges. Your hosts welcome you to enjoy the ambience of their architecturally designed home, set within landscaped grounds. You are part of the quiet, peaceful country life that is rural New Zealand; yet are only two kilometres from the CBD of Dannevirke. With the choice of two bedrooms, private bathroom and guest lounge, we are able to offer the opportunity to relax at the end of your day's journey, enjoying tea/coffee and home-baking. From a refreshing night's sleep, awake to birdsong and the aroma of a full English breakfast. Continental breakfast is also available.

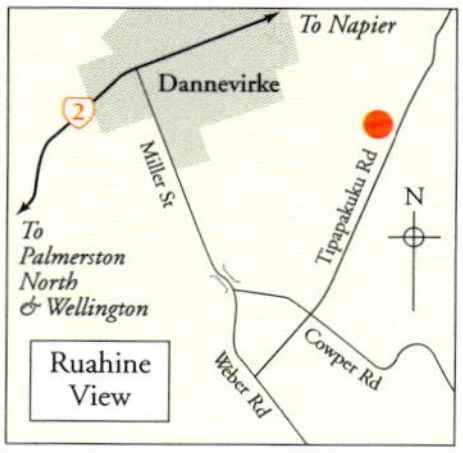

ANNDION LODGE

143 Anzac Parade, Wanganui
Ph (06) 343 3593, Fax (06) 343 3056
email: *info@anndionlodge.co.nz*
www.anndionlodge.co.nz

Tariff : N.Z. Dollars	
Double	$75-120
Single	$60
Child	

Bedrooms	Qty
Double	7
Twin	3
Single	2
Bed Size	**Qty**
Super King	1
King	
Queen	2
Double	5
Single	9
Bathrooms	**Qty**
Ensuite	1
Private	
Guest Share	4

Bed & Breakfast Homestay

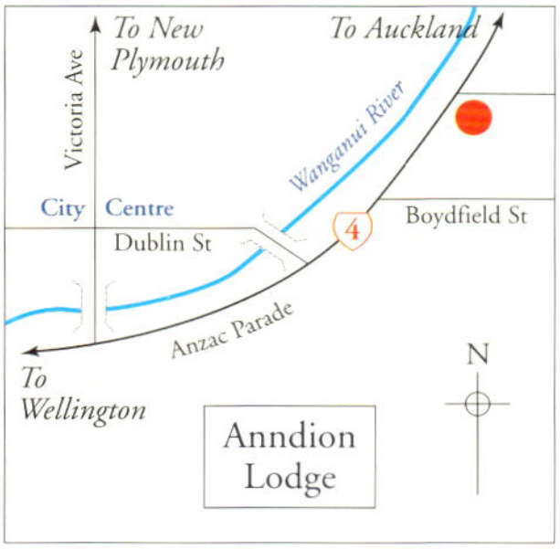

Features & Attractions

- *Genuine Kiwi Hospitality*
- *Laundry Facilities*
- *Licensed Mini Bar*
- *Scooter Hire*
- *Salt-Water Swimming pool & Spa*
- *Free 24hr high speed internet*
- *Physiotherm Infrared Sauna*
- *Sunny Balcony Overlooking River*

Stunning river views and a warm welcome awaits you at the **Anndion Lodge**, located on the banks of the Whanganui River, just a short drive from the city centre, offering superior, affordable accommodation. Relax in the salt-water swimming pool, or perhaps with a drink on the balcony taking in the views of the majestic Whanganui River or talking to friends or making new friends around the BBQ or simply just enjoying the sunset at the end of your day sitting in the steaming outdoor spa. Your hosts Anne and Dion will make your stay most memorable while providing you with 'home-away-from-home' comfort. **The Lodge** offers three living areas with Sky TV and a DVD/video library, an indoor and outdoor dining area, computers with free high-speed internet as well as a slate pool table for your leisure. In the large, modern, fully equipped self-catering kitchen guests can prepare meals at their leisure. We have a courtesy vehicle, and also offer secure motorcycle garaging.

Ashley Park

SH 3, PO Box 36, Waitotara 5180, South Taranaki
Ph (06) 346 5917, Fax (06) 346 5861
email: *ashley_park@xtra.co.nz*
www.ashleypark.co.nz

Features & Attractions

- *Peaceful country setting*
- *Pet farm animals & aviaries*
- *Park, lake & farm walks*
- *Antique and tea-shop*
- *Swimming pool*
- *Tennis and mini golf*

Farmstay Bed & Breakfast and Self-contained Chalets

$	
Double	$90-130
Single	$80
Child	

Relax and enjoy the peace of the country with views of Mt. Egmont. Hand-feed our pet farm animals, stroll around the park and lake or take a more strenuous farm walk. Be tempted with Devonshire teas in the antique shop, and a visit to our 'memory lane' museum. Partake in a round of mini golf or tennis. Dinner available.

I look forward to welcoming you into my home.

Guests comment – *"Feels like we belong here, very welcoming and friendly".*

Bedrooms	Qty
Double	1
Twin	2
Single	
Bed Size	**Qty**
King	
Queen	1
Double	
Single	4
Bathrooms	**Qty**
Ensuite	1
Private	
Guest Share	1

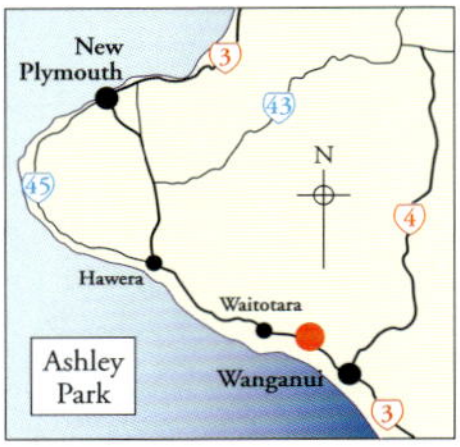

Arles Bed & Breakfast

50 Riverbank Road, SH4, Wanganui
Ph (06) 343 6557, Fax (06) 343 6557
Mobile 021-257 8257, Skype sueday1234
email: *sue@arles.co.nz*
www.arles.co.nz

Features & Attractions

- *Sumptuous full breakfast*
- *Tea/coffee in rooms*
- *Toiletries and fresh flowers*
- *Central heating*
- *Broadband/wireless/skype*
- *Salt water pool and BBQ*

DIRECTIONS: **Arles** is on SH4 as you enter/exit the city from/to National Park. A printable map can be found on the web site.

Historic Bed & Breakfast and Modern Apartment

$	
Double	$120-160
Single	$100-120
Child	$20-30

At **Arles** you will find affordable luxury. Every need is taken care of, from rooms with comfortable beds, tea/coffee facilities, toiletries and fresh flowers to complimentary internet, kitchen and laundry facilities. Breakfast features homemade breads and jams, fresh fruit and a full cooked breakfast option. **Arles**, built in the late 1880's, is the first accommodation house as you reach Wanganui from the north on SH4. It features an original kauri staircase and rimu-panelled lounge. The spacious grounds, adjacent to the Whanganui River, feature the southernmost Queensland Kauri. The guest lounge has a piano, organ, TV/CD/DVD and complimentary wine. The library is well-stocked with books, board games and jigsaw puzzles, and a computer with internet facilities. **Arles** offers spacious double rooms, a two bedroom suite, plenty of off-road parking and two acres of lawns and gardens to relax in. Stay 3 nights or more and receive a discount.

Bedrooms	Qty
Double	4
Twin	2
Single	
Bed Size	**Qty**
King	1
Queen	2
Double	1
Single	4
Bathrooms	**Qty**
Ensuite	2
Private	2
Guest Share	

KEMBALI

26 Taranaki Street, Wanganui
Phone (06) 347 1727
Mobile 027-244 4347
email: *wespalmer@xtra.co.nz*

Features & Attractions

- *Exclusive - one party only*
- *Central, quiet and friendly*
- *Overlooks wetlands - trees*
- *Guest lounge with tea/coffee*
- *Cooked breakfast*
- *Off-street parking*

$	
Double	$100
Single	$70
Child	n/a

Bed & Breakfast Homestay

Bedrooms	Qty
Double	1
Twin	1
Single	
Bed Size	**Qty**
King	
Queen	1
Double	
Single	2
Bathrooms	**Qty**
Ensuite	
Private	1
Guest Share	

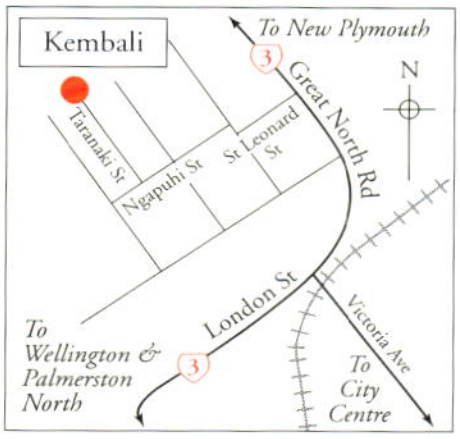

Welcome to **Kembali**, our modern, centrally heated home. As we take only one group/party at a time, the sunny guest lounge, bedrooms and bathroom are for your exclusive use. These upstairs rooms overlook trees and wetlands, where native birds roam. The lounge has television, refrigerator, tea and coffee making facilities. We are semi-retired, our children married, and we offer a relaxing, peaceful stay. We enjoy people, gardens, books, travel and have Christian interests. Five minutes drive will take you to a variety of restaurants, shops, art and craft, and walks. Historic Wanganui with its river is a lovely place to visit. Our tariff includes a cooked/continental breakfast and laundry facilities are available. We look forward to meeting you.

MISTY VALLEY FARMSTAY

97 Parihauhau Rd, Wanganui
Ph (06) 342 5767
email: *linda.garry.wadsworth@xtra.co.nz*

Features & Attractions

- *Quiet, rural location*
- *Large country garden*
- *Families welcome*
- *Near Whanganui River Park*
- *Short drive to Wanganui*
- *Dinner by arrangement*

$	
Double	$80
Single	$50
Child	$20

Farmstay Self-contained

Bedrooms	Qty
Double	2
Twin	1
Single	
Bed Size	**Qty**
King	
Queen	
Double	2
Single	2
Bathrooms	**Qty**
Ensuite	
Private	
Guest Share	1

Misty Valley is an organic farm of nine hectares, set in the picturesque Parihauhau Valley. We are twenty five kilometres north of the historic river city of Wanganui, on State Highway 4, and fifteen minutes from the Whanganui River National Park turn-off. We have people-friendly farm animals for you to meet, including our Brittany dogs and two cats. All our animals live outside year round. Children visit the farm regularly and yours will be made very welcome. We are non-smoking, but offer pleasant deck areas for those who do. Start your day with our hearty farm breakfast before exploring Wanganui, the surrounding area and famous River Park. We can help you make the best of your time with us. In the evenings we can prepare a three-course dinner for you (by arrangement), using our own produce when possible. Alternatively you can prepare your own in the kitchen facilities available.

Drovers' Retreat

2697 Cheltenham/Hunterville Road, SH 54, Feilding
Ph (06) 328 9068, Fax (06) 328 9065
email: *droversretreat@xtra.co.nz*
nanbob@airstream.net.nz

Features & Attractions

- *Million dollar views*
- *Cosy, rustic, separate cabin*
- *Wander in our gardens*
- *Midway Taupo/Wellington*
- *Small farmlet, friendly folk*
- *Country pub 3km*

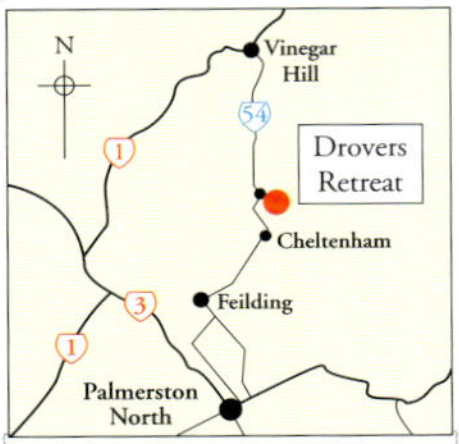

DIRECTIONS:
South turn off SH1 onto SH54 at Vinegar Hill, 27km on L. North turn L. at Cheltenham on Kimbolton Rd, 3 km on R.

Countrylife Bed & Breakfast Homestay

Double	$100
Single	$50
Child	$10

Enjoy our 'Million Dollar Views' from Ruapehu in the north to Kapiti in the south. Located on SH54, Vinegar Hill Road, with good access and parking. Our **Drovers' Cabin** is self-contained with separate queen and double beds, suitable for small family or two couples. In our home we have queen and twin bedrooms with private guest bathroom. Within 20 minutes drive is Feilding with good cafés, restaurants, gardens, parks and historic stock sale yards or visit Cross Hills or Heritage Rhododendron Gardens, Te Apiti and Tararua Wind farms. **Drovers'** is an easy 2.5 hrs drive from Taupo or Wellington. We guarantee a friendly, warm, comfortable stay with breakfast included. Dinner is available on request for a small extra charge.

Bedrooms	Qty
Double	3
Twin	1
Single	1
Bed Size	**Qty**
King	
Queen	2
Double	1
Single	3
Bathrooms	**Qty**
Ensuite	1
Private	1
Guest Share	

Rothesay

10 Bruce Street, Hunterville
Ph (06) 322 8122
email: *d-r.mcnie@xtra.co.nz*
www.rothesaybnb.co.nz

Tariff : N.Z. Dollars	
Double	$110-150
Single	$90
Child	neg

Bedrooms	Qty
Double	3
Twin	1
Single	
Bed Size	**Qty**
Super King	
King	
Queen	3
Double	1
Single	1
Bathrooms	**Qty**
Ensuite	2
Private	
Guest Share	1

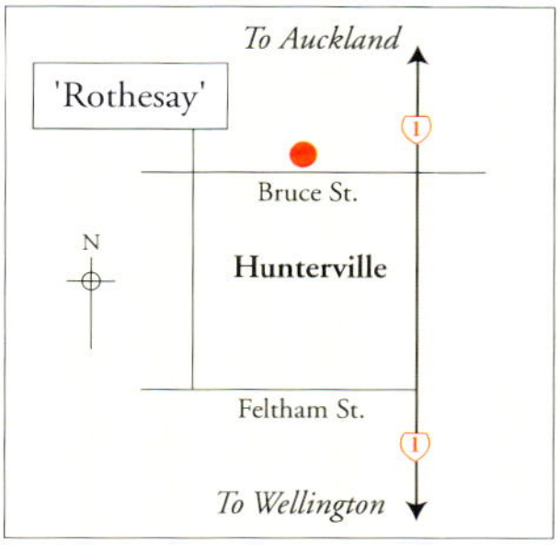

Historic Bed & Breakfast

Features & Attractions

- *Golf courses*
- *Trout fishing*
- *Skiing*
- *Bungy jumping*
- *Jet boating, river rafting*
- *Antique and craft shops*
- *Historic restored Post Office*
- *Dinner by arrangement*

Rothesay, previously the Hunterville Post Office, was built in 1903. A heritage building, listed with the Historic Places Trust Category One. This lovely old building, close to State Highway One, has been tastefully renovated and converted to superior guest accommodation on the first floor with large comfortable bedrooms and separate guest lounge. Our garden with stream is a perfect place to relax in after a day of travel. Your hosts Robyn and Duncan welcome you and invite you to experience the ambience of a bygone era. The atmosphere at **Rothesay** is friendly, relaxed and informal. A hearty breakfast is included and dinner is provided by arrangement. Hunterville is centrally located in the lower North Island, close to the ski fields and is a convenient two hour drive from Taupo and Wellington, making it an ideal stopover for the inter-island ferry. The Rangitikei district offers stunning scenery, many attractive gardens to visit as well as numerous other activities throughout the area.

Palmerston North — YOUR HOSTS: **Lyndall and John Whitelock** — Ph: (06) 353 3749

LARKHALL

42 The Strand, Palmerston North
Ph (06) 353 3749, Fax (06) 353 3748
Mobile 0274-416 890
email: *jlwhitelock@inspire.net.nz*

Features & Attractions

- *First class accommodation*
- *Quiet, peaceful location*
- *Indoor heated pool*
- *Private luxury facilities*
- *Outstanding views*
- *Close to City and University*

Luxury Accommodation Homestay Bed & Breakfast

$	
Double	$175-200
Single	$120
Child	

Bedrooms	Qty
Double	1
Twin	1
Single	
Bed Size	**Qty**
King	1
Queen	
Double	
King Single	1
Bathrooms	**Qty**
Ensuite	2
Private	2
Guest Share	

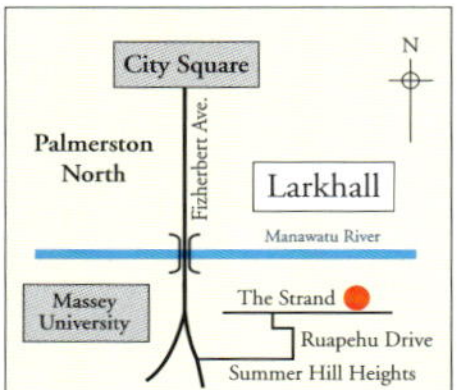

A stunning, newly created up-market home with picturesque views of Palmerston North City and the Manawatu region. Your hosts, John and Lyndall, have a wealth of local knowledge and international experience. They can assist and direct you to a wide selection of sights and activities. Palmerston North, apart from local attractions, is on the central pathway leading to Wellington. Palmerston North is a centre of major agricultural, educational (Massey University and International Pacific College), business and sporting (Adidas Rugby Academy and museum) activities and interests. Palmerston North Airport offers domestic and international services. John and Lyndall invite you to enjoy the scenery and native dell as you take in the views from the patio. A warm welcome awaits you.

Woodville - Tararua — YOUR HOSTS: **Sue and Del Trew** — Ph: (06) 376 4603

OTAWA LODGE

132 Otawhao Road, Kumeroa, RD 1, Woodville
Ph (06) 376 4603, Fax (06) 376 5042
Mobile 027-230 1327
email: *rest@otawalodge.co.nz*
www.otawalodge.co.nz

Features & Attractions

- *Gourmet four course dinner*
- *Te Apiti windfarm visits*
- *Fishing & Hunting*
- *Woodville antique shopping*
- *Hill & native bush walks*
- *Gottfried Lindauer studio*

Historic Country Lodge

$	
Double	$230-275
Single	$220-265
Child	n/a

Bedrooms	Qty
Double	2
Twin	
Single	
Bed Size	**Qty**
King	1
Queen	1
Double	
King/Single	2
Bathrooms	**Qty**
Ensuite	
Private	2
Guest Share	

DIRECTIONS:
Please phone for easy directions.

Rest, relax, rejuvenate in our magnificent 1914 historic homestead and garden, nestled in 70 acres of rolling hills a short drive from Woodville. Be enchanted by the Edwardian elegance of wood panelling, stained glass windows, unique Art Nouveau plasterwork and authentic period furniture. Take a walk in the mature gardens, or wander through the walnut grove to the stream accompanied by native birds. Unwind in the privacy of the spacious guest sitting room, or the sunny octagonal library. Dine on the award winning four course dinner, featuring fish and organic cuisine, with a selected wine list. Be warmed by the hot water radiators, which ensure comfort in all seasons. At the end of the day sleep peacefully in one of two luxurious bedrooms, each with its own private bathroom. In the morning arise refreshed to birdsong and a hearty breakfast. Above all indulge yourself in historic opulence and friendly service.

The Ambers

58A McMaster Street, Greytown, Wairarapa
Ph (06) 304 8588, Fax (06) 304 8590
Mobile 027-499 4394
email: *ambershomestay@xtra.co.nz*
www.ambershomestay.co.nz

Tariff : N.Z. Dollars	
Double	$120
Single	$75
Child	$25

Bedrooms	Qty
Double	4
Twin	
Single	1
Bed Size	**Qty**
Super King	
King	1
Queen	2
Double	1
Single	1
Bathrooms	**Qty**
Ensuite	3
Private	
Family Share	1

VISA MasterCard

Boutique Accommodation
Bed & Breakfast

DIRECTIONS:
Please phone for easy directions.
Advance booking is recommended

Features & Attractions

- *Quiet peaceful surrounds*
- *Cafés & antique shops*
- *Fine dining*
- *Close to Martinborough vineyards*
- *Beautiful breakfast*
- *Themed romantic bedrooms*
- *Self-contained serviced apartment*
- *Great for honeymooners*

The new **Ambers** is a 1920s two storey home originally from Lowry Bay in Wellington, moved over the Rimutaka Ranges and set on a lovely private section with mature trees. We offer spacious accommodation in this new home. The Cherub Room has a large ensuite bathroom, queen bed, television and coffee making facilities, french doors opening onto the deck. The Vintage Suite provides a large ensuite bathroom, king bed, private lounge with television and coffee making facilities, a single bed for extra guests or children in the same group. The Oak-Aged Room has a shared bathroom, double bed. This room is ideal for any overflow or big groups wishing to stay together. **The Ambers** now offers a serviced apartment "Petite Maison" with own outdoor area. Great for romantic weekends. Facilities include a mini kitchen, bathroom, lounge area with television and sofa bed for the kids, a queen bed, bathroom and a woodburner.

If you desire the ultimate privacy or a "romantic getaway", we offer a "blissful" cottage set in its own private garden featuring lovely old trees. **Ambrosia Cottage** has two double bedrooms with own amenities including fire and bath. For tariff please contact Marilla.

Martinborough ▶ YOUR HOSTS: **Lorraine and David Murray** Ph: (06) 306 9708

The Martinborough Connection

80 Jellicoe Street, Martinborough, Wairarapa
Ph (06) 306 9708, Fax (06) 306 9706
Mobile 0274-381 581
email: *martinboroughconnection@xtra.co.nz*
www.martinboroughconnection.co.nz

Tariff : N.Z. Dollars	
Double	$130
Single	$110
Child	

Bedrooms	Qty
Double	4
Twin	
Single	
Bed Size	**Qty**
Super King	
King	
Queen	4
Double	
Single	
Bathrooms	**Qty**
Ensuite	4
Private	
Guest Share	

Historic Bed & Breakfast
Boutique Accommodation

Features & Attractions

- *Restored heritage building*
- *Guest lounge, open fire*
- *Garden furniture/swing*
- *Wine tours arranged*
- *6 minute walk to cafés*
- *Wineries & olive groves*
- *Cape Palliser Lighthouse*
- *Fur seal colony 55 min*

Warm and friendly hospitality awaits you at this stunningly restored original home and boot store built in 1889 for Alexander McLeod. **The Martinborough Connection** exudes character and provides a relaxed ambience, enhancing your stay in Martinborough with its award winning vineyards, olive groves, and variety of outdoor activities like kayaking, jetboating, quadbikes, horseriding, fishing and claybird shooting. Soak up the warmth of the open fire in the spacious guest lounge with its native timber panelling and New Zealand artworks.

Sky digital television, tea and coffee making facilities, books and magazines available.

Sip a wine in the sun on the outdoor deck or in the shade of the tortured willows on the garden swing. Commence your day with a scrumptious breakfast including fresh fruit and homebaked bread. Our interests include bridge, art, wine, travel, sport and we look forward to sharing our home with you.

The Vicarage

94 Jellicoe Street, Martinborough, Wairarapa
Ph (06) 306 8596, Fax (06) 306 8597
Mobile 021-472 794
email: *mike.cooper@paradise.net.nz*
www.thevicarage.co.nz

Tariff : N.Z. Dollars	
Double	$150
Single	$150
Child	

Bedrooms	Qty
Double	1
Twin	1
Single	
Bed Size	**Qty**
Super King	
King	
Queen	1
Double	
King Single	2
Bathrooms	**Qty**
Ensuite	
Private	1
Guest Share	

Boutique Cottage

DIRECTIONS:
Please phone for easy directions.
Advanced booking recommended.

Features & Attractions

- *1890's restored vicarage*
- *Short walk to Town Square*
- *Close to wineries*
- *Gas barbeque*
- *Sky digital television*
- *Gas log fire*
- *Fully equipped kitchen*
- *Laundry facilities*

Historic early 1890's cottage built as the Anglican Vicarage in Wanganui. Relocated to Martinborough in 2001 and completely restored so as to preserve the original character. Renovated and appointed to the highest standards of convenience and warmth. Set in a peaceful discreet sunny location alongside similar character cottages immediately behind the First Presbyterian Church in Jellicoe Street, Martinborough.

It's just a short walk to Martinborough Square with its shops, bars, cafés and restaurants. Within easy reach of the vineyards and olive groves. Martinborough is an excellent base for wine tours, walking (hill and rugged coastline), hill country quad biking, jet boating, golfing, great meals and just plain relaxing. Tariff includes breakfast provisions.

Managed by M and Jays Homestays (021 036 1436).

Martinborough ▶ YOUR HOSTS: **Dawn and Bob Knight** Ph (06) 306 9912

MARTINBOROUGH EXPERIENCE B & B

84 Venice Street, Martinborough
Ph (06) 306 9912
Mobile 027-445 8266
email: *info@martinboroughexperience.co.nz*
www.martinboroughexperience.co.nz

Features & Attractions

- *Peaceful locality*
- *5 min. walk to village*
- *Café & vineyards*
- *Large rooms & ensuites*
- *Spa bath unit*
- *Family unit available*

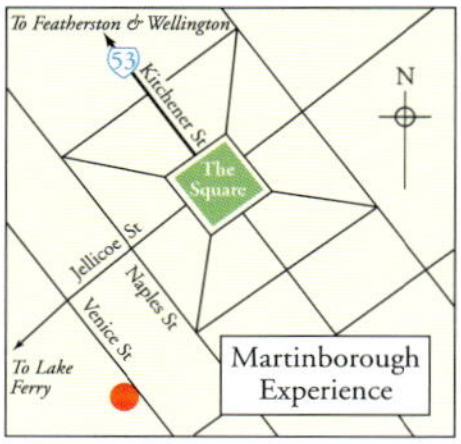

Boutique-style Bed & Breakfast Accommodation

Double	$100-150
Single	$80-120
Child	$10-20

Experience a night of luxury in one of our beautiful self-contained suites, followed by a scrumptuous breakfast. Our boutique-style Bed & Breakfast accommodation is situated on a half-acre section, five minutes walk to village square, restaurants, cafés, art and crafts. We are also close to the vineyards and olive groves that Martinborough is famous for. Our three main guest rooms have super-king size beds, their own ensuite (one with spa-bath), tea and coffee making facilities, fridge, couch and TV. The beds can convert to singles if required. Fold-away beds and a port-a-cot are available on request.
We also have available a three bedroom family unit.

Bedrooms	Qty
Double	5
Twin	1
Single	
Bed Size	**Qty**
King	3
Queen	2
Double	
Single	2
Bathrooms	**Qty**
Ensuite	3
Private	
Family Share	1

Levin ▶ YOUR HOST: **Heather Watson** Ph: (06) 368 9011

FANTAILS ACCOMMODATION

40 MacArthur Street, Levin,
Ph (06) 368 9011, Fax (06) 368 9279
email: *fantails@xtra.co.nz*
www.fantails.co.nz

Features & Attractions

- *Antique shops, organic winery*
- *'De Molen' working windmill*
- *Gardens, vintage cars, museums*
- *Wetlands/Kapiti Is. bird tours*
- *Tramping, walks*
- *River rafting, horse riding*

Self-Contained Cottages Bed & Breakfast

Double	$115-150
Single	$80-110
Child	neg

The perfect place to experience genuine hospitality, **Fantails** is a lovely haven in a hectic world.
"Wanting something different?"
Beautiful themed gardens of two acres.
Very comfortable beds, quiet surroundings – to assure a good night's sleep. Security – organic food a speciality – in a totally relaxing environment.
Lovely self-contained cottages (home-away from home), laundry facilities. "Simply the best value" say returning guests.
We look forward to your visit and will give you a memory to last a life time and a wonderful experience guaranteed.

DIRECTIONS: Please Phone for easy directions

Bedrooms	Qty
Double	3
Twin	1
Single	
Bed Size	**Qty**
King	1
Queen	2
Double	1
Single	
Bathrooms	**Qty**
Ensuite	3
Private	1
Guest Share	

Serendipity Bed & Breakfast

86 MacArthur St, Levin
Ph (06) 368 6766, Fax (06) 368 6764
Mobile 027-413 1504
email: *relax@serendipitynz.co.nz*
www.serendipitynz.co.nz

Tariff : N.Z. Dollars	
Double	$120
Single	$120
Extra pp	$30

Bedrooms	Qty
Double	2
Twin	
Single	
Bed Size	**Qty**
Super King	1
King	
Queen	1
Double	
Single	1
Bathrooms	**Qty**
Ensuite	1
Private	1
Guest Share	

Bed & Breakfast
Homestay

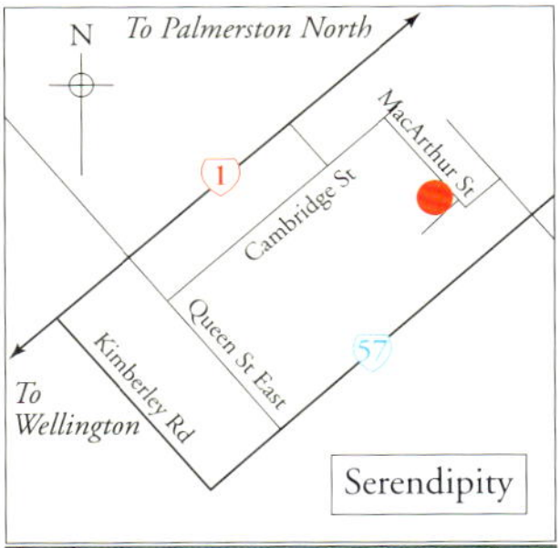

Features & Attractions

- *Superb uncrowded beaches*
- *River rafting, horse riding*
- *Vintage cars, museums, gardens*
- *Birdlife and sanctuaries*
- *Public indoor swimming pool*
- *Golf courses, mountain biking*
- *Arts and crafts*
- *Great range of restaurants*

Experience Kiwi heartland hospitality on the Nature Coast – stop, relax and take your time. Chris and Barbara invite you to unwind at **Serendipity** – in a quiet corner of town. A pleasant 30-minute walk, or 5 minute drive from the centre – close to the theatre and restaurants. The Nature Coast is ideally located to explore the lower North Island. 1½ hours to Wellington, 40 minutes to Palmerston North, 3 hours to the Hawkes Bay or Taranaki. Discover the pleasures of the Nature Coast – take your time to enjoy the fine foods, produced in the 'market garden' of New Zealand, the talented local artisans and craftspeople. Historic Otaki, the Foxton Windmill and museums, the Manawatu Estuary and Lake Papaitonga for birdlife, are all within a ½ hour drive.

Visit the unspoiled beaches, enjoy the fantastic sunsets, picnic by rivers, tramp in the Tararua Ranges, go white-water rafting or take a 4X4 motorcycle excursion. With prior notice we can arrange permits and passage to Kapiti Island. A world-class vintage car museum and several golf courses are all within easy distance.

Awatea Lodge

19 Hadfield Rd, Peka Peka, RD 1, Waikanae
Ph (04) 293 2404, Mobile 027-2427572
email: *brent@awatealodge.co.nz*
www.awatealodge.co.nz

Tariff : N.Z. Dollars	
Double	$120-150
Single	$90-100
Child	

Bedrooms	Qty
Double	1
Twin	1
Single	
Bed Size	**Qty**
Super King	
King	
Queen	1
Double	
Single	2
Bathrooms	**Qty**
Ensuite	
Private	1
Guest Share	

A Relaxing Farmstay/Homestay Bed & Breakfast

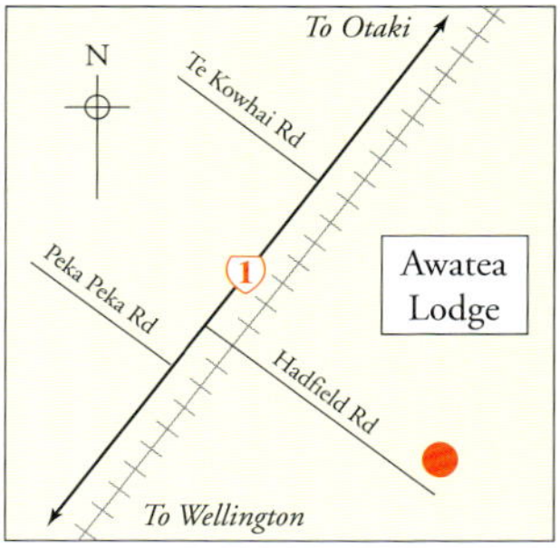

Features & Attractions

- *Restful, friendly atmosphere*
- *Panoramic views/sunsets*
- *Private spa pool*
- *Gourmet breakfast*
- *Bush or beach walks*
- *Great local restaurants*
- *Spinning/weaving studio*
- *45 min. to Wellington*

We welcome you! Take time to relax and enjoy eight acres of garden and beautiful natural surroundings. Unwind in the hammock on the deck, or walk around the farm and meet the friendly alpacas and llamas.
A spectacular way to enjoy a beautiful Kapiti Island sunset is to either stroll up the back hill or wander along the beach – or you may just prefer to "chill-out" in the spa pool.
Local eco-tourism includes coastal, river and bush walks, or a special day trip to the Kapiti Island. Other popular attractions include the 'Kapiti Arts Trail', Maori Arts gallery and golf courses.

Our specialty is "slow-food" using where possible our own fresh, organic produce. We can prepare delicious home-made dinners and hampers on request. A cooked or continental breakfast is included in the tariff.
Guests' comments:
"An extremely wonderful and relaxing setting, lovely food, comforts and company". Lower Hutt.
"Our stay here was the highlight of our trip". UK.

YOUR HOSTS: **Glenys and Brian Daw** Ph: (04) 902 8530 ***Waikanae - Kapiti Coast***

AT SUDBURY ESTATE

39 Manu Grove, Waikanae, Kapiti Coast
Ph (04) 902 8530
Mobile 021-129 6970
email: *stay@sudbury.co.nz*
www.sudbury.co.nz

Tariff : N.Z. Dollars	
Double	$150-195
Single	$120-195
Child	

Bedrooms	Qty
Double	3
Twin	
Single	
Bed Size	**Qty**
Super King	
King	
Queen	3
Double	
Single	
Bathrooms	**Qty**
Ensuite	
Private	2
Guest Share	

VISA MasterCard

DIRECTIONS:
At Waikanae turn off SH 1 at BP Service Station (Ngaio Rd) then 1st right into Parata St, 2nd left into Sylvan Ave, 4th right into David St, 1st left into Hurunui St, 1st right into Manu Grove. **Sudbury Estate** is signposted at the end of the Grove.

Delightful Boutique Cottage & Homestay in Unique Garden Setting

Features & Attractions

- *Ample safe off-street parking*
- *Room safes*
- *Internet facilities*
- *Laundry available*
- *Four golf courses nearby*
- *Beach and bush walks*
- *Pétanque piste*
- *Complimentary bicycles*

"The place to stay in Kapiti."

Experience sincere Kiwi hospitality in a superb location only 50 minutes from Wellington City and ferry.
Arrive at **Sudbury** and enter another world. Nestled in a beautiful secluded 2 acre garden surrounded by trees and natural bush with a large lily pond the peacefulness will astound you.
The cosy **Frangipani** and **Magnolia** rooms have French doors opening onto the garden, private lounge and large private bathroom with spa bath. Self-contained **Camellia Cottage**, a romantic hideaway with private courtyard, fully equipped kitchenette and entertainment centre provides that extra dimension for a very special stay. All rooms have quality queen-size beds, are charmingly furnished and include many little luxuries for your comfort. Awake to birdsong and enjoy a leisurely breakfast with a fresh fruit platter, freshly baked pastries, home-made preserves, choice of teas or freshly brewed coffee. Excellent village restaurants 1km. Dinner available by prior arrangement. Come as a stranger but leave as a friend.

Broadeaves

24 Ngarara Road, Waikanae, Wellington
Ph (04) 293 1483, Fax (04) 293 1583
Mobile 027-554 5175
email: *stay@broadeaves.co.nz*
www.broadeaves.co.nz

Tariff : N.Z. Dollars	
Double	$145-250
Single	$125-180
Child	$25-50

Bedrooms	Qty
Double	2
Twin	1
Single	
Bed Size	**Qty**
Super King	
King/Twin	1
Queen	2
Double	
Single	
Bathrooms	**Qty**
Ensuite	1
Private	1
Guest Share	1

Elegant Accommodation

Features & Attractions

- *Park-like tranquil gardens*
- *Separate guest wing*
- *Relaxed friendly atmosphere*
- *Wellington 45 min/beach 4 min*
- *Children very welcome*
- *Cater for everyone - holiday or business*
- *Weekend packages available*
- *Activities plentiful*

DIRECTIONS:
Take SH 1 to Waikanae, turn at Harcourt lights into Te Moana Road, take 3rd street on right - Ngarara Road.

Looking for a night or two away, on your own or with family? You'll find **Broadeaves** is the answer. Join us in a relaxed atmosphere, where time is your own. Join us for refreshments and feel yourself quickly unwind.

Our separate guest wing includes large luxurious bedroom, ensuite and French doors leading to private spa area, with an adjacent twin room for families or friends travelling together. Flat screen TV, DVD, tea and coffee facilities in room.

After a great night's sleep you'll enjoy a freshly prepared breakfast, al fresco beside the pool or in the dining room. Visit local tourist attractions, have a game of pétanque, sit in the garden with a book, dine in great restaurants and most of all – relax. The apartment-style Pool House is great for those wanting a little more privacy. Dinners available on request. We invite you to share our paradise with our two children, two dogs and the cat. **See you soon.**

"What a treat to stay in such a peaceful spot".

Country Patch

18 Kea Street, Waikanae
Ph (04) 293 5165, Fax (04) 293 5164
Mobile 027-457 8421
email: *stay@countrypatch.co.nz*
www.countrypatch.co.nz

Tariff : N.Z. Dollars	
Double	$135-210
Single	
Child	$20-25

Bedrooms	Qty
Double	2
Twin	1
Single	1
Bed Size	**Qty**
Super King Twin	2
King	
Queen	1
Double	
Single	2
Bathrooms	**Qty**
Ensuite	3
Private	
Guest Share	

Self-contained Bed & Breakfast

Features & Attractions

- *Delightful country style*
- *Magnificent views*
- *Cosy and comfortable*
- *Good restaurants close by*
- *2 minutes drive from SH 1*
- *Wellington commuter train 7 min*
- *Villa has large verandah and wheelchair access*

It's the little extras... that keep guests staying an extra night. Our visitor book glows with appreciative accolades. Two delightful self-contained accommodation sites...

Country Patch Studio, with its own entrance and deck, has a queen bed with ensuite and twin beds on the mezzanine floor of the kitchen-lounge.

Country Patch Villa has an open fire and large verandah with magical views. It is wheelchair accessible and the two bedrooms, each with ensuite, have super-king beds that can unzip to make twins.

Set on 2½ acres in the Waikanae foothills with breathtaking views over the Kapiti Coast and historic Kapiti Island, the property is handy to Wellington and the Manawatu. Bush walks can be enjoyed from over the back fence.

Hosts Brian and Sue display an infectious hospitality. **A treat you can't beat!**

Waikanae Sands

8 Waiheke Street, Paraparaumu Beach, Waikanae
Ph (04) 293 4601
Mobile 027-306 9336
email: *enquiry@waikanaesands.co.nz*
www.waikanaesands.co.nz

Tariff : N.Z. Dollars	
Double	$130-220
Single	$85-110
Child	neg

Bedrooms	Qty
Double	2
Twin	
Single	1
Bed Size	**Qty**
Super King	
King	
Queen	2
Double	
King/Single	1
Bathrooms	**Qty**
Ensuite	2
Private	
Guest Share	1

BB **Self-contained Luxury Bed & Breakfast** SC

VISA MasterCard

Features & Attractions

- *Private beach access*
- *Kapiti Island and river views*
- *Good local restaurants*
- *Bedrooms with ensuites/seaviews*
- *Safe and quiet setting*
- *Full kitchen and laundry*
- *Guest lounge with fireplace*
- *Double garaging*

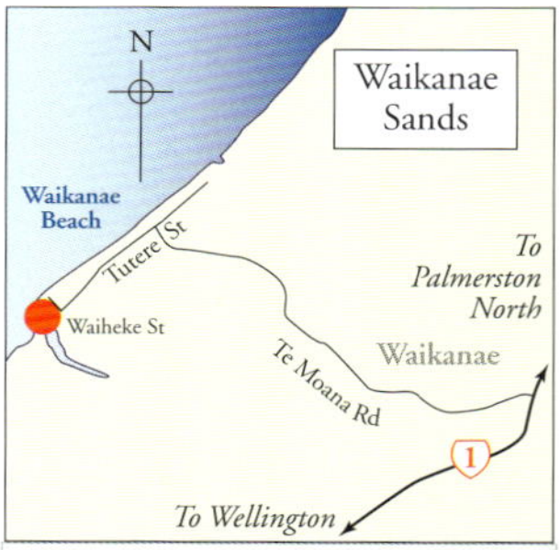

DIRECTIONS: From north, take south-bound SH1. Turn right into Te Moana Road. Turn left into Tutere Street. Go to the end of the street to find Waiheke Street.
From Wellington, take north-bound SH1. Turn left into Te Moana Road. From here same as above.

Located in the finest spot of the Kapiti Coast, **Waikanae Sands** offers the best in Bed & Breakfast (holiday home) for for a wide variety of guests. From its private entrance you have access to kayaking, swimming or strolls in the park or along the lagoon next to the beach. **Waikanae Sands** offers our guests spectacular views of the Kapiti Island from all bedrooms. It also overlooks the Waikanae River. At night, you can observe breathtaking views of the sunset. The accommodation is also minutes from local cafés and restaurants with a variety of cuisine-styles. **Waikanae Sands** is also close to a range of activities and attractions within the region including golf courses, arts and crafts and the Lindale Farm, which is famous for its Kapiti Cheese(s).
Set in a quiet and safe cul-de-sac area, this is ideal for a wide range of guests, including a family with children. Everyone will enjoy this warm and friendly home.

Helen's Waikanae Beach B&B/Homestay

115 Tutere St, Waikanae Beach, Kapiti Coast
Ph (04) 902 5829, Fax (04) 902 5840
Mobile 021-259 3396
email: *waikanaebeachbandb@paradise.net.nz*
www.waikanaebeachbandb.net

Tariff : N.Z. Dollars	
Double	$110-130
Single	$90-110
Child	neg

Bedrooms	Qty
Double	2
Twin	
Single	
Bed Size	**Qty**
Super King	
King	
Queen	2
Double	
Single	
Bathrooms	**Qty**
Ensuite	1
Private	1
Guest Share	

A Relaxing Seaside Homestay/ Bed & Breakfast

DIRECTIONS:
From Wellington travel north on SH1, cross Waikanae Bridge, then left into Te Moana Road. Follow road down, keep left where road splits. At T-intersection turn left into Tutere St.

Features & Attractions

- *Warm, friendly hospitality*
- *Delicious dinners by arrangement*
- *Awesome sea views and sunsets*
- *All day tea/coffee making facilities*
- *Direct beach access*
- *Good local restaurants*
- *Tennis courts for hire nearby*
- *Petanque, bicycles, racquets av.*

Helen's Waikanae Beach B&B is situated on a beautiful sandy, safe swimming beach, approx. 55 minutes drive north of central city Wellington. With spectacular views of Kapiti Island and all the way to the South Island, you will find this the perfect relaxing location away from all the hustle and bustle of life. At night, marvel at the brightest stars you have ever seen and be lulled to sleep by the soothing sound of the ocean. Sheer magic! In the morning, tuck into a delicious breakfast, followed by a leisurely walk on the beach. Visit my website for suggestions of what to do and see on the Kapiti Coast. Why not treat someone special (e.g. Mum and Dad) to a weekend stay (dinner included – Helen's speciality!)

Guests' comments...

"A wonderful experience–your home truly welcomes *guests* that leave as *friends*."–USA "5 Star! A very relaxing 2 days."–UK "Everywhere in NZ is wonderful, but this is the best. Unrivalled position and hospitality."–UK "We loved our stay, very beautiful, and a wonderful welcome."–Hamburg

Kapiti Coast - Waikanae

YOUR HOSTS: **Karen and Peter Anderson** Ph (04) 293 5908

Reikorangi Country Cottage

154 Akatarawa Road, R.D. Waikanae, Kapiti Coast
Ph (04) 293 5908, Fax (04) 293 5908
Mobile 021- 214 0654
email: *the.country.cottage@xtra.co.nz*

Features & Attractions

- *Peaceful country setting*
- *Veranda BBQ area*
- *Golf & beach shops 7min.*
- *5min/5km from SH1*
- *120 acres of tranquillity*
- *Cooked meals available*

Self-contained Cottage Bed & Breakfast

$	
Double	$120-160
Single	$90-130
Child	neg

Bedrooms	Qty
Double	1
Twin	
Single	
Bed Size	**Qty**
King	
Queen	
Double	1
Single	
Bathrooms	**Qty**
Ensuite	
Private	1
Guest Share	

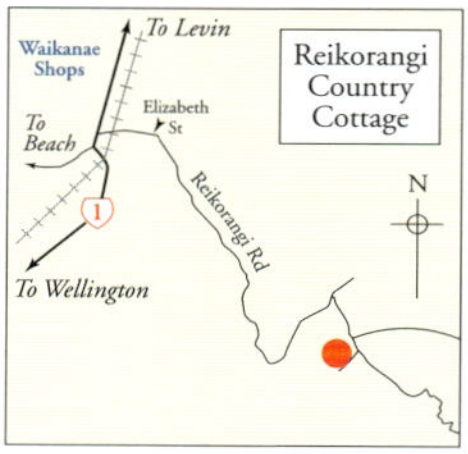

Superb, quiet Countrystay in a newly built self-contained cottage only 5 minutes/5km from Waikanae State Highway 1. The cottage comprises of a kitchen/dining/lounge and bedroom open plan area with a private bathroom and toilet. Outside is a veranda and deck BBQ area. We have 120 acres of farm with river and bush walks on the property as well as sheep, calves, pigs, chooks and a big vegie garden, orchard and berries. Cooked breakfast and evening meals are available in traditional Kiwi style with most ingredients grown on the farm.

Waikanae has many restaurants, shops, golf course and safe beach. Wellington is 50 minutes away. On arrival it's our pleasure to show you around and point out the best day tours to make your stay most enjoyable.

Waikanae - Wellington

YOUR HOSTS: **Eppie and Paul Murton** Ph: (04) 293 1936

Riverstone Garden

111 Ngatiawa Road, Waikanae, Kapiti Coast
Ph (04) 293 1936, Fax (04) 293 1936
email: *riverstone@paradise.net.nz*

Features & Attractions

- *Rural self-contained*
- *Local dining out*
- *River and bird song*
- *Bush and local walks*
- *Shops, beach, Lindale*
- *Golf and car museum*

Rural Cottage Bed & Breakfast

$	
Double	$100-120
Single	$70
Child	$45

Bedrooms	Qty
Double	1
Twin	1
Single	
Bed Size	**Qty**
King	
Queen	1
Double	
Single	2
Bathrooms	**Qty**
Ensuite	
Private	1
Guest Share	

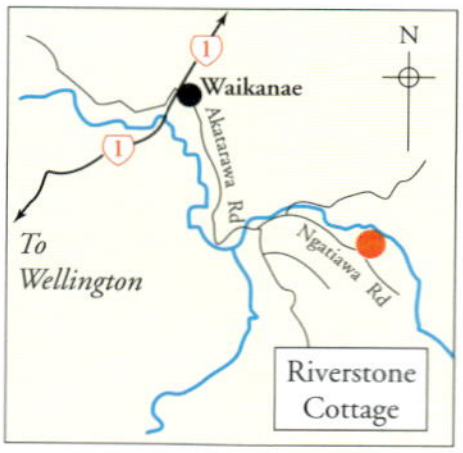

The cottage has self-contained accommodation with bedrooms, bathroom, lounge and kitchenette. Courtyard and barbecue area with views of river and bush. Continental or full breakfast. Paul is an engineer and writer, and Eppie sketches and paints. Laundry facilities. Local café, pottery and birdpark with river walks and you can swim in the river. There are more restaurants in Waikanae village, six minutes drive, and in Paraparaumu, ten minutes towards Wellington. Craft shops and boutiques at Lindale and general shopping at Paraparaumu. Beaches and swimming pools in both centres. The capital city Wellington is forty-five minutes away and has the airport, inter-island ferries, modern shops, art galleries and museums.

DIRECTIONS: Turn off SH 1 across railway lines onto Akatarawa Road. At 5km turn left before small church into Ngatiawa Road. 1km to **Riverstone** on left.

Anchor at the Pier

4 Seaview Rd, Paraparaumu Beach, Kapiti Coast
Ph (04) 293 2875, Fax (04) 293 1583
Mobile 027-554 5175
email: *stay@anchoratthepier.co.nz*
www.anchoratthepier.co.nz

Tariff : N.Z. Dollars	
Double	$250-350
Single	
Child	$25

Bedrooms	Qty
Double	2
Twin	
Single	
Bed Size	**Qty**
Super King	
King	
Queen	1
Double	
Single	2
Bathrooms	**Qty**
Ensuite	1
Private	1
Guest Share	

VISA MasterCard

Executive Self-contained Apartment

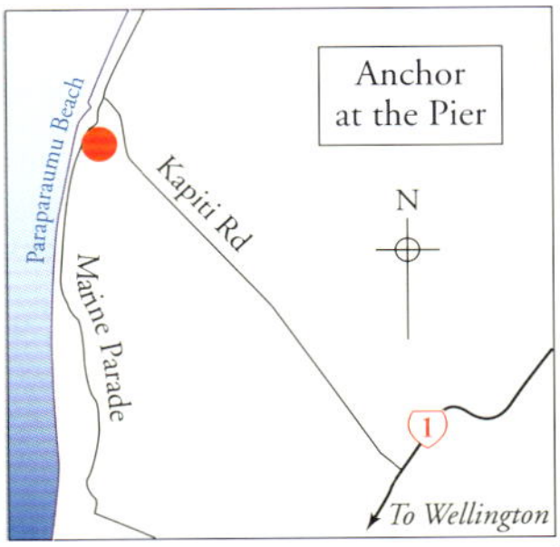

Features & Attractions

- *Kapiti Island views*
- *Two x 2-bedroom apartments*
- *Heated swimming pool*
- *Variety cafés and restaurants*
- *Underground car parking*
- *Secure entry to complex*
- *Quality furnishings and linen*
- *Full kitchen and laundry*

Anchor at the Pier is on the Kapiti Coast, just one hour north of Wellington, and three and a half hours south of Taupo.

Touring New Zealand? Family gathering? Spoil yourselves, take a break and relax in one of our two new stunning apartments in 'The Pier' complex, overlooking the conservation island of Kapiti. Situated in the enviable beachfront location on Paraparaumu Beach, just minutes from the ferry to Kapiti Island and the buzz of local cafés, restaurants, and shopping. Close to the links golf course, Paraparaumu Airport, Southwards vintage car museum and nature reserves.

Each apartment has two bedrooms and two bathrooms and is tastefully furnished with stylish drapes and quality linen. Use the fully equipped kitchen and dine formally or alfresco on the private patio (with electric barbeque) overlooking the heated pool or enjoy the stunning views from the private balcony. The stylish lounges are spacious and comfortable with underfloor heating, flat screen TVs and DVD/CD players. There is a secure proximity entry system with designated underground parking. Minimum of two nights or rent for a week or more. Enjoy the beach holiday feel.

The Boathouse

39 Matatua Rd, Raumati Beach, Kapiti Coast, Wellington
Ph (04) 293 1483, Fax (04) 293 1583
Mobile 027-554 5175
email: *stay@theboathouse.co.nz*
www.theboathouse.co.nz

Tariff : N.Z. Dollars	
Double	$180-250
Single	–
Child	–

Bedrooms	Qty
Double	1
Twin	1
Single	
Bed Size	**Qty**
Super King	
King	
Queen	1
Double	
Single	2
Bathrooms	**Qty**
Ensuite	
Private	1
Guest Share	

Self-contained
Bed & Breakfast

Features & Attractions

- *Walk to beach & cafés*
- *Nautical theme*
- *Sole occupancy*
- *TV, DVD, CD*
- *40 min to Wellington*
- *Full kitchen & laundry*
- *Full breakfast provisions*
- *Caters for holiday or business*

DIRECTIONS:
Please telephone for easy directions.
Advance booking recommended

The Boat House is a selfcontained romantic holiday cottage with only a 4 minute walk to Raumati Beach and a 4 minute walk to a variety of restaurants. A large deck overlooks the eastern hills, you get to see the sunrise. French doors open onto deck for great outdoor entertaining. Aquarium toilet – spot all the fish – bathroom and full laundry. Stylish kitchen with all modern convenienes, even a dishwasher. You'll find a 28ft whale chaser boat right next to the house. Take a walk up the garden path and you'll find not only a double hammock between the trees, but an *outdoor bath* with hot and cold running water. Quality linens and furnishings. Refreshments and breakfast provisions provided. Outdoor furniture and a gas BBQ.
Sleeps four, so bring the kids along too. Take the time to stop and relax. Play golf, walk the beach or simply read a book.

Beach Haven

26 Pukerua Beach Road, Pukerua Bay, Porirua
Ph (04) 239 9384, Fax (04) 239 9553
email: *Pukerua.Glass@xtra.co.nz*

Features & Attractions

- *Sea & Kapiti Island views*
- *Modern spacious guest wing*
- *Handy to SH1, ferry, public transport*
- *German spoken*
- *Beaches, coastal walks*
- *Off-street parking*

$		
	Double	$190
	Wing	$350

Boutique Bed & Breakfast Stunning Sea Views

Bedrooms	Qty
Double	2
Twin	
Single	
Bed Size	**Qty**
Super King	1
Queen	
Double	
King/Single	2
Bathrooms	**Qty**
Ensuite	1
Private	
Guest Share	

Enjoy the best of both worlds - Pukerua Bay is a coastal village in a region that boasts a wide range of outdoor activities and yet is only a thirty minute drive from Wellington and all the attractions of the capital city. Visit wildlife sanctuaries, art and craft galleries, walk in the bush or tramp in the nearby Tararua Ranges. Local sports include golf, fishing, wind-surfing, paragliding, sailing and swimming.
Ideal for a group of one to four people, the guest wing in our large modern home has two bedrooms, which share a bathroom. Both rooms are sunny and have stunning sea views. The largest room has a balcony. We only take one group at a time, so you can be sure of privacy. Share an upstairs lounge with open fire and large deck with us, as well as our landscaped private courtyard surrounded by native bush. We provide meals on request. Laundry facilities available.

Boating Club Point Bed & Breakfast

Whale Cottage, 9 Gordon Road, Karehana Bay,
Plimmerton, Wellington
Ph (04) 233 9690, Mobile 027- 354 8832
email: *lizpeter@actrix.co.nz*

Features & Attractions

- *Superb sea panorama*
- *Unique décor*
- *Beach, bush & coastal walks*
- *1 min. walk to safe beach*
- *Private spa bath*
- *No stairs, extra sofa bed*

$		
	Double	$120
	Single	$95
	Child	Half price

Panoramic Sea View, Privacy and a Tale to Tell

Bedrooms	Qty
Double	1
Twin	
Single	1
Bed Size	**Qty**
King	
Queen	1
Double	
Single	1
Bathrooms	**Qty**
Ensuite	
Private	1
Guest Share	

Your self-contained wing of our character home, Whale Cottage, has breathtaking views of harbour and sea from every window. Rest in your comfortable rooms or fill your spa bath to unwind. The house has a unique nautical décor of NZ maritime history, ship fittings, curiosities and seagoing books. Your sitting-room has a telescope, easy chairs, double sofa, music, TV/video, m/w, fresh coffee, tea and breakfast (continental, self-service). On upper level, parking at your door. 2km from traffic lights on SH1. Wellington 25 minutes away - we can help plan your visit. Will meet commuter train. Enjoy the ever-changing blues of the sea. Relax watching the boats or go fishing from the jetty. At night a thousand pretty lights shine across the harbour. Good village cafés and takeaways.

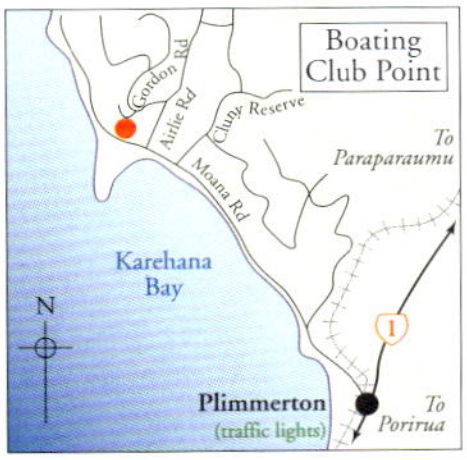

Aquavilla

16 Steyne Avenue, Plimmerton
Ph (04) 233 1146
Mobile 027-231 0141
email: *aquavilla@paradise.net.nz*
www.aquavilla.co.nz

Features & Attractions

- *Beach, a few steps away*
- *Safe off-street parking*
- *Gourmet full breakfasts*
- *Walk to cafés and shops*
- *Easy 20mins to Wellington*
- *Garden setting*

Self-Contained Seaside Accommodation

Double	$150-170
Single	$150
Child	neg

Breathe deep the sea-scented air and treat yourself, mind, body and soul at our seaside haven. In the gorgeous garden of our character villa, your architecturally-designed accommodation features a delightful courtyard – and comfort plus. Guests love the little touches, crisp cotton sheets, flowers, home-made biscuits and artistic details inside and out. Best of both worlds here: explore Wellington by easy car or rail ride, or savour the serenity of this very special retreat. Forest and beach walks right at hand, as is great golfing, galleries, shopping, windsurfing and diving. You'll relish our scrumptuous breakfasts: muesli, yoghurt and fruit or choose from the full cooked menu including blueberry pancakes and sweet-corn fritters. Later, watch the sun set before strolling to excellent cafés and restaurants, or use your kitchenette and barbeque. Warm, welcoming and widely-travelled, we're art and nature lovers with a patch of paradise we love to share. Off-street parking at your door.

Bedrooms	Qty
Double	1
Twin	
Single	
Bed Size	**Qty**
King	
Queen	1
Double	
Single	1
Bathrooms	**Qty**
Ensuite	
Private	1
Guest Share	

DREAMWATERS

9A Gordon Road, Karehana Bay, Plimmerton
Ph (04) 233 2042, Fax (04) 233 2072
Mobile 027-688 8371
email: *relax@dreamwaters.co.nz*
www.dreamwaters.co.nz

Tariff : N.Z. Dollars	
Double	$150-180
Single	$150
Child	$20

Bedrooms	Qty
Double	1
Twin	
Single	
Bed Size	**Qty**
Super King/Twin	1
King	
Queen	
Double/Sofa bed	1
Single	
Bathrooms	**Qty**
Ensuite	
Private	1
Guest Share	

Self-contained Seaside Accommodation

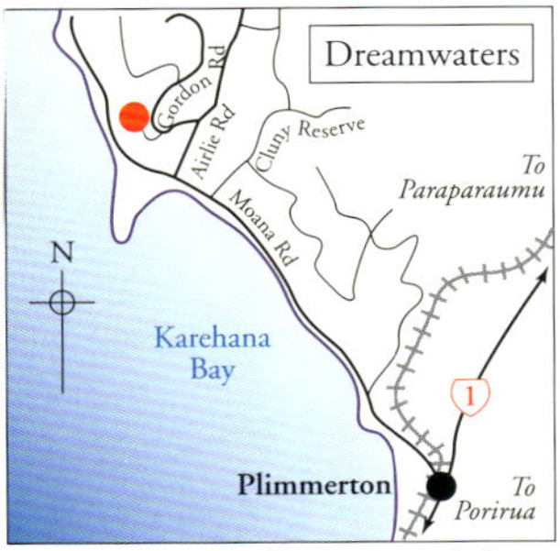

Features & Attractions

- *Awesome sea views*
- *Architecturally designed*
- *Ideal for honeymooners*
- *Sky television & phone*
- *Just 25 min. to Wellington*
- *Listen to the waves*
- *Off-street parking*
- *Private and safe*

"We absolutely loved it. Outstanding views, situation, facilities and hosts. Thank you - so much!"

Enjoy the holiday feel of this stunning Bed & Breakfast, just 20-25 minutes away from Wellington. Spectacular sea, island and coastal views from your private accommodation in our new architecturally designed home. Elevated sea front location overlooking rocks and waves only a stone's throw away. Spacious lounge, bathroom and fully equipped kitchen. Skylights, double-glazed, tinted glass and heated floor tiles for your comfort. We provide a tasty and substantial continental breakfast for you to enjoy whenever it best suits you. Listen to the sigh of the sea as you relax indoors with books, music and Sky TV. Marvel at the sunsets from your lounge or the deck. Breathe the salt air, stroll along the beach, dine in the village cafés. It's all yours. Kiwi/American hosts. Porirua City 8km. Golf courses within 10 minutes drive. ***"An excellent weekend - we'd love a ten trip ticket".***

PENRYN COVE

32 Penryn Drive, Paremata, Wellington
Ph (04) 233 8265, Fax (04) 233 8265
Mobile 027-481 5525
email: *JWClark@xtra.co.nz*

Tariff : N.Z. Dollars	
Double	$150-170
Single	$150
Child	neg

Bedrooms	Qty
Double	2
Twin	
Single	
Bed Size	**Qty**
Super King	
King	
Queen	2
Double	
Single	
Bathrooms	**Qty**
Ensuite	
Private	1
Guest Share	1

Homestay
Bed & Breakfast

Features & Attractions

- *Peaceful and tranquil location*
- *Adjoins native bush reserve*
- *Bird sanctuary*
- *Private access to beach*
- *NZ cooked or continental breakfast*
- *Close to café and restaurants*
- *2 min SH 1, 20 min Wellington*
- *Private and spacious guest area*

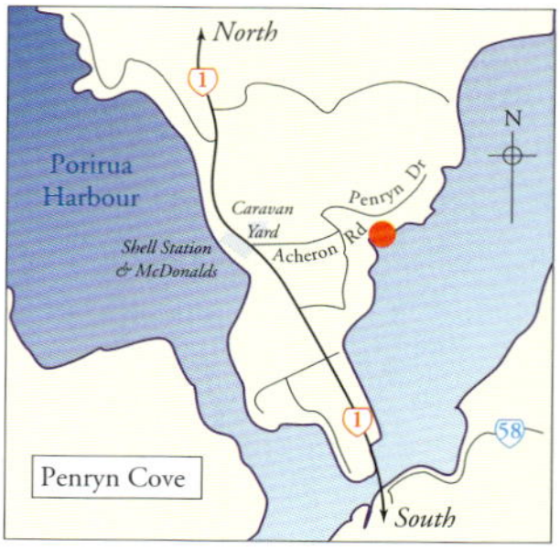

DIRECTIONS:
Two minutes from SH 1.
Please phone for easy directions.

We extend a warm welcome to our guests. Enjoy the tranquil, peaceful setting of Penryn Cove, surrounded by native bush reserve, set on the edge of a peninsula, overlooking the picturesque Pauatahanui inlet and bird sanctuary. Private and easy access onto inlet walkway will provide you with some relaxing recreation, or simply relax and enjoy the garden, peace, sun and views on the decks or in our private courtyard and pergola. We have travelled extensively and enjoy meeting and sharing our home with fellow travellers. Your home away from home. Easy walking distance to café, restaurants, shops, rail and historic Plimmerton village and beach. Private, spacious guest area with magical views, private deck.

Eirené Retreat

1029 Akatarawa Road, Birchville, Upper Hutt
Ph (04) 526 3638, Fax (04) 526 3628
Mobile 021-107 6949
email: *beachen@paradise.net.nz*
www.eirene.co.nz

Tariff : N.Z. Dollars	
Double	$150-185
Single	$130-165
Child	$40

Bedrooms	Qty
Double	2
Twin	
Single	
Bed Size	**Qty**
Super King	
King	
Queen	1
Double	
Single	2
Bathrooms	**Qty**
Ensuite	
Private	1
Guest Share	

Advance booking recommended

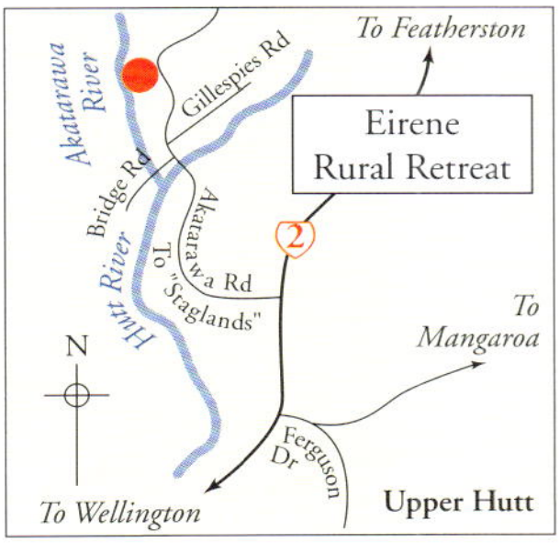

Rural Retreat
Self-contained Accommodation

Features & Attractions

- *Single-party bookings*
- *Quiet, peaceful surrounds*
- *Private river access*
- *Outdoor ozone spa pool*
- *Sumptuous breakfasts*
- *Two bedrooms, sleep four*
- *Sky Television*
- *30 min. to ferry*

'Time Out' – it sounds so familiar, doesn't it? But somewhere in our busy lives it's become a distant memory. We all need time out. You simply need the space to recharge and refresh your soul. Welcome to **Eirené Retreat**. No crowds, just a gentle rural pace.

Our guests say:
'Charming place, lovely hosts, an unforgettable experience' – France
'A special spot for the weary traveller' – USA
'Delightful, relaxing place' – UK
'Amazing, we have been spoilt, thank you so much' – UK
'Lovely piece of paradise' – Singapore
'Thank you for sharing your paradise with us. We could not have started the New Year better' – USA
'Delightful stay, very relaxing and sumptuous breakfasts. A lovely place to relax and explore the area' – Germany
'This place is magic' – Australia

DUNGARVIN

25 Hinau Street, Woburn, Lower Hutt, Wellington
Ph (04) 569 2125, Fax (04) 569 2126
Mobile 021-252 2933
email: *t.b.cudby@clear.net.nz*
www.bnbnz.com

Tariff : N.Z. Dollars	
Double	$105-120
Single	$80-100
Child	n/a

Bedrooms	Qty
Double	1
Twin	
Single	
Bed Size	**Qty**
Super King	
King	
Queen	1
Double	
Single	
Bathrooms	**Qty**
Ensuite	
Private	1
Guest Share	

Homestay
Bed & Breakfast

Features & Attractions

- *Bountiful breakfasts*
- *Totally relaxing environment*
- *20 min to Te Papa Museum*
- *15 min to ferries & stadium*
- *Variety of cafés/restaurants*
- *Secluded garden setting*
- *Dinner by prior arrangement*
- *Laundry and email facilities*

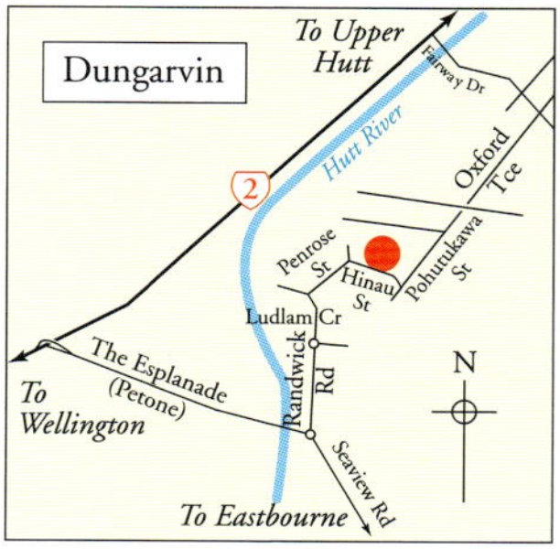

Our 75-year-old character cottage has been fully refurbished whilst retaining its original charm. We have a secluded property landscaped for quiet living, with ample off-street parking. Our home is centrally heated and has space for you to relax, read, listen to our CD collection or watch television. The sunny guest bedroom has windows opening over our well-established garden and pétanque court. The bed has an electric blanket and a wool duvet, and the private bathroom is equipped with a hairdryer, robes and toiletries.
Dinner is available by arrangement and vegetarians are catered for. Our main interests are travel, music, gardening, shows, entertaining and enjoying New Zealand wines. We will help you to plan local trips and enjoy your stay in this lovely area.

At The Bay

Marine Drive, Sorrento Bay, Eastbourne
PO Box 3717, Wellington
Ph/Fax (04) 568 4817, Mobile 027-4500 670
email: *at.the.bay@ihug.co.nz*

Tariff : N.Z. Dollars	
Double	$95-130
Single	$70-105
Child	neg.

Bedrooms	Qty
Double	1
Twin	
Single	1
Bed Size	**Qty**
Super King	
King	
Queen	
Double	1
Single	1
Bathrooms	**Qty**
Ensuite	
Private	1
Guest Share	

Homestay
Bed & Breakfast

DIRECTIONS:
Please phone, fax
or email us for directions

Features & Attractions

- *Awesome harbour & city views*
- *Bush and beachfront setting*
- *Sleep to lapping waves*
- *Awaken to birdsong*
- *Relaxed peaceful atmosphere*
- *Friendly hosts and cat*
- *20 min to ferry and CBD*
- *Single party bookings*

Jennifer, Ken and our neighbour's friendly cat Ginger look forward to giving you a warm welcome to our homestay, **At The Bay**. It is nestled amongst native bush on the beachfront at Sorrento Bay. Share with us the magical views of Wellington's picturesque harbour and city, and the tranquility of lapping waves in the evening and birdsong in the morning.

We invite you to join us for a drink on a deck in summer, or in front of a cosy fire in winter.

We are on the bus route and only twenty minutes by vehicle from Wellington's CBD, close enough to enjoy the vibrancy of the city but far enough away to relax from its hustle and bustle. Cafés and shops are close by in Eastbourne Village and historic Petone.

We hope to make your stay a memorable one, where you arrive as strangers but leave as friends. No smoking inside, please.

Johnsonville - Wellington ▶ YOUR HOSTS: Joy and Autry Kawana Ph (04) 478 1747

Paparangi Homestay

145 Helston Road, Johnsonville, Wellington
Ph (04) 478 1747
Mobile 0274-856432
email: *autry.joy@xtra.co.nz*

Features & Attractions

- *Airp/Ferry pickup by arrangement*
- *Train/shops/restaurants 2km*
- *Secluded garden setting*
- *10 min. to city/ferry*
- *20 min. to airport*
- *Off-street parking*

Secluded Garden Setting

$	
Double	$95
Single	$60
Child	neg

Paparangi Homestay is a restored cottage, over 100 years old and set in over 1 acre of cottage gardens. We are situated only 2 km from Johnsonville Railway Station and shopping centre. We have a friendly dog, 2 cats, ducks and hens, so you can have free range eggs for breakfast if desired. We enjoy sharing a pre-dinner drink with our guests and you are very welcome to have dinner with us. Ample parking is available. Bedrooms have TV/Radio and Sky TV is available in the lounge. Autry is a keen hunter and golfer and could arrange a game. We also enjoy watching rugby. We can accommodate a small dog by arrangement and have a small secure kennel. Children are welcome and smoking is okay on the verandah. Autry and Joy enjoy the company of other nationalities and our home is your home while you are with us.

DIRECTIONS: From the north from SH1 motorway take Johnsonville turn-off, sharp right around roundabout. Sharp right next roundabout , over bridge which brings you to Helston Road.

Bedrooms	Qty
Double	1
Twin	1
Single	1
Bed Size	**Qty**
King	
Queen	1
Double	1
Single	2
Bathrooms	**Qty**
Ensuite	
Private	1
Family Share	1

Petone - Wellington ▶ YOUR HOSTS: Alasdair and Christopher Ph: (04) 586 6868

Devenport Estate

1 Korokoro Road, Korokoro,
Petone, Wellington
Ph (04) 586 6868. Fax (04) 586 6869
email: *devenport_estate@hotmail.com*
http://homepages.paradise.net.nz/devenpor

Features & Attractions

- *Edwardian-style charm*
- *Unrivalled sea views*
- *Close to Picton Ferry*
- *Free Internet*
- *Continental breakfast*
- *Bohemian restaurants*

Boutique Vineyard Private Bed & Breakfast

$	
Double	$115-145
Single	$100-115
Child	neg.

Stay at the closest vineyard to the capital. Only 15 minutes to Interisland ferry, city and stadium yet with the privacy and quietness of a country retreat. An Edwardian-styled homestead overlooking Wellington harbour, built at the turn-of-the-century (2000!) based upon the MacDonald family home in Scotland. Nestled amongst native bush we have planted 400 Pinot Gris/Pinot Noir grapevines in our hobby vineyard. Guests enjoy stunning sea, bush and garden views. Bedrooms contain queen sized bed, writing desk, chairs, television, tea-making services, hairdryer, electric blanket with either ensuite or private bathroom. Free internet access, laundry service for 2 or more night stays and Petone Railway Station pick-up (see Devenport's website as limits apply). Ample off-street parking. Enjoy the gardens, play pétanque or sink back into a deck chair and admire Somes Island. Alasdair, Christopher and our two cocker spaniels, welcome you to a comfortable stay in Wellington on our vineyard estate.

Bedrooms	Qty
Double	1
Triple	2
Single	
Bed Size	**Qty**
King	
Queen	3
Double	
Single	2
Bathrooms	**Qty**
Ensuite	2
Private	1
Guest Share	

Sea Breeze

4 Green Park Lane, Korokoro, Petone, Wellington
Ph (04) 586 0025, Fax (04) 586 0026
Mobile 021-453 743 or 021-877 333
email: *bronnie@seabreezehomestay.co.nz*
www.seabreezehomestay.co.nz

Tariff : N.Z. Dollars	
Double	$275
Single	$175 p.p.
Child	

Bedrooms	Qty
Double	1
Twin	1
Single	
Bed Size	**Qty**
Super King	
King	1
Queen	
Double	
King Singles	2
Bathrooms	**Qty**
Ensuite	1
Private	1
Guest Share	

Luxury Accommodation
Bed & Breakfast

Features & Attractions

- *Stunning harbour & city views*
- *Fax & email access*
- *Inter Island Ferry 6-10 min*
- *Close to bush walks/beaches*
- *Beauty Therapist on site*
- *Close to shops and cafés*
- *Rental car available*
- *Peaceful & tranquil setting*

Sea Breeze features one of the world's most beautiful panoramic views of the ocean, bush and Wellington City. This three-level Mediterranean style house welcomes you with balconies opening from every room for ultimate views of Wellington, including all day sun.

Sea Breeze has all the elements of a secluded executive, romantic or business retreat, yet being only ten minutes along the motorway from the bright lights of Wellington City for shopping and entertainment, or for the more outdoor type there are golf courses, beaches and bush walks. Bronnie and Craig also host half or full day tours as well as four-wheel driving. Bronnie is a Beauty Therapist and offers a full range of inhouse beauty treatments.

Evening meals, lunches and picnic hampers available on request. We love it here and you will too.

Ngaio Homestay

56 Fox Street, Ngaio,
Wellington
Ph (04) 479 5325, Fax (04) 479 4325
email: *jennifer.timmings@clear.net.nz*

Tariff : N.Z. Dollars	
Double	$130-140
Single	$100-130
Child	neg

Bedrooms	Qty
Double	2
Twin	1
Single	1
Bed Size	**Qty**
Super King	
King	
Queen	1
Double	1
Single	3
Bathrooms	**Qty**
Ensuite	3
Private	1
Guest Share	

Homestay
Self-contained Accommodation

Features & Attractions

- *Family home atmosphere*
- *Safe, quiet surroundings*
- *Off-street parking*
- *Extensive views*
- *2 min walk to local train station*
- *Ferry 5 min, city 10 min by car*
- *Internet facilities available*
- *Music salon*

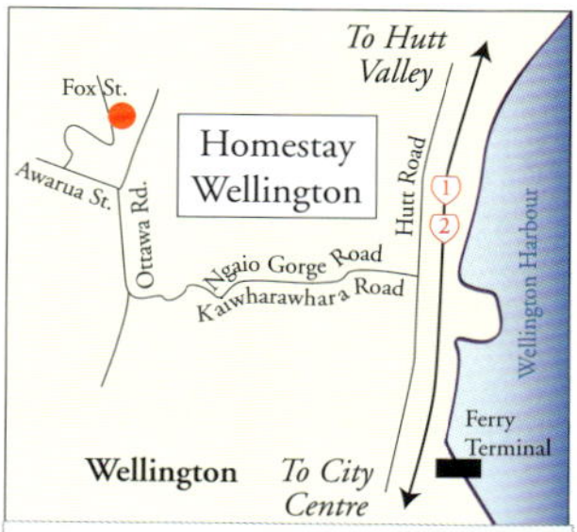

DIRECTIONS: From ferry take north exit, left at first traffic lights – Ngaio Gorge Road, at roundabout take Ottawa Road fork, at shops turn left Awarua Street – Fox Street is second on right. Use driveway at No.56.

Welcome to Wonderful Wellington! Share your visit with us and enjoy helpful personal hospitality! Our unusual multi-level open plan character home (built1960) is in the suburb of Ngaio. Guests may leave their car here and take the train to CBD (10 min). Our double room has tea/coffee facilities, quality bedding, tiled ensuite and French doors opening onto a deck and private "jungle" garden. Breakfast is continental. Evening meals an optional extra. Adjacent to our property, two self-contained apartments, one queen, one twin, are comfortable, convenient, tastefully furnished and recently redecorated. Each apartment has a couch with a fold out bed in lounge, fully equipped kitchen, shower, bath, laundry facilities, cable television, telephone and internet (small fee). There is a large garden with trees, birds and views. Jennifer plays harp at home and live piano music daily in NZ's top department store. Our adult son Christopher lives at home and is a computer whiz. Compliment from guest "This is a home where there is beautiful music, art and love". Please phone before 11am or after 3pm or fax or email.

KHANDALLAH BED & BREAKFAST

50 Clark Street, Khandallah, Wellington
Ph (04) 479 5578
email: *fairhall@paradise.net.nz*
www.travelwise.co.nz

Tariff : N.Z. Dollars	
Double	$250
Single	$220
Child	neg

Bedrooms	Qty
Double	2
Twin	1
Single	
Bed Size	**Qty**
Super King	
King	
Queen	2
Double	
Single	2
Bathrooms	**Qty**
Ensuite	2
Private	1
Guest Share	

Superior Bed & Breakfast

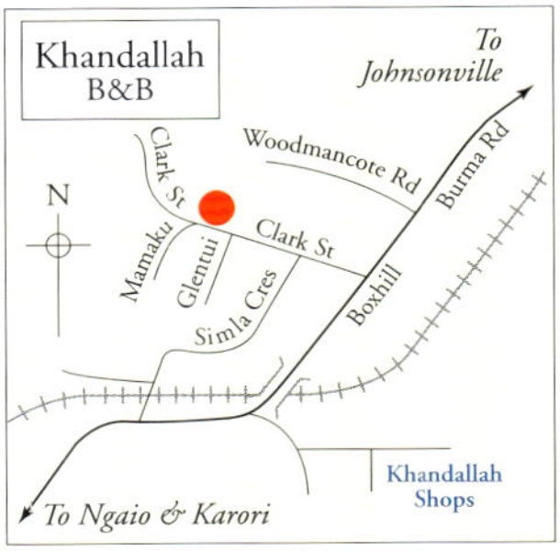

DIRECTIONS: From SH 1 motorway take Johnsonville exit and follow signs for Khandallah & Karori. Turn right off Box Hill into Clark Street (4 km from SH 1).

Features & Attractions

- *Quiet and tranquil setting*
- *8 min to Interisland Ferry*
- *Spacious bedrooms with balconies*
- *Heated swimming pool*
- *10 min to the city*
- *Off street parking*
- *Excellent local dining*
- *Tennis court*

Khandallah Bed & Breakfast is set in large grounds with formal rose gardens and box hedging. There is a heated swimming pool and tennis court which guests are welcome to use. Tim has a large model of the German Black Forest Railway set in the 1930s, which he is delighted to show to guests. The bedrooms include television, tea/coffee, home baking, refrigerator with fresh milk, wine and lemon cordial, electric blankets, bathrobes, heating and hair dryers. Full breakfast is served in the formal dining room which includes fresh fruit salad, homemade muffins and jam. The house is filled with antiques and New Zealand art. We have a voluptuous black cat, Samantha, who loves meeting the guests.
We enjoy sports, especially golf, and can arrange a game.

HARBOUR VISTA

24 Kilsyth Street, Karori, Wellington
Ph (04) 476 2477, Fax (04) 476 2479
Mobile 021-139 0606
email: *pgsisson@xtra.co.nz*
www.harbourvista.co.nz

Tariff : N.Z. Dollars	
Double	$140-200
Single	$120
Child	–

Bedrooms	Qty
Double	2
Twin	
Single	
Bed Size	**Qty**
Super King	
King	1
Queen	1
Single	
Bathrooms	**Qty**
Ensuite	1
Private	1
Guest Share	
Family Share	

Quality Homestay Bed & Breakfast

Features & Attractions

- *Quiet cul-de-sac*
- *City 8-10 minutes*
- *Magnificent harbour views*
- *Well travelled hosts*
- *Free pick-up and drop-off*
- *Free internet, laundry*
- *German spoken*
- *Scrumptuous breakfast*

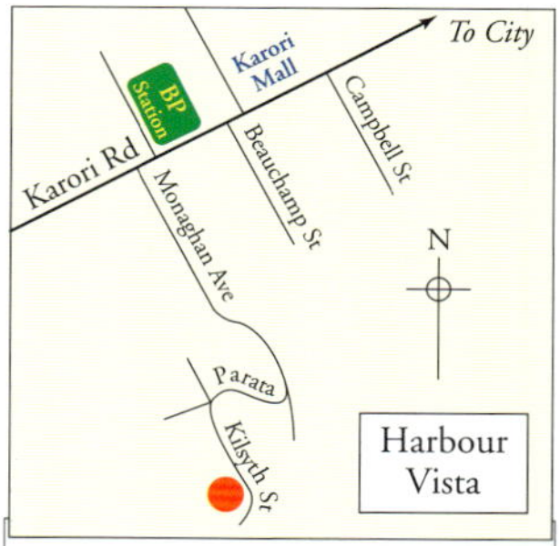

DIRECTIONS:
From Wellington on SH1 to Karori past botanical gardens, through tunnel. 50m past Karori Shopping Mall: BP Station on right, immediately after turn left into Monaghan Ave. Continue up street till you see large green space on left, turn right ino Paparata, left into Kilsyth, we are on the right.

Welcome to our home, situated in a quiet cul-de-sac with awesome views of our suburb, hills and our beautiful harbour. We are 5-10 minutes from the Cable Car, botanical gardens, the world renowned 'Bird Sanctuary' and the city. We have travelled extensively ourselves and enjoy meeting and sharing our home with fellow travellers. Rooms have tea and coffee making facilities, electric blankets, hair dryer and bathrobes. Extremely comfortable beds and a warm welcome awaits you. We encourage you to relax and enjoy our lovely lounge with its views, books, music and a piano. A scrumptious breakfast is served in our elegant dining room. Free internet and laundry facilities, off-street parking. – 'Home-away-from-home'.

Harbour Lodge Wellington

200 Barnard Street, Wadestown, Wellington
Ph (04) 976 5677, Mobile 021-032 6497
email: *lou@harbourlodgewellington.com*
www.harbourlodgewellington.com

Tariff : N.Z. Dollars	
Double	$180-260
Single	$160-240
Child	neg

Bedrooms	Qty
Double	4
Twin	
Single	
Bed Size	**Qty**
Super King	
King	4
Queen	
Double	
Single	
Bathrooms	**Qty**
Ensuite	4
Private	
Guest Share	

BB **Luxury Bed & Breakfast** LA

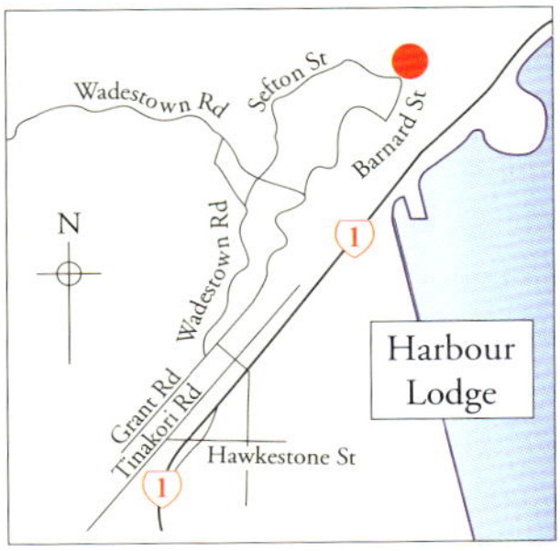

DIRECTIONS: From north - take Hawkestone St exit off motorway. Turn right onto bridge, right again onto Tinakori Rd. Follow signs to Wadestown (3rd on left), follow Wadestown Rd up hill for 2 min, turn right into Sefton St (changes name to Barnard St). Look for our sign on left. Drive down driveway to the bottom.

Features & Attractions

- *Fabulous harbour views*
- *Heated indoor pool*
- *Spa pool & sauna*
- *Beautiful bush setting*
- *2 km to central city*
- *Close to ferry & stadium*
- *Rooms with balconies*
- *Large lounge with woodburner*

Harbour Lodge is situated on a quiet hillside amongst beautiful native bush, with all day sun and sweeping harbour views, yet only three minutes drive from central Wellington, Wellington Stadium and the ferry terminal. Admire the fabulous views of Wellington Harbour from the large sunny deck. Idly watch as the ferries curve in and out of the harbour and the yachts drift by. Enjoy a dip in the heated pool, treat yourself to a sauna or spa, or on cooler evenings warm up around a crackling fire in the spacious guest lounge. The guest rooms have been refurbished to the highest quality with king size beds and snowy white linen. Each room has a private bathroom and views to the native bush-clad hills or harbour. Cable television, tea /coffee making facilities are available in each room.
Let your stresses be gently lulled away in the luxurious comfort of this beautiful new lodge.

You might never want to leave.

Villa Vittorio

6 Hawker Street, Mt. Victoria, Wellington
Ph (04) 801 5761, Fax (04) 801 5762
Mobile 027-432 1267
email: *villa@villavittorio.co.nz*
www.villavittorio.co.nz

Tariff : N.Z. Dollars	
Double	$180-220
Single	$120-135
Child	

Bedrooms	Qty
Double	1
Twin	
Single	
Bed Size	**Qty**
Super King	
King	
Queen	1
Double	
Single	
Bathrooms	**Qty**
Ensuite	
Private	1
Guest Share	

Boutique Bed & Breakfast
Restored 1870 Villa

Features & Attractions

- *Historic suburb*
- *5 minute walk to cafés etc*
- *Sitting room with balcony*
- *Italian-styled courtyard*
- *Gourmet breakfasts*
- *Dinner by arrangement*
- *Good shopping nearby*
- *Close to Te Papa Museum*

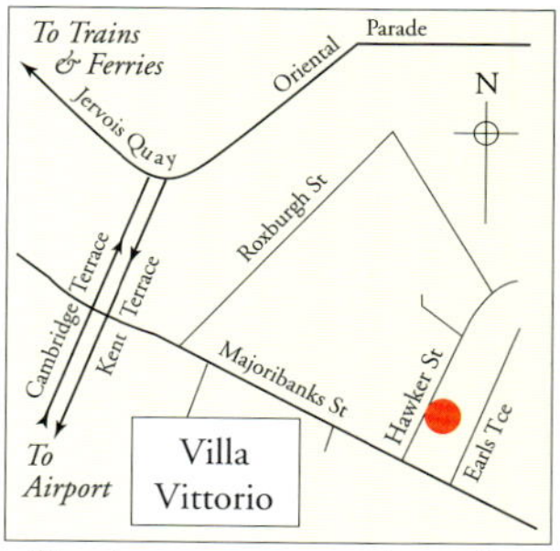

Built in 1870 and recently renovated, Villa Vittorio offers a guest bedroom with television, tea and coffee making facilities and an adjoining sitting room with balcony with city views. You have your own luxurious bathroom with shower and bath. Te Papa National Museum, shopping, theatres, restaurants and the upgraded Oriental Bay Beach are all within easy walking distance. Westpac Stadium is within a thirty minute walk. The café scene at Courtenay Place is only a short stroll. We cater for special occasions and small intimate weddings. We also offer dinner by arrangement, including a complimentary bottle of New Zealand wine. Recent guests have recorded in our visitors book: "Beautiful home, wonderful breakfast, superb hospitality". Garaging, internet and laundry are available at a small charge. Parking is also available. No children or pets please. Reservations are recommended – please phone, fax, email or write. We have travelled extensively ourselves and enjoy having guests. We hope your stay with us will be memorable.

Lambton Heights Boutique Bed & Breakfast

20 Talavera Terrace, Kelburn, Wellington
Ph (04) 472 4710, Fax (04) 472 4715
Mobile 027-693 1952
email: *lambtonheights@paradise.net.nz*
www.lambtonheights.co.nz

Tariff : N.Z. Dollars	
Double	$180-250
Single	$160-200
Child	

Bedrooms	Qty
Double	3
Twin	2
Single	
Bed Size	**Qty**
Super King	3
King	
Queen	
Double	
Single	4
Bathrooms	**Qty**
Ensuite	3
Private	
Guest Share	

Luxury
Bed & Breakfast

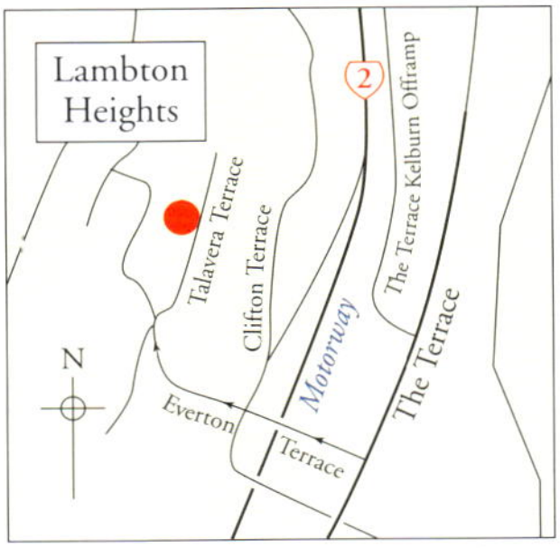

Features & Attractions

- *Beautiful heritage home*
- *Private and peaceful*
- *Stroll to the C.B.D.*
- *Garden spa pool*
- *Views of city and harbour*
- *Two min walk to the cable car*

Lambton Heights offers Boutique Bed & Breakfast accommodation two minutes off the motorway and a short walk from the CBD. **Lambton Heights** is a heritage home in Wellington's inner suburb of Kelburn with sweeping views of city and harbour. Our guest lounge overlooks the garden. Facilities include a small library and tea/coffee making facilities with delicious home-made baking. The olde-world charm and character of **Lambton Heights** has been enhanced with new, modern bathroom facilities. Our luxurious suites include super-king beds, quality linen, bath-robes, toiletries, hair dryer and Sky TV. Internet access available if required. Enjoy the sound of New Zealand's native tui in the morning, the short stroll to the botanic gardens, historic cable car, parliament buildings, Te Papa and Victoria University. Breakfast includes fresh fruit salad, cereals, bread and preserves accompanied by a delicious gourmet-cooked course. Complimentary pick-up from airport or ferry terminals if requested. We are proud to be smoke free.

Mount Victoria Homestay

11 Lipman Street, Mount Victoria, Wellington
Ph (04) 802 4886, Fax (04) 802 4877
email: *stay@mountvictoria.co.nz*
www.*mountvictoria.co.nz*

Tariff : N.Z. Dollars	
Double	$230
Single	$180
Child	

Bedrooms	Qty
Double	2
Twin	
Single	
Bed Size	**Qty**
Super King	
King	
Queen	2
Double	
Single	
Bathrooms	**Qty**
Ensuite	2
Private	
Guest Share	

Bed & Breakfast Homestay

Features & Attractions

- *Walk to restaurants*
- *Close to Te Papa Museum*
- *Private court yard*
- *Complimentary refreshments*
- *Walk to café district*
- *Central city*
- *All rooms ensuite*
- *Pre-dinner wine & canapés*

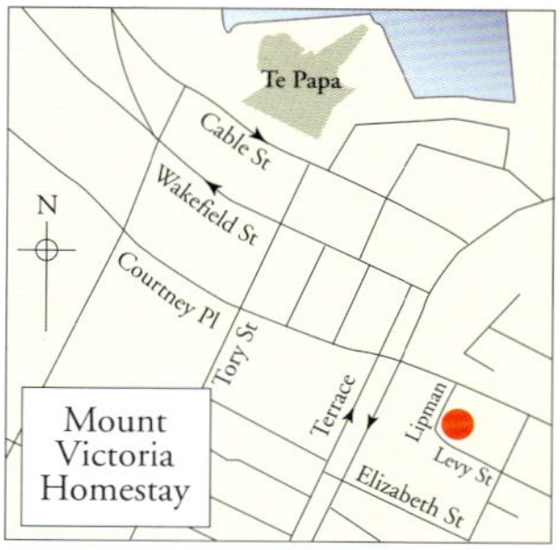

Located in the heart of Wellington City we are a short walk from Wellington's cafés and a few minutes walk from Wellington's major attractions such as Te Papa Museum and the Oriental Bay beaches. We are also a short walk from some of Wellington's best restaurants and cafés. We offer two double rooms with ensuite and television in a luxuriously renovated Edwardian villa for discerning travellers who desire comfort and personal hospitality of the highest quality. Staying this close to the attractions of Wellington you will not require transport locally. Your room will have TV and complimentary tea, coffee and cookies. Full English breakfast is included.

Dinners can be provided by arrangement, but if you choose to dine out, enjoy pre-dinner refreshments with your hosts. We will be pleased to make arrangements for guided tours, theatres or other events either before you arrive or during your stay.

Austinvilla Bed & Breakfast

11 Austin Street, Mt. Victoria, Wellington
Ph (04) 385 8334, Fax (04) 385 8336
email: *info@austinvilla.co.nz*
www.austinvilla.co.nz

Features & Attractions

- *Top location*
- *Easy walk to inner city*
- *Sun and beautiful views*
- *Private entrance & courtyard*
- *Off-street parking/laundry facilities*
- *Self-contained and private*

$	
Double	$120-160
Single	$100-120
Child	

Boutique Bed & Breakfast & Self-contained Accommodation

Bedrooms	Qty
Double	2
Twin	
Single	
Bed Size	**Qty**
King	
Queen	2
Double	
Single	
Bathrooms	**Qty**
Ensuite	2
Private	
Guest Share	

Top location: A warm welcome to one of Mt Victoria's most elegant turn of the century villas.

Set amongst beautiful gardens and only a few minutes walk to theatres, restaurants, Oriental Bay and Te Papa. Close to public transport and short drive to airport, ferries and Westpac Stadium.

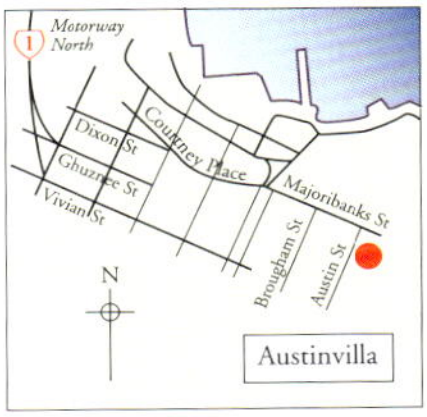

Two spacious, self-contained apartments offer sun, privacy and include kitchen, queen bed, ensuite with bath and shower, lounge, cable TV and phone. Apartments have french doors to private courtyard and private entrance way. Laundry facilities and off-street parking available. Continental breakfast provided. Children welcome. Smoke-free.

Matai House

41 Matai Road, Hataitai, Wellington
Ph (04) 934 6985, Fax (04) 934 6987
email: *matai@paradise.net.nz*
www.mataihouse.co.nz

Features & Attractions

- *City/Airport 5mins, Ferry 10mins drive*
- *Boutique & character home*
- *Gourmet breakfast at a time to suit*
- *Fabulous sea views*
- *Digital/Sky TV*
- *Broadband Internet/Email*

$	
Double	$225-275
Single	$225-275
Reservations essential	

Superior Bed & Breakfast Beautiful Sea Views

Bedrooms	Qty
Double	2
Twin	
Single	
Bed Size	**Qty**
King	2
Queen	
Double	
Single	
Bathrooms	**Qty**
Ensuite	2
Private	
Guest Share	

Originally built circa 1913 as a private residence, this fine character villa offers purpose-built guest suites refurbished in harmony with the era of the home. Each suite is tastefully decorated, including; heavenly king-size beds, thick pillow-top mattress, crisp linen, goose-down covers, plump pillows, local art-work and fresh flowers. Ensuites feature hair dryer, toiletries, bathrobes and heated towel rail. French doors open onto decking overlooking a garden of NZ native plants. With a private entrance, the guest lounge provides tea and coffee making facilities, refrigerator, broadband internet/email, laundry and ironing facilities. Off-street car park available. Breakfast includes espresso coffee, muesli, seasonal berries and cooked options. Enjoy a local wine on the deck during the warmer evenings or by an open fire during winter. Phone and fax facilities available.

DIRECTIONS: On SH 1 follow airport signs until exiting Mt. Victoria tunnel, (2nd tunnel) drive ahead into Hataitai, left and then right into Waitoa Rd. Drive up Waitoa Rd and 2nd left into Matai Road. From airport Highway 1 turn right at lights into Evans Bay Parade, 2nd left into Rata Rd, left and left again into Matai Rd.

TOP O' T'ILL

2 Waitoa Road, Hataitai, Wellington
Ph (04) 976 2718, Fax (04) 976 2719
Mobile 025-716 482
email: *top.o.hill@clear.net.nz*
www.topotill-homestay.co.nz

Tariff : N.Z. Dollars	
Double	$110-130
Single	$70-110
Child	

Bedrooms	Qty
Double	2
Twin	1
Single	1
Bed Size	**Qty**
Super King	
King	
Queen	2
Double	
Single	3
Bathrooms	**Qty**
Ensuite	2
Private	1
Guest Share	1

Homestay / Bed & Breakfast
Self-contained

Features & Attractions

- *Friendly and helpful hosts*
- *Attractive warm rooms*
- *Popular suburb near city*
- *Efficient local bus service*
- *Continental/cooked breakfast*
- *Excellent local restaurants*
- *Self-contained, serviced studio*
- *Studio – long-term rates available*

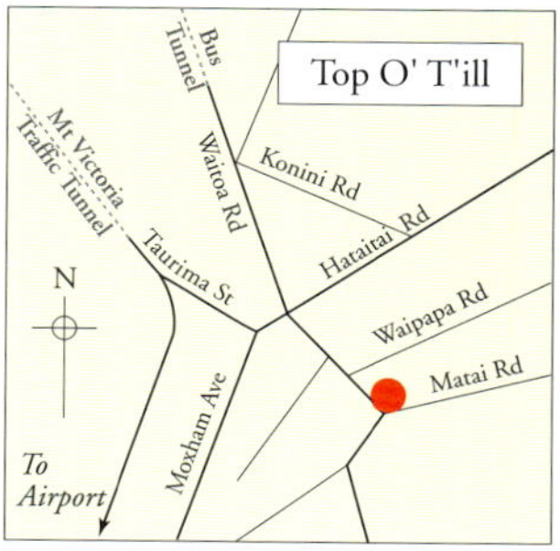

Hataitai 'breath of the ocean' is situated in the eastern suburbs of Wellington, midway between Airport and City. A homely atmosphere is provided for guests in our comfortable 1919 two storey home, which has been in our family over 60 years. From the bedrooms there are views of Evans Bay, Hataitai Village and Mount Victoria. The charming studio Áit Siocháin –Peaceful Place, is fully appointed, including kitchenette, ensuite, cable television, phone line, private entrance and patio. We enjoy the beauty of our vibrant harbour city, including its cultural life and range of superb restaurants. Distance to the CBD, airport, ferry, Te Papa National Museum and sporting venues is 5-10 min by bus or car. We have travelled widely overseas and in New Zealand, and share interests in music, the arts, historic places and meeting people. We will be glad to help you make the most of your visit to Wellington. **Unsuitable for young children. @home NEW ZEALAND approved.**

Buckley Homestay

51 Buckley Road, Melrose, Wellington
Ph (04) 934 7151, Fax (04) 934 7152
Mobile 025-607 1853
email: *willy.muller@paradise.net.nz*
www.buckleyhomestay.co.nz

Tariff : N.Z. Dollars	
Double	$95-140
Single	$80-95
Child	neg.

Bedrooms	Qty
Double	3
Twin	2
Single	1
Bed Size	**Qty**
Super King	1
King Single	2
Queen	1
Double	
Single	3
Bathrooms	**Qty**
Ensuite	1
Private	1
Guest Share	

VISA MasterCard

Bed & Breakfast Homestay and Self-contained Suite with Views

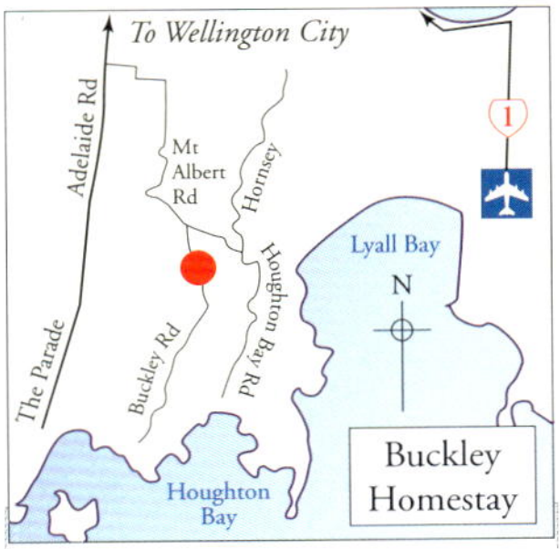

DIRECTIONS: From Newtown go straight to end of Newtown past Hospital, McDonalds. Take right hand fork at roundabout, up the hill on Russell Tce. past hockey stadium to top of hill, then right into Buckley Rd. From Island Bay up the hill through Mersey St. then Melrose Rd. to Buckley Rd.

Features & Attractions

- *Private and peaceful*
- *Te Papa Museum 4km*
- *Close to golf course*
- *Sleeps up to 6*
- *Close to Red Rocks and seals*
- *Handy to airport, on bus route*
- *Close to restaurants and zoo*
- *Also available 2-storey town house*

Buckley Homestay is a large and sunny two storey home with spectacular scenery and beautiful views over Wellington, Cook Strait and the surrounding mountains. Sit in the award winning garden or join me in my home. I am a trained nurse, love cooking and gardening, have travelled extensively and I do speak Dutch. Alternatively you may like to stay in the modern, tastefully decorated self-contained guest suite with private entrance and balcony. I also offer a wide variety of extra facilities. Also a 2 level fully furnished townhouse, S/C, opposite the Homestay with queen and single bed, kitchen, off-street parking and on bus routes. Dinners by arrangement. Take time out to surf or swim at our safe local beach or enjoy complimentary tea and coffee with a good book. A wide range of restaurants is available nearby. Whether you desire company or privacy – the choice is yours.

Homestay at Evans Bay

4/378 Evans Bay Parade, Wellington
Ph (04) 386 1504, Fax (04) 386 1503
Mobile 021-043 5683
email: *leishas@xtra.co.nz*
www.homestayevansbay.co.nz

@ home NEW ZEALAND

Tariff : N.Z. Dollars	
Double	$190-230
Single	$190
Extra pp	$75

Bedrooms	Qty
Double	1
Twin	1
Single	
Bed Size	**Qty**
Super King	
King	
Queen	1
Double	
King/Singles	2
Bathrooms	**Qty**
Ensuite	1
Private	1
Guest Share	

BA

Luxury Homestay/Bed & Breakfast with Stunning Harbour Views

H

American Express, JCB, MasterCard, VISA

Features & Attractions

- *Collected from airport*
- *5 min. from city & airport*
- *Drive to the door*
- *Email & internet facilities*
- *City bus in front*
- *Gourmet breakfast*
- *Dinner by arrangement*
- *Stylish & comfortable home*

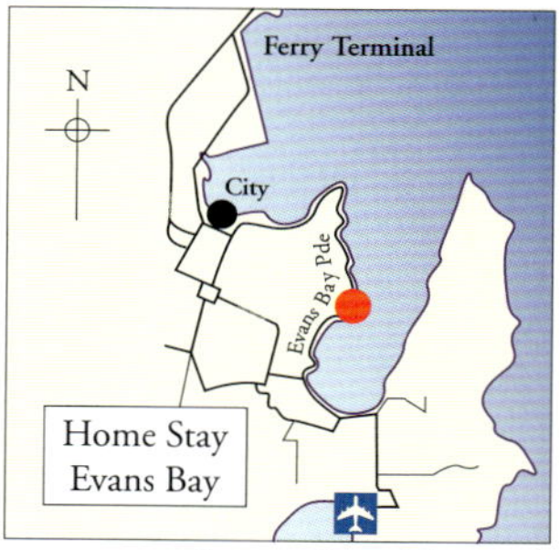

Homestay at Evans Bay is a luxury Boutique Bed & Breakfast, overlooking the bay, swimming beach and canoe club. Restaurants and golf course nearby. Elisabeth is a watercolour artist, has travelled extensively and speaks Dutch.

The home is luxuriously decorated, sunny and comfortable with indoor/outdoor living. The bedrooms are on a separate floor, thus very private. They overlook the bay and have coffee/tea/chocolate making facilities with complimentary biscuits, chocolates and mineral water. The home is comfortably heated and there are electric blankets on the beds. Robes, toiletries, hairdryers and heated towel rails in bathrooms. We serve an extensive gourmet breakfast at your convenience, either in the dining room or alfresco in our private rose garden. Sky television in bedrooms and a large screen in the lounge. Negotiable out-of-season rates. See our website.
Mentioned in Frommers and also @ home New Zealand approved.

MA MAISON

9 Tamar Street, Island Bay, Wellington
Ph (04) 383 4018, Fax (04) 383 4018
Mobile 025-242 9827
email: *bedandbreakfast@paradise.net.nz*
www.nzwellingtonhomestay.co.nz

Tariff : N.Z. Dollars	
Double	$130
Single	$110
Child	

Bedrooms	Qty
Double	2
Twin	
Single	
Bed Size	**Qty**
Super King	
King	
Queen	2
Double	
Single	
Bathrooms	**Qty**
Ensuite	1
Private	1
Guest Share	

Advance booking recommended.

Charming Romantic Boutique Accommodation

Features & Attractions

- *A place of style and comfort*
- *Warmth and hospitality*
- *Luxurious, romantic bedrooms and bathrooms*
- *Only 8 minutes to City Centre*
- *Really comfortable beds*
- *Plump down duvets*
- *Quiet, peaceful garden setting*

Ma Maison offers you Boutique Homestay Bed & Breakfast accommodation in our 1920's home, decorated with a French flavour, set in a lovely garden with drive to front door. Two romantic guest rooms, both with queen posturepaedic beds, tea and coffee making facilities, television, quality white linen, featherdown duvets, electric blankets – in fact, everything to make your stay as comfortable as possible. One room has a private bathroom with shower and claw foot bath, the other room, which has an ensuite, has its own private entrance. Delicious cooked breakfast is served at a time to suit you.

Ma Maison is within easy walking distance to excellent local restaurants or eight minutes drive to swinging Courtenay Place, in the centre of Wellington, with a great variety of places to eat. Close by are a golf course and private and public hospitals. We are very handy to public transport. Island Bay has an excellent bus service into Wellington City, Te Papa, Stadium, shopping and theatres.

Seatoun - Wellington ▶ YOUR HOSTS: Karen Cronin and Wren Green Ph (04) 934 5913

THE ADMIRAL'S BREAKFAST BOUTIQUE B&B

97 Inglis St, Seatoun, Wellington
Ph (04) 934 5913, Fax (04) 934 5923
Mobile 021- 304 524
email: *enquiries@admiralsbreakfast.co.nz*
www.admiralsbreakfast.co.nz

MasterCard VISA

Features & Attractions

- *New luxury apartment*
- *Private entrance garage*
- *Self-catering breakfast*
- *Beautiful seaviews*
- *Broadband Internet, SKY TV*
- *Airport 5 min, city 12 min.*

$	
Double	$175
Single	$155
Child	

Superior B&B Self-contained Apartment with Sea Views

Bedrooms	Qty
Double	1
Twin	
Single	
Bed Size	**Qty**
King	
Queen	1
Double	
Single	
Bathrooms	**Qty**
Ensuite	1
Private	
Guest Share	

Enjoy the luxury of a spacious studio apartment in Seatoun, Wellington's premier seaside village. Quiet, coastal location yet only 5 minutes to the airport. Start the day with a hearty breakfast, fit for an admiral, on the sunny terrace overlooking the sea. The apartment is completely self-catering with a fully equipped kitchen, laundry and internal access garage. Private entrance and courtyard with wonderful harbour and mountain views. Excellent restaurants and cafés close by, along with swimming beaches, sailing, golf, stunning coastal walks and boutique shopping. Our street is named Inglis after a Scottish Rear Admiral. We welcome travellers from near and far to join us for short or long stays. Corporate rates available. Complimentary champagne gift basket on arrival.

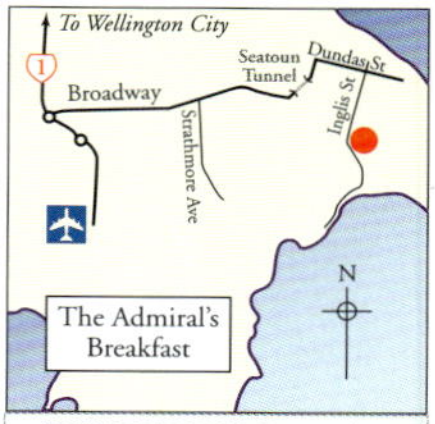

DIRECTIONS: From city, follow arrows to airport. At roundabout, turn left onto Broadway. Drive through Strathmore to Seatoun Tunnel. Take 1st right, Ludlam St, then 2nd right onto Inglis St.

Miramar - Wellington ▶ YOUR HOSTS: Sherryn and Ray Strickland Ph (04) 380 8367

KAURI COTTAGE

78 Kauri Street, Miramar, Wellington
Ph (04) 380 8367, Fax (04) 380 8467
Mobile 021 038 7367
email: *sheray@clear.net.nz*

Features & Attractions

- *2 min. to airport*
- *Private and spacious*
- *Close to Miramar Links*
- *8 min. to city*
- *Fully equipped kitchen*
- *Extended stay options*

Self-contained Bed & Breakfast

$	
Double	$120
Single	$100
Child	neg

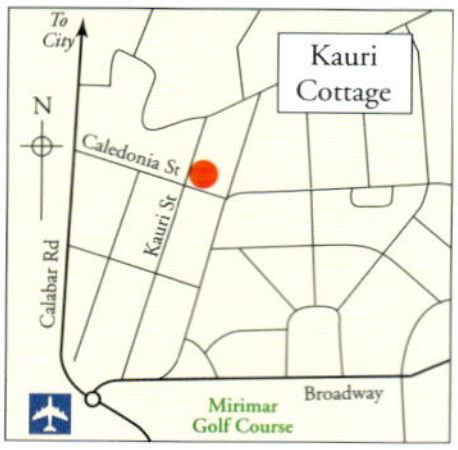

This early 20th century-style residence is private, with your own deck, entrance, full kitchen, lounge/dining, and bedroom with ensuite.
A selection of breakfast foods, snacks and basic cooking needs are provided. It is a short stroll to the golf links, film studios, supermarket and medical centre.
Miramar is an ideal starting point for exploring the coast, harbour and capital city. Your Wellington hosts have brochures and maps waiting for you.
An iron and board is provided and washing machine available on request.

Bedrooms	Qty
Double	1
Twin	
Single	
Bed Size	**Qty**
King	1
Queen	
Double	
Single	
Bathrooms	**Qty**
Ensuite	1
Private	
Guest Share	

NATURE'S TOUCH GUEST HOUSE

25A Happy Valley Road, Owhiro Bay, Wellington
Ph (04) 383 6977, Fax (04) 383 6977
Mobile 027-559 0966
email: *info@naturestouchguesthouse.com*
www.naturestouchguesthouse.com

Tariff : N.Z. Dollars	
Double	$100-120
Single	$90-100
Child	$45

Bedrooms	Qty
Double	1
Twin	
Single	
Bed Size	**Qty**
Super King	
King	1
Queen	
Double	
Single	1
Bathrooms	**Qty**
Ensuite	
Private	
Family Share	1

Just Nature
Bed & Breakfast

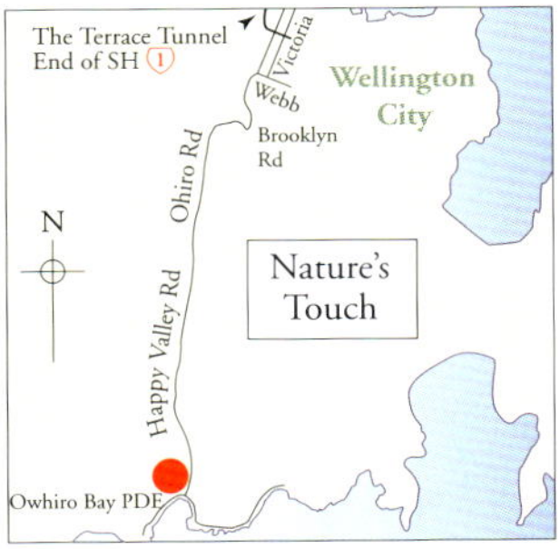

DIRECTIONS:
Feel free to give us a call for easy directions.

Features & Attractions

- *Free seals tour (option)*
- *Private lounge & double bedroom*
- *Ever changing seaviews*
- *Peaceful stream sounds*
- *10% off after 3 nights*
- *Gourmet breakfast*
- *Free pick up / drop off*
- *Japanese meals available*

"Thank you again for a wonderful visit to your home. Your meal was stupendously prepared and we often regret that our appetites were not up to the generous portions! We loved our seal hunt,…" Leslie, Mike, Zealand and Scotland from USA.

"…thank you both for a wonderful stay. Your B&B is very beautiful and homely. The views are spectacular. The trip out to the seals was wonderful even though we didn't see a seal… The scenery is outstanding and different. Now about your wonderful breakfast. They are the best we have had in NZ and I must admit in the world…" Margie & Joe from Australia.

A warm welcome from us and our friendly dog, Lucky! We are just a short stroll to the beach and reserve. Only 10 minutes drive to the city, 15 minutes drive to ferry terminal and airport. Whole of upstairs is yours to enjoy elevated views as well as privacy.

South Island

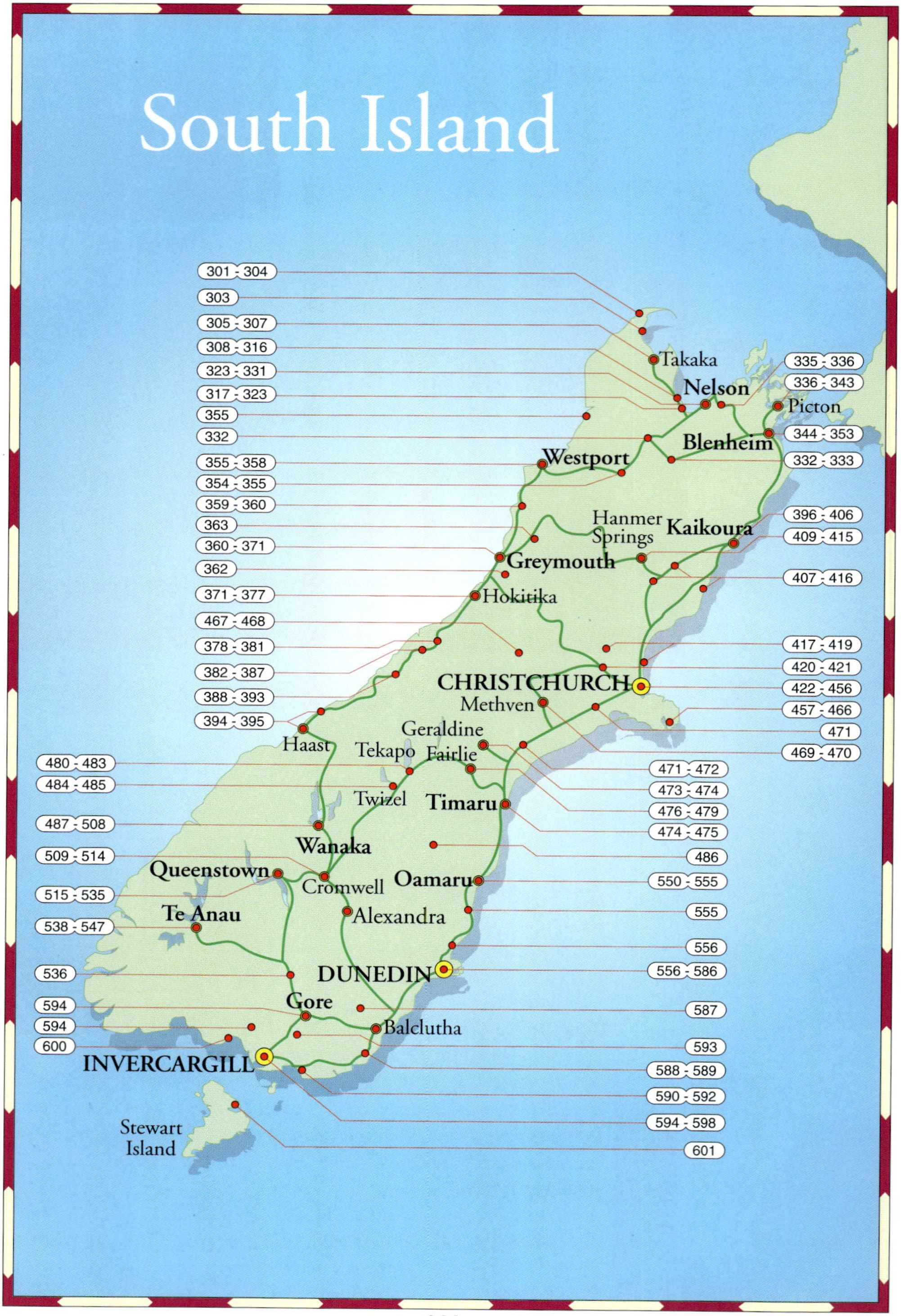

Clemmiec

1737 Collingwood-Puponga Road,
Pakawau, Collingwood
Ph (03) 524 8787, Fax (03) 524 8785
Mobile 027-262 2947
email: *clemmiec@goldenbay.net.nz*

Tariff : N.Z. Dollars	
Double	$150
Single	$120
Child	neg

Bedrooms	Qty
Double	2
Twin	1
Single	
Bed Size	**Qty**
Super King	
King	
Queen	2
Double	2
King/Single	2
Bathrooms	**Qty**
Ensuite	
Private	2
Guest Share	

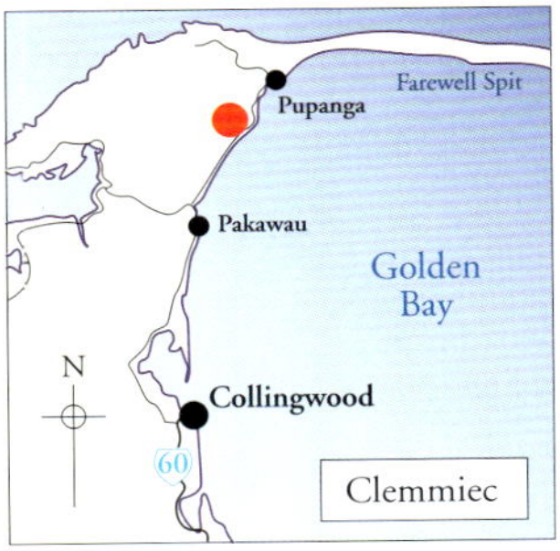

DIRECTIONS: From Collingwood, follow the signs north through Pakawau to Farewell Spit. **Clemmiec** is just 6 km north of Pakawau. Turn left at our sign and drive 300m up the driveway.

Homestay Bed & Breakfast

Features & Attractions

- *Quiet peaceful location*
- *Stunning beaches*
- *Birdwatchers' dream*
- *Walking tracks*
- *Excellent rural views*
- *Comfort plus*
- *Barbeque available*
- *Dinners by arrangement*

Clemmiec – the homestead of the children of the Matriarch Clem. As in the early 16th century **Clemmiec** is today a homestead of family and friends. Stay at **Clemmiec** and become part of that family or enjoy solitude, as you wish. Our house is your house with a choice of three large bedrooms, a lounge and reading area. Bathrooms are private and adjacent to the bedrooms. A full breakfast menu is provided with dinners by arrangement at a small additional cost. We are situated just 4 km from Farewell Spit, an internationally renowned wetland and bird sanctuary, Kahurangi National Park is literally at our back door. Use **Clemmiec** as a base to explore the many beaches and walkways in the immediate area and the greater Golden Bay, to enjoy a horse trek, go fishing or to visit some of the many craft galleries in our region. We can organise your tour of Farewell Spit with pick-ups at our gate.

Westhaven Retreat

Te Hapu Road, Collingwood
Ph (03) 524 8354, Fax (03) 524 8354
Mobile 027-220 3941
email: *westhave@ihug.co.nz*
www.westhavenretreat.com

Tariff : N.Z. Dollars	
Double	$175-225
Single	$155-225
Child	

Bedrooms	Qty
Double	3
Twin	2
Single	
Bed Size	**Qty**
Super King	1
King	2
Queen	
Double	
King/Single	4
Bathrooms	**Qty**
Ensuite	3
Private	1
Guest Share	1

Boutique Accommodation and Self-contained Cottage

Features & Attractions

- *Private peninsula of 1000 acres*
- *New luxury accommodation*
- *Total privacy, peace & freedom*
- *Plus our graceful 50 llamas!*
- *Unique Nikau rain forest*
- *Breathtaking scenery*
- *8 km of private coastline*
- *Exquisite cuisine*

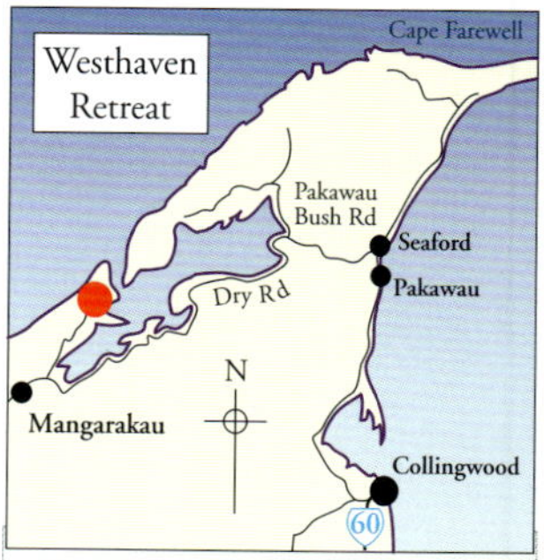

DIRECTIONS: From Collingwood travel towards Farewell Spit. Turn right to Pakawau and continue 12km. Turn left towards Westhaven Inlet. 2km before Mangarakau turn right to Westhaven Retreat at end of road.

Westhaven, a privately owned peninsula, is a very special place of outstanding ecological values and enjoys the most spectacular views in the whole region. Surrounded by the Tasman Sea, the Westhaven Entrance, the Whanganui Inlet (Marine Reserve) and Kahurangi National Park, the natural beauty with all its variety of scenery and landscapes creates a setting you cannot find anywhere else. Enjoy endless beaches, swim, go fishing or discover magnificent rock formations, caves, palm groves and rain forests. Watch the bird life and our peaceful, gentle llamas with their young crias or look out for seals and dolphins. In the newly built retreat with splendid and spectacular views, the guest rooms as well as the Cottage are spacious and modern, furnished with the highest quality king/california-size beds. With our delicious food, from seafood, fish, vegetarian meals or European cuisine, we will please your individual taste.

Twin Waters Lodge

Totara Avenue, PO Box 33, Collingwood
Ph (03) 524 8014, Fax (03) 524 8014
Mobile 027-242 8778
email: *twin.waters@xtra.co.nz*
www.twinwaters.co.nz

Tariff : N.Z. Dollars	
Double	$180
Single	$160
Child	

Bedrooms	Qty
Double	1
Twin	1
Single	
Bed Size	**Qty**
Super King	
King	
Queen	1
King/Single	1
Single	
Bathrooms	**Qty**
Ensuite	2
Private	
Guest Share	

Boutique Accommodation
Bed & Breakfast

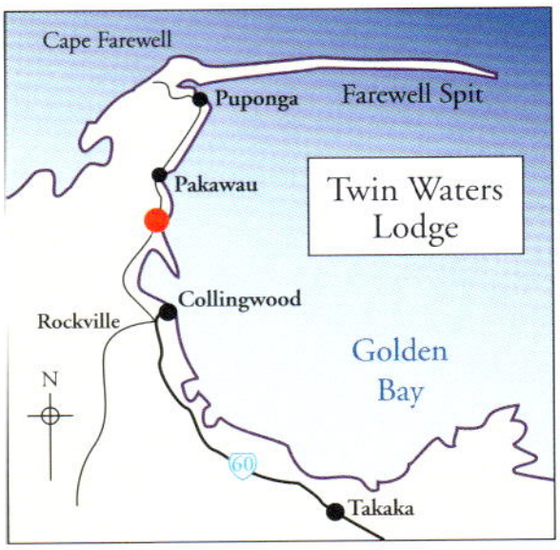

Features & Attractions

- *Booking and pick-up point for Farewell Spit Tours*
- *50m to sandy beach*
- *Peaceful setting*
- *Abundant birdlife*
- *Guest lounge with woodburner*
- *Comfortable beds*
- *Evening meals by arrangement*

Nestled harmoniously beside a tidal estuary, **Twin Waters Lodge** features curved timber ceilings, floor to ceiling windows and multi-level decks. The ensuite rooms open onto private decks, and the spacious guest lounge has pleasant views of the estuary and forested hills. **Twin Waters Lodge** is a great base to explore the Golden Bay region. Wander the wild West Coast beaches, take a tour of Farewell Spit, a bird sanctuary of world renown, visit Kahurangi and Abel Tasman National Parks, try your hand at gold panning, horse trekking or sea kayaking. Indulge your passion for walking, tramping, tennis or golf. Visit the local art galleries and find out what it is about Golden Bay that inspires them. Waking to the sound of tuis, breakfasting in the sun, sipping wine on the decks, or savouring a delicious dinner, there's sure to be a special moment to remember your stay. Trish and Mike have many interests and are widely travelled. They look forward to welcoming you to their paradise at **Twin Waters**.

HERON'S REST B & B

23 Gibbs Road, Collingwood, Golden Bay
Ph (03) 524 8987, Fax (03) 524 8987
email: *stay@herons-rest.co.nz*
www.herons-rest.co.nz

Tariff : N.Z. Dollars	
Double	$90-110
Single	$65
Extra pp	$15

Bedrooms	Qty
Double	2
Twin	1
Single	2
Bed Size	**Qty**
Super King	
King	
Queen	1
Double	1
Single	2
Bathrooms	**Qty**
Ensuite	2
Private	1
Guest Share	

Bed & Breakfast & Self-contained Accommodation

VISA MasterCard

Features & Attractions

- *Panoramic views of mountains & sea*
- *Farewell Spit Eco Tours/bird-watching*
- *Pottery & Pacific Carver's Studio*
- *4 min. bush walk to eateries, beach*
- *Friendly & welcoming hosts*
- *Landscaped, private gardens*
- *Large deck with BBQ facility*
- *Spacious lounge; Sky TV*

Situated in a unique, unspoilt location, your welcoming hosts enjoy making guest stays comfortable and memorable. We offer home-made and locally-produced foods and complimentary hot drinks. Hairdryer, laundry and internet available. A wide choice of outdoor activities cater for all fitness levels. Excellent walks. Farewell Spit, Abel Tasman and Kahurangi National Parks are nearby, as is access to the Heaphy Track. Guests can follow the trail of Golden Bay's many artisan outlets sampling, en route, our interesting cafés and restaurants (including *The Mussel Inn*), or merely relax on the deck, nearby sandy beaches or in the garden. **Heron's Rest** is a peaceful location, yet very convenient to amenities in Collingwood.

In addition, our charming, self-contained **Treetops' Cottage** (sea vistas from each bed) gives combined choices of the above options and offers a double bed, single and pullout, sleeping up to 4 persons. It has an ensuite bathroom, hairdryer, small private deck looking down onto superb sea/mountain/estuary views, TV, some kitchen appliances including fridge and microwave; we provide breakfasts.

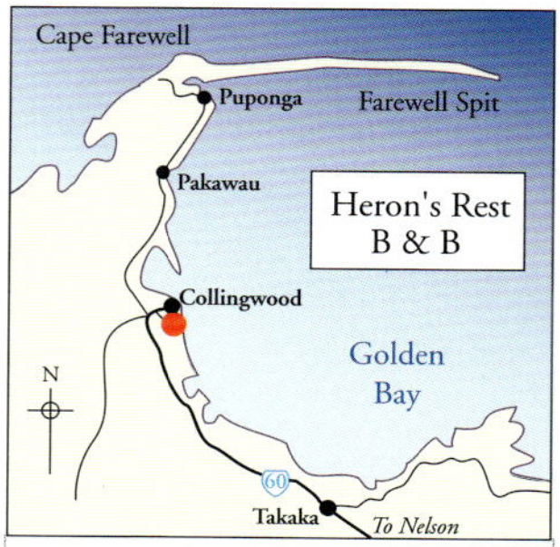

DIRECTIONS: Just before Collingwood township, turn right up Lewis St, left into Washington Rd, then left into Gibbs Rd. Proceed to end, taking left fork of (level) gravel road - to end . We're on the headland overlooking Collingwood.

Bay Vista House

Paradise Way, Pohara, Golden Bay
Ph (03) 525 9772, Fax (03) 525 9772
Mobile 021-378 736
email: *hosts@bayvistahouse.co.nz*
www.bayvistahouse.co.nz

Tariff : N.Z. Dollars	
Double	$195-250
Single	$175-200
Child	

Bedrooms	Qty
Double	3
Twin	
Single	
Bed Size	**Qty**
Super King	
King	1
Queen	2
Double	
Single	
Bathrooms	**Qty**
Ensuite	3
Private	
Guest Share	

Luxury Accommodation with Panoramic Sea Views

Features & Attractions

- *Views across Golden Bay*
- *Spacious rooms*
- *TV, fridge, tea/coffee in rooms*
- *Spa pool*
- *Walk to 3 restaurants*
- *5 min. walk to beach*
- *Abel Tasman National Park*
- *Farewell Spit & walking tracks*

Bay Vista House sits above Pohara Beach with spectacular sea and mountain views across Golden Bay to Farewell Spit. Our spacious rooms all enjoy the panoramic views and open to the terrace. Each room has its own ensuite, lounge furniture, TV, fridge, tea and coffee making facilities. Three restaurants are within 5 minutes easy walk for a good choice of evening meals featuring local produce and seafood.

All the natural features of Golden Bay are within easy reach, including Abel Tasman National Park, Farewell Spit, Pupu Springs, forests, waterfalls and spectacular coastlines. Sea kayaking, horse trekking, fishing, birdwatching, Spit tours and coastal boat trips can be readily arranged and there are many bush and coastal walks through the national parks and conservation reserves. The northern loop of the fabled Abel Tasman National Park Coastal Walkway can be walked from **Bay Vista House** in a single day. Active local artists and potters abound and can be visited in their studios.

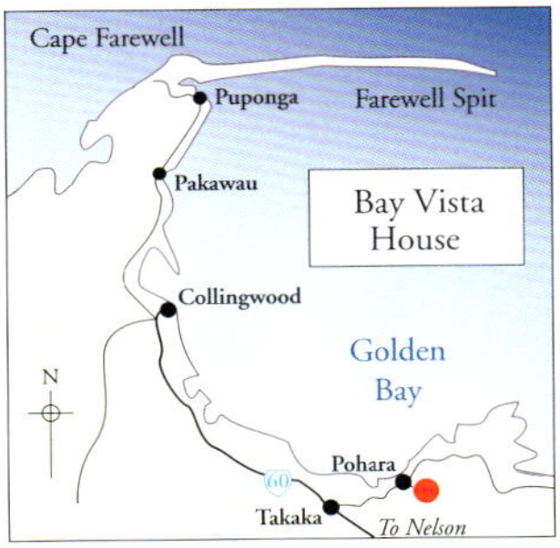

DIRECTIONS: From SH60 turn right on entry to Takaka (Motupipi St) and follow signs to Pohara, 8km. Turn right up Richmond Road opposite camping ground entrance (sign), and left to Paradise Way (sign).

Beautiful Patons Rock

Sea & Beachview Homestay

Patons Rock, RD 2, Takaka, Golden Bay
Ph (03) 525 7230, Fax (03) 525 7231
email: *kaliswj@clear.net.nz*

Tariff : N.Z. Dollars	
Double	$85
Single	$50-55
Exta pp	$13

Bedrooms	Qty
Double	3
Twin	
Single	
Bed Size	**Qty**
Super King	
King	1
Queen	1
Double	
Single	5/6
Bathrooms	**Qty**
Ensuite	
Private	2
Guest Share	

Homestay Bed & Breakfast & Self-contained Accommodation

Features & Attractions

- *View over whole of Golden Bay*
- *Private lounge/kitchen/balcony*
- *Separate shower and bathroom*
- *Safe, clean beach 2 min*
- *Good log burner*
- *Very comfortable & cosy*

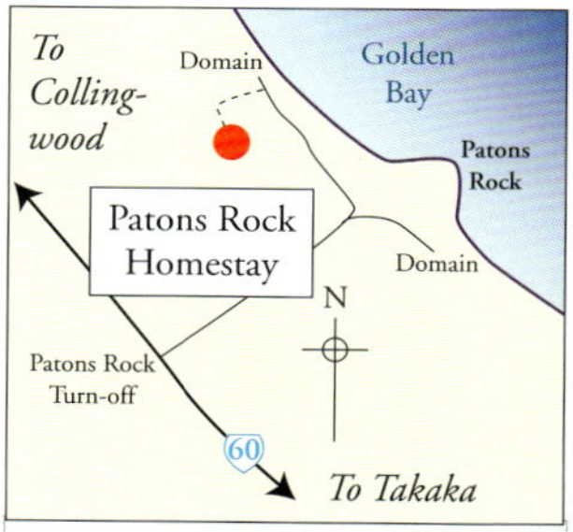

DIRECTIONS: From Takaka Post Shop drive 10 km towards Collingwood, take Patons Rock turn-off. At end of Road take private track "Byders Terrace" We are last house on left.

Our separate upper floor gives a beautiful view over the Bay from Farewell Spit to Separation Point. We are only two minutes from a safe, clean, good walking beach. You will enjoy our big lounge with log burner and television. Bathroom, toilet and shower are separate. A balcony on three sides gives ample room to sit and enjoy the views. Patons Rock area has about 100 houses and no shops. In Takaka or Collingwood you find facilities like restaurants, pubs and shops, only twelve kilometres away. Golden Bay has plenty to offer with its variable scenery and good walkways. We can pick you up from the Tasman or Heaphy Track or in Takaka or drop you off at Collingwood for a Farewell Spit Safari. Kayak, windsurfer and barbeque available.

Self-contained option:
Our downstairs self-contained flat comprises of an open-plan kitchen/ living area and has one bedroom with queen-size bed and one bedroom with 3 single beds. Divan in lounge. Tariffs per night: $45 for double and $35 for single, extra person $13. Breakfast is available ($5 per person)

Garden Retreat Bed & Breakfast

598 State Highway 60, Puramahoi RD 2, Takaka
Ph (03) 525 6121, Fax (03) 525 6121
Mobile 027-272 4200
email: *info@gardenretreat.co.nz*
www.gardenretreat.co.nz

Features & Attractions

- *Only 8 km from Takaka*
- *Orchard and sheep farm*
- *Many arts, crafts & walks*
- *National parks vicinity*
- *Swimming and fishing*
- *Picnic lunches available*

$	
Double	$115-165
Single	$90-100
Child	5+ neg

Take Time To Unwind

Bedrooms	Qty
Double	2
Twin	1
Single	
Bed Size	**Qty**
King	
Queen	2
Double	
Single	2
Bathrooms	**Qty**
Ensuite	1
Private	1
Guest Share	1

Surrounded by lush sub-tropical gardens, **Garden Retreat** is the perfect place for the weary traveller to relax and unwind. All rooms are located upstairs, are sunny, light and have lovely garden views. The guest breakfast lounge has a self-service home-made continental breakfast available at your convenience. **Garden Retreat** is en-route to such wonderful attractions as Farewell Spit with its internationally renowned wetlands and bird sanctuary, the spectacular Wharariki Beach and the famous Heaphy Track. Patons Rock Beach, popular for swimming and fishing, is only minutes away. Diane and Alan are happy to share their knowledge of the local attractions, eateries, artists, walks and other points of interest in the glorious Golden Bay to help make your stay extra enjoyable.

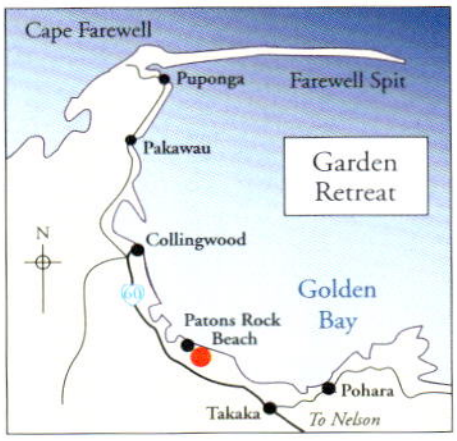

Golden Bay Homestays

Dodson Road, RD 1,
Takaka, Golden Bay
Ph (03) 525 9593, Fax (03) 525 9593

Features & Attractions

- *Warm hospitality*
- *Excellent cuisine*
- *Peaceful countryside*
- *Gateway to Farewell Spit*
- *Two National Parks nearby*
- *Beautiful beaches abound*

$	
Double	$90-100
Single	$75
Child	

Homestay Bed & Breakfast

Bedrooms	Qty
Double	1
Twin	2
Single	1
Bed Size	**Qty**
King	
Queen	1
Double	
Single	5
Bathrooms	**Qty**
Ensuite	
Private	1
Guest Share	1

A warm welcome awaits you at **Glendale**, our rural homestay, just three minutes drive from Takaka township in beautiful Golden Bay. Situated on six hectares of peaceful countryside, including a large garden and small kiwifruit orchard, we offer rest and relaxation, warm hospitality, excellent cuisine and a base from which to explore the many attractions of the area. We are close to both the Abel Tasman and Kahurangi National Parks, beautiful beaches for swimming and fishing, safari tours to famous Farewell Spit, tramping, horse trekking or farm visits. We provide tastefully furnished double or twin rooms with private facilities, including own lounge area and welcome family groups. By arrangement we can provide a delicious evening meal and cater for any dietary requirements. We are Kiwihosts and look forward to meeting you.

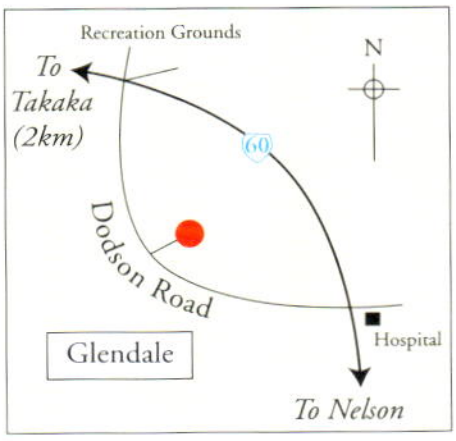

Abel Tasman National Park ▶ YOUR HOSTS: Suzanne Win and John Ayling Ph: (03) 527 8487

Split Ridge

Toko Ngawa Drive, Split Apple Rock, RD 2, Motueka
Ph (03) 527 8487, Fax (03) 527 8497
Mobile 027-229 6729
email: *split.ridge@xtra.co.nz*

Features & Attractions

- *Set amongst native bush*
- *Use of swimming pool*
- *Quiet & peaceful*
- *Expansive sea views*
- *Spacious rooms*
- *Close to national parks*

Expansive Sea Views
Bed & Breakfast

$	
Double	$130-160
Single	$120-140
Child	

Split Ridge sits above the picturesque and turquoise waters of the Abel Tasman National Park, with expansive sea views to the north and mountains to the south.

Each room has its own ensuite or private bathroom, tea and coffee making facilities and outdoor terraces.

You are free to walk around our extensive gardens, enjoy the use of our swimming pool or walk to the Split Apple Rock and adjacent beaches.

Alternatively visit the local national parks or visit the many vineyards, craft outlets or local cafés and restaurants.

Dinner (including wine) is shared with hosts and is available by arrangement.

Bedrooms	Qty
Double	2
Twin	
Single	
Bed Size	**Qty**
King	1
Queen	
Double	1
Single	
Bathrooms	**Qty**
Ensuite	1
Private	1
Guest Share	

DIRECTIONS:
4 km past the well marked Kaiteriteri Beach, turn right into Toko Ngawa Drive. **Split Ridge** is at the top on right (1km)

Kaiteriteri ▶ YOUR HOSTS: Avis Kemp and Tim Rich Ph (03) 527 8090

Bayview B & B

Bayview Heights, Kaiteriteri, RD2 Motueka
Ph (03) 527 8090, Fax (03) 527 8090
Mobile 027-454 5835
email: *book@kaiteriteribandb.co.nz*
www.kaiteriteribandb.co.nz

Features & Attractions

- *Gateway to Abel Tasman*
- *Kayaking trips organised*
- *Hiking trips arranged*
- *Sea views from your room*
- *Golden sand beaches*
- *Restaurants close by*

$	
Double	$165-195
Single	$130-160
Child	

Purpose Built B&B
with Views to Die for

Bedrooms	Qty
Double	1
Twin/Double	1
Single	
Bed Size	**Qty**
King	1
Queen	
Double	
King/Single	1
Bathrooms	**Qty**
Ensuite	2
Private	
Guest Share	

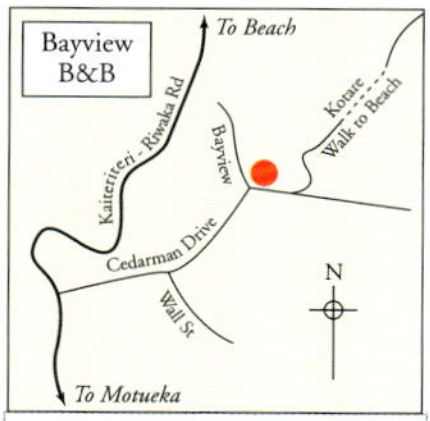

DIRECTIONS: 8km north of Motueka on HW60 turn right into Kaiteriteri Rd. After 4km take 2nd right into Cederman Drive. **Bayview** is 200mtrs on right.

We welcome you to paradise. Kaiteriteri Beach, the gate way to the Abel Tasman National Park with the most beautiful coastline in New Zealand and the sunniest weather. Here we can offer you Bed & Breakfast at its best. Your rooms are large and beautifully furnished with extensive views of the bay. You have a comfortable sitting area, outside terrace, ensuite with heated towel rail and hair dryer, fridge, tea/coffee making facilities, radio and TV. Laundry, phone, fax and email are available. You are welcome to share our living area, terraces, extensive collection of books or be as private as you wish. Kayak adventures and water taxi services leave from our pristine beach. We recommend a minimum 2 night stay to explore this unique area.

BELLBIRD LODGE

Sandy Bay Road, RD 2, Kaiteriteri, Motueka
Ph (03) 527 8555, Fax (03) 527 8556
Mobile 021-057 1470
email: *stay@bellbirdlodge.com*
www.bellbirdlodge.com

Tariff : N.Z. Dollars	
Double	$180-250
Single	$150-180
Child	

Bedrooms	Qty
Double	2
Twin	1
Single	
Bed Size	**Qty**
Super King	1
King	
Queen	1
Double	
Single	4
Bathrooms	**Qty**
Ensuite	1
Private	1
Guest Share	

Luxury Boutique Accommodation
Panoramic Sea Views

DIRECTIONS: From Kaiteriteri Beach follow the road up the hill towards Marahau for approx 1.5 km. At the **Bellbird Lodge** sign, turn right into our private road. We are the 3rd house.

Features & Attractions

- *Panoramic sea views*
- *Relaxed and friendly*
- *Spacious and comfortable*
- *Lounge with TV, video, CD & piano*
- *Phone, fax, email available*
- *Laundry and barbeque*
- *Art, craft and wine trails*
- *Winter specials*

Welcome to Bellbird Lodge, where warm friendly hospitality, superb food and fine accommodation await you. Nestled on the hillside in a tranquil setting with panoramic sea views, Bellbird Lodge is close to Kaiteriteri Beach with its stunning golden sands, the gateway to Abel Tasman National Park. The tastefully furnished guest rooms are on the ground floor and have either ensuite or private bathrooms. All have tea/coffee making facilities, hairdryers, electric blankets, bathrobes and have sea or bush views and outdoor terraces. Wake to the songs of bellbird and tui and marvel at the sunrise over Tasman Bay. Enjoy a delicious buffet breakfast with fresh local produce and homemade muesli, bread and preserves and featuring a hot gourmet special of the day, served in the dining room or alfresco on the terrace. The area has much to offer all year round. Walk the coastal track, take a scenic cruise, water taxi or kayak and discover the unspoiled beauty of the Abel Tasman National Park. Excellent restaurants are a few minutes drive away. Dinner available by prior arrangement (May-October). We look forward to welcoming you soon.

KAIRURU FARMSTAY COTTAGES

1792 Takaka Hill, Highway 60,
(*or* Private Bag), Motueka
Ph/Fax (03) 528 8091, Mobile 027-433 7457
email: *kairuru@xtra.co.nz*
www.kairurufarmstay.co.nz

Tariff : N.Z. Dollars	
Double	$130-160
Single	$130-145
Child	$15-30

Bedrooms	Qty
Double	3
Twin	3
Single	
Bed Size	**Qty**
Super King	
King	
Queen	2
Double	1
Single	2
Bathrooms	**Qty**
Ensuite	
Private	3
Guest Share	

Farmstay
Self-contained Cottages

Features & Attractions

- *Breakfast provisions optional*
- *Spectacular views*
- *Peaceful and private*
- *Children welcome*
- *Self-contained cottages*
- *Farm animals and - activities*
- *Abel Tasman National Park*
- *Gateway to Golden Bay*

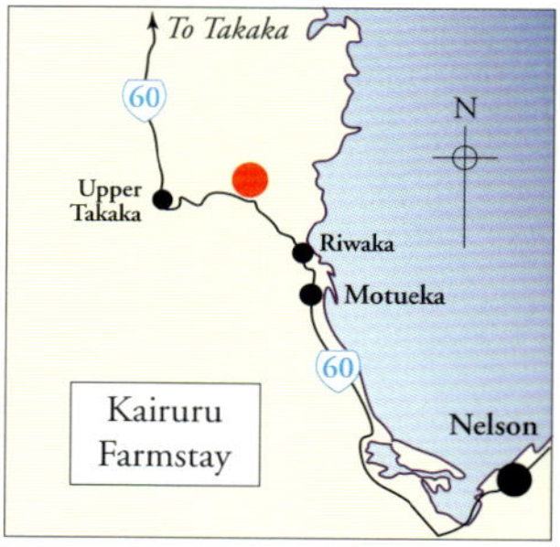

DIRECTIONS:
From Motueka travel north-west towards Takaka. We are 17 km from Motueka on the rights side of the road. **Kairuru** sign at gate.

Guests' accommodation is offered in three self-contained, comfortable, fully equipped cottages. 'Kea Cottage' has three bedrooms, sleeping up to six. 'Pipit Cottage' has two bedrooms, sleeping up to five and 'Canaan Cottage' is one bedroom, suitable for two. All cottages have full kitchens, sitting/dining, laundry, telephone, TV, microwave, BBQ and great views. **Kairuru** is a working sheep and cattle farm of 4000 acres on the unique Takaka Hill. Perfectly situated between the Abel Tasman National Park and Golden Bay. Relax in the privacy, peace and quiet of your own cottage or enjoy the many attractions of the area. Dinners are available by prior arrangement, at $55 per adult, either in our home or delivered to your cottage. We are 3rd generation farmers who enjoy sharing their farm with others and happy to assist you to experience the local attractions.

The Resurgence

Riwaka Valley Road, RD 3, Motueka
Ph (03) 528 4664, Fax (03) 528 4605
email: *info@resurgence.co.nz*
www.resurgence.co.nz

Tariff : N.Z. Dollars	
Double	$295-495
Single	$280-445
Child	

Bedrooms	Qty
Double	5
Twin/Double	3
Single	
Bed Size	**Qty**
Super King/Twin	3
King	
Queen	5
Double	
Single	
Bathrooms	**Qty**
Ensuite	8
Private	
Guest Share	

Five Star Nature

DIRECTIONS: Follow SH 60 from Motueka, through Riwaka and past the two turnings towards Abel Tasman National Park. After 2 km, just as SH 60 starts to go uphill, turn left down Riwaka Valley Rd. Continue towards the source of the river for 5.7 km.

Features & Attractions

- *Swimming pool and spa pool*
- *Gourmet dining*
- *Wilderness with bush tracks*
- *Sorry, no children under 18*
- *Abel Tasman National Park 15 mins*
- *Nelson art and wine trails*
- *Golden Bay day trips*
- *Guided walks & eco tours*

Perfect for couples who love nature, the outdoors and good food.

The Resurgence is a tranquil haven alive with native birdsong overlooking the Kahurangi wilderness. An excellent base for three or four days exploring the Nelson-Tasman region and just fifteen minutes from the start of the Abel Tasman track.

Your well-travelled hosts, Clare and Peter, are keen conservationists and outdoor enthusiasts; they will help you select the very best local activities to make your stay truly memorable.

The welcoming **Lodge** provides informal luxury in four well-appointed ensuite guest rooms with balconies and views. **Lodge** tariff includes full cooked breakfast with free-range eggs, home baking and espresso coffees plus cocktails and four-course dégustation dinner with fresh local produce. Licensed with fine Nelson wines.

Escape the world in our unique self-contained **Bush Cottage** and **Chalet Suites**. Luxurious and very private with BBQ, kitchen and large deck. Serviced daily, tariff includes a wholesome breakfast hamper. Ideal for honeymoons and longer stays. Dinner by reservation.

We are 50 minutes from Nelson airport and 15 minutes from Motueka.

FRASER HIGHLANDS

Riwaka - Sandy Bay Road, RD 2, Motueka
Ph (03) 528 8702
Mobile 027-3150688
email: *fraserhighlands_nz@hotmail.com*

Features & Attractions

- *Abel Tasman National Park*
- *Crafts, wineries, cafés*
- *Bordering Golden Bay*
- *Boating, biking, tramping*
- *Kaiteriteri/Motueka 14min.*
- *Transport & tours available*

Spectacular Views Tasman Bay Bed & Breakfast

Double	$105-145
Single	$85-125
Child	

Welcome to **Fraser Highlands**, where we offer Bed & Breakfast with a 'Scottish' atmosphere 180 metres above sea level. The peaceful native bush property offers spectacular sights of Tasman Bay and surrounding mountainous areas. A resident bagpiper and dancer could provide a wee bit of extra entertainment! Comfortable accommodation includes two queen bedrooms with ensuites, TV, tea/coffee facilities, and email access. A separate guest lounge is available, but hosts, Jim and Sue Fraser, would be happy for you to settle in the bigger lounge with an open log fire. Full English or continental breakfast provided and evening meals can be arranged. 5-15 minutes from **Fraser Highlands**, you could be enjoying a great variety of activities – parks, rivers, beaches, aircraft, golf link, town or mountains.

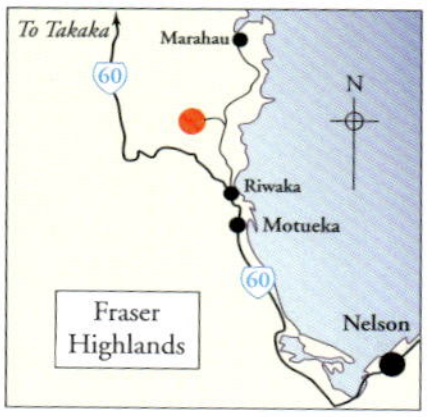

DIRECTIONS: 2nd driveway on left from turn onto Riwaka - Sandy Bay Rd.

Bedrooms	Qty
Double	2
Twin	
Single	1
Bed Size	**Qty**
King	
Queen	2
Double	
Single	1
Bathrooms	**Qty**
Ensuite	2
Private	
Guest Share	1

Photo Ian Trafford

Olives @ Mariri Bed & Breakfast

2597 Coastal Highway, Mariri, Tasman
Ph (03) 526 6775, Fax (03) 526 6775
Mobile 021-163 7610
email: *stay@olivesatmariri.co.nz*
www.olivesatmariri.co.nz

Tariff : N.Z. Dollars	
Double	$160
Single	+$60
Child	$20

Bedrooms	Qty
Double	1
Twin	
Single	
Bed Size	**Qty**
Super King	
King	
Queen	1
Double	
Single	1
Bathrooms	**Qty**
Ensuite	1
Private	
Guest Share	

Countrystay
Bed & Breakfast

Features & Attractions

- *Yours Exclusively*
- *Peaceful rural setting*
- *Quality Accommodation*
- *Superb restaurants 10 min.*
- *Vineyards*
- *Day trips to Abel Tasman*
- *Local potters & artists*
- *Golf course nearby*

You will be our exclusive guests when you stay at **Olives @ Mariri,** our 90 year old farmhouse, situated among olive and fruit trees. The elegant, comfortable suite with bathroom opens through French doors to the patio and lovely garden. It includes tea/coffee making facilities, refrigerator, TV and a comfortable sofa bed for a third person. Wake to bird-song and a leisurely breakfast of home baking, fresh fruit and vegetables from the garden. Walk in the olive grove, relax with a book and a glass of wine, or use the telescope to explore the Milky Way Galaxy on those beautiful dark starlit nights. **Olives @ Mariri** is a convenient staging post for Abel Tasman and Kahurangi National Parks and close to beaches, wineries, potters and artists. We have travelled or worked in most continents and would love to share our little bit of paradise with you. You are assured of a warm welcome.

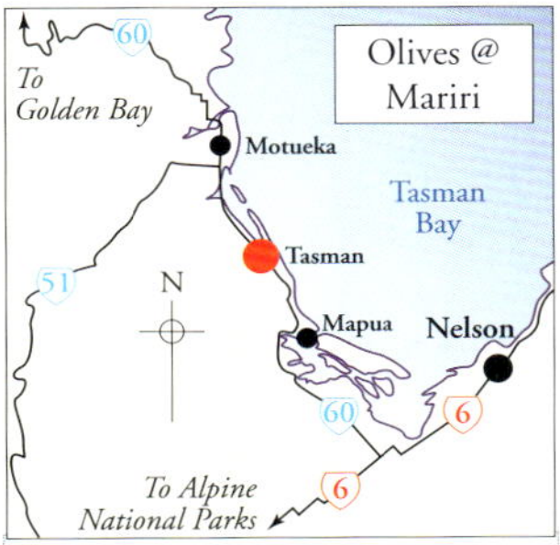

DIRECTIONS:
Between Tasman and Motueka, 300 metres north of Harley Road on Highway 60, take the unsealed loop road and follow the signs.

Centre Ridge Farmstay

Blackbird Valley 176,
RD 2, Upper Moutere, Nelson
Ph (03) 543 2882, Fax (03) 543 2882
email: *centreridge@xtra.co.nz*

Features & Attractions

- *Spacious family home*
- *Welcoming cuppa*
- *Amazing sheep dogs*
- *Beaches & sea kayaking*
- *Excellent restaurants nearby*
- *Help with local sightseeing*

$	
Double	$90-100
Single	$60
Child	neg

Farmstay
Bed & Breakfast

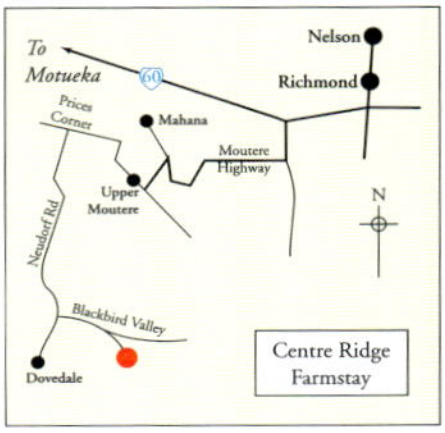

Bedrooms	Qty
Double	1
Twin	
Single	
Bed Size	**Qty**
King	1
Queen	
Double	
Single	
Bathrooms	**Qty**
Ensuite	
Private	1
Guest Share	

For 14 years we have welcomed guests to our 95 year old family home where we invite you to enjoy our sunny deck, our garden, the birds and the valley views. Feel free to go walking on our sheep farm, or a farm tour can be arranged. **Centre Ridge** is halfway between Nelson City and the Abel Tasman National Park, in an area of award winning wineries. Stay a night or more. Meet Millie and Smooch, our cats, and Luke, our farm dog. Enjoy an evening meal with us (by arrangement) $25pp. Sample farm food, home-made bread and jams with a cooked or continental breakfast. Our king room has a spa in the bathroom.

DIRECTIONS: 1.5 km south of Richmond turn right. After 6 km turn left (Moutere Highway). After 17 km turn left at Prices Corner. Travel 4.4 km to Blackbird Valley, turn left. Find us after 1.76 km.

Lemonade Farm

99 Roses Road, Upper Moutere , RD2, Nelson
Ph (03) 543 2686, Mobile 021-059 0464
email: *stay@lemonadefarm.co.nz*
www.lemonadefarm.co.nz

Features & Attractions

- *Vineyard region*
- *Abel Tasman NP 35 min.*
- *Arts and crafts area*
- *Private deck and lawn*
- *Beautiful countryside*
- *Barbeque available*

Luxury Country Retreat

$	
Double	$130-150
Extra pp	$40
Child	4-12 $20

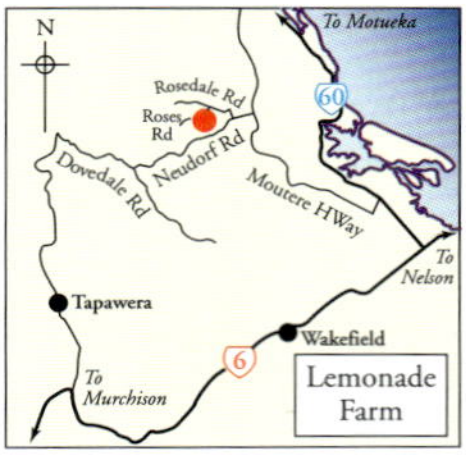

Your farm apartment is a little bit special. A spacious, private and sunny self-contained luxury country retreat. Ideally situated 35 minutes from the start of the Abel Tasman National Park, stunning beaches and Nelson City, yet you're in the heart of Moutere wine country. This is a great base for your holiday. You'll enjoy a fully equipped kitchen and the substantial 'cook-your-own' breakfast basket which includes bacon or sausages, free-range eggs, home-baked goodies and fresh fruit. Your apartment is separate from the main house with its own deck, lawn and driveway. Expect style and quality; cotton sheets, big towels, freshly ground coffee, and a great bed. All our guests say it's relaxing.
Please check the website www.lemonadefarm.co.nz for more.

Bedrooms	Qty
Double	2
Twin	
Single	
Bed Size	**Qty**
King	
Queen	2
Double	
Single	2
Bathrooms	**Qty**
Ensuite	
Private	1
Guest Share	

Larchwood House

1 Dicker Road, Tasman,
RD 1, Upper Moutere 7152
Ph/Fax (03) 526 6204, Mobile 025-527 249
email: *larchwood.house@paradise.net.nz*
www.larchwoodhousetasman.co.nz

Tariff : N.Z. Dollars	
Double	$170-210
Single	$170-210
Child	neg

Bedrooms	Qty
Double	2
Twin	
Single	
Bed Size	**Qty**
Super King	
King	
Queen	1
Double	1
King/Single	
Bathrooms	**Qty**
Ensuite	
Private	1
Guest Share	

Stylish CountryHomestay Bed & Breakfast

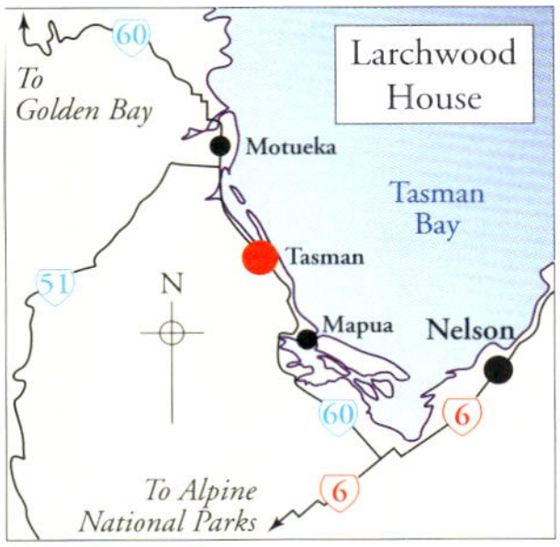

Features & Attractions

- *Genuine Kiwi hospitality*
- *Bird watchers delight*
- *World class trout fishing*
- *15 min from Abel Tasman*
- *3 golf courses nearby*
- *Superb alfresco dining*
- *Private guest entrance*
- *Beaches & sea kayaking*

Larchwood House is a sanctuary of gardens, wonderful home grown fruit and vegetables, with BBQs and intimate dining. Your guest room is beautifully furnished, sunny, spacious with a writing desk, quality cotton bed linen, bathrobes, hair dryer your own refrigerator, tea and coffee, andTV. French doors open onto wide decks and verandahs overlooking the gardens, ornamental pond and views to the mountains beyond. The excitement of exploring the region is balanced by coming home to the tranquility of **Larchwood House** each day. Complimentary drinks are served at 6pm followed by a BBQ or quiet meal in-house or at a local award-winning restaurant. Our focus is quality. This has been reflected in some of the written guest comments: *"Heavenly accommodation... perfect hosts... 5-star hotel in a lovely country garden... we expected to stay 2 nights and stayed 5... glad we found you, perfect stay"*. Expect to find this same care and quality at Larchwood House when you stay with us.

Four Acre Park

Permin Rd, Tasman, Nelson
Ph (03) 540 2756, Mobile 021-153 9980
email: *info@fouracre.co.nz*
www.fouracre.co.nz

Features & Attractions

- *Peaceful country setting*
- *Warm, helpful hospitality*
- *New, fully equipped cottage*
- *Central to beaches, Abel Tasman*
- *Cafés, wineries, art & craft*
- *Original paintings for sale on site*

Self-contained Cottage

$	
Double	$120-200
Single	
Child	

Richard and Karyn welcome you to **Four Acre Park**. Our quality, affordable cottage is part of our peaceful rural park. Let us help you plan your stay. Relax and feed the ducks at the pond. The beach is within walking distance. We are centrally located to Nelson, Mapua, Abel Tasman. Our spacious double-glazed cottage is tastefully decorated. Facilities include well-equipped kitchen, laundry, heated towel-rails, hairdryer, heaters, electric blankets, TV and DVD player. We have a large selection of DVDs you are welcome to use. Tea, herbal tea, coffee complimentary. Continental breakfast available. Serviced. Children welcome and baby-sitting service available. Karyn, a water-colour artist has original paintings of local vistas for sale.

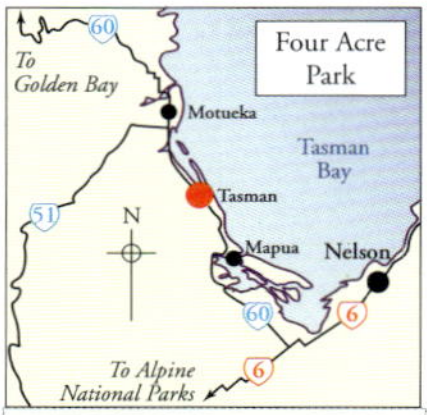

DIRECTIONS: From HW60, turn into Permin Rd, then 1st right. Four Acre Park signposted from Permin Rd.

Bedrooms	Qty
Double	1
Twin	1
Single	
Bed Size	**Qty**
King	1
Queen	
Double sofa bed	1
Single	2
Bathrooms	**Qty**
Ensuite	
Private	1
Guest Share	

Harakeke Lodge Chalets

Cnr. Moutere Highway/Harley Road, Harakeke,
RD 2, Upper Moutere, Nelson
Ph (03) 543 2588, Fax (03) 543 2588
email: *harakekelodge@paradise.net.nz*

Features & Attractions

- *Peaceful garden setting*
- *Three National Parks*
- *Guided walks*
- *Art, craft and wine trails*
- *Excellent restaurants nearby*
- *Trout fishing, kayaking, golf*

Countrystay Bed & Breakfast

$	
Double	$95-120
Single	$70-90
Child	neg

Harakeke Lodge offers you quiet, comfortable and very affordable accommodation in a peaceful country-garden setting with extensive rural views towards Kahurangi National Park. Our aim is to allow you to feel at home in your private well-appointed, separate lodge and to meet any special needs that you require. Each lodge is equipped with self-catering facilities, including microwave, refrigerator, television etc. Email available. A wholesome continental breakfast is provided for you to enjoy at your leisure. There are a wide variety of award winning restaurants situated locally to cater for your discerning tastes. The central location of our lodge makes **Harakeke** an ideal base from which to explore the surrounding National Parks, beaches, wine and craft trails. Be assured of a very warm welcome.

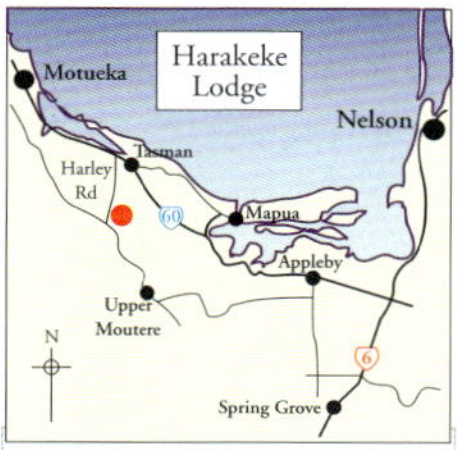

DIRECTIONS:
On SH 60 to Motueka, 26 km from Richmond (Nelson) turn left into Harley Road at Tasman. **Harakeke Lodge** is 5 km on left.

Bedrooms	Qty
Double	1
Twin	2
Single	
Bed Size	**Qty**
King	
Queen	1
Double	
Single	5
Bathrooms	**Qty**
Ensuite	2
Private	
Family Share	1

YOUR HOSTS: **Doris Lindegger and Peter Bullock** Ph: (03) 543 2472 **_Motueka - Nelson_**

Neudorfs Gingerbread House

Neudorf Road, Upper Moutere, Nelson
Ph (03) 543 2472
email: *dandp@gingerbreadhousenz.com*
www.gingerbreadhousenz.com

Features & Attractions

- *German & Italian spoken*
- *Vineyards, cafés, beaches*
- *Abel Tasman National Park*
- *Organic Swiss breakfast*
- *Romantic wild gardens*
- *Good beds, email, laundry*

$		
	Double	$95-130
	Single	$75-100
	Child	neg

Organic Bed & Breakfast
Self-contained Countrystay

Bedrooms	Qty
Double	3
Twin	1
Single	3
Bed Size	**Qty**
SuperKing/Twin	1
Queen	3
Double	
Single	2
Bathrooms	**Qty**
Ensuite	1
Private	1
Guest Share	1

Seeking privacy and relaxation or company and activity? Whichever, enjoy what you like best. Let magic colours and scents, birds' song and thousands of stars take you into a world away from life's daily rush and stress. Join your Swiss/Kiwi hosts in their homely country kitchen, sharing stories, local knowledge and good laughter by the smell of home-made bread. Or relax on the sunny veranda of your self-contained, eco-friendly cottage. Beautiful views and wild romantic gardens invite you to unwind. Our central location helps you to make the most out of your precious holiday time. We offer you a perfect gateway to the region's attractions. Guests comments: *"We were made so welcome. Beautiful setting. A delightful place to stay".*

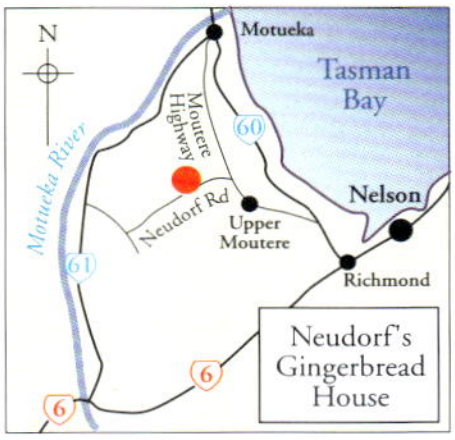

DIRECTIONS:
From **Richmond** 6 km on SH 60, turn left into Moutere Highway. After 17 km turn left, then 3.4 km along Neudorf Road. From SH 61 please contact us for directions

YOUR HOSTS: **Julie and Phil Booth** Ph (03) 543 2233 **_Upper Moutere - Nelson_**

Serendipity

7 Neudorf Road, Upper Moutere RD 2, Nelson
Ph (03) 543 2233Mobile 021-043 9031
email: *asimov02@ihug.co.nz*
www.serendipityb&b.net.nz

Features & Attractions

- *Newly decorated home*
- *Art, crafts, wine trail*
- *Barbecue available*
- *Three national parks close by*
- *Home cooking using local produce*
- *Large garden setting*

$		
	Double	$90-120
	Single	$70-90
	Child	

Countrystay
Bed & Breakfast

Bedrooms	Qty
Double	
Twin	1
Single	1
Bed Size	**Qty**
King	
Queen	
Double	
Single	3
Bathrooms	**Qty**
Ensuite	
Private	1
Guest Share	

Serendipity means 'the gift of making fortunate discoveries by accident'. We aim to make our guests feel fortunate in staying in our home to enjoy the beautiful area in which we live. Our home is newly decorated and surrounded by over 2 acres of garden which we began to develop 4 years ago. Our guest room is light and comfortable overlooking the garden and the Mt. Arthur range in the Kahurangi National Park. A private bathroom is appointed to a high standard with bath, shower cubicle, vanity unit and separate toilet. A continental or cooked breakfast is available to include home-baking and local and home-grown produce when in season. We also have a barbecue and outdoor dining area in the garden courtyard area which guests are welcome to use to prepare an evening meal, or we have a variety of restaurants/ wine bars and takeaways in the area.

DIRECTIONS:
From Richmond on SH60 towards Motueka. Turn left at signpost 'Moutere Highway'. Approx. 17km to Upper Moutere Village (SARAU). Through village to Neudorf Rd junction (Prices corner). 1st house left on Neudorf Rd.

Mahana Escape Bed & Breakfast

750 Old Coach Rd, Mahana, RD 1 Upper Moutere, Nelson
Ph (03) 540 3090, Fax (03) 540 3090
Mobile 027-289 0060
email: *gloria@mahanaescape.co.nz*
www.mahanaescape.co.nz

Tariff : N.Z. Dollars	
Double	$250-350
Single	$350
Child	

Bedrooms	Qty
Double	3
Twin	2
Single	
Bed Size	**Qty**
Super King	
King	1
Queen	2
King-Single	2
Single	2
Bathrooms	**Qty**
Ensuite	1
Private	2
Guest Share	

Luxury Accommodation in Stunning Setting

Features & Attractions

- *Alpacas on property*
- *Golf courses nearby*
- *Local potteries & art studios*
- *Dinner available on request*
- *Mapua village & restaurants 6 min*
- *Walking/kayaking in Abel Tasman & Kahaurangi National Parks*
- *Small weddings catered*

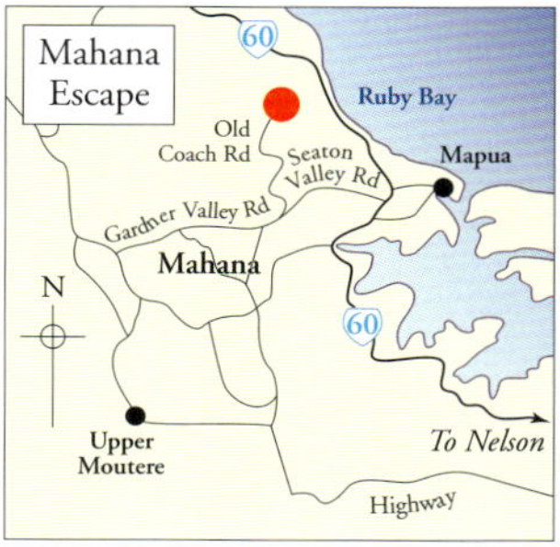

Upon arrival at your ridge top escape you will be rewarded with stunning views of the Tasman Bay. Relax and enjoy a platter of local produce and wine. With four beautiful rooms and suites your comfort is of prime importance to us at **Mahana Escape**. In all suites nothing has been spared when it comes to comfort, so each day's outing will end in a deep revitalising slumber. Sumptuous breakfast awaits you. Your day will begin with a wonderful gourmet breakfast in the dining room, on the patio or in the privacy of your suite.

Mahana Escape is in the heart of the Tasman district, where artisans are abundant. Walk the Abel Tasman and Kahurangi National Parks. Small groups and conferences are our speciality. This is also a fabulous honeymoon destination, where every luxury is provided for you in the King Suite.

Facilities include... private parking, barbecue area, petánque, new developing gardens and walkways. Families and children are welcome.

MAPUA "SEAVIEW" BED & BREAKFAST

40 Langford Drive, Mapua Village, Nelson
Ph/Fax (03) 540 2006
email: *seaview@mapua.co.nz*
www.mapua.co.nz

Features & Attractions

- *Abel Tasman Park 30 min*
- *Walk to restaurants/wharf*
- *Nelson City 30 min drive*
- *Panoramic views - peaceful*
- *Quality bedding/furnishings*
- *Off-street parking*

$	
Double	$135-145
Single	$135-145
Child	

Bed & Breakfast Homestay

Bedrooms	Qty
Double	2
Twin	
Single	
Bed Size	**Qty**
King	
Queen	2
Double	
Single	
Bathrooms	**Qty**
Ensuite	2
Private	
Guest Share	

Thirty minutes from Nelson, **Mapua "Seaview" Bed & Breakfast** is nestled in the coastal village of Mapua. Our new home offers uninhibited panoramic views overlooking the Waimea Estuary and the Richmond mountain vista beyond. A five minute stroll takes you to four picturesque waterfront licensed restaurants, to Leisure Park and popular beaches. Being central within the Nelson Bay's coastal region makes us an ideal base to explore Abel Tasman National Park, Farewell Spit and many other well known attractions. We have sought to create a homely friendly atmosphere with the accent on comfort. Our cosy guest rooms offer comfortable quality queen beds with feather duvets, television and private bathrooms. Coffee/tea and homebaking always available. Cooked/continental breakfast provided with fresh local fruit. The numerous leisure activities, sightseeing highlights and sunshine should cater for everyone's interests and tastes. The regions vineyards, arts and craft studios surround us.

TUIVALE BED & BREAKFAST

76 Higgs Road, Mapua, Nelson
Ph/Fax (03) 540 3300, Mobile 021-152 9310
email: *tuivale@actrix.co.nz*
www.tuivale.co.nz

Features & Attractions

- *Relaxed & friendly*
- *Rural views to sea*
- *Wheelchair entrance*
- *Private access to Rimu Room*
- *Quality bedding*
- *Special diets catered for*

Bed & Breakfast Homestay

$	
Double	$85-120
Single	$65-90
Child	

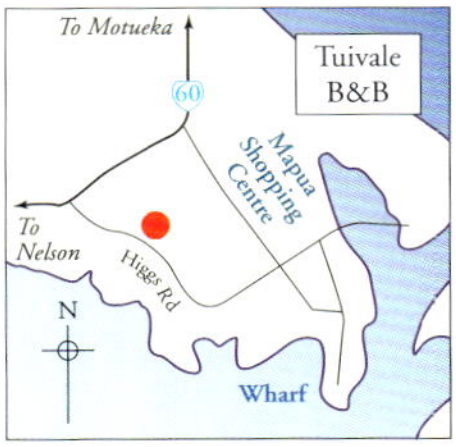

Relaxation starts here... **Tuivale Bed & Breakfast** offers you a real home away from home. Situated in the picturesque village of Mapua, **Tuivale** is the ideal location from which to explore the beautiful Nelson/Tasman Region. It is also the perfect place to kick back, relax and recharge. Guests are invited to enjoy the genuine southern hospitality of Vesper and Max Harrison.

The Rimu Room is large with queensize bed and ensuite with heated tile floor. The ranchslider door opens to private balcony and alternative access. The Kowhai Room is also a double. Both have tea and coffee making facilities, televisions and hairdryers. Delicious gourmet breakfasts are a feature. We look forward to your company.

Bedrooms	Qty
Double	2
Twin	
Single	
Bed Size	**Qty**
King	
Queen	1
Double	1
Single	
Bathrooms	**Qty**
Ensuite	1
Private	
Family Share	1

Clayridge House & Cottages

72 Pine Hill Rd, Ruby Bay, RD 1, Upper Moutere, Nelson
Ph (03) 540 2548, Fax (03) 540 2541
Mobile 027- 447 2099
email: *enquiries@clayridge.co.nz*
www.clayridge.co.nz

Tariff : N.Z. Dollars	
Double	$165-195
Single	$120-160
Child	neg

Bedrooms	Qty
Double	5
Twin	3
Single	
Bed Size	**Qty**
Super King	3
King	2
Queen	
Double	
Single	
Bathrooms	**Qty**
Ensuite	1
Private	3
Guest Share	

BA **Quiet Country Cottages and Homestay** C

VISA MasterCard

Features & Attractions

- *360 degree views*
- *Peaceful & private country stay*
- *Email & high speed internet*
- *Comfortable guest lounge*
- *35 min. Abel Tasman National Park*
- *Minutes from restaurants, crafts, wineries*
- *Golf clubs for loan*
- *Personalised day trips organised*

DIRECTIONS: On Coastal Highway (SH 60) 20 min from Richmond or 15 min from Motueka, turn into Pine Hill Road. Drive 700m up the valley to the **Clayridge House** and Cottage sign on the left. Then proceed up the drive to the top of the hill.

A stunning setting – Nestled on a ridge at Ruby Bay, in the heart of the beautiful Nelson Province, is **Clayridge House and Cottages**. Providing classic country accommodation, with panoramic views of Tasman Bay, rolling hills and the nearby mountain ranges. **Clayridge** is the ideal place to relax in peace and privacy. The Mt Arthur room in the house offers DVD, radio, robes, toiletries, broad band internet, computer, tea and coffee making facilities and local art. You will enjoy the comfortable guest lounge with an inviting open fire, and a sunny serving area for your delicious **Clayridge** breakfast. The sun-filled two bedroom cottages offer space and privacy. Choose to self-cater or enjoy a breakfast tray delivered to your cottage. Equipped with a full kitchen, TV, DVD, radio, linen, hairdryers, electric blankets, robes, towels and toiletries, heat pumps, washing machine and access to broadband internet. Take a walk through our landscaped gardens or enjoy a game of croquet or petanque. A friendly Labrador and two Llamas are our resident pets.

KIMERET PLACE

Bronte Rd East, Nr Mapua,
RD 1, Upper Moutere, Nelson
Ph (03) 540 2727, Fax (03) 540 2726
email: *stay@kimeretplace.co.nz*
www.kimeretplace.co.nz

Tariff : N.Z. Dollars	
Suites	$225-340
Apartments	$150-200
Cottage	$275-335

Bedrooms	Qty
Double	4
Twin	
Single	
Bed Size	**Qty**
California King	1
King	3
Queen	
Double	
Single	
Bathrooms	**Qty**
Ensuite	4
Private	
Guest Share	

Boutique Bed & Breakfast

Features & Attractions

- *Stunning views*
- *Swimming pool & spa*
- *Self-contained cottage*
- *Craft & wine trails*
- *Space, peace, privacy*
- *Elegant rooms & suites*
- *Award winning restaurants*
- *National Parks & beaches*

At **Kimeret Place** the emphasis is on comfort and relaxation. Enjoy the peace of our secluded two acres overlooking the Waimea Inlet. Soak up the sun and the stunning views from our heated pool and terrace or escape to the hammock and the shade of mature trees. Then, in the evening, after a fabulous meal at a local restaurant, soak in the spa under the star-filled southern sky. What better way to recharge the batteries?

Situated in the heart of Nelson's wine and craft area, **Kimeret Place** is an ideal base to explore the diversity of the region, from the beautiful beaches of the Abel Tasman NP to the dramatic mountains of Kahurangi NP. Our accommodation options include two luxurious suites and two stylish adjoining apartments (which can be booked together as a two bedroom cottage, ideal for families or groups). All have tea/coffee facilities, fridge, hair dryers, toiletries, sitting-area with TV and Hi-fi and views from either balcony or deck. Also available light meals, internet and laundry.

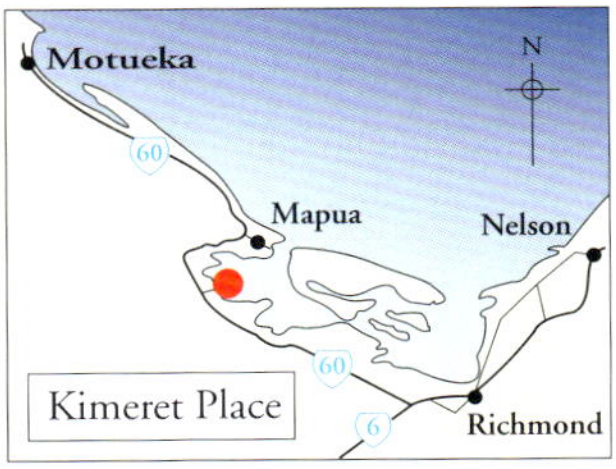

DIRECTIONS: From Richmond on SH 60 turn right after 12 km into Bronte Road East. From Mapua: 4 km on left.

Felbridge Cottage & House

6 Pitfure Rd, Wakefield, 7181, Nelson
Ph (03) 541 8505
Mobile 021-022 42540
email: *dplatt33@hotmail.com*
www.felbridge.co.nz

Features & Attractions

- *Welcome basket*
- *Local attractions*
- *Relaxing spa*
- *Fishing, golf, horse riding*
- *15 min. from Nelson*
- *Pets welcome by prior arrangement*

Boutique & Self-contained Accommodation

$	
Double	$150-185
Single	
Child	

Welcome – Haere Mai. Sheryle and Dave are proud owners of historic **Felbridge House & Cottage**, a magnificent Victorian house with wrap-around verandas and the cottage a 'Dutch Barn', fully equipped self-catering accommodation. Queen and double-size beds and choice of breakfasts from fresh local produce. Wakefield Village is in a prime location for all that the Nelson region has to offer – fishing, golf, local wineries, arts and crafts, horse trekking. Our local beaches are just a short drive away. Steam railway, historic churches or a relaxing stroll in 'Faulkner Bush Reserve' with native trees in abundance, play area and BBQ facilities. A friendly community awaits with a fresh bakery, butcher, mini market and 'Chateau Rhubarbe', our local café, with local wines and excellent cuisine. All the ingredients for a relaxing stay.

DIRECTIONS: **From Nelson** SH6 Wakefield Village sign - fork left into Pitfure Rd, we are 600 metres on left. **From Christchurch** SH 6 enter Wakefield Village 1st turn right Edward St, 3rd turn left, we are on the right.

Bedrooms	Qty
Double	2
Twin	
Single	
Bed Size	**Qty**
King	
Queen	1
Double	1
Single	
Bathrooms	**Qty**
Ensuite	
Private	
Family Share	1

Lansfield Bed & Breakfast Homestay

133, 88 Valley RD1, Wakefield
Ph (03) 541 9789, Fax (03) 541 9780
Mobile 021- 131 3415
email: *mdtillier@xtra.co.nz*

Features & Attractions

- *Warm, friendly hospitality*
- *Generous breakfasts*
- *Great golf course nearby*
- *Join us for dinner*
- *Beautiful views*
- *Purpose built homestay*

Countrystay Bed & Breakfast

$	
Double	$130-150
Single	$90
Child	

Welcome to our lovely new home, all rooms enjoying rural views over the valley. Expect comfortable beds, well appointed ensuites, a delicious breakfast and dinner by prior arrangement. Home baking is part of the welcome, with tea and coffee making facilities available in your room. We are also handy to Nelson and Tasman Bay. A great golf course and café are nearby. Gardening and classic cars are interests. Pheobe is our friendly Burmese cat. We look forward to meeting you.

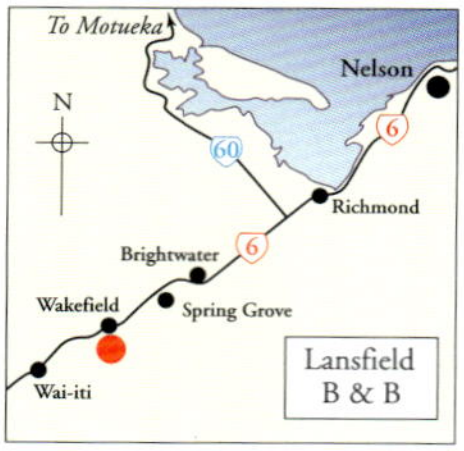

DIRECTIONS: Directly south on the outskirts of Wakefield Village on SH6. 88 Valley Rd is clearly signposted. We are 1km from the turn-off to your left on the lower slope of the hill.

Bedrooms	Qty
Double	3
Twin	
Single	
Bed Size	**Qty**
Super King	1
Queen	2
Double	
Single	
Bathrooms	**Qty**
Ensuite	3
Private	
Guest Share	

Westleigh

Waimea West Road, RD, Brightwater, Nelson
Ph (03) 542 3654
email: *westleigh@paradise.net.nz*

Features & Attractions

- *Secluded park-like setting*
- *Close to good beach*
- *Great dinner available*
- *Near 3 good golf courses*
- *On wine & craft trail*
- *Relax & smell the roses*

$		
	Double	$100-120
	Single	$80-100
	Child	

Countrystay Bed & Breakfast

Bedrooms	Qty
Double	2
Twin	
Single	
Bed Size	**Qty**
King	
Queen	1
Double	
Single	2
Bathrooms	**Qty**
Ensuite	1
Private	
Guest Share	

Westleigh is a relaxing home set on 27 acres. An ideal base to explore all that the Nelson province has to offer. The house has evolved from an old farmhouse and is now surrounded by a woodland garden visited by many birds including wild ducks taking advantage of the large pond. We are a short drive from two good golf courses and an uncrowded safe beach.

There is a selection of good restaurants nearby, or you can enjoy a home cooked meal by arrangement.

Nelson has much to offer including on average seven hours of sunshine a day. Share our corner of paradise.

Our email address is accurate!

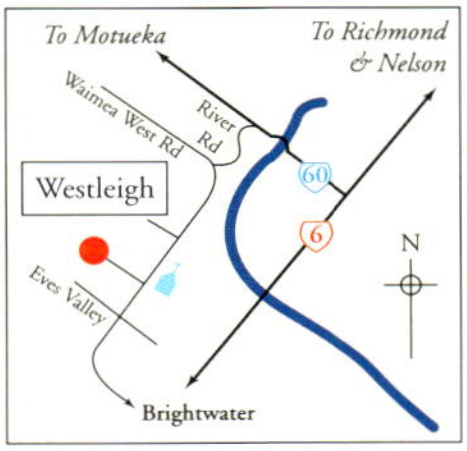

Idesia

14 Idesia Grove, Richmond, 7002, Nelson
Ph (03) 544 0409, Fax (03) 544 0402
Mobile 027-632 7869
email: *idesian@xtra.co.nz*
www.idesia.co.nz

qualmark ★★★★ guest & hosted

@ home NEW ZEALAND

Features & Attractions

- *National parks & beaches*
- *Dinner by arrangement*
- *Ample off-street parking*
- *Central to Nelson/Tasman Region*
- *Abel Tasman Booking Agent*
- *Local & South Island knowledge*

$		
	Double	$100-115
	Single	$80-85
	Child	

Homestay Bed & Breakfast

Bedrooms	Qty
Double	2
Twin	
Single	
Bed Size	**Qty**
S King/ Twin	1
Queen	1
Double	
Single	
Bathrooms	**Qty**
Ensuite	1
Private	1
Guest Share	

A warm welcome to our home centrally located to explore the Nelson region. **Idesia Bed & Breakfast** is two kilometres from Highway 6, in a quiet grove.

Our modern house is elevated to catch the sun and views.

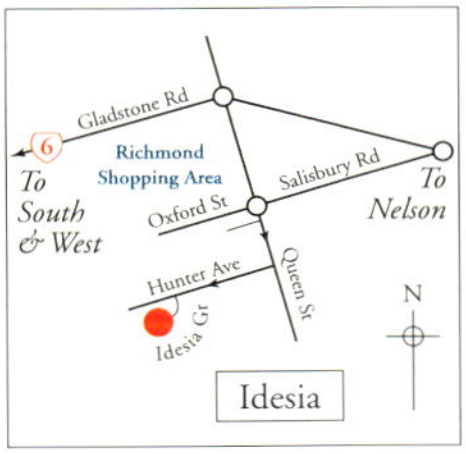

Your choice of full or continental breakfast will include local and home-made produce. Join us for dinner, by prior arrangement; however, Richmond's restaurants are within two kilometres. Pet-free. Smoke-free. Broadband access. Off-road parking.

With our local experience our aim is to enable you to enjoy our regions' attractions for a truly memorable stay.

ALMOND COTTAGE

3/60 Songer Street, Stoke, Nelson
Ph/Fax (03) 547 9486
Mobile 025-652 2418
email: *almond.cottage@paradise.net.nz*

Features & Attractions

- *Lovely breakfast*
- *Airport pick-up*
- *Quiet location*
- *Ample off-street parking*
- *Agents for Abel Tasman Adventure Trips*
- *8 km to Nelson City centre*

Homestay Bed & Breakfast

Double	$95
Single	$70
Child	

We are centrally located in the Nelson area, 8 kilometres from Nelson City, close to all amenities and restaurants. We are situated down a long driveway, where you are assured of a quiet stay. An elegant cottage, with warm, homely atmosphere, a private garden and close to the 'new' Monaco Village. Have dinner at the 'Honest Lawyer', our romantic olde English pub and restaurant, overlooking the Monaco inlet, 200 metres away. Relax in our private lounge or sunroom with complimentary tea/coffee. Our queen room has a private guest bathroom. There is tea/coffee making facilities, bathrobes and hair dryer in this room. The twin room has ensuite, tea/coffee making facilities and hair dryer. We serve you with a lovely breakfast, our own home preserves and jams, fresh home-grown berries in season and home-made yoghurt. **Almond Cottage**, a wonderful starting point to explore this beautiful area.

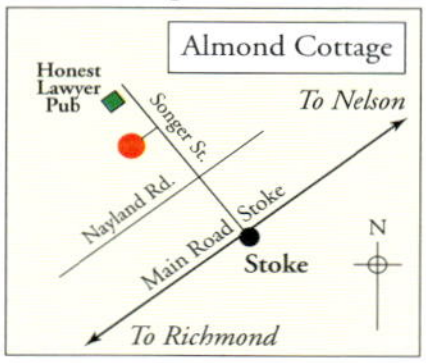

Bedrooms	Qty
Double	1
Twin	1
Single	
Bed Size	**Qty**
King	
Queen	1
Double	
Single	2
Bathrooms	**Qty**
Ensuite	1
Private	1
Guest Share	

ARAPIKI

21 Arapiki Road, Stoke, Nelson
Ph (03) 547 3741
email: *wisechoice@nelsonparadise.co.nz*
www.nelsonparadise.co.nz

VISA MasterCard

Features & Attractions

- *Centrally located in Nelson area*
- *Fully self-contained units*
- *Continental breakfast $7.50 pp*
- *Attractive garden setting*
- *Private deck or balcony*
- *Off-street parking*

Self-contained Homestay Units in Attractive Garden Setting

Double	$75-110
Single	$70-90
Child	

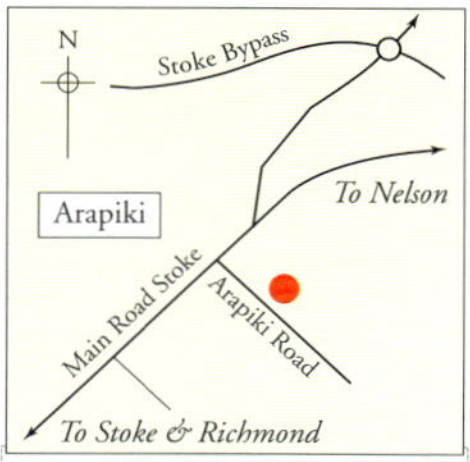

DIRECTIONS:
From the Stoke Shopping Centre Arapiki Road is on the right approx. 1 km north along the Main Road Stoke. It is approx. 6 km from Central Nelson.

Enjoy a relaxing holiday in the midst of your trip. The two self-contained smokefree units in our large home offer you comfort and privacy and are also very suitable for longer stays. These quality units in an attractive garden setting are centrally located in the Nelson area which has NZ's highest sunshine hours. Unit 1, which is larger, is in a pleasant and private garden setting. A ranchslider opens out to a deck with outdoor furniture for your use. It contains an electric stove, microwave, television, auto washing machine, phone and outdoors barbeque.

Unit 2 has a balcony setting with seating to enjoy sea and mountain views. It contains a television, microwave and phone. At present our affordable prices offer excellent value for money for the 'home away from home' accommodation provided.

Bedrooms	Qty
Double	2
Twin	
Single	
Bed Size	**Qty**
King	
Queen/Double	2
Double	
Single	1
Bathrooms	**Qty**
Ensuite	2
Private	
Guest Share	

YOUR HOSTS: **Gay and Derek Ball** Ph (03) 547 3556 **Stoke - Nelson**

MOERAKI

724 Main Rd, Stoke, Nelson
Ph (03) 547 3556, Fax (03) 547 3556
Mobile 027-4855 181
email: *d.g.ball@xtra.co.nz*

Features & Attractions

- *Elegant spacious room*
- *Tranquil private setting*
- *Pool and tennis court*
- *Artist's studio*
- *Ample off-street parking*
- *Airport pick-up*

$	
Double	$125-140
Single	$90
Child	

Much more than Bed & Breakfast

Bedrooms	Qty
Double	1
Twin	
Single	
Bed Size	**Qty**
King	
Queen	
Double	1
Single	
Bathrooms	**Qty**
Ensuite	
Private	1
Guest Share	

Come and enjoy a unique experience in our elegant, Edwardian homestead, set in secluded park-like grounds with swimming pool and tennis court.
Relax beside the pool or go exploring the near-by cafés, beaches, vineyards and craft studios. Take advantage of private access to walking and biking trails, or spend time viewing Derek's sculpture.
Choose breakfast in the large conservatory with garden views, on the pool patio, or in your sunny bedroom. Join Derek and Gay for a complimentary drink on the verandah at the end of the day.
Guests are encouraged to use the outdoor facilities during their stay.

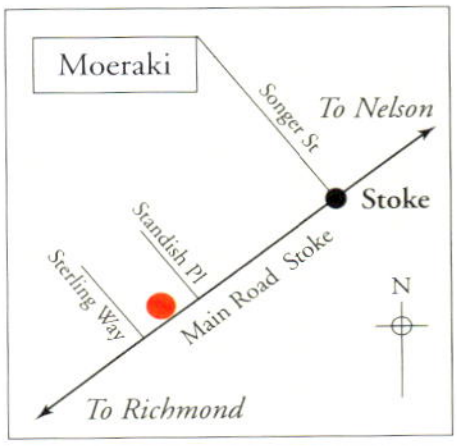

YOUR HOSTS: **Fumio and Sayuri Noguchi** Ph (03) 547 0229 **Stoke - Nelson**

SAKURA BED & BREAKFAST

604 Main Road, Stoke, Nelson
Ph (03) 547 0229, Fax (03) 547 0229
Mobile 021-547 022
email: *fumio.noguchi@paradise.net.nz*
www.sakura-nelson.co.nz

Features & Attractions

- *Special Japanese breakfast*
- *Quiet & peaceful location*
- *Off -street parking*
- *Wine & craft trails*
- *Close to Mac's Brewery*
- *Bone carving artist's residence*

$	
Double	$150
Single	$85-110
Child	neg

Bed & Breakfast

Bedrooms	Qty
Double	1
Twin	1
Single	1
Bed Size	**Qty**
King	1
Queen	
Double	
Single	3
Bathrooms	**Qty**
Ensuite	1
Guest Share	1
Family Share	1

Sakura Bed & Breakfast is named after two cherry trees in our garden. Cherry tree or blossom is called 'Sakura' in Japanese. We are friendly Japanese hosts and also serve Japanese traditional breakfast, which is tasty and healthy (or you may prefer to choose European style breakfast). **Sakura Bed & Breakfast** is only 5 minutes from Nelson Airport and 10 minutes from the city centre. The house, situated in a quiet cul-de-sac off the main road, is modern, sunny and comfortable with a peaceful garden. Complimentary tea/coffee, Japanese green tea and home-made biscuits are available at all times. We follow the Japanese custom of no shoes in the house. Fumio is a bone-carving artist and his works are displayed at our B&B.

Nelson ▶ YOUR HOSTS: Ann and Nick James Ph (03) 548 0554

Annick House

29 Cleveland Terrace, Nelson
Ph (03) 548 0554, Fax (03) 548 0505
Mobile 021-1342 808
email: *nick.james@xtra.co.nz*
www.annickhouse.co.nz

Features & Attractions

- *5 min. easy walk to city*
- *Self-contained/off street parking*
- *Breakfast essentials included*
- *Quiet and peaceful area*
- *Internet/laundry facilities*
- *Free use of bicycles*

Quality and Affordable Self-contained

Double	$110-140
Single	$100-120
Child	neg

Bedrooms	Qty
Double	1
Twin	1
Single	
Bed Size	**Qty**
King	1
Queen	1
Double	
Single	2
Bathrooms	**Qty**
Ensuite	
Private	2
Guest Share	

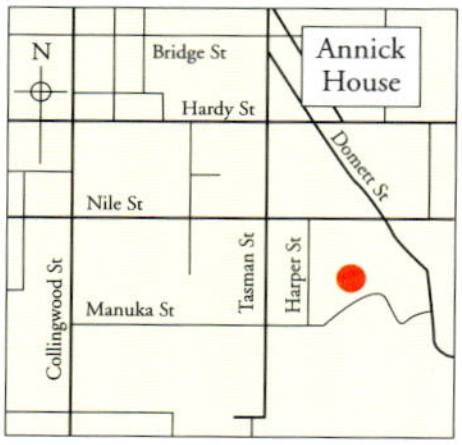

Welcome to **Annick House**. We offer a self-contained studio and guest wing. Both are tastefully furnished and have private entrances and are fully equipped. Weekly rates are available. Our central location allows you to explore the region's many attractions. Walk the nearby tracks or ride bicycles to the beach. We have hosted foreign students for 12 years and enjoy travelling in New Zealand and other countries. We are happy to assist you with tour planning. Our hobbies include miniatures, brewing, sewing and fishing. Nelson is a beautiful place and we look forward to meeting you and sharing our city and country.
You can be sure of a warm, friendly welcome from our two Tokinese cats and a comfortable stay.

Nelson City ▶ YOUR HOSTS: Deirdre and Wally Olykan Ph (03) 546 9913

Shakespeare Cottage

5 Shakespeare Walk, Nelson
Ph (03) 546 9913, Fax (03) 546 9913
Mobile 021-215 6950
www.shakespearecottage.co.nz

Features & Attractions

- *5 min. walk to city*
- *Riverside location*
- *Golf course, beach*
- *Fully self-contained*
- *Close to bus, info centre*
- *Off-street parking*

Inner City Self-contained & Self-catering Accommodation

Double	$120-150
Single	$100-150
Child	$10

Bedrooms	Qty
Double	2
Twin	
Single	
Bed Size	**Qty**
SuperKing/Twin	4
Queen	
Double-sofabed	1
Single	
Bathrooms	**Qty**
Ensuite	2
Private	2
Guest Share	

Shakespeare Cottage and **Villa Apartment** are situated by the Maitai River, only a few minutes walk from the city centre with its wonderful variety of restaurants and cafés, galleries and gardens, the centre of New Zealand, river and bush walks plus a heated swimming pool just a stroll away. The cottage and apartment are completely self-contained and can sleep up to four people each.
The apartment is situated in a character villa, circa 1890. There is one spacious bedroom with large bay window area, bathroom with underfloor heating and washing machine, separate lounge with kitchenette, river views, private entrance and OSP. The cottage is situated in a private garden setting at the rear of villa. It is completely self-contained, fridge/freezer, dishwasher, underfloor heating, private sunny and fenced. Both the **Apartment** and **Cottage** are equipped with wireless internet and telephone access. Tea, real coffee and basic breakfast essentials are included.

Ambleside Luxury Bed & Breakfast

237 Annesbrook Drive, Tahunanui, Nelson
Ph (03) 548 5067
Mobile 021-147 0898
email: *ambleside@paradise.net.nz*
www.amblesidenelson.co.nz

Tariff : N.Z. Dollars	
Double	$140-170
Single	$140-170
Child	

Bedrooms	Qty
Double	2
Twin	2
Single	
Bed Size	**Qty**
Super King	
King	
Queen	2
King/Single	2
Single	2
Bathrooms	**Qty**
Ensuite	4
Private	
Guest Share	

Homestay Boutique Accommodation
Luxury Bed & Breakfast

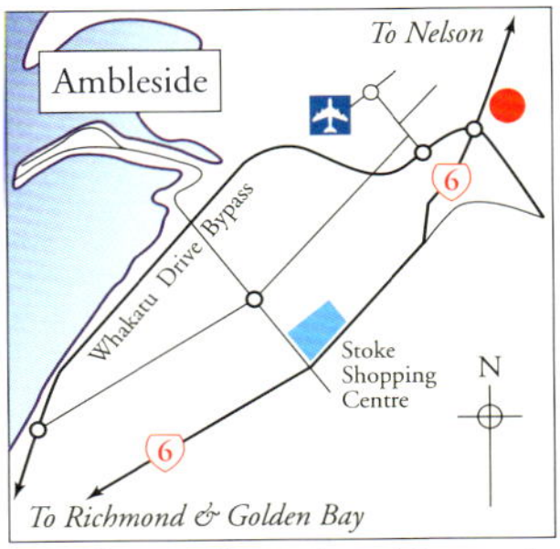

Features & Attractions

- *Purpose-built guest wing*
- *Off-street parking*
- *Gourmet breakfasts*
- *Gateway Abel Tasman Park*
- *Tea/coffee, refreshments*
- *Laundry facilities*
- *Email/Internet*
- *5 minutes to airport*

Ambleside, like its namesake in England, has a typical 'olde worlde' charm. The new, purpose-built guest wing is luxuriously appointed, exuding comfort, style and ambience that belie the 'little cottage' frontage. Guests have own private entrance off the deck, separate lounge and each room, tastefully decorated, has its own ensuite. Breakfasts, according to our guests, are *"second to none"*, served on the deck, sunny courtyard or dining room. Choose from the extensive menu and and dine at the time of your choice. Settle in with a cuppa and yummy home-made baking.

Complimentary refreshments are served throughout your stay. A spirit of gracious hospitality sets **Ambleside** apart and you are assured of warm and friendly, (in guest's words) *"six-star service!"* In addition to our extensive brochure display, we are happy to help you make the most of your stay in the Nelson Region. Our central location affords you close proximity to Nelson City, beaches, world-class restaurants and beautiful Abel Tasman Park.

Nelson ▶ YOUR HOSTS: **Victoria and David Los** Free Ph 0800 868 687

SUSSEX HOUSE BED & BREAKFAST

238 Bridge Street, Nelson
Ph (03) 548 9972, Fax (03) 548 9975
Mobile 027-478 4846
email: *reservations@sussex.co.nz*
www.sussex.co.nz

Features & Attractions

- *5 min. walk to city*
- *130-year-old residence*
- *Overlooking botan. gardens*
- *Riverside location*
- *Off-street parking*
- *Fluent French spoken*

VISA MasterCard

Quality Bed & Breakfast

$	
Double	$120-160
Single	$110-140
Child	

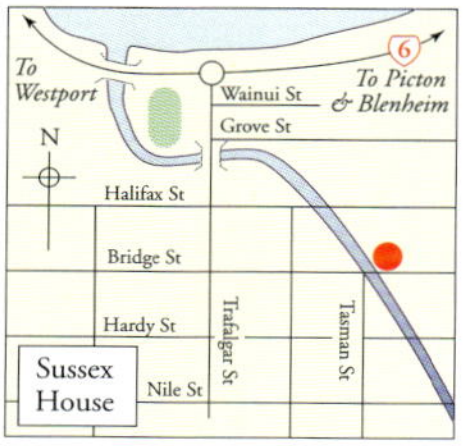

Situated beside the beautiful Maitai River, our charming Victorian family home has retained its original character and ambience. It is only minutes walk from central Nelson's award-winning restaurants and cafés, the Queen's Gardens, Suter Art Gallery, Botanical Hill (The Centre of New Zealand) and numerous river and bush walks. The five sunny bedrooms all have TV and are spacious and tastefully decorated. All rooms have access to the verandah and complimentary tea and coffee facilities are provided. Breakfast includes fresh and preserved fruits, home-made bread, hot croissants, home-made yoghurt, cheeses and a large variety of cereals. Our facilities include: a wheelchair suite, free email/Internet station, fax, laundry and complimentary port. We speak French, having lived for 25 years in New Caledonia.

Bedrooms	Qty
Double	3
Twin	2
Single	
Bed Size	**Qty**
King	
Queen	5
Double	
Single	2
Bathrooms	**Qty**
Ensuite	4
Private	1
Guest Share	

Nelson ▶ YOUR HOSTS: **Shirley and Bruce Lauchlan** Free Ph: 0800 546 604

HAVENVIEW HOMESTAY

10 Davies Drive, Walters Bluff, Nelson
Ph (03) 546 6045, Mobile 027-420 0737
email: *havenview@paradise.net.nz*
www.havenview.co.nz

MasterCard VISA

Features & Attractions

- *Nearby walks to gardens*
- *Cooked breakfast*
- *Panoramic views*
- *Sky television*
- *3 min to city centre*
- *Private double spa bath*

$	
Double	$120-145
Single	$90
Child	

Homestay Bed & Breakfast

Bedrooms	Qty
Double	2
Twin	
Single	1
Bed Size	**Qty**
King	
Queen	2
Double	
King/Single	1
Bathrooms	**Qty**
Ensuite	1
Private	1
Guest Share	

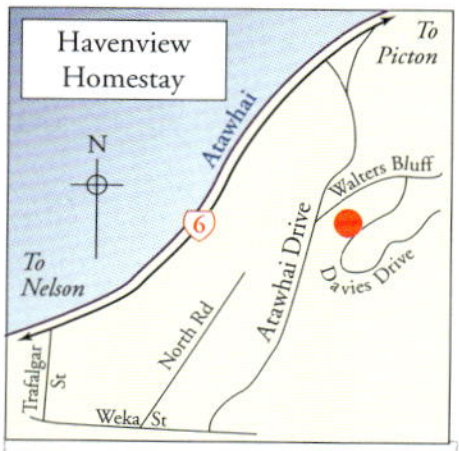

DIRECTIONS: Exit motorway at Founders Park sign, 700 m turn left up Walters Bluff, right into Davies Drive, look for homestay sign after 3rd house on right. (We are down right of way).

Welcome to our sunny, modern home, only three minutes from the centre of Nelson.
Relax on our deck sipping a complimentary local wine and nibbles each evening while enjoying the panoramic views across the bay to Able Tasman Park (see photo). Join us for an evening meal or dine at one of Nelson's fine restaurants. We serve a light cooked breakfast at a time to suit you; and then during the day visit the National Park; do a wine tour; or have a game of golf. We both play golf and can recommend various courses.
Our large queen ensuite has sea views, while our second queen room has a view of our garden. Come and let us make your stay a friendly, pampered experience.

A Culinary Experience

71 Tresillian Ave, Atawhai, Nelson
Ph (03) 545 1886, Fax (03) 545 1869
Free Ph: 0800-891 886
email: *kpastorius@xtra.co.nz*
www.a-culinary-experience.com

Tariff : N.Z. Dollars	
Double	$175-225
Single	$160-210
Child	

Bedrooms	Qty
Double	2
Twin	
Single	
Bed Size	**Qty**
Super King/Twin	2
King	
Queen	
Double	
Single	
Bathrooms	**Qty**
Ensuite	2
Private	
Guest Share	

Luxury B&B Homestay
A Culinary Experience

Features & Attractions

- *Pampered holiday package*
- *Sea and mountain views*
- *Therapy massage and spa*
- *National parks and beaches*
- *Art, laughter, great food*
- *Gourmet cooking classes*
- *Email, laundry facilities*
- *Sculpture & herb garden*

Welcome to our lovely home, filled with original art, laughter and great food. Awake to the sensory pleasure of freshly baked bread. Enjoy a cappuccino while your sumptuous breakfast is prepared. Indulge yourself with a leisurely soak in the spa. Celebrate sensational sunsets, bay/mountain views with your complimentary glass of wine. Choose the sun-drenched garden or patio to read a book. Quaff the aroma of edible flowers or organic herbs, grown for meals and cooking classes. Explore Nelson's wineries, restaurants, museums, galleries and national parks.

Your hosts lead gourmet tours on four continents. Joe, a naturopath, offers therapeutic massage. Kay, author and former cooking school owner, provides delightful dinners and cooking classes. This boutique accommodation has two rooms, **Chambre de Provence** and **Tuscan Room** with king-size beds and ensuites with warmed tile floors. Accommodations are smoke-free. Private parking and Internet access are provided. Pets, laundry and courtesy transfers are by arrangement. With so much to do in the region, 3 or more nights are recommended. Please see our website for: European and/or New Zealand food and wine tours, B&B Indulgence Weekends and Pampered Stay options.

Atawhai Homestay
Mike's Bed & Breakfast

4 Seaton Street, Atawhai, Nelson
Ph (03) 545 1671
email: *cooperkent@actrix.co.nz*

Features & Attractions

- *Easy access to Nelson City*
- *Gateway to West Coast*
- *Gateway to National Parks*
- *Ferries less than 2 hours*
- *Access to the BoulderBank*
- *Only 200m from the sea*

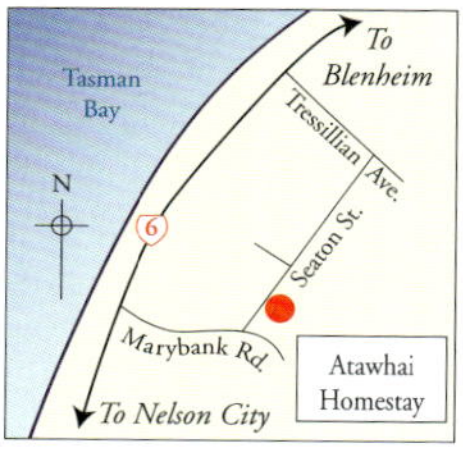

Homestay
Bed & Breakfast

Only five minutes by car from Nelson city centre, we give you a warm welcome to our comfortable home in a safe, quiet neighbourhood with superb views over Tasman Bay and out to the mountains beyond.

Our guest accommodation is almost self-contained and is well equipped with two ensuite bedrooms, a small kitchenette with fridge/freezer, microwave and complimentary tea and coffee making facilities; a lounge, holding some of our large book collection, which you are welcome to use, and a TV. Complimentary laundry facilities are available. Besides books and our rose garden, our main interests include travel, education, sea fishing and our beautiful Schnauzer dog.

$	
Double	$70-80
Single	$70
Child	neg

Bedrooms	Qty
Double	2
Twin	
Single	
Bed Size	**Qty**
King	
Queen	2
Double	
Single	
Bathrooms	**Qty**
Ensuite	2
Private	
Guest Share	

Parautane Lodge

137 Parautane Way, Wakapuaka, RD 1 Nelson
Ph (03) 545 2959, Fax (03) 545 2958
Mobile 021-052 6842
email: *parautaneinfo@paradise.net.nz*
www.nelsonlodge.co.nz

Tariff : N.Z. Dollars	
Double	$180-340
Single	
Child	

Bedrooms	Qty
Double	4
Twin	
Single	
Bed Size	**Qty**
Super King	
King	1
Queen	3
Double	1
Single	1
Bathrooms	**Qty**
Ensuite	4
Private	
Guest Share	

Country Luxury Lodge

Features & Attractions

- *Stylish Luxury Lodge*
- *10 acres lifestyle block*
- *180° sea and mountain views*
- *Ocean view from spa & rooms*
- *Art, craft & wine trails*
- *Beaches & town 12 min.*
- *Abel Tasman Nat. Park 1hour*
- *Hike, kayak, hunt, fish*

Parautane Lodge is an exquisite Bed & Breakfast in an idyllic country setting – the uttermost combination of peace and tranquillity while still catering to your every need. Situated just 12 minutes drive from Nelson City, Candace and Alan provide luxurious rooms, breathtaking views and generous breakfasts. It is the perfect retreat for a weekend away from the stresses of life or for a taste of New Zealand culture. From the comfort of your bed the rooms offer beautiful sea and mountain views. Each room accesses expansive decking from where you can wander down to the garden gazebo for a spa. Our 10-acre section allows you the opportunity to stroll about enjoying the tranquillity of the country. Lounge around the house or experience all the wonderful things Nelson has to offer, be it arts/festivals, beaches, sporting activities or wonderous cafés and eateries. Close to Abel Tasman and Kahurangi National Parks it is the perfect location to spend a week or two exploring the Nelson/Marlborough Region. Offering amazing comfort, romance and seclusion, the **Lodge** is also ideal for honeymooners and those seeking a retreat.

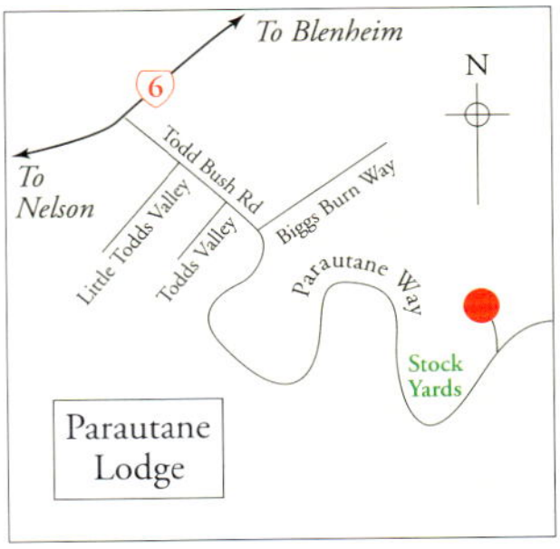

DIRECTIONS: Leave Nelson towards Blenheim on SH 6. After 10 km turn right into Todd Bush Rd. Landmark: Church on sweeping corner. We are 2 km from here. Follow off the end of Todd Bush Rd. onto Parautane Way, climb uphill until you see our sign on the left.

The Log House

Main Road, Motupiko
Ph (03) 522 4260, Fax (03) 522 4240
email: *jimandshiela@theloghouse.co.nz*
www.theloghouse.co.nz

Features & Attractions

- *American style loghouse*
- *6 acres parklike grounds*
- *Friendly llamas and sheep*
- *Shiatsu/reiki treatments*
- *Garden hot tub/spa*
- *Vegetarian household*

Homestay Bed & Breakfast

Double	$150
Single	$135
Child	

Enjoy the warm, friendly feeling of being surrounded by the logs when you stay at **The Log House**, set in 6 acres with a mix of native, ornamental and fruit trees, flower gardens and a labyrinth. Relax on the decks or let your cares float away in the hot spa pool. Indulge in a Shiatsu/Reiki massage with Sheila, a trained practitioner. At the end of the day sleep well in comfortable beds and awake to a delicious breakfast. Vegetarian evening meals and picnic lunches are available on request. We are well situated for days out exploring national parks, beaches, wineries and potteries. Jim, Sheila, friendly dogs, llamas and sheep look forward to welcoming you to their little corner of paradise.

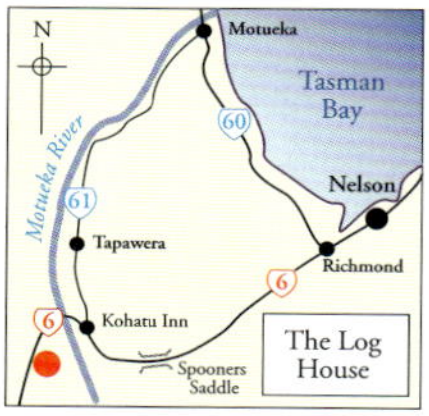

DIRECTIONS: From Richmond follow SH6 south. **The Log House** is exactly 3km on left beyond the curved bridge at the junction with Motueka Valley Highway at the Kohatu Inn. Approx. 45km from Richmond.

Bedrooms	Qty
Double	1
Twin	1
Single	
Bed Size	**Qty**
King	
Queen	1
Double	
King/Single	2
Bathrooms	**Qty**
Ensuite	1
Private	1
Guest Share	

Triple Tui

2454 Dry Weather Road, Glenhope, RD 2, Nelson
Ph (03) 548 4481, Fax (03) 548 4491
Mobile 027-517 1923
email: *stay@tripletui.co.nz*
www.tripletui.co.nz

Features & Attractions

- *Bush & river walks*
- *Peaceful & private*
- *Log fire in cabins*
- *Great trout fishing nearby*
- *Hunt, ski & white water raft*
- *Backs onto Kahurangi N Park*

Self-contained Log Cabins

Double	$160-180
Single	$160-180
Extra pp	$40-60

Triple Tui's log cabins provide a central base from which many varied outdoor activities are on your doorstep. World class fly fishing is but a short cast away with rivers including the Buller, Wairau, Gowan, Owen and Motueka, lakes include Rotoiti and Rotoroa. If getting wet is an option, there is white water rafting and kayaking available in nearby Murchison. In the winter season skiing at St Arnaud and Rainbow ski fields might attract, with feet up on your return and a glass of wine in front of a roaring manuka fire. Our 50 acres, with the Hope Range behind us, allows plenty of privacy and tranquility. An ample breakfast basket, with tea and coffee, awaits in your log cabin, enough for every day of your stay. Visit our website.

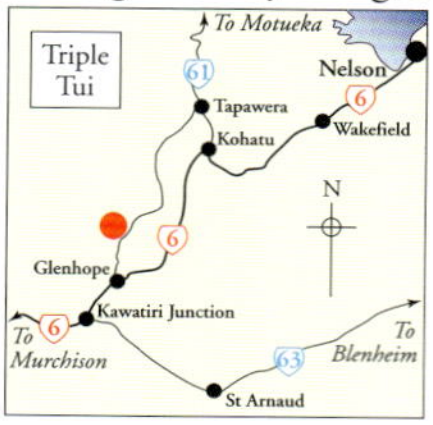

DIRECTIONS: SH6 1hr south of Nelson, 30min north of Murchison. Dry Weather Rd (Glenhope-Tadmore Rd) is at the bottom of Hope Saddle. We are 4.5 km up road on left.

Bedrooms	Qty
Double	2
Twin	
Single	
Bed Size	**Qty**
King	
Queen	2
Double	2
Single	
Bathrooms	**Qty**
Ensuite	
Private	2
Guest Share	

Avarest Bed & Breakfast

1 Kerr Bay Road, PO Box 20, St Arnaud, Nelson Lakes 7053
Ph (03) 521 1864, Fax (03) 521 1865
Mobile (027) 430 5036
e-mail: *avarestbnb@xtra.co.nz*
www.avarestbnb.co.nz

Tariff : N.Z. Dollars	
Double	$220-260
Single	$195-235
Child	

Bedrooms	Qty
Double	2
Twin	
Single	
Bed Size	**Qty**
Super King	
King	
Queen	1
Double	1
Single	1
Bathrooms	**Qty**
Ensuite	
Private	1
Guest Share	

DIRECTIONS:
Enter Kerr Bay Road from SH63, travel past the Dept of Conservation HQ towards the lake. We are the last driveway on the left.

VISA MasterCard

Boutique Accommodation
Bed & Breakfast

Features & Attractions

- *1 min. walk to lake edge*
- *Single party bookings*
- *Comfortable and private*
- *Rhododendron gardens*
- *Overlooking Lake Rotoiti*
- *Bush walks, fishing, hunting*
- *Among mature native forest*
- *Relaxed atmosphere*

Situated in the heart of Nelson Lakes National Park, **Avarest** is the perfect luxury mountain retreat for people who wish to relax in style and comfort. Overlooking Lake Rotoiti, we are nestled among mature native forest filled with the sound of bellbirds and tuis.

Underneath the beech canopy are over 130 rhododendrons which flower progressively from September to January.

Guest rooms are comfortable and tastefully decorated with private luxury amenities, including separate toilet, shower and ladies' vanity room. A separate lounge with television, music, books and art is available for guests. Breakfast at **Avarest** can be as simple or elaborate as your appetite requires.

We are 70km from Nelson on SH 6, 80km from Blenheim on SH 63, 300km from Christchurch on SH 7. The National Park has world renowned tramps and walks available for all levels of fitness. You will be welcomed by our cat Kiri.

MUDBRICK LODGE

150 Rimu Gully Rd, PO Box 92, Rai Valley, Marlborough
Ph (03) 571 6147, Fax (03) 571 6147
Mobile 027-251 3867
email: *tania@mudbricklodge.co.nz*
www.mudbricklodge.co.nz

Tariff : N.Z. Dollars	
Double	$220-260
Single	$190-210
Child	

Bedrooms	Qty
Double	2
Twin	
Single	
Bed Size	**Qty**
Super King	2
King	
Queen	
Double	
Single	
Bathrooms	**Qty**
Ensuite	2
Private	
Guest Share	

Self-contained Luxury

Features & Attractions

- *Blissful country retreat*
- *Spa pool in garden*
- *Self-contained suites*
- *Open fire, luxury lounge*
- *40 minutes to Nelson*
- *40 minutes to Marlborough*
- *Art, craft & wine trails*
- *Great base to explore*

DIRECTIONS:
Take French Pass turn-off from Rai Valley on SH 6 halfway between Blenheim and Nelson. We are 5 km from this turn-off, signposted on each turn. Take 1st right across Carluke Bridge, next right. Then 1st left up Rimu Gully.

Your host Tania searched the whole of New Zealand for a setting that would enable her to create a lifestyle she could share with others. **Mudbrick Lodge**, with its two luxury guest rooms, is the result. Tania's background as a professional chef with a passion for fine wines, along with her local Marlborough and Nelson connections, make her the ideal host for your exploration of this, one of New Zealand's most beautiful regions. Starting each day with a superb home-cooked breakfast, you decide just how energetic or relaxing your day will be by choosing from the endless array of activities the area provides. Whether you wish to tour the famous Marlborough vineyards, fish for the notoriously cunning trout in one of the local streams, horse ride through stunning scenery, hunt for deer and wild pig, kayak the beautiful Tennyson Inlet accompanied by dolphins, picnic on your own 'desert island' in the Sounds, bush walk to the crystal clear waters of the Emerald Pools, cast a line into one of the secret salt water fishing spots or just wish to relax on the patio with a good book and a crisp Chardonnay, **Mudbrick Lodge** is perfectly equipped to make each day a memorable one.

Ngaio Bay Homestay and B&B

Ngaio Bay, French Pass Road, RD 3, Rai Valley,
Marlborough Sounds
Ph (03) 576 5287 Fax (03) 576 5287
email: *homestay@ngaiobay.co.nz*
www.ngaiobay.co.nz

Tariff : N.Z. Dollars	
Double	$225
Single	$140
Child	$70

Bedrooms	Qty
Double	2
Twin	
Single	
Bed Size	**Qty**
Super King	
King	
Queen	2
Double	
Single	3
Bathrooms	**Qty**
Ensuite	
Private	2
Guest Share	

eftpos MasterCard VISA

Remote Marlborough Sounds Homestay and Bed & Breakfast

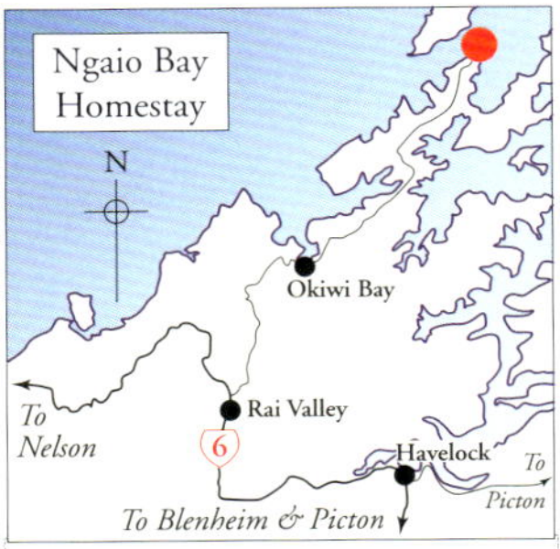

DIRECTIONS:
Please phone for easy directions.

Features & Attractions

- *Sandy private beach*
- *Outdoor fire-heated bath*
- *Kayaks & dinghies*
- *Dolphins & seabirds abound*
- *Bush & farm walks nearby*
- *Charter boats available*
- *Organic garden & orchard*
- *Stunning sunsets*

Experience something special at **Ngaio Bay**, with its own private beach, situated in a truly remote part of the Marlborough Sounds. Breathtaking wilderness and physical beauty, warm, welcoming hosts, scrumptious food, peace and tranquility, fresh seafood, own homegrown organic veggies and fruit when available, beautiful garden, stunning sunsets, comfortable, private, separate accommodation. Views of the awesome waters of French Pass. Ideal for a romantic honeymoon, relaxing holiday, family get-together or wilderness adventure. Your stay at **Ngaio Bay** will be an authentic Kiwi experience. The 'Garden Cottage', with small private deck, is hidden in the garden and overlooks the beach. The loft-style 'Rose and Dolphin' is sunny and spacious. A small verandah overlooks a stream, bush and beach. A favourite speciality is our private outdoor bath enjoyed at sunset, or under sun, rain or stars, prepared by your hosts. Dinner is included in tariff. Three loveable labradors. ***Arrive as strangers, leave as friends.***

Pelorus Bridge - Marlborough ▶ YOUR HOSTS: Roz and Jack Ph (03) 574 2841

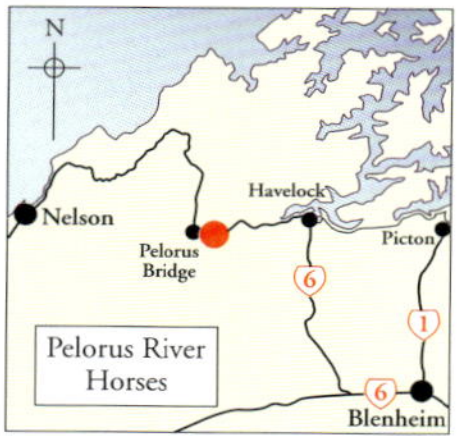

Pelorus River Horses

5677 SH6, Pelorus Bridge, Marlborough
Ph (03) 574 2841, Fax (03) 574 2842
email: *riverhorses@xnet.co.nz*
www.pelorusriverhorses.co.nz

Features & Attractions

- *Stunning scenery*
- *Baths with a view*
- *Lots to do*
- *Comprehensive complimentary comforts*
- *Memorable magical horserides*
- *Really rather relaxing*

C **Genuine Kiwi Flavour** SC

$	
Double	$185
Single	$150
Child	

Bedrooms	Qty
Double	1
Twin	
Single	1
Bed Size	**Qty**
King	
Queen	1
Double	
Single	3
Bathrooms	**Qty**
Ensuite	
Private	2
Guest Share	

Why not take the time and come on over?
"Give y'self a treat!"
A couple of days of stayin' with us is pretty hard to beat!

Our Ranchhouse is the place to stay with crockery and linen.
While Blenheim's not too far away,
The wine, the Sounds with fish'n.

And Nelson is quite close as well with access to the sea.
A feed of fish, a nice cold beer and the local sunset's free.

And while you're here take a ride, if our horses are your thing.
Or read a book, or take a walk and hear the fantails sing! *Jack*

Kenepuru Sound ▶ YOUR HOSTS: Alison and Robin Bowron Ph: (03) 573 4432

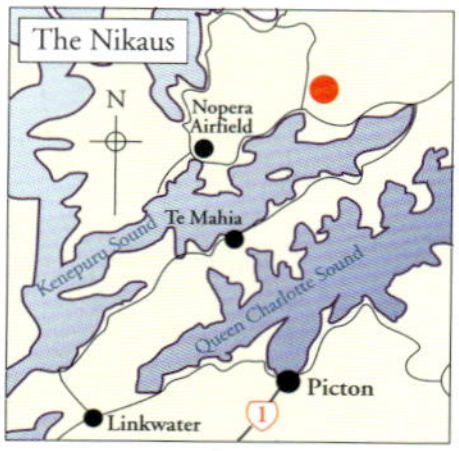

The Nikaus

86 Manaroa Road, Waitaria Bay,
Kenepuru Sound, RD 2, Picton 7372
Ph/Fax (03) 573 4432, Mobile 027-454 4712
email: *info@thenikaus.co.nz*
www.thenikaus.co.nz

Features & Attractions

- *Genuine NZ farm experience*
- *Central location in Kenepuru and Pelorus Sounds*
- *Evening meal $30 pp*
- *Golf, fishing, water taxi*
- *Large country garden*

F **Farmstay Bed & Breakfast** BB

$	
Double	$120
Single	$60
Child	

Bedrooms	Qty
Double	1
Twin	2
Single	
Bed Size	**Qty**
King	
Queen	1
Double	
Single	4
Bathrooms	**Qty**
Ensuite	
Private	
Guest Share	1

The Nikaus sheep and cattle farm in Waitaria Bay, Kenepuru Sound, is 2.5 hours drive from Blenheim via Picton or Havelock. We offer friendly, personal service in our comfortable, spacious home. The large gardens contain many rhododendrons, roses, camellias, lilies and perennials with big sloping lawns and views out to sea.
We are interested in farming, boating, fishing and gardening and have pet cats, Minnie (Jack Russell) and farm dogs, donkeys, pet wild pigs, turkeys, hens, peacocks, sheep and cattle. We offer good, hearty country meals using home-grown produce. Local operators are available for fishing trips and water taxis. Tariff for full farmstay with Dinner, Bed & Breakfast is $90.00 per person per day.
Prior booking essential please phone/fax.

TIRIMOANA HOUSE

257 Anakiwa Road, Tirimoana, RD 1, Picton
Ph (03) 574 2627, Fax (03) 574 2647
Mobile 021-167 2342
email: *bookings@tirimoanahouse.com*
www.tirimoanahouse.com

Tariff : N.Z. Dollars	
Double	$140-220
Single	$110-175
Child	$70

Bedrooms	Qty
Double	4
Twin	
Single	
Bed Size	**Qty**
Super King	
King	1
Queen	3
Double	
Single	
Bathrooms	**Qty**
Ensuite	4
Private	
Guest Share	

This Is Our View!
Luxury Waterfront Accommodation

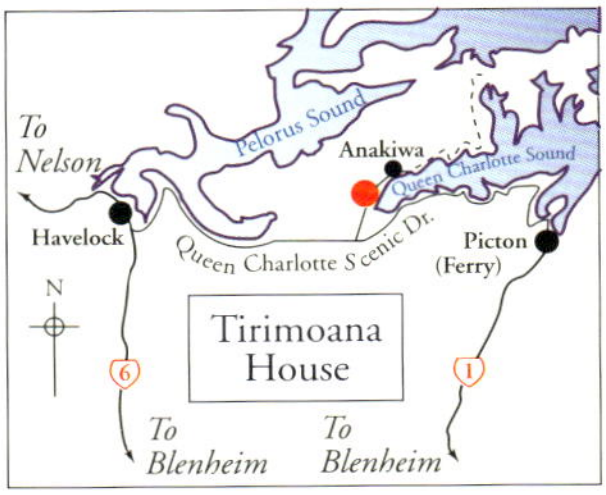

Features & Attractions

- *Swimming pool*
- *Local walks & boat trips*
- *Stunning sea views*
- *Picton - only 30 min*
- *Wine trails arranged*
- *Great home cooking*
- *Spa pool*
- *Queen Charlotte Track*

Enjoying superb sea views of the Marlborough Sounds, **Tirimoana House** is located a convenient 30 min drive from both Picton and the Marlborough wineries. Our two-storey home sits on an elevated waterfront site once occupied by historic Tirimoana Hotel. Our sumptuous bedrooms are all ensuite, all have antique French double beds (one has a 1789 four poster), antique bedside cabinets and chandeliers. One suite is self catering and sleeps four. Our home has antique furniture throughout and many works of art (John and Michelle are both artists) collected by your hosts on their travels. Close by is the renowned Queen Charlotte Track (walk out - water taxi back), kayaking, mountain biking and of course those famous wineries. Relax afterwards in our spa and swimming pools before enjoying a gourmet dinner of local fare and wines. The Blistered Foot café is open from 11am-4pm for guests, those walking the Queen Charlotte Track or waiting for the water taxi.

"Arrive as guests, leave as friends" is our maxim.

Kenepuru Sound — YOUR HOSTS: Flora, Melva and Glenda Robb — Ph: (03) 573 4086

St Omer House

Kenepuru Road, Kenepuru Sound, RD 2, Picton
Ph (03) 573 4086, Fax (03) 573 4586
email: *stomer.house@xtra.co.nz*
www.stomerhouse.co.nz

Features & Attractions

- *Mussel farm & nature cruises*
- *Photographer's dream*
- *Crafts, books & paintings for sale*
- *Bird watcher's paradise*
- *9 hole golf course*
- *Shipwreck, glow worms*

Historic Guest House
Cottage & New Motels

Double	$140
Single	$70
Child	$35

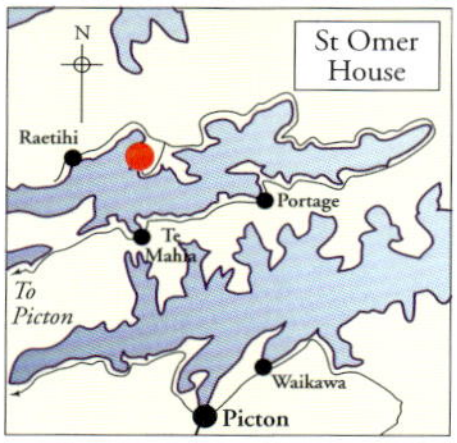

We welcome you to our peaceful bay where the lawns run down to the shelly beach, surrounded by native bush. Sun-bathe, swim, kayak or go boating and catch a fish. Ramble through our large Victorian garden or take a bush walk and listen to the birdsong. Tennis court, games room, nine hole golf course and shipwreck to explore. Fishing trips and Pelorus Sound cruises arranged. Shop and licensed restaurant. Enjoy our homecooked meals including wild game, seafood and delectable sweets and local wines in our historic dining room. Take the scenic 2½ hour drive from Picton or Havelock, fly with Sounds Air to Nopera Airfield, float plane from Picton or Porirua, or arrive by water taxi. Ask for particulars.

Bedrooms	Qty
Double	9
Twin	6
Single	2
Bed Size	**Qty**
King	1
Queen	3
Double	5
Single	14
Bathrooms	**Qty**
Ensuite	6
Private	1
Guest Share	4

Marlborough Sounds — YOUR HOSTS: Linda and Stephen Hearn — Ph (03) 574 2080

Tanglewood

1744 Queen Charlotte Dve, The Grove, RD 1, Picton
Ph (03) 574 2080, Fax (03) 574 2044
Mobile 027-481 4388
email: *tanglewood.hearn@xtra.co.nz*

Features & Attractions

- *5km Queen Charlotte Walkway*
- *Glow worms / native gardens*
- *Dinner by arrangemt $35.00pp*
- *Self-cont. accommodation*
- *Warm, friendly hospitality*
- *Private garden spa pool*

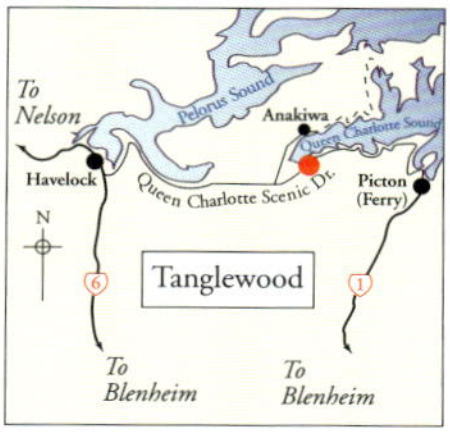

Bed & Breakfast
Self-contained Accommodation

Double	$125
Single	$90
Child	

Come and enjoy our paradise nestled amongst the native ferns overlooking Queen Charlotte Sounds. 16km from Picton on scenic Queen Charlotte Drive and Nelson only 1 hour's drive away.

Our self-contained, private guest wing includes spacious rooms with ensuites, lounge, kitchenette and private BBQ area. Relax in our spa surrounded by our beautiful native garden, listen to the birds or take a walk with us to view the glow worms.

For privacy, relaxation, fishing, kayaking, mountain biking, dolphin watching, walking the Queen Charlotte Track or exploring the Marlborough Wineries. Enjoy a delicious, generous breakfast before your day's pursuits.

Kiwi hospitality at its best, we look forward to making you welcome.

Bedrooms	Qty
Double	1
Twin	1
Single	
Bed Size	**Qty**
Super King	2
Queen	
Double	
King/Single	2
Bathrooms	**Qty**
Ensuite	2
Private	
Guest Share	

Sennen House Luxury Accommodation

9 Oxford Street, Picton, Marlborough
Ph (03) 573 5216, Fax (03) 573 5216
Mobile 021-035 9956
email: *enquiries@sennenhouse.co.nz*
www.sennenhouse.co.nz

Tariff : N.Z. Dollars	
Double	$275-425
Single	$220-350
Child	neg

Bedrooms	Qty
Double	5
Twin	2
Single	
Bed Size	**Qty**
Super King	1
King	2
Queen	2
Double	
Single	3
Bathrooms	**Qty**
Ensuite	5
Private	
Guest Share	

Magnificent Heritage Colonial Villa
Unique Accommodation

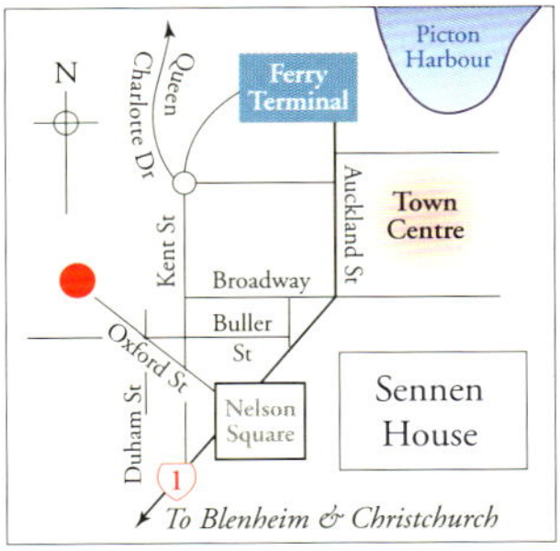

Features & Attractions

- *Queen Charlotte Track & cruises*
- *Luxurious character apartments*
- *Courtesy transfers/internet/phone*
- *Five acre private setting*
- *Short stroll to Picton's amenities*
- *Winetours Marlborough*

Experience the timeless elegance, luxurious comforts and Victorian charm of **Sennen House**, a magnificent 1886 Heritage-registered 2-storey colonial villa, restored in keeping with its gracious style and era, to offer superior accommodation in 5 acres of mature gardens and native bush, only a short stroll to Picton's restaurants, ferries and foreshore. Three elegant apartments and two luxurious suites, three with private lounge and all with ensuite, kitchen facilities and private entrance, offer individual character, historic features, luxury linens, satellite TV, DVD, robes, telephone and wireless internet. Sumptuous daily provisions for leisurely breakfasts on sunny verandahs with views, seclusion, tranquillity and romantic timeless grandeur. Courtesy transfers, pre-dinner drinks, guest office and luggage storage. Superbly situated to explore the magnificent Marlborough Region.

Picton ▶ YOUR HOSTS: Nan and Malcolm Laurenson Ph: (03) 573 7692

RIVENHALL

118 Wellington Street, Picton
Ph (03) 573 7692, Fax (03) 573 7692
email: *rivenhall.picton@xtra.co.nz*

Features & Attractions

- *Town centre 4 min walk*
- *Full breakfast*
- *Ferry & bus pick-up*
- *Easy walk to restaurants*
- *Dinner on request*
- *Laundry*

Homestay Bed & Breakfast

$	
Double	$140
Single	$100
Child	neg

Rivenhall, a gracious home with all the warmth and comfort of a bygone era, is up the rise on the left at the top of Wellington Street. Picton, a small town with many cafés and restaurants is within easy walking distance from **Rivenhall**, but if a relaxing meal with the hosts is more to your needs, Nan will, with sufficient warning, provide dinner at a cost of $35 per head. Not just a stopover at the beginning or end of your South Island tour, Picton can be a destination of its own.

With Sound's activities and tours all running from the bottom of our street, suggested one day activities, wine tours, kayaking, return trip to Kaikoura for whale or dolphin watching (own transport), day trip to Nelson (two hour drive each way) or walking the Queen Charlotte track (one to four days) plus walks and shopping around town.

Bedrooms	Qty
Double	2
Twin	
Single	
Bed Size	**Qty**
King	
Queen	1
Double	1
Single	1
Bathrooms	**Qty**
Ensuite	
Private	2
Guest Share	

Picton - Marlborough ▶ YOUR HOSTS: Alex and Colette Wilson Ph: (03) 573 7192

WHATAMONGA HOMESTAY AT WATERS EDGE

425 Port Underwood Road, RD 1, Picton
Ph (03) 573 7192, Fax (04) 472 4085
email: *info@whsl.co.nz*
www.whsl.co.nz

Features & Attractions

- *Magnificent views*
- *Set in native bush*
- *Direct access to water*
- *Dinner by arrangement*
- *20 min to ferry terminal*
- *Minimum 2 night stay*

Luxury Self-contained Accommodation

$	
Double	$112-180
Single	$100-150
Child	

Bedrooms	Qty
Units	2
Double	2
Single	
Bed Size	**Qty**
Super King	2
King	1
Double	
Single	2
Bathrooms	**Qty**
Ensuite	2
Private	2
Guest Share	

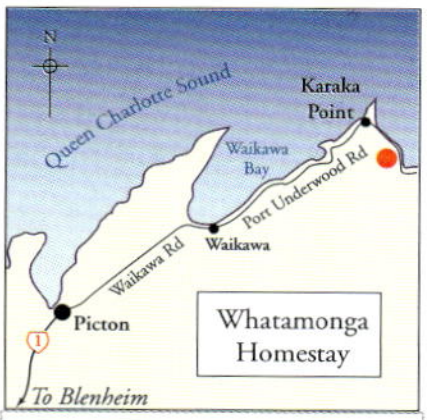

DIRECTIONS: From Picton take Waikawa Rd. From Waikawa shop take Port Underwood Rd past Karaka Pt. After 2 km **Whatamonga Homestay** sign is on the left.

Your hosts at **Whatamonga Home Stay** are Alex and Colette Wilson. The homestay offers accommodation in secluded units, or in two separate bedrooms with own bathroom and deck under the main house. The homestay has been specifically designed by one of Marlborough's leading designers to face north for best sun and allowing guests to enjoy the view and their seclusion, or enjoy the interaction with the sea offered by accommodation with direct access to the water. Evening meals are served in the main house as are cooked breakfasts. Continental breakfasts can be delivered to the units or downstairs bedrooms by prior arrangement. Bookings are essential, especially during the summer months of October to May.

A Sea View

424 Port Underwood Road, Whatamonga Bay,
RD 1, Picton 7372
Ph/Fax (03) 573 8815, Mobile 021-155 1890
email: *info@aseaview.co.nz*

Tariff : N.Z. Dollars	
Double	$149-199
Single	$140-160
Child	

Bedrooms	Qty
Double	3
Twin	
Single	
Bed Size	**Qty**
Super King	2
King	
Queen	1
Double	
Single	
Bathrooms	**Qty**
Ensuite	3
Private	
Guest Share	

VISA MasterCard

Self-contained Bed & Breakfast

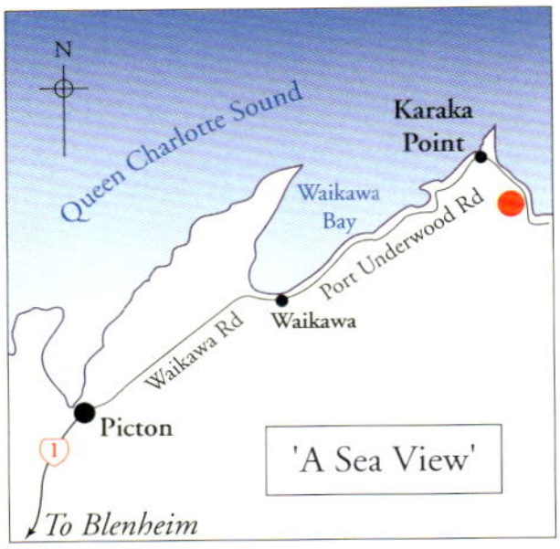

Features & Attractions

- *Breathtaking views*
- *Secluded terraced garden*
- *Self-catering units*
- *2 tonne mooring*
- *Courtesy pick-up from Picton*
- *Outdoor activities & wine tours*
- *Delicious full breakfast*
- *Private entrance to rooms*

You will feel welcome and relaxed at **A Sea View** which is nestled among the trees and just above the water of the Sounds. It offers unsurpassed, awe-inspiring views of the water and mountains of the Sounds from all guest rooms. Here you will experience the ever changing moods of the Queen Charlotte Sound and the peaceful tranquility of the large garden with its great variety of plant and bird life. While enjoying the view from the deck, partake of a generous cooked breakfast which includes homemade jams, yoghurt, muesli and bread. We also offer dinner or lunch, by request. All rooms are warm with large comfortable beds, ensuites, and a cot or extra bed is available for families. We would be pleased to help you discover the many activities that Marlborough is famous for: wine tasting, kayaking, boating, fishing, diving and trekking the Queen Charlotte Walkway, or a gentle cruise on the Sounds visiting the many beautiful bays.

DIRECTIONS: From High St in Picton take Waikawa Bay Rd for 9km, continue for 1km past Karaka Point until you see **Sea View** sign on your right (12-15 min from Picton)

VUE POINTE

PO Box 12, Waikawa Bay, Picton
Ph (03) 573 7621, Fax (03) 573 7621
Mobile 027-205 1664 / 021-041 1740
email: *j_roberts@xtra.co.nz*

Tariff : N.Z. Dollars	
Double	$275
Single	$275
Child	n/a

Bedrooms	Qty
Double	1
Twin	
Single	
Bed Size	**Qty**
Super King	
King	1
Queen	
Double	
Single	
Bathrooms	**Qty**
Ensuite	1
Private	
Guest Share	

Luxury Self-contained Accommodation

Features & Attractions

- *Magical views*
- *Very private and peaceful*
- *15 min drive from Ferry Terminal*
- *Golf, boating, vineyards, plus, plus*
- *Air conditioning & heating*
- *Continental breakfast basket*
- *Discounts for second and subsequent nights*

DIRECTIONS:
Accessed via private road 7 km from Picton.
Please phone for easy directions.

BOOKINGS ESSENTIAL

Vue Pointe is in an elevated position, private and set in native bush. 180° panoramic views of the Marlborough Sounds (Waikawa Bay, Marina and Queen Charlotte Sound).

Relax on any of the extensive deck areas, watch the boat traffic from on high and generally enjoy this special vantage point with its ever changing views. This is also a great base from which to enjoy the region's attractions – excellent vineyards (wine tasting and restaurants), golf, sailing, boat trips, sea kayaking and walking or to just take an extended break before heading south or taking the ferry to Wellington.

Luxury acommodation is provided in a modern self-contained suite with private entrance, consisting of a large double bedroom opening onto a private deck area, an ensuite, partially tiled open plan bathroom with shower, bidet and undertile heating, and a large lounge and dining/kitchen area offering end to end views with access to your private deck area from one end and to a patio area at the other. A generous continental breakfast basket is provided, at your leisure and in the privacy of your own suite.

OYSTER BAY LODGE

1474 Port Underwood Rd, Port Underwood, Picton
Ph (03) 579 9644, Fax (03) 579 9645
Mobile 0274-363 363
email: *enquiries@oysterbaylodge.co.nz*
www.oysterbaylodge.co.nz

Tariff : N.Z. Dollars	
Double	$180
Single	$150
Child	

Bedrooms	Qty
Double	3
Twin	2
Single	
Bed Size	**Qty**
Super King	
King	1
Queen	2
Double	
Single	3
Bathrooms	**Qty**
Ensuite	1
Private	2
Guest Share	

Bed & Breakfast
Homestay

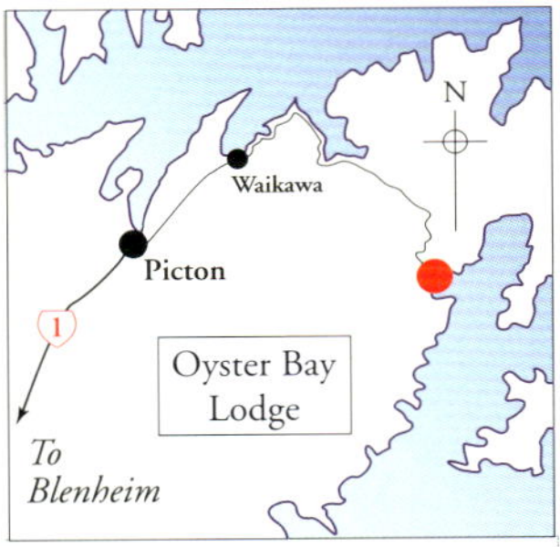

DIRECTIONS:
14 km from Waikawa Bay, Picton on the Port Underwood Road. Keep following the road to the right. Sign posted in the bay.

Features & Attractions

- *Fishing/diving - compressor available*
- *Wonderful views*
- *Bush walks & native birds*
- *Direct water access*
- *Dinner by arrangement*
- *Outdoor activities available*
- *Spa & games room*
- *2 ton mooring available*

Our lodge is set in picturesque Oyster Bay. We have an uninterrupted view over the bay in a charming and historical part of the Marlborough Sounds. Your hosts share an enjoyment of the outdoors and marine environment. Our 8metre boat can offer access to a full range of marine activities in comfort and safety. Personally guided tours and activities of your choosing available at the lodge. Relax in comfort and tranquility on expansive decks or be massaged in the luxury spa and enjoy the amazing array of wildlife and native birds in the garden. 3 course meals are $60 per person, local wines and beer included. Multiple night discount available. We welcome you to enjoy with us at **Oyster Bay Lodge** our unique lifestyle and opportunity.

A two bedroom self-contained unit is now also available. Tariff: $160 - 1 room, $190 - 2 rooms

Koro Park Lodge

779 State Highway 1, Koromiko, RD 3 Blenheim
Phone (03) 573 5542
email: *koropark@xtra.co.nz*

Features & Attractions

- *Private and peaceful*
- *In lovely Koromiko Valley*
- *Close to Picton/Blenheim*
- *Comfortable and friendly*
- *Close to ferry and airport*
- *Art, craft and wine trails*

Bed & Breakfast

$	
Double	$125-195
Single	$105-175
Child	n/a

Situated in the lovely Koromiko Valley, 9 kilometres south of Picton on State Highway 1, **Koro Park Lodge** is an ideally located base from where you may enjoy the many wineries, art and crafts, restaurants, shopping facilities, golfing, scenic boat trips and walking tracks available in wonderful Marlborough.
Close to the Picton ferry terminal and airport, **Koro Park Lodge** is set on almost a hectare of park-like grounds, with mature trees and rural views of the valley and surrounding bush-clad hills.
Jackie and Ted's guests just love to relax in their comfortable private suites.
A delicious breakfast of your choice is served in the guest lounge.

Bedrooms	Qty
Double	2
Twin	
Single	1
Bed Size	**Qty**
King	
Queen	2
Double	
Single	1
Bathrooms	**Qty**
Ensuite	2
Private	
Guest Share	

DIRECTIONS: 9 km south of the Picton ferry terminal on State Highway 1, Koromiko. Sign at the gate.

Blenheim YOUR HOSTS: **Jenny and Phil McAuslin** Ph: (03) 570 5593

The Stream Estate Cottage

856 Rapaura Road, Rapaura, PO Box 772, Blenheim
Ph (03) 570 5593 Mobile 0274-365 554
email: *cozzy@xtra.co.nz*
www.thestreamestate.co.nz

Features & Attractions

- *Self-contained privacy*
- *Located in vineyard*
- *Set beside natural spring*
- *Trout fishing at cottage door*
- *Town and airport 10 min*
- *Heart of wine trail region*

Self-contained Vineyard Cottage

$	
Double	$200-250
Single	
Child	

Set beside a natural spring creek, renowned for its fantastic trout fishing, **The Stream Estate Cottage** offers total privacy within the vineyard. From the front patio, surrounded by vines and the natural fast flowing spring, the views are breathtaking. The Stream Estate Cottage is self-contained and well appointed with separate lounge, dining and kitchen area, featuring a large open fire and double doors which open onto the front patio from the lounge and main bedroom. Two double bedrooms, plus a shared ensuite complete the cottage. Being very centrally located on the Rapaura Road, the 'Golden Mile' of the Marlborough wine industry, **The Stream Estate Cottage** is within ten minutes of most wineries, restaurants and the town centre of Blenheim.

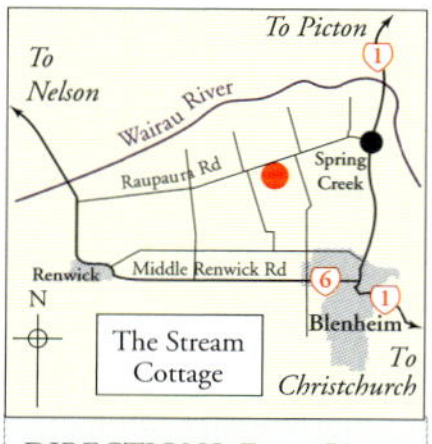

DIRECTIONS: From Picton (SH 1), take Rapaura Road towards Nelson. From Nelson (SH 6) turn left into Rapaura Road, immediately after Main Wairau River Bridge.

Bedrooms	Qty
Double	1
Twin	1
Single	
Bed Size	**Qty**
King	
Queen	1
Double	
King/Single	2
Bathrooms	**Qty**
Ensuite	
Private	1
Guest Share	

Blue Ridge Estate

50 O'Dwyers Road, Rapaura, RD 3, Blenheim
Ph (03) 570 2198, Fax (03) 570 2199
email: *stay@blueridge.co.nz*
www.blueridge.co.nz

Tariff : N.Z. Dollars	
Double	$175-200
Single	$160-185
Child	

Bedrooms	Qty
Double	2
Twin	1
Single	
Bed Size	**Qty**
Super King	
King	
Queen	2
Double	
Single	2
Bathrooms	**Qty**
Ensuite	1
Private	2
Guest Share	

Boutique Vineyard Homestay

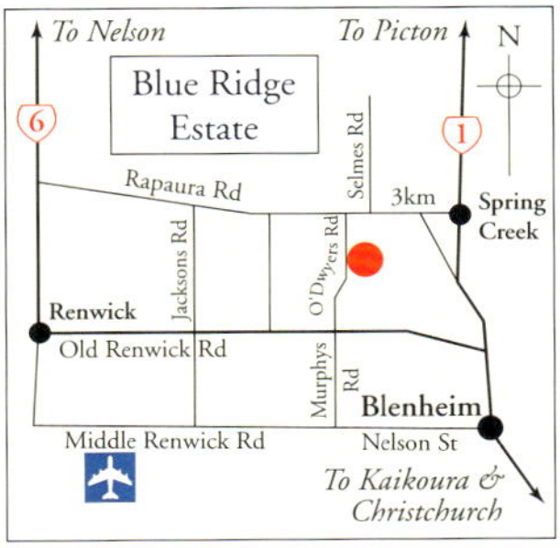

Features & Attractions

- *Quiet and peaceful*
- *Stunning rural views*
- *Dinner by arrangement*
- *Excellent restaurants nearby*
- *Award winning home*
- *Comfort and privacy*
- *Tastefully furnished*
- *Heart of the wine region*

Set on a twenty acre purpose-designed homestay property, **Blue Ridge Estate**, 2002 Master Builders' House of the Year, enjoys a rural setting with stunning views across vineyards to the Richmond Range. Close to many of Marlborough's fine wineries, restaurants, gardens; only twenty five minutes from Picton, and seven minutes to the airport or Blenheim. Bedrooms and bathrooms are tastefully furnished – electric blankets, tea and coffee facilities, high quality linen, hair dryer, heated towel rail. Spend a winter evening in front of our open fire. Our home has proven popular with both international and New Zealand visitors. Come and share our home, where comfort and privacy will ensure your Marlborough visit is indeed a memorable one.

Reservations essential.

ANGLESEA HOUSE BED & BREAKFAST

4 Anglesea Street, Renwick, Blenheim
Ph (03) 572 8520, Fax (03) 572 8521
Mobile 021-703 545
email: *info@angleseahouse.co.nz*
www.angleseahouse.co.nz

Features & Attractions

- *Wineries nearby*
- *World class restaurants*
- *Off-street parking*
- *Close to airport & Picton Ferry*
- *Private lounges, spacious grounds*
- *2 queen rooms with ensuites*

Boutique Bed & Breakfast

$	
Double	$185
Single	$100
Child	neg

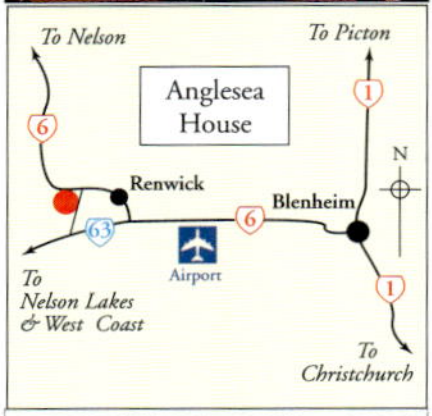

DIRECTIONS: Follow SH 6 from Blenheim/Nelson for 10 km and pass through main street of Renwick. Turn left into Anglesea St (last street on left) Anglesea House is 2nd on right.

This gracious Edwardian residence is set in spacious grounds and situated in the very heart of the famed Marlborough Wine District.
The combination of a tastefully furnished and stylish décor with modern amenities creates an ambience that is both pleasant and comfortable for guests to relax in. Renwick is a central location and a convenient spring board for visiting vineyards, either by car, cycling, arranged ½ or full day tours, while a few are close enough to stroll to. A range of eateries to choose from includes world class restaurants on the doorstep and local pubs and cafés. Easy access to the Kenepuru and Queen Charlotte Sounds means water pleasures such as kayaking and fishing are on offer.

Bedrooms	Qty
Double	3
Twin	1
Single	1
Bed Size	**Qty**
Super King	1
Queen	2
King/Single	2
Single	1
Bathrooms	**Qty**
Ensuite	2
Guest Share	1
Family Share	1

BAXTER HOMESTAY

28 Elisha Drive, Blenheim, Marlborough
Ph (03) 578 3753, Fax (03) 578 3796
Mobile 021-129 2062
email: *baxterart@xtra.co.nz*
www.baxterhomestay.com

Features & Attractions

- *Panoramic views*
- *Private, peaceful, quiet*
- *Close to wineries*
- *4 min from town centre*
- *Attractive gardens*
- *Brian Baxter Art Gallery*

$	
Double	$120-160
Single	
Child	

Homestay Bed & Breakfast

Bedrooms	Qty
Double	3
Twin	
Single	
Bed Size	**Qty**
Super King	1
Queen	1
Double	1
Single	
Bathrooms	**Qty**
Ensuite	2
Private	
Guest Share	1

Brian, a well known New Zealand artist, and Kathy welcome you to their spacious, sunny, modern home and art gallery. You will enjoy magnificent panoramic views over Blenheim and nearby vineyards or explore our terrace gardens-chosen for Hunter's Garden Marlborough 2006 tours.
Share our spacious lounge with original paintings, large screen TV and piano or relax in the privacy and luxury of your "room with a view" upstairs. We are happy to help you arrange visits to wineries, restaurants, gardens, golf courses, art and craft trails, etc.
Our interests include travel, gardening, music, photography, video production and meeting people. TV in all bedrooms. Tea and coffee making and laundry facilities, wireless internet connection, fax and DVD player available.

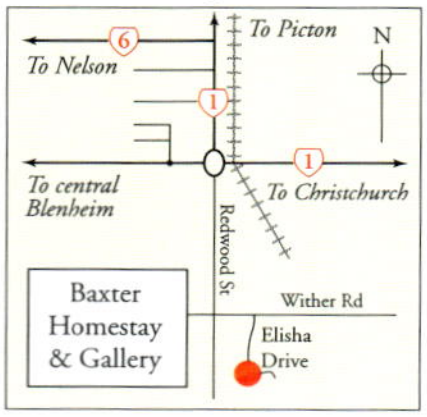

Tamar Vineyard

67 Rapaura Road, RD 3, Rapaura, Blenheim
Ph (03) 572 8408, Fax (03) 572 8405
email: *tamar.vineyard@xtra.co.nz*
www.tamarvineyard.co.nz

Features & Attractions

- *A romantic retreat*
- *Four poster bed*
- *Sumptuous breakfast*
- *Heart of the wine trail*
- *15 min to Blenheim*
- *30 min to Picton*

$	
Double	$175-200
Single	$150
Child	half price

Self-contained Vineyard Cottage

Bedrooms	Qty
Double	1
Twin	
Single	
Bed Size	**Qty**
King	
Queen	1
Double	
Single	1
Bathrooms	**Qty**
Ensuite	
Private	1
Guest Share	

Situated in the heart of the wine region, **Tamar** is one of Marlborough's oldest vineyards. Your newly-built cottage is a secluded, warm, romantic retreat with an ornately carved four-poster bed, featherdown duvet and classic leather couch. From the wide verandah you have breathtaking views through the vines to the Richmond Ranges. Our sumptuous three-course breakfasts feature homegrown produce and preserves. As we are an easy stroll from several wineries and restaurants you may choose to lunch or dine out, or cater for yourself in your fully equipped kitchenette. Clive and Yvonne enjoy showing you round the vineyard and we can help arrange winery tours or trips to the Marlborough Sounds (30 min drive) and Rainbow Skifield (60 min drive). We look forward to welcoming you for a memorable stay.

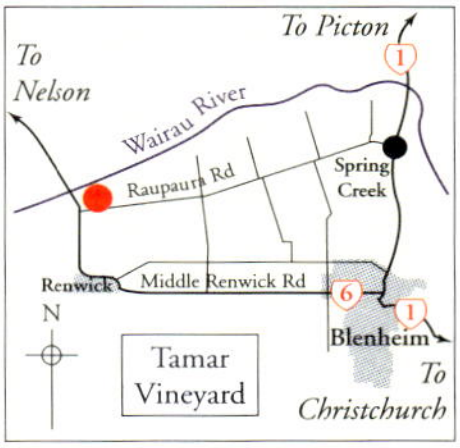

Creekside

774 Rapaura Road, RD 3, Blenheim
Ph (03) 579 8018, Fax (03) 579 8218
On-site Ph (03) 570 5338
email: *janhood@xtra.co.nz*
www.creekside.co.nz

Features & Attractions

- *Wine & olive oil tasting*
- *All rooms with ensuite*
- *Beside Tennis Club*
- *Expansive, mature gardens*
- *Just minutes to Blenheim*
- *Close to Marlborough Airport*

$	
Double	$160-200
Single	
Child	

In the Heart of Blenheim's Wine and Olive Oil Country

Bedrooms	Qty
Double	3
Twin	
Single	
Bed Size	**Qty**
King	1
Queen	2
Double	
Single	2
Bathrooms	**Qty**
Ensuite	3
Private	
Guest Share	

Our beautiful Bed & Breakfast adjoins both the spring-fed stream and the popular Rapaura Tennis Club with access off both Rapuara Road and Giffords Creek Lane. Set back from the road amidst Blenheim's wine and olive oil producing area, it is centrally located not far from Marlborough's Airport. The 8 ha property comprises of a 6 ha producing vineyard, 1 ha of producing olive trees.

Set back on the remaining land, which includes a stream boundary, is **Creekside** residence and Bed & Breakfast. Enjoy expansive, mature gardens with wildlife aplenty and numerous plantings of fruit and specimen trees. The main house consists of three ensuited bedrooms, a terrace and the breakfast room. The 100 sq. m. **Olive Room** is used for entertaining. It's only a few minutes to Blenheim's shopping centre and 30 min. to the Marlborough Sounds. Or just stay on the property, recover, rest and enjoy wine and olive tasting.

REDWOOD HEIGHTS

245 Redwood Street, Blenheim
Ph/Fax (03) 578 0143, Mobile 027-680 3125
email: *k.besley@xtra.co.nz*
www.redwoodheights.co.nz

Tariff : N.Z. Dollars	
Double	$110-175
Single	$70
Child	

Bedrooms	Qty
Double	2
Twin	1
Single	
Bed Size	**Qty**
Super King	
King	1
Queen	1
Double	
Single	2
Bathrooms	**Qty**
Ensuite	1
Private	1
Guest Share	

Quality Bed & Breakfast

Features & Attractions

- *Comfort and privacy*
- *Easy to find*
- *4 min. from town centre*
- *25 min. from Picton Ferry*
- *Close to wineries*
- *Golf courses nearby*
- *Spectacular views*
- *Laundry facilities*

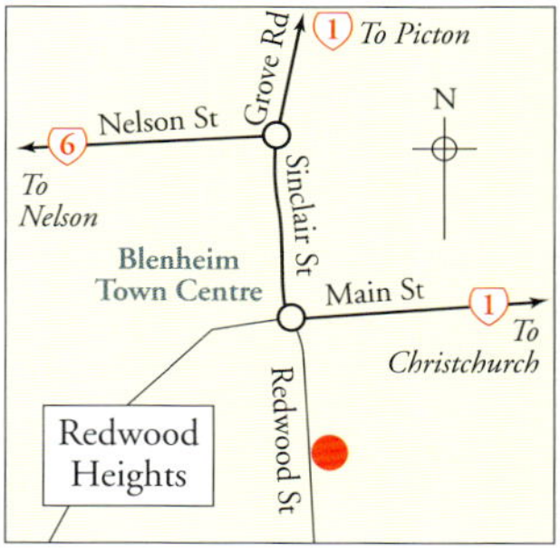

A warm welcome awaits you at **Redwood Heights**. Relax in private, modern, quality accommodation. Enjoy the quiet, peaceful country atmosphere and extensive views from our spacious **Stream Reserve** king bedroom with ensuite, refreshment-making facilities and fridge. All guest accommodation is upstairs and separate from hosts with a guest lounge and balcony for your use and TV in all rooms.

We are close to many of Marlborough's fine wineries and restaurants and we can help arrange winery tours or bicycle tours through the vineyards with pick-up and delivery from **Redwood Heights**.

We are adjacent to the Marlborough Wither Hill walkways, bike tracks and farm park. We are ideally situated to be a perfect base for day trips to the Marborough Sounds, Nelson or Kaikoura. Enjoy a full breakfast, warm hospitality and personal service. We look forward to meeting you.

Green Gables

St Andrews, 3011 SH 1, R D 4, Blenheim
Ph (03) 577 9205, Fax (03) 577 9205
Mobile 021-078 2142
email: *relax@greengablesbedandbreakfast.co.nz*
www.greengablesbedandbreakfast.co.nz

Tariff : N.Z. Dollars	
Double	$160-180
Single	$100-120
Child	

Bedrooms	Qty
Double	2
Twin	2
Single	
Bed Size	**Qty**
Super King	1
King	
Queen	
Double	2
Single	2
Bathrooms	**Qty**
Ensuite	3
Private	
Family Share	1

Secluded Bed & Breakfast

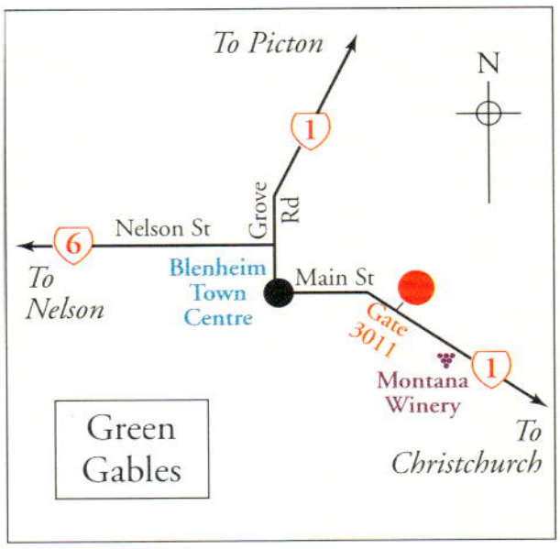

Features & Attractions

- *Peaceful rural setting*
- *Close to town centre 1.5km*
- *Sited on banks of Opawa River*
- *Variety of restaurants*
- *Wine tasting*
- *River fishing*
- *Wireless connection*
- *Email & fax facilities*

Situated on the banks of the Opawa River, close to Blenheim town centre, **Green Gables** provides spacious, peaceful riverside accommodation, set in one acre of landscaped gardens, offering superb rural views. Guest accommodation comprises four well appointed bedrooms, three with ensuite bathrooms and access to a guest lounge and balcony. The **Willowmere Room** sleeps three and has its own private sitting area and balcony. The **Idlewild** and **Garden Rooms** have French doors opening to a patio, or balcony. The **Birchpath Room** has both, a separate bath and separate shower. Rooms are equipped with coffee/tea facilities, televisions, clock radio, hair dryers and heating. For breakfast choose either full English or light continental, or if you prefer, a delectable combination of both, served with delicious home-made jams and preserves. Dinner is available by arrangement. The picturesque Opawa River meanders past the boundary. Try your hand at eeling, whitebaiting or trout fishing. You are welcome to use our mountain bikes or the dingy. We offer facilities to suit the modern day traveller including a wireless connection, internet, email and fax.

Blenheim — YOUR HOSTS: Jill Crisp and Royce Lanaway Ph: (03) 578 2764

TROTTERS REST

27 Dillons Point Road, Blenheim
Ph (03) 578 2764, Fax (03) 578 2764
email: *trotters-rest@xtra.co.nz*

Features & Attractions

- *Tranquil surroundings*
- *Art, craft & wine trails*
- *Close to town centre*
- *Dinner by arrangement*
- *Warm & welcoming*
- *Borders onto Opawa River*

Homestay Bed & Breakfast

$	
Double	$95
Single	$70
Child	neg

Welcome, come share with us a slice of tranquility only moments from town. Our adobe block and timber home is warm in winter and cool in summer. Enjoy the garden, take time out to rest in a shady spot at the river's edge, in the gazebo or under a leafy tree.
Marlborough has plenty to offer you and we are happy to advise on activities and make bookings for you. We offer tea/coffee making facilities, facsimile, internet and laundry facilities. Dinner is by prior arrangement, breakfast is bountiful with a choice of continental or English, served with homemade preserves and home grown fruit. We love to meet new people and can't wait to meet you.

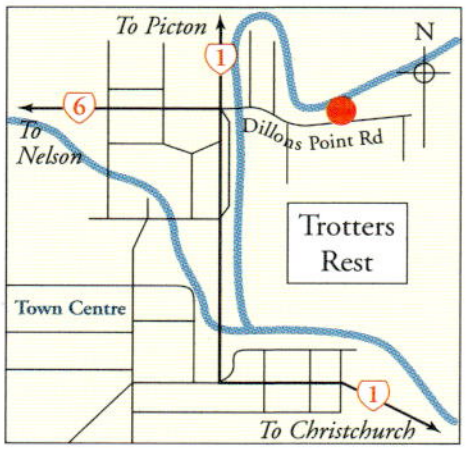

Bedrooms	Qty
Double	3
Twin	1
Single	
Bed Size	**Qty**
King	
Queen	3
Double	
Single	2
Bathrooms	**Qty**
Ensuite	
Private	1
Guest Share	1

Blenheim — YOUR HOSTS: Catherine Healy and Lindsay Grenfell Ph(03) 579 3451

VIEWFORTH

5 Glenhill Drive, Blenheim
Ph 03) 579 3451, Mobile 021-152 9406
email: *viewforth@xtra.co.nz*
www.viewforth.co.nz

Features & Attractions

- *Extensive gardens*
- *Dinner by arrangement*
- *Complimentary email/internet*
- *Solarium with garden views*
- *Handy to winery tours*
- *Restaurants nearby*

Cape Cod Comfort in Gorgeous Garden Setting

$	
Double	$150
Single	
Child	

Welcome to **Viewforth** on Glenhill our Cape-Cod style home. We are situated in sunny Blenheim in the heart of Marlborough which is New Zealand's largest grape growing and wine making region.
The **Greenpark Suite** is upstairs in our home and enjoys a northern aspect outlook to our north and west gardens. The ensuite bathroom is equipped with a double bath, shower, vanity and toilet, heated towel rail and hair dryer. Next to this room is a walk-in wardrobe and dressing room. The suite has a super-king bed, a leisure area with a two seater sofa for relaxing, a radio/disc player, tea and coffee making facilities and a refrigerator. Laundry facilities by request. We hope you will enjoy your visit with us. We are happy to advise on places to see and activities in and around Marlborough, Kaikoura, Picton and Nelson. Stay a while and enjoy the country.

Bedrooms	Qty
Double	1
Twin	
Single	
Bed Size	**Qty**
Super King	1
Queen	
Double	
Single	
Bathrooms	**Qty**
Ensuite	1
Private	
Guest Share	

Omaka Heights
Bed & Breakfast Countrystay

199 Brookby Road, Omaka Valley, RD 2, Blenheim 7272
Ph (03) 572 7402, Fax (03) 572 7403
email: *omakaheights@ts.co.nz*
www.omakaheights.co.nz

@ home NEW ZEALAND

Tariff : N.Z. Dollars	
Double	$160-195
Single	$120-150
Child	neg

Bedrooms	Qty
Double	1
Twin	1
Single	
Bed Size	**Qty**
Super King	
King	
Queen	1
Double	
Single	2
Bathrooms	**Qty**
Ensuite	2
Private	
Guest Share	

VISA MasterCard AMERICAN EXPRESS

Countrystay Bed & Breakfast

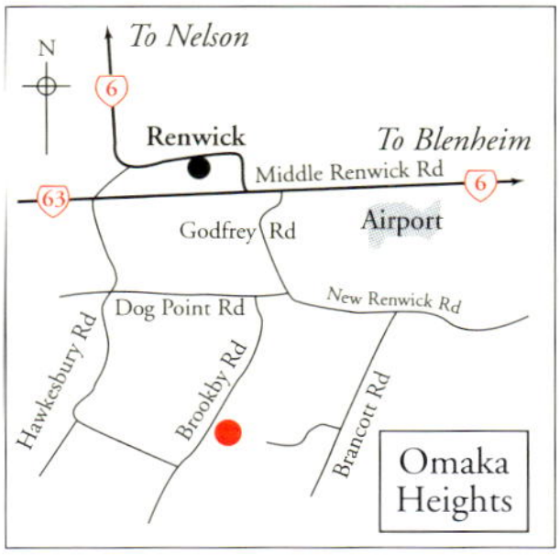

DIRECTIONS:
From Blenheim take Middle Renwick Rd, after passing the airport take 1st left into Godfrey Rd. Then take 1st right into Dog Point Road and first left into Brookby Rd.

Features & Attractions

- *Outstanding views*
- *Wine & sightseeing tours*
- *Art and craft visits*
- *Scenic flights*
- *Golf, fishing, boating*
- *Whale & dolphin watching*
- *Skiing and tramping*
- *Excellent dining nearby*

Positioned in the picturesque Omaka Valley, just 12 km from Blenheim, our purpose-built hilltop Countrystay offers outstanding panoramic views over vineyards and farmland through to the Richmond Range in the distance. We are within a few minutes drive of over thirty wineries. There are numerous restaurants and cafés, offering world class cuisine, located within Blenheim town and the surrounding vineyard area. Our self-contained Countrystay wing offers two guest rooms with private ensuite facilities and private decks plus a guest lounge. The twin room/ensuite is completely wheelchair accessible. The lounge provides tea/coffee making facilities, refrigerator and television. The bedrooms are fully equipped with hairdryer and electric blankets. Guests are offered a hearty breakfast and complimentary pre-dinner beverages. Evening meals are available by arrangement. You may enjoy a stroll around our eight hectare property on which we farm alpacas.

JEFFERSWOOD

Camerons Road, RD 1, Havelock,
Marlborough
Ph (03) 572 8081, Fax (03) 572 8091
email: *jefferswood.sewell@xtra.co.nz*
www.jefferswood.co.nz

Tariff : N.Z. Dollars	
Double	$240
Single	$185
Child	

Bedrooms	Qty
Double	2
Twin	
Single	
Bed Size	**Qty**
Super King	1
King	
Queen	1
Double	
King/Single	2
Bathrooms	**Qty**
Ensuite	2
Private	
Guest Share	

Bed & Breakfast
Homestay

- *Historic Havelock*
- *2 hectare arboretum on site*
- *Fishing, boating & golf*
- *Local bush walks & gardens*
- *Delicious breakfasts*
- *Organic vegetable garden*
- *Spacious warm homestead*
- *Hosted farm visits*

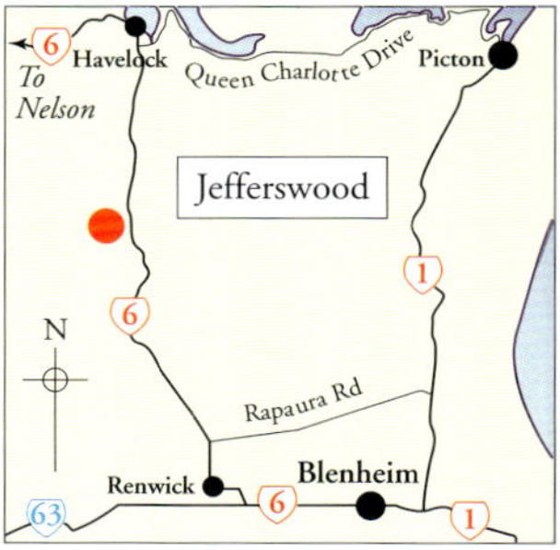

Jefferswood is an eco-friendly elegant adobe mudbrick homestead, set on 4ha of rural splendour between Blenheim and Havelock. The property includes a large pond which attracts a range of wildlife; hundreds of trees, an organic orchard and many restful spots to relax on the summer seats provided. Picnic hampers and BBQ can be arranged. **Jefferswood** offers peaceful, comfortable accommodation 5-15 minutes from restaurants, cafés/wineries, shopping and the local airport. Guest accommodation comprises of generous rooms, sumptuous beds with fine linen, plenty of wardrobe and storage space. Pampering ensuites have huge walk-in showers with abundant solar heated water. Toiletries and bathrobes are provided. Each bedroom opens into the gallery where cosy two-seater couches invite you to sit and read or just take in the spectacular surroundings. A large sundrenched sitting room with extensive music selection, bookcase and daily newspapers. Refreshments and home baking are available during the day. Join us for pre-dinner Marlborough wine and nibbles.

TERRACE BROOK COTTAGE

Terrace Brook, Peakes Road, Onamalutu, RD 5, Marlborough
Ph (03) 572 9623, Fax (03) 572 9623
Mobile 027-473 4373
email: *terracebrook@ihug.co.nz*
www.terracebrookcottage.co.nz

Tariff : N.Z. Dollars	
Double	$175
Single	$120
Child	n/a

Bedrooms	Qty
Double	2
Twin	
Single	
Bed Size	**Qty**
Super King	1
King	
Queen	1
Double	
King/Single	1
Bathrooms	**Qty**
Ensuite	
Private	
Guest Share	1

**Countrystay
Bed & Breakfast**

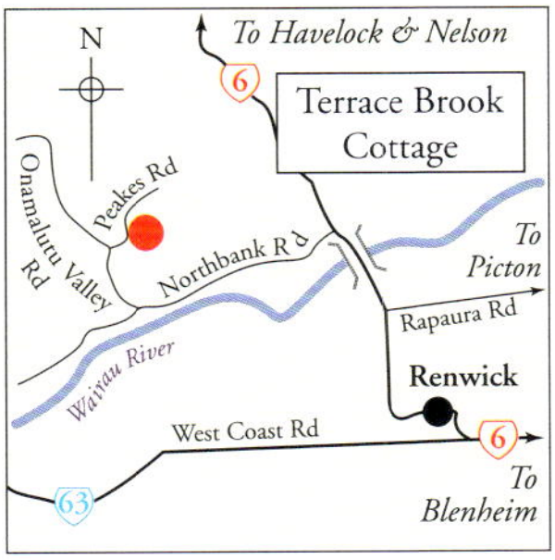

DIRECTIONS:
From S.H.6 Nelson/Blenheim Highway turn into Northbank Rd, drive 5km. Take Onamalutu Valley Rd, drive 2km. Peakes Rd R.H. side, cross bridge **Terrace Brook** 2nd gateway on right.

Features & Attractions

- *Peaceful country setting*
- *Golf and fishing*
- *Skiing and tramping*
- *Quality restaurants nearby*
- *Lavender farm*
- *Vintage vehicles*
- *Art & craft trails*
- *Wine & sightseeing tours*

Terrace Brook offers a peaceful environment and commanding views of the Onamalutu Valley and Richmond Ranges. Your hosts on the 24 acre farmlet offer warm, homely hospitality. The guest cottage has private decks for you to take time to relax and enjoy your surroundings. It contains two bedrooms, complimentary teas and coffee in foyer, heated towel-rails in each room, hairdryer, underfloor heating, personal robes, and fine linen. Laundry, B.B.Q, e-mail facilities available. You're on holiday, so breakfast when it suits! Cooked or continental. A 'home-away-from-home' – enjoy.

Centrally situated between Blenheim and Havelock, both 20minutes. Picton and inter-island ferry 35 minutes. Nelson 1 hour.

"Strangers are friends we have yet to meet."

MURCHISON LODGE

15 Grey Street, Murchison
Ph (03) 523 9196, Fax (03) 523 9197
Mobile 021-266 7016
email: *info@murchisonlodge.co.nz*
www.murchisonlodge.co.nz

Tariff : N.Z. Dollars	
Double	$145-175
Single	$115-160
Child	

Bedrooms	Qty
Double	2
Twin	1
Single	1
Bed Size	**Qty**
Super King	
King	1
Queen	2
Double	
King/Single	1
Bathrooms	**Qty**
Ensuite	3
Private	1
Guest Share	

Quality B&B Lodge with Character

VISA MasterCard

Features & Attractions

- *Peaceful setting*
- *Easy walk to pubs & cafés*
- *Fishing, rafting, golf*
- *Meals by arrangement*
- *Wireless internet access*
- *Comfy beds – really!*
- *Hosts in own cottage*
- *Children over 12 welcome*

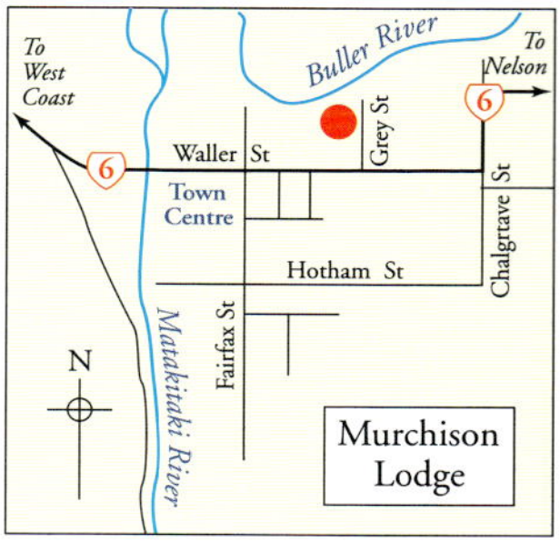

DIRECTIONS:
To find Grey Street when entering town:
From south & west take 2nd left.
From north & east take 1st right.

At **Murchison Lodge** you will find warm and relaxed hospitality combined with comfortable beds and hearty breakfasts. Uniquely crafted from local timber, the Lodge is set in three acres of mature wooded gardens, surrounded by rivers and mountains. You feel miles from anywhere, yet you're less than ten minutes walk from Murchison's historic pubs and cafés. The area is renowned for its fly-fishing and white-water activities. There's also golf, bush walks and biking or try gold-panning at NZ's longest swing bridge. Alternatively, just relax with a book in a hammock! Many guests take the opportunity to stop and unpack their bags for a while. Murchison's central location makes it a great base for exploring three national parks. Try a different direction every day, then return home to familiar accommodation and friendly faces. Come home to a cold beer on the veranda or a wine in front of the log fire and…yumm…fresh baking!

Awapiriti Farmstay

State Highway 65, PO Box 36,
Murchison, Nelson
Ph (03) 523 9466, Fax (03) 523 9777
email: *awapiriti@ihug.co.nz*

Features & Attractions

- *Quiet, peaceful surroundings*
- *Breathtaking scenery*
- *Pets welcome by arrangement*
- *Fishing guides arranged*
- *Tours/activities arranged*
- *Swimming/fishing on site*

$	
Double	$170
Single	$120
Child	n/a

Farmstay Bed & Breakfast

Bedrooms	Qty
Double	2
Twin	1
Single	
Bed Size	**Qty**
King	
Queen	1
King/Single	1
Single	2
Bathrooms	**Qty**
Ensuite	2
Private	1
Guest Share	

Share our little slice of paradise beside the Maruia River in the scenic Murchison District. **Awapiriti** is a deer farm with the usual domestic animals, dogs, cats, horses etc. We enjoy walking with our guests through the unspoilt forest that surrounds the farm. Relax in the convivial atmosphere of our country home over pre-dinner drinks followed by locally produced food and New Zealand wines. We are easily reached from Christchurch, the West Coast, Picton and Nelson, and we are happy to help with any further travel plans. Murchison offers many adventure activities as well as golf, horse trekking, gold panning, New Zealand's longest swing bridge and much more. **Awapiriti** is a haven for adults. Children over the age of fifteen welcome.

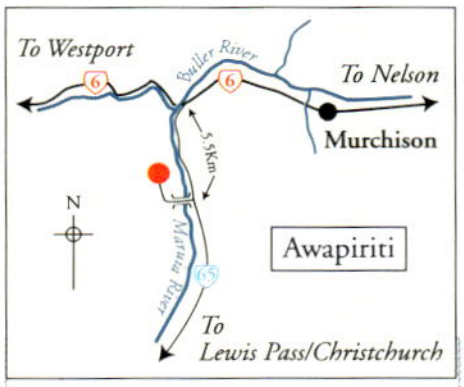

DIRECTIONS: From north: 5.5 km past SH 65 turn-off, turn right over bridge. From south: 5 km from Maruia Falls turn left over bridge. **Awapiriti** signposted

Beachfront Farmstay

Karamea, State Highway 67
Ph/Fax (03) 782 6762, Mobile 021-782 676
email: *farmstay@xtra.co.nz*
www.westcoastbeachaccommodation.co.nz

Features & Attractions

- *Peaceful rural setting*
- *Special full breakfast*
- *Dinner by arrangement*
- *Close to famous Heaphy Track*
- *Trout fishing, golf, forest walks*
- *Mountain & sunsets*

$	
Double	$130-150
Single	$100
Child	$35

Farmstay Bed & Breakfast

Bedrooms	Qty
Double	2
Twin	
Single	1
Bed Size	**Qty**
King	1
Queen	1
Double	
Single	1
Bathrooms	**Qty**
Ensuite	2
Private	
Family Share	1

Welcome to a spectacular area of the West Coast. Our home is a 2 minute walk to an unspoiled beach with wonderful sunsets. Relax in our spacious home and garden. The ensuite rooms are tastefully decorated with every convenience. We are a working farm with 420 cows and interesting pasture development.

Join us for delicious country cuisine, organic vegetables, home-made desserts and New Zealand wine. Farmhouse special breakfasts include freshly baked bread, whitebait, yoghurt and home preserves. Visit the impressive Limestone Arch and Honeycomb Caves, stroll the numerous walks in the Kahurangi National Park. Also available: trout fishing, golf, kayaking, mountain biking.

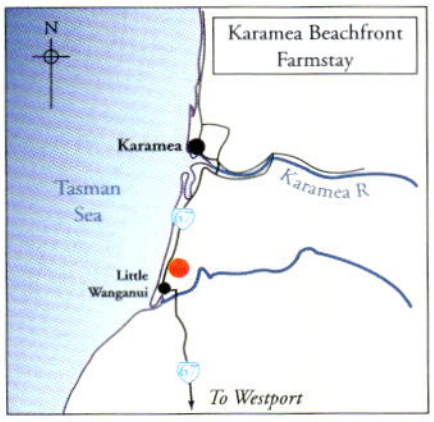

DIRECTIONS:
Karamea Beachfront Farmstay is 84 km north of Westport and 3 km north of Little Wanganui.

RIVERLEA COTTAGE

89 Snodgrass Road, RD 2, Westport
Ph (03) 789 8655, Fax (03) 789 8655
Mobile 027-245 7258
email: *marg.b@xtra.co.nz*

Features & Attractions

- *Quiet peaceful setting*
- *Glorious views & sunsets*
- *Riverside walks & fishing*
- *Warm friendly helpful hospitality*
- *Ever changing river and bird life*
- *Delicious breakfast*

SC **Self-contained Cottage Bed & Breakfast** BB

$		
	Double	$100-150
	Single	$100-150
	Child	neg

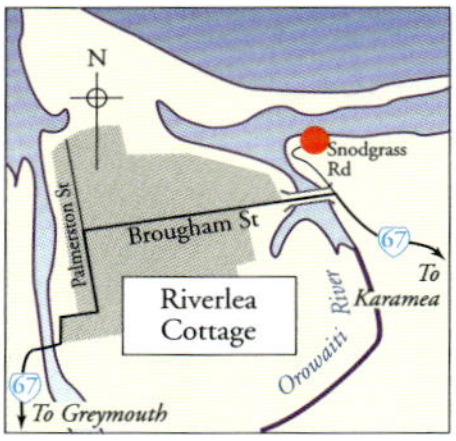

Riverlea Cottage, situated on the northern side of the Orowaiti River, is one of Westport's most peaceful and tranquil areas. You will want to and are most welcome to stay awhile. Marg offers a warm welcome with friendly, relaxed accommodation. End your day with a short walk along the river edge or enjoy a wine while watching the moon come up over the hills and water.

For the more active – try some night spear-fishing. Your host has lived all her life in the area and will help with attractions and numerous activities available. A self-catering unit is available as well as Bed & Breakfast. Always a plentiful breakfast to start your day.

DIRECTIONS: Enter Westport on Palmerston St., turn right into Brougham St., continue over Orowaiti Bridge, turn left on 1st bend into Snodgrass Rd, follow around to white picket fence, No.89.

Bedrooms	Qty
Double	2
Twin	1
Single	
Bed Size	**Qty**
King	
Queen	2
Double	
Single	2
Bathrooms	**Qty**
Ensuite	
Private	2
Family Share	1

HAVENLEE HOMESTAY

76 Queen Street, Westport
Ph (03) 789 8543, Fax (03) 789 8502
email: *info@havenlee.co.nz*
www.havenlee.co.nz

@ home NEW ZEALAND

MasterCard VISA

Features & Attractions

- *Warm friendly welcome*
- *'At home' atmosphere*
- *Peace and tranquility*
- *A garden oasis*
- *Local area information*
- *300m from Town Centre*

BB **Best Choice for First Class Hospitality** H

$		
	Double	$100-150
	Single	$90
	Child	neg

DIRECTIONS: Along Palmerston Street turn right at Wakefield Street, left at Queen Street, 1st home on left.

Peace in Paradise - this is **Havenlee.** From the moment you arrive you will feel at home right away. A warm, welcoming greeting at our relaxed, spacious, quality homestay will introduce you to the fine hospitality you will receive during your stay with us. We were born and bred in the Westport area and are very proud of our West Coast heritage. Havenlee is centrally located: an idyllic base from which to explore the environmental wonderland, share local knowledge or just take time out. Check out the numerous adventure experiences and local attractions. Soak up the nature to rest and restore body and soul. As our guest you will enjoy a healthy, nutritous continental-plus breakfast. What a way to start the day! A well appointed private bathroom or guest share facilities. Shower room, toilet and bathroom (with large tub) each separate. Laundry facilities available. Treat yourself - stay a while and feel exhilarated.

Bedrooms	Qty
Double	2
Twin	1
Single	
Bed Size	**Qty**
King	
Queen	2
Double	1
Single	1
Bathrooms	**Qty**
Ensuite	
Private	1
Guest Share	1

River View Lodge

SH 6 Lower Buller Gorge, PO Box 229, Westport
Ph/Fax (03) 789 6037, Mobile 027-405 5359
email: *info@rurallodge.co.nz*
www.rurallodge.co.nz

Tariff : N.Z. Dollars	
Double	$220
Single	$180
Child	n/a

Bedrooms	Qty
Double	4
Twin	
Single	
Bed Size	**Qty**
Super King	
King	3
Queen	1
Double	
Single	
Bathrooms	**Qty**
Ensuite	4
Private	
Guest Share	

Luxury Rural Bed & Breakfast

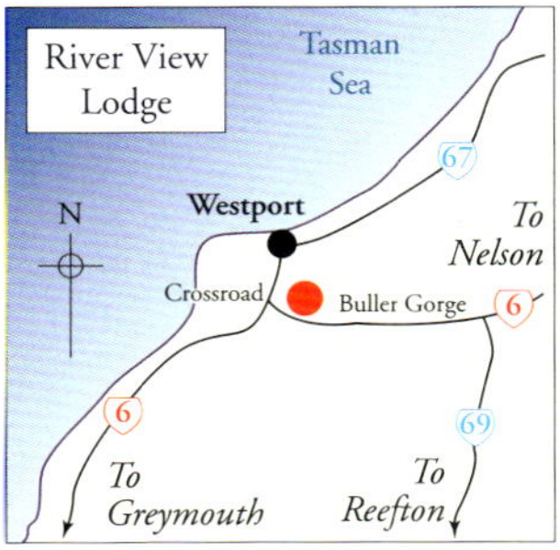

Features & Attractions

- *Quiet peaceful surroundings*
- *Spacious comfortable rooms*
- *Dinner by arrangement extra*
- *Off season rates May-August*
- *Wonderful large garden*
- *Rooms with garden and river views*
- *Friendly NZ born host*
- *Discount for over 2 nights stay*

Situated above the Buller River, purpose-built **Riverview Lodge** is seven kilometres from Westport. Off the main road with picturesque views of the Buller River and country, overlooking a large garden for you to wander in and relax, or play a game of tennis on the grass court.
The four rooms are comfortable and tastefully decorated, all with ensuites and three open onto a large deck overlooking the river and garden.
Tariff includes a full breakfast in the dining room. Dinner is by arrangement only. Laundry is available. Discount for more than two nights and off-season rates available. We offer helpful, friendly advice on local activities and can recommend restaurants in the town.

Birds Ferry Lodge

Birds Ferry Rd, 8 km north of Charleston, Westport
Free Ph 0800 212 207
Mobile 021-337 217
email: info@birdsferrylodge.co.nz
www.birdsferrylodge.co.nz

Tariff : N.Z. Dollars	
Double	$150-250
Single	$130-230
Child	neg

Bedrooms	Qty
Double	2
Twin	1
Single	
Bed Size	**Qty**
Super King	
King	
Queen	2
Double	1
Single	1
Bathrooms	**Qty**
Ensuite	3
Private	
Guest Share	

Tranquil Bush Setting
Dinner, Bed & Breakfast

Features & Attractions

- *Log fire & house bar*
- *Mountain & ocean views*
- *2 km from highway*
- *Spa overlooking ocean*
- *Fabulous dinners*
- *Stay 3 nights for price of 2*
- *Friendly resident Norfolk Terrier*
- *Lakeside cottage available*

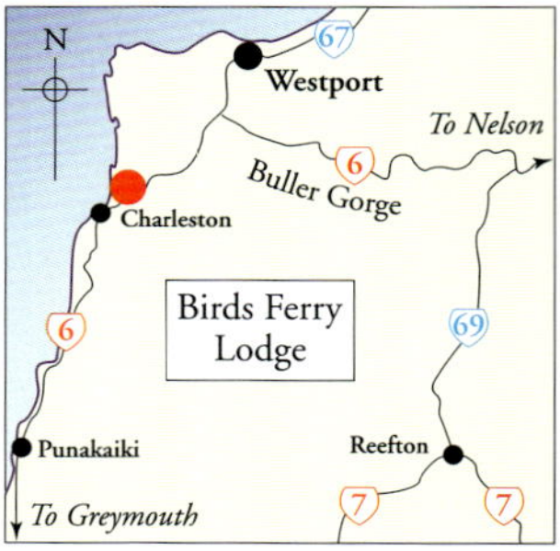

DIRECTIONS:
17km south of Westport on SH 6. – 8km north of Charleston on SH6. Turn off the highway at our sign and drive for 1.7km.

Allow yourselves to relax and unwind at **Birds Ferry Lodge**. Along with native birdlife, you will enjoy an exceptionally tranquil spot with panoramic views of Paparoa Mountains, Tasman Sea and forest. Privately accessed guest accommodation with bath and shower. Tariff includes refreshments, laundry service, internet and cooked breakfast. Home-produced vegetables and free-range eggs are used wherever possible. Alison and André are keen gardeners. House bar, with New Zealand wines. Historic Buller has a multitude of activities, accessible areas of dense, luxuriant forest, rich bird-life and a wild coastline – something for everyone. On arrival, many guests ask to extend their visit to more than one night. Why? On arrival you will discover the answer to this. 5 minutes away visit an exhibition gold mine. 10 minutes away take the Charleston Nile River Forest Train. 30 minutes away is Punakaiki. A day trip distance north of us you can visit Heaphy Track, Karamea, Oparara Arches and historic Denniston.

The Rocks Homestay

Hartmount Place, Community Box 16, Punakaiki
Ph (03) 731 1141, Fax (03) 731 1142
email: *therocks@minidata.co.nz*
www.therockshomestay.com

Features & Attractions

- *Pancake Rocks, Blowholes*
- *Adjoins National Park*
- *Spectacular panoramas*
- *Relaxed and friendly*
- *Dinner by arrangement*
- *Bush walking & beaches*

$	
Double	$145-195
Single	$110-195
Child	

Wilderness Homestay
Luxury Isolation

Bedrooms	Qty
Double	2
Twin	1
Single	
Bed Size	**Qty**
King	
Queen	2
Double	
Single	2
Bathrooms	**Qty**
Ensuite	3
Private	
Guest Share	

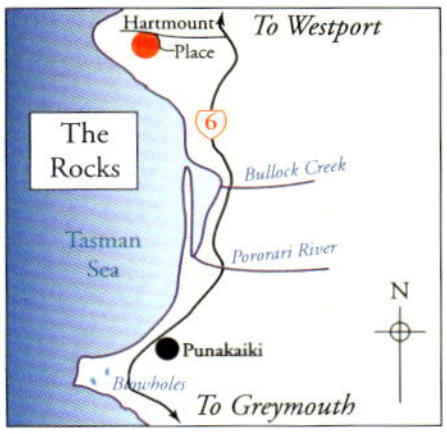

Forget cute and delightful! Think wild coast, isolated beaches, sculptured crags, Nikau Palms, stunning views and tangled fern-filled rainforest to the doorway. Welcome to **The Rocks Homestay at Punakaiki**, Paparoa National Park, between Greymouth and Westport on the amazing untamed West Coast. Forget cellphones. Enjoy ensuite rooms, heated towel rails, hairdryers, minibars, electric blankets, conservatories and an extensive library of New Zealand books. Forget street lamps and traffic. Experience forest tracks and river walks, Pancake Rocks and Blowholes, beach rambles and memorable sunsets, environmental care and sustainable impact. Relish healthy breakfasts, fruit, muesli, yoghurt, home baking, and home-cooked evening meals with wine (by arrangement). Forget confusion! Accept our warm invitation to share our environmentally sensitive home nestled in the wilderness.

Beach Hideaway

Glen Road, RD 1 Barrytown, Westland
Ph/Fax (03) 731 1120, Mobile 021-529 418
email: *relax@beachhideaway.co.nz*
www.beachhideaway.co.nz

Features & Attractions

- *Peaceful, private, relaxing*
- *Antipasto platters & sweet treats*
- *Beach walks, bush walks*
- *Cedar hot tub*
- *Jade carving, local art*
- *10 acres, private setting*

$	
Double	$150-230
Single	$150-230
Child	$10

Panoramic Sea Views
Luxury Beach Hideaway

Bedrooms	Qty
Double	3
Twin	
Single	
Bed Size	**Qty**
Super King	3
Queen	
Double	
King/Single	6
Bathrooms	**Qty**
Ensuite	2
Private	
Guest Share	

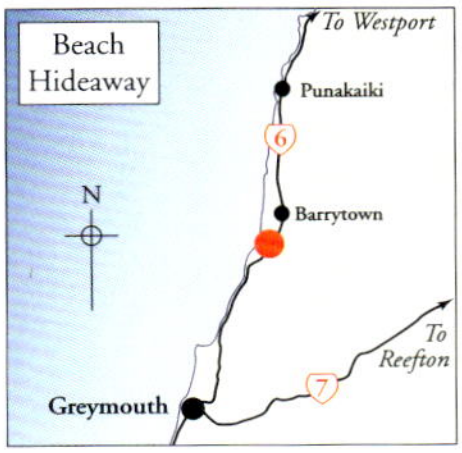

Follow the scenic Coast Road to find the 'hidden gem' that is **Beach Hideaway**. Set with a backdrop of regenerating bush and expansive sea views, you can relax and enjoy the privacy in your new, well-appointed luxury villa. The grounds include extensive native landscaping, pétanque/volleyball court and a meandering creek with small bush walks.

Relax in the private cedar hot tub or sit around the fire pit and toast marshmallows while you watch the stunning West Coast sunsets. Stroll along the beach or walk one of the many tracks in the Paparoa National Park.

Sweet treats, antipasto and breakfast platters available to order. Be spoilt, relax and enjoy!!

Kally House

13 Cargill Road, Barrytown, Runanga, RD 1, Westland
Ph (03) 731 1006, Fax (03) 731 1106
email: *kallyhouse@xtra.co.nz*
www.travelwise.co.nz

Features & Attractions

- *Sea views & sunsets*
- *Two licensed restaurants*
- *Pancake Rocks close by*
- *Fishing, walking, tramping*
- *Paparoa Adventure Park*
- *Lapidary stone beach*

Bed & Breakfast Homestay

Double	$110-125
Single	$75
Child	

Our unique elevated location reveals a multitude of exciting adventure activities. Pancake Rocks in the national park just fifteen minutes north. Fishing, walks, tramping, canoeing, restaurants, lapidary stone beach are all close by. Our spacious home is six years old, centrally heated, well appointed, quiet and with views of the sea and bush. We have two queen bedrooms upstairs with television. Guest share bathroom. Family share lounge with widescreen television. Continental breakfast with hosts. We also have a self-contained flat downstairs. It has a queen bedroom with twin beds in a spacious living area. Full kitchen, washing and drying facilities. Parking and separate entrance. We have a frost-free micro climate to enjoy.

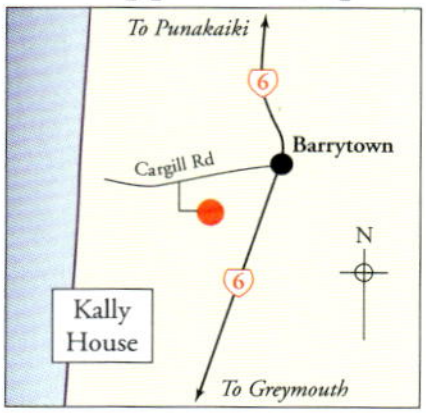

Bedrooms	Qty
Double	3
Twin	1
Single	
Bed Size	**Qty**
King	
Queen	3
Double	
Single	2
Bathrooms	**Qty**
Ensuite	
Private	1
Guest Share	2

Barrytown-Greymouth YOUR HOSTS: **Russell Johns and Sandy Passant** Ph (03) 731 1460

Ti Kouka

2522 Coast Road, SH 6 Barrytown, West Coast.
Ph (03) 731 1460, Fax (03) 731 1460,
Mobile 027-438 5951
email: *russan@paradise.net.nz*
www.Tikoukahouse.co.nz

Features & Attractions

- *National Park on boundary*
- *Sub-tropical rain forest*
- *Beach and bush walks*
- *15 min south of Punakaiki*
- *All rooms have sea view*
- *Free beer tomorrow!*

Boutique Country Bed & Breakfast

Double	$190-230
Single	$190
Child	

Our recently completed, architecturally designed home is packed with character, having used old hardwood bridge beams, old church windows and doors, and 100-year-old recycled Matai and Rimu timber flooring to create the charm of the old and warmth and comfort of new. **Ti Kouka** is nestled against a backdrop of sub-tropical rain forest on the edge of the Paparoa National Park, enjoying ocean views and fabulous sunsets from every window. We would like to invite you to spend some time to enjoy beach and bush walks. There's no shortage of Wild West Coast to enjoy. Excellent local restaurants, art and crafts to please all tastes and a good home-cooked breakfast to start your day. Come and enjoy genuine West Coast hospitality.

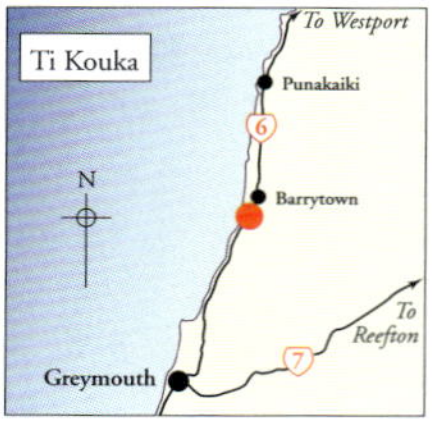

Bedrooms	Qty
Double	2
Twin	1
Single	
Bed Size	**Qty**
King	
Queen	2
Double	
Single	2
Bathrooms	**Qty**
Ensuite	3
Private	
Guest Share	

Westway

58 Herd Street, Dunollie, Greymouth
Ph (03) 762 7077, Fax (03) 762 7377
Mobile 027-495 2844
email: *westway@xtra.co.nz*
www.westway.co.nz

Tariff : N.Z. Dollars	
Double	$110-120
Single	$85-95
Child	neg

Bedrooms	Qty
Double	2
Twin	1
Single	
Bed Size	**Qty**
Super King	
King	
Queen	2
Double	
Single	2
Bathrooms	**Qty**
Ensuite	1
Private	1
Guest Share	1

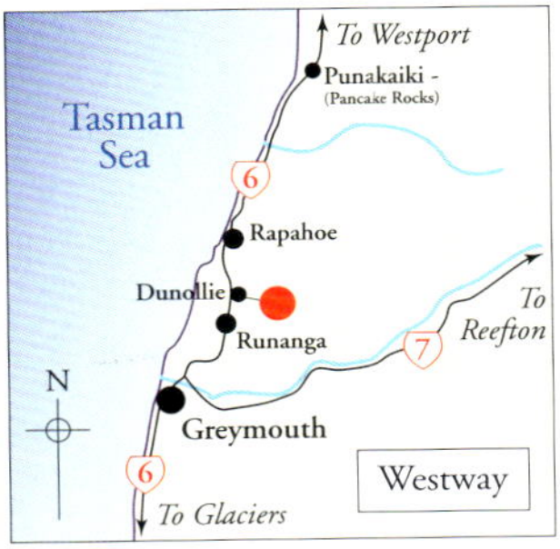

Rural Homestay
Bed & Breakfast and Dining

Features & Attractions

- *Tranquil & private places*
- *Glow worms - Native bush*
- *Bush walking from* ***Westway***
- *Mountains, rivers & lakes*
- *Evening meals from Wayne's kitchen*
- *Powered site for Camp-a-van*
- *The Homestay for all seasons*
- *Winter wonderland - group bookings*

Just minutes from Greymouth, Westway is situated in a native forest clad valley. An historic tunnel on the property dates from 1902 when New Zealand's first state-owned coalmine operated further up the valley – glow worms live around the entrance. There are private places in the garden where you can experience nature and the tranquility of **Westway**.

We're only five minutes drive from the sandy swimming beach at Point Elizabeth, the start of the famous Coastal Road.
We have a friendly and relaxing lifestyle; take pleasure in sharing our local knowledge and in creating an environment that visitors can enjoy.
There's space for your leisure equipment. Evening meals are available. Complimentary transport when appropriate.

"Come and let us spoil you."

Breakers Seaside Bed & Breakfast

Nine Mile Beach, Coast Road, SH 6,
PO Box 188, Greymouth
Ph (03) 762 7743, Fax (03) 762 7733
email: *stay@breakers.co.nz*
www.breakers.co.nz

Features & Attractions

- *Fabulous sea views*
- *Incredible sunsets*
- *Beach access*
- *National Park close by*
- *Great hospitality*
- *Dinner by arrangement*

$	
Double	$180-250
Single	
Child	n/a

Seaside Bed & Breakfast

Bedrooms	Qty
Double	2
Twin	2
Single	
Bed Size	**Qty**
King	2
Queen	2
Double	
Single	2
Bathrooms	**Qty**
Ensuite	4
Private	
Guest Share	

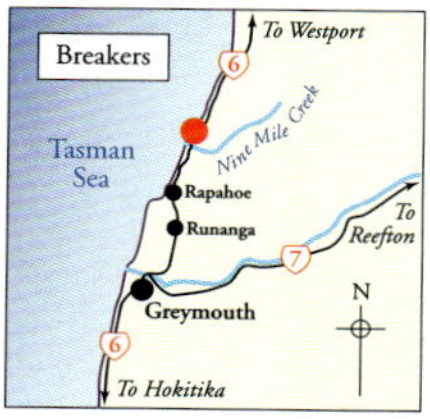

Spectacular location is one of the comments made about **Breakers.** Overlooking the Tasman Sea, at Nine Mile Beach on the Coast Road (SH 6), **Breakers** is located 14 km north of Greymouth and 30 km south of the Pancake Rocks at Punakaiki. **Breakers** is nestled on the edge of the Paparoa National Park amongst two acres of native bush and garden, with all rooms overlooking the sea.

Wander down the track to the beach, collect driftwood, stones and sometimes find pounamu (jade) pebbles. Or just sit on your verandah/deck, and watch the waves, enjoy the view, you may never want to leave. A good range of eating places within a short drive or enjoy our hospitality with pre-arranged gourmet dinners.

Lancewood

2177 Arnold Valley Road,
Moana, Lake Brunner
Ph (03) 738 0844, Mobile 0274-369 706
email: *lancewood.upon.moana@paradise.net.nz*
www.lancewood.co.nz

Features & Attractions

- *Gold panning*
- *Float plane charter*
- *Secure off-street parking*
- *Trout fishing*
- *Scenic walkways*
- *Lake cruises*

Homestay Bed & Breakfast

$	
Double	$215
Single	$195
Child	neg

A very warm welcome awaits you at 'Lancewood'. Relax with us enjoying captivating views of Lake Brunner, amidst a scenic backdrop of the Southern Alps. Spend time enjoying bush walks, gold panning, trout fishing or a scenic launch trip. Your accommodation is a double queen bed with ensuite, complimentary tea and coffee facilities plus television and fridge. Breakfast is served at a time suitable to you. A bunk room is also available for older children. We look forward to sharing our piece of paradise with you. Please refer our website.

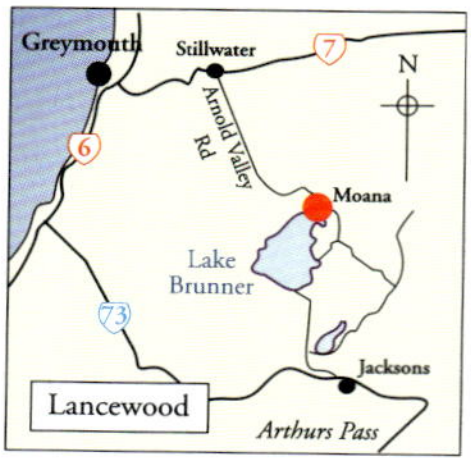

Bedrooms	Qty
Double	1
Twin	
Single	
Bed Size	**Qty**
King	
Queen	1
Double	
Single	
Bathrooms	**Qty**
Ensuite	1
Private	
Guest Share	

Chalet Pininoa

State Highway 7, Matai, Grey Valley, RD Dobson
Ph (03) 732 3408
Mobile 021-052 9160
email: *pininoa@xtra.co.nz*
www.pininoa.co.nz

Tariff : N.Z. Dollars	
Chalet	$225-375
Single	
Child	

Bedrooms	Qty
Double	1
Twin	1
Single	
Bed Size	**Qty**
Super King	
King	
Queen	1
Double	
Single	2
Bathrooms	**Qty**
Ensuite	
Private	1
Guest Share	

Unique Self-contained Country Chalet

Features & Attractions

- *Secluded, rural setting*
- *Evening dinner BA*
- *Native bush & glow worms*
- *Smoke free property*
- *Queen and twin rooms*
- *Exclusive one party only*
- *Internet connection available*
- *Not suitable for children*

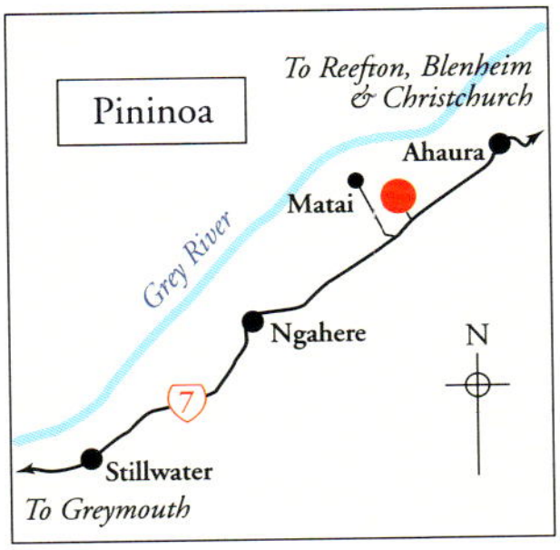

DIRECTIONS: 20 mins nth of Greymouth, 30 mins sth of Reefton

Chalet Pininoa offers quality boutique accommodation in our purpose-designed country chalet with polished matai floors, native timber walls and cathedral ceiling, quality furnishings, warm comfy beds, freshly ironed linen, fluffy duvets, towels and robes and bathroom toiletries. A special breakfast basket including our free-range eggs and a loaf of fresh homemade bread is delivered to you in the evening, so you may breakfast at your leisure. The kitchenette has a selection of teas, coffee etc, also a small selection of provisions if you wish to make an evening meal. Enjoy birdsong, green fields, star-filled skies and expansive views across the valley to the Paparoa Mountains. Relax with a drink in your secluded garden and watch the sun set, curl up in your cosy chalet with a book, or you are welcome to join us for a walk, a drink, a chat or even a BBQ on a warm summers evening. The choice is yours. Our two dogs, Mo and Tai, delight in welcoming our guests and so do we.

Oak Lodge

Coal Creek, State Highway 6, Greymouth
(3 km north of Greymouth)
Ph (03) 768 6832, Fax (03) 768 4362
email: *oaklodgenz@xtra.co.nz*

Tariff : N.Z. Dollars	
Double	$140-260
Single	$110
Child	

Bedrooms	Qty
Double	4
Twin	3
Single	
Bed Size	**Qty**
Super King	2
King	
Queen	2
Double	
Single	3
Bathrooms	**Qty**
Ensuite	4
Private	1
Guest Share	

Homestay
Bed & Breakfast

Features & Attractions

- *Rural setting*
- *Spa/jacuzzi*
- *Sauna*
- *Swimming pool*
- *Extensive gardens*
- *Tennis court*
- *Billiards room*
- *Black sheep, hens, donkey*

DIRECTIONS:
3 km north of Greymouth
State Highway 6.
Oak Lodge is on the right,
an elevated section.

This 100 year old farmhouse is full of character, and only three minutes drive from Greymouth. It is surrounded by extensive gardens containing over 400 rhododendrons and azaleas. Pathways are interlaced throughout the garden for wandering and exploring.

The guest accommodation is upstairs and includes a spacious guest lounge with television and tea & coffee making facilities. You can sit on the balcony sipping your drink and gaze over the surrounding farmland and mountains; or rejuvenate yourself in the spa pool or sauna. For the more energetic there is a tennis court, swimming pool, or stroll over the eighteen acre farmlet. Our donkey, Finias, welcomes any snack and some patting, as does our black ram called Pete - he will always come to the sound of sheep nuts being rattled in the tin! We also have a collection of multi coloured sheep on the property, and a few hens to provide eggs for your farmhouse breakfast. Colette and Brian, who have travelled themselves, extend a very warm welcome to you. Guest comment: *"We came as guests and leave as friends"*

JIVANA RETREAT

8 Leith Crescent, PO Box 143, Greymouth
Ph (03) 768 6102, Fax (03) 768 6108
email: *sandie@jivanaretreat.co.nz*
www.jivanaretreat.co.nz

Tariff : N.Z. Dollars	
Double	$120-160
Single	$110
Child	$20

Bedrooms	Qty
Double	3
Twin	2
Single	
Bed Size	**Qty**
Super King	1
King	
Queen	3
Double	
Single	2
Bathrooms	**Qty**
Ensuite	1
Private	1
Guest Share	1

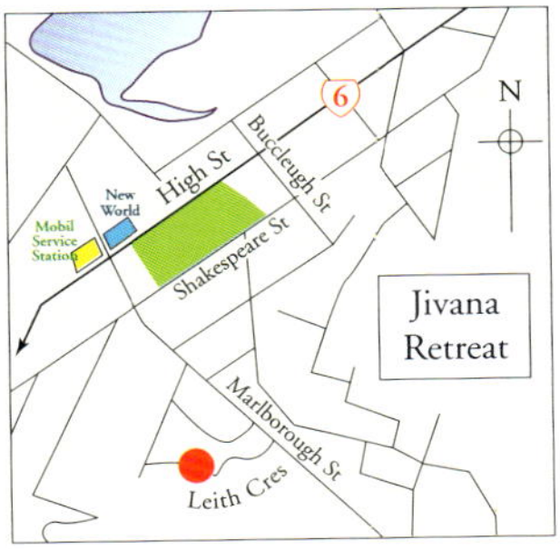

Organic Bed & Breakfast
Boutique Self-contained

Features & Attractions

- *Free infrared sauna*
- *Massage & reflexology*
- *Yoga & pilates*
- *Specialised health programmes*
- *Dinner by arrangement*
- *Spacious, yet cosy*
- *Mountains, lakes & rivers*
- *Guided tours available*

Jivana is a serene, affordable, quality haven. Sandie spoils you with a home-made organic breakfast menu of your choice, served indoors in the sunny conservatory, or lush outdoors. Special diets catered for. You may enjoy a spacious, comfortable super king, or cosy queen ensuite, guest share, or private chalet. The fully equipped yoga / pilates studio is available for guests, meditation, fitness, or simply just a tranquil place to relax, listen to CDs or quietly read. Take the time to relax in a herbal outdoor bush bath under the stars, or allow yourself to be pampered with an aromatherapy herbal massage / reflexology session, or a beneficial health program.

Sandie is a certified health practitioner, and yoga tutor with a passionate love for the outdoors. Brent is a local trades contractor, with a keenness for boating, and fishing.

"*Jivana Retreat has been a wonderful experience of nurturing and nourishment. I definitely got what I came for – rest and rejuvenation.*" T Williams.

Rosewood Bed & Breakfast

20 High Street, Greymouth
Ph (03) 768 4674, Fax (03) 768 4694
Mobile 027-242 7080
email: *rosewoodnz@xtra.co.nz*
www.rosewoodnz.co.nz

Tariff : N.Z. Dollars	
Double	$150-200
Single	$110-150
Child	$25

Bedrooms	Qty
Double	4
Twin	2
Single	1
Bed Size	**Qty**
Super King	1
King	
Queen	4
Double	
Single	1
Bathrooms	**Qty**
Ensuite	3
Private	1
Guest Share	

Superior Bed & Breakfast

Features & Attractions

- *Character home*
- *Spacious rooms*
- *Separate guest lounge*
- *Courtesy pick-ups*
- *10-15 min walk to restaurants*
- *Ensuite or private facilities*
- *German spoken*
- *Off-street parking*

Whether you've just got off the Trans Alpine or are travelling through Greymouth between Christchurch, Nelson or the Glaciers, or just want a few days away, **Rosewood Bed & Breakfast** is the ideal place to stop and recover from your journey and the activities of the day. Rhonda and Stephan await you with a warm friendly welcome in their restored 1920's character home that has retained its grand features of wood panelling and leadlight windows. You will enjoy relaxing in the window seat in the guest lounge/ dining room with a cup of tea or coffee and some of Rhonda's home-made biscuits before taking a wander into town for dinner in one of the cafés or restaurants. Spacious, well equipped bedrooms with private facilities will let you have a great night's sleep in a very comfortable bed. Full continental and cooked breakfast awaits you next morning to give you that perfect start to the day. Rhonda and Stephan appreciate all that the West Coast region has to offer, and would love to make your stay a memorable one for you!

Maryglen Homestay

20 Weenink Road, Karoro, Greymouth
Ph (03) 768 0706, Fax (03) 768 0599
Mobile 027-438 0479
email: *seaview@bandb.co.nz*
www.bandb.co.nz

Features & Attractions

- *Seaview in bush setting*
- *Off main road*
- *Dinner available*
- *Own entrance off deck*
- *Relaxed and friendly*
- *Tours can be arranged*

$	
Double	$110-140
Single	$85-125
Child	neg

Homestay
Bed & Breakfast

Bedrooms	Qty
Double/Twin	2
Double	1
Single	
Bed Size	**Qty**
King/Twin	2
Queen	1
Double	
Single	1
Bathrooms	**Qty**
Ensuite	3
Private	
Guest Share	

Picture relaxing on our seaview deck amidst native bush - an oasis after your travels. Our homestay is on a hillside off the main road. Two rooms open to the deck and have their own entrance. Amazing sunsets can be enjoyed from the deck or while relaxing in the spa pool. Dinner is often served outside where the native bird sounds serenade us while we dine. Having lived on the West Coast for over twenty years now, we have some delightful spots, bush walks and drives to share – Punakaiki Pancake Rocks, Lake Brunner, Glaciers, Trans Alpine Train (complimentary pick up). Bridge players welcome – a game is a possibility.

DIRECTIONS: Approximately 3 km south of town centre. Weenink Road - is on the east side of main road.

Kia Ora Homestay

15 Keith Road, Paroa, Greymouth
Ph (03) 762 6770, Mobile 021-041 3021
email: *almorley@xtra.co.nz*
www.kiaora-homestay.co.nz

Features & Attractions

- *Tranquil setting*
- *Sea view & sunsets*
- *Gold panning*
- *Off-street parking*
- *Coastal & bush walks*
- *Dinner by arrangement*

$	
Double	$90-100
Single	$65-70
Child	neg

Bed & Breakfast
Homestay

Bedrooms	Qty
Double	1
Twin	1
Single	1
Bed Size	**Qty**
King	
Queen	1
Double	
Single	3
Bathrooms	**Qty**
Ensuite	
Private	
Guest Share	1

Kia Ora means "greetings", "welcome". We are set in a very quiet area off the main road, where the sound of the sea and bird song predominate. A place to relax and unwind. Guest rooms are quiet and peaceful. The large lounge opens out onto the deck, where you can relax with a complimentary beer enjoying the sea view and stunning sunsets. We are within 5minutes of town centre and the historic village of Shantytown. There are many attractions nearby. Having travelled the South Island extensively, we are able to help with forward planning. Laundry facilities, hairdryer, off-street parking and a delicious cooked or continental breakfast. Guest comments: *"Really beautiful and relaxing"; "Excellent accommodation – would like to have stayed longer"*. We offer you a warm welcome.

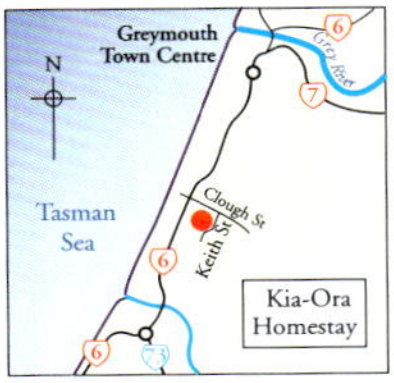

Greymouth ▶ YOUR HOST: Pam Sutherland Ph: (03) 762 6769

Paroa Homestay

345 Main South Road, Greymouth
Ph (03) 762 6769, Fax (03) 762 6765
Mobile 027-323 3118
email: *paroahomestay@xtra.co.nz*

Features & Attractions

- *Home away from home*
- *Off street parking*
- *Superb breakfast*
- *Seaview and mountain views*
- *Three minutes walk to beach*
- *Will organise tours (fishing etc)*

Homestay Bed & Breakfast

Double	$110-135
Single	$79-99
Child	neg

Bedrooms	Qty
Double	2
Twin	
Single	1
Bed Size	**Qty**
Super King	1
King	1
Double	1
Single	
Bathrooms	**Qty**
Ensuite	1
Private	1
Guest Share	1

Imagine relaxing on twin terraces, overlooking Tasman Sea, enjoying incredible sunsets and mountain views. Just three minutes walk to the beach. Listen to chorus of native birds nesting amongst towering trees and native shrubs. Relax in the luxurious and spacious guest lounge in classic style home. Excellent restaurants are between three to six minutes drive.

Pam enjoys people, collects antiques and china, loves organic gardening and bush walking. Experience superb continental breakfast. Baking and cooking are Pam's forté (previously owning Greymouth's busiest cafés/bar). Pam has NZQA food hygiene qualifications. Being West Coast-born, Pam's vast local knowledge is invaluable. On arrival and for supper enjoy home-made cakes/biscuits.

Guests comments *"incredible breakfast (best in New Zealand)", "Beautiful home away from home - did not want to leave."*

Looking forward to sharing my lovely home with you.

Greymouth ▶ YOUR HOSTS: Jill and Russell Fairhall Ph (03) 762 6616

Sunsetview Homestay

335 Main South Road, Greymouth, Westland
Ph (03) 762 6616, Fax (03) 762 6616
email: *sunsetview@xtra.co.nz*

Features & Attractions

- *Sea & mountain views*
- *Short walk to beach*
- *Swimming pool/barbeque*
- *Relaxed & friendly*
- *Children welcome*
- *Generous breakfasts*

Homestay Bed & Breakfast

Double	$100-140
Single	$90-100
Child	neg

DIRECTIONS:
Approx 5km South of town centre

Bedrooms	Qty
Double	4
Twin	
Single	
Bed Size	**Qty**
Super King	1
King	2
Queen	1
King/Single	2
Bathrooms	**Qty**
Ensuite	2
Private	1
Guest Share	

Welcome to our sunny home with amazing sea and mountain views. We offer well appointed queen and king bedrooms with Sky TV.

Full continental and cooked breakfasts, other home cooked meals available by prior arrangement. Our home is centrally heated. Internet, laundry/dryer facilities available. We have for your use an indoor pool which is heated from November till April. Beach is a 3min walk.

Downstairs we offer an apartment with its private entrance and two bedrooms, ensuite, kitchen/ dining/ lounge area. It can sleep up to 5 and can be enjoyed either as a regular B&B facility or as a self-catered basis. Fishing trips can be arranged. Courtesy car service to and from local restaurants and travel centres. Plenty of off-street parking.

Piners Homestay

75 Main South Road, Karoro,
Greymouth
Ph (03) 768 5397, Fax (03) 768 5396
email: *tpiner@paradise.net.nz*

Tariff : N.Z. Dollars	
Double	$85-95
Single	$60-65
Child	neg

Bedrooms	Qty
Double	1
Twin	1
Single	
Bed Size	**Qty**
Super King	
King	
Queen	
Double	1
Single	2
Bathrooms	**Qty**
Ensuite	
Private	
Guest Share	1

Homestay
Bed & Breakfast

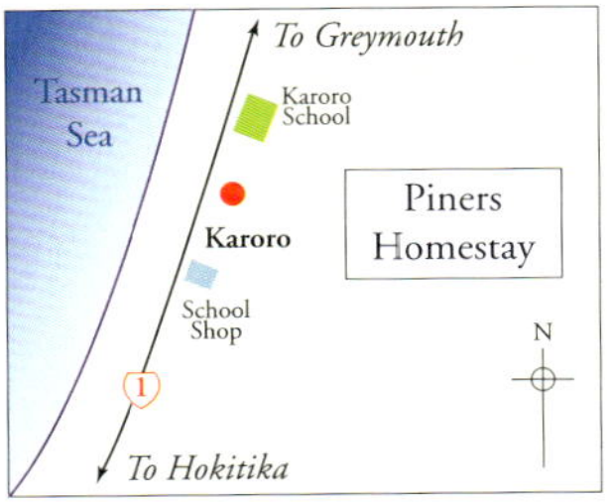

Features & Attractions

- *Tariff includes extensive continental breakfast*
- *Special diets no problem*
- *Knowledgeable & friendly hosts*
- *5 minutes walk to seaside*
- *Very comfortable beds*
- *Off-street parking*
- *Rental Cars arranged*

We have been welcoming guests to our home for over thirteen years now and would love to share it with you. You will be very comfortable with a warm bed and a cosy fire in the winter. You will be able to enjoy delicious food made from our home grown and local produce. Dinner available with complimentary wine and pre-dinner drinks. Tea, coffee and home baking available at any time. Laundry facilities available for a small charge. We only take a maximum of four guests so you will have our total attention to making your stay in our lovely district everything you would wish for. As well as lots of local knowledge, we can also help you plan your activities when you journey to your next destination. You will be near the seaside and will see beautiful sunsets and mountain views. There is off-street parking. Courtesy pick up from Trans Alpine or bus. We are four kilometres south of the town centre. There is a second toilet adjacent to the bedrooms. We have two spoilt cats. There is much more we could say but space does not allow. Why not come and see for yourself? See you soon!

AWATUNA HOMESTEAD

9 Stafford Road, Awatuna, RD 2
Hokitika, Westland
Ph (03) 755 6834, Fax (03) 755 6876
email: *rest@awatunahomestead.co.nz*
www.awatunahomestead.co.nz

Tariff : N.Z. Dollars	
Double	$190-300
Single	$175
Child	neg

Bedrooms	Qty
Double	3
Twin	2
Single	
Bed Size	**Qty**
Super King	1
King	
Queen	2
King Single	2
Single	2
Bathrooms	**Qty**
Ensuite	3
Private	1
Guest Share	

Classic Country Accommodation & Self-contained

Features & Attractions

- *Cultural talks & story telling*
- *Vintage Morris 8 cars*
- *Private hot tub in bush setting*
- *Helipad glacier/snowfields flights*
- *Dinner by request*
- *Extensive wine list*
- *Continental or special Breakfast*
- *Garden walks & beach fossicking*

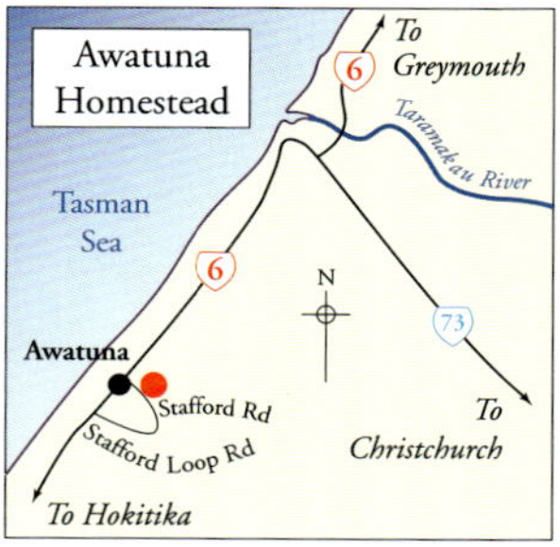

Awatuna Homestead offers old-fashioned New Zealand hospitality with classic country accommodation, set in extensive park-like gardens, featuring native trees and shrubs. Elegant native timber interiors and an open fire in the guest lounge complement the beautifully appointed, superior guest rooms, which have French doors opening into wide verandahs. Pauline, Hemi, Eleanor and Peter welcome you to experience wood-stove warmth, country cooking, continental or special breakfasts and time spent sharing your hosts' traditional cultural knowledge of Polynesia and the West Coast. Take a walk on the wild West Coast beach, fossick for precious stones and driftwood treasures or enjoy the other activities offered. Masie and Poppy, our 2 small dogs, 2 horses, 2 cats and some sheep complete the family welcome. The Piper's Flat self-catering apartment (queen bedroom, twin bedroom and sofa-bed) has private access, exclusive deck with views to the mountains, the sea and gardens. Apartment tariff: $200 double, $25 each extra person. Breakfast $18pp extra by request. Recommend two nights stay.

YOUR HOSTS: **Sharon and Michael Pugh** Ph: (03) 762 6678 ***New River - Greymouth***

New River Bluegums

985 Main South Road, New River, Greymouth
Ph (03) 762 6678, Fax (03) 762 6678
Mobile 027-438 5324
email: *mail@bluegumsnz.com*
www.bluegumsnz.com

Features & Attractions

- *Unique owner-built log house*
- *Two self-contained log cottages*
- *Courtesy pickups*
- *Relaxing farm setting*
- *10 min. walk to beach*
- *Floodlit tennis court*

$		
	Double	$125-180
	Single	$95-120
	Child	$25

Countrystay and Self-contained B&B

Bedrooms	Qty
Double	3
Twin	1
Single	
Bed Size	**Qty**
King	1
Queen	2
Double	
Single	2
Bathrooms	**Qty**
Ensuite	2
Private	1
Guest Share	

Sharon, Michael and baby Harry welcome you to the warmth and comfort of their log and stone home on a small farmlet, set in the heart of the scenic West Coast. Enjoy friendly hospitality and knowledge of the coast while relaxing in front of the big stone open fireplace, sampling a local ale, cup of tea or coffee and home-made cookies. Stroll around the paddocks amongst the cattle, feed the sheep or say hello to Piggy, the Kune Kune, and Coco, our chocolate Labrador. The main house offers a huge king room with its own balcony and a lovely twin room. Our new self-contained cottages are superbly appointed, cosy and secluded overlooking the tennis court. Wake to the morning birdlife and enjoy a delicious breakfast. You will find us on the main highway (SH 6) between Greymouth and Hokitika. *"Beautiful setting! Delightful home! Your relaxed and welcome manner made us feel like we were somewhere special and we certainly were - thank you!"* G&K – Guest book.

YOUR HOSTS: **Janice Da-Via and Des McEnaney** Ph: (03) 755 5393 ***Awatuna - Hokitika***

Awatuna Beachside Bed & Breakfast

State Highway 6, Awatuna, RD 2, Hokitika
Ph (03) 755 5393, Fax (03) 755 5390
email: *mcenvia@clear.net.nz*

Features & Attractions

- *Scenic coastal views*
- *Historic gold trail walks*
- *Adventure activities arranged*
- *A taste of the country*
- *10 min from town*
- *Beach walks*

$		
	Double	$165
	Single	$120
	Child	

Bed & Breakfast Homestay

Bedrooms	Qty
Double	2
Twin	1
Single	
Bed Size	**Qty**
King	1
Queen	1
Double	
Single	2
Bathrooms	**Qty**
Ensuite	3
Private	
Guest Share	

Awatuna Beachside Bed & Breakfast is nestled between the highway and the beach, in park-like grounds and with splendid views of the coastline and the Alps. We offer indoor and outdoor relaxation and ease. Walk along a lonely beach, or just soak up the views from our veranda, while enjoying a quiet drink.

For the more active there is tramping, exploring the gold field trails, or a spot of fishing. A host of activities can be arranged.

The best of country living within minutes of town. Our house has been purpose-built – mixing modern living with traditional West Coast hospitality, offered by two traditional West Coasters, who really know the district and its people. We may even have a tale or two to tell, especially if prodded with a little moonshine...

DIRECTIONS: 20 minutes south of Greymouth, 10 minutes north of Hokitika, 2 hours from the Glaciers, 1 hour from Paparoa National Park, and 3 hours from Christchurch International Airport.

Bushline Retreat Bed & Breakfast

Bluespur Rd, RD2, Hokitika
Ph. (03) 755 8557 Day, (03) 755 6603 Evening
Mobile 027-403 3406
email: *bushlinebnb@xtra.co.nz*
www.bushline.co.nz

Features & Attractions

- *Great fishing & bush walks*
- *Private spa bathroom*
- *Pancake Rocks 75 min*
- *Families welcome*
- *Restaurant 5 min drive*
- *1¾ hours to Glaciers*

Bed & Breakfast
Hosted Accommodation

$	
Double	$95-180
Single	$90-120
Child	$35

MasterCard VISA

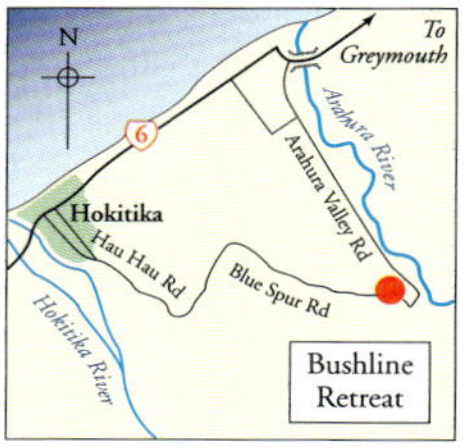

Bushline Retreat is just a ten minutes scenic drive from Hokitika, in the heart of greenstone country 'Blue Spur'. Experience the true feeling of retreat with our peaceful surroundings, native birds and native bush setting.
Enjoy a relaxing breakfast taking in the views down the valley to the Tasman Sea. Unwind in our outdoor spa under a blanket of stars, after a short walk to our glow worm dell. Discount for multi night stays, families very welcome. With so much to do in the area why not stay an extra day or two. Handfeed the native Weka birds or try your hand at goldpanning.
At **bushline** we are more than happy to help with all your forward bookings. Award winning restaurant 5 minutes drive.

Bedrooms	Qty
Double	4
Twin	
Single	
Bed Size	**Qty**
King	1
Queen	3
Double	
Single	3
Bathrooms	**Qty**
Ensuite	2
Private	1
Guest Share	1

Stopforth Dynasty Homestay

105 Weld Street, Hokitika,
Ph (03) 755 7615, Fax (03) 755 5262
email: *info@vacationnewzealand.co.nz*
www.vacationnewzealand.co.nz

Features & Attractions

- *Close to town centre*
- *Underfloor heating in bathrooms*
- *Punakaiki/Glaciers 1½ hours*
- *Lake Kaniere & Hokitika Gorge 20 minutes*

Bed & Breakfast
Homestay

$	
Double	$120
Single	$65
Child	$10

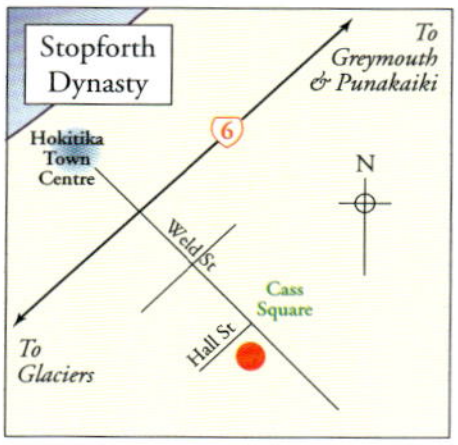

Anne and Spencer welcome you to their slice of Heaven. This is where visitors from all over New Zealand and the world come to experience the "Hokitika Food Festival" held opposite, at the park. Spencer has been a goldminer and can show you a nugget or two.
An easy five minute walk to the town centre where you will find a choice of top restaurants. Our guests enjoy a continental breakfast with extras (homemade bread), comfortable beds and underfloor heating in the bathrooms. Children are welcome. Make our home your place away from home and stay more than one night.

Bedrooms	Qty
Double	1
Twin	1
Single	1
Bed Size	**Qty**
King	
Queen	2
Double	1
Single	
Bathrooms	**Qty**
Ensuite	2
Private	1
Guest Share	

Hokitika Heritage Lodge

46 Alpine View, PO Box 176, Hokitika
Ph (03) 755 7357, Fax (03) 755 8760
Mobile 027-437 1254
email: *hokitikaheritage@xtra.co.nz*
www.hokitikaheritagelodge.co.nz

Tariff : N.Z. Dollars	
Double	$185-225
Single	$185
Child	

Bedrooms	Qty
Double	3
Twin	
Single	
Bed Size	**Qty**
Super King	
King	1
Queen	2
Double	
Single	1
Bathrooms	**Qty**
Ensuite	3
Private	
Guest Share	

Luxury Accommodation

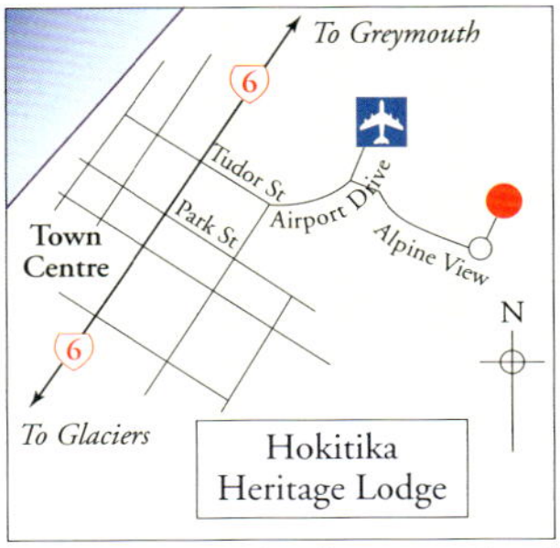

Features & Attractions

- *NZ-born hosts*
- *Heritage character home*
- *Magnificent sea vistas*
- *Bush setting spa*
- *Spectacular mountain views*
- *Two minutes to glow worms*
- *Two minutes to restaurants*
- *Dinner by arrangement*

Dianne (literacy teacher) and Chris (property consultant and Rotarian) warmly welcome you to their lodge, built two years ago and situated in a quiet, private location overlooking Hokitika, Tasman Sea and Southern Alps, including Mount Cook. Soak up the atmosphere and views in our stylish, comfortable lounge with huge windows or while sitting on our terrace; relax in the bush-setting spa or in one of our heritage themed bedrooms: **Gold**, **Jade** and **Heritage**, reflecting the West Coast history. All guest rooms are quiet and spacious with high-quality bedding, ensuites, superb views, tea/coffee making and Sky TV. Broadband internet and wireless network are available. Stay and explore Lake Kaniere, Hokitika Gorge, Glow-worm Dell, craft-galleries, bush and historic walks, restaurants, or visit the Glaciers (1.5 hours) or Punakaiki (1.25 hours). Take a scenic flight. We can help you with all arrangements. Guests comments: "Outstanding hospitality and facilities, superb accommodation, beautiful house, warm welcome, best cooked breakfast, the BEST night that we have had in New Zealand." Four-course dining can be enjoyed in our stunning dining room with prior arrangement.

WOODLAND GLEN LODGE

96 Hau Hau Rd, Blue Spur, Hokitika
Ph/Fax (03) 755 5063, Mobile 027-201 6126
email: *l.anderson@xtra.co.nz*
www.hokitika.net.nz

Tariff : N.Z. Dollars	
Double	$140-250
Single	$130-180
Child	—

Bedrooms	Qty
Double	5
Twin	2
Single	
Bed Size	**Qty**
Super King	
King	
Queen	5
Double	
Single	2
Bathrooms	**Qty**
Ensuite	3
Private	
Guest Share	1

Luxury Bed & Breakfast

Features & Attractions

- *Quiet private surroundings*
- *Only 2 km to Hokitika*
- *Lake Kauiere & Hokitika Gorge*
- *Courtesy car to local restaurants for dinner*
- *Wonderful gardens*
- *Helicopter scenic tours*
- *Heli fishing & hunting*
- *Honeymoon packages*

DIRECTIONS:
From Main St into Hokitika turn east into Hampden St. Proceed straight for approximately 2km until sign on right.

Advance booking recommended.

Laurie and Janette welcome you to **Woodland Glen Lodge**, located on the outskirts of Hokitika. The gateway to Franz Joseph and Fox Glaciers, **Woodland Glen** is more than a home away from home. Our 6,500 square foot lodge is located on 21 acres and is surrounded in native Kahikatea trees which provide complete quiet and privacy. A great place for a retreat or just time out. We specialise in honeymoon package deals. Laurie is a fourth generation West Coaster, a retired 30 year police veteran with an aviation background as a commercial pilot on both helicopters and aeroplanes. Laurie has a wealth of knowledge of the region and its people. Janette is originally from Edinburgh Scotland and is presently employed as a health professional. She is actively involved in a local quilting group and has an interest in most crafts. **Woodland Glen Lodge** is an excellent base for local and regional tourist attractions so allow for at least 2 nights stay. From the lodge we provide helicopter scenic tours, guided heli fishing and hunting.

Teichelmann's Bed & Breakfast

20 Hamilton Street, PO Box 156, Hokitika
Ph (03) 755 8232, Fax (03) 755 8239
email: *teichel@xtra.co.nz*
www.teichelmanns.co.nz

Tariff : N.Z. Dollars	
Double	$175-240
Single	$165-185
Child	

Bedrooms	Qty
Double	5
Twin	2
Single	1
Bed Size	**Qty**
Super King	4
King Single	3
Queen	
Double	
Single	
Bathrooms	**Qty**
Ensuite	5
Private	1
Guest Share	

Bed & Breakfast

DIRECTIONS:
Turn left at Town Clock, then first right.
Booking in advance is recommended.

Features & Attractions

- *Quiet, central location*
- *Close to restaurants/cafés*
- *Craft & heritage trails*
- *Walks, golf and fishing*
- *Warm, friendly service*
- *Walk to beach & shops*
- *Interesting craft galleries*
- *Magnificent sunsets*

Frances and Brian pride themselves in offering friendly, informal hospitality within the comforts of a warm character home. It gives guests the opportunity to 'Catch Your Breath and Breakfast' after a long day travelling. **Teichelmann's**, located in the heritage area of Hokitika, is a large home built for Dr Ebenezer Teichelmann in 1897.

Its layout gives our guests privacy if they wish or to relax in the comfort of a separate guest's lounge. The house has been refurbished to include very comfortable beds, quality furnishings and excellent ensuite bathroom facilities. Join other guests for a substantial continental or cooked breakfast at our elegant table which seats ten and enjoy swapping experiences and stories with people from all parts of the world.

Children over ten years of age are welcome.

Our home is smoke free.

Hokitika

YOUR HOSTS: **Jacque Evans & Peter Schwass** Ph: (03) 755 5151

Braeside Farmstay

445 Lake Kaniere Road, Hokitika
Ph (03) 755 5151, Fax (03) 755 5151
Mobile 021-371 161
email: *braeside@xtra.co.nz*

Features & Attractions

- *Superb views*
- *Peaceful surroundings*
- *Fishing lakes 10 min*
- *Close to Hokitika Airport*
- *Dinner by arrangement*
- *Beautiful Lake Kaniere*

Farmstay Bed & Breakfast

DIRECTIONS: Please phone for easy directions.

Double	$100
Single	$60
Child	$30

Relax and enjoy time out at **Braeside,** where the views are superb and peace is paramount. Where it is only ten minutes drive to anywhere, fishing, lakes, town, airport or any interests you may have.
If the season is right, try your luck at "Whitebaiting", a traditional fishing sport, enjoyed by many West Coasters. Restaurants abound in Hokitika or by prior arrangement you can try our homecooked meal for an additional $24 per person.
We can advise you on places of interest to visit. Our home is warm and comfortable, set on a hill overlooking our property and surrounding area. You can find it by following the road to Lake Kaniere and looking for the swinging sign on your left just one minute from Kaniere Village.

Bedrooms	Qty
Double	1
Twin	1
Single	
Bed Size	**Qty**
King	
Queen	1
Double	
Single	2
Bathrooms	**Qty**
Ensuite	
Private	
Guest Share	1

Ruatapu - Hokitika

YOUR HOSTS: **Eileen and Roger Berwick** Ph: (03) 755 7876

Berwicks Hill Countrystay

106 Ruatapu Ross Rd, SH 6,RD 3, Hokitika
Mobile 025-673 7387
Ph (03) 755 7876, Fax (03) 755 7870
email: *berwicks@xtra.co.nz*
www.berwicks.co.nz

Features & Attractions

- *Lake Mahinapua*
- *Beach walks*
- *Bush walks*
- *Sea and mountain views*
- *Breakfast from our menu*
- *Dinner by arrangement*

Countrystay Bed & Breakfast

Double	$100-120
Single	$70
Child	

We offer you a warm and friendly welcome to our comfortable home situated on the property that was settled by the Berwick family in 1907. The Tasman Sea and Southern Alps are seen from the living areas, the sunrises and sunsets are uniquely beautiful. We have sheep, cattle, and hens and grow pine trees on our hobby farm, with one farm dog, a cat and a house dog. Beautiful Lake Mahinapua is only minutes away with many interesting bush walks. We are only a short distance from the beach and golf course. Hokitika is a ten minute drive with its jade (pounamu) carvers and many other arts, crafts and walks. We look forward to spending time with you and sharing our love of the West Coast.

DIRECTIONS: Travel over the Hokitika Bridge on State Highway 6 for 12 km, on the right just past the southern Ruatapu turnoff.

Bedrooms	Qty
Double	1
Twin	1
Single	
Bed Size	**Qty**
King	
Queen	1
King/Single	2
Single	
Bathrooms	**Qty**
Ensuite	1
Private	1
Guest Share	

Paramata Lodge

554 Bold Head Road, RD1, Ross, South Westland
Ph (03) 755 4290
Mobile 027-367 2699
email: *stay@paramatalodge.co.nz*
www.paramatalodge.co.nz

Tariff : N.Z. Dollars	
Double	$200-350
Single	$180-250
Child	n/a

Bedrooms	Qty
Double	3
Twin	
Single	
Bed Size	**Qty**
Super King	2
King	
Queen	1
Double	
Single	
Bathrooms	**Qty**
Ensuite	3
Private	
Guest Share	

Ecological Sanctuary
Warm and Friendly

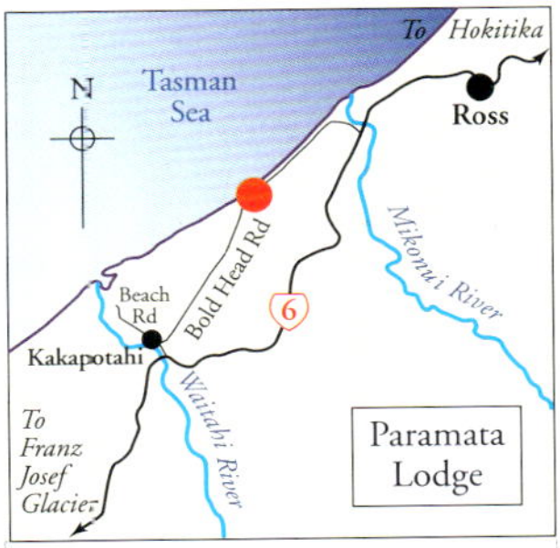

DIRECTIONS: **Paramata Lodge** is situated 5.5km from either turn-offs from SH6

Features & Attractions

- *Coast/forest eco tours*
- *Conservation projects*
- *New Zealand treaty history*
- *Bird watching/fishing*
- *Eclectic mix of art*
- *Library, lounges and decks*
- *Piano and CD collection*
- *Wireless internet*

Here is the most spectacular natural landscape in New Zealand, unaltered indigenous forest from the Southern Alps to the Tasman Sea. And on the coast of Te Wai Pounamu, where wind and ocean collide with this mountainous island, rocks, waterways and wildlife create unique dramas. Yet today, along the Hokitika Haast Highway, there are few places to access these scenes. **Paramata Lodge,** situated within a sheltered proximity to the beach, is an artfully designed New Zealand home, where fine hospitality and comforts are provided, so guests can absorb the special features of rare ancient forest, coastal wetlands and miles of remote sandy beach at leisure. The name **Paramata** has been

lodge to acknowledge the Ngai Tahu Maori historic presence. Short ecological and histc conducted daily with longer excursions on foot or by canoe, at extra charge.
Dinner and lunch with selected wines are also extra, and two nights minimum is recon

Matai Lodge

Whataroa, South Westland, South Island
Ph/Fax (03) 753 4156, Mobile 021-395 068
email: *jpurcell@xtra.co.nz*

Tariff : N.Z. Dollars	
Double	$150-180
Single	$120
Child	half price

Bedrooms	Qty
Double	2
Twin	1
Single	
Bed Size	**Qty**
Super King	1
King	1
Queen	
Double	
King/Single	2
Bathrooms	**Qty**
Ensuite	1
Private	1
Guest Share	

**Farmstay
Bed & Breakfast**

Features & Attractions

- *Glacier flights*
- *Forest & glacier walks*
- *3-course dinner $40 pp*
- *Stunning location*
- *Fishing - salmon and trout*
- ***White heron** bird sanctuary*
- *Golf, kayaking, horse riding*
- *Peaceful farm setting*

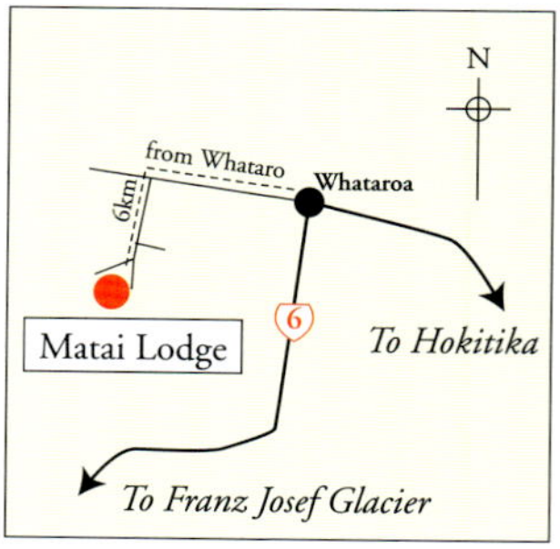

DIRECTIONS:
Whataroa is 20 minutes north of Franz Josef Glacier. 3km west of SH 6: Blue B & B sign.

If you are coming to see the Glaciers, walk in the World Heritage Park, the coastal track at Okarito or visit the White Heron Bird Sanctuary in Whataroa, you are warmly welcome to share with us our tranquil, rural retreat in our modern, spacious home on a 400 acre farm of sheep, cows and a farm dog.
Upstairs is a suite of two bedrooms, conservatory and private bathroom and downstairs a king size ensuite.
You are welcome to join us for a home-cooked dinner with New Zealand wine ($40 per person).

Our motto is: *"A stranger is a friend we have yet to meet".*
Glenice speaks Japanese and has taught felting, spinning and weaving in Japan. Glenice also plays golf.

YOUR HOSTS: **Beverleigh and Grant Muir** Free Ph: 0800 WAPITI **Harihari - South Westland**

Wapiti Park Homestead

SH 6, Harihari, South Westland
Ph (03) 753 3074, Fax (03) 753 3024
email: *wapitipark@xtra.co.nz*
www.wapitipark.co.nz

Tariff : N.Z. Dollars	
Double	$295-545
Single	$245-495
Child	n/a

Bedrooms	Qty
Double	4
Twin	4
Single	
Bed Size	**Qty**
Super King	3
King	1
Queen	
Double	
Single	2
Bathrooms	**Qty**
Ensuite	3
Private	1
Guest Share	

Boutique Country Lodge
Luxury Farmstay

Features & Attractions

- *Quiet, peaceful surroundings*
- *Superior comfort beds*
- *5 course dinner by arrangement*
- *Evening glow worm tour*
- *Large, spacious rooms & lounges*
- *Traditional hospitality*
- *Morning elk farm tour*
- *Guided hunting/fishing available*

DIRECTIONS:
On the west side of State Highway 6
at southern approach to Harihari.
Look for the sign.

Nestled under the foothills of the Southern Alps at the northern gateway to the Glacier region, **Wapiti Park Homestead** stands on the site of the original Harihari Post Office and Accommodation House.

Owner hosts, Grant and Bev, invite you to discover the special experience of a stay at their luxurious colonial-style Boutique Country Lodge, which offers guests a unique blend of ambience and traditional West Coast hospitality.

Relax in complete comfort while enjoying the privacy of either the Rose Suite with private sitting room and hydro-spa ensuite, or one of the 3 spacious, individually decorated first floor rooms. Extensive indoor/outdoor living areas provide the opportunity to enjoy the tranquillity of the rural location. Wander the award winning gardens, relax on the deck, or just catch up on some sleep. Be sure to reserve a legendary 5-course Lodge Dinner.

Wapiti Park is now a destination. Allow a mininum 2 or 3 night stay to experience these in-house activities: elk farm, glow-worm tours and the superb guided brown trout fis'

The Lodge is non-smoking and unsuitable for young children.

Mount Adam Lodge

State Highway 6, RD 1, Whataroa, South Westland
Ph (03) 753 4030, Fax (03) 753 4264
Mobile 021-170 2502
email: *mtadamlodge@paradise.net.nz*
www.mountadamlodge.co.nz

Tariff : N.Z. Dollars	
Double	$115-135
Single	$85-105
Child	

Bedrooms	Qty
Double	3
Twin	2
Single	2
Bed Size	**Qty**
Super King	
King	
Queen	2
Double	1
Single	6
Bathrooms	**Qty**
Ensuite	5
Private	
Guest Share	1

F

Quality Lodge
Majestic Scenery

BB

Features & Attractions

- *Quiet, peaceful surroundings*
- *White Heron Bird Sanctuary*
- *35 min north of Franz Josef*
- *Licensed restaurant with home cooking*
- *Stay on a real farm*
- *Friendly hosts*
- *Farm and river walks*
- *Stunning location*

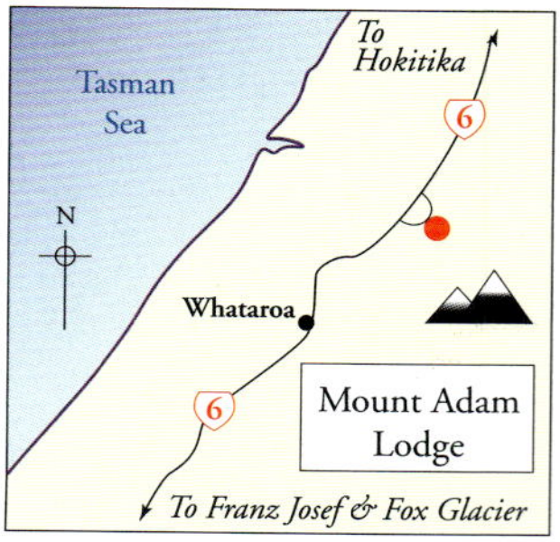

If you are wanting to escape the crowds in the busy tourist centres, then we are the ideal place for you to stay. Just a short thirty-five minute drive north of Franz Josef Glacier. We are situated on our farm at the foot of Mount Adam, surrounded by farmland and beautiful native bush with breathtaking mountain views. Our lodge offers comfortable accommodation and a fully licensed restaurant with tasty home cooked meals. You can stroll along our farm tracks and river bank meeting our variety of farm animals on the way. We will be happy to provide details or make reservations for helicopter flights, walks, or helihikes at the glaciers and also the White Heron Bird Sanctuary at Whataroa. Elsa and Mac look forward to meeting you. You will find us on State Highway 6, half way between Harihari and Whataroa. Seventy minutes south of Hokitika, thirty-five minutes north of Franz Josef.

Heritage Gateway Bed & Breakfast

State Highway 6, PO Box 18, Whataroa
Ph (03) 753 4158, Fax (03) 753 4159
email: *heritage.gateway@xtra.co.nz*
www.heritage-gateway.co.nz

Tariff : N.Z. Dollars	
Double	$110-130
Single	$70-100
Child	

Bedrooms	Qty
Double	2
Twin	
Single	
Bed Size	**Qty**
Super King	
King	
Queen	2
Double	
Single	
Bathrooms	**Qty**
Ensuite	2
Private	
Guest Share	

Bed & Breakfast Homestay

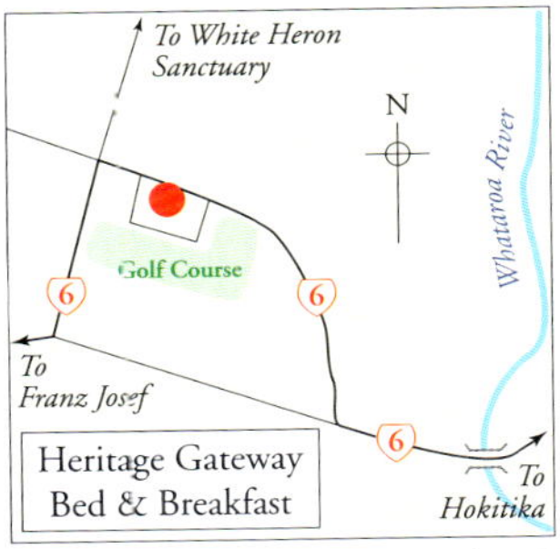

Features & Attractions

- *Genuine hospitality*
- *Relaxed, comfy accommodation*
- *Guest lounge*
- *Close to activities and amenities*
- *Glacier flights & walks*
- *White heron sanctuary*
- *Laundry facilities*
- *Continental breakfast*

We welcome you to our home in Whataroa, a scenic drive 25 minutes north of Franz Josef Glacier. We offer a friendly, genuine retreat from the busy Glacier Towns in our comfortable spacious home. Clare is a fourth generation member of a pioneering family, who settled on the West Coast in 1871. Rob, formerly from Auckland, has been mining gold in this area for the past thirty years. **Heritage Gateway** is a 1930's home and is the former doctors' surgery and residence of South Westland's medical practitioner. Guest rooms have quality linen, electric blankets, heaters, hairdryers and clock radios. Guest lounge contains Sky TV, complimentary tea, coffee and home baking, adjoining outdoor patio with bar-b-que and mountain backdrop. Continental breakfast included with homemade jams and muffins. Activities include glacier flights and walks, White Heron Sanctuary, 9-hole golf course, fishing, kyaking, coastal and rainforest walks. We look forward to your visit and are happy to assist you with booking your activities.

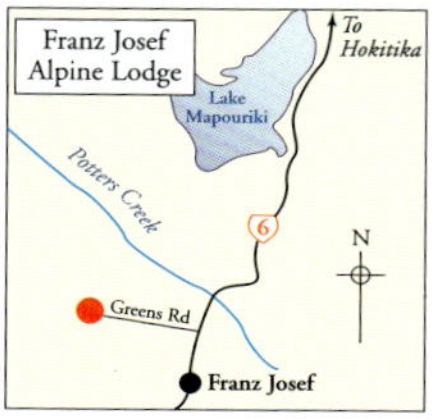

Franz Josef Alpine Lodge

117 Greens Road, Franz Josef, South Westland
Ph (03) 752 0688, Fax (03) 752 0688
Mobile 021-767 024
email: *jacque@franzlodge.com*
www.franzlodge.com

Features & Attractions

- *Franz Josef Glacier*
- *Guided walks*
- *Hunting & fishing*
- *Kayak Lake Mapourika*
- *Private ensuites*
- *Helicopter scenic flights*

Homestay
Bed & Breakfast

Double	$180
Single	$100
Child	

Bedrooms	Qty
Double	3
Twin	1
Single	

Bed Size	Qty
Super King	1
King	1
Queen	1
Single	

Bathrooms	Qty
Ensuite	3
Private	
Guest Share	1

Jacque and Brian invite you to their home which adjoins 13 acres of rural land surrounded by Westland National Park. We are situated 1km off State Highway 6, just 7km north of the Franz Josef township. If you are looking for a peaceful setting to unwind, then this is the place for you. Brian is a helicopter pilot and you can do your scenic flight from your doorstep at your leisure. We also offer guided hunting and fishing tours. We enjoy meeting people and look forward to sharing our West Coast hospitality with you. **Franz Josef Alpine Lodge** is home to amazing native birdlife and in close proximity to Lake Mapourika and Lake Pratt.

Holly Homestead B&B

State Highway 6, PO Box 35, Franz Josef Glacier
Ph (03) 752 0299, Fax (03) 752 0298
email: *stay@hollyhomestead.co.nz*
www.hollyhomestead.co.nz

Tariff : N.Z. Dollars	
Double	$200-290
Single	$170-260
Child	n/a

Bedrooms	Qty
Double	2
Twin	2
Single	
Bed Size	**Qty**
Super King/Twin	2
King	
Queen	2
Double	
Single	
Bathrooms	**Qty**
Ensuite	4
Private	
Guest Share	

Quality Bed & Breakfast
Fine Accommodation

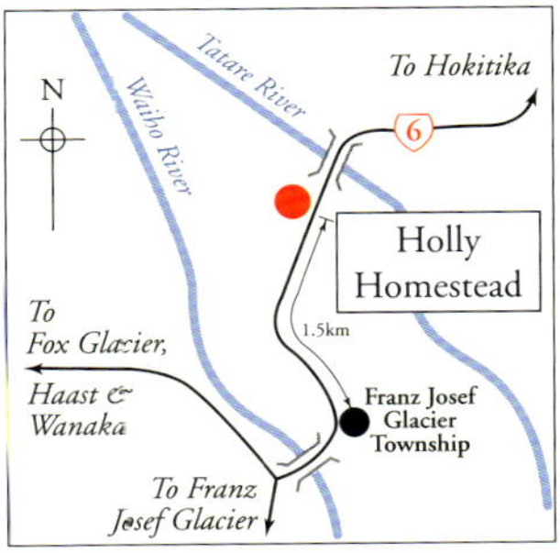

Features & Attractions

- *Friendly NZ-born hosts*
- *Central heating & log fire*
- *Glacier carpark 10 min.*
- *Restaurants 2 min. drive*
- *Character home*
- *Generous breakfast*
- *Off-street parking*
- *Year round activities*

Greetings from glorious Franz Josef. In 2000 Gerard and Bernie became the proud owners of one of the area's finest old timber homes, originally built for an Italian family in 1926. We invite you to share the charm and ambience of this impressive colonial homestead. Recent renovations and extensions have carried on the warm timber theme. Relax in our cosy guest lounge after your adventures. Spend a restful night in comfortable beds with quality linen, wool duvets and electric blankets. All guest rooms have ensuite bathrooms, hairdryers and toiletries – and the comfort of wooden toilet seats! Socialise with other guests while enjoying a hearty continental and cooked breakfast. Enjoy a spectacular alpine view from the large breakfast table – clouds permitting! We offer helpful, friendly advice on local activities and are happy to assist you with bookings. Courtesy transport for guests travelling by coach. Children over twelve welcome. Allow yourself time to unw magnificent region. We recommend a two night minimum. Don't be disappointed, book no

FRANZ JOSEF GLACIER COUNTRY RETREAT

State Highway 6, Lake Mapourika, PO Box 11, Franz Josef
Ph (03) 752 0012, Fax (03) 752 0021
Mobile 027-545 1198
email: *stay@glacier-retreat.co.nz*
www.glacier-retreat.co.nz

Tariff : N.Z. Dollars	
Double	$195-295
Single	$175-275
Child	

Bedrooms	Qty
Double	10
Twin	2
Single	
Bed Size	**Qty**
Super King	5
King	
Queen	5
Double	
King/Single	4
Bathrooms	**Qty**
Ensuite	11
Private	2
Guest Share	

Boutique Bed & Breakfast
Luxury Lodge

Features & Attractions

- *Hosts 4th generation locals*
- *Mountain & lake views*
- *The quietest accommodation*
- *Free activity booking service*
- *Guest lounge with open fire*
- *Rooms all centrally heated*
- *DVD players, Sky TV in all rooms*
- *Guest laundry facilities*

DIRECTIONS: On State Highway 6, located 5 minutes drive north of the village, near Lake Mapourika.

We are delighted to welcome you to **Franz Josef Glacier Country Retreat.** Our retreat is set in 200 acres of peaceful farmland where our pioneer family has resided for over 100 years. Our building's design was inspired by a historical West Coast homestead. This unique accommodation offers traditional hospitality in luxurious surroundings, looking towards picturesque Lake Mapourika, 5 minutes drive north of Franz Josef village. Our 12 luxury rooms have been individually decorated, named and themed after local pioneers' families. All rooms are centrally heated, with tea/coffee making facilities, fridge, private ensuite with shower and toilet, SKY (satellite) TV, DVD player, telephone, console table and chairs. All rooms have French doors opening onto a balcony with magnificent views of the lake or mountains.

We also have a special honeymoon suite with a four poster bed and an old fashioned claw-foot bath. Relax in the guest lounge with large gas open fire or in our spa-bathroom. Also have guest laundry and outdoor open fire/BBQ for all guests to use.

We look forward to sharing with you our special place.

Knightswood Lodge Bed & Breakfast

State Highway 6, PO Box 70, Franz Josef Glacier
Ph (03) 752 0059, Fax (03) 752 0061
Mobile 027-433 0312
email: *info@franzjosefaccommodation.com*
www.franzjosefaccommodation.com

Tariff : N.Z. Dollars	
Double	$160-210
Single	$130-170
Child age dependent	

Bedrooms	Qty
Double	3
Twin	2
Single	
Bed Size	**Qty**
Super King	4
King	2
Queen	1
Double	
Single	1
Bathrooms	**Qty**
Ensuite	2
Private	
Family Share	1

Bed & Breakfast
Countrystay

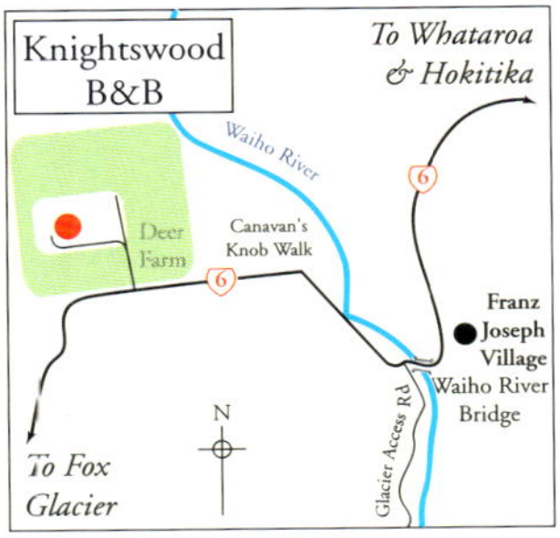

DIRECTIONS:
On main SH 6, 3 km south of Franz Josef. Travelling from the north we are on the right, from the south on the left side.

Features & Attractions

- *Spectacular alpine views*
- *Peaceful rural setting*
- *Private native bush*
- *Many native birds*
- *Own entrance to ensuite rooms*
- *Comfortable beds*
- *Children welcome*
- *Glacial flights/hikes*

Enjoy this modern home alongside a forest and alpine splendor. Although **Knightswood Lodge** is located only minutes from town and Franz Josef Glacier, be assured peace and tranquility.

Gerry, a former helicopter pilot and wildlife ranger, welcomes good conversation. Enjoy an interpretive guided walk within a private native forest or venture further toward the grand alpine expanse. Explore glaciers, the forest and perhaps the wilderness coast, or kayak and fish amongst lake and estuary.

Guest rooms have private entrance / outside verandah space. Be welcomed upstairs with evening / afternoon drinks - breakfast to suit. Courtesy transport available 3km to/from village.

Westwood Lodge

SH 6, PO Box 37, Franz Josef Glacier 7552
Ph (03) 752 0112, Fax (03) 752 0111
email: *info@westwoodlodge.co.nz*
www.westwoodlodge.co.nz

WESTWOOD LODGE
FRANZ JOSEF GLACIER - WEST COAST

qualmark ★★★★ plus guest & hosted

Tariff : N.Z. Dollars	
Grand Suite	$370
Suites	$320
Child	$150

Bedrooms	Qty
Double	9
Twin	
Single	
Bed Size	**Qty**
Super King	9
King	
Queen	
Double	
King/Single	
Bathrooms	**Qty**
Ensuite	9
Private	
Guest Share	

BB **Luxury Accommodation Bed & Breakfast** LA

VISA MasterCard eftpos AMERICAN EXPRESS

- *Glacier flights and walks*
- *Mountain views*
- *Coastal rainforest walks*
- *Spacious guest rooms*
- *Sumptuous lounge*
- *Billiard room*
- *Quiet, rural garden setting*
- *Quad bike adventures*

DIRECTIONS:
On main State Highway 6,
The Lodge is 2 km north of the
village of Franz Josef.

Welcome to our premier Bed & Breakfast in Franz Josef Glacier. Set in a native bush garden with views to the forests and mountains of the Southern Alps, **Westwood Lodge** offers you superior comfort and service.

Main House Suites all include relaxing French bath tubs. The Main House Grand Suite also features its own separate lounge. Coach House Suites offer stunning alpine views. All rooms are superbly comfortable, open plan super-king suites (or generous twin option) with underfloor-heated ensuite bathrooms, electric blankets, electric heating, tea & coffee making facilities and modem compatible phones. The warmth of natural timber throughout **Westwood Lodge** reflects the West Coast forest environment and complements the traditional hospitality for which the region is famed. Relax in the Sumptuous Lodge Lounge and Bar with impressive fire and magnificent views or enjoy the outdoors in any weather from within the Conservatory. Withdraw to the Billiard Room and take your cue. Start your day with a continental and cooked breakfast from our delectable menu and then set off on your day of discovery.

Ribbonwood Retreat

26 Greens Road, PO Box 30, Franz Josef
Ph (03) 752 0072, Fax (03) 752 0272
email: *ribbon.wood@xtra.co.nz*
www.ribbonwood.net.nz

Tariff : N.Z. Dollars	
Double	$180-245
Single	$100-120
Child	

Bedrooms	Qty
Double	3
Twin	
Single	
Bed Size	**Qty**
Super King	
King	1
Queen	2
Double	
Single	
Bathrooms	**Qty**
Ensuite	1
Private	2
Family Share	1

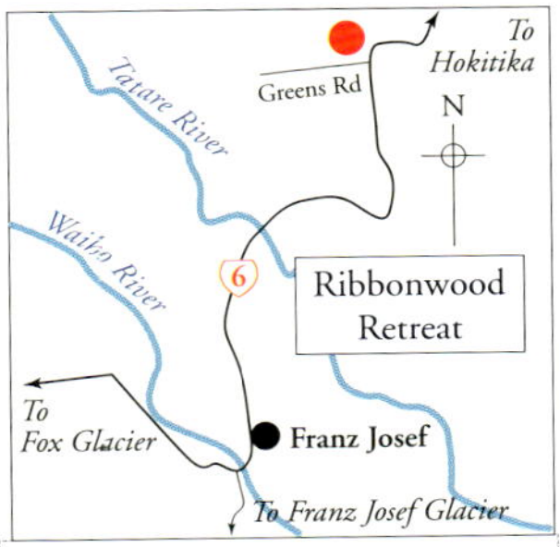

DIRECTIONS: 5 km north of Franz Josef (towards Hokitika), **Ribbonwood** is situated on the corner of Greens Rd and SH 6. Look for 2-storey house with blue roof set back 100 m from highway, surrounded by trees.

Bed & Breakfast
Homestay

Features & Attractions

- *Glacier views*
- *5 min to Franz Josef & restaurants*
- *Spectacular mountain scenery*
- *Self-contained cottage*
- *Contemporary home*
- *Relaxing rural outlook*
- *Modern bathrooms*
- *Scenic flights, glacier walks*

Guests commented: *"Thank you for the friendly welcome to your lovely, spacious home and for your fund of knowledge on the local environment and wildlife"*, Keith & Audrey, Hampshire UK.

We are both Kiwis – Julie is a schoolteacher on sabbatical to work with endangered Okarito brown kiwi and Jo, a conservation ranger, specialises in flora and fauna, especially native birds. We cater for just a few guests at **Ribbonwood**, because we want you to feel completely at home. We pride ourselves on our knowledge of the region and offer friendly, personalised advice.

You will be warmly welcomed into our clean, sunny, modern home. Our 2 guest rooms have comfortable new beds with electric blankets and luxury bathrooms featuring powerful showers. The new self-contained cottage has timber-panelled walls, and a large deck looking out to the mountains and farmland. Breakfast includes fresh fruit crepes, freshly ground coffee and delicious home-made bread. With stunning views of mountains, glaciers and forests, **Ribbonwood** is 5 min. drive from glacier walks, scenic flights and restaurants.

Fox Glacier Lodge

Sullivan Road, PO Box 22, Fox Glacier
Ph (03) 751 0888, Fax (03) 751 0888
email: *foxglacierlodge@xtra.co.nz*
www.foxglacierlodge.co.nz

Tariff : N.Z. Dollars	
Double	$110-250
Single	$90-180
Child	$40

Bedrooms	Qty
Double or Twin	6
Twin	
Single	
Bed Size	**Qty**
Super King	
King	1
Queen	5
Double	
Single	4
Bathrooms	**Qty**
Ensuite	6
Private	
Guest Share	

Alpine Chalet Lodge
Bed & Breakfast

Features & Attractions

- *Warm & friendly hospitality*
- *Magestic mountain views*
- *Tranquil rainforest setting*
- *Guided walks*
- *Double spa bath units available*
- *Mountain bikes available*
- *Central to cafés, restaurants & shops*
- *Scenic helicopter flights arranged*

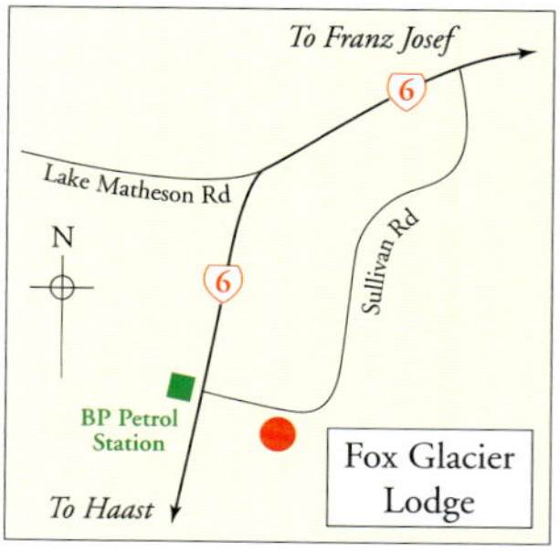

DIRECTIONS: Sullivan Road is off SH 6, opp BP Petrol Station.

Experience our warm hospitality, mountain views and awake to the smell of freshly made bread and filter coffee. Our modern, solid timber, purpose-built lodge is in the heart of Fox Glacier Village. We are the closest accommodation to the glacier and only a one minute stroll to all cafés, restaurants and shops. Enjoy our tranquil setting, surrounded by unique temperate rainforest with majestic mountain views. Close by glow worm forest walk. We would be more than happy to offer our local knowledge in helping you book any local activities like glacier walks and scenic helicopter/fixed wing flights. Laundry facilities and mountain bikes are available for your use. We have 3 new apartment-style units, completed late 2005, all fully self-contained with spa bath. We will endeavour to make your stay a comfortable and memorable experience. We look forward to meeting you and sharing our little slice of heaven.

Misty Peaks
Boutique Bed & Breakfast

130 Cook Flat Road, PO Box 65, Fox Glacier
Ph (03) 751 0849, Fax (03) 751 0849
email: *davidbentley@xtra.co.nz*
www.mistypeaks.co.nz

Tariff : N.Z. Dollars	
Double	$280-350
Single	$280-330
Child	

Bedrooms	Qty
Double	5
Twin	
Single	
Bed Size	**Qty**
Super King/Twin	5
King	
Queen	
Double	
Single	
Bathrooms	**Qty**
Ensuite	5
Private	
Guest Share	

Boutique Accommodation
A La Carte Dinner

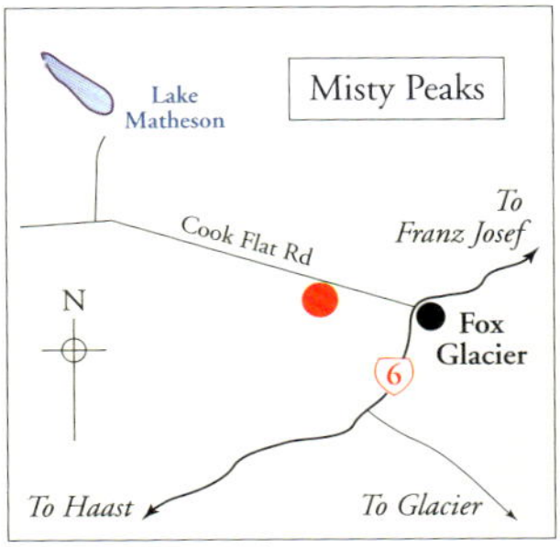

Features & Attractions

- *A la carte dinner*
- *Laundry & internet*
- *Complimentary nibbles & drink*
- *Full cooked breakfast*
- *Lake Matheson*
- *Gillespies Beach*
- *Glacier walks*
- *Helicopter flights*

Lea and Dave welcome you to **Misty Peaks**, our new purpose-built boutique accommodation offering you the very best in quality, comfort and genuine Kiwi Bed and Breakfast hospitality. **Misty Peaks** offers 4 private guest suites, each with luxurious bedding, private ensuites, hairdryers and TV. Each suite has double opening doors to veranda, double glazing and individual guest access. The veranda around **Misty Peaks** provides a comfortable setting to take in breathtaking views of Mt Cook and Mt Tasman, stunning sunsets and the delightful ever-changing rural setting. A well appointed guest lounge with wood fire provides a quality atmosphere to relax in and enjoy a complimentary drink with other guests. An 'A La Carte' dinner offering quality fresh NZ produce and wines is available every evening with all guests dining together. Breakfast is available at a time to suit your plans for the day, full cooked or continental. Tea or coffee available at all times.

REFLECTION LODGE

Cook Flat Road, PO Box 46, Fox Glacier
Ph (03) 751 0707, Fax (03) 751 0707
email: *raelene@reflectionlodge.co.nz*
www.reflectionlodge.co.nz

Tariff : N.Z. Dollars	
Double	$150-180
Single	$150
Child	$45

Bedrooms	Qty
Double	2
Twin	1
Single	
Bed Size	**Qty**
Super King	
King	
Queen	2
Double	
Single	
Bathrooms	**Qty**
Ensuite	1
Private	
Family Share	1

Homestay
Bed & Breakfast

Features & Attractions

- *Spectacular views*
- *Peaceful and tranquil*
- *Lake Matheson nearby*
- *Stunning scenic walks*
- *We arrange helicopter flights & heli-hikes*
- *Breakfast with lake views*

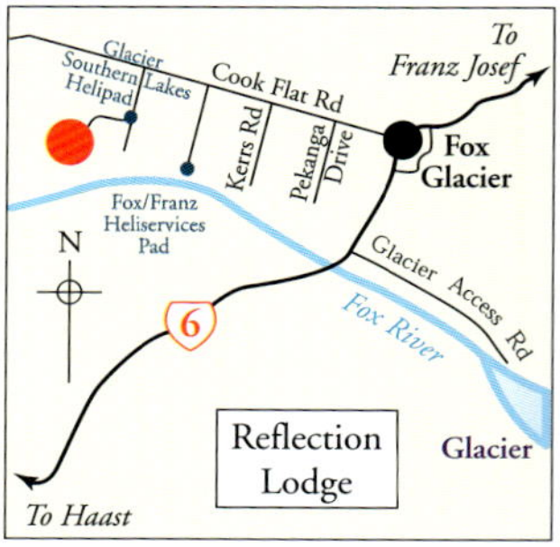

Welcome to the 'Glacier Region'. **Reflection Lodge** offers panoramic views of Mount Cook and Mount Tasman. New Zealand's two highest peaks reflecting in our very own private lake. Colin, a local helicopter pilot, and Raelene are fourth generation 'West Coasters' and have lived and worked in the glacier region for over 12 years. We invite you to share the comfort of our home and gardens. We are more than happy to assist you with any activities in our picturesque region. We enjoy meeting people and look forward to sharing our wonderful piece of paradise with you.

"Leave everything the way it is. You cannot improve the perfect." Wolfgang Hebs, Wipperfuerth, Germany

"I feel comfortable. Just like I'm staying in my home." Yuko Sekiguchi, Nagoya, Japan

"Wonderful – we'll come again!" Peter & Billy Constable, Cincinnatti Ohio, USA

Ropatini's Homestay B&B

81 Cook Flat Road, Box 15, Fox Glacier
Ph (03) 751 0779, Fax (03) 751 0789
email: *ropatinis@xtra.co.nz*

Tariff : N.Z. Dollars	
Double	$130-230
Single	
Child	

Bedrooms	Qty
Double	4
Twin	1
Single	
Bed Size	**Qty**
Super King	3
King	
Queen	1
Double	
Single	2
Bathrooms	**Qty**
Ensuite	3
Private	
Guest Share	1

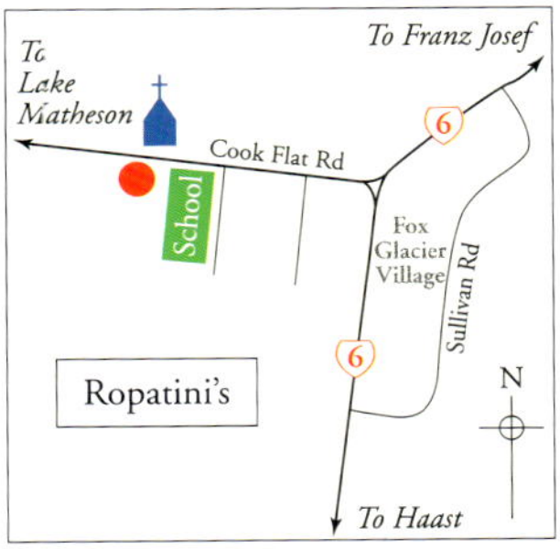

Quality Bed & Breakfast
Self-contained & Cottages

Ropatini's

- *Ensuite or guest share*
- *Unique dining room table*
- *Great views of Mt Cook*
- *Dinner by arrangement*
- *Large gardens*
- *Free wireless broadband*
- *Free email access*
- *Glacier & Lake Matheson nearby*

Haere mai and welcome to our warm, comfortable home. We enjoy our large peaceful gardens and the spectacular views of the Southern Alps and Mount Cook. Travellers are always welcome here and we try to make them feel as comfortable as we do. The separate garden studios, with mountain views are ideal for those who like a little space of their own, and have super king beds, cosy bedding, turbo showers, heater, TV, fridge, tea and cofffee facilities. In the main house choose either an ensuite room or one of the two rooms which share a bathroom. Our dining room has this view of Mt Cook and a special unforgettable table. Refreshments and home baking are always available. We can help plan your day with local attractions and activities – from a peaceful fifteen minute walk to the thrill of ice climbing. Join us for pre dinner drinks served with genuine Kiwi hospitality and chat about your travels – stay for dinner or restaurants nearby. You are welcome to stay for a night or longer .

The White Fox

4 State Highway 6, PO Box 82, Fox Glacier
Ph (03) 751 0717, Mobile 027-306 6759
email: *thewhitefox@xtra.co.nz*
www.thewhitefoxbandb.co.nz

Tariff : N.Z. Dollars	
Double	$130-160
Single	$100-130
Child	neg by age

Bedrooms	Qty
Double	1
Twin	
Single	
Bed Size	**Qty**
Super King	
King	
Queen	1
Double	
Single	1
Bathrooms	**Qty**
Ensuite	1
Private	
Guest Share	

**Genuine NZ Family
Quality Homestay B&B**

Features & Attractions

- *Native bush & birdlife*
- *Local hosts, local knowledge*
- *Itinerary planning/booking*
- *Warm, friendly, relaxed*
- *Tea/coffee/home-baking*
- *Email/internet/laundry*
- *Stroll to restaurants and shops*
- *5 km to Fox Glacier & Lake Matheson*

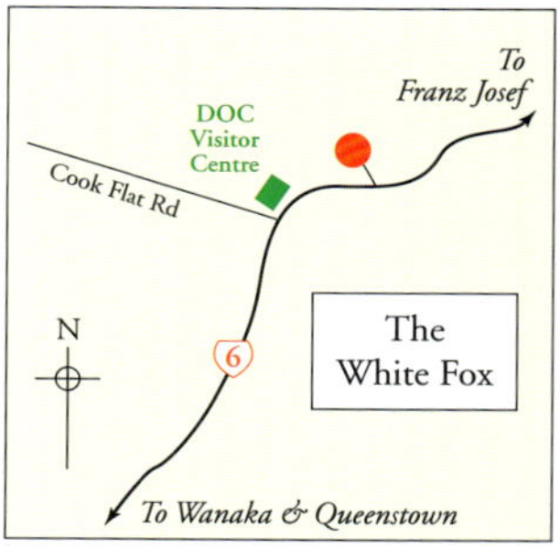

The White Fox offers you the convenience of a central location where you can relax and enjoy the genuine hospitality of a real New Zealand family home. Our property combines the peaceful outlook of Westland National Park bush and birdlife with an easy to find location on the Main Road. Your room has a superior comfort bed, quality linen, electric blankets and TV. The modern ensuite includes toiletries and hairdryer. Our house is sunny and warm and heated by a wood burner on the occasional rainy West Coast day! Our 'Continental Plus' breakfast includes cereals, fruits, yoghurt, home baked bread plus eggs or French Toast. Coffee lovers can linger over a hot, creamy latte. Experience a real home coming welcome by our young daughters Meghan (3) and Isla (1), Triumph Bonneville the tabby cat and an occasional Border Collie dog (Jess).

"An excellent homestay, lovely family, lovely food, good advice on what to do and where to go" - David and Janet Martin, Yorks, UK.

THE HOMESTEAD

Cook Flat Road, PO Box 25, Fox Glacier
Ph (03) 751 0835, Fax (03) 751 0805
email: *foxhomstd@xtra.co.nz*

@ home NEW ZEALAND

Tariff : N.Z. Dollars	
Double	$140-175
Single	
Child	

Bedrooms	Qty
Double	2
Twin	1
Single	
Bed Size	**Qty**
Super King	
King	1
Queen	1
Double	
King/Single	2
Bathrooms	**Qty**
Ensuite	2
Private	1
Guest Share	

DIRECTIONS:
On Cook Flat Road **The Homestead** is the 5th house on the right, 450m back from road.

Farm Retreat Amidst Stunning Scenery

Features & Attractions

- *Stained glass windows*
- *Stunning mountain views*
- *Delicious breakfast*
- *Peaceful rural retreat*
- *Guest lounge*
- *A place to unwind*
- *Children 7+ welcome*
- *Close to village facilities*

Kevin and Noeleen Williams welcome you to our 2200 acre sheep, beef-cattle farm. Beautiful native bush clad mountains surround our paradise, and we enjoy a view of Mount Cook. Our spacious 100-year-old character home, built for Kevin's grandparents, has fine stained glass windows. The breakfast room overlooks the house paddocks, and you are served homemade jams, marmalade, yoghurt, hot scones etc. Our guest lounge has a beautiful timbered ceiling, with an open fire for cooler nights. A variety of teas and coffees are provided.

The Homestead is a rural retreat within walking distance of village facilities. Famous Lake Matheson (Mirror Lake) and glacier are nearby.

It is our pleasure to help you with your helicopter flights, glacier walks and onward reservations.

Mahitahi Lodge

SH 6, P O Box 130, Bruce Bay, South Westland
Ph (03) 751 0095, Fax (03) 751 0195
email: *stay@mahitahilodge.co.nz*
www.mahitahilodge.co.nz

Features & Attractions

- *Genuine West Coast hospitality*
- *Within walking distance of beach*
- *Dinner available*
- *Short drive to glaciers*
- *Veranda from each bedroom*
- *Activities available*

Boutique Accommodation

$	
Double	$245-295
Single	$195-245
Child	

Situated only 30 minutes south of Fox Glacier and 50 minutes north of Haast, and surrounded by the magnificent South Westland landscape, this Boutique Lodge featuring various West Coast native timbers, provides an intimate atmosphere, where guests are treated to the utmost hospitality. All guest rooms have ensuite bathrooms complete with heated floors and mirrors, bathrobes, hairdryers and toiletries. There is also a fully self-contained suite available suitable as a family unit. Enjoy our selection of local cuisine, fine NZ wines and John's complimentary interpretation tour of the area. It's all here – fishing, hunting, bush walking, the beach and wonderful photographic opportunities – and it's peaceful as well.

Bedrooms	Qty
Double	3
Twin	2
Single	
Bed Size	**Qty**
Super King	2
Queen	1
Double	
Single	2
Bathrooms	**Qty**
Ensuite	3
Private	
Guest Share	

DIRECTIONS:
Bruce Bay is approximately 35 minutes south of Fox Glacier and 50 minutes north of Haast. **Mahitahi Lodge** is situated on SH 6 directly opposite the historic Bruce Bay Hall.

Okuru - Haast ▶ YOUR HOSTS: **Marian and Derek Beynon** Ph: (03) 750 0719

Okuru Beach

Okuru, Haast, South Westland
Ph (03) 750 0719, Fax (03) 750 0722
email: *okurubeach@xtra.co.nz*
www.okurubeach.co.nz

Features & Attractions

- *Walking distance to beach*
- *Fiordland Crested Penguins*
- *Enjoyable forest walks*
- *Good trout fishing*
- *Craft shop for guests*
- *Friendly and relaxed*

$	
Double	$85
Single	$55
Child	$25

Self-contained: $85-95 per night
Extra person: $10-15. Sleeps 10

Homestay Bed & Breakfast

Bedrooms	Qty
Double	4
Twin	3
Single	
Bed Size	**Qty**
Twin	6
Queen	
Double	4
Single	4
Bathrooms	**Qty**
Ensuite	1
Private	2
Guest Share	1

Okuru Beach gives you the opportunity to stay in a unique part of our country where time moves slowly. Enjoy the coastal beaches with interesting driftwood and shells. On a walk in the rainforest a variety of native birds can be viewed. In the season, Fiordland Crested Penguins can be seen within walking distance along a rocky beach, near Jackson's Bay, a 30-minute drive away. We and our friendly labrador dogs enjoy sharing our comfortable home and local knowledge of the area. With prior notice we can serve dinner at $25 per person, BYO, vegetarian is available. Our interests are handcrafts, coin collecting, fishing and tramping. We enjoy the chance to meet new people from New Zealand and overseas. Complimentary tea or coffee on arrival.

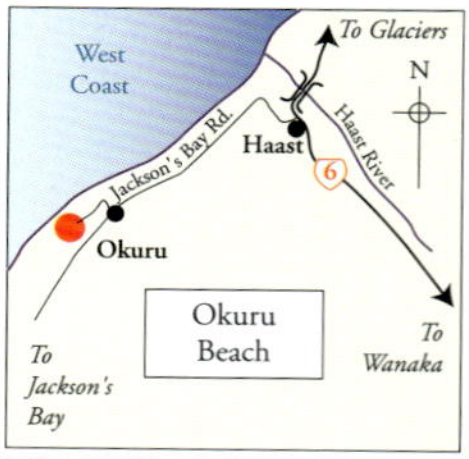

Collyer House

Jackson Bay Road, PO Box 63, Haast
Ph (03) 750 0022, Fax (03) 750 0023
email: *collyerhouse@xtra.co.nz*
www.collyerhouse.co.nz

Tariff : N.Z. Dollars	
Double	$250
Single	$200
Child	

Bedrooms	Qty
Double	3
Twin	1
Single	
Bed Size	**Qty**
Super King	1
King	
Queen	1
Double	1
Single	2
Bathrooms	**Qty**
Ensuite	4
Private	
Guest Share	

Bed & Breakfast
Luxury Accommodation

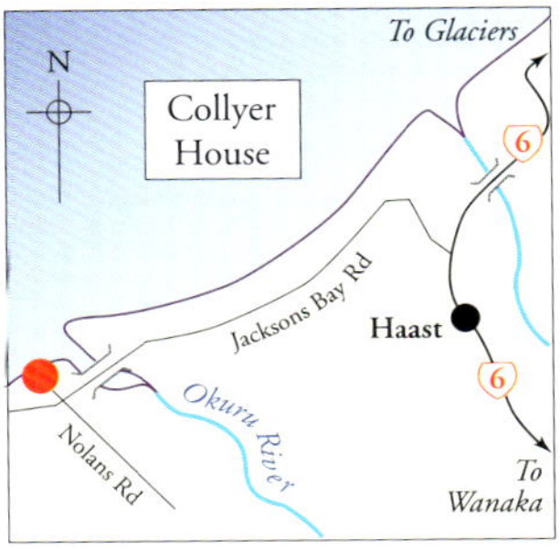

Features & Attractions

- *Genuine hospitality*
- *Peace & quiet*
- *Stunning sea views*
- *Dinner by arrangement*
- *Scenic flights*
- *Jet boating*
- *World heritage area*
- *Antiques & quality fittings*

Collyer House has been purpose built on this isolated coastline, to offer comfort along with peace and quiet to travellers. It has been tastefully furnished, using antiques and quality fittings, and the spacious living areas are dominated by a large open fire made from local stone, a perfect place to relax. The well appointed bedrooms all have French doors leading to the verandah and the ensuites all have baths, bathrobes, heated towel rails, hair dryers and toiletries.

Every room in the house has a magnificent view of the river estuary and the Tasman Sea. I am the fourth generation of a pioneering family and enjoy sharing my knowledge and the history of this special place. After 28 years of travel and working in the city I have returned here to carry on a family tradition of great hospitality.

ARDARA LODGE

233 Schoolhouse Road, Kaikoura
Ph (03) 319 5736, Fax (03) 319 5732
email: *aemboyd@xtra.co.nz*
www.ardaralodge.com

@home NEW ZEALAND

Tariff : N.Z. Dollars	
Double	$110-135
Single	$100-120
Cottage	$140-250

Bedrooms	Qty
Double	6
Twin	2
Single	2
Bed Size	**Qty**
Super King	
King	
Queen	7
Double	
Single	4
Bathrooms	**Qty**
Ensuite	6
Private	
Guest Share	

Bed & Breakfast
Self-contained Accommodation

Features & Attractions

- *Spectacular mountain view*
- *Whalewatch/dolphins 5min*
- *Quiet & tranquil*
- *Hot-tub / Spa*
- *Walk to 'Donegal House', Irish restaurant and bar*
- *Guest lounge with Sky TV*
- *Off-street parking*

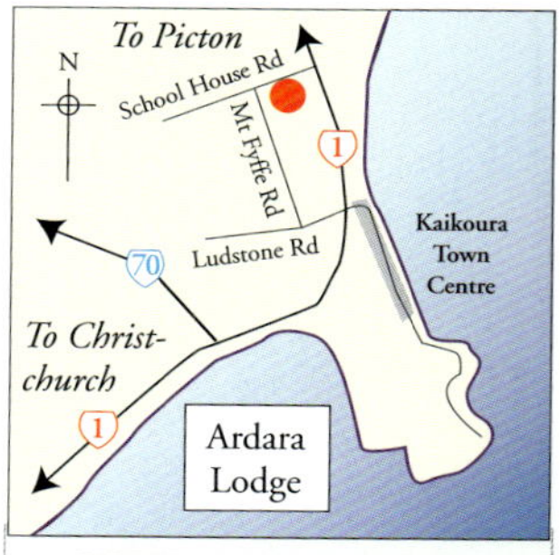

DIRECTIONS: Driving north from Kaikoura on SH 1 (Atheney Road) turn left into **Schoolhouse Road** 1.5 km to **Ardara Lodge**.

You will enjoy a relaxed and peaceful stay in a beautiful rural setting near the magnificent Kaikoura mountains. Relax on our deck, view the mountain panorama, and enjoy Alison's colourful garden. Use our outdoor hot-tub (spa), read in our new guest lounge. **Cottage** (designed and built by Ian in 1998): upstairs bedroom, queen bed/two single beds. Downstairs, queen bed, bathroom with shower, lounge and kitchen. Private deck with a mountain view. **House**: Five ensuite rooms, queen beds, two triple rooms, one two bedroom unit. All units have TV, fridge, settee, coffee/tea facilities and private entrance. Come and go as you please. Guest lounge, laundry facilities, off-street parking. Ian's great-great uncle came from Ardara, Ireland, in 1883 and settled on this land in Kaikoura. Ian's brother, Murray, has Donegal House, an Irish Bar and Restaurant, which is within walking distance. Ian is a retired teacher and Alison a retired librarian. No smoking indoors please. We look forward to your company.

AUSTIN HEIGHTS

19 Austin Street, Kaikoura
Ph (03) 319 5836, Fax (03) 319 6836
email: *austinheights@xtra.co.nz*
www.austinheights.co.nz

Tariff : N.Z. Dollars	
Double	$160-240
Single	$150-180
Child	neg

Bedrooms	Qty
Double	2
Twin	
Single	
Bed Size	**Qty**
Super King	1
King	
Queen	1
Double	
Single	2
Bathrooms	**Qty**
Ensuite	2
Private	1
Guest Share	

Boutique Bed & Breakfast on the Peninsula

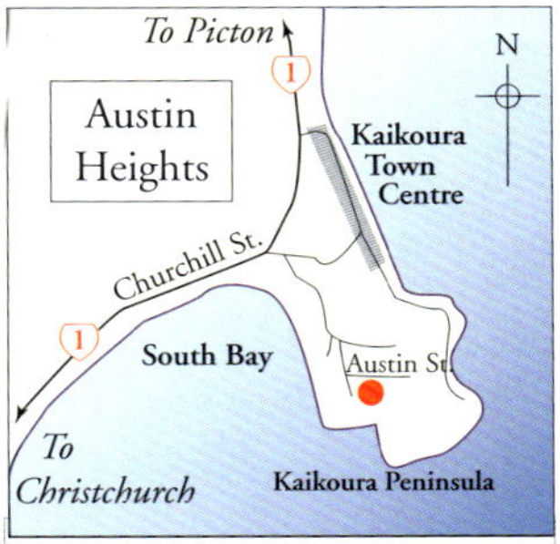

DIRECTIONS: From the south turn right before town centre into Scarborough St. 2 km Austin St is 2nd on left. From north by-pass town centre & turn left into Scarborough St.

Features & Attractions

- *Central to all major attractions*
- *Panoramic sea & mountain views*
- *Beautiful coastal walks*
- *Courtesy bus/train transfer*
- *Luxury outdoor spa*
- *Balcony from each room*
- *Guests private entrance*
- *Prize winning gardens*

Lynne, John and Oscar our friendly Ragdoll cat welcome you to **Austin Heights.** Situated on a prime elevated site on the Kaikoura peninsula with stunning views of the sea and Kaikoura ranges capped with snow most of the year. You will be central to whalewatch, dolphin encounters, the seal colony, local winery, town centre and the beach is only a short walk away. You have a choice of a super-king or a queen bed in the apartments. The rooms are sunny and have great views. Each opens out directly onto a balcony where you can relax. Each apartment has a flat screen TV, DVD, movies, stereo, CD player, local books, refrigerator, microwave, tea/coffee facilities, biscuits, chocolates, kitchenette, heating, hair-dryer , toiletries, bathrobes and heated towel rails. The most comfortable beds, (our guests always say) with quality bedding, electric blankets and woolrests. We serve a generous continental breakfast in the privacy of your room or with hosts in dining area. A cooked breakfast is available on request.

Admiral Creighton Bed & Breakfast

191 Beach Rd, Kaikoura
Ph (03) 319 7111, Fax (03) 319 7111
Free Ph: 0800 742 622
email: *admiral.creighton.b2b@ihug.co.nz*
www.admiral-creighton.com

Tariff : N.Z. Dollars	
Double	$120-160
Single	
Child	

Bedrooms	Qty
Double	4
Twin	1
Single	
Bed Size	**Qty**
Super King	
King	
Queen	4
Double	
King/Single	1
Bathrooms	**Qty**
Ensuite	3
Private	2
Guest Share	

Quality Bed & Breakfast Fine Accommodation

Features & Attractions

- *Whale watching & dolphin swim*
- *Set on stream boundary*
- *Level off-street parking*
- *Golf, fishing, arts & crafts*
- *Peaceful, rural setting*
- *Fishing and albatross tours*
- *Scenic flights, horse trek*
- *Walking distance to town*

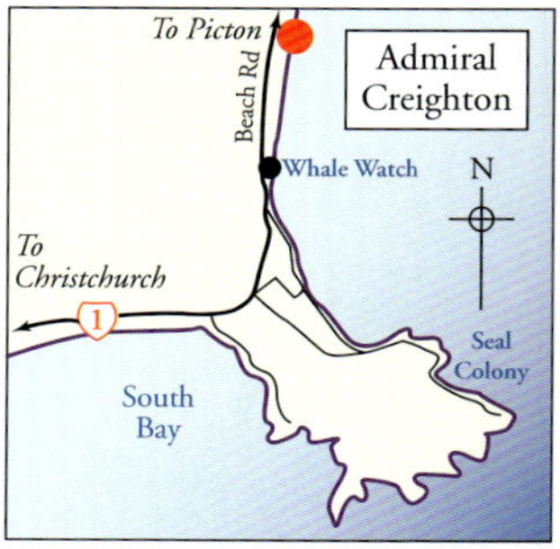

Where the mountains meet the sea.
You will enjoy staying at this lovely Bed & Breakfast. Peace and tranquility ensure that you will relax in the stunning surroundings which make the **Admiral Creighton** such a special place. Enjoy a cooked or continental breakfast, select from our menu.

While enjoying your complimentary drink, relax in the large lounge or outside living area. Enjoy the local wildlife in our stream as the ducks, trout and eels are fed. Creighton, our well behaved cockatoo, will welcome you warmly.

At the **Admiral Creighton**, we are always happy to assist with bookings for Kaikoura's attractions. Finding the best place to dine out is always a challenge. We will help you with your transport requirements. The property is fully government compliant for your health and safety. The one-level property is set back from the main highway with plenty of parking.

Awatea Country Bed & Breakfast

29 Skevingtons Road, RD 1, Kaikoura
Ph (03) 319 7075, Fax (03) 319 7075
Mobile 021-318 759
email: *info@awatea.co.nz*
www.awatea.co.nz

Features & Attractions

- *Amazing mountain & sea views*
- *Minutes to town, Whale Watch etc*
- *Spacious guest lounge*
- *Close to good restaurants*
- *Tranquil, quiet, private*
- *Walking distance to beach*

$		
	Double	$160
	Single	$100
	Child	neg

Bed & Breakfast

Bedrooms	Qty
Double	3
Twin	1
Single	
Bed Size	**Qty**
King	
Queen	3
Double	
King/Single	2
Bathrooms	**Qty**
Ensuite	4
Private	
Guest Share	

Only minutes from all of Kaikoura's tourist attractions, with spectacular mountain and sea views, **Awatea** offers quiet country accommodation for the discerning traveller. Relax by the fire in the spacious guest lounge or enjoy your cup of tea on the sunny patio. All rooms have ensuite facilities, TV, electric blankets, hairdryers and are warm and welcoming. Laundry done at your request. You can walk to the beach on quiet country roads. There is a courtesy car service and I will help you arrange your activities so that you don't miss a thing while in Kaikoura. Travelling with your horse? Grazing is available and there is plenty of parking for floats or horse trucks. Is your dog with you? Kennels are available. **Awatea** is a pet friendly place to stay.

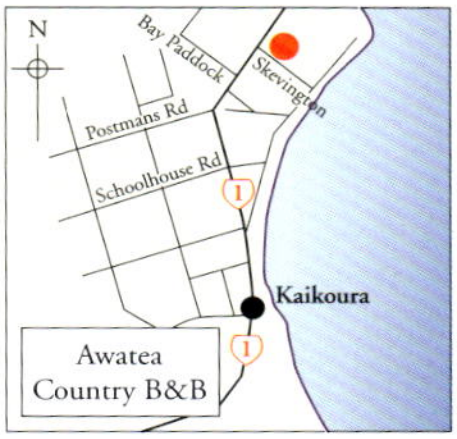

Carrickfin Lodge B & B Lodge

Mill Road, Kaikoura
Ph (03) 319 5165, Fax (03) 319 5162
Mobile 025- 315 076
email: *rogerboyd@xtra.co.nz*
www.carrickfinlodge.co.nz

Features & Attractions

- *Stunning view of Kaikoura Mts.*
- *Whale watch*
- *Dolphin swimming*
- *Bird-watching trip*
- *Horse trekking*
- *Peninsula walks*

$		
	Double	$120-130
	Single	$120
	Child	

Bed & Big Irish Breakfast
Self-Contained Cottage

DIRECTIONS: Mill Rd is 3km north of the township on No1 Highway. Easy to find and hard to leave! **Carrickfin Cottage** is located 90m from the **Lodge**.

Bedrooms	Qty
Double	5
Twin	
Single	1
Bed Size	**Qty**
King	
Queen	5
Double	
Single	1
Bathrooms	**Qty**
Ensuite	6
Private	
Guest Share	

Welcome to Kaikoura. My name is Roger and I am the 4th generation 'Boyd' to live and farm **Carrickfin** which has been home of the Boyds since 1867. My great grandfather bought and settled on this land in 1867 for 100 gold sovereigns. The **Lodge** is built on 100 acres adjoining Kaikoura township. It was built well back from the road amidst 2 acres of lawn, shrubs and trees, making it private and peaceful. Most rooms have stunning views of Kaikoura Mountains which are home to a unique variety of wildlife. Two large lounges with open fire, guest bar (BYO) and 24 hour coffee/tea making facilities make it most welcoming. The main feature of the **Lodge** is the '**Big Irish Breakfast**', which is legendary. We are 3km from the Whale Watch, Dolphin Encounter and some of the best restaurants. To view the **Lodge** and **Carrickfin Cottage** (great for families) go to the website and you will love it!

BENDAMERE HOUSE BED & BREAKFAST

BED & BREAKFAST AND HOMESTAY
37 Adelphi Terrace, Kaikoura 8280
Free Ph: 0800 107 770, Fax (03) 319 7337
email: *bendamerehouse@xtra.co.nz*
www.bendamere.co.nz

Tariff : N.Z. Dollars	
Double	$130-190
Single	$100-130
Child	neg

Bedrooms	Qty
Double	6
Twin	
Single	
Bed Size	**Qty**
Super King	
King	
Queen	6
Double	
Single	5
Bathrooms	**Qty**
Ensuite	6
Private	
Guest Share	

Bed & Breakfast
Scenic Homestay

Features & Attractions

- *5 min. walk to township*
- *Large gardens & lawns*
- *Quiet, private & peaceful*
- *Ample sealed off-street parking*
- *Five bedrooms enjoy sea views*
- *Large family dining room*
- *Enjoy local seafood, & dine alfresco*
- *Courtesy transfers*

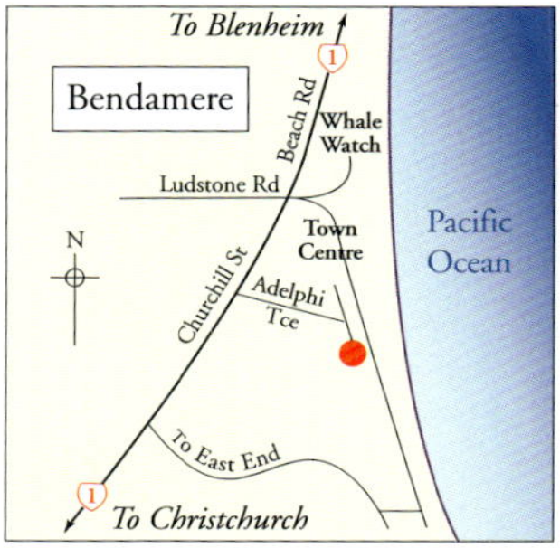

We are fourth generation Kaikourians with an extensive knowledge of the area. **Bendamere House**, with its large lawn and gardens is just 5 minutes walk to the township, beach, restaurants and various local attractions, and takes in incredible views of the Pacific Ocean and Kaikoura Ranges. We have the **Fairweather Room**; and have added our four new boutique rooms, which were completed December 2005. The **Langman** and **Hampden Rooms** on the ground floor with the **Hampden** having wheelchair facilities. The **Hartnell** and **Harrington Rooms** are on the first floor. All rooms have first class facilities with large ensuites, queen and single beds, TV, tea and coffee making, bath robes, electric blankets and heat pumps. Special breakfast is served in our dining room. A cooked breakfast is also available on request. These new rooms all have panoramic views with balconies opening out to lawns and gardens. We offer home-made cookies and a courtesy car is available to meet public transport.

Bush & Sea Boutique Bed & Breakfast

14 Takahanga Terrace, Kaikoura
Ph (03) 319 6789, Fax (03) 319 6709
Mobile 027-4813150
email: *info@bushandsea.co.nz*
www.bushandsea.co.nz

Tariff : N.Z. Dollars	
Double	$165-230
Single	$165-220
Child	

Bedrooms	Qty
Double	2
Twin	
Single	
Bed Size	**Qty**
Super King	1
King	
Queen	1
Double	
Single	
Bathrooms	**Qty**
Ensuite	2
Private	
Guest Share	

Panoramic Sea Views
Indulgent Accommodation

Features & Attractions

- *Delicious breakfast menu*
- *Guided photography trips*
- *5 min. walk to town, cafés, etc*
- *On-site massage therapy*
- *Stunning sea views over bush reserve*
- *Intimate B&B with just 2 suites*
- *Whale watch & dolphin swimming*
- *Guest decks and outdoor furniture*

DIRECTIONS: On Churchill St (SH1) turn into Deal St, then 1st right into Takahanga Tce

Our home is nestled above a bush reserve with fabulous sea views yet is only minutes walk into Kaikoura's township with its busy café scene. We are well travelled Kiwi hosts, who enjoy the outdoors, music, family and friends and our Bed & Breakfast! Hence we have only two suites, so we can offer great service to our guests.

Our suites are purpose built with tiled ensuites and underfloor heating. They are sound insulated and have CD/DVD players, silent fridges, tea/coffee (fresh) making facilities, hair dryers, electric blankets, private access and decks with outdoor furniture. The wonderful comfort of our beds is always mentioned by our guests!

John and Diane Mellows, UK: "One of the highlights of our trip was undoubtedly our stay with you, in particular the wonderful crayfish, which Scott prepared for us."

Chantal Fisher, Paris: "Beautiful room, spectacular views from the deck and great welcome from a lovely couple!"

Bush & Sea Bed & Breakfast is an excellent base for local and regional tourist attractions, so allow for two nights stay. (Check our website for current package deals).

Churchill Park Lodge

34 Churchill Street, Kaikoura
Ph (03) 319 5526, Fax (03) 319 5526
email: *cplodge@ihug.co.nz*
www.churchillparklodge.co.nz

Features & Attractions

- *Awesome views*
- *Central location*
- *Friendly hospitality*
- *Quality accommodation*
- *Smoke-free rooms*
- *Private guest balcony*

Superb Bed & Breakfast Accommodation

$	
Double	$95-120
Single	$95-120
Child	$20

We proudly offer two upstairs suites with ensuite bathrooms, TV, fridge, settee, tea/coffee making facilities, heater and electric blankets.
We believe the sea and mountain views we offer from your room are unbeatable in Kaikoura. Watch the sun rise out of the sea from your balcony while enjoying your continental breakfast, or relax over your complimentary wine and nibbles. Take a five minute walk through Churchill Park to the town where you will find a selection of shops. We are in close walking distance to the beach, Whalewatch, Dolphin Encounter and are happy to book tours.
We are a Christian couple and like Muffy, our cat, are friendly and welcoming and look forward to making your stay a time to remember.
Laundry facilities, off-street parking. Courtesy pick-up from train or bus station.

Bedrooms	Qty
Double	1
Twin	1
Single	
Bed Size	**Qty**
King	
Queen	1
Double	1
Single	1
Bathrooms	**Qty**
Ensuite	2
Private	
Guest Share	

ENDEAVOUR HEIGHTS BED & BREAKFAST

1 Endeavour Place, Kaikoura
Phone (03) 319 5333, Fax (03) 319 5333
Mobile 027-224 0549
email: *dreavers@xtra.co.nz*
www.endeavourheights.co.nz

Tariff : N.Z. Dollars	
Double	$160-220
Single	$150
Child	neg

Bedrooms	Qty
Double	2
Twin	
Single	
Bed Size	**Qty**
Super King	
King	2
Queen	
Double	
Single	
Bathrooms	**Qty**
Ensuite	1
Private	1
Guest Share	

Boutique Bed & Breakfast

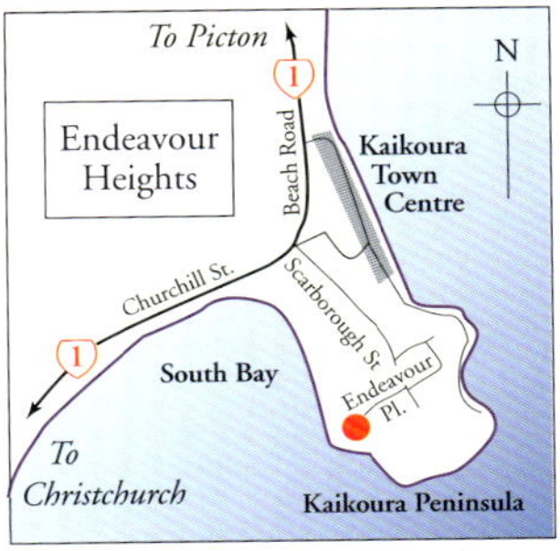

Features & Attractions

- *Stunning sea & mountain view*
- *Elevated views*
- *Luxury bathrooms with baths*
- *Cafés, restaurants & shops nearby*
- *Private balconies – outdoor living*
- *Overlooking Peninsula Walkway*
- *Private and peaceful*
- *Warm kiwi hosts*

Endeavour Heights truly portrays excellence in hospitality,quality accommodation and scenic views. Nestled within the Kaikoura Peninsula, guests will experience a warm welcome from their kiwi hosts, Janice and Grant. **Endeavour Heights** is centrally located amidst Kaikoura's major tourist attractions, such as the popular Seal Colony, Peninsula Walkway and the Kaikoura township, all of which are accessible by foot. Guests may choose between the **Te Moana** suite, a luxury private apartment, or the **Te Maunga** suite with a large private bathroom and separate level living. Both rooms offer king beds, luxury bed linen, deep baths and comfortable surroundings.

Embrace the magnificence of the breathtaking views of *"Kaikoura, where the mountains meet the sea"* from your room and own private balcony. We welcome you to **Endeavour Heights,** warm, relaxing and peaceful. Easy to find but hard to leave.

Lemon Tree Lodge

31 Adelphi Terrace, Kaikoura
Ph (03) 319 7464, Fax (03) 319 7467
Mobile 027-648 0670
email: *info@lemontree.co.nz*
www.lemontree.co.nz

Tariff : N.Z. Dollars	
Double	$140-240
Single	$140-240
Child	n/a

Bedrooms	Qty
Double	4
Twin	
Single	
Bed Size	**Qty**
Super King	
King	1
Queen	3
Double	
Single	
Bathrooms	**Qty**
Ensuite	4
Private	
Guest Share	

Boutique Bed & Breakfast

Features & Attractions

- *Spectacular ocean & mountain views*
- *Whale-watch & dolphins 2 minutes*
- *Relaxed atmosphere*
- *Cafés, restaurants, shops nearby*
- *Classic and contemporary design and furnishings*
- *Luxury hot tub*
- *All rooms with ensuite*

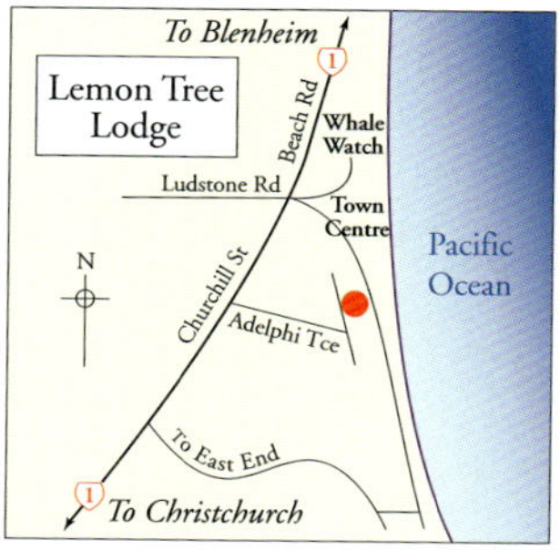

Overlooking Kaikoura with spectacular ocean and mountain views. We are centrally situated and in easy walking distance of all the major activities, cafés and shops. Our four classic contemporary designed non-smoking rooms have shower ensuite facilities, television, hair dryers, iron & ironing boards, bathrobes, mini fridges, beverage facilities, heating, and complimentary fruit & chocolate. Two of the rooms have elevated magnificent sea and mountain views and have their own private balconies. The other two are set in a relaxing garden environment with their own private deck. To the front of the building is a luxury 5/6-person hot tub and viewing deck where our guests can relax and soak up the views and atmosphere. A freshly made continental breakfast can be served in the morning to your room or you can book in on a room only basis (cooked breakfast is available). We cater for singles, couples and small groups. Not suitable for children.

Old Convent Bed & Breakfast

Mt Fyffe Road, Kaikoura
Ph (03) 319 6603, Fax (03) 319 6690
email: *o.convent@xtra.co.nz*
www.theoldconvent.co.nz

Tariff : N.Z. Dollars	
Double	$120-185
Single	$95
Child	

Bedrooms	Qty
Double	15
Twin	7
Single	15
Bed Size	**Qty**
Super King	4
King	
Queen	5
Double	5
Single	11
Bathrooms	**Qty**
Ensuite	15
Private	
Guest Share	

Bed & Breakfast
"Where the Whales Are"

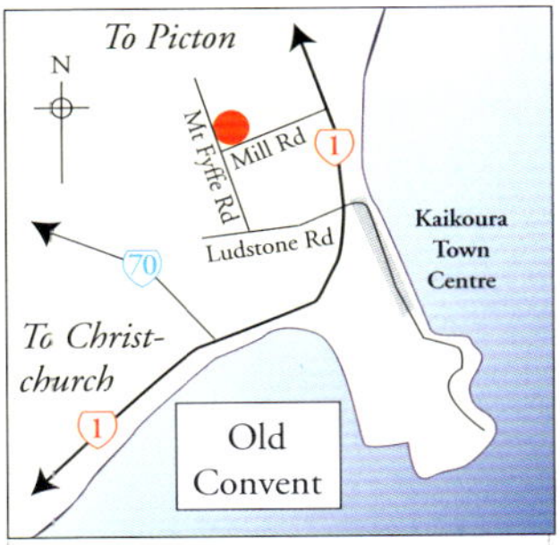

DIRECTIONS: Turn off SH1 at Mill Rd or take Ludstone Rd, then Mt Fyffe Rd.

Features & Attractions

- *Glorious garden setting*
- *Peaceful, tranquil*
- *Divine food*
- *4 min. to town/whales*
- *Cooked breakfast*
- *Indoor/outdoor dining*
- *Great dawn chorus*
- *Family friendly*

The **Old Convent** is reminiscent of a warm, lively country inn, where there is top-class food, including Kaikoura crayfish, venison and lamb and the famous chocolate cake, good conversation and a friendly atmosphere. The Chapel, now the lounge, the sunny deck and the travellers' bar are lovely places to sit and read or chat.
The owners, with backgrounds in journalism, human rights, aid work and heritage building restoration, have a wealth of knowledge of New Zealand. Their families settled in the Kaikoura and Otago areas in the 1850s.

"Before Gordon handed us the keys we knew we wanted to stay another night." – Guest 2006.

PACIFIC ALLURE HEIGHTS

278 Scarborough St, Kaikoura
Ph/Fax (03) 319 5669, Mobile 021-319 735
email: *accommodation@pacificallure.co.nz*
www.pacificallure.co.nz

Tariff : N.Z. Dollars	
Double	$160-200
Single	$120-180
Child	$15

Bedrooms	Qty
Double	1
Twin	1
Single	
Bed Size	**Qty**
Super King	
King	2
Queen	
Double	
Single	
Bathrooms	**Qty**
Ensuite	2
Private	
Guest Share	

BB **Boutique Accommodation with Stunning Views** BA

VISA MasterCard eftpos

Features & Attractions

- *Spectacular ocean & mountain views*
- *15 min. walk from renowned Peninsula walkway*
- *Close to town*
- *Contemporary design and furnishings*
- *All rooms have private courtyard and gardens*
- *All rooms are self-contained with bathroom and kitchen*
- *Private entrance to each room*

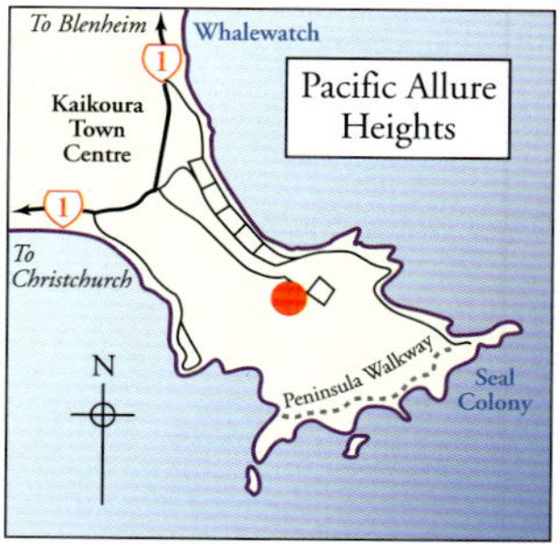

Stunning inside and out! Relax in comfort in modern, self-contained apartments which open onto private courtyards with sweeping views of the Pacific Ocean and the Seaward Kaikoura Ranges.

Pacific Allure Heights is located on the Kaikoura Peninsula, nestled amongst beautiful gardens just a short walk from both the Kaikoura township and the popular Peninsula Walkway.

We offer king rooms with private ensuites, TV, tea/coffee making facilities, microwave, double glazing and off-street parking. Tariff includes continental breakfast.

Bookings can be arranged for popular local activities such as whale watching, dolphin, bird and seal swimming.

Your hosts, Judy and Alan, care about your comfort and are committed to making your stay a memorable one.

Gore Bay Lodge

716 Gore Bay Road, R D 3, Cheviot
Ph (03) 319 8870, Fax (03) 319 8871
email: *gorebaylodge@xtra.co.nz*
www.gorebaylodge.co.nz

Tariff : N.Z. Dollars	
Double	$140-160
Single	
Child	

Bedrooms	Qty
Double	2
Twin	1
Single	
Bed Size	**Qty**
Super King	
King	
Queen	3
Double	
Single	1
Bathrooms	**Qty**
Ensuite	3
Private	
Guest Share	

Sea-Side Luxury Bed & Breakfast

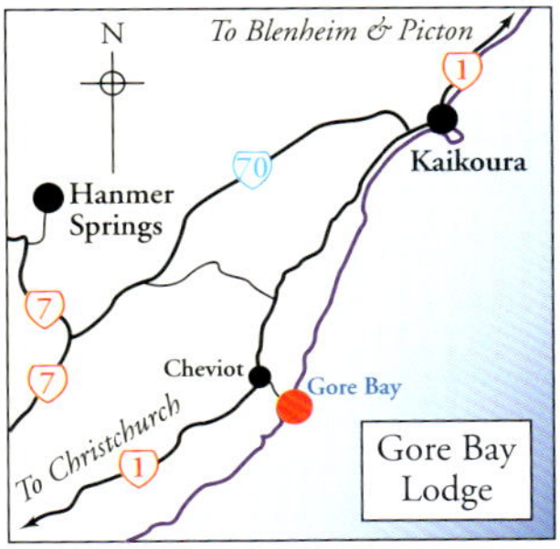

Features & Attractions

- *Swimming, surfing, fishing*
- *Golfing, bush walks*
- *1 hour drive to Hanmer*
- *1 hour drive to Kaikoura*
- *1¼ hour drive to Christchurch*
- *Waipara winery 45 minutes*
- *Excellent restaurants 8 minutes*
- *Micro climate (no frosts)*

Your hosts, Jillian and Lyndon, welcome you to **Gore Bay Lodge**, located right on the beachfront of one of New Zealand's most popular surfing and swimming beaches. The unique microclimate (no frosts) ensures year round beach walks, tennis, bush walks, golf and fishing. Built in 2005, **Gore Bay Lodge** provides three self-contained suites, each with uninterrupted sea views, a private deck and a kitchenette to enable guests to self-cater if desired.

Each guestroom has an ensuite bathroom with toiletries and bathrobes. A games room has a pool table, TV and lounge suite overlooking the beach. We have available a guests' barbecue area, fax, email, and shared self-service laundry facilities. Tea, coffee, filtered water, TV and fridge available in all bedrooms and a continental breakfast is served in guestrooms.

"The Lodge that Friends recommend to Friends".

Bell Bird Haven

20 Lulu's Lane, Mt Lyford, RD Waiau
Ph (03) 315 6411, Fax (03) 315 6442
Mobile 021-931 990
email: *info@mt-lyford.com*
www.mt-lyford.com

Tariff : N.Z. Dollars	
Double	$180
Single	$150
Child	

Bedrooms	Qty
Double	2
Twin	
Single	
Bed Size	**Qty**
Super King	
King	
Queen	2
Double	
Single	
Bathrooms	**Qty**
Ensuite	2
Private	
Guest Share	

Bed & Breakfast
Homestay

Features & Attractions

- *Stunning views/spectacular location*
- *Newly built post & beam log home*
- *Underfloor heating/double glazing*
- *Two guest rooms with ensuite*
- *Back country 4WD tours*
- *Golf, fishing*
- *Skiing/snow boarding*
- *Horse treks, hiking, walking*

You will be warmly welcomed in one of the most spectacular locations in the country.

This newly built post and beam log home is a delight to look at and live in. Situated for the sun and views with underfloor heating, double glazing and furnished to a high standard, you will be comfortable in every season.

You can stay in touch with the world via internet, fax and phone or just relax and enjoy the peace.If it's adventure you crave then this is a great place to base yourself with many activities including skiing in the winter, horse riding, 4WD tours and just a short distance to a range of golf courses, whale and dolphin encounters or thermal hot pools. This is a central place to enjoy all that North Canterbury has to offer.

Alpine B&B Hanmer

21A Leamington Street, Hanmer Springs
Ph (03) 315 5051, Fax (03) 315 5051
email: *gavinandco@callplus.net.nz*

Features & Attractions

- *Short level walk to hot pools*
- *Overlooks reserve & bush walks*
- *Handy to restaurants & shops*
- *Quality breakfast*
- *Tea & coffee facilities in room*
- *Fantastic golf course nearby*

$	
Double	$120-145
Single	$100-120
Child	

Superior Bed & Breakfast Accommodation

Bedrooms	Qty
Double	2
Twin	
Single	
Bed Size	**Qty**
King	1
Queen	1
Double	
Single	
Bathrooms	**Qty**
Ensuite	2
Private	
Guest Share	

We invite you to come and stay at our purpose designed brand new Bed & Breakfast home which opened in February 2005. We are in a tree-lined residential street with views across the Hanmer Valley to the mountains and a short level walk to the famed Hot Springs, forest walks, restaurants and shops. Each of our two ensuite guest rooms has television, private entrance, deck, tea and coffee making facilities. The king bed can be split into two singles if you wish. Breakfast will be served in your room. Your hosts (New Zealand and Dutch) have been moteliers for 15 years and, having travelled widely themselves, believe they can offer you complete unobtrusive hospitality in our delightful 'Tranquility Capital of New Zealand'. Hanmer Springs offers many activities which cater for all ages and capabilities, all to be enjoyed at your own pace without pressure. See you soon!

DIRECTIONS: Turn right at Tussock Peak Motor Lodge, go 150m down Leamington St. where you will see our sign on the right. We are 40m down the drive with parking by the house.

Mira Monte

324 Woodbank Road, Hanmer Springs
Ph (03) 315 7604, Fax (03) 315 7604
Mobile 021-129 9339
e-mail: *relax@miramonte.co.nz*
www.miramonte.co.nz

Features & Attractions

- *Village centre 5min drive*
- *Swimming pool*
- *Quiet and peaceful*
- *Large garden with mountain views*
- *Grand piano, selection CD's*
- *Golf course nearby*

$	
Double	$140-150
Single	$110
Child	neg

Delightful Countrystay Bed & Breakfast

Bedrooms	Qty
Double	2
Twin	
Single	
Bed Size	**Qty**
King	2
Queen	
Double	
Single	1
Bathrooms	**Qty**
Ensuite	2
Private	
Guest Share	

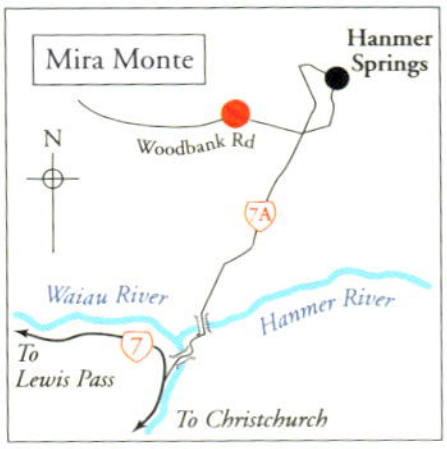

Tastefully peaceful – the ideal place to relax and enjoy a unique part of New Zealand. Near Hanmer Springs, a popular sub-alpine tourist resort, we offer delightful, warm, affordable accommodation. Lovely country garden setting. Relax in our swimming pool and enjoy the mountain outlook. We have it all! Our rooms are attractively decorated with your comfort in mind. Withdraw to your own sittingroom or join us for a coffee, wine or chat. After 20 years in the hospitality trade we know how to pamper you.

We have travelled widely and have many interests. Music, tramping and golf are some of our hobbies. We speak Dutch and German. Mindy, our Jack Russell, is part of our family. We'd love you to stay with us!

ALBERGO HANMER LODGE & ALPINE VILLA

88 Rippingale Road, Hanmer Springs,
PO Box 79, North Canterbury
Ph (03) 315 7428, Fax (03) 315 7428
email: *albergo@paradise.net.nz*
www.albergohanmer.com

Tariff : N.Z. Dollars	
Double	$150-250
Single	from $120
S/C Villa	$250-525

Bedrooms	Qty
Double	4
Twin	
Single	
Bed Size	**Qty**
Amer.King/Twin	1
Super King/Twin	3
Queen	1
Double	
Single	
Bathrooms	**Qty**
Ensuite + Spa	2
Ensuite + Bidet	1
Ensuite	1

Albergo Alpine Villas & Eclectic B&B Lodge

Features & Attractions

- *All day sun, views from all windows*
- *3-course breakfast, over 10 choices*
- *Perfect fusion of NZ & Swiss cuisine*
- *Hot pools, cafes & shops 2 min.*
- *S/C villa with cinema & hot tub*
- *Underfloor heat & aircon*
- *Fine dining by arrangement*
- *A place where magic happens*

The Wellness & Cuisine Haven in Hanmer Springs

DIRECTIONS:
At junction before main village, 300m past Caltex Garage, take Argelins Rd (centre branch), take 2nd left Rippingale Rd Albergo Hanmer is 800m down on left (sign at drive).

Arrive to dramatic alpine views, blitz your senses in fresh n' fun eclectic interiors with whimsical touches. Stretch out on super-king beds in main lodge rooms, with TV/fridge/teas and spacious ensuites – choose the spa one for that bubble bath delight! Relax in cosy corners or Feng Shui courtyard with soothing waterfall. Your dedicated hosts have spent 8 years refining this accommodation experience by creating the stylish Alpine Villa, with 'wow' views from the high panorama window, while you shower. Slip on a fluffy bathrobe and wander out to the private jacuzzi and soak up Hanmer's starry night skies. Awesome cinema (great DVD library), American king bed and kitchen/lounge. **Served at a time to suit you, Albergo's** breakfast features: Designer fruit platters or Swiss Birchermuesli, French fluffy omelettes, wafer-thin crepes, 'Albergo Egg Nests', all with crunchy Swiss bread and Italian coffee! *"Albergo is the most warmest, adorable and fun place I have ever visited. Your kindness and spirit shine through in everything"* Marcia & Paul, Colorado, USA

CHARWELL LODGE

Medway Road, PO Box 227, Hanmer Springs
Ph (03) 315 5070, Fax (03) 315 5071
Mobile 021-347 905
email: *charwell.countrystay@xtra.co.nz*
www.charwell.co.nz

Tariff : N.Z. Dollars	
Double	$210-260
Single	$190
Child	n/a

Bedrooms	Qty
Double	3
Twin	
Single	
Bed Size	**Qty**
Super King	1
King	1
Queen	1
Double	
Single	
Bathrooms	**Qty**
Ensuite	3
Private	
Guest Share	

Homestay & Countrystay

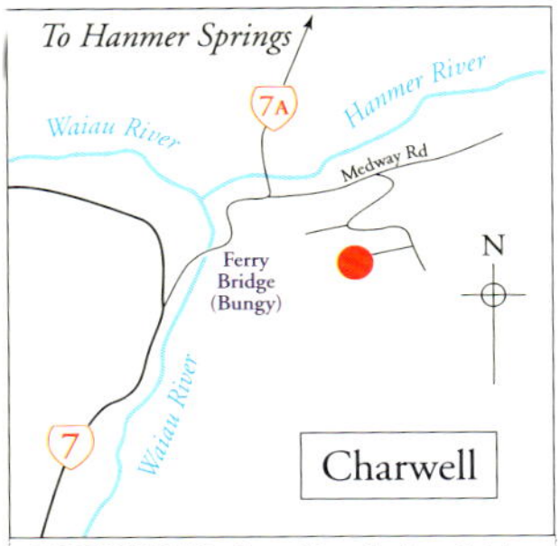

DIRECTIONS: Cross historic ferry bridge over Waiau River. 1km turn right before Hanmer River bridge, signposted to Charwell Lodge. 100m from campground take steep drive on right. Keep left on drive at fork, we are 1st turn-off on right.

Features & Attractions

- *A view from every room*
- *Tasty home cooking*
- *Large open fire*
- *8 mins to hot pools*
- *Private & peaceful*
- *Sheep dog demo avail*
- *Well travelled delightful hosts*
- *Magical alpine retreat*

A little off the beaten track, on a sunny, private hillside in the Hanmer Basin, **Charwell Lodge** offers the perfect place to relax and enjoy a little luxury. Situated 1½ hours from Christchurch Garden City and International Airport, 8 minutes from Hanmer Springs Village and Thermal Resort, 1½ hours from Kaikoura Whale Watch activities on the Alpine Pacific Triangle and 40 minutes from the Waipara wine-growing region. Ours is the perfect place to base yourselves for your visit to the South Island, be it holiday or honeymoon. The views from your ensuite room are awesome. On warm evenings you may sit on your private patio and soak in the scenery. In the winter months you can sit in front of our large open log fire and enjoy a complimentary glass of wine before sampling an evening meal at one of the many excellent restaurants in Hanmer Springs. A visit to our website www.charwell.co.nz will explain all the services we provide to make your stay an enjoyable experience.

 YOUR HOSTS: **Maree and Len Earl** Ph (03) 315 7545

CHELTENHAM HOUSE

13 Cheltenham Street, Hanmer Springs
Ph (03) 315 7545, Fax (03) 315 7645
email: *enquiries@cheltenham.co.nz*
www.cheltenham.co.nz

Tariff : N.Z. Dollars	
Double	$180-220
Single	$150-180
Child	neg

Bedrooms	Qty
Double	4
Twin	2-4
Single	
Bed Size	**Qty**
Super King/Twin	2
King	
Queen	5
Double	
Single	1
Bathrooms	**Qty**
Ensuite	5
Private	1
Guest Share	

Boutique Heritage Bed & Breakfast

Features & Attractions

- *200m to pools, restaurants, etc.*
- *Tranquil setting on park-like grounds*
- *NZ hosts in Heritage Home*
- *Evening wine in Billiard Room*
- *Breakfast in your own suite*
- *Extensive breakfast menu*
- *Centrally heated throughout*
- *Outdoor spa*

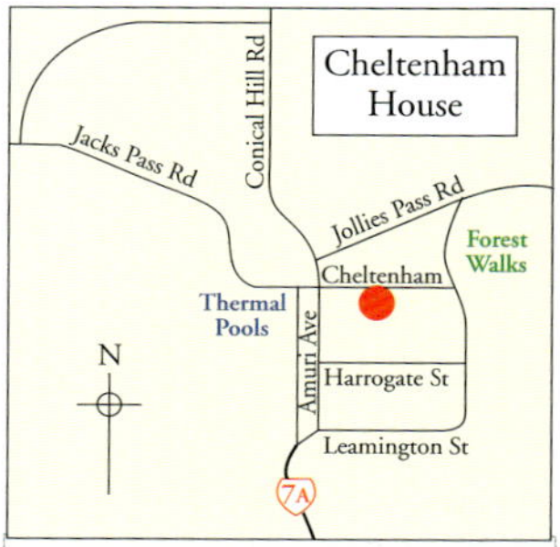

DIRECTIONS: Take Highway 7a into Hamner Springs Village, on to Amuri Ave, Cheltenham Street is third to your right. **Cheltenham House** is the 4th property on the right hand side.

Relax in the warmth and tranquillity of our romantic 1930s character home. **Cheltenham House** is situated on extensive grounds, just 200 metres from thermal pools, forest walks, restaurants and shops in this picturesque alpine resort. We renovated this gracious home with our guests' comfort paramount. There are four spacious, sunny suites in the house and two cottages situated in the garden. All are centrally heated and provide comfortable seating and dining areas, quality bedding, fridge, television and tea/coffee making facilities. An open fire enhances the atmosphere in the billiard room, where we share a local wine with our guests in the evening. Awake to a delicious cooked breakfast in the privacy of your own suite. **Cheltenham House** has received widespread acclaim for its comfort and genuine NZ hospitality: *"This B&B is superb"* Lonely Planet. *"Best B&B in town"* Rough Guide to NZ. *"Great style at an unbelievably good price"* Frommer's NZ.

Cheshire House

164C Hanmer Springs Road, Highway 7A
Hanmer Springs
Ph (03) 315 5100
Mobile 021-269 2737
email: *janandchris@xtra.co.nz*

Tariff : N.Z. Dollars	
Double	$130-160
Single	$110-120
Child	neg

Bedrooms	Qty
Double	2
Twin	1
Single	
Bed Size	**Qty**
Super King	
King	
Queen	2
Double	
Single	2
Bathrooms	**Qty**
Ensuite	3
Private	
Guest Share	

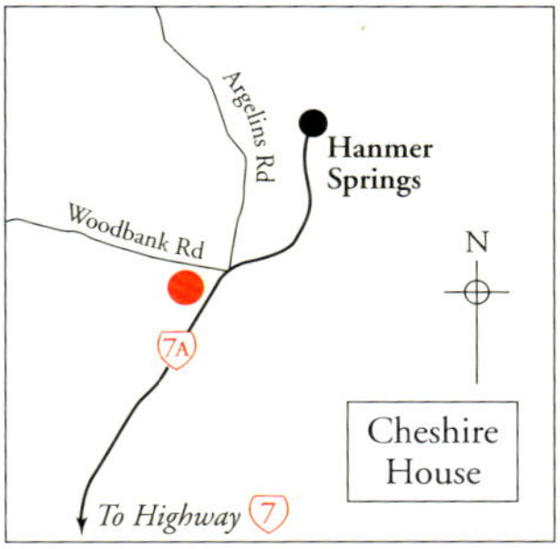

DIRECTIONS: Cheshire House is located just after the Welome sign to Hanmer Springs opposite the Highway B&B sign.

Bed & Breakfast
Luxury Accommodation

Features & Attractions

- *Hot thermal pools*
- *Relaxing forest walks*
- *Tranquil setting*
- *Lovely mountain views*
- *English hospitality*
- *Continental & English breakfast*
- *English breakfast, gluten free on request*
- *Superb restaurants nearby*

Cheshire House is conveniently situated a one minute drive from Hanmer Springs township. Come and experience a memorable stay here with outstanding English hospitality and relax to your heart's content in one of our three beautifully furnished ensuite bedrooms. Our bedrooms have stunning mountain views and you also have your private guest entrance with an outdoor decking area for relaxing 'al fresco' if you wish.

For a great start to your day enjoy our continental and freshly cooked English breakfast, which is truly 'mouthwatering' and then, if you wish, choose from various activities which Hanmer has to offer, including horse-trekking, gorgeous forest walks, hiking, 'Thrillseekers' and much more!

Jan and Chris take pride in everything they have to offer and will ensure that your stay is perfect in every way and quite unforgettable!

Hanmer View Bed & Breakfast

8 Oregon Heights, Hanmer Springs
Mobile 021-040 6609
Ph (03) 315 7947
email: *hanmerview@xtra.co.nz*
www.hanmerview.co.nz

Tariff : N.Z. Dollars	
Double	$170-185
Single	$140-150
Child	n/a

Bedrooms	Qty
Double	2
Twin	1
Single	
Bed Size	**Qty**
Super King	1
King	
Queen	2
Double	
Single	2
Bathrooms	**Qty**
Ensuite	3
Private	
Guest Share	

Bed & Breakfast
Boutique Accommodation

Features & Attractions

- *Panoramic views of forest' village & mountains beyond*
- *Tasteful, warm, spacious rooms*
- *Warm, friendly hospitality*
- *Delicious homemade breakfasts*
- *Walk to hot pools, restaurants etc*
- *Enjoy Hanmers forest walks*
- *Short drive to 2 ski fields*

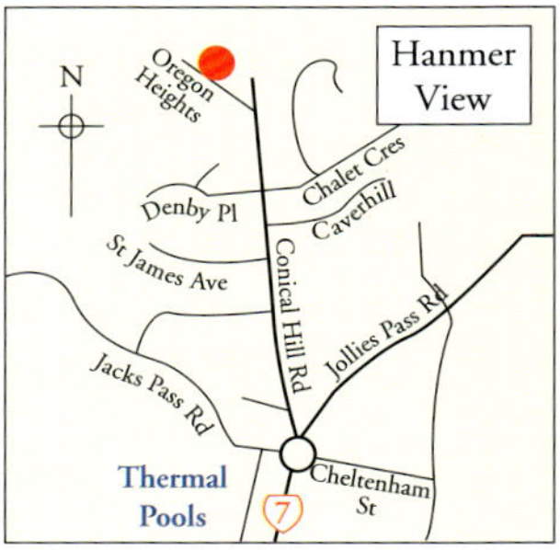

Come and relax in the ambience of our purpose-built Bed & Breakfast. Enjoy the privacy of your own studio room, designed with television, ensuite and tastefully decorated with your comfort in mind. Laze on the deck or in our guest lounge absorbing the fantastic views while watching the native birds that are frequent visitors to our garden.

Your needs are well provided for at **Hanmer View Bed & Breakfast.**
Tea, coffee and home baking are always available.
Our generous breakfasts set you up for the day.
The Village Centre and Hot Thermal Pools are a short walk away. Jet boating, rafting, mountain biking, horse trekking, bungy jumping and skiing in winter are for the energetic.
You may just wish to walk in the forest or play a round of golf at our picturesque 18-hole course or simply soak in the hot pools.

Oakview Bed & Breakfast

46 Jacks Pass Road, Hanmer Springs
Ph (03) 315 7757, Fax (03) 315 7746
Mobile 021-577 570
email: *stay@oakview.co.nz*
www.oakview.co.nz

Features & Attractions

- *250 metres to thermal pools*
- *Continental or cooked breakfasts*
- *Alpine exotic forest walks*
- *Trout fishing & jet boating*
- *Good shopping and golf*
- *Great selection of restaurants*

$		
	Double	$160-200
	Single	$110-120
	Child	

LA

Delightful Alpine Outlook in Hanmer Springs

BB

Bedrooms	Qty
Double	3
Twin	1
Single	
Bed Size	**Qty**
King	1
Queen	2
Double	
Single	2
Bathrooms	**Qty**
Ensuite	2
Private	
Guest Share	

Oakview provides well appointed accommodation with private entrances within a modern, gracious home overlooking large gardens and, through a vista of oak trees, the golf course. Enjoy a delightful, alpine, rural outlook while also being within the heart of the village. Only 250 metres easy walk to the internationally acclaimed thermal pools with their various health and beauty treatments. Your hosts, Jenny and Michael, have been in the hospitality field over many years and have a good knowledge of what experiences should make your stay enjoyable and memorable. The choice of accommodation varies from two bedroom self-contained apartments with kitchen to one bedroom suites, all with their own spa baths and showers. Breakfasts can either be continental, delivered to your accommodation, or a shared full cooked breakfast. Our aim is to make you feel welcome and cater for your individual requirements to the highest standard, so that you leave with happy memories of **Oakview** and Hanmer Springs.

Ballindalloch

95 Long Plantation Road, Culverden, RD 2
North Canterbury
Ph (03) 315 8220, Fax (03) 315 8220
Mobile 027-437 3184

Features & Attractions

- *Quiet, peaceful surroundings*
- *Dinner by arrangement, $35pp*
- *Excellent trout/salmon fishing*
- *Magnificent mountain views*
- *Complimentary farm tour*
- *30 min to Hanmer Springs*

$		
	Double	$120
	Single	$70
	Child	$35

BB

Farmstay Bed & Breakfast

F

Bedrooms	Qty
Double	1
Twin	1
Single	
Bed Size	**Qty**
King	
Queen	1
Double	
Single	1
Bathrooms	**Qty**
Ensuite	
Private	
Guest Share	1

Welcome to **Ballindalloch**, a 2090 acre irrigated farm 3 km south of Culverden. We milk 1500 cows in a floating rotary and a new 70 bale rotary dairy. We also have a 400 head Corriedale sheep stud. Our home is set amongst lawns and gardens with a swimming pool. Panoramic views of the hills and mountains surround us. Our home is centrally heated in winter and has a log fire. Culverden is situated between two excellent fishing rivers.

We are 100 km north of Christchurch, ½ hour to Hanmer Springs thermal pools and 1½ hours to Kaikoura Whale Watch. We have travelled extensively overseas and appreciate relaxing in a homely atmosphere and extend this to all our guests. Complimentary farm tour. Please ring or fax for reservations. We have one cat Thomas, and guests are welcome to smoke outdoors.

PAHAU DOWNS

RD 2, Culverden, North Canterbury
Ph (03) 315 8224, Fax (03) 315 8224
email: *pahaudowns@xtra.co.nz*
www.pahaudowns.co.nz

Features & Attractions

- *Self-contained private cottage*
- *Excellent local fishing*
- *Sheep & beef farm, walks & tours*
- *Heated swimming pool*
- *High quality furnishings*
- *Dinner by arrangement*

Luxury Self-contained Cottage

Double	$230
Single	$180
Child	neg

This romantic self-contained cottage is superbly furnished and available for your exclusive use as a base for fishing, walking and trips to local attractions such as Hanmer Springs, Mount Lyford Ski Centre and Kaikora. **Pahau Downs** is a tranquil hill farm set amidst stunning scenery between the Hurunui and Waiau rivers, famous for their excellent trout and salmon fishing (guides can be arranged). The cottage is superbly equipped with two large bedrooms, a shower and bathroom and a sunny sitting/ dining room with woodburner. Enjoy the mountain views from the heated outdoor swimming pool, walk over the 6,000 acre farm or tour the working sheep and beef station with the owner.

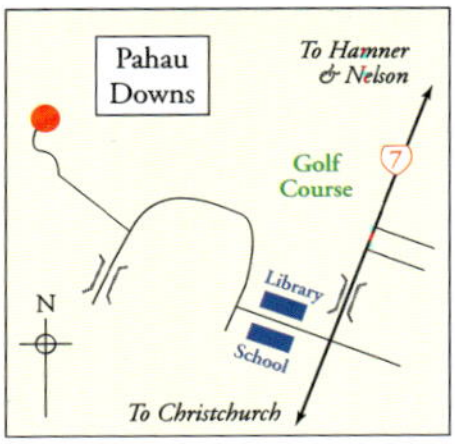

Bedrooms	Qty
Double	1
Twin	1
Single	
Bed Size	**Qty**
King	
Queen	1
Double	
Single	2
Bathrooms	**Qty**
Ensuite	
Private	1
Guest Share	

DIRECTIONS: In Culverden turn past school till you reach a T-junction; turn right and follow the road till you reach a sign 'Pahau Downs Road', follow unsealed road till you reach the farm. (30 min from Hanmer Springs)

Hawarden-North Canterbury ▶ YOUR HOSTS: **Sue and Wylie Evans** Ph (03) 314 4221

TARUNA

230 Taruna Road, Hawarden, North Canterbury
Ph (03) 314 4221, Fax (03) 314 4670
email: *ow.sm@paradise.net.nz*

Features & Attractions

- *Excellent local fishing*
- *Mountain bike trails*
- *Golf, hiking, horse treks*
- *Boutique wineries & wine trail*
- *Peace, space, privacy*
- *Gateway to Hurunui Lakes*

Farmstay Bed & Breakfast

Double	$120
Single	$60
Child	POA

Hawarden is a rural village 1¼ hours drive from Christchurch Airport and ¾ hours drive from Hanmer Springs. **Taruna** is a sheep and beef hill country farm situated 12km west of Hawarden in the foothills of the Southern Alps.
The separate guest accommodation adjoins the house with doors opening to a private garden patio. It has an ensuite bathroom with heated towel rail and hair dryer. Fresh home-baking is included with the tea and coffee making facilities.
We encourage guests to relax in our sunny home and enjoy panoramic mountain views. Laundry and internet access available. A farmstyle evening meal with garden fresh vegetables and New Zealand wines is available by prior arrangement, $30pp.
As well as a background in farming we have an interest in classic cars and home-built aircraft. We have two affectionate terriers, Ed and Biggles.
Please phone, fax or email for reservations and easy directions.

Bedrooms	Qty
Double	1
Twin	
Single	
Bed Size	**Qty**
Super King	1
Queen	
Double	
Single	
Bathrooms	**Qty**
Ensuite	1
Private	
Guest Share	

Bredon Downs

Bredon Downs, Amberley, RD 1, North Canterbury
Ph (03) 314 9356, Fax (03) 314 9357
Mobile 027-290 3067
email: *lucy.lucy@xtra.co.nz*
www.bredondownshomestay.co.nz

Features & Attractions

- *Amidst English-style garden*
- *Dinners by arrangement*
- *Delicious & filling breakfast*
- *Visit our ostriches*
- *Start of Waipara wine trail*
- *Less than 2 hr to whales at Kaikoura*

$	
Double	$110-130
Single	$75
Child	$30

Homestay Bed & Breakfast

Bedrooms	Qty
Double	1
Twin	1
Single	1
Bed Size	**Qty**
King	
Queen	1
Double	
Single	3
Bathrooms	**Qty**
Ensuite	1
Private	1
Guest Share	

Our drive leads off State Highway One, so we are conveniently located enroute to and from the Inter-Island Ferry and just forty minutes north of Christchurch – very easy to find. The house is a very comfortable 100-year-old farmhouse, extensively renovated and restored, and surrounded by an English-style garden with swimming pool which guests are welcome to use. We are close to the Waipara Wine Trail, the beach, an attractive golf course, and the hot thermal pools at Hanmer are only an hour away. We breed ostriches, which we are pleased to show visitors, and we have chicks hatching each week during the summer. We have travelled extensively and lived in Africa before coming from England to live here thirty five years ago and enjoy welcoming local and overseas visitors into our home. We share our lives with a Labrador, a Newfoundland, two geriatric donkeys and Hugo, the cat.

Purple Patch Lavender and B&B

42 Greney's Lane, Amberley, North Canterbury
Ph (03) 314 8611, Fax (03) 314 7149
email: *info@lavenderbeds.co.nz*
www.lavenderbeds.co.nz

Features & Attractions

- *Working lavender farm*
- *Peaceful mountain views*
- *Wineries close by*
- *Warm hospitality*
- *Giftshop on site*
- *City & airport 45 min.*

$	
Double	$105
Single	$60
Child	

Lavender Farm Bed & Breakfast

Bedrooms	Qty
Double	1
Twin	1
Single	
Bed Size	**Qty**
King	
Queen	
Double	1
Single	2
Bathrooms	**Qty**
Ensuite	
Private	
Guest Share	1

"Where your eyes see the beauty and your senses feel the dream."
Relax and enjoy a tranquil break in the country in our comfortable home, where you are assured of a warm welcome. We are ideally located for many temptations – minutes to Waipara Valley wineries, 45 min. Christchurch and the airport, 1 hr Hanmer Springs thermal reserve, 1.5 hrs. Kaikoura Whalewatch.

Browse in our on-farm lavender giftshop and purchase a beautiful reminder of your visit or a souvenir for friends back home. If the field of purple has been harvested (mid January), there are still the display gardens to stroll in, where you can view dozens of different lavenders. Have a game of pétanque or checkers on our giant board among the lavender or just relax surrounded by awesome scenery.
We look forward to your company.

Springbank Vineyard

1035 Oxford Road, RD1, Rangiora
Ph (03) 312 5653, Fax (03) 312 5623
email: *springbankvineyard@hotmail.com*

Features & Attractions

- *Peaceful & secluded*
- *Close to golf & fishing*
- *Friendly and relaxed*
- *Good restaurants nearby*
- *Genuine historic home*
- *Children welcome*

Countrystay Boutique Accommodation

$	
Double	$150-175
Single	$75
Child	neg

Bedrooms	Qty
Double	2
Twin	2
Single	1
Bed Size	**Qty**
King	
Queen	2
Double	
Single	5
Bathrooms	**Qty**
Ensuite	1
Private	2
Family Share	1

Welcome to beautiful **Springbank Homestead**, originally one of New Zealand's great estates and the second sheeprun ever established in Canterbury. Today the 145 year old historic homestead still stands proudly overseeing a vineyard, a genuine country home featuring large, high living rooms and spacious upstairs bedrooms charmingly furnished with countrystyle antiques and colonial paintings.

For a taste of true **Springbank** hospitality, tell me about your travels over a blazing open fire and a complementary glass of wine. Breakfast is included in the tariff and a delicious home-cooked dinner is available on request. Ideally situated on Scenic Highway 72, **Springbank Vineyard** is close to many local attractions including fishing and golf. Christchurch Airport or Waipora's Vineyards are just a short half hour's drive away, whilst Rangiora offers good shopping and a choice of restaurants just 10km down the road. Experience **Springbank** for yourself. I look forward to meeting you soon.

Hielan House Countrystay B&B

74 Bush Road, Oxford
Ph (03) 312 4382, Fax (03) 312 4382
Free Ph 0800 279 382
email: *hielanhouse@ihug.co.nz*
www.hielanhouse.co.nz

Features & Attractions

- *Dinner by arrangement, home-grown meat/vegetables in season*
- *Laundry, internet, sauna, spa*
- *Gateway to everywhere!*
- *Peaceful quality setting*
- *Golf clubs available*

Countrystay Bed & Breakfast

$	
Double	$130-150
Single	$120
Child	$0-35

Bedrooms	Qty
Double	2
Twin	1
Single	
Bed Size	**Qty**
Super King	1
Queen	1
Double	
Single	2
Bathrooms	**Qty**
Ensuite	1
Private	1
Guest Share	

Shirley and John offer quiet quality accommodation just three minutes from the main street of Oxford. Elevated above the township our home enjoys beautiful views.

Come, relax, enjoy a peaceful night's sleep in comfortable beds. Wake up to bird song and enjoy delicious continental and/or cooked breakfast from our menu. Two well appointed upstairs guest areas include relaxing areas, ensuites, TVs, tea/coffee making facilities.

Our grounds are yours to enjoy. Check out the farm animals, if you wish. Dinner available (even at short notice with home-grown meat/vegetables from the garden in season). Laundry, internet, sauna, spa, inground swimming pool (summer), cot. We have ladies' and men's golf clubs available for your use. We would love to host you.

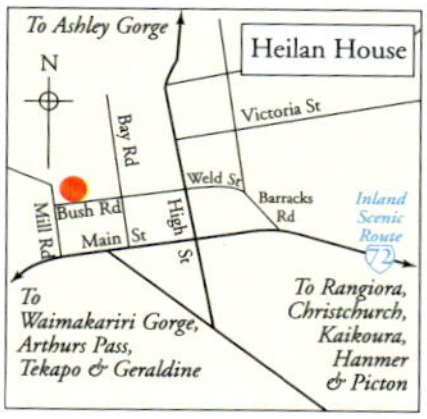

San Dona Lodge

100 Siena Pl, Ohoka, RD 2, Kaiapoi
Ph (03) 312 6346, Fax (03) 312 6342
Mobile 021-799 922
email: *info@sandonalodge.co.nz*
www.sandonalodge.co.nz

Features & Attractions

- *Quiet rural setting*
- *Spacious modern rooms*
- *Home grown delicacies*
- *20 min from Christchurch City*
- *Relaxed friendly atmosphere*
- *Corporate & International specialists*

$	
Double	$130-150
Single	$85
Child	POA

Olive Grove Bed & Breakfast

Bedrooms	Qty
Double	3
Twin	
Single	
Bed Size	**Qty**
King	1
Queen	1
Double	
Single	1
Bathrooms	**Qty**
Ensuite	
Private	2
Guest Share	1

San Dona Lodge is a new purpose built home. Surrounded by 200 acres of olive trees and farmland yet only a short drive to restaurants and the city centre. Your hosts are a young professional couple who themselves have travelled extensively, so fully understand what it is that makes the difference in delivering service and a warm friendly environment. Our beds are super comfortable, breakfasts to die for and local activities limitless. High pressure showers, large satellite TV and internet. Bookings essential. We would love to have you. Visit our website for more information.

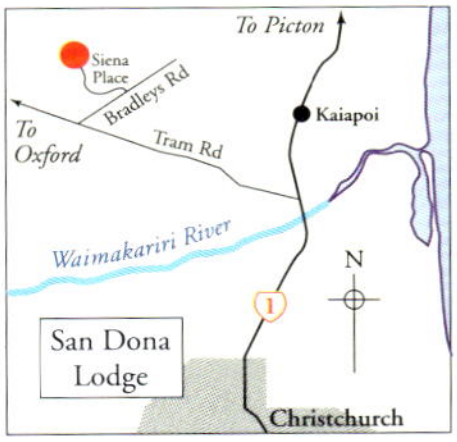

DIRECTIONS: Once in Siena Place drive to end at roundabout. Good signage and yellow letter box

VISA MasterCard

Rossburn

Spark Lane, Rangiora
Ph (03) 313 7427, Fax (03) 313 7421
Mobile 027-430 0420
email: *sparkfarm@xtra.co.nz*
www.northbrookmuseum.co.nz

Features & Attractions

- *Working dairy farm*
- *Children very welcome*
- *Country hospitality*
- *Extensive colonial museum*
- *Rangiora 1 kilometre*
- *Christchurch & airport 25 min.*

$	
Double	$110
Single	$75
Child	$25

Farm and Museum Bed & Breakfast

Bedrooms	Qty
Double	3
Twin	
Single	1
Bed Size	**Qty**
King	
Queen	2
Double	1
Single	2
Bathrooms	**Qty**
Ensuite	1
Private	
Guest Share	1

Our home, **Rossburn**, is a large 102 year-old homestead, surrounded by park-like gardens and mature trees. Richard and Dawn, ex dairy farmer and kindergarten teacher, operate a function centre in conjunction with their extensive colonial museum, possibly NZ's largest private museum. This could be your trip highlight, you'll be amazed at the collections. Entry included in tariff. We enjoy entertaining people from all walks of life and sharing travel experiences. Our interests include our family of six adult children, grandchildren, farm and church life, pets and collecting NZ's social history. Beaches, wineries, and a superb lakeside walk are nearby (conservation winner).
Please share a 3-course evening meal with us at $25.00pp (advise when booking).
Welcome to **Rossburn**.

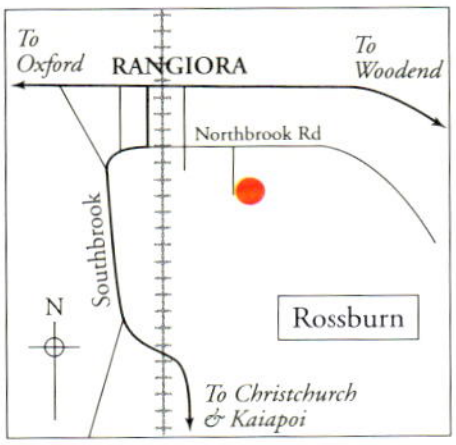

THE OAKS HISTORIC HOMESTEAD

Corner SH 73 & Clintons Road,
Darfield, RD 1, Canterbury
Ph (03) 318 7232, Fax (03) 318 7236
Mobile 027-241 3999
email: *theoaks@quicksilver.net.nz*
www.theoakshomestead.co.nz

Tariff : N.Z. Dollars	
Double	$150-275
Single	$140
Child	FOC

Bedrooms	Qty
Double	3
Twin	
Single	1
Bed Size	**Qty**
Super King	
King	
Queen	3
Double	
Single	1
Bathrooms	**Qty**
Ensuite	1
Private	2
Guest Share	

Boutique Bed & Breakfast
Historic Homestay

Features & Attractions

- *Boutique accommodation*
- *Open fires*
- *Home-baked meals*
- *35 minutes to Airport*
- *Private/ensuite bathrooms*
- *Ski fields & golf courses nearby*
- *Large garden/sunny verandahs*
- *Stunning Southern Alps scenery*

The Oaks Historic Homestead is surrounded by the stunning scenery of the Southern Alps on State Highway 73 to the West Coast.
Nestled between the Waimakariri and Rakaia River Gorges, it has all major Canterbury ski fields, golf courses and tourist attractions on its doorstep and is only a leisurely 35 min drive from Christchurch and the airport.
The homestead features four guest rooms (3 queen size and 1 single including a cot) with ensuite and private bathrooms. The separate guest dining room and stunning living room, complete with an inviting open fire, make your stay a memorable one. Relax on our beautiful verandas with a book, entertain some close friends, or simply take deep breaths of fresh, clean air amidst the beautiful tranquil setting.
Our traditional large homestead kitchen is heated by the original Atlas coal range. Enjoy a delicious freshly baked breakfast in the kitchen, in the elegant dining room or in the sun on the veranda.
There is ample parking with large grounds for the children.
Dinner reservations can be made at point of booking.

Meychelle Manor

SH 73, Main West Coast Road,
Darfield, Kirwee, Canterbury
Ph (03) 318 1144, Fax (03) 318 1965
email: *stay@meychellemanor.co.nz*
www.meychellemanor.co.nz

Tariff : N.Z. Dollars	
Double	$120-220
Single	$100-140
Child	$10-50

Bedrooms	Qty
Double/Twin	3
Twin	
Single	
Bed Size	**Qty**
King/Single	3
King	
Queen	
Double	
Single	2
Bathrooms	**Qty**
Ensuite	3
Private	
Guest Share	

Luxury Farmstay Bed & Breakfast

Features & Attractions

- *Award-winning home*
- *Stunning views*
- *Outstanding facilities*
- *Private beautiful rooms*
- *Communications, full laundry*
- *Delicious breakfast*
- *Extensive grounds on "farm park"*
- *Restaurants, shopping, train 4 min*

5th Generation Kiwis.

Meychelle Manor Luxury Bed & Breakfast offers you a warm and friendly environment in magnificent, award-winning accommodation with outstanding facilities, only 30 min from Christchurch City/Airport, only 4 min from Darfield (SH 73), the gateway to several ski, golf and recreational opportunities. Facilities include heated pool, gym, two guest lounges with DVD, music, telescope, guest bar, barbeque and many complimentaries. The home is centrally heated throughout. Family needs are catered for. Outside activities include a farm tour, feeding of animals and birds, putting green and playground. From beautifully appointed guest rooms, with all conveniences, you can overlook stunning mountain and farmland views, deer grazing, extensive grounds in a "farm park" setting, our lake of trout and goldfish, birds roaming and a selection of exotic and farmyard animals. Choose your breakfast from our scrumptious menu selection. In the evening enjoy complimentary NZ wine, taste the highly recommended local cuisine (courtesy transport available) or enjoy conversation with Michelle and Brian, who want to assure you of a special experience.

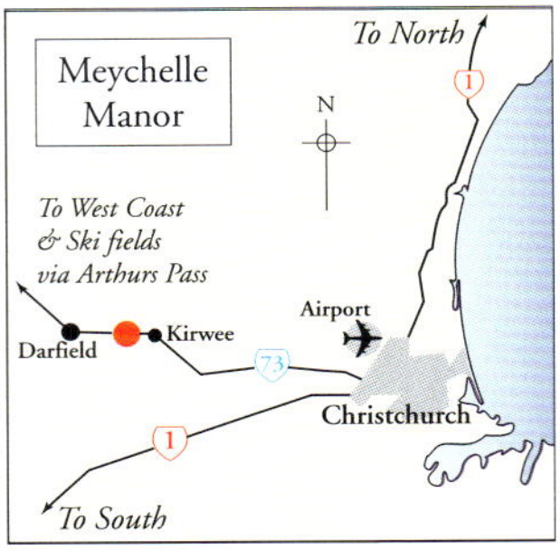

Highsted Homestead

132B Highsted Road, Harewood, Christchurch
Ph (03) 359 6486, Fax (03) 359 6490
Mobile 025-676 4625
email: *enquiries@highstedhomestead.co.nz*
www.highstedhomestead.co.nz

Tariff : N.Z. Dollars	
Double	$130-150
Single	$90-110
Child	

Bedrooms	Qty
Double	1
Twin	1
Single	
Bed Size	**Qty**
Super King	
King	
Queen	1
Double	
Single	3
Bathrooms	**Qty**
Ensuite	2
Private	
Guest Share	

Boutique Accommodation
Bed & Breakfast

Features & Attractions

- *Airport 5 min, city 10 min*
- *Courtesy airport transfers*
- *Secure off-street parking*
- *Real New Zealand hospitality*
- *Antarctic Centre 5 min*
- *Excellent local restaurants*
- *Kiwi-breeding park nearby*
- *Peaceful garden setting*

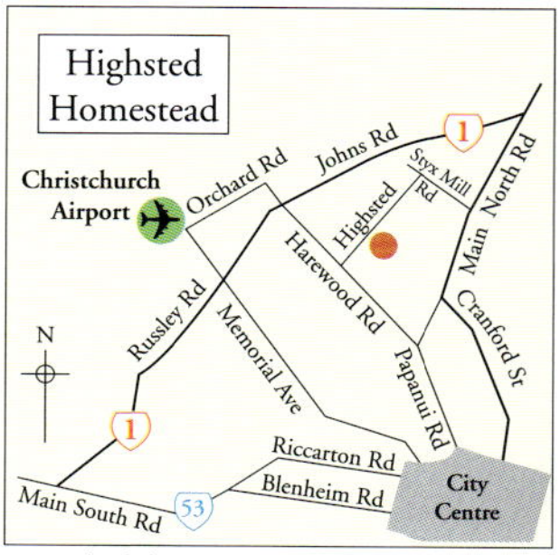

Welcome to our large colonial-style home, situated on a secluded half acre property surrounded by gardens. Be pleasantly surprised as you drive through our gates. We invite you to get to know our family and get a real glimpse of New Zealand life. We have two teenage children.

Our very spacious upstairs room has a queen and single bed with ensuite bathroom (new 2005). This room also has a couch, coffee table and fridge. Both guest rooms have tea/coffee making facilities. We are happy to do your laundry for you while you are out sightseeing. E-mail facilities available.

Guest comments: – *"Delightful place to stay for our last days in New Zealand. Loved your family."*
– *"We came back for seconds. Started and ended our travels here. It was like coming home, superb."*
– *"Charming and obliging hosts, well appointed rooms and a beautiful garden setting."*

Belmont on Harewood

37 Harewood Road, Papanui, Christchurch
Ph (03) 354 6890, Fax (03) 354 6895
Mobile 021-388 670
email: *janalltd@paradise.net.nz*

Tariff : N.Z. Dollars	
Double	$95-140
Single	$70-115
Child	$25

Bedrooms	Qty
Double	3
Twin	
Single	
Bed Size	**Qty**
Super King	
King	
Queen	3
Double	
Single	
Bathrooms	**Qty**
Ensuite	1
Private	
Guest Share	2

Bed & Breakfast

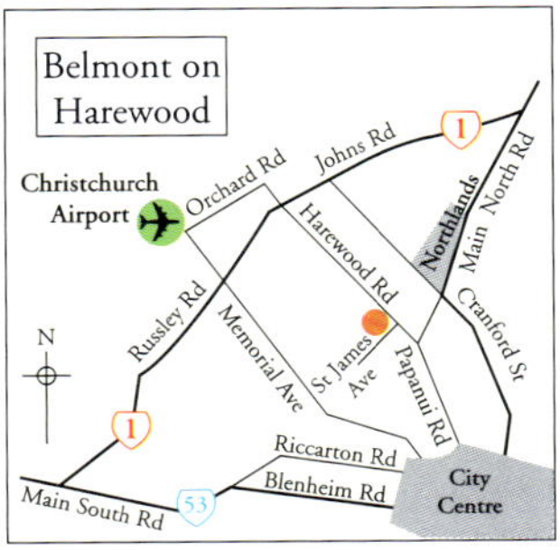

Features & Attractions

- *Edwardian Villa*
- *Central heating*
- *Quality bedding, generous rooms*
- *Disabled facilities*
- *Family cat , 'Possum'*
- *Email, internet and fax facilities*
- *Walk to restaurants, cafés, mall*
- *Excellent bus routes*

Jan and Alan welcome you to **Belmont on Harewood**. Our home has the beauty of yesteryear with ornate plaster cornices, ceiling roses, and beautiful rimu timber work. Enjoy the three metre high ceilings, crystal chandeliers, central heating, rimu furniture and very comfortable queen beds. Television and hairdryer in all rooms. Full disabled facilities are available.

Our mature gardens have a wonderful array of camellias and rhododendrons. A large paved BBQ area and off-street parking are provided for guests.

A five minute stroll takes you to a magnificent choice of multi cultural restaurants, boutique bars and the South Island's largest shopping mall at 'Northlands' complete with cinema and Irish Pub. Across the road from our home, you can wander through St James Park or alternatively, enjoy the glorious award-winning Sanitarium show gardens.

A few doors from our gate, bus-stops link you to the city centre, the airport, and all the major shopping malls in Christchurch.

EVANSLEIGH

344 Gardiners Road, Harewood, Christchurch
Ph (03) 359 8872, Mobile 021- 299 4424
email: *evansleighbb@hotmail.com*
www.evansleigh.com

Features & Attractions

- *Close to airport & city*
- *Victorian villa and garden*
- *Guest entrance & -lounge*
- *Full a-la-carte breakfast*
- *Restaurants & golf courses*
- *Wildlife & leisure parks*

Boutique Bed & Breakfast

$		
	Double	$110-140
	Single	$90-110
	Child	neg

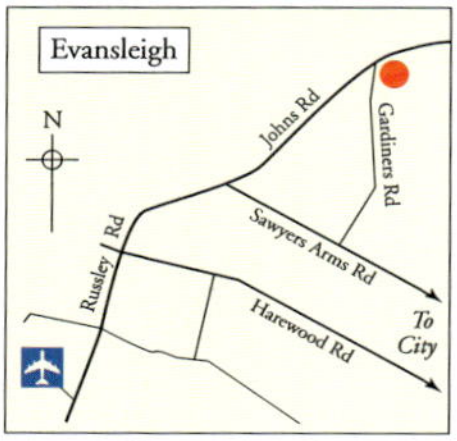

Evansleigh offers luxury B&B accommodation in a private rural setting. Enjoy old-fashioned hospitality in a Victorian villa, set in a large English garden on a 12 acre farmlet just 5 minutes from the airport and 15 minutes to the city centre. Clearwater International Golf Resort, the Antarctic Centre, wildlife reserves, award-winning restaurants, recreation areas with fishing, shops and vineyards are only minutes away. A gourmet a-la-carte breakfast is served in your room or al fresco on the veranda. All guests benefit from complimentary tea/coffee. I am happy to help with planning your excursions and dinner options by arrangement. I have travelled extensively, have three grown children and enjoy cooking and entertaining. I share my property with my grown daughter and partner, our dog, cat and horses. Children welcome, cot available.

Bedrooms	Qty
Double	2
Twin	1
Single	
Bed Size	**Qty**
King	
Queen	2
Double	
Single	2
Bathrooms	**Qty**
Ensuite	1
Private	
Guest Share	1

Burnside - Christchurch ▶ YOUR HOSTS: **Margaret and Tony Spowart** Ph: (03) 358 3264

STABLEFORD AIRPORT BED & BREAKFAST

2 Stableford Green, Burnside, Christchurch
Ph (03) 358 3264
Mobile 027-415 0834
email: *stableford@xtra.co.nz*
www.stableford.co.nz

Features & Attractions

- *Closest B&B to airport*
- *Off-street parking*
- *Good restaurants nearby*
- *Courtesy airport transfers*
- *Friendly, relaxed, comfortable*
- *Adjacent Russley Golf Course*

Airport Bed & Breakfast

$		
	Double	$130
	Single	$120
	Child	

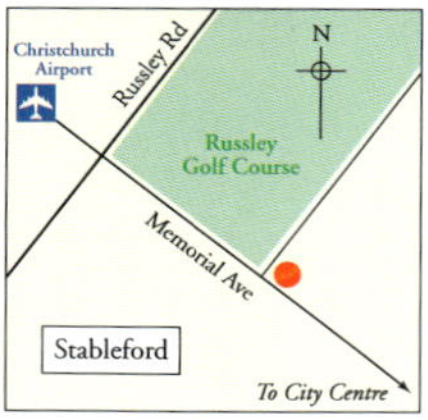

Welcome to **Stableford**, the closest Bed & Breakfast to Christchurch Airport, making it ideal for arriving or departing visitors. City bus-stop at door.
We are situated adjacent to the prestigious Russley Golf Club. Let us know if you require a tee booking at the Russley Golf Course. **Stableford** is new, clean and comfortable with a separate guest lounge. Airport transfer available. Full breakfast, continental and cooked. Good restaurants nearby or dinner by arrangement.
Our interests are travel, sport, music, and antiques.
Luxury room and ensuite available with minimum three nights. Own entrance and spa bath. $190 double per night.

Bedrooms	Qty
Double	2
Twin	1
Single	
Bed Size	**Qty**
King	
Queen	2
Double	
Single	2
Bathrooms	**Qty**
Ensuite	2
Private	1
Guest Share	

Russley 302

302 Russley Road, Avonhead, Christchurch
Ph (03) 358 6510, Fax (03) 358 6470
Mobile 021-662 016
email: *haduck@ducksonrussley.co.nz*
www.ducksonrussley.co.nz

Tariff : N.Z. Dollars	
Double	$120-130
Single	$70-120
Child	

Bedrooms	Qty
Double	1
Twin	1
Single	1
Bed Size	**Qty**
Super King	1
King	1
Queen	
Double	
Single	3
Bathrooms	**Qty**
Ensuite	1
Private	1
Guest Share	1

Boutique Accommodation
Bed & Breakfast

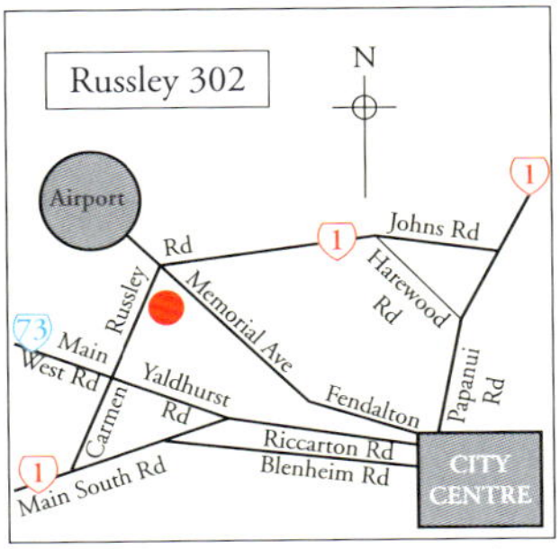

Features & Attractions

- *Christchurch Airport 3 min*
- *Central city 15 min*
- *Courtesy airport transfers*
- *Christchurch - the Garden City*
- *Private spacious bedrooms*
- *Fax & email facilities*
- *Golf courses/driving range*
- *Antarctic exhibition*

You are assured of a warm welcome and friendly hospitality at **Russley 302** - an ideal location for visitors to Christchurch. With abundant and secure off-street parking **Russley 302** has lovely well appointed guest rooms offering tea/coffee making facilities, fridge, TV and electric blankets. Laundry options are available upon request and you are welcome to use email and fax facilities. We are fortunate to be situated near the urban/rural boundary on a ten acre farmlet with sheep and chickens. Alfresco dining on summer evenings and a log fire in winter enhance a very relaxing atmosphere. Christchurch, the Garden City, has much to offer and is an ideal base for excursions to Canterbury's hinterland. Fishing, gardening, travel, vintage motor cars and convivial company are what we enjoy. Let us assist you with travel or sightseeing plans and further accommodation.

Lavender Towers (Airport)

11 Kedleston Drive, Avonhead, Christchurch
Ph (03) 358 4387, Mobile 021-261 5927
email: *sandy@inet.net.nz*

Tariff : N.Z. Dollars	
Double	$130
Single	$110
Child	

Bedrooms	Qty
Double	1
Twin	
Single	1
Bed Size	**Qty**
Super King	
King	
Queen/Double	1
Double	
Single	1
Bathrooms	**Qty**
Ensuite	
Private	1
Family Share	1

Homestay
Bed & Breakfast

Features & Attractions

- *Courtesy pick-up, airport 3 min.*
- *Restaurant/shops/parks closeby*
- *Beautiful cottage garden*
- *On bus route to city – 20 min.*
- *Continental breakfast*
- *Friendly family home*
- *Snacks by arrangement*
- *Off-street parking*

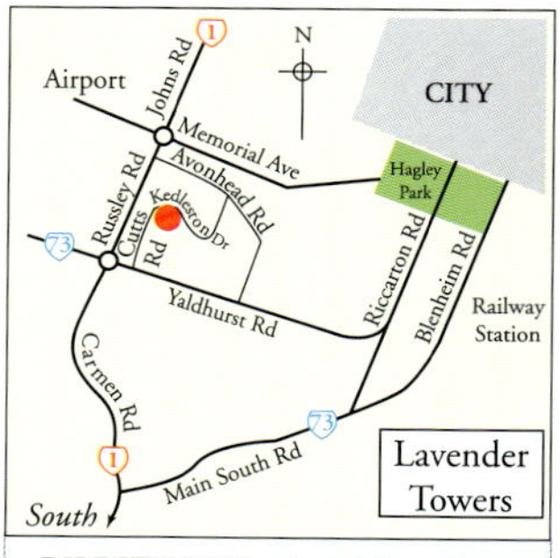

DIRECTIONS: Travel south from city on Riccarton Rd, turn right into Yaldhurst Rd. After 2 km turn right into Cutts Rd/Apsley Drive. We are 3rd street on left.

We would like to welcome you to our Garden City and would like to make your holiday as comfortable and as memorable as possible. We are situated in the northwest, in a quiet, safe suburb –3 km to the airport and 7 km to the city. Just a short walk to a shopping mall, restaurant and two beautiful parks. We have travelled extensively throughout New Zealand and are happy to help you with your sightseeing/garden tours etc. Our interests include – boating, gardening, doll-making, sport, travel and animals. A continental breakfast will be served at your leisure, which includes cereal, fruit, yoghurt, toast, home-made jams/muffins and tea/coffee. We have an outdoor area for you to enjoy in the summertime and a lovely warm fire in winter. There is also a guest lounge if you need a quiet time with tea, coffee and cookies. Laundry/email facilities at a small cost. And if you are an animal lover, we have two very adorable/very friendly samoyed dogs and one cat.

A very warm 'Kiwi' welcome awaits you.

Ambience on Avon

45 Totara Street, Fendalton, Christchurch
Ph (03) 348 4537, Fax (03) 348 4837
Mobile 027-433 3627
e-mail: *lawsonh@xtra.co.nz*
www.ambience-on-avon.co.nz

qualmark ★★★★ plus guest & hosted

@ home NEW ZEALAND

Tariff : N.Z. Dollars	
Double	$140-190
Single	$120-150
Child	

Bedrooms	Qty
Double	2
Twin	1
Single	
Bed Size	**Qty**
Super King	
King	
Queen	2
Double	
Single	2
Bathrooms	**Qty**
Ensuite	3
Private	
Guest Share	

Luxury Boutique Hosted Bed & Breakfast

Features & Attractions

- *Luxury air-conditioned home*
- *Guest lounge, large fire*
- *Quiet, secluded street*
- *Tranquil Avon River garden*
- *Airport, city, rail 8 min.*
- *Courtesy transfers*
- *Special breakfast, home-baking*
- *Wireless LAN, email available*

Peace, tranquility and a warm welcome await you at **Ambience on Avon**, with park-like garden on 26 metres Avon River frontage in the heart of quiet, leafy suburb Fendalton. Helen and Lawson, your gracious hosts, look forward to welcoming you into their new architecturally designed, luxurious home with elegant, comfortable understated furnishings, guest lounge, large open fire and TV. Only 4 minutes walk to Riccarton Mall, banks, bus stop, university and easy walk to Hagley Park, botanical gardens and city centre. Guests may like to enjoy complimentary refreshments and home-baking in our peaceful garden and share a local wine before dining out. Art, comfortable beds, fine linen, electric blankets, air conditioning and all modern conveniences are here for a relaxing friendly-hosted stay. Close to city centre, airport, Tranz Alpine. Off-street parking. High speed broadband internet, laundry available. Lawson and Helen enjoy art, walking, garden, fine food, wine, singing around the vintage pianola. – Travel home and abroad, holiday planning, accommodation and travel bookings available.

Russley - Christchurch ▶ YOUR HOSTS: Joanne and Allan Ph: (03) 342 5201

CASTLEREAGH

368A Yaldhurst Road, Russley, Christchurch
Ph (03) 342 5201, Fax (03) 342 3030
Mobile 027-499 3881
email: *castlereagh@xtra.co.nz*

Features & Attractions

- *Restful, friendly atmosphere*
- *Easy city/airport access*
- *Russley Golf Course 5 min*
- *Bus route to city*
- *Quiet garden setting*
- *Courtesy Car to/from airport*

Homestay Bed & Breakfast

Double	from $100
Single	from $65
Child	

Welcome to our single storey five bedroom, three bathroom home, situated on a main route to the city, within five minutes of the international airport and easy access to the West Coast and main routes north and south. Free pick-up and delivery from airport or any other public transport. Breakfast is cooked or continental. Dinner on request. We have off-street parking. Spacious bedrooms offer electric blankets, heaters and hairdryers. Laundry facilities if requested. Separate guest lounge with TV and access to picturesque English-style garden with outdoor privacy on rear section. Complimentary tea, coffee, biscuits, fruit. We would enjoy helping plan your South Island eperience. Allan and Jo-Anne have a wide range of interests, which they will share with you. Our aim is to make your stay with us an absolute pleasure.

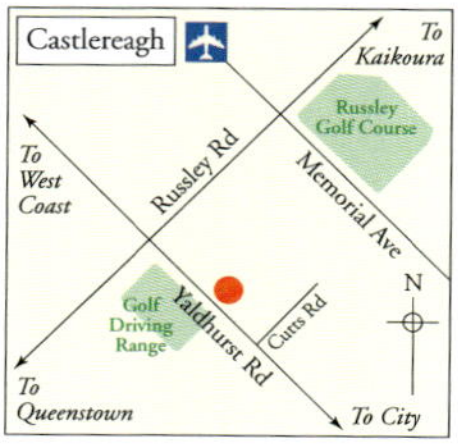

Bedrooms	Qty
Double	2
Twin	2
Single	
Bed Size	**Qty**
King	
Queen	2
Double	
Single	4
Bathrooms	**Qty**
Ensuite	1
Private	
Guest Share	1

Bryndwr - Christchurch ▶ YOUR HOSTS: Patricia and Win Clancey Ph (03) 351 6092

ROWAN HOUSE

89A Aorangi Road, Bryndwr, Christchurch
Ph (03) 351 6092, Fax (03) 351 6092
Mobile 027- 666 2006
email: *wclancey@xtra.co.nz*
www.geocities.com/w_clancey/

Features & Attractions

- *Airport 10min, city 10min.*
- *Courtesy transfers*
- *On city bus route*
- *Warm, friendly hospitality*
- *Quiet, peaceful surroundings*
- *4 local restaurants*

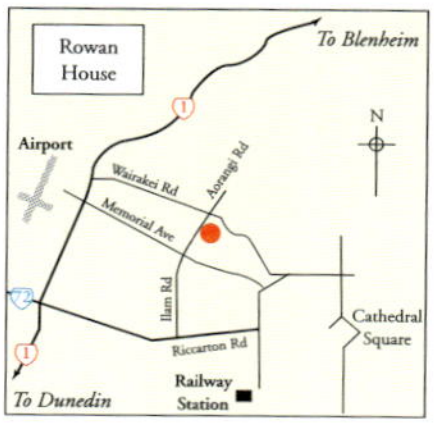

DIRECTIONS:
Take SH 1, by-passing Christchurch, (Russley Rd). At Wairakei Rd roundabout (close to airport) drive towards Bryndwr, east along Wairakei Rd. At second group of shops, turn right along Aorangi Rd. 89A is soon on the left.

Quality Homestay Bed & Breakfast

Double	$130-140
Single	$90-100
Child	

We offer warm, friendly hospitality in our sunny, spacious, comfortable home on a very quiet back section. There are two guest rooms, each with ensuite bathroom. One room opens to a balcony overlooking a swimming pool and the other opens into secluded gardens. Each room has TV, electric heating, and tea/coffee making facilities. A comfortable sunroom is available as a private lounge. Breakfasts are delicious and home-baking is always available. Four excellent restaurants are only ten minutes walk away.
We have both travelled, have a wide range of interests and are happy to help you plan your New Zealand trip.
Courtesy airport pick-up, laundry facilities and off-street parking are available.

Bedrooms	Qty
Double	2
Twin	
Single	
Bed Size	**Qty**
King	
Queen	2
Double	
Single	
Bathrooms	**Qty**
Ensuite	2
Private	
Guest Share	

AMBARS

23A Jeffrey's Road, Fendalton, Christchurch 5
Ph (03) 351 7330, Fax (03) 351 8967
Mobile 027-432 2390
email: *mw.glh@xtra.co.nz*

Features & Attractions

- *Courtesy pick-up*
- *Tranquil garden setting*
- *Email & laundry facilities*
- *Banks & restaurants short walk*
- *Secure off-street parking*
- *Dinner by arrangement $30 pp*

$	
Double	$150
Single	$120
Child	

Bed & Breakfast Homestay

Bedrooms	Qty
Double	1
Twin	
Single	1
Bed Size	**Qty**
King	1
Queen	
Double	
Single	1
Bathrooms	**Qty**
Ensuite	1
Private	1
Guest Share	

Our spacious colonial property is situated in a very private tranquil garden setting. We are midway between the airport and city centre, ten minutes from either by car. A warm welcome awaits you, we offer a complimentary pick-up from the airport, railway or bus stations. Our bedrooms are sunny with television, electric blankets, heaters and tea/coffee facilities. A fine breakfast is served in a charming dining room and we are happy to advise you on sightseeing or travel within the country. There are banks and restaurants within a short walk. You are welcome to smoke, but please do so outdoors. Please telephone, fax or email for reservations. We look forward to meeting you.

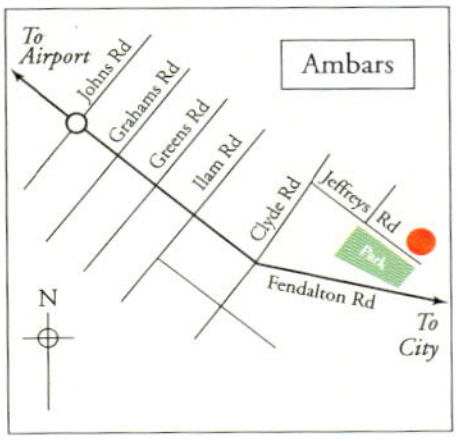

40 THORNYCROFT STREET BED & BREAKFAST

40 Thornycroft Street, Fendalton, Christchurch
Ph (03) 351 8228, Fax (03) 351 8820
Mobile 027-431 3348
e-mail: *bbthornycroft@clear.net.nz*
www.thornycroft.co.nz

Features & Attractions

- *Airport 5min, city 10min*
- *Delicious cooked breakfast*
- *Extremely quiet*
- *Walk to restaurants, shops*
- *Close to university, park*
- *Fax and email facilities*

$	
Double	$130-180
Single	$115-160
Child	

Boutique Accommodation Bed & Breakfast

Bedrooms	Qty
Double	2
Twin	
Single	
Bed Size	**Qty**
Super King/Twin	1
Queen	1
Double	
Single	
Bathrooms	**Qty**
Ensuite	1
Private	1
Guest Share	

40 Thornycroft Street Bed & Breakfast is located in a peaceful cul-de-sac in the suburb of Fendalton, one of Christchurch's most appealing areas. It is a very sunny, modern house with double-glazed windows and underfloor heating (necessary in winter!) and is set in an attractive established garden with an enticing courtyard to relax in at any time of the day. The guest bedrooms are attractively and comfortably appointed. Each has its own private bathroom, TV, tea and coffee making facilities and many extra touches. A private reading/sitting room is provided for those requiring time out, and complimentary New Zealand wine before dinner is always popular. A delicious gourmet cooked breakfast caters for all tastes and if the weather is perfect, you may choose to enjoy this in the courtyard. Knowledgeable assistance with travel plans is offered.

DIRECTIONS: From the airport drive down Memorial Ave. Continue into Fendalton Road. Turn 2nd left into Glandovey Road, then 1st left into Thornycroft Street.

Anselm House

34 Kahu Road, Fendalton, Christchurch
Ph (03) 343 4260, Fax (03) 343 4261
email: *anselm@paradise.net.nz*
www.anselmhouse.co.nz

Tariff : N.Z. Dollars	
Double	$140-190
Single	$100-120
Child	n/a

Bedrooms	Qty
Double	2
Twin	
Single	
Bed Size	**Qty**
Super King	
King	
Queen	2
Double	
Single	
Bathrooms	**Qty**
Ensuite	2
Private	
Guest Share	

Boutique Accommodation
Bed & Breakfast

Features & Attractions

- *Secure off-street parking*
- *Outdoor tables by Avon River*
- *Free transport to/from airport*
- *Friendly family atmosphere*
- *Banks, mall, restaurants short walk*
- *Free Tranz Alpine transfer*
- *Handy to University and Mona Vale*
- *Walk to Hagley Park, Bot. Gardens*

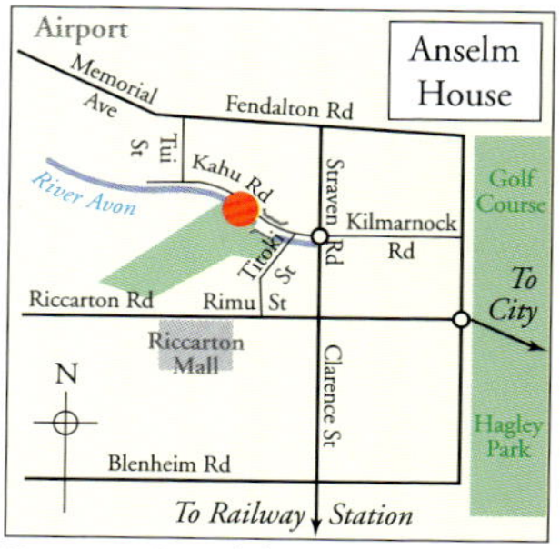

"Kia ora!"

Anselm House is a landmark building beside the Avon River. Designed by the famous architect Heathcote Helmore, it is one of the few homes in Christchurch built of Hanmer Marble. Bay windows overlook the Avon River. Guests can relax in our peaceful riverside garden, or cross over the brick bridge to view historic Riccarton House and walk through Deans Forest. Remnants can be seen of the original kahikatea trees and native forest which once covered much of the Canterbury Plains. Delicious continental or cooked breakfasts are served in the formal dining room, in the family room or outside on the terrace by the Avon River. New Zealand wine and cheese are shared in the late afternoon. An evening meal is available by arrangement. We have wide experiences and interests including agriculture, horticulture, medicine, rugby, sport, education and travel. We are happy to share information and to help you plan your Canterbury, South Island or New Zealand experience.

Leinster Bed & Breakfast

34b Leinster Road, Merivale, Christchurch
Ph (03) 355 6176, Fax (03) 355 6176
Mobile 027-433 0771
email: *brian.kay@xtra.co.nz*

Tariff : N.Z. Dollars	
Double	$130-135
Single	$120
Child	

Bedrooms	Qty
Double	2
Twin	1
Single	1
Bed Size	**Qty**
Super King	
King	
Queen	1
Double	1
Single	1
Bathrooms	**Qty**
Ensuite	1
Private	1
Guest Share	

Bed & Breakfast
Homestay

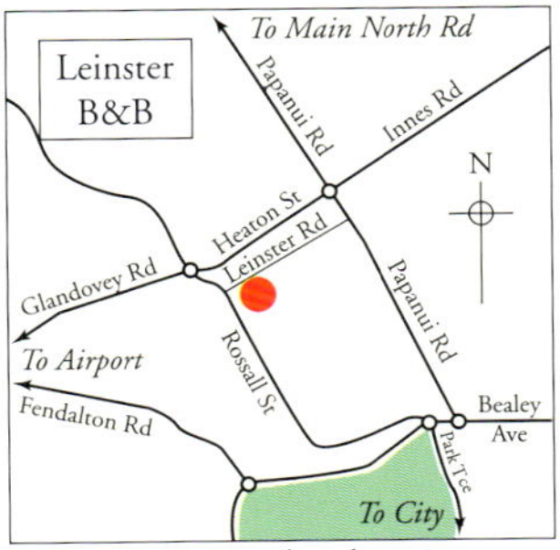

- *Centrally located*
- *Easy to find*
- *Quiet comfortable rooms*
- *Excellent local restaurants*
- *Courtesy transfers*
- *Off-street parking*
- *Laundry & email facilities*
- *Gluten-free food on request*

At **Leinster Bed & Breakfast** we offer a friendly, hospitable stay in our modern, sunny home. We pride ourselves on creating a relaxed, friendly atmosphere. Comfortable quiet rooms with television, tea & coffee, electric blankets and heaters. Having travelled to many countries and most places in New Zealand, we enjoy meeting like-minded travellers and helping with their ongoing travel plans. This can be done around the breakfast table or in the evening whilst enjoying a good wine (or two). By car we are only five minutes to all the city attractions and ten minutes from the airport. For evening dining convenience there are excellent restaurants and wine bars at Merivale Village which is a leisurely stroll to the end of the street. So why not come and stay and see if you can agree with Jim and Jo from Colorado, who wrote and said: "Kay and Brian are a big #10. I hope we get to visit them again. We stayed longer than intended because of them and because of the beauty of Christchurch".

GREATSTAY BED & BREAKFAST

33 Kilmarnock Street, Riccarton, Christchurch
Ph (03) 343 1377, Fax (03) 343 1357
Mobile 027-622 0788
email: *ruske.greatstay@xtra.co.nz*
www.greatstay.co.nz

Tariff : N.Z. Dollars	
Double	$180-190
Single	$120-130
Child	neg

Bedrooms	Qty
Double	2
Twin	1
Single	
Bed Size	**Qty**
Super King	
King	
Queen	2
Double	
King/Single	1
Bathrooms	**Qty**
Ensuite	3
Private	
Guest Share	

Bed & Breakfast

Features & Attractions

- *Courtesy pick-up*
- *No smoking policy*
- *Quiet, restful environment*
- *Close large shopping complex*
- *Close to city centre*
- *Variety top restaurants*
- *Off-street parking*
- *Easy walk to town*

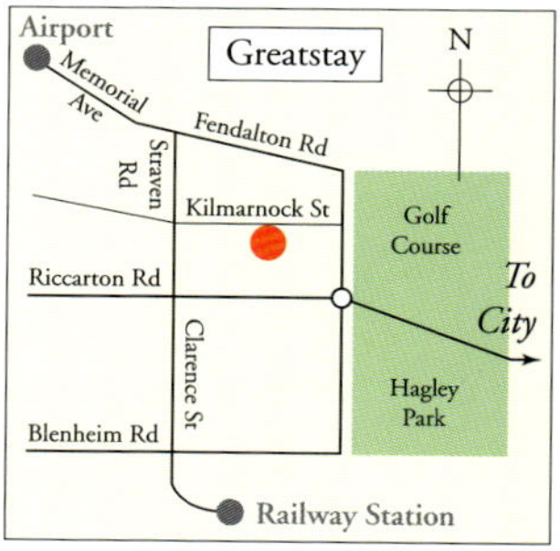

A wonderful home to begin your holiday. Courtesy transport on your arrival. Luxury, spacious, clean, quiet ensuited accommodation. Indulge yourself with a cooked/continental breakfast. Guest lounge for a quiet social time before going out for dinner. Our home is quiet and restful, and an easy picturesque walk to all attractions through Hagley Park and Botanic Gardens.
A car is not a necessity while staying with us, as public transport is at the gate. See our website for more details. We would be pleased to assist planning your holiday. **"Come as a guest, leave as a friend"**.

Comments: *"Warm, vibrant people"* Sally & Ward (USA), *"Perfect host and hostess"* Don & Andrea (Canada), *"Don't change anything – spot on – 5 stars"* Bob & Frieda (UK).

Springfield Cottages

137 Springfield Road, St. Albans, Christchurch
Ph (03) 377 1368
email: *relax@springfieldcottage.co.nz*
www.springfieldcottage.co.nz

Tariff : N.Z. Dollars	
Double	$150-250
Single	$150-250
Child	

Bedrooms	Qty
Double	1
Twin	
Single	
Bed Size	**Qty**
Super King	
King	
Queen	1
Double	
Single	
Bathrooms	**Qty**
Ensuite	
Private	1
Guest Share	

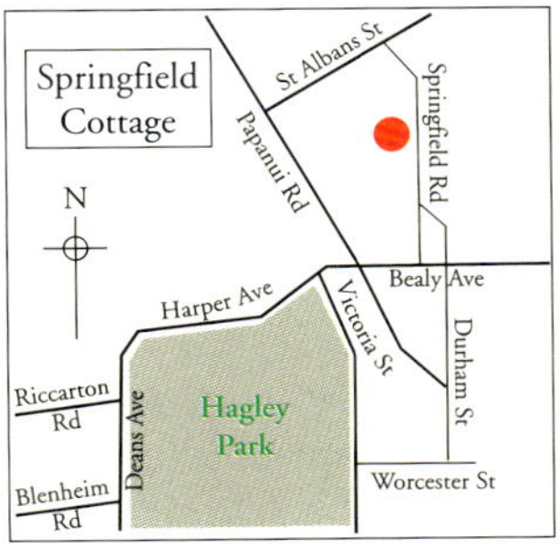

Self-contained Boutique Accommodation

Features & Attractions

- *Self-contained and private*
- *2 km to city centre*
- *Heritage cottage*
- *All modern comforts*
- *Romantic hideaway*
- *Private garden with BBQ*
- *Quality bed linen*
- *Breakfast hamper available*

If you are looking for Boutique Accommodation in central Christchurch, **Springfield Cottages** offer a uniquely different experience with self-contained heritage cottages designed to be romantic, peaceful, private hideaways within two kilometres of the city centre.

All the cottages have been recently refurbished to a very high standard offering a delightful combination of classic colonial charm and modern comforts. They include a full, modern kitchen, (if you like to do a bit of home-cooking, supermarket and shops are close by), washing machine/dryer (to catch up on the laundry), and a home theatre system to watch the DVD's and listen to CD's. The bedroom has fresh flowers and a queen-size bed with fine linen. The bathroom has a shower and heated towel rail. Outside you can enjoy the tranquility of the cottage garden complete with a courtyard barbeque and garden furniture. You can order a breakfast hamper of provisions for continental and cooked breakfasts. Minimum stay two nights, bookings essential.

The Lilac Rose

172 Blighs Road, Strowan, Christchurch
Ph (03) 354 6500, Fax (03) 354 6500
Mobile 027-437 3940
email: *lilacrose@xtra.co.nz*
www.lilacrose.co.nz

Tariff : N.Z. Dollars	
Double	$185-225
Single	$150
Child	

Bedrooms	Qty
Double	3
Twin	
Single	
Bed Size	**Qty**
Super King	
King	1
Queen	2
Double	
Single	
Bathrooms	**Qty**
Ensuite	1
Private	2
Guest Share	

Boutique Accomodation
Bed & Breakfast

Features & Attractions

- *Courtesy airport transfers*
- *Close by Merivale Village*
- *Walking distance to restaurants*
- *Off-street parking*
- *Complimentary laundry*
- *Picnic hampers by arrangement*
- *Vineyards, golf, Arts Centre*
- *Barbeque facilities*

DIRECTIONS:
Please phone for easy directions.
Advanced booking recommended.

Welcome to **Lilac Rose**. We offer warm hospitality and hope your stay with us will be memorable. We are easily found being just minutes from the Main North road and 7 min. by car from Christchurch Arts Centre and the city. Our charming villa has been completely renovated to offer luxury accommodation. Three beautifully furnished guest rooms have televison, tea making facilities, fresh flowers, chocolates and toiletries. The three rooms have spacious, fully tiled bathrooms with high pressure showers. The new 'Attic Suite' is totally private and has a separate lounge with television and a DVD player. The elegant 'Attic Bedroom' has been furnished with rich burgandy silk and has views to the Port Hills – a perfect retreat for a honeymoon or those wanting a little more privacy. At the end of the day relax in the elegantly furnished guest lounge and enjoy a complimentary glass of great New Zealand wine. Breakfast is a main event with temptations such as Grand Marnier French Toast, creamy scrambled eggs, seasonal fruits and home-made muesli. We are experienced hosts, who look forward to being part of your journey. We share our home with a Cocker Spaniel.

Riverview Lodge

361 Cambridge Terrace, Christchurch Central
Ph (03) 365 2860, Fax (03) 365 2845
email: *riverview.lodge@xtra.co.nz*
www.riverview.net.nz

Tariff : N.Z. Dollars	
Double	$170-225
Single	$100-160
Child	neg

Bedrooms	Qty
Double	4
Twin	1
Single	1
Bed Size	**Qty**
Super King	
King	
Queen	4
Double	1
King/Single	1
Bathrooms	**Qty**
Ensuite	5
Private	1
Guest Share	

Christchurch Central

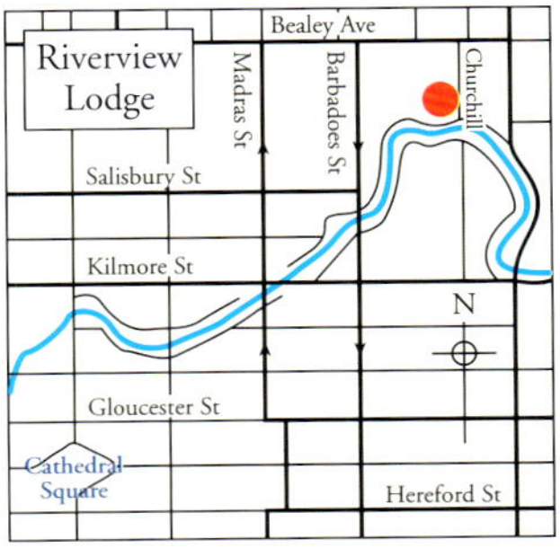

Features & Attractions

- *10 min. river walk into Central Business District*
- *Romantic river setting*
- *Historic residence*
- *Swimming pool 10 min. walk*
- *Bicycles, kayaks, golf clubs for guests to use*
- *Fine dining 8 min. walk*

Riverview Lodge is a restored Edwardian residence that reflects the grace and style of the period with some fine carved Kauri and Rimu features. It is ideally situated on the banks of the Avon River in the tranquil setting surrounded by an old English garden with mature trees. Guest rooms are elegant combining modern facilities with colonial furnishings. All rooms have ensuite/private facilities, TV and heating. Balconies provide superb river views. Breakfast is a house speciality with a choice of cooked and continental fare. As experienced travellers and tour operators we'll be happy to provide you with all the information that will make your stay in Christchurch and New Zealand memorable. We are multilingual.

We do operate a few self-contained cottages and character apartments nearby for those who like to stay more independently and/or for longer times. See www.moacottages.co.nz

Home Lea Bed & Breakfast

195 Bealey Avenue, Christchurch
Ph (03) 379 9977, Fax (03) 379 4099
email: *homelea@xtra.co.nz*
www.homelea.co.nz

@home NEW ZEALAND

Tariff : N.Z. Dollars	
Double	$105-145
Single	$85-120
Child	neg

Bedrooms	Qty
Double	1
Twin	3
Single	1
Bed Size	**Qty**
Super King	
King	1
Queen	3
Double	
Single	4
Bathrooms	**Qty**
Ensuite	2
Private	2
Guest Share	1

H **Bed & Breakfast Homestay** BB

VISA MasterCard AMERICAN EXPRESS

Features & Attractions

- *Central location*
- *Easy to find*
- *Warm & friendly atmosphere*
- *Gluten free food available*
- *Walk to city attractions*
- *Off-street parking*
- *Children welcome*
- *Grand piano for musicians*

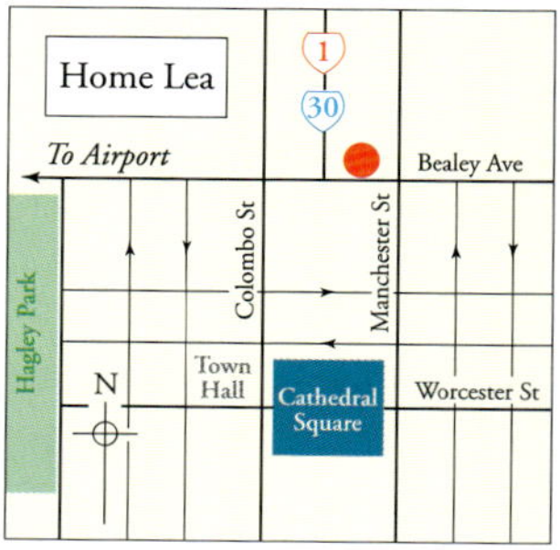

DIRECTIONS:
Please phone for direct route from airport.
Advance reservation recommended.

Home Lea offers the traveller a comfortable and enjoyable stay. Built in the early 1900's, **Home Lea** has the charm and character of a large New Zealand home of that era: Rimu panelling, leadlight windows, and a large lounge with a log fire. Tea, coffee, biscuits and fruit are available at all times. **Home Lea Bed & Breakfast** is centrally located within walking distance of Cathedral Square, Art Gallery, Botanic Gardens and a large variety of restaurants. We are easy to find arriving from any direction into Christchurch, situated on the north side of Bealey Avenue near Colombo Street, Christchurch's main street.

Off street parking, and email/fax facilities available for guests. Pauline and Gerald are happy to share their knowledge of local attractions and their special interests are travel, sailing and music.

Devon Bed & Breakfast Hotel

69 Armagh Street, Christchurch
Ph (03) 366 0398, Fax (03) 366 0392
email: *bandbdevonhotel@xtra.co.nz*
www.devonbandbhotel.co.nz

Tariff : N.Z. Dollars	
Double	$125-165
Single	$89-125
Child	$35

Bedrooms	Qty
Double	6
Twin	3
Single	2
Bed Size	**Qty**
Super King	
King	
Queen	6
King/Single	1
Single	14
Bathrooms	**Qty**
Ensuite	6
Private	1
Guest Share	4

Bed & Breakfast Guest House

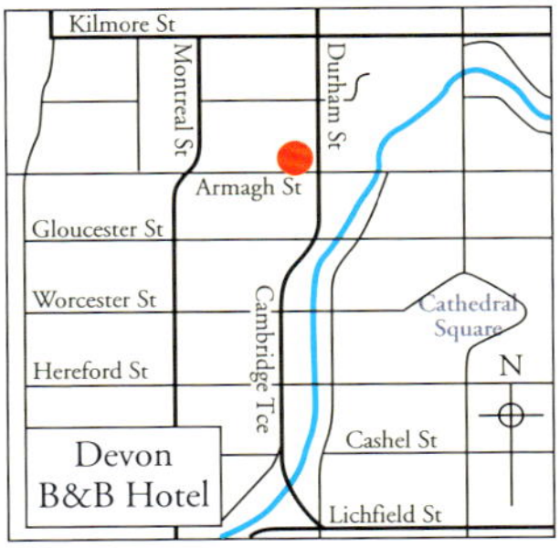

Features & Attractions

- *Central City*
- *Olde Worlde English Manor*
- *Edwardian architecture*
- *Elegant & comfortable*
- *Close to Hagley Park*
- *Hearty breakfasts*
- *Spacious guest lounge*
- *On historic tram route*

Located in the heart of beautiful Christchurch City, The **Devon** offers elegance and comfort in the style of an Olde Worlde English Manor. The historic Christchurch Tramway, re-established in 1994, runs past the front door. A short walk will take you to Hagley Park where you can relax, enjoy the frequent outdoor entertainment or just stroll through the beautiful Botanical Gardens. The **Devon** has retained its grace and dignified appearance for almost a century. The beautiful panelled entrance hall and dining room have a warm ambience that evokes the feel of a bygone era. Nowadays you can luxuriate in a comfortable queen-sized bed. Enjoy a hearty breakfast before venturing forth to take in the many attractions of our delightful garden city with its truly English atmosphere. The Christchurch Cathedral, Town Hall, Arts Centre, Christchurch Art Gallery, live theatre, movie theatres, the Casino, Museum, Hospital and excellent shopping are all within easy walking distance. Wireless Internet access/ + Internet access available.

We look forward to welcoming you!

HAMILTONS

307 Cambridge Terrace, Christchurch 8001
Ph (03) 366 9993
Mobile 021-150 1228
email: *camb307@xtra.co.nz*

Tariff : N.Z. Dollars	
Double	$135-160
Single	$110-125
Child	

Bedrooms	Qty
Double	1
Twin	
Single	
Bed Size	**Qty**
Super King	
King	
Queen	1
Double	
Single	1
Bathrooms	**Qty**
Ensuite	
Private	1
Guest Share	

City Bed & Breakfast

Features & Attractions

- *Architectural design*
- *Avon River views*
- *5 minutes to cafés etc.*
- *Guest sitting room*
- *A great place to stay*
- *A central city site*
- *Private guest facilities*
- *Underfloor heating*

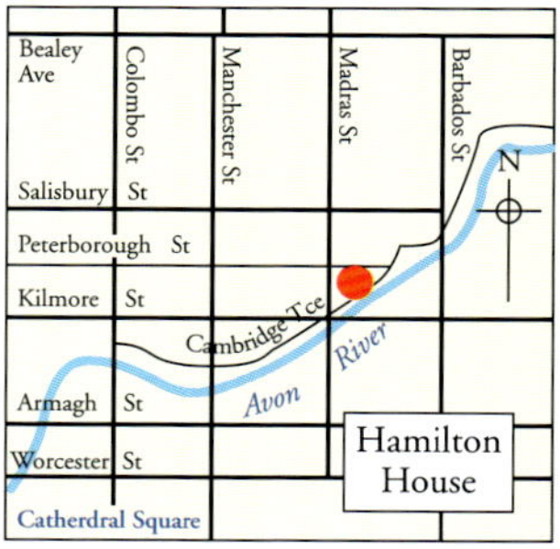

This much admired architecturally designed home offers guests prime comfort and convenience. The home is situated in a quiet cul-de-sac yet it is just a short walk to the city through our unique poplar-tree lined river walk; a delight in any season and an absolute gem in autumn. The fireman's memorial is nearby. Conveniently located to many amenities and attractions the city offers. A delicious breakfast is served at a time to suit. In summer guests may enjoy breakfast alfresco on the spacious balcony overlooking the Avon River or in the private, sunny courtyard. In winter, you may decide to have your breakfast, tea or coffee beside the log fire. Tea and coffee facilities. Parking available. Garage and laundry facilities available at a small charge. I aim to provide that special Christchurch accommodation experience. Reservations recommended; please phone, email or write.

The Close

10 Jane Deans Close, Christchurch
Ph (03) 343 5907, Fax (03) 343 5907
Mobile 021-402 427
email: *pandkmurray@xtra.co.nz*
www.theclose.co.nz

@ home NEW ZEALAND

Features & Attractions

- *Courtesy pick-up*
- *Close to city centre*
- *Many top restaurants*
- *Email facility*
- *Safe parking*
- *Great food*

$	
Double	$150-175
Single	$100-125
Child	

Bed & Breakfast Homestay

Bedrooms	Qty
Double	2
Twin	
Single	
Bed Size	**Qty**
King	1
Queen	1
Double	
Single	
Bathrooms	**Qty**
Ensuite	1
Private	1
Guest Share	

The Close, as its name suggests, is situated in a leafy secluded close, within a 5 minute bus ride into the city centre. Alternatively you could walk through our beautiful Hagley Park via the botanic gardens, past the popular Art Centre into the city, a 25 min walk. We are also near two historic homesteads, Mona Vale and Deans Bush, and within walking distance of a golf course and tennis courts. Also within 5 min walk are a large shopping complex and a huge variety of restaurants. We offer a courtesy pick-up as we are close to the airport and train station. Paul and I are 50+ with two grown daughters, one in San Francisco and one in Melbourne. We have travelled extensively and always enjoy meeting new people. Our aim is to make your stay as comfortable as possible, indulge you with good food and hopefully good conversation, should you wish it.

Central City B&B

31 Peacock Street, Christchurch
Ph (03) 377 8750, Fax (03) 377 8760
Mobile 021-134 4122
email: *trish.barry@actrix.co.nz*

Features & Attractions

- *Friendly hosts*
- *Delicious breakfasts*
- *Spa pool*
- *Very central location – walk to city, gardens, Hagley park*
- *Dinner by arrangement*

$	
Double	$120
Single	$90
Child	neg

Homestay Bed & Breakfast

Bedrooms	Qty
Double	2
Twin	
Single	
Bed Size	**Qty**
King/Twin	1
Queen	1
Double	
Single	
Bathrooms	**Qty**
Ensuite	
Private	1
Family Share	1

We are well travelled, fun loving and really enjoy meeting people. We provide a relaxing atmosphere and look forward to making your stay a happy and memorable one. We welcome you to our modern home, right in the city. It is tastefully and stylishly decorated and opens to a lovely lawn surrounded by olive trees and native grasses. Walk to all the inner city attractions.

Delicious continental and/or cooked breakfast is available at a time to suit you. Complimentary tea, coffee and home-baking is available at any time. We are keen sportspeople and love especially tennis, golf, and skiing. We are happy to help you organise your sporting activities. Relax in the garden in summer and by the fire in the winter.

DIRECTIONS:
Peacock Street is parallel to Bealey Ave and runs between the two one-way streets - Durham and Montreal Streets.

The Chester

Apt. 3, 173 Chester Street East, Christchurch
Ph (03) 366 5777, Fax (03) 365 6314
Mobile 021-365 495
e-mail: *thechester@clear.net.nz*
www.thechester.com

Features & Attractions

- *Spacious & private*
- *Large comfortable suite*
- *1km from City Center*
- *Quiet location*
- *Historic building*
- *Ample parking*

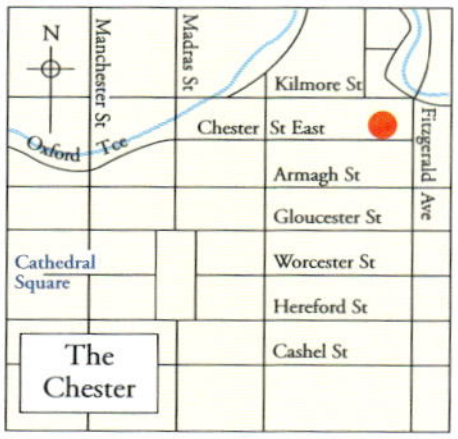

Boutique Accommodation Bed & Breakfast

Double	$95-120
Single	$65-75
Child	

The Chester Bed & Breakfast Apartment in Christchurch, New Zealand, offers all modern comforts and amenities. It is within close walking distance of the city centre, restaurants, banks, town hall, Arts Centre, Casino and Convention Centre. Perfect for holiday or business. Your hosts, Jan and Jennifer van den Berg, will ensure your stay is comfortable and memorable.

Airport transfers, theatre and concert bookings can be arranged on request.

The Chester is situated in the historic Old Wards Brewery Building. This heritage building, which dates back to the 1850's, has now converted into elegant apartments.

Bedrooms	Qty
Double	1
Twin	
Single	1
Bed Size	**Qty**
Super King	1
Queen	
Double	
King/Single	1
Bathrooms	**Qty**
Ensuite	2
Private	
Guest Share	

Christchurch Central ▶ YOUR HOSTS: **Tracey and Des Ramsay** Free Ph: 0800 932 850

The Grange Guest House/Serviced Apartments

56 Armagh Street, Christchurch
Ph (03) 366 2850, Fax (03) 374 2470
Mobile 025-297 6920
email: *reservations@thegrange.co.nz*
www.thegrange.co.nz

Features & Attractions

- *On the tourist tram route*
- *Friendly service*
- *Broadband internet access*
- *Air conditioned comfort*
- *Generous breakfast*
- *Art gallery & gardens close*

Bed & Breakfast Guest House

Double	$125-160
Single	$110-140
Child	$15

The Grange Guesthouse, a gracious Victorian mansion, is situated within walking distance from most of Christchurch's favourite spots, including Cathedral Square, the Art's Centre, Art Gallery and Museum, also the Botanical Gardens, Hagley Park and Mona Vale. Built before the turn of last century and now tastefully refurbished, The Grange Guesthouse offers a high standard of accommodation. You can relax in the guest lounge. During your stay you will be treated to comfortable accommodation, complimentary tea and coffee, email and Broadband internet access, laundry services and complimentary bicycles.

Sightseeing tours and onward travel can be arranged. Banks, shops, restaurants, night clubs and cafés are all within easy walking distance. Des and Tracey will ensure your stay is pleasurable and relaxed. All tariffs include GST and full cooked breakfast.

Please enquire about our winter rates (1st May to 1st October).

Bedrooms	Qty
Double	16
Twin	
Single	
Bed Size	**Qty**
Super King	2
Queen	5
Double	1
King/Single	6
Single	3
Bathrooms	**Qty**
Ensuite	16
Private	

Devon on the Park

13 B Devon Street, Beckenham, Christchurch
Ph (03) 337 1518, Fax (03) 962 5998
Mobile 021-743 814
email: *devononthepark@hotmail.com*

Tariff : N.Z. Dollars	
Double	$110-135
Single	$100
Child	

Bedrooms	Qty
Double	1
Twin	1
Single	
Bed Size	**Qty**
Super King	
King	
Queen	1
Double	
Single	2
Bathrooms	**Qty**
Ensuite	
Private	
Guest Share	1

Quality Bed & Breakfast on the Park

DIRECTIONS:
From Cathedral Square travel south on Colombo St towards the 'Port Hills' for about 2.5km. Turn right into Devon St. at Countdown Supermarket.
Please phone for directions if required.

Features & Attractions

- *Walk to cafés and shops*
- *Select breakfast menu*
- *Quiet park setting*
- *Off-street parking*
- *Private rooms with a view*
- *Warm hospitality-smoke free*
- *Courtesy transfer-air/rail/bus*
- *City & Botanic Gardens 5min*

Picture a typical English summer in the park. The clear, mellow sound of the Song Thrush as the occasional butterfly flits by. The lads all in white playing cricket on a Saturday afternoon. This is the scene from **Devon on the Park.** A modern 'terrace style' townhouse with two spacious upstairs bedrooms furnished with your home comforts in mind. A choice of continental or sumptuous cooked breakfast awaits you each morning. Frequent bus services take you to or around the city and suburban malls, arts and crafts, botanic gardens, museum, art gallery, Ferrymead Historic Park, many golf courses and wineries. A short drive to the foot of Mt Cavendish and a brief 'Gondola' ride to the top gives a spectacular 360 degree view of Christchurch City, Banks Peninsula, Pegasus Bay and the fascinating little port town of Lyttelton. Ross and Claire have a special interest in flowers and things horticultural and would welcome the opportunity to share with you or to assist you to organise as much or as little of your interests as you desire.

POOL HOUSE

57 Aynsley Terrace, Murray Aynsley, Christchurch
Ph (03) 337 0380
email: *entwistle@slingshot.co.nz*

Tariff : N.Z. Dollars	
Double	$125
Single	$90
Child	neg

Bedrooms	Qty
Double or Twin	1
Twin	
Single	
Bed Size	**Qty**
Super King	
King/Single	2
Queen	1
Double	
Single	
Bathrooms	**Qty**
Ensuite	1
Private	
Guest Share	

Bed & Breakfast
Self-contained Accommodation

Features & Attractions

- *Ten minutes to city centre*
- *Separate living area*
- *Cosy under-floor heating*
- *River walks*
- *Swimming pool*
- *TV and DVD player*
- *Adjacent to Hansen Park*
- *Port Hills walking tracks*

The **Pool House** is a cosy self-contained weatherboard guest house. The comfortable, separate living and sleeping areas are kept beautifully warm with under-floor heating, as is the well appointed ensuite shower room.
Children can be accommodated by arrangement on the sofa-bed in the living area. Facilities include a fridge and microwave in addition to tea and coffee making, TV and DVD player. Ample continental breakfast can be enjoyed inside or out in the sheltered courtyard sun trap.
Our 1920's villa overlooks Hansen Park and the Heathcote River offering gentle riverside walks and a children's playground. There are frequent buses into the city and to the Port of Lyttelton.
Local sandy beaches are ten to fifteen minutes by car. The Rapaki Track gives walking access to the Port Hills which are close behind the house. Our border collie, Shadow, will join us in giving you a warm welcome to Christchurch and its many attractions.

SEASIDE HAVEN

165F Rockinghorse Road, Southshore, Christchurch
Ph (03) 388 2177, Fax (03) 388 2177
Mobile 021-136 2770
email: *irwmethven@hotmail.com*

Features & Attractions

- *Sea and mountain views*
- *Immediate access to beach*
- *Wave ski, swimming, surfing*
- *Friendly, hospitable hosts*
- *Breakfast on the deck*
- *Single-party bookings*

$		
	Double	$130-150
	Single	
	Child	

Seaside Boutique Bed & Breakfast

Bedrooms	Qty
Double	1
Twin	
Single	
Bed Size	**Qty**
King	
Queen	1
Double	
Single	1
Bathrooms	**Qty**
Ensuite	
Private	1
Guest Share	

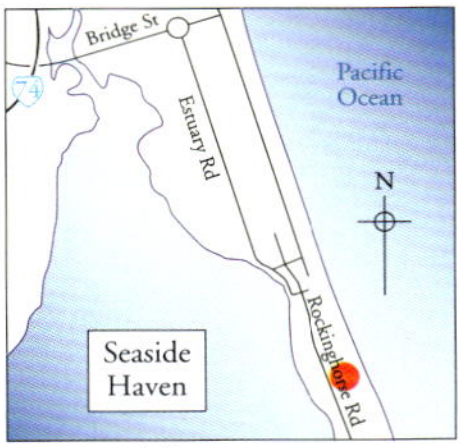

The sea and sand is our front garden. Guests will enjoy a delicious al fresco breakfast as they take in the breathtaking views over the Pacific Ocean, extending from Kaikoura to Banks Peninsula. Relax on the deck with a coffee as you listen to the surf roll in. Step out of your room onto the soft sand, into the surf, or sit and watch the sun rise over the horizon. Sea kayak, wave ski, boogie board, fish, swim or just stroll along this beautiful coastline, and all of this is only 20 min. from Christchurch city centre. Friendly, hospitable hosts offer you comfortable accommodation with all amenities in their beach home. There is an indoor swimming pool for summer use. Reservations for this Boutique Accommodation are recommended. Plenty of parking available. Meals on request. We look forward to your stay with us.

ON THE SHORE

126B Rocking Horse Road, South Shore, Christchurch
Ph (03) 388 5505
Mobile 021-202 2211
email: *enquiries@ontheshore.co.nz*
www.ontheshore.co.nz

Features & Attractions

- *Absolute waterfront*
- *Spa, views to Southern Alps*
- *Twelve minutes to city centre*
- *Private entrance*
- *Watersport equipment available*
- *Cafés and pub short walk*

$		
	Double	$199
	Single	$175
	Child	< 2 free

Boutique Waterfront 180 Degree Views

Bedrooms	Qty
Double	1
Twin	
Single	
Bed Size	**Qty**
King	
Queen	1
Double	1
Single	
Bathrooms	**Qty**
Ensuite	1
Private	
Guest Share	

On The Shore is located in a beautiful seaside area in Christchurch. South Shore is unique in that it is bounded by the Pacific Ocean on one side and the estuary on the other. Our home is situated on a 1415 square metre landscaped property on the waterfront overlooking the estuary and bird sanctuary, all within metres of the surf beach of South New Brighton. From the outside spa, your bedroom and from the balcony you have beautiful views of the Port Hills, Christchurch City and the Southern Alps beyond. Enjoy beautiful sunsets over the water.

On The Shore offers you a tranquil oasis, but if you like, a drive of only 12 minutes takes you to the city centre. Off-street parking. Home-made evening vegetarian meals by prior arrangement. Extra per person $50. Kids and pets live here.

MT. PLEASANT BED AND BREAKFAST

14 Hobday Lane, Mt. Pleasant, Christchurch
Ph (03) 384 9220, Fax (03) 384 9235
Mobile 021-070 3076
email: *kristiansen@xtra.co.nz*
www.mtpleasantbandb.co.nz

Features & Attractions

- *Full-sized private kitchen*
- *Private sauna (holds six)*
- *Christchurch Gondola 5 min.*
- *Views of City/Southern Alps*
- *Use of two mountain bikes*
- *King-size cast-iron bath*

$	
Double	$130
Single	
Child	Free

Self-contained Accommodation with Spectacular Views

Bedrooms	Qty
Double	1
Twin	
Single	
Bed Size	**Qty**
King	
Queen	1
Double	
Single	
Bathrooms	**Qty**
Ensuite	1
Private	
Guest Share	

This unique home offers a friendly and relaxed stay in your private suite. Enjoy your spacious and comfortable queen bedroom and ensuite bathroom with king-size vintage cast-iron bath (such bliss our guests tell us!). Sitting room with private entrance can accommodate extra sleeping facilities, leading to deck and sauna (takes six). Private full-sized kitchen facilities.

Explore the huge rambling garden – fascinating with waterwheel, plentiful trees and abundant bird life. Conveniently situated 15 min. from city, 10 min. to popular Sumner beach, 5 min. to paragliding, windsurfing, Gondola, walking and mountain-bike tracks. You will love it!

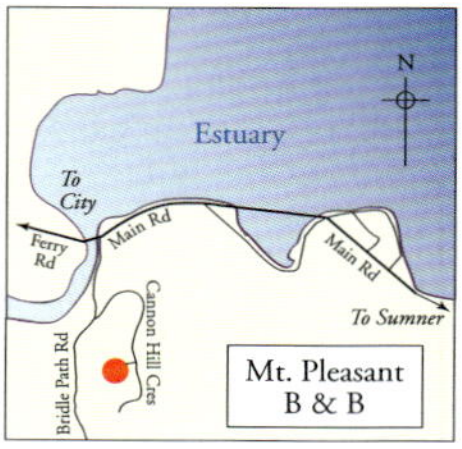

DIRECTIONS:
Once over Ferrymead Bridge turn right into Bridle Path Rd. Then 2nd left Cannon Hill Cresc., 2nd right Hobday Lane. Drive into no. 14 (last house at end of driveway on left).

Coastal Cliffs

11 Balmoral Lane, Redcliffs, Christchurch 8
Ph (03) 384 2247, Fax (03) 384 2205
Mobile 021-1082977
email: *coastalcliffs@xtra.co.nz*
www.coastalcliffs.co.nz

Tariff : N.Z. Dollars	
Double	$140
Single	$80
Child	

Bedrooms	Qty
Double	2
Twin	1
Single	
Bed Size	**Qty**
Super King	
King	
Queen	1
Double	
King Single	2
Bathrooms	**Qty**
Ensuite	2
Private	1
Guest Share	

DIRECTIONS:
Drive towards Sumner and after causeway turn right into McCormacks Bay Road and Balmoral Lane is on your left immediately after 1st house.
Advance booking is recommended

Redcliffs Christchurch

Features & Attractions

- *Warm, sunny Beach House*
- *Estuary bird sanctuary*
- *Yachting, wind-surfing, kayaks*
- *Unique interior design*
- *Close to beach, cafés, cinema*
- *Walk down woodland garden track to McCormacks Bay & walking tracks*
- *Fantails, kingfishers, bellbirds*

Coastal Cliffs provides a quiet hideaway – coastal living in an easy, relaxed and casual atmosphere. A large solar-heated swimming pool is surrounded by sheltered timber decks. Upstairs, the decks from the house offer uninterrupted views of the city and Southern Alps.

Nelly, our chocolate Labrador and Molly and Stella, our beautiful cats, add extra warmth. Our four white doves seem to show off when they fly, as they look so dramatic!

Self-contained apartment provides Television with DVD, microwave, fridge, tea and coffee facilities. Delicious breakfast can be served in your own room or enjoyed in the sunroom or on the outside decks.

Coastal Cliffs is 15 minutes from the city centre. – Laundry facilities are available.

Mt Pleasant Homestay

106A Mt Pleasant Road, Mt Pleasant, Christchurch
Ph (03) 384 1940, Fax (03) 384 1940
email: *mtpleasantbnb@xtra.co.nz*

Tariff : N.Z. Dollars	
Double	$120-140
Single	$90-100
Child	neg

Bedrooms	Qty
Double	1
Twin	1
Single	
Bed Size	**Qty**
Super King	
King/Twin	1
Queen	1
Double	
Single	
Bathrooms	**Qty**
Ensuite	
Private	2
Guest Share	

Bed & Breakfast Homestay
Panoramic Sea Views

Features & Attractions

- *Sea and mountain views*
- *Rest, comfort, peace*
- *Courtesy transfers*
- *Friendly, hospitable host*
- *Stylish, contemporary design*
- *Purpose-built guest accomm*
- *Guest lounge and kitchen*
- *Delicious breakfasts*

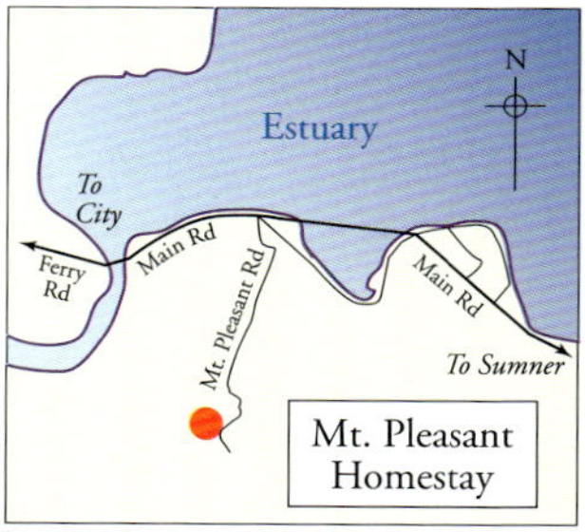

Jan welcomes you to **Mt Pleasant Homestay**. Simply park your car at the front door and then enjoy great hospitality plus the warmth and comfort of a new, modern, purpose-built home with breath-taking views of Pegasus Bay as far as the Kaikoura Mountain Range. All rooms open onto the patio and the garden, which is young but blooming! A guest lounge has full cooking facilities. Laundry, facsimile, internet available.

Sumner, the most popular beach in Christchurch (five minute drive) and its wonderful cafés will delight you and draw you back. The Christchurch gondola is minutes away as is the Ferrymead Heritage Park. Scenic walks and historical sights abound. If you wish, your host will happily introduce you to information to make the most of your time here and help with plans for further travel. Christchurch City Centre with its many attractions is ten minutes by car. You can be sure of a friendly and comfortable stay, plus sumptuous breakfasts at **Mt Pleasant Homestay**.

YOUR HOSTS: **Helen Mackay and Brian Lamb** Ph (03) 326 6209 **Sumner - Christchurch**

TIROMOANA

89 Richmond Hill Road, Sumner, Christchurch 8
Ph (03) 326 6209, Fax (03) 326 6208,
Mobile 021-107 0790
email: *relax@tiromoana.co.nz*
www.tiromoana.co.nz

Features & Attractions

- *Sea and mountain views*
- *Garden setting*
- *Close to restaurants & cafés*
- *Bath outside under the stars*
- *15 min. to city*
- *Friendly and relaxed*

$	
Double	$120-140
Single	$90-120
Child	$25

Boutique Homestay Bed & Breakfast

Bedrooms	Qty
Double	2
Twin	
Single	1
Bed Size	**Qty**
King	1
Queen	1
Double	1
King/Single	2
Bathrooms	**Qty**
Ensuite	1
Private	1
Guest Share	

Tiromoana is one of the original homes of Sumner, built in 1904 in a spectacular position overlooking the beach. The atmosphere is friendly, relaxed and informal, providing guests' lounge with kitchen facilities.
A fresh and generous breakfast is included in the tariff – weather permitting it can be taken on the deck looking out towards the sea. Wander the garden, have a bath outside under the stars and sleep to the sound of the sea. Make yourself at home.
Tiromoana is within walking distance of the village cafés, movie theatres and beach. Sumner is only 15 minutes from the city, a perfect spot to relax. We're happy to share our local knowledge to help you maximise your stay. Laundry facilities are available.
We look forward to welcoming you.

DIRECTIONS: Drive towards Sumner. Turn right at Surf Club building (on beach) to Nayland Street, 1st right to Richmond Hill Road. We are on second sharp corner with flat access.

YOUR HOSTS: **Rowena and Max Dorfliger** Ph (03) 329 9118 **Lyttelton-Christchurch**

BERGLI HILL FARM

265 Charteris Bay Rd, Teddington, Lyttelton Harbour, RD1
Ph(03) 329 9118, Fax (03) 329 9118
Mobile 027-482 9410
email: *bergli@ihug.co.nz*
www.vmacgill.net/bergli

Features & Attractions

- *Harbour views*
- *Friendly animals*
- *Interesting hosts*
- *Spa*
- *Self-built log house*
- *German & Japanese spoken*

$	
Double	$125-150
Single	$85-110
Triple	$195-220

Farmstay Bed & Breakfast

日本語出来ます

Bedrooms	Qty
Double	4
Twin	1
Single	
Bed Size	**Qty**
SuperKing/twin	1
Queen	1
Double	2
Single	4
Bathrooms	**Qty**
Ensuite	2
Private	
Guest Share	1

Enjoy the panoramic views of the inner Lyttelton Harbour from the log house we built ourselves. We are both self-employed (wood worker and shadow puppeteer) and enjoy sharing the occassional sail on Max's yacht.

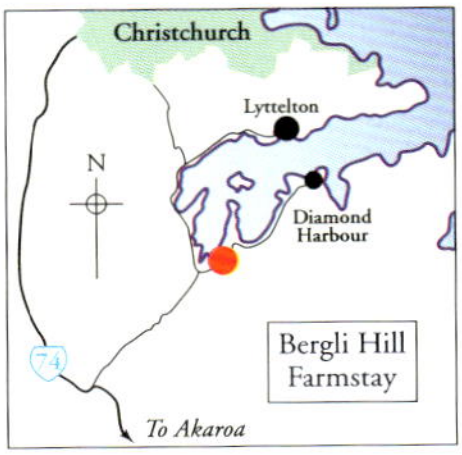

Our 100 acre farm has forests, sheep, cows and alpacas. Rowena also offers wool-fun and workshops. Golf, horse-trekking and walking tracks are nearby.
Bergli is ideally situated for sightseeing in Christchurch (30 minutes), Akaroa (1 hour 10 minutes) and Banks Peninsula.

Broad Oaks Vista

4 Swanton Drive, Broad Oaks, Cashmere, Christchurch
Ph (03) 332 5724, Fax (03) 332 5724
Mobile 025-224 6537
email: *brianmor@clear.net.nz*
www.christchurchbandb.co.nz

Tariff : N.Z. Dollars	
Double	$180
Single	$160
Child	$120

Bedrooms	Qty
Double	2
Twin	2
Single	2
Bed Size	**Qty**
Super King/Twin	2
King	
Queen	
Double	
Single	
Bathrooms	**Qty**
Ensuite	2
Private	
Guest Share	

Bed & Breakfast
Fine Accommodation

Features & Attractions

- *A warm & happy place to stay*
- *10 minutes to city centre*
- *Full or continental breakfast*
- *Private off-street parking*
- *Internet and laundry facilities*
- *Pre-evening drinks*
- *Stunning sunsets*
- *Outstanding views from every room*

DIRECTIONS:
Proceed along Colombo Street to bottom of hill. Turn left at the roundabout into Centaurus Rd. Travel along Centaurus Rd 0.9 km and turn right into Major Aitken Drive. Carry on up the hill and turn right at Kenmure Reserve. Proceed along Kenmure Drive and turn right at Swanton Drive. Turn into first lane on right.

Our unique new home, situated on the Cashmere Hills in Christchurch, offers something special to all our guests. Each guest room, with super king or twin beds, is ideally sited to give individual privacy and modern comforts. Satin-jet showers, heated mirrors, hair dryers and personal robes compliment your ensuite setting. Your luggage can be conveniently placed in your own walk-in wardrobe. Each guest room looks out through glass doors to amazing views over Christchurch and beyond. Relax on your own outdoor patio and seating. Val and Brian enjoyed staying in B & B's so much they decided to design their own. Val is the keen gardener while Brian does the spade work. Brian is also active in Rotary and International Fellowship. We offer pre-evening drinks and take pride in our New Zealand wines. Close by are a number of dining cafés and restaurants. Beaches, estuary, vineyards, golf courses and walking tracks are all close by. Your hosts will assist you in every way with travel planning and transport. We thoroughly recommend at least a 3-night stop over to really appreciate what the Garden City of Christchurch has to offer.

Andaview

18 Woodlau Rise, Huntsbury, Christchurch
Ph (03) 332 5522, Fax (03) 332 5592
Mobile 027-433 2769
email: *andaview@xtra.co.nz*
www.andaview.co.nz

Tariff : N.Z. Dollars	
Double	$170-230
Single	$150-175
Child	n/a

Bedrooms	Qty
Double	2
Twin	
Single	
Bed Size	**Qty**
Super King/Twin	1
King	1
Queen	
Double	
Single	
Bathrooms	**Qty**
Ensuite	1
Private	1
Guest Share	

VISA MasterCard eftpos

Bed & Breakfast
Absolute Ambience

DIRECTIONS:
Please phone, fax, or email for easy directions.
Advance bookings recommended.

Features & Attractions

- *Stunning views, day and night*
- *Purpose-built for guests*
- *Separate guest lounge, balcony*
- *Evening hospitality hour*
- *Super comfortable beds*
- *Luxurious double spa bath*
- *Scrumptuous breakfasts*
- *Complimentary hi-speed internet*

We invite you to **Andaview** to experience genuine Kiwi hospitality just 10 minutes from the city centre. Our beautifully decorated guest rooms offer TV/DVDs, feather duvéts, super comfy pillows and beds, electric blankets, hair dryers, large, fluffy towels, luxurious bathrobes, fresh flowers and a choice of coffees, teas and homemade treats.

Your breakfast can be served on a tray in your room, on your balcony or at the dining table – it's up to you.
We have a comprehensive knowledge of Christchurch, the South Island and its many attractions, for example, 15 golf courses within 30 minutes drive, 5 ski fields within 2 hours drive, Akaroa, our French village, 1¼ hrs and Hanmer Springs thermal resort 1½ hrs.
In the evening relax in our guest lounge (warm fire in winter, sunny balcony in summer), with a New Zealand wine and watch the sun set behind the mountains.
We have ample off-street parking and a guest laundry. Late flight arrivals happily catered for.

Christchurch ▶ YOUR HOSTS: **Jenny and Bob Wilkinson** Free Ph: 0800 352 7564

ONUKU BED & BREAKFAST

27 Harry Ell Drive, Christchurch
Ph (03) 332 7296
email: *bob.wilkinson@paradise.net.nz*
www.onukubedandbreakfast.co.nz

Features & Attractions

- *Families welcome*
- *Hill walks*
- *Hiking tours arranged*
- *Golf & bridge arranged*
- *Warm friendly hospitality*
- *Dinner by arrangement*

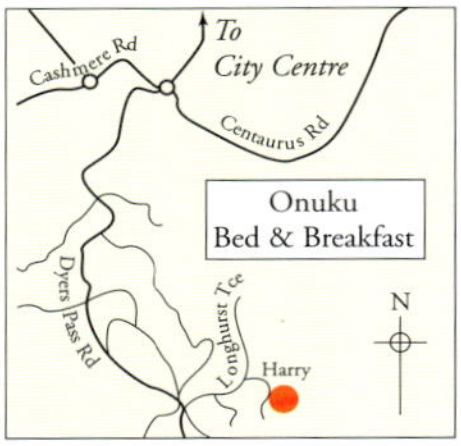

H **Luxury Bed & Breakfast** BB

$	
Double	$150-175
Single	$100
Child	

Onuku Bed & Breakfast is a stunning, newly created upmarket home, specifically designed for the comfort of guests. It has panoramic views from Banks Peninsula over the city and plains to the sea and mountains. The ground floor (with two bedrooms, two bathrooms and living area) is most suitable for a family or group. Bob is involved in the tourism industry and can arrange and accompany guests on golf and hiking tours.

Jenny is a New Zealand bridge representative and is happy to arrange a friendly game of bridge either at home or in one of the local clubs. We have both travelled extensively and promise fellow travellers a warm and friendly welcome along with our labrador, Max and cat, Tao.

Bedrooms	Qty
Double	2
Twin	1
Single	
Bed Size	**Qty**
King	
Queen	2
Double	
Single	2
Bathrooms	**Qty**
Ensuite	2
Private	1
Guest Share	

Westmorland - Christchurch ▶ YOUR HOSTS: **Georgie and Ron McKie** Ph: (03) 339 6170

SLIPPERS

66 Penruddock Rise, Westmorland, Christchurch
Ph (03) 339 6170, Fax (03) 339 6170
Mobile 021-022 97650
email: *mckiepic@paradise.net.nz*
www.slippersbnb.co.nz

Features & Attractions

- *Single-party booking*
- *Special diets catered for*
- *Gourment dinners with wine*
- *7km to city, bus at gate*
- *Photographic facilities*
- *Complimentary internet*

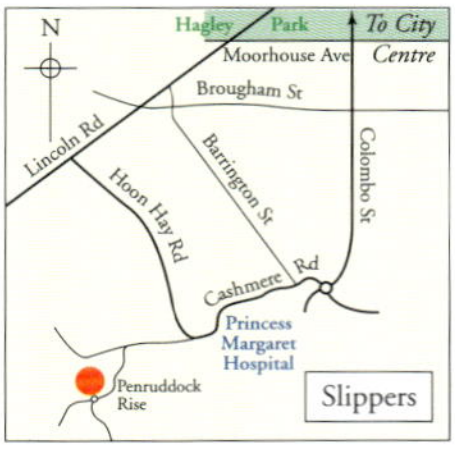

H **Homestay Bed & Breakfast** BB

$	
Double	$190
Single	$120
Child	neg

Pure New Zealand wool slippers are ready for you when you arrive at **Slippers**. Relax in a beautiful Port Hills home and enjoy the stunning views of the Alps, the Canterbury Plains and the city.

Your suite of rooms includes two bedrooms, a lounge, private bathroom and secluded patio and balcony areas, all with the highest standard of appointments. Home-baking, fruit bowl, a selection of teas and Papua New Guinean plunger coffee are always available.

Photographic guests are welcome to use a chemical darkroom and our digital facilities. Allow us and our two cats, to assist you with your travel plans and to get the most from your Christchurch stay. Check our website.

Bedrooms	Qty
Double	1
Twin	
Single	1
Bed Size	**Qty**
King	1
Queen	
Double	
Single	1
Bathrooms	**Qty**
Ensuite	
Private	1
Guest Share	

WILLERSLEY COTTAGE

85 Sutherlands Road, Halswell, Christchurch
Ph (03) 322 7225
Mobile 021-102 1775
email: *willersley@inet.net.nz*

Tariff : N.Z. Dollars	
Double	$120
Single	$100
Extra PP	$20

Bedrooms	Qty
Double	1
Twin	1
Single	
Bed Size	**Qty**
Super King	
King	
Queen	1
Double	
Single	2
Bathrooms	**Qty**
Ensuite	
Private	1
Guest Share	

BA

Self-contained Cottage in Unique Garden Setting

SC

Features & Attractions

- *Tranquil rural atmosphere*
- *Cottage exclusively yours*
- *Scenic drive to local wineries*
- *Walk to Halswell Quarry Park*
- *8km to city centre*
- *5 min to shopping centre*
- *Self catering*
- *Unique garden setting*

Willersley Cottage is situated on a 6 acre smallholding in a rural area on the outskirts of Christchurch, yet is only a 12 minute drive to the city centre. The cottage is set on its own in a peaceful secluded garden, 75 metres from the main house.

The sunny open plan living area has french doors which open onto the cottage garden. Fully equipped kitchen, TV, bathroom with shower and vanity. Separate toilet. Washing machine and clothesline. All linen provided. We have created our own corner of paradise from a piece of bare land and invite guests to stroll through the various areas of the garden. You will find a large potager and adjoining apple orchard, which have been managed on organic principles for the past 20 years. There are some interesting architectural features, in fact the garden would appeal to keen gardeners or environmentalists. The cottage is conveniently located for exploring the Christchurch area and scenic Banks Peninsula.

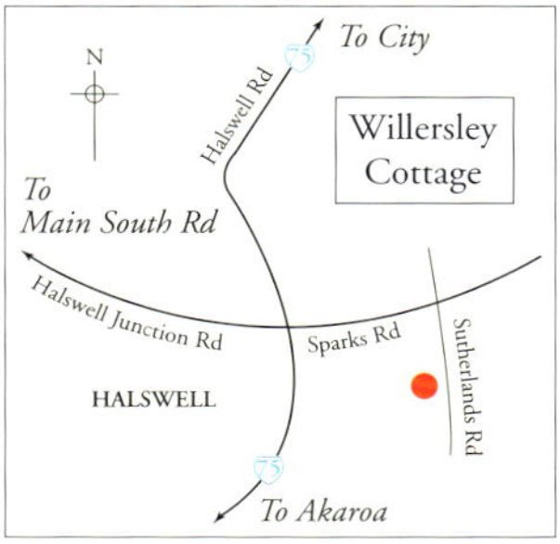

DIRECTIONS: When you reach No 85 please drive through the brick entrance and along the tree-lined drive until you reach the house.

Huntingdon Grange

Shands Road, RD 6, Broadfield, Christchurch
Ph (03) 344 5899, Fax (03) 344 5599
Mobile 027-446 6144
email: *stay@huntingdongrange.co.nz*
www.huntingdongrange.co.nz

Tariff : N.Z. Dollars	
Double	$120-200
Single	$90
Child	neg

Bedrooms	Qty
Double	4
Twin	1
Single	
Bed Size	**Qty**
Super King	
King	1
Queen	3
Double	
King Single	2
Bathrooms	**Qty**
Ensuite	3
Private	
Guest Share	1

Bed & Breakfast
Countrystay

Features & Attractions

- *Beautiful country estate*
- *Expansive gardens*
- *Generous, stylish rooms*
- *Hearty breakfasts*
- *Swimming pool*
- *Tennis, boules, croquet*
- *Outside bath*
- *Wineries, golf, shopping*

DIRECTIONS:
Driving south from Christchurch City on State Highway 1, at Hornby turn left over the railway line into Shands Road. At 6.5 km look to see **Huntingdon Grange** sign on the right.

Enjoy the ambience of our small country estate. Superb choices of rooms including 'The Smithy' – a delightful hideaway and 'The Stablecroft' – a fully self-contained, queen bedroom apartment. Full breakfast. Tea, coffee, milk, sugar and cookies also provided. Unwind in the stylish lounge around the open fire or on the covered barbeque terrace. Quality furnishings and tasteful décor enhance your relaxation. Enjoy tennis, pétanque or croquet, swim in our pool (summer) or relax in the expansive gardens. Just fifteen minutes from Christchurch City, ten minutes from the airport and five minutes to Lincoln University. Golf courses, wineries, restaurants and shopping are close by, and within an hour you can ski or snowboard at one of over a dozen Canterbury ski areas, or we'll transfer you to the Tranz Alpine train for 'one of the greatest train journeys in the world'. **Huntingdon Grange** also offers **stabling** and full size **all-weather dressage arena** as well as a seminar room for sales meetings or board meetings.

The Paddock

Weedons Road, RD 5 Broadfield, Christchurch
Ph (03) 347 4142
email: *thepaddock@xtra.co.nz*

Tariff : N.Z. Dollars	
Double	$150-198
Single	$150-198
Child	

Bedrooms	Qty
Double	3
Twin	
Single	
Bed Size	**Qty**
Super King	
King	
Queen	3
Double	
Single	
Bathrooms	**Qty**
Ensuite	2
Private	1
Guest Share	

VISA MasterCard

BB **Country Bed & Breakfast** F

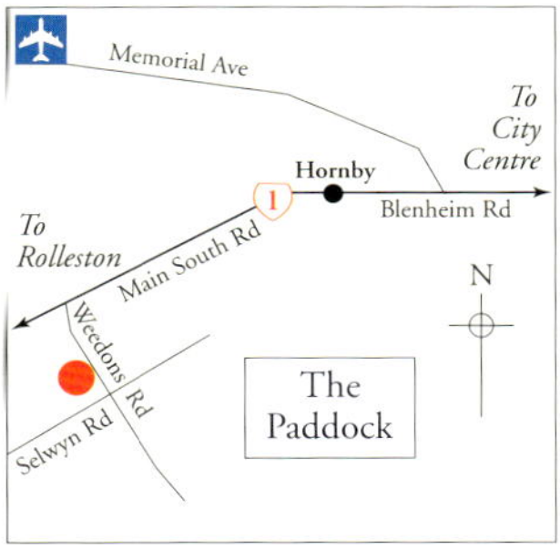

Features & Attractions

- *Luxurious, rural retreat*
- *Idyllic, peaceful gardens*
- *Private garden spa pool*
- *Working orchard*
- *All-weather tennis court*
- *Popular wineries nearby*
- *Close to city & airport*
- *Tranz-Alpine link – 3 min.*

We have purpose-built our home to be a luxury rural retreat, which we would now like to share with you. The rooms are spacious and attractive, opening out to a private veranda overlooking walnut, cherry and apple orchards. We also grow a wide variety of produce and where possible all meal ingredients are home-grown including: apple juice, cider, vegetables and fruit. A hearty cooked breakfast will be prepared for you each morning and will include bacon and eggs, cereals, breads and juices. Wander through the orchards and gardens and explore our property, complete with a variety of interesting pets. We are only 20 minutes from the city centre and international airport, with easy access to all main routes. Our 10 acre property is close to many of the well-known wineries and restaurants popular in Canterbury including Trent's Vineyard, Larcomb's Vineyard, The Raspberry Café and Drury's Wine Shed.

Cedarview Farm

33 Barters Road, Templeton, Christchurch RD 5
Ph (03) 349 7491, Fax (03) 349 7755
Mobile 027-433 5335
email: *cedarviewfarm@xtra.co.nz*
www.cedarviewhomestay.com

Tariff : N.Z. Dollars	
Double	$110-150
Single	$95-110
Child	neg

Bedrooms	Qty
Double	2
Twin	1
Single	
Bed Size	**Qty**
Super King	
King	
Queen	1
Double	1
Single	2
Bathrooms	**Qty**
Ensuite	1
Private	1
Guest Share	1

Farmstay Bed & Breakfast
"Where town meets country"

Features & Attractions

- *Airport 10min, City Centre 20min*
- *Highways, north, south, west, nearby*
- *Relaxed, tranquil atmosphere*
- *Restaurants, wineries, golf*
- *Factory outlet shopping*
- *Modern smoke-free home*
- *Lovely garden setting*
- *Antarctic experience*

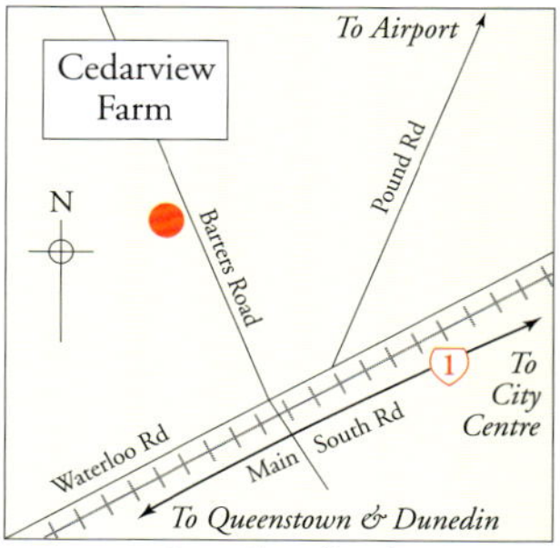

Welcome to New Zealand. We moved here from the UK in 1986 and simply love our lifestyle. Our modern home is situated on a small farm close to central Christchurch. We keep beef cattle, hens and occasionally a lamb or two. If animals interest you then an extra hand at feeding time is always appreciated. Especially when bottle feeding a baby calf! Take a trip to the ski fields (pick up at gate) then back home for a long hot soak in our spa pool.

Shopping, motor racing, golf, wineries and restaurants (enjoy a meal and see the kiwis at Willowbank Wildlife Reserve). Whatever your passion then we are close to it. Enjoy Carol's home-made bread, jams and preserves. Free-range eggs (providing the girls get busy and lay some of course) and even our own honey.
We look forward to getting to know you over a coffee, glass of wine or beer and helping you make the most of your stay in charming Christchurch.

Menteith Country House

Rapid No 961, Springs Road, RD 6, Christchurch
Ph (03) 325 2395
Mobile 021-131 5523
email: *stay@menteith.co.nz*
www.menteith.co.nz

Tariff : N.Z. Dollars	
Double	$150-190
Single	$135-170
Child	neg

Bedrooms	Qty
Double	3
Twin	
Single	
Bed Size	**Qty**
King	2
or KingSingle	4
Queen	1
Double	
Single	
Bathrooms	**Qty**
Ensuite	3
Private	
Guest Share	

Quality Country Bed & Breakfast

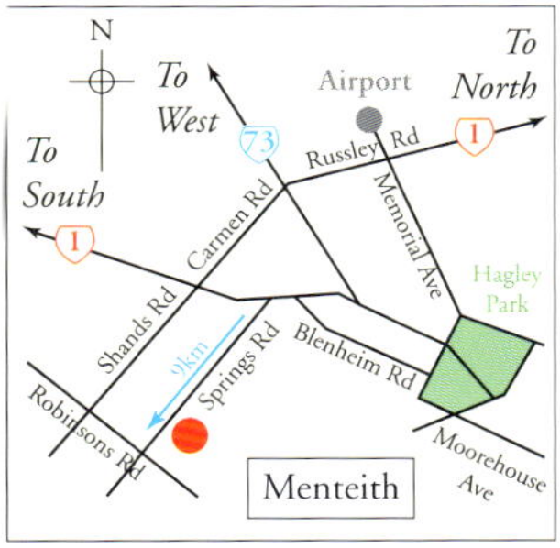

Features & Attractions

- *Heated swimming pool (summer)*
- *Country tranquility*
- *Delightful local restaurants*
- *Lincoln university 3km*
- *Indoor spa pool*
- *City/airport 15 min.*
- *Safe off-street parking*
- *Email/laundry facilities*

Menteith, named after an ancient Scottish Graham clan, nestles among mature trees with great views of hills and mountains. Awake to morning birdsong from your warm, spacious room or catch the world's news on your in-room TV while sipping your morning tea or coffee. In summer a pre-breakfast swim invigorates the body before a day of adventure exploring Christchurch, Akaroa or a return journey across the Alps by train. While enjoying your hearty breakfast in our sunny dining room, Stephen will enlighten you on the specialty honeys produced by the family, while you savour the flavours. Fay is an avid spinner of differing fibres and is happy to demonstrate her craft – you are very welcome to try your hand! Our **Port Hills** room with its magical view from the queen-sized bed collects the morning sun while the **Copland** and **Elie** rooms with flexible king or twin beds look out onto the garden. After a life in tourism, mainly at Franz Josef Glacier, our retirement interests include skiing, golf, Rotary, genealogy, travel and our grandchildren. Welcome to **Menteith**.

Rolleston-Christchurch ▶ YOUR HOSTS: Anne and Ron Finch Ph (03) 347 7605

Cedar Park Gardens

"Cedar Park", 101B Lowes Rd, Rolleston, Christchurch
Ph (03) 347 7605, Mobile 027-436 5156
email: *anne@cedarparkgardens.co.nz*
www.cedarparkgardens.co.nz

Features & Attractions

- *Secluded 1.5 acre garden*
- *Warm, friendly hosts*
- *Close to airport/city*
- *Secure off-road parking*
- *Superb breakfast menu*
- *Dinner by arrangement*

Quality Bed & Breakfast
Relaxing Homestay

$	
Double	$100-165
Single	$90-130
Child	

DIRECTIONS: At Rolleston BP Station, turn from SH 1onto Tennyson St, continue 1.5 km through stop sign to roundabout, turn right onto Lowes Rd. We are 300m on left, at **end** of lane.

Welcome to **Cedar Park Gardens.** Enjoy a relaxing stay in our modern, sunny home, set in beautiful, **prize-winning gardens**, less than 25 min. from central Christchurch. We're conveniently located 2 km off SH 1 and within easy reach of many Canterbury ski-fields, Lincoln University, Akaroa, wineries, golf courses, Christchurch attractions and airport, yet away from the hustle and bustle of city life. An excellent restaurant is only 10 min. walk away. Our main guest room has a private entrance and park-like outlook, tea/coffee facilities, TV, ensuite, and many extras.
A twin room is also available. Dine inside, or in our lovely garden. Transport to/from airport and TranzAlpine is available on request. Our hobbies include gardening, cooking, crafts, sailing, photography, and NZ travel. We can advise on activities and make bookings for you. Along with 'Tigger', our cat, we look forward to welcoming you.

Bedrooms	Qty
Double/Triple	1
Twin	1
Single	
Bed Size	**Qty**
King	
Queen	1
King/Single	1
Single	2
Bathrooms	**Qty**
Ensuite	1
Private	
Family Share	1

Lincoln - Christchurch ▶ YOUR HOSTS: Diane and Rick Fraser Ph (03) 325 3362

Hazelview

1153 Springs Road, Lincoln, Canterbury
Ph (03) 325 3362
email: *enquiry@hazelview.co.nz*
www.hazelview.co.nz

Features & Attractions

- *Secluded orchard setting*
- *City/airport 17 minutes*
- *Superb nearby restaurants*
- *Off-road covered parking*
- *1 km Lincoln University*
- *Courtesy pick-up*

Quality Bed & Breakfast
Countrystay

$	
Double	$120
Single	$105
Child	

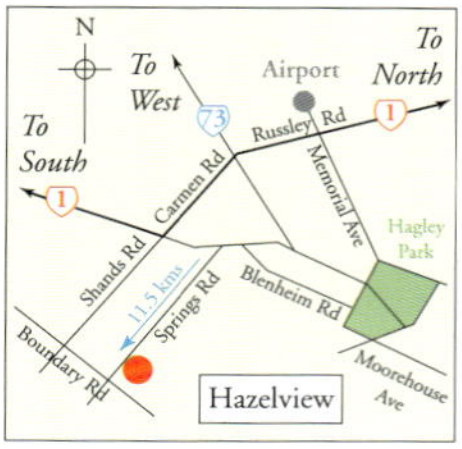

Welcome to **Hazelview.** Experience the quiet of the country just a short drive from the airport and city. Your spacious self-contained and well-appointed apartment assures a great stay. Dine out at the excellent nearby restaurants and wineries or prepare your own evening meal in the apartment kitchen. Take a stroll around the nut orchard (walnuts, hazelnuts, almonds, chestnuts, plus many different fruits and herbs) or simply relax in front of the TV, watch a video or read a book from the guest library. The spacious king-size bedroom, spa bath, and fine linen assure a great night's rest. Enjoy either a continental breakfast or by arrangement have a full cooked breakfast. Complimentary coffee, teas and nibbles.

Bedrooms	Qty
Double	1
Twin	
Single	
Bed Size	**Qty**
King	1
Queen	
Double	
Single	
Bathrooms	**Qty**
Ensuite	1
Private	
Guest Share	

Bossu Farm

Wainui, Akaroa, RD 2, Banks Peninsula
Ph (03) 304 8421, Fax (03) 304 8421
email: *bossu@xtra.co.nz*
www.bossufarmstay.co.nz

Tariff : N.Z. Dollars	
Double	$165
Single	$110
Child	neg

Bedrooms	Qty
Double	1
Twin	1
Single	
Bed Size	**Qty**
Super King	
King	
Queen	1
Double	
Single	2
Bathrooms	**Qty**
Ensuite	
Guest Share	1
Family Share	1

DIRECTIONS:
First property on seaward side after Wainui with a stone entrance.

Farmstay
Bed & Breakfast

Features & Attractions

- *Panoramic views of Akaroa Harbour*
- *Viewing dophins & sea birds*
- *French farm winery nearby*
- *Drinks, dinner & good company*
- *Farm tour & walks*
- *Hand feed pet sheep*
- *Golf course nearby*
- *Grass tennis court*

Our farm which has 2 km of coastline overlooks the beautiful harbour of Akaroa with panoramic views to the historic town of Akaroa. Our house is situated near this coastline with a large garden, and a well used grass tennis court surrounded by lovely mature trees. The property runs sheep, cattle, some forestry and two small vineyards. We have been hosting guests since 1977 so obviously, love having people to stay, and taking them, we think, on an interesting farm tour. From our motor boat we offer viewing of nesting sea birds, hector dolphins and penguins. There are lovely walks and interesting bays to visit on Banks Peninsula. Our interests include tennis, golf (Akaroa golf course is nearby) and bridge and many of our guests come with us to our local club. We have both travelled extensively so enjoy hearing about other countries. We have a small well behaved Jack Russell terrier. Most guests join us for dinner where we offer pre-dinner drinks and our locally grown wine for $35 per person. We look forward to your enquiry and hopefully meeting you.

DECANTER BAY HOMESTEAD 1851

386 Decanter Bay Rd, Akaroa RD3
Ph (03) 304 8949, Fax (03) 304 8949
email: *rejuvenate@relaxnz.co.nz*
www.relaxnz.co.nz

Tariff : N.Z. Dollars	
Double	$175-220
Single	$140-175
Child	neg

Bedrooms	Qty
Double	2
Twin	
Single	
Bed Size	**Qty**
Super King	
King	
Queen	1
Double	1
Single	
Bathrooms	**Qty**
Ensuite	2
Private	
Guest Share	

Secluded Beachside Retreat

Features & Attractions

- *Coastal, rural paradise*
- *Transport available*
- *Scenic walks*
- *Outdoor bath*
- *Swiss-German spoken*
- *Playful outdoor dog*
- *Woodworking studio*
- *Tai Chi workshops*

A scenic thirty minute drive on the way to Akaroa or one hour fifteen minutes from Christchurch. Relax in our comfortable 1851 homestead, restored and stylishly decorated to reflect the past. Our rural 2 acre property extends to the foreshore of a picturesque, private bay. Dramatic wilderness vistas from two Boutique guest suites, each with private entrance, sitting room with open fire, study, verandah sunroom. Music, books, interesting art, musical instruments and handcrafted antiques throughout the homestead. Established, secluded gardens for your enjoyment. Relax to lapping waves or unwind by learning gentle Tai Chi movements with Chris on the beach or in the studio. Kayaking and swimmining. Wholesome, generous, continental breakfast. The dinner menu (by arrangement) specialises in seafood; organic vegetarian dishes and special diets, served in a location of your choice or join the table of your well travelled hosts. Afternoon tea served on arrival and noon checkout. Stay one night or several.

DIRECTIONS: From Christchurch take Highway 75. At "Hilltop" take Scenic Summit Rd to Eastern Bays. Turn off Little Akaloa Bay Road, follow signs to Decanter Bay-2km.

Kokopu Estate

Rapid No 155, Grehan Valley Road, PO Box 61, Akaroa
Ph (03) 304 7427, Fax (03) 304 7777
Mobile 021-399 169
email: *bradlez@paradise.net.nz*
www.akaroa-holidays.co.nz

Tariff : N.Z. Dollars	
Double	$140-185
Single	$105-150
Child	

Bedrooms	Qty
Double	3
Twin	1
Single	1
Bed Size	**Qty**
Super King	
King	
Queen	3
Double	
Single	3
Bathrooms	**Qty**
Ensuite	1
Private	1
Family Share	1

Countrystay Bed & Breakfast
Self-contained Accommodation

- *Panoramic views of hills & sea*
- *Self-contained cottage & apartment*
- *80 min drive from Christchurch*
- *Delightful country setting*
- *2 min drive to restaurants/cafés*
- *37 acre farm in the hills*
- *Magnificent open fire*
- *Some French spoken*

Relax in the tranquil surroundings of our 37 acre estate set on the volcanic rim of panoramic Akaroa Harbour. Our home and cottage are the result of many years' work, cleaning old recycled beams, bricks and antique windows, building and extensive landscaping. **The Apartment** is a timber lover's dream with a Matai floor and vaulted macrocarpa ceiling. It has a spacious bedroom with a luxurious queensize bed and ensuite bathroom plus a kitchenette with refrigerator, microwave, etc. Downstairs is a sunny sitting room with large desk and couch/sofa bed opening out through French doors into a private brickwalled and stone courtyard. You can have breakfast delivered, join us, or make your own. Our menu includes crepes, croissants, and homemade muesli, fruit from our orchard and bacon and eggs. **The Green Room** in the main house has a private sumptuous marble and Kauri bathroom with an old-fashioned cast iron bath for two. There are some wonderful walking tracks to explore, or the town is only two minutes' drive. We also have a private self-contained cottage, shown in picture to the right, with gardens, orchard, and stream. It has an open fire inside and a bush bath, also wood-fired. We enjoy meeting new people and have a relaxed informal atmosphere.

KAWATEA FARMSTAY

'Kawatea', Okains Bay,
Banks Peninsula 8161
Ph (03) 304 8621, Fax (03) 304 8621
email: *kawatea@xtra.co.nz*

Tariff : N.Z. Dollars	
Double	$115-140
Single	$75-95
Child	neg

Bedrooms	Qty
Double	1
Twin	2
Single	
Bed Size	**Qty**
Super King	
King	
Queen	3
Double	
Single	2
Bathrooms	**Qty**
Ensuite	1
Private	1
Guest Share	1

Historic Homestead
Quality Accommodation & Dinner

Features & Attractions

- *1400 acre sheep & beef farm*
- *Creative dinners, NZ wine*
- *Warm country hospitality*
- *Peaceful romantic retreat*
- *Safe swimming beach*
- *Seals, dolphins, birdlife*
- *Coastal walks, kayaks, golf*
- *Akaroa Village 20 min*

DIRECTIONS:
Take Highway 75 from Christchurch through Duvauchelle. Turn left at signpost marked Okain's Bay. Kawatea is 11 km on right.

Escape to the beauty and tranquillity of the country. Enjoy a unique holiday experience in a gracious historic homestead set in beautiful mature gardens, and surrounded by land, farmed by our family for five generations. **Kawatea** is an elegant, carefully renovated home, built in 1900 from native timbers; it features stained glass windows, handcrafted furniture and much olde world charm. Enjoy a relaxing day with a book on the verandah, or participate in seasonal farm activities and feed the pet sheep. Wander our hillside farm enjoying the panoramic views of Banks Peninsula, or walk along the scenic coastline to secluded swimming beaches and a seal colony. Learn about Maori culture and the life of early settlers at the acclaimed Okain's Bay Museum or visit Akaroa with its French influence, cafés and craft shops. Join us for dinner savouring seafood from the bay and creative country fare from our garden, whilst sharing experiences with fellow travellers. We have been hosting since 1988 and pride ourselves on thoughtful, personal attention and friendly hospitality in a relaxed atmosphere.

YOUR HOSTS: **Ross, Lynette, Kirsty, & Matt Curry** Ph: (03) 304 5804 **_Barrys Bay - Akaroa_**

Rosslyn Estate

SH 75, Rapid #5797,
Main Christchurch - Akaroa Road,
Barry's Bay, RD 2, Akaroa
Ph (03) 304 5804, Fax (03) 304 5804
email: *Rosslyn@xtra.co.nz*

Tariff : N.Z. Dollars	
Double	$120-140
Single	$100
Child	neg

Bedrooms	Qty
Double	2
Twin	
Single	
Bed Size	**Qty**
Super King	
King	
Queen	2
Double	
Single	
Bathrooms	**Qty**
Ensuite	2
Private	
Guest Share	

Historic Farm Homestead
Bed & Breakfast

DIRECTIONS:
State Highway 75 **Rosslyn Estate** sign behind picket fence (left travelling to Akaroa) in Barry's Bay. The house is 400m from the entrance.

Features & Attractions

- *Working dairy farm*
- *Situated in extinct volcano*
- *Bush-lined streams*
- *Abundant bird life*
- *Share NZ family table*
- *Refreshments on arrival*
- *3 km to winery & restaurants*
- *70 km to Christchurch*

Rosslyn is a large, historic homestead, built in the 1860's of native timbers milled on the property, set on a working dairy farm amid the rolling hills of Banks Peninsula overlooking the serene Akaroa Harbour. Our family home of four generations is situated within informal gardens and offers the tranquillity of farm life, while our entrance is conveniently situated on the main road between Christchurch and 12 km before Akaroa, allowing you to explore this intriguing volcanic peninsula with ease.
While with us, you will have a large ground floor bedroom, firm queen bed, ensuite bathroom, antiques, central heating and screened windows. A spa room, pool, and laundry are also available at no charge. Breakfast ranges from fresh fruit to full cooked. We take pride in offering quality home-grown and prepared produce and preserves, served at the family table in the farm-style kitchen. We invite you to join us for dinner ($35 per person). We look forward to welcoming you with a refreshing tea, coffee or cool drink, served with home baking.

Banks Peninsula ▶ YOUR HOSTS: Angela and Luis Thacker Ph (03) 304 8615

DIRECTIONS: Take HW 75 from Christchurch through Duvauchelle, turn left at signpost marked Okains Bay. Rowandale is 9km on right

Rowandale Homestead

Rowandale Box 49, Okains Bay, Banks Peninsula
Ph/Fax (03) 304 8615, Mobile 027-667 0003
email: *rowandalefarm@xtra.co.nz*
www.rowandalehomestead.co.nz

Features & Attractions

- *French tub on balcony*
- *Stunning craftsmanship*
- *Late checkout*
- *20 min. to local tourist activities*
- *World-renowned museum*
- *Coastal walks/secluded bush/beaches*

Discover What You've Been Missing!

$		
	Double	$195-225
	Single	$120-145
	Child	

Bedrooms	Qty
Double	4
Twin	1
Single	1
Bed Size	**Qty**
King	
Queen	3
Double	1
Single	2
Bathrooms	**Qty**
Ensuite	
Private	1
Guest Share	1

Indulge yourself in the **Rowandale Experience**. We welcome you to this magnificent 1916 historic homestead, characterizing an original elegant/shabby-chic style that has matured graciously with time (like a good wine!). Located on 5th generation hillside farmland, we offer you spacious relaxation and the privacy of an untouched world. Treat yourself to the decadence of room service, private dining, delicious homestead menu of organically grown produce, sumptuous breakfast and late checkout. Self-service bar, NZ wine, complimentary facilities, nibbles on arrival, served to you on original antique silver and china. Relax and enjoy siestas on our very popular luxury balcony beds, with a French tub to soak in with the sunset. Sleep with the stars and awake to the music of dawn. Featuring large bath, bedroom fires, billiards and grand piano/music room. Specializing in exclusive stays, weekend get-away and retreats with friends, party and wedding venue. 5 double rooms. Formal garden, rolling lawn and native bush.

Akaroa ▶ YOUR HOSTS: Alison and Gavin Porteous Ph (03) 304 7121

Lavaud House

83 Rue Lavaud, Akaroa
Ph (03) 304 7121, Fax (03) 304 7125
Mobile 021-442 718
email: *stay@lavaudhouse-akaroa.co.nz*
www.lavaudhouse-akaroa.co.nz

Features & Attractions

- *Magnificent harbour views*
- *Gourmet continental breakfast*
- *Close to restaurants/shops*
- *Superior rooms*
- *Historic home*
- *Central, but private*

Boutique B&B in Historic Home

$		
	Double	$185-230
	Single	
	Child	

Bedrooms	Qty
Double	3
Twin	
Single	
Bed Size	**Qty**
King	1
Queen	2
Double	
Single	
Bathrooms	**Qty**
Ensuite	2
Private	1
Guest Share	

Situated in a wonderful sunny garden, our historic home offers the perfect setting for your stay in idyllic Akaroa. Restaurants, cafés, the beach and activities based in the town are all a short stroll away. Comfortable, well appointed bedrooms and a relaxing ambience will leave you with the best memories of what New Zealand has to offer. Rest in our guest lounge – watch TV, listen to music, read a book or simply enjoy the magnificent harbour view. Upstairs are the popular **Charlotte Rose** and **Harbour View** bedrooms with splendid sea vistas, and downstairs is the **Woodland** bedroom with a view out onto a secluded garden. A full continental breakfast is served in the separate guest dining room with sea views or al fresco on the front lawn overlooking the harbour.

Chez Fleurs

15 Smith Street, Akaroa, Banks Peninsula
Ph (03) 304 8674, Fax (03) 304 8974
Mobile 021- 155 7727
email: *chezfleurs@xtra.co.nz*
www.chezfleurs.co.nz

Tariff : N.Z. Dollars	
Double	$160
Single	$140
Child	n/a

Bedrooms	Qty
Double	2
Twin	1
Single	
Bed Size	**Qty**
Super King	
King	
Queen	2
Double	
King/Single	2
Bathrooms	**Qty**
Ensuite	2
Private	
Guest Share	

Homestay
Bed & Breakfast

Features & Attractions

- *Stunning waterfront views*
- *3 min walk to cafés & shops*
- *Beautiful, tranquil garden*
- *Laundry & BBQ available*
- *150 metres to beach*
- *Own private balcony*
- *Delicious breakfast*
- *Off-street parking*

DIRECTIONS:
Stay on Beach Rd, take Smith St,opposite main beach, 2nd street on left,past the BNZ.

Bonjour! Welcome to **Chez Fleurs**. We are situated 150 metres from the beach and 3 minutes walk from the cafés, galleries, restaurants and shops. Enjoy our stunning waterfront views and beautiful garden while relaxing on our guest balcony.

We offer superior accommodation with tea/coffee home-baking treats,fridge, TV, hairdryers and fresh flowers in your suite. Your delicious continental breakfast, using fresh home-grown produce, is served alfresco on your private balcony. Park up , relax and soak up the magic scenery, or take the short walk to explore our historic village.

Drive around our picturesque bays and beaches,learning of our colonial,French and Maori heritage on the way. Entertain yourself at our local wineries or cheese factory, or wander through our quaint, narrow streets. Our majestic harbour is a feast of scenic and wildlife encounters . Choose to cruise, fish, sail, kayak or swim with our famous hector dolphins, the smallest and rarest in the world. We also have salmon and paua pearl farms, penquins, fur seals and amazing birdlife. 'A Bientot' – See you soon.

AKA-VIEW

5 Langlois Lane, PO Box 100, Akaroa
Ph (03) 304 8008, Fax (03) 304 8008
Mobile 027-459 6042
email: *aka-view@xtra.co.nz*
www.aka-view.co.nz

Tariff : N.Z. Dollars	
Double	$160-185
Single	$125-150
Child	n/a

Bedrooms	Qty
Double	3
Twin	1
Single	
Bed Size	**Qty**
Super King	
King	
Queen	3
Double	
Single	2
Bathrooms	**Qty**
Ensuite	2
Private	1
Guest Share	

Luxury Bed & Breakfast

Features & Attractions

- *Breathtaking view from all guest rooms*
- *Telephone, fax and email available*
- *10 min walk to shops & restaurants*
- *Scrumptious breakfast*
- *Quality bed linen*
- *Toiletries, hair dryers, robes*
- *Romantic Akaroa*
- *Relaxing atmosphere*

Do you dream of a place "with a view"?
Elegant bedrooms, just made for two
Comfortable study - still "with a view"
Books, music, good coffee too -
A gourmet breakfast - sheer delight
Perfect - after a restful night
In a large country house
That's just all "brand new"
*Fulfill your dreams at - **Aka-View.***

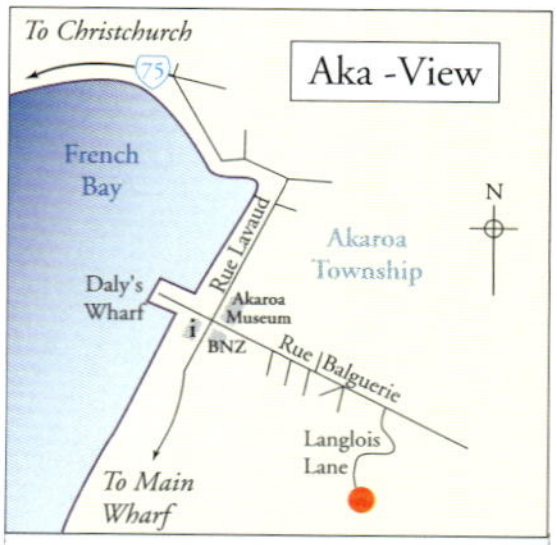

DIRECTIONS: On Rue Lavaud - main village street - turn left at BNZ corner into Rue Balguerie - then up to Langlois Lane, fifth on right.

Aka-View is a purpose built Mediterranean styled Bed & Breakfast. The upper level features two queen suites, one twin, private guest study, separate tea/coffee facilites, all with unprecedented harbour views. In addition, guests may choose to use the formal lounge, with cosy fire, stylish but comfortable furnishings.

A romantic option is our lower level garden studio - private courtyard, sunny, queen with ensuite, lounge, television, full tea/coffee making facilities. Breakfast is a full gourmet surprise, either in the well appointed kitchen or a hamper delivered to your garden studio. For total relaxation enjoy our fine teas, superb coffee, tasty treats, CDs, in the guest study and garden studio.

GARTHOWEN

7 Beach Road, Akaroa 8161
Ph/Fax (03) 304 7419, Mobile 027-437 1096
email: *info@garthowen.co.nz*
www.garthowen.co.nz

Tariff : N.Z. Dollars	
Double	$240
Single	$200
Child	$90

Bedrooms	Qty
Double	3
Twin	1
Single	
Bed Size	**Qty**
Super King	4
King	
Queen	
Double	
Single	2
Bathrooms	**Qty**
Ensuite	4
Private	
Guest Share	

Luxury Waterfront Accommodation

Guests comments:
"Wonderful, caring, gracious hosts"
Jeremy & Wendy Lezin, USA

Features & Attractions

- *Panoramic sea views*
- *Warm, friendly hospitality*
- *Superior rooms with sea views*
- *2 min. walk to shops & restaurants*
- *Scrumptuous cooked breakfasts*
- *Purpose-built home*
- *Finest linen, flowers, robes*
- *Complimentary wine, nibbles*

Sometimes you discover a very beautiful place. Akaroa is such a place. When you visit, **Garthowen** will provide you with the perfect setting in which to relax, unwind and feel pampered.
Situated right on the water front of Akaroa's main street, purposely built to the original 1890's Guest House, **Garthowen** opened in December '05 – an absolutely stunning home with harbour views. From your own dining room and lounge you can view the harbour or sit by the fire with a good book. Enjoy a delicious breakfast from our scrumptious menu served in the dining room or on the balcony while smelling the sea air. All rooms have TV, DVD's, air conditioning, underfloor heating, personalized gowns, tea/coffee, chocolates, quality linen, flowers and super-king beds.
Join us with a complimentary glass of wine and nibbles before sampling an evening meal at one of Akaroa's fine restaurants – only a 2 minute stroll away.
We will make your stay a memorable one!
Bonnie and Jessie, our Jack Russells, love being spoiled by our guests.

Penlington Views B & B Akaroa

13 Penlington Place, Akaroa, Banks Peninsula
Ph (03) 304 8996, Mobile 027-699 9217
email: *penlingtonviews@xtra.co.nz*
www.penlingtonviews.co.nz

VISA MasterCard

Features & Attractions

- *Scenic walks for all levels*
- *Quiet, beauty and peaceful*
- *Guest lounge*
- *Quality bed linen*
- *90 min. from Christchurch*
- *Wineries*

Bed & Breakfast
Self-contained Accommodation

$	
Double	$145-190
Single	$85
Child	

You will be warmly welcomed with fresh flowers, chocolates and beautiful views of the harbour or garden from either a self-contained king flat, a king-size balcony room, a queen-size garden room or a double room (suitable for one person). Admire the magical views and sunsets over the harbour from a sun-drenched balcony.

On a warm summer's night, enjoy a BBQ in the garden area, or in winter cuddle up with a good book and watch a movie in the lounge by the log burner. We offer Sky television, continental or cooked breakfast, spa bath, dressing gowns and any other specific requirements. Located within walking distance from all the major activities, jewellery and beauty therapy facilities, restaurants and shops.

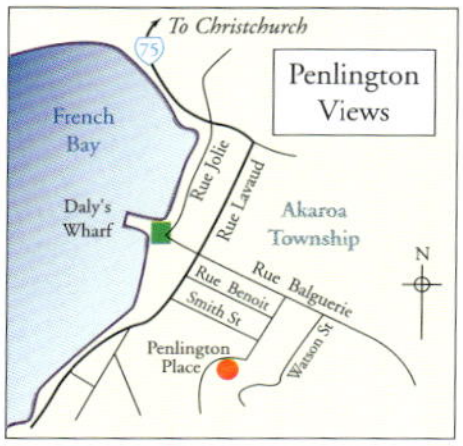

Bedrooms	Qty
Double	3
Twin	
Single	1
Bed Size	**Qty**
King	2
Queen	1
Double	1
Single	
Bathrooms	**Qty**
Private	1
Guest Share	1
Family Share	1

The Maples

158 Rue Jolie, Akaroa, Banks Peninsula
Ph (03) 304 8767, Fax (03) 304 8767
email: *maplesakaroa@xtra.co.nz*
www.themaplesakaroa.co.nz

Features & Attractions

- *Historic house*
- *3 min walk to cafés*
- *Delightful garden*
- *Quiet and peaceful*
- *Guest lounge*
- *Relaxed & friendly*

VISA MasterCard

Homestay
Bed & Breakfast

$	
Double	$130-150
Single	$95
Child	

Built in 1877, **The Maples** is one of Akaroa's charming historic two-storey houses. We have tastefully decorated the interior and have combined modern comforts with yester-year charm. You can choose from our two queen rooms upstairs or our delightful separate garden room with a single and a queen bed. All our rooms are ensuited.

NZ HISTORIC PLACES TRUST POUHERE TAONGA

A delicious cooked and continental breakfast, which includes freshly baked croissants and home-made jams, is included in the tariff. We have a separate guest lounge, where complimentary tea and coffee is available. We also have a pretty cottage garden that you can sit and relax in. Centrally situated but quiet, it is only a three minute stroll to the water front and some of Akaroa's many excellent restaurants and cafés. We invite you to share our beautiful historic home and hope we can make your stay relaxed and special.

Bedrooms	Qty
Double	3
Twin	
Single	
Bed Size	**Qty**
King	
Queen	3
Double	
Single	1
Bathrooms	**Qty**
Ensuite	3
Private	
Guest Share	

Ryton Station

Harper Road, RD 2, Darfield,
Lake Coleridge, Canterbury
Ph (03) 318 5818, Fax (03) 318 5819
email: *ryton@xtra.co.nz*
www.ryton.co.nz

Tariff : N.Z. Dollars	
Double	$280-320
Single	$150-170
Child	neg

Bedrooms	Qty
Double/Twin	7
Twin	
Single	
Bed Size	**Qty**
Super King	
King	
Queen	6
Double	1
Single	
Bathrooms	**Qty**
Ensuite	7
Private	
Guest Share	

High Country Station Stay
Dinner, Bed & Breakfast

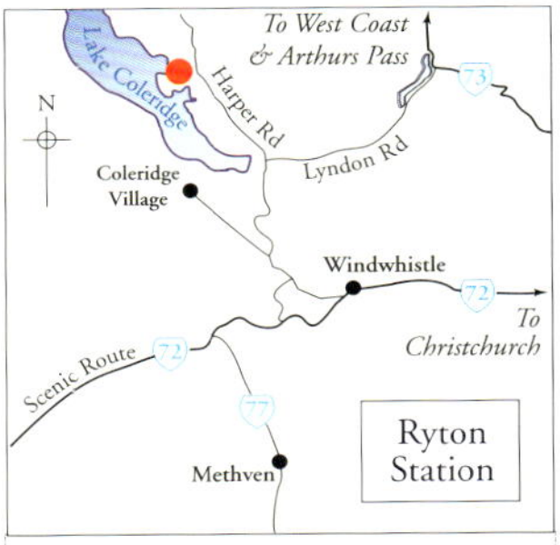

DIRECTIONS: Follow Ryton signposts from either SH 72 at Windwhistle or SH 73 at Lake Lyndon, approximately ½ hour. On the north side of Lake Coleridge, 10 min once on Harper Road

Features & Attractions

- *High country merino sheep station*
- *37,000 acres (14,000 hectares)*
- *Superb views overlooking Lake Coleridge*
- *Sample high country life*
- *Trout, salmon fishing*
- *Walks and tramps*
- *Private ensuite chalets*
- *Horse trekking/jet boating*

Adventure and hospitality in the South Island high country. **Ryton Station** is a wonderful place for a personal experience of home hospitality on a 37,000 acre high country merino sheep station. The scenery is magnificent, overlooking Lake Coleridge, the air and water crystal clear.

1½ hours inland from Christchurch, accessible all year round. Abundance of fishing, walks, tramping, station activities. Jet boat and 4X4 trips available. Skiing at Mt Hutt (60 minutes away), Porter Heights and Mt Olympus. Local golf courses nearby.

Relax and enjoy the native flora and fauna in the peacefulness of our environment. Office, Sky television and laundry facilities available at the homestead.

Ensuite chalet accommodation includes dinner with the family. Self-catering lodge accommodation also, next to the homestead.

Lake Coleridge Lodge

Hummock Rd, P O Box 18, Lake Coleridge
Ph (03) 318 5002, Fax (03) 318 5004
email: *lakecoleridge@paradise.net.nz*
www.lakecoleridgelodge.co.nz

Tariff : N.Z. Dollars	
Double	$190-220
Single	$110-125
Child	neg

Bedrooms	Qty
Double	5
Twin	4
Single	
Bed Size	**Qty**
Super King	
King	
Queen	1
Double	4
Single	8
Bathrooms	**Qty**
Ensuite	2
Private	
Guest Share	3

Alpine Retreat
Dinner Bed & Breakfast

Features & Attractions

- *Cafe & bar on site*
- *9 hole chip & putt golf*
- *2-course Lodge dinner included*
- *Gas Heated outdoor baths*
- *Historic power station*
- *Fishing, hunting, skifields*
- *Quiet, peaceful village atmosphere*
- *5 skifields nearby*

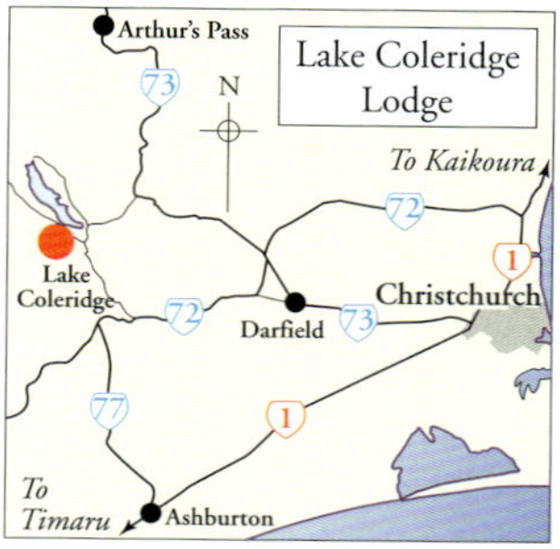

Built in the early 1930's to accommodate workers on the nearby historic Power Station, **Lake Coleridge Lodge** has been refurbished to cater for visitors to the area. Situated in a secluded back country village, the lodge overlooks the braided Rakaia River against a stunning mountain backdrop. The lodge also features a rich pictorial and written history dating back to the early 1900's, with many photographs from the era adorning the walls and hallways. Open daily onsite are a licensed café with indoor/ outdoor seating and an internet café. The villages' little known Arboretum with one of the worlds' best collections of conifers is a treat for tree lovers. A range of activities can be arranged for the more adventurous: jet boating, horse treks, 4x4 tours (including 'Lord of the Rings' tour), hot air ballooning. An international golf course is only 10 min away.

DIRECTIONS:
From Christchurch, drive out Yaldhurst Road towards Darfield through West Melton. Turn off to **Hororata.** At Hororata round-about steer left to Lake Coleridge. At stop sign at Windwhistle drive straight through to Lake Coleridge Township, don't turn off to Lake. Drive through township, around S-bend and up the Hill (Hummocks Road). The Lodge is situated on this corner.

Tyrone Deer Farm

Mt. Hutt Station Rd, Alternative Route
Methven to Rakaia Gorge
Ph (03) 302 8096, Fax (03) 302 8099
email: *tyronedeerfarm@xtra.co.nz*

Tariff : N.Z. Dollars	
Double	$140-150
Single	$100
Child	neg

Bedrooms	Qty
Double	3
Twin	1
Single	
Bed Size	**Qty**
Super King	1
King	
Queen	1
Double	1
Single	1
Bathrooms	**Qty**
Ensuite	2
Private	1
Guest Share	

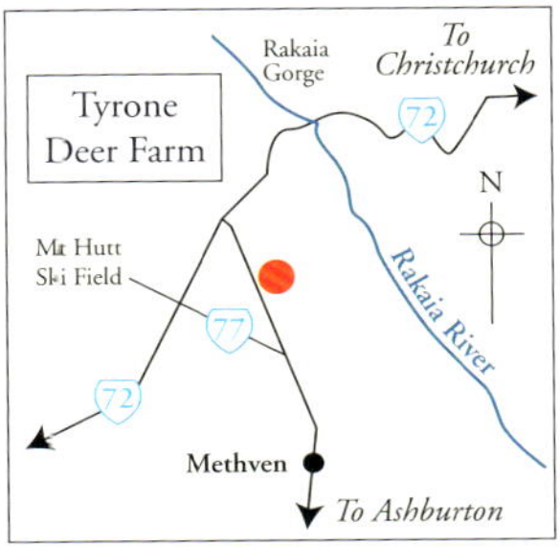

Countrystay
Bed & Breakfast

Features & Attractions

- *Centre of South Island*
- *Golf 18-hole courses, club hire*
- *Skiing MtHutt & heli-skiing*
- *Jet boating/hot air ballooning*
- *1 hour Christchurch Airport*
- *Tramping, alpine & bush walks*
- *Fishing, hunting guides available*
- *Mountain views*

Welcome to **Tyrone Deer Farm**, centrally situated in the Mt.Hutt, Rakaia Gorge, Methven area, 5km from the Inland Tourist Route (SH72), making **Tyrone** an ideal stopover heading south to Queenstown. Our home is positioned with mountain views (Mt Hutt) and deer grazing metres away. We have ensuite bedrooms with electric blankets, wool underlays and duvet, also heaters and hair dryers. The lounge has an open fire, television, tea/coffee facilities and guest fridge. Come, meet 'Gus', our pet deer, her daughter '$$s' and '10.30' our cat. Laze in the garden, swim in the pool, relax. Evening meal served with New Zealand wine by arrangement. We are able to arrange professional guides for fishing (trout and salmon) and for hunting, especially Tahr, Red Deer and Chamois.

On Main Street Methven (Mt. Hutt Village) are 2 self-contained townhouses, tariff (2 persons) $140.00. $20.00 extra person, $10.00 child. Not @home accredited. (Summer rate.)

Alaska Park & Tranquil House

703 Pudding Hill Road, Methven, RD 12, Rakaia
Ph (03) 302 9335, Fax (03) 302 9335
email: *ppjm@xtra.co.nz*
www.tranquilhouse.co.nz

Tariff : N.Z. Dollars	
Double	$120-160
Single	
Child	

Bedrooms	Qty
Double	4
Twin	1
Single	1
Bed Size	**Qty**
Super King	
King	
Queen	2
Double	2
Single	3
Bathrooms	**Qty**
Ensuite	
Private	1
Guest Share	1

C **Bed & Breakfast or Self-contained Accommodation** BB

Features & Attractions

- *Alaska Park:*
- *Complimentary farm tour*
- *3-course wine & dine $40pp*
- *Farmhouse ambience*
- *Tranquil House:*
- *Close to Mt Hutt ski field*
- *Self-catering*
- *Minimun 2 night stay*

Alaska Park House and **Tranquil House** are based on about 350 acres of a park-type working beef and sheep farm near the base of the Mount Hutt ski field and only 7km from Methven.
Alaska Park House, a renovated early New Zealand farm house with rimu wood panelling and wood archways and the warmth of modern day central heating, offers executive Bed & Breakfast accommodation. Two double bedrooms share a large bath and shower room. There's also a guest sitting/sun room.
Guests are welcome to sit and dine or share a glass of wine with us in our large family farmhouse kitchen (the hub of the farm). Three course evening meals are available (prior booking essential). A farm tour is included in your stay.

SC **Tranquil House** is self-contained, with accommodation for up to 7, private garden and a BBQ area. The tastefully designed living and dining areas are all centrally heated, with a modern, well equipped kitchen. Bedrooms are cosy. The modern bathroom and toilet are separate. The laundry is fully equipped. The garage has ski waxing facilities and a heated cupboard for ski wear. Minimum 2 nights stay.

St Ita's Guesthouse

11 Barrhill - Methven Road, Rakaia
Ph (03) 302 7546, Fax (03) 302 7564
Mobile 027-488 8673
email: *stitas@xtra.co.nz*
www.stitas.co.nz

Features & Attractions

- *40 min. to Christchurch*
- *Historic convent school*
- *Salmon fishing*
- *Small New Zealand town*
- *Spacious grounds*
- *River walks*

$	
Double	$120
Single	$70
Child	$30

Bed & Breakfast Guesthouse

Bedrooms	Qty
Double	2
Twin	1
Single	
Bed Size	**Qty**
King	
Queen	1
Double	1
Single	3
Bathrooms	**Qty**
Ensuite	3
Private	
Guest Share	

A warm welcome is assured at **St Ita's Guesthouse**. This former convent school was built in 1912, set in spacious grounds and is full of comfort and charm.
All three guest rooms have ensuites and garden views. Large lounge and games room for use. **St Ita's** is situated on the western fringe of Rakaia, opposite the domain, just past the catholic church. A range of sports gear is available. Nearby: salmon fishing, golf, tennis, visiting local pubs and craft shops. Within 30 minutes drive, skiing, bushwalks, jetboating and more.
Evening three-course meal includes local produce and New Zealand wine or walk down to the local café. Full breakfast. Share the open fire with our cat.

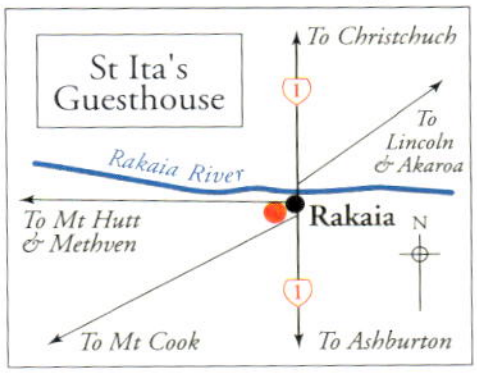

The Gardeners Cottage

Coniston, 30 Methven Highway, SH 77
Ph (03) 307 8189, Fax (03) 307 8179
Mobile 027-435 4705
e-mail: *coniston@xtra.co.nz*
www.coniston.co.nz

Features & Attractions

- *5.5 acres of garden*
- *Sheep, highland cattle and crops*
- *1hr Christchurch, 3hrs Mt Cook*
- *Restaurants 3 min.*
- *Private and peaceful setting*
- *Breakfast extra charge*

$	
Double	$110
Single	$80
Child	$10

Historic Farm Cottage Self-contained

DIRECTIONS:
Turn off SH1 onto SH77 to Methven at McDonalds corner. Coniston 3.1 km from SH1.

Bedrooms	Qty
Double	1
Twin	2
Single	1
Bed Size	**Qty**
King	
Queen	
Double	1
Single	5
Bathrooms	**Qty**
Ensuite	
Private	1
Guest Share	

The Gardeners Cottage, built in 1870, is situated on the edge of 5.5 acres of established gardens. **The Cottage** features 4 bedrooms including 1 double and 1 twin bedroom downstairs and 1 twin attic bedroom. There is also a small room with a single bed next to the double bedroom.
All beds have electric blankets. The kitchen/dining room has a log fire and is fully equipped. The lounge has an open fire, TV, video, CD player and board/card games for family entertainment. The bathroom features shower and original claw-foot bath. There is a separate laundry.
Outside you will find a barbecue area with gas barbecue and a tree swing and plenty of room for the children to play outdoor games. Portacot, highchair, stroller and bicycles provided. Continental and cooked breakfast provisions available (extra charge). Relax and enjoy the peace and quiet in this rural setting. A warm welcome awaits you.

Cricklewood House

120 Johnstone Street, Tinwald, RD 4, Ashburton
Ph (03) 3071980, Fax (03) 3071985
Mobile 027-2231939
email: *gdrobins@clear.net.nz*

Tariff : N.Z. Dollars	
Double	$140-170
Single	$100
Child	

Bedrooms	Qty
Double	2
Twin	1
Single	
Bed Size	**Qty**
Super King	
King	1
Queen	1
Double	
Single	2
Bathrooms	**Qty**
Ensuite	1
Private	
Guest Share	1

Country Stay
Boutique Accommodation

Features & Attractions

- *Golf – two courses handy*
- *One hour south of Christchurch*
- *Three-course dinner available*
- *Email facilities*
- *Quiet, comfortable rooms*
- *Smoke-free inside*
- *Local restaurants nearby*
- *Friendly hosts*

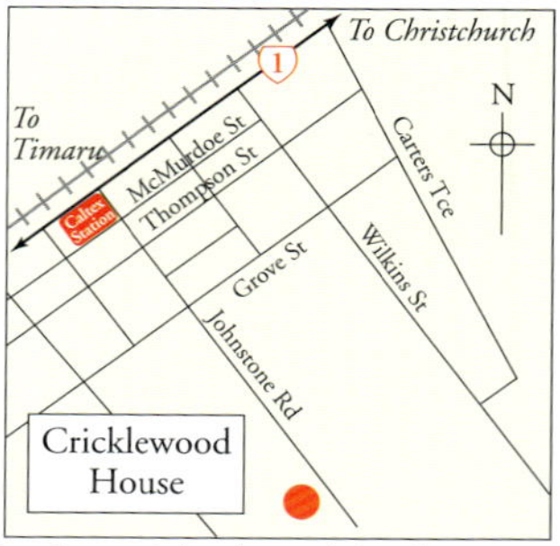

Cricklewood House is a new house, purpose-built with guests' total comfort catered for. Formal dining room with period furniture makes our home very relaxing. We have one king-size bedroom with ensuite, one queen-size bed with shared guest bathroom, and one room with two single beds also with shared bathroom. There is also a separate sitting room for you to relax in.

When you arrive you will be greeted with a hot drink, and a very warm welcome. We will serve dinner with twenty four hour notice, alternatively you are only five to eight minutes to some fine Ashburton restaurants. We are situated just off Highway One, one hour south of Christchurch, well suited to travelling north or to Mount Cook, the Southern Lakes and Queenstown. We can also direct you to various activities in the district and further afield.

Our interests are gardening, sports, embroidery, and cooking. We are retired farmers who have been in the hosting business for over twenty years. We look forward to having your company at our place.

THE DOWNS BED & BREAKFAST

5 Ribbonwood Road, The Downs, RD 21, Geraldine
Ph (03) 693 7388, Fax (03) 693 7388
Mobile 021-675 249
email:thedownsbnb@xtra.co.nz
www.thedowns.co.nz

Tariff : N.Z. Dollars	
Double	$150-250
Single	$150-250
Child	

Bedrooms	Qty
Double	3
Twin	1
Single	
Bed Size	**Qty**
Super King	
King	
Queen	3
Double	
Single	2
Bathrooms	**Qty**
Ensuite	3
Private	1
Guest Share	

Bed & Breakfast Homestay

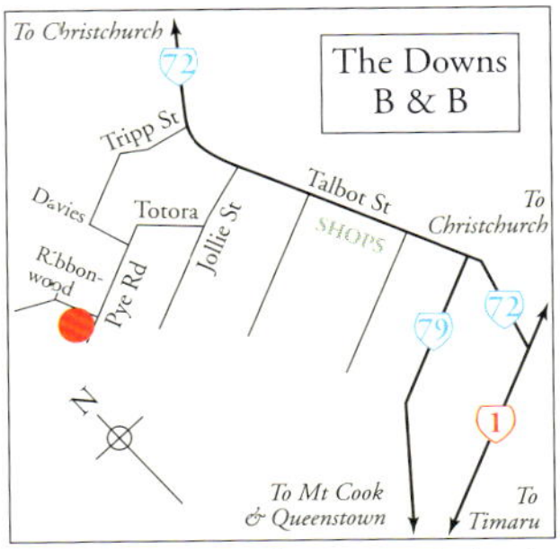

Features & Attractions

- *Large garden setting*
- *Complimentary bar*
- *Free guest laundry*
- *Skiing, golf*
- *Tranquil surroundings*
- *Handy shops, restaurants*
- *Art studios*
- *High standard of facilities*

The Downs B &B offers you quality accommodation in our large, modern home. A wander round the beautiful park-like garden is a lovely way to unwind after your journey. Peace, tranquillity and bird song are part of the surroundings here. The guest rooms are spacious. Each has its own TV, comfortable armchairs and ensuites, all furnished to a very high standard. A full Kiwi and continental breakfast is served in the guest lounge or on the balcony overlooking the garden. There is also a complimentary self-service bar and tea and coffee making facilities and home-baked cookies are available at all times. The region of Geraldine has much to offer in the way of arts, crafts, dining experiences, golf, fishing, 4 WD tours and skiing. We are only too pleased to assist you with your further sightseeing plans and accommodation if necessary.

Geraldine	YOUR HOSTS: **Leigh and Gerald Basinger**	Free Ph: 0800 537 533

Victoria Villa

55 Cox Street, Geraldine, 7930
Ph (03) 693 8605, Fax (03) 693 8605
Mobile 027-482 1842
email: *jbasinger@xtra.co.nz*

Features & Attractions

- *Ensuites or private bathroom*
- *Town & bush walks 7 min*
- *Modern heat & plumbing*
- *Private entrance & lounge*
- *Restored 100-year-old villa*
- *Molded ceilings & original wood*

BA **Boutique Accommodation & Attached Studio** SC

$	
Double	$100-125
Single	$80-100
Child	neg

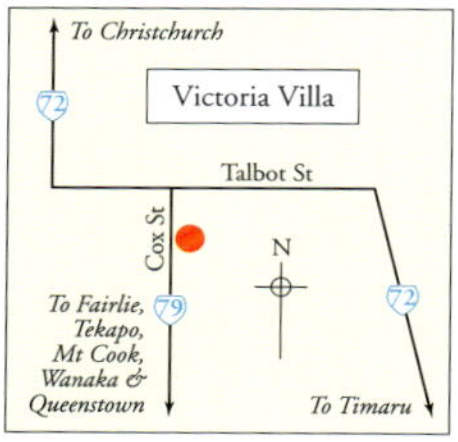

We welcome you to our historic villa which was built in 1900 and has been completely refurbished. Each guest room has a television, tea and coffee facilities. A detached studio has three beds, ensuite, a light kitchen facility; ideal for family up to five people. We are only seven minutes stroll from Geraldine's main street which has boutique movie theatre, fine restaurants, cafés, sports pub, auto museum, antiques, world class glass blower, stained glass artists and boutique shops. Geraldine has two golf courses, only twenty minutes from Peel Forest, Rangitata River and 75 minutes from Mt Hutt and Dobson ski fields. Your hosts are well travelled and will assist to make your stay enjoyable. Continental or cooked breakfast provided.

Bedrooms	Qty
Double	4
Twin	
Single	
Bed Size	**Qty**
King	
Queen	3
Double	2
Single	2
Bathrooms	**Qty**
Ensuite	3
Private	1
Guest Share	

Temuka	YOUR HOSTS: **Wendy and Ray Pearson**	Ph: (03) 615 6157

Ashfield House Bed & Breakfast

71 Cass Street, Temuka, South Canterbury
Ph (03) 615 6157
email: *ashfield@paradise.net.nz*
www.ashfield.co.nz

@ home NEW ZEALAND

Features & Attractions

- *Spacious gardens*
- *Close to ski fields*
- *Trout & salmon fishing*
- *Warm hospitality*
- *Close to Timaru*
- *Email & internet access*

BA **Victorian Boutique Bed & Breakfast Homestay** BB

$	
Double	$100-150
Single	$80-100
Child	

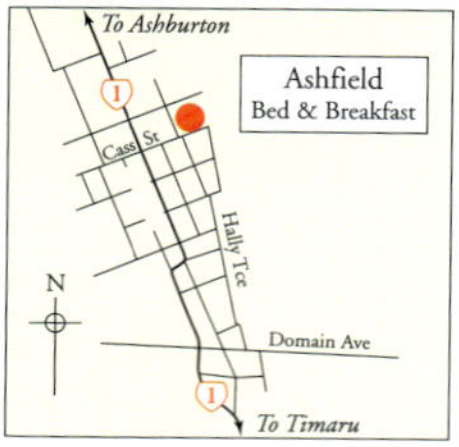

DIRECTIONS:
200m from SH 1

Ashfield, built in 1883, is set in four acres of gardens and woodland, which we share with our two Newfoundland dogs. You are assured of warm hospitality. We aim to make your stay enjoyable.

Temuka is only twenty minutes from Timaru and 1¾ hours from Christchurch. Close by is the Rangitata River, which is noted for its fly fishing, not to mention the salmon! No visit to Temuka would be complete without a visit to its famous pottery outlet. If you just want to relax, then **Ashfield** has lovely gardens and a stream, which is host to ducks and trout. Some of the redwood trees are believed to be over three hundred years old. Currently being assessed by NZ Historic Places Trust as a heritage building.

Bedrooms	Qty
Double	4
Twin	
Single	
Bed Size	**Qty**
King	
Queen	4
Double	
Single	
Bathrooms	**Qty**
Ensuite	1
Private	
Guest Share	1

BLUEBERRY COTTAGE

72A High Street, Timaru
Ph (03) 684 3115, Fax (03) 684 3172
Mobile 027-636 4301
email: *relax@blueberrycottage.co.nz*
www.blueberrycottage.co.nz

Features & Attractions

- *Quiet sea-front setting*
- *Friendly home hospitality*
- *Sea to mountain views*
- *Gateway to Southern Alps*
- *Stroll to beach-walkways*
- *Relaxation at its best*

Bed & Breakfast Homestay

$	
Double	$85
Single	$60
Child	neg

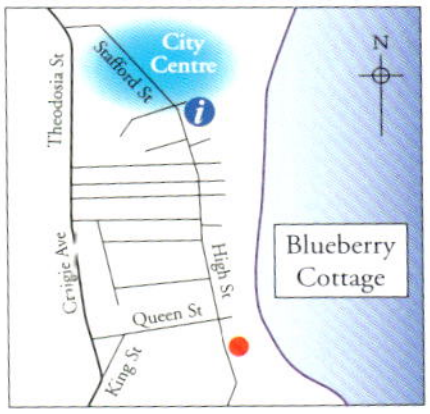

DIRECTIONS: Timaru South on SH 1. Turn into Queen Street. Pass hospital and right into High Street. **Blueberry Cottage** entrance on left.

Our recently delightfully up graded 1950s brick home exudes comfort with spectacular close-up views of the ocean and inland to Mt Cook. We feel it is a delight living here and would like to share this with others. The tastefully furnished rooms have television with access to separate outside patios. Handy to hospital and gardens. It is a comfortable walking distance to shops, cafés, bars, or eating place of your choice. Timaru is centrally situated on the east coast of the South Island, allowing easy access to many scenic spots, i.e. day trips to lakes, skiing in winter, Mount Cook, fishing rivers, bush walks, vineyards and other interesting towns. Shops display our high quality wool products and gifts of interest to overseas' visitors.

Bedrooms	Qty
Double	1
Double/Twin	1
Single	
Bed Size	**Qty**
S.King/Twin	1
Queen	
Double	
Single	2
Bathrooms	**Qty**
Ensuite	
Private	
Guest Share	1

SEFTON HOMESTAY

32 Sefton Street, Seaview, Timaru
Ph (03) 688 0017, Fax (03) 688 0042
Mobile 027-473 7366
email: *trish@seftonhomestay.co.nz*
www.seftonhomestay.co.nz

Features & Attractions

- *2 hours from Christchurch*
- *Restaurants 5 min. easy walk*
- *Guest sitting room*
- *Email & internet access*
- *Quiet & peaceful bedrooms*
- *Full cooked breakfast*

$	
Double	$120
Single	$100
Child	½ price

Homestay Bed & Breakfast

Bedrooms	Qty
Double	2
Twin	
Single	1
Bed Size	**Qty**
Super King/Twin	1
Queen	1
Double	1
Single	
Bathrooms	**Qty**
Ensuite	1
Private	1
Guest Share	

Conveniently located, just a few minutes walk from the Bay Hill restaurants, Caroline Bay and the Stafford Street shops. Once you arrive in Timaru, you can park your car off-street and explore the city on foot.

Relax in our superbly appointed and spacious two storey character brick home with sweeping views from the mountains to the sea. Refurbished with the feel of yesteryear, but with ambience and style you will love. There is a separate sitting room upstairs for guests to enjoy a quiet read, hot drink or glass of wine and unwind. Start or finish your holiday in New Zealand on a high note. We are just a couple of hours south of Christchurch Airport. We also have a passenger service license and do personal tours.

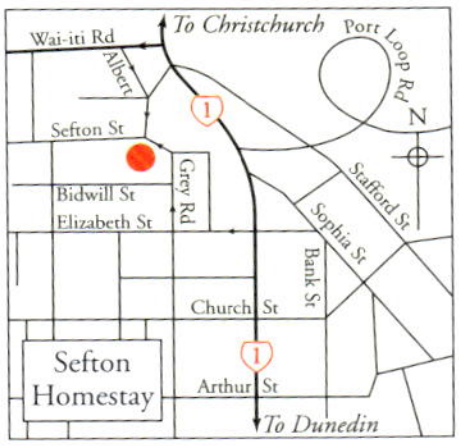

Centre Hill Cottage

59 Howell Road, Totara Valley, RD 12, Pleasant Point
Ph (03) 614 7385, Fax (03) 614 7380
Mobile 027-420 1120
email: *centre.hill@paradise.net.nz*
www.centrehillcottage.com

Tariff : N.Z. Dollars	
Double	$250
Extra person	$50
Child	under 5 free

Bedrooms	Qty
Double	1
Twin	1
Single	
Bed Size	**Qty**
Super King	
King	
Queen	1
Double	
Single	2
Bathrooms	**Qty**
Ensuite	
Private	1
Guest Share	

Luxury Farmstay Retreat

DIRECTIONS:
Coming from Pleasant Point, at the Pleasant Point Hotel, turn into Te Ngawai Road, over bridge, turn left into Totara Valley, next left into Howell Road and **Centre Hill Cottage** is first on the left, 5 km from Hotel turn-off.

Features & Attractions

- *Smoke-free environment*
- *Complimentary food hamper & wine*
- *Private chef available (bookings essential)*
- *Swimming pool, farm walks, tennis*
- *Laundry facilities*
- *Covered access from garage*
- *Sampling organic produce*
- *Gas BBQ available*

Experience bliss at **Centre Hill Farm**. Your host, Ian Blakemore, invites you to experience this idyllic part of South Canterbury. Centre Hill Cottage Farm Stay Retreat offers a cosy charm for those wanting to get away and relax in an atmosphere of tranquility and peaceful purity. **The Farm**: Drenched with stunning views, **Centre Hill Organic Farm** sits elevated above the fertile farmland of Totara Valley, Pleasant Point. Since 1968 Ian has farmed Centre Hill, gaining full organic status in 1990, running deer, beef cattle and sheep, also growing potatoes, for the New Zealand organic market. **Centre Hill Cottage** is quaint and stylish. It features a large, warm living area and modern kitchen, two bedrooms and a luxury bathroom with heated floor tiles and a three-person raised spa-bath with a view. With the backdrop of the Southern Alps and surrounded by so much serenity, it is hard not to feel serene in yourself. It is two hours drive south of Christchurch City and a fifteen minute drive from Timaru Airport.

Rivendell Lodge

15 Stanton Road, Kimbell, RD 17, Fairlie
Ph (03) 685 8833, Fax (03) 685 8825
Mobile 027-4819 189
email: *rivendell.lodge@xtra.co.nz*
www.fairlie.co.nz/rivendell

Tariff : N.Z. Dollars	
Double	$110-140
Single	$70-90
Child	neg

Bedrooms	Qty
Double	4
Twin	2
Single	
Bed Size	**Qty**
Super King	
King	
Queen	3
Double	1
Single	2
Bathrooms	**Qty**
Ensuite	2
Private	
Guest Share	2

Country Homestay

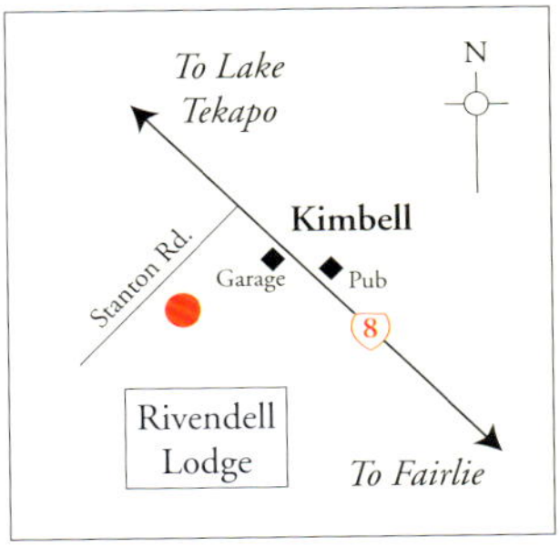

Features & Attractions

- *Peaceful rural retreat*
- *Great home cooking*
- *Skifield 5 km*
- *Spa bath available*
- *Magnificent alpine scenery*
- *Guided walking & tramping*
- *Families welcome*
- *Ensuite rooms also have balconies*

"They stayed long in Rivendell and found it hard to leave. The house was perfect whether you liked sleep, or work, or storytelling, or singing, or just sitting and thinking best, or a pleasant mixture of them all. Everyone grew refreshed and strong in a few days there. Merely to be there was a cure for weariness, fear and sadness." - Tolkien.

DIRECTIONS:
100m up Stanton Road at Kimbell on SH 8, 8km west of Fairlie.

Welcome to my one acre of paradise – a haven of peace and tranquility offering quality country comfort and hospitality.

As a well travelled writer I am passionate about mountains, literature and good conversation. I enjoy cooking and gardening, and delight in sharing home-grown produce. Take time out from the Christchurch-Queenstown route and enjoy our magnificent countryside. Fishing, walking, golf, watersports or skiing nearby.
Relax in the garden, complete with stream and cat, or come exploring with me. Complimentary refreshments on arrival. Laundry and email available. Dinner $40.00pp by arrangement.

BRAELEA ALPINEVIEW FARMSTAY

279 Highway 79, RD 17, Fairlie, South Canterbury
Ph (03) 685 8366, Fax (03) 685 8943
Mobile 021-070 9375
email: *braelea@xtra.co.nz*
www.alpineviewfarmstay.com

@ home NEW ZEALAND

Tariff : N.Z. Dollars	
Double	$125-140
Single	$80
Child	$10+age

Bedrooms	Qty
Double/Twin	4
Twin	
Single	
Bed Size	**Qty**
Super King/Twin	4
King	
Queen	
Double	
Single	
Bathrooms	**Qty**
Ensuite	
Private	2
Family Share	1

Farmstay Experience

Features & Attractions

- *Complimentary farm tour at dusk*
- *One group per guest wing*
- *Mt Cook 90 min, Christchurch 2 hrs*
- *Winter central heating*
- *Feed sheep, cattle, deer & hens*
- *Dinner often available*
- *Free email, laundry and BBQ*
- *Close to skiing, golf, fishing*

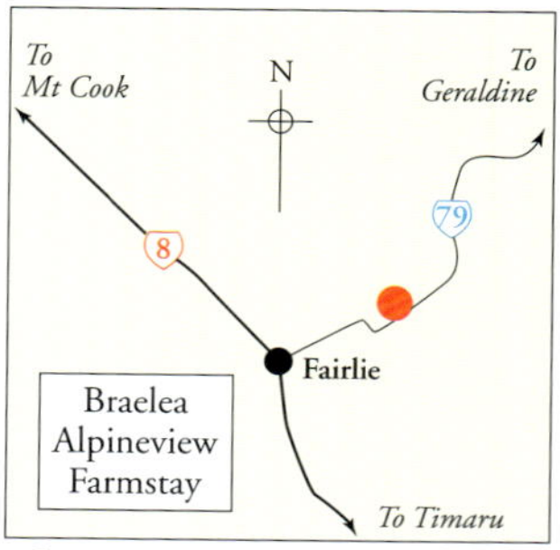

Break your journey between Christchurch and Queenstown with a farmstay at Fairlie. Enjoy the tranquility and spectacular views as you wander the gardens, amble around the farm or laze on the veranda. Indulge in the privacy of your guest wing; join us for a cuppa before your farm tour; sample a local wine/beer before dinner.

Our modern home has two guest wings, each with two bedrooms, bathroom and lounge; each can accommodate up to six. Tariff – extra per person $25-35.

Our small farm has been in the extended family since it was established in 1911. The seasonal feeding regime gives variety. Les' interests include local thar and wallaby hunting, tramping, photography, building and country driving. Sandra's interests include developing the gardens and gerontology.

"We loved it – we will be back" – Our latest Australian guests.

"Many thanks for two magical stays" – Family from Singapore –'06.

Ashgrove B & B

Mt Cook Road, Fairlie, South Canterbury
Ph (03) 685 8797, Fax (03) 685 8795
Mobile 027-289 5323
email: *maria@ashgrove.co.nz*
www.ashgrove.co.nz

Features & Attractions

- *Restful stopover*
- *3 Ski fields close by*
- *Mt. Cook 90 mins drive*
- *Queenstown 3hrs drive*
- *Fishing and hunting guides*
- *Golf and walks*

$	
Double	$125
Single	$85
Child	neg

Countrystay Bed & Breakfast

Bedrooms	Qty
Double	2
Twin	
Single	
Bed Size	**Qty**
Super King	1
Queen	1
Double	
Single	
Bathrooms	**Qty**
Ensuite	1
Private	1
Guest Share	

Welcome to **Ashgrove**, your home away from home.
Our Guest Facilities for the Super king room include a spacious private sitting room with TV, fridge, tea and coffee making facilities, microwave, toaster and dishes etc and also a comfortable sofa bed to sleep 1 adult or 2 children in the separate sitting room. The super king may also be made into 2 singles.
The Queen bedroom with ensuite has a spacious sitting area with TV, fridge, tea and coffee making facilities, toaster and dishes etc and a comfortable sofa bed to sleep 1 adult or 2 children.
At an extra cost, I offer a cooked breakfast with eggs from our free-range chickens. We have sheep and lambs from October to March. Top quality restaurants 2 mins drive or 15 mins walk. We are two hours drive from Christchurch, one and a half from Mt. Cook and three hours to Queenstown.

DIRECTIONS: In the 80kph zone Tekapo end of Fairlie. The second Blue B&B sign leaving, and the first Blue B&B sign entering Fairlie.

Allandale Lodge

555 SH 79, RD 17, Fairlie
Ph (03) 685 8722, Fax (03) 685 8722
email: *info@allandalehall.co.nz*
www.allandalehall.co.nz

Features & Attractions

- *Heritage style building*
- *Smoke house tastings*
- *Spectacular scenery*
- *Great cafés/restaurants*
- *Ski fields, golf, lakes*
- *Mt. Cook 90min. drive*

$	
Double	$130
Single	$80
Child	neg

Heritage Style Bed & Breakfast Boutique Smokehouse

Bedrooms	Qty
Double	2
Twin	
Single	
Bed Size	**Qty**
King	
Queen	2
Double	
Single	
Bathrooms	**Qty**
Ensuite	
Private	
Family Share	1

Welcome to historic **Allandale Lodge**. Our unique home is nestled on five acres of farmland and only five kilometres from Fairlie. Originally built as a school in 1911, it has now been lovingly renovated and offers two double bedrooms. Each room furnished with a queen size bed and hand basin. The original school room has been transformed into the living area with polished New Zealand native timber floors and log fire. We also operate a boutique smokehouse (Fat Albert Smokehouse) based on a traditional Scottish recipe. Specialising in smoked venison, pork, duck and also salmon. We look forward to sharing **Allandale Lodge** with you and to promote Fairlie and the Mackenzie Country as a unique and memorable stay.

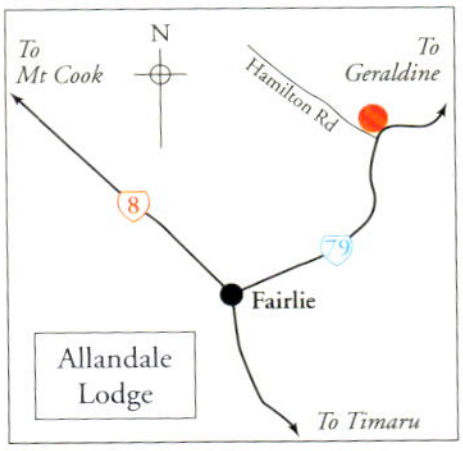

DIRECTIONS: Situated on SH79, 5km north of Fairlie on the Geraldine-Fairlie route.

Alpine Vista Bed & Breakfast

12 Hamilton Drive, Lake Tekapo
Ph (03) 680 6702, Fax (03) 680 6707
Mobile 021-415 544
email: *info@alpinevista.co.nz*
www.alpinevista.co.nz

@ home NEW ZEALAND

qualmark ★★★★ guest & hosted

Tariff : N.Z. Dollars	
Double	$170-240
Single	$120-195
Child	

Bedrooms	Qty
Double	2
Twin	1
Single	
Bed Size	**Qty**
Super King	
King	2
Queen	
Double	
Single	2
Bathrooms	**Qty**
Ensuite	3
Private	
Guest Share	

BB **Delightful Bed & Breakfast** LA

JCB VISA MasterCard AMERICAN EXPRESS eftpos

Features & Attractions

- *Warm hospitality*
- *Magnificent scenery*
- *Cooked breakfast*
- *Mount Cook 1 hour*
- *Restaurants 10 min walk*
- *Trout fishing*
- *Golf (clubs available)*
- *Christchurch/Queenstown 3 hrs*

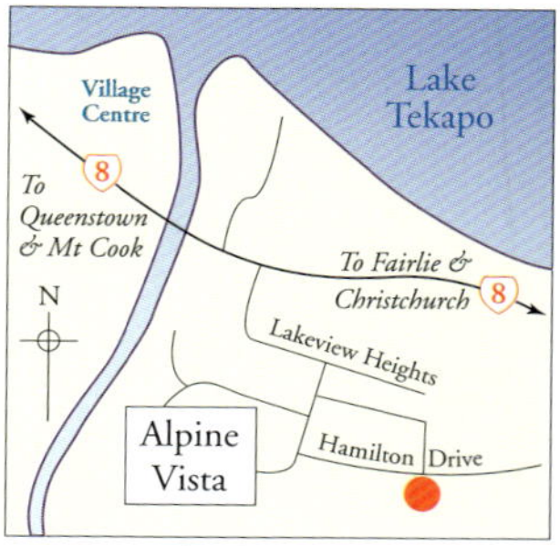

Pete and Jill welcome you to **Alpine Vista**, our large, modern home offering amazing views of the Southern Alps, beautiful Lake Tekapo and the Richmond Range. Our home offers 3 guest bedrooms, each with an ensuite, tea/coffee making facilities, email and fax access. Our home is situated in a quiet location and being double glazed, a peaceful night's sleep is guaranteed. A full continental and English cooked breakfast is served in our large country-style kitchen. Each evening guests are invited to join us in the lounge for pre-dinner drinks. Lake Tekapo is halfway between Christchurch and Queenstown and is an ideal location to base yourself for a day trip to explore the Mt Cook National Park as it is only a one hour drive away. Lake Tekapo offers many attractions including golf, trout fishing, tramping, star gazing, snow skiing, (2 skifields within 40 minutes drive), scenic flights around Mt Cook – or just take in the peace and tranquillity.

FREDA DU FAUR HOUSE

1 Esther Hope Street,Lake Tekapo,
South Canterbury
Ph (03) 680 6513
email: *dawntek@xtra.co.nz*
www.fredadufaur.co.nz

Tariff : N.Z. Dollars	
Double	$130-140
Single	$80-90
Child	neg

Bedrooms	Qty
Double	2
Twin	1
Single	
Bed Size	**Qty**
Super King	
King	
Queen	1
Double	1
Single	2
Bathrooms	**Qty**
Ensuite	2
Private	1
Guest Share	

Bed & Breakfast Homestay

DIRECTIONS:
From SH 8 turn into Lakeview Heights and follow green B&B sign into Barbara Hay Street. Turn right and see our sign.

Features & Attractions

- *Snowcapped mountains*
- *Crystal blue lakes*
- *Beautiful gardens & water feature*
- *Fishing and small game guide*
- *Handy to ski fields*
- *5 min to shops, restaurants*
- *1 hour from Mt. Cook*
- *Peaceful and quiet*

When you come to this area you will experience Tekapo's tranquility and a touch of mountain magic. Dawn and Barry extend to you a warm and friendly welcome. Our home with beautiful mountain and lake views is warm and comfortable. Rimu panelling, heart timber furniture and an attractive decor are blending in with the McKenzie Country.

All guest bedrooms in their private wing are overlooking the garden, two are opening onto a balcony.

Enjoy light refreshments on our patio surrounded by the scent of lavender and roses or view the ever-changing panorama from the lounge. In the morning you have the choice of either continental or special breakfast.

A five minute walk takes you to the centre with shops and restaurants. There are several lovely walkways nearby and Mount Cook is only a one hour scenic drive from Lake Tekapo.

 YOUR HOSTS: **Jennifer and Peter Rayne** Free Ph: 0800 573 364

TEKAPO HOUSE

8 O'Neill Place, Lakeview Heights, Lake Tekapo
Ph (03) 680 6607, Fax (03) 680 6691
Mobile 027-240 4974
email: *rayntek@xtra.co.nz*
www.tekapoholidayhomes.co.nz

Tariff : N.Z. Dollars	
Double	$130-150
Single	$80
Child	$35

Bedrooms	Qty
Double	2
Twin	1
Single	
Bed Size	**Qty**
Super King	1
King	
Queen	1
Double	
Single	
Bathrooms	**Qty**
Ensuite	1
Private	
Guest Share	1

Bed & Breakfast
Boutique Accommodation

Features & Attractions

- *Outstanding lake views*
- *Excellent walking tracks*
- *Excellent choice of restaurants*
- *Christchurch/Queenstown, 3 hr. drive*
- *Fishing*
- *Round hill ski field*
- *Amazing clear skies*
- *Generous cooked breakfast*

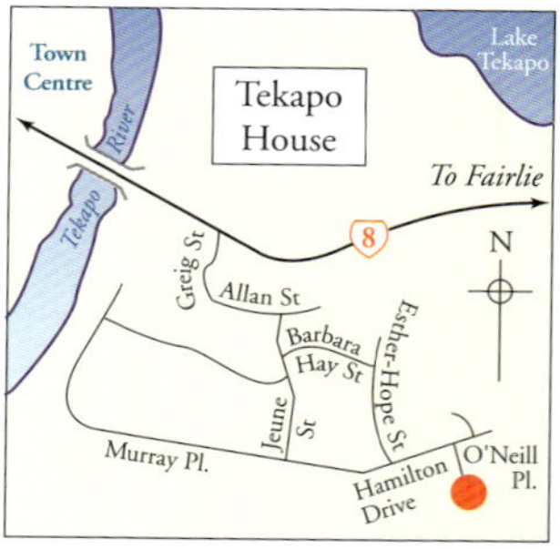

Treat yourself to Tekapo. Just three hours from Christchurch and three hours from Queenstown, Lake Tekapo is one of New Zealand's most celebrated beauty spots. The ever-changing colours of the lake with snow capped mountains beyond draw artists and photographers from around the world every season.

Take time to relax at **Tekapo House**, with stunning views from almost every room and hearty breakfasts to start your day. Enjoy warmth, comfort and home-style hospitality. Jenny and Peter used to run a farm and still have a small flock of sheep you can hand-feed. They know the area well and can advise on all local attractions. At Lake Tekapo you can fish, hike, bird-watch, horse-trek, take scenic flights over the Alps, and ski and skate in winter. Or simply take in the beauty of the environment. Treat yourself to memories at **Tekapo House**.

Creel House

36 Murray Place, PO Box39, Lake Tekapo
Ph (03) 680 6516, Fax (03) 680 6659
Mobile 021-137 9787
email: *creelhouse.l.tek@xtra.co.nz*
www.laketekapoflyfishing.co.nz

Features & Attractions

- *Church of the Good Shepherd*
- *Scenic flights glaciers/Mt. Cook*
- *Easy access to walking tracks*
- *Stargazing on clear evenings*
- *Skiing/ice-skating - winter*
- *Great outdoors*

$		
	Double	$150-160
	Single	$80
	Child	

Creel House
Bed & Breakfast

Bedrooms	Qty
Double	2
Twin	1
Single	
Bed Size	**Qty**
King	
Queen	2
Double	
Single	2
Bathrooms	**Qty**
Ensuite	1
Private	2
Guest Share	

"Welcome." Our home, built by Grant, has three storeys with panoramic views of Lake Tekapo, Mt. John, Southern Alps and surrounding mountains, and has a native garden. There is a separate guest lounge and guest entrance, and all rooms are spacious. Walking distance to shops and restaurants is 10-15 minutes. We have one secondary school daughter living at home and two cats. Our living quarters are on the ground floor with guest's accommodation on the middle and upper floor. Breakfast is a lavish, healthy continental with home-made produce.
Grant is a registered member of the NZ Fishing and Guides Association. He is available for guided fly fishing for day tours and packages are available. Details on website.

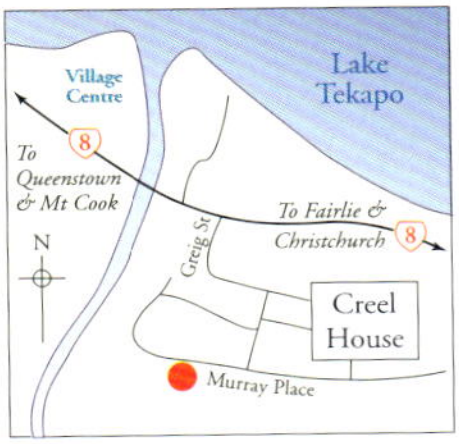

YOUR HOST: **Rayna Clarke** Ph (03) 680 6673 **Lake Tekapo**

Lakeview Bed & Breakfast & Studio Unit

7 Hamilton Drive, PO Box 118, Lake Tekapo
Ph (03) 680 6673
Mobile 027-202 3419
email: *lakeviewlaketekapo@xtra.co.nz*
www.tekapolakeview.co.nz

Features & Attractions

- *Kiwi hospitality*
- *Picturesque lake views*
- *Fantastic night sky*
- *Tremendous walking tracks*
- *Close to lake & restaurants*
- *Mount Cook 1 hour*

$		
	Double	$110-140
	Single	$80-90
	Child	

Bed & Breakfast Homestay
& Self-contained Studio Unit

Bedrooms	Qty
Double	2
Twin	1
Single	
Bed Size	**Qty**
King	
Queen	2
Double	
Single	2
Bathrooms	**Qty**
Ensuite	1
Private	
Guest Share	1

Rayna welcomes you with genuine Kiwi hospitality to **Lakeviews** and is happy to share her local knowledge with you.
Enjoy the peace and tranquility at our unique location. From our elevated position you can look at beautiful Lake Tekapo, renowned for its aquamarine colour, and further up towards the surrounding mountain ranges. In the evening watch when the setting sun turns Mt. Edward into a glowing gold. Lake Tekapo is famous for its fantastic night sky. From our large balcony, which is ideal for stargazing, you may like to watch the Milkyway and the Southern Cross later in the evening .
You have the choice of staying as a Bed & Breakfast guest or enjoy your self-contained studio unit with private entrance. **Lakeviews** is close to the lake and restaurants. Mount Cook is one hour's drive away.

Artemis Bed & Breakfast

33 North West Arch, PO Box 78, Twizel,
Mackenzie Country
Ph (03) 435 0388, Fax (03) 435 0377
email: *artemistwizel@paradise.net.nz*

Features & Attractions

- *Stunning alpine views*
- *Guest sitting room*
- *Private tea/coffee making*
- *Special continental breakfast*
- *3 minute drive to restaurants*
- *45 minutes to Mount Cook*

Bed & Breakfast Homestay

Double	$125
Single	$95
Child	

Bedrooms	Qty
Double	2
Twin	1
Single	

Bed Size	Qty
King	
Queen	2
Double	
Single	1

Bathrooms	Qty
Ensuite	1
Private	1
Guest Share	

Jan and Bob welcome you to the magnificent Mackenzie Basin and the Mount Cook National Park. Our modern home, which is situated on a hectare of land, has stunning mountain views along with space and tranquility. We are a forty-five minute drive to Mount Cook and only three minutes drive to several local restaurants. There is a guest sitting room and balcony, with complimentary tea, coffee, snacks and television.

Our special continental breakfast includes juices, fruits, cereals, cheeses, home-made croissants, jams and toast. There is also a selection of teas and coffees. We look forward to sharing our home with you and are only too happy to discuss your New Zealand itineraries and sightseeing.

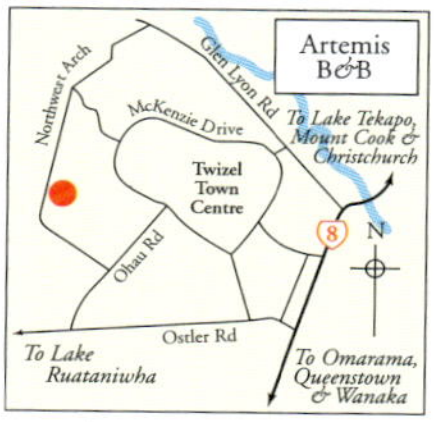

Hunters House

58 Tekapo Drive, Twizel
Ph (03) 435 0038, Fax (03) 435 0038
email: *annehunter@xtra.co.nz*

Features & Attractions

- *Lovely peaceful views*
- *Close to Mt Cook*
- *Fishing opportunities*
- *Riverside walks*
- *6 min walk to town*
- *Sightseeing trips arranged*

$	
Double	$150
Single	$100
Child	

Bed & Breakfast Homestay & Self-contained Cottage

Bedrooms	Qty
Double	2
Twin	
Single	
Bed Size	**Qty**
Super King	2
Queen	
Double	
Single	
Bathrooms	**Qty**
Ensuite	2
Private	
Guest Share	

"Cead mille fuilte".

Hunters House was built in 2003. It is architecturally designed for guests and features every comfort and a warm welcoming environment. It overlooks the native tussocks and trees of the green belt on the township boundary with the mountains as a backdrop. All rooms are tastefully decorated with all facilities and french doors opening to the peaceful outdoors sited for the sun and views. We also have a self-contained cottage, fully equiped with all home comforts and same views as **Hunters House**, situated on its own private setting. Available short or long term. "Cead mille failte"

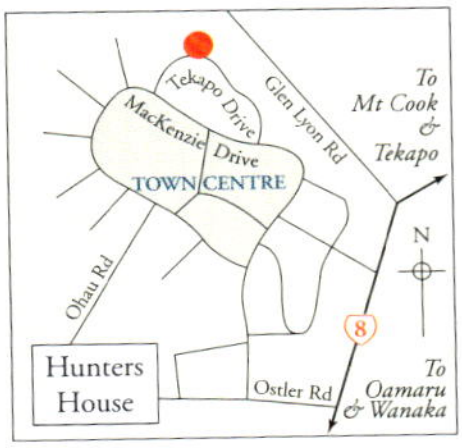

Heartland Lodge

19 North West Arch, Twizel, South Canterbury
Ph (03) 435 0008, Fax (03) 435 0387
Mobile 025-688 6944
www.heartland-lodge.co.nz

Features & Attractions

- *Spectacular mountain views*
- *Sightseeing trips arranged*
- *Self-catering option*
- *Fly fishing guide*
- *Spa and sauna*
- *Peaceful rural setting*

$	
Double	$200-220
Single	$150
Child	neg

Homestay - Bed & Breakfast and Self-Service 'Loft'

Bedrooms	Qty
King/Twin	4
Twin	
Single	
Bed Size	**Qty**
Super King	
King	1
Queen	1
King/Single	2
Bathrooms	**Qty**
Ensuite	4
Private	
Guest Share	

Welcome to our lovely, large Homestay Lodge, only forty minutes from the Aoraki/Mt Cook World Heritage Park. Luxurious guest rooms feature ensuites with spa baths or therapeutic saunas. We are a short drive from the township of Twizel, which has all services including a bank and restaurants. Relax with your friendly Kiwi hosts. Kerry is of Maori descent and would love to share her culture and history with you, and Steve is a world renowned fly fishing guide. We also offer **The Loft** – a large self-service apartment above our garage, which sleeps up to six. From $120 double.

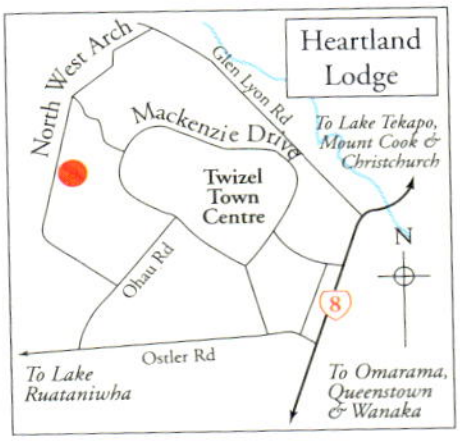

Reaper & Binder Farm Cottage

Windsor Downs, Hakataramea Valley, RD, Kurow
Ph (03) 436 0649, Fax (03) 436 0949
Mobile 027-479 2760
email: *mccaw@reaperandbinder.co.nz*
www.hakatarameariver.co.nz

Tariff : N.Z. Dollars	
Double	$95-150
Single	
Child	

Bedrooms	Qty
Double	2
Twin	
Single	
Bed Size	**Qty**
Super King	
King	1
Queen	1
Double	
Single	
Bathrooms	**Qty**
Ensuite	
Private	2
Guest Share	

Self-contained Accommodation

Features & Attractions

- *40mins from SH 1*
- *Breath taking views*
- *Good fishing*
- *Central to Mt Cook & Queenstown*
- *Cropping farm with sheep*
- *Peaceful & relaxing*
- *Time to meet the country people*
- *A warm welcome awaits you*

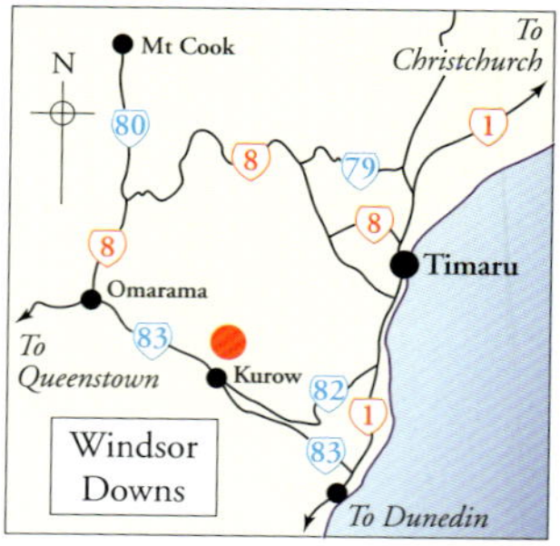

DIRECTIONS: At Kurow cross to northern side of Waitaki River and turn left onto Hakataramea Valley Road over Haka Hill into Haka Valley. Milne Road is 10 min into the valley on left. After 3 km our entrance is on right.

Wide, expansive, open country – air so clear, you can look into a 50 km valley of mountains rolling fans and a river threading its way to the sea. Yellow tussock, alpine grasses and a necklace of grazing sheep against a blue sky. Here a pocket of loamy soils, lush green with grain growing crops awaiting the summer harvest.

We offer unique self-catering accommodation for two at the **Reaper & Binder Cottage**, where you can indulge yourself in peace and solitude and where birdsong meets your breakfast and re-kindles your spirit. Fully equipped with bedroom, bathroom and kitchen living area. A comfortable king-size bed, TV, radio and laundry. Outdoor living area with a private garden and road entrance. Outdoor barbeque with food available.

– Bed & Breakfast accommodation is available at the nearby farmhouse, with large bedroom and seating area (tea coffee making facilities) and a private bathroom. Time to meet a southern breed of people and share their place under the sun.

Bellbird Cottage

121-125 Noema Terrace, Lake Hawea
Ph (03) 443 7056 or (03) 443 8676
Fax (03) 443 1807
email: *marge@xtra.co.nz*
www.bellbirdcottage.co.nz

Tariff : N.Z. Dollars	
Double	$125
Single	$125
Child	n/a

Bedrooms	Qty
Double/Twin	1
Twin	
Single	1
Bed Size	**Qty**
Super King	
King	
Queen	1
Double	
Single	1
Bathrooms	**Qty**
Ensuite	1
Private	
Guest Share	

DIRECTIONS:
Please telephone for easy directions.
Advance booking recommended.

Self-contained Luxury Accommodation

Features & Attractions

- *Seven-day-dining close by*
- *Microwave & dishwasher*
- *Two television sets*
- *Fully equipped kitchen*
- *Full private laundry*
- *Log fire, stereo, video*
- *Central to activities*
- *Co-operative hosts*

Our modern, self-contained cottage is situated in beautiful Lake Hawea village, surrounded by majestic mountains. We are just 12 km from Lake Wanaka in the centre of the Lakes District of Central Otago. With Queenstown just an hour away, less than two hours to Mount Cook, you are close to all attractions. We are located about thirty minutes from two major ski fields – Treble Cone and Cadrona. Lake Hawea is renowned for fishing with guides available. Horse riding, nature walks, adventure trips, canoeing, paragliding are just some of the local attractions. The cottage construction is timber and rammed earth. The bedroom has a double and single bed and there is a double sofa sleeper in the lounge. If required on occasions we have a double self-contained bedroom adjacent complete with ensuite. A typical comment from our guest book is: "This is an outstanding cottage, cosy, tastefully decorated and thoughtfully well equipped. Together with warm hospitality this has perfected our holiday in New Zealand." Hosts are Marjorie Goodger, who has had a career in hotel management, and her sister Sheila McCaughan from a farming background. Should you wish, your log fire will be burning on your return from skiing. Dinner by arrangement hosted by Marjorie, Sheila and Brian McCaughan. Easy to find – Noema Terrace leads off the main road, Capell Avenue, where you are welcome at 121 & 125.

Matagouri Cottage

37 Elizabeth Street, Lake Hawea
Ph (03) 443 1987
email: *info@matagouricottage.co.nz*
www.matagouricottage.co.nz

Tariff : N.Z. Dollars	
Double	$130-150
Single	$100-120
Child	neg

Bedrooms	Qty
Double	1
Twin/Double	1
Single	
Bed Size	**Qty**
Super King	
King	
Queen	2
Double	
Single	1
Bathrooms	**Qty**
Ensuite	2
Private	
Guest Share	

Bed & Breakfast Homestay

Features & Attractions

- *Purpose built cottage*
- *Secluded location*
- *Off-street parking*
- *5 min. walk to lake*
- *Relax on the verandah*
- *Dinner by arrangement*
- *Full breakfast*
- *17km to Wanaka*

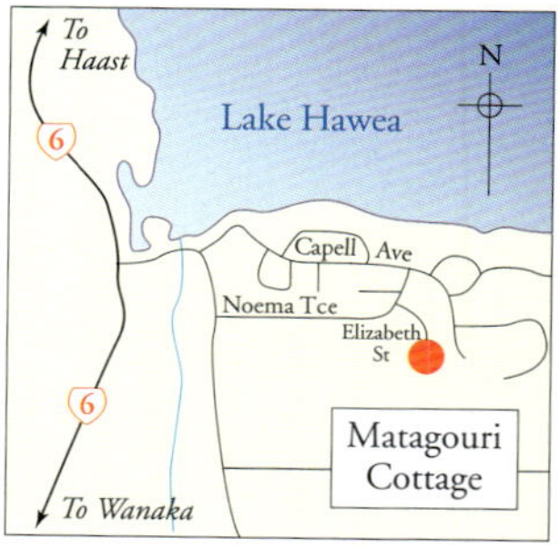

Ian and Judith welcome you to charming **Matagouri Cottage**, which is nestled in trees in a tranquil part of Lake Hawea village.

Judith has come back to the district where she was raised on a sheep station, still in family hands and close by for visits. Ian trained as a quantity surveyor and has lived in Hong Kong and also in England, where he was involved in the running of a Bed & Breakfast. He's lived in New Zealand since 1987.

Matagouri Cottage, apart from the fact of its peaceful location, is the centre of an area famed for its diversity. Ski fields abound, mountains and lakes with their immense opportunities are a great attraction, a vibrant wine growing industry virtually on the doorstep and a world-renowned gliding centre nearby.

Matagouri Cottage has two charmingly appointed ensuite bedrooms and all the comforts of a New Zealand country home including an open fire in the sitting room and wood burner in the kitchen/dining room.

RIVERSONG

5 Wicklow Terrace Albert Town, No 2 RD, Wanaka
Ph (03) 443 8567, Fax (03) 443 8564
Mobile 021-113 6397
email: *info@happyhomestay.co.nz*
www.happyhomestay.co.nz

Tariff : N.Z. Dollars	
Double	$130-160
Single	$100
Child	$25

Bedrooms	Qty
Double	1
Twin	1
Single	1
Bed Size	**Qty**
Super King	1
King	
Queen	1
Double	
King/Single	1
Bathrooms	**Qty**
Ensuite	1
Private	1
Guest Share	

VISA MasterCard

BB **Homestay Bed & Breakfast** H

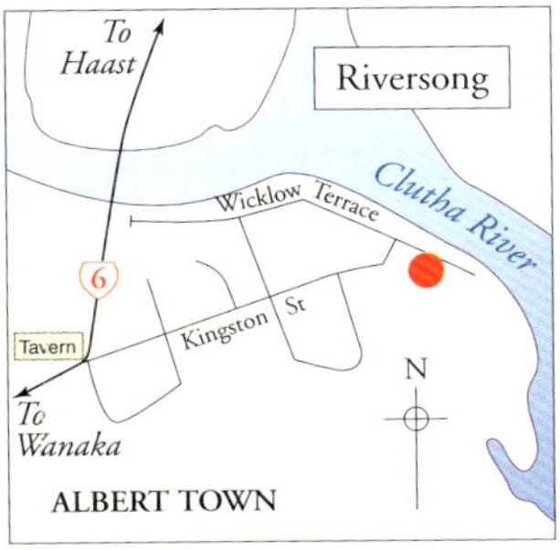

DIRECTIONS:
Kingston St joins SH6 opposite Albert Town Tavern. Travel the length of Kingston St to Wicklow Terrace, which runs parallel to the Clutha River. Turn right into Wicklow Terrace. **Riversong** is the 2nd last house.

Features & Attractions

- *Outstanding natural views*
- *Historic riverside setting*
- *Wireless/broadband facility*
- *Bedrooms with balconies*
- *Trout fishing opportunities abound*
- *Riverside walk to lake outlet*
- *Dinner by arrangement with hosts*
- *Book lovers and gardeners delight*

Riversong is an enchanting home in a stunning setting, and is one of Albert Town's most admired and historic homes. Situated on the banks of the Clutha River and a few minutes drive from Wanaka, it lies at the heart of Central Otago's unique scenic beauty, trout fishing, ski fields and entry to Mount Aspiring National Park. The guestrooms all command stunning river, mountain and garden views. Privacy and full home comforts are assured and provided. Ann's background is in healthcare, Ian's law. Ian is happy to provide guests with the benefit of his local fishing knowledge and guidance services. Three ski fields are located within close distance. Otherwise just relax, walk or golf if you prefer, and take in the unsurpassed vista. All travellers are warmly welcome.

Ferryman's Cottage (Circa 1870)

4 Arklow St, Albert Town, Wanaka
Ph (03) 443 4147, Mobile 021-144 7513
email: *ferrymanscottage@xtra.co.nz*
www.ferrymanscottage.co.nz

Features & Attractions

- *Fragrant cottage garden*
- *Fisherman's paradise*
- *Fine food, crisp linen*
- *Scenic walks*
- *Stunning landscape*
- *Dinner by arrangement*

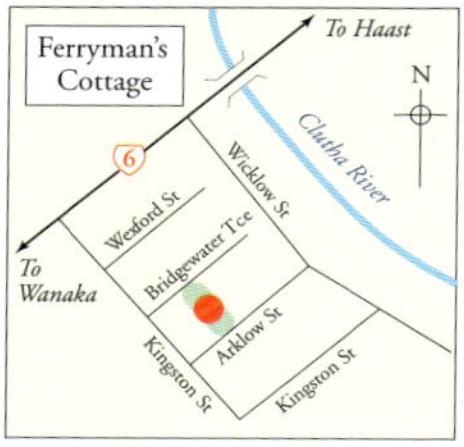

Bed & Breakfast Homestay

Double	$150-165
Single	$95-115
Child	

Ferrymans is our recently renovated historic cottage, located 5 minutes from Wanaka, on the banks of the beautiful Clutha River (one of New Zealand's foremost fishing rivers). The warmth, peace and tranquillity of our home has been created for you and us to enjoy. A unique breakfast experience from Marie's kitchen awaits you. Following this you can either relax in our traditional cottage garden or partake of all the outdoor recreational activities that are available in our corner of paradise. We look forward to meeting you and ensuring that you have a memorable stay with us. Our cat 'Indy' left her previous home and adopted us. Let us pamper you in your 'home-away-from home'. – "Take time to smell the roses."

Bedrooms	Qty
Double	2
Twin	
Single	
Bed Size	**Qty**
King	
Queen	2
Double	
Single	
Bathrooms	**Qty**
Ensuite	1
Private	
Guest Share	

Wanaka YOUR HOSTS: **Dorothy and Ian McDonald** Ph: (03) 443 6362

Greystones

219 Beacon Point Road, Wanaka
Ph (03) 443 6362, Fax (03) 443 6062
email: *iandorothy@paradise.net.nz*

Features & Attractions

- *Stunning lake & mountain views*
- *Close to restaurants & galleries*
- *Private courtyard & BBQ area*
- *Warm, friendly, relaxed*
- *Close to lake*
- *Pick-up from coach*

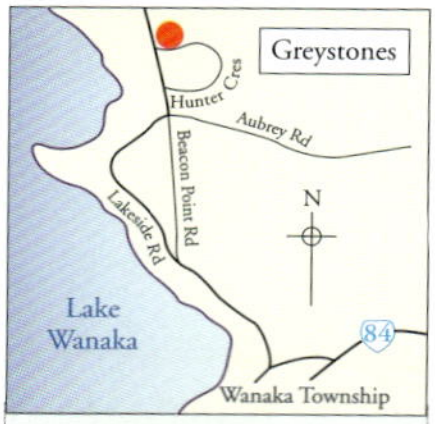

DIRECTIONS: From town – take Lakeside Rd to Beacon Point Rd. You will find us on the corner of Hunter Crescent.

Homestay Bed & Breakfast

Double	$120-140
Single	$80-90
Child	

Dorothy and Ian extend a warm and friendly welcome to you at **Greystones**, our charming two storey home, with wonderful lake and mountain views. Guests are spoiled with friendly service in intimate surroundings. In summer your breakfast is served in our courtyard. In the colder months curl up by the open fire with a pre-dinner drink. At our back door are the three main ski fields: Treble Cone, Cardrona and Waiorau. There is also walking and boating for the summer enthusiasts. It's a casual stroll to restaurants, galleries and shops. We come from a farming background and we both enjoy golf, bridge (happy to have a game), music, walking and handcrafts. Ian is a keen fisherman. We will delight in sharing our home with you and make every effort to make your stay with us enjoyable and memorable.

Bedrooms	Qty
Double	1
Twin	1
Single	
Bed Size	**Qty**
King	
Queen	1
Double	
Single	2
Bathrooms	**Qty**
Ensuite	
Private	1
Guest Share	1

Riverview Terrace

31 Matheson Crescent, Albert Town, Wanaka
Ph (03) 443 7377, Fax (03) 443 7377
Mobile 027-609 0650
email: *pphiggins@slingshot.co.nz*
www.riverviewterrace.co.nz

Tariff : N.Z. Dollars	
Double	$195-250
Single	
Child	

Bedrooms	Qty
Double	3
Twin	
Single	
Bed Size	**Qty**
Super King/Twin	1
King	2
Queen	
Double	
Single	
Bathrooms	**Qty**
Ensuite	3
Private	
Guest Share	

Bed & Breakfast
Luxury Accomodation

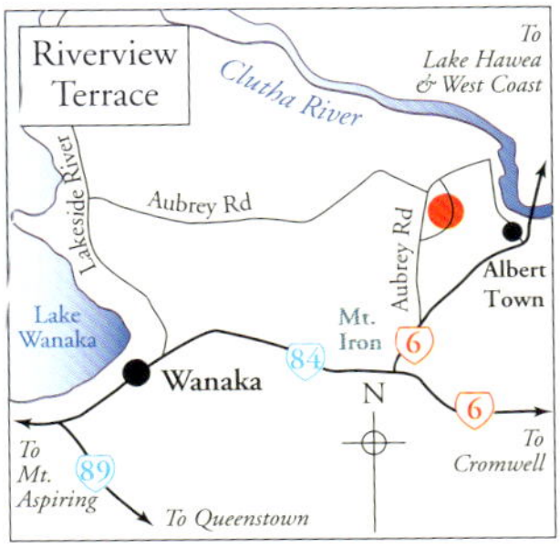

Features & Attractions

- *New luxury accommodation*
- *Stunning 360° views*
- *3 min. drive to Wanaka*
- *Courtesy car to restaurants*
- *Private guest lounge and patio*
- *Complimentary drinks and nibbles*
- *Close to ski fields*
- *Warm, friendly hospitality*

Wake up to amazing views and a generous cooked or continental breakfast, served in our dining room or on the patio.
Your friendly hosts, Peter and Pam, can help to plan your kind of day at your pace.
Choices include numerous walking and biking trails, fishing (bikes and rods available), alpine sightseeing flights, boating, golfing, kayaking, horse trekking, skiing, wine tasting, day spa or enjoying a latté in the sun. These are some of the popular options in and around the Lake Wanaka area.

Riverview Terrace is located above the picturesque Clutha River. It has a rural atmosphere and offers 3 large, spacious bedrooms with ensuites (one with a spa bath), all beautifully appointed and with electric blankets, hair dryers, mirror demisters, robes and writing desks. Our guests are welcome to enjoy watching DVDs and Sky TV. Other facilities available include ski storage and drying room, internet access plus ample off-street parking.
Opening January 2007.

52 on Willowridge

52 Willowridge, Wanaka
Ph (03) 443 1330, Fax (03) 443 1338
email: *stay@willowridgehouse.co.nz*
www.willowridgehouse.co.nz

Tariff : N.Z. Dollars	
Double	$195-245
Single	$195-245
Child	

Bedrooms	Qty
Double	3
Twin	1
Single	
Bed Size	**Qty**
Super King	
King	
Queen	3
Double	
Single	2
Bathrooms	**Qty**
Ensuite	1
Private	1
Guest Share	

Luxury Bed & Breakfast and Self-contained Apartment

Features & Attractions

- *Tranquil & private setting*
- *Stunning views*
- *Garden & balconies to enjoy*
- *Warm hospitality*
- *Five ski fields close by*
- *Golf course 5 min. drive*
- *500m walk to lake*
- *Internet and email access*

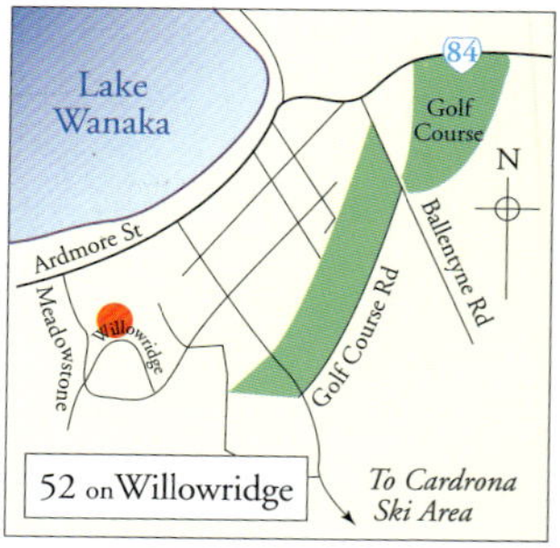

DIRECTIONS:
SH 84 into Ardmore Street,
left into Meadowstone Drive,
then 2nd left into **52 onWillowridge**.

Gorgeous house, delightful garden, wonderful views and superb Kiwi hospitality all at **52 on Willowridge**. The **Bed & Breakfast Suite** on the top level is strictly 1 party booking only. Ideal for up to 4 people.
The **Suite** has 2 large bedrooms with cotton linen, wool duvets, electric blankets, robes and hairdryer. Your own lounge area has a TV, radio, CD player, fridge, tea & coffee making facilities.
The **Apartment** with its indoor/outdoor living is as ideal for couples as it is for families. Self-catering allows for total independence. Comprises 2 bedrooms with electric blankets, wool duvets, hairdryer, a fully equipped kitchen, TV, video, CD player, radio and laundry with ski drying and storage.
Your entrance is security lit and privacy is assured.

AMPHALAW BOUTIQUE LODGE

50 Mount Aspiring Road, Wanaka 9305
Ph (03) 443 4070, Fax (03) 443 4070
Mobile 027- 487 5494
email: *amphalaw.wanaka@xtra.co.nz*
www.amphalaw.co.nz

Tariff : N.Z. Dollars	
Double	$165-225
Single	$150
Child	

Bedrooms	Qty
Double	1
Twin	1
Single	
Bed Size	**Qty**
Super King	1
King	1
Queen	
Double	
Single	
Bathrooms	**Qty**
Ensuite	
Private	1
Guest Share	

Bed & Breakfast
Boutique Accommodation

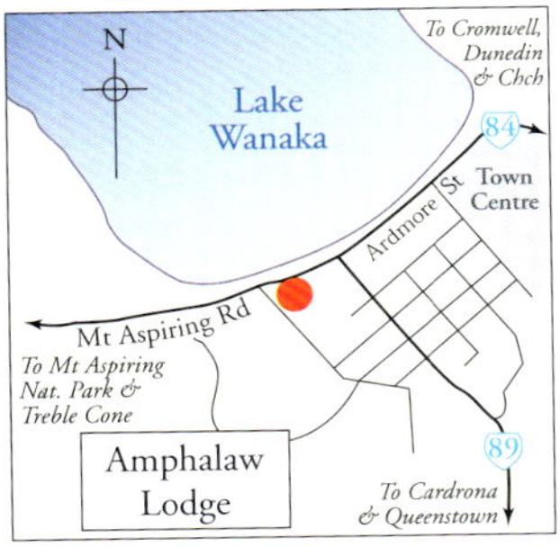

Features & Attractions

- *Charming lakefront home*
- *Guests' private entrance*
- *Peaceful mountain/ lake outlook*
- *Walk to town & vineyard*
- *Lovely gardens and tennis court*
- *Cooked breakfast – silver service*
- *Walking tracks and 3 skifields*
- *Warm and friendly hospitality*

Nestled just metres from the gentle lapping shores of Lake Wanaka and a short walk to the township. This comfortable, elegant home offers private, independent accommodation on the first floor, comprising of one bedroom with a king-size bed offering stunning views of the lake and mountains with a second bedroom with twin/ king bed looking over the tennis court and garden to the majestic splendour of Mt. Barker and the Cardrona Valley.

Also offered is a library/sitting room with kitchenette for making refreshments or light meals. **Amphalaw Boutique Lodge** is tastefully furnished with antiques and there is a tennis court for your use.

During the summer months the lake is easily accessible for swimming and picnics with a lakefront walkway leading to a local vineyard, and secluded beaches, while the premier snow fields of Queenstown, Cardrona, Snow Farm and Treble Cone are all within an hour's drive for the active in winter.

Atherton House

3 Atherton Place, Wanaka
Ph (03) 443 8343, Fax (03) 443 8343
Mobile 027-228 1982
email: *Roy.Kate@xtra.co.nz*
www.atherton.co.nz

Tariff : N.Z. Dollars	
Double	$195-250
Single	$150
Child	

Bedrooms	Qty
Double	2
Twin	
Single	
Bed Size	**Qty**
Super King	
King	
Queen	1
Double	
King Single	1
Bathrooms	**Qty**
Ensuite	2
Private	
Guest Share	

Luxury Lakeside Bed & Breakfast

Features & Attractions

- *Stunning lake and mountain views*
- *Quiet and peaceful*
- *Lakeside walk to township*
- *Complimentry aperitifs*
- *Warm hospitality*
- *Free laundry facilities*
- *Generous breakfast incl.*
- *Dinner available with hosts*

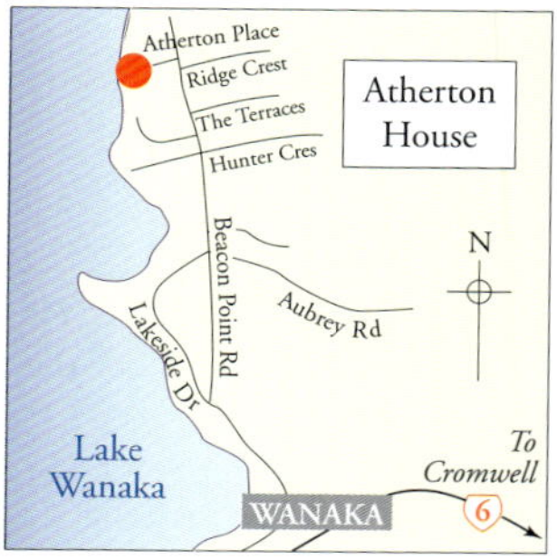

Welcome to our home offering luxurious comfort and warm Kiwi hospitality, set in an acre of lawns and gardens on the shores of beautiful Lake Wanaka. Visitors can unwind in their own spacious and tastefully appointed private wing, which opens out to a peaceful courtyard and landscaped grounds running down to the lake. Our guests are welcome to share our living areas with its collections of antiques and New Zealand Art or just relax in their own private lounge with tea/coffee facilities, Sky TV, a New Zealand library and writing desk. Enjoy the lakeside walk to the township accessible from our home.

After extensive experience hosting farm-stays we built **Atherton House** to provide tranquil and comfortable surroundings perfect for relaxing and enjoying the views. We enjoy art, antiques, travel, all sports especially golf, good food and wine, meeting and helping guests experience our wonderful part of the world.

Beaconfield B&B

251 Beacon Point Road, Wanaka
Ph (03) 443 2737,
Mobile 021- 056 2996
email: *mikerackley@xtra.co.nz*

Tariff : N.Z. Dollars	
Double	$150-195
Single	$125-150
Child	

Bedrooms	Qty
Double	2
Twin	
Single	

Bed Size	Qty
Super King	
King	
Queen	2
Double	
Single	

Bathrooms	Qty
Ensuite	2
Private	
Guest Share	

VISA MasterCard

Bed & Breakfast
Homestay

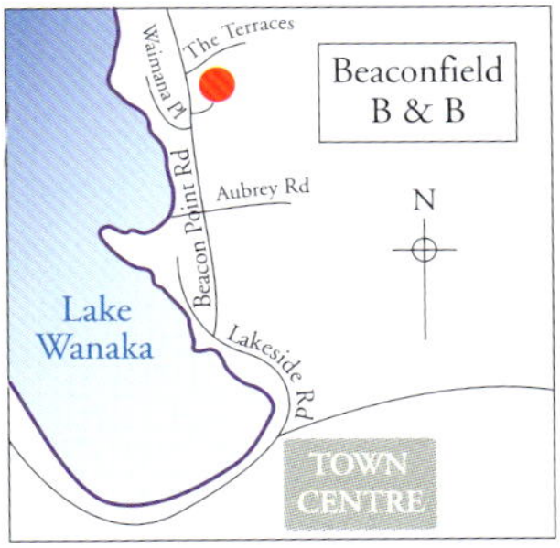

Features & Attractions

- *Breathtaking views*
- *New, architect designed home*
- *Warm, friendly hospitality*
- *Delicious, healthy breakfast*
- *Private and peaceful*
- *Well travelled hosts*
- *Complimentary refreshments*
- *Local knowledge*

Welome to our lovely, brand new home set on one acre amidst a boutique vineyard and with breathtaking lake and mountain views. We invite you to share our Kiwi hospitality and local knowledge. Your guest room with ensuite has French doors opening to a sunny verandah with stunning views. You will never tire of the beauty and tranquility. Share our interests of food, wine, music, local art, antiques, travel and sports. Carla is an RN and Michael was a lawyer and hospital manager. We are both widely travelled and have lived in the UK, USA and Australia. A delicious, healthy breakfast and refreshments are included. Laundry and email facilities are available without charge as is the use of our home cinema.

Black Peak Lodge

38 Kings Drive, Wanaka
Ph (03) 443 4078, Fax (03) 443 4038
Mobile 021-295 0046
email: *relax@blackpeaklodge.co.nz*
www.blackpeaklodge.co.nz

@ home NEW ZEALAND

Tariff : N.Z. Dollars	
Double	$140-200
Single	$130
Child	neg

Bedrooms	Qty
Double	3
Twin	1
Single	
Bed Size	**Qty**
Super King	
King	
Queen	3
Double	
King/Single	1
Bathrooms	**Qty**
Ensuite	2
Private	2
Guest Share	

Boutique Lodge
Bed & Breakfast

Features & Attractions

- *Mountain & lake views to die for*
- *Full business & internet facilities*
- *Decking and barbeque area*
- *Central Otago wineries close by*
- *Relaxing outdoor hot tub*
- *3 ski mountains within 30 min*
- *Architecturally designed*
- *Elegant furnishings*

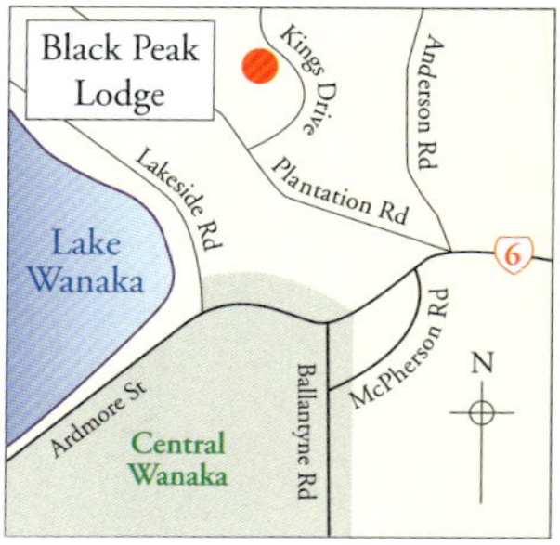

Bed & Breakfast accommodation with a stunning view – **Black Peak Lodge** is the place to stay. Enjoy warmth, comfort and home-style hospitality, where our aim is to make your visit as unforgettable and relaxing as possible. Come, soak up the ambience, from the hot tub on the deck to the guest rooms.

The lodge, fitted with elegant furnishings, has four bedrooms. Each contains quality bedding and electric blankets, TV, DVD and CD player along with lush spa robes. In winter you may curl up with a complimentary aperitif in front of the feature fire place, while in warmer months the living room opens up onto the decking, ideal for barbeques and admiring the sunset. Inclusive of facilities include laptop computer, fax and internet for your complimentary use. In the morning we serve a delicious gourmet breakfast at a time that suits guests, so you can plan your day around your needs. Come and share the most beautiful part of the world.

DRUMMONDS ON WANAKA

137 Anderson Road, Wanaka
Ph (03) 443 1961, Fax (03) 443 1964
Mobile 027-244 8243
email: *stay@drummonds.co.nz*
www.drummonds.co.nz

Tariff : N.Z. Dollars	
Double	$265-325
Single	
Child	neg

Bedrooms	Qty
Double	5
Twin	
Single	
Bed Size	**Qty**
King/Twin	1
King	1
Queen	3
Double	
Single	
Bathrooms	**Qty**
Ensuite	4
Private	
Guest Share	1

Fine Accommodation

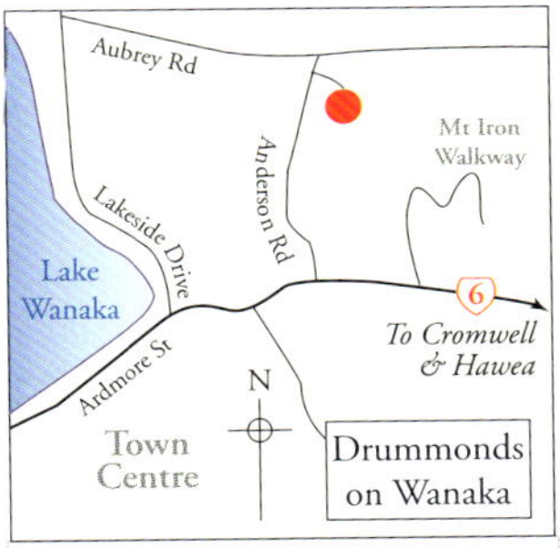

DIRECTIONS: From SH 84 drive almost to the end of Anderson Road at the T-junction with Aubrey Road. Look for the B&B sign on the right before the T-junction.

Features & Attractions

- *Genuine Kiwi hospitality*
- *Luxurious, centrally heated*
- *Fine cuisine & wine available*
- *Skype & Broadband available*
- *Private guest lounge*
- *NZ gifts & artwork available to buy*
- *Fabulous mountain views*
- *Just minutes to town & ski fields*

Drummonds on Wanaka was purpose-built in 2003 as a luxury guest house. Just minutes from Lake Wanaka and the township, **Drummonds** is situated in a sunny position on a broad 2 acres. The alpine environment is well framed in the architectural design with sweeping picture windows capturing the panoramic views of the lofty Harris Mountain Range and World Heritage Listed Mount Aspiring Park. When your hosts, Sally and Duncan Drummond conceived of **Drummonds on Wanaka**, their aim was to offer the very best in regional wine, home-cooked cuisine and fine accommodation. Sally, the highly-acclaimed **Drummonds** 'family chef', offers innovative, wholesome, home-cooked cuisine from fine dining to casual alfresco barbeques. You may choose meals and beverages in addition to your lodging. Duncan is the affable host, with an expansive character and passions for fishing, Bonsai, and photography. Jess and Hal, the Labradors, are always keen for extra company (or a walk). George, the cat, is always looking for a willing lap.

Lake Wanaka Home Hosting

19 Bill's Way, Wanaka, Central Otago
Ph (03) 443 9060, Fax (03) 443 1626
Mobile 027-228 9160
email: *lex.joy@xtra.co.nz*
www.lakewanakahomehosting.co.nz

Tariff : N.Z. Dollars	
Double	$110-150
Single	$70
Child	$25

Bedrooms	Qty
Double	2
Twin	1
Single	
Bed Size	**Qty**
Super King	1
King	
Queen	1
Double	
Single	2
Bathrooms	**Qty**
Ensuite	
Private	2
Guest Share	

Homestay - Bed & Breakfast

Features & Attractions

- *Peaceful lake walks*
- *A little luxury*
- *Meals on request*
- *Lovely patio garden*

- *Spacious, relaxing decor*
- *Mountain and lake views*
- *15-20 min. walk to shops*
- *Close to Rippon Vineyard*

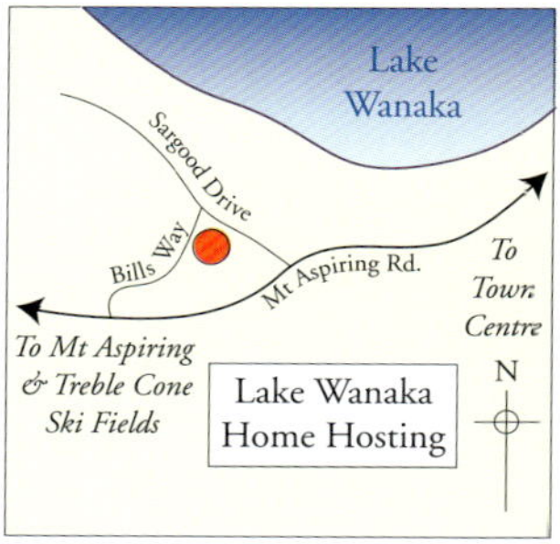

We welcome visitors to Lake Wanaka and enjoy sharing our natural surroundings with others. We have a large, peaceful home where our guests can experience not only the awesomeness of the lake and mountains around, but also experience the ambience of Wanaka itself. The picturesque twenty to thirty minute walk to Wanaka Town is very worthwhile. Our guest room upstairs has the super king size bed with an adjoining lounge with tea and coffee making facilities, refrigerator, television and a private bathroom. Our double guestroom also has a private bathroom. We have smoke alarms, central heating and electric blankets in all beds. Good laundry facilities. We have no children living at home and no pets. Our interests are sport, gardening, boating, farming and good cuisine. Lex and I enjoy your company.

Collinsons Cottage

67 Manuka Crest, Wanaka
Ph (03) 443 7089, Fax (03) 443 7088
Mobile 027-443 0180
email: *stay@collinsonscottage.co.nz*
www.collinsonscottage.co.nz

Features & Attractions

- *Warm hospitality*
- *Relaxed location*
- *Off-street parking*
- *Garden setting*
- *Painting gallery*
- *Golf experience*

Homestay Bed & Breakfast
SC. Studio & Apartment

$	
Double	$125
Single	$85
Studio	$135

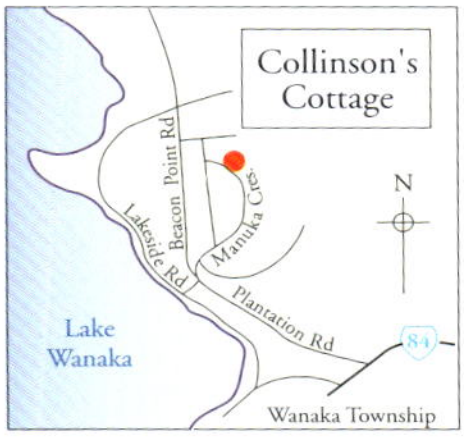

Your hosts Brian and Susanne welcome you to our relaxing home and garden. Situated minutes from the town centre with thirty odd restaurants at your disposal. A quiet walk around our large garden will entice your camera and with a painting gallery to view local scenery. All the perks of home are enjoyed at the Collinsons - tea/coffee making facilities with filtered water on tap, plus television in your own lounge, and a secluded hideaway courtyard to enjoy in the summer evenings. Our interests are gardening, painting, sport and meeting people. Our passion is golf. The kids are gone and only our cat (Cambo) is in residence. You may arrive as a guest but hopefully you will leave as friends having enjoyed all that Wanaka has to offer.

Bedrooms	Qty
Double	1
Twin	1
Single	
Bed Size	**Qty**
King	
Queen	1
Double	
Single	2
Bathrooms	**Qty**
Ensuite	
Private	1
Guest Share	

Hunt's Homestay

56 Manuka Crescent, Wanaka
Ph (03) 443 1053, Fax (03) 443 1355
Mobile 027-427 2780
email:*relax@huntshomestay.co.nz*
www.huntshomestay.co.nz

Features & Attractions

- *New house in large garden*
- *Access to many activities*
- *Free laundry facilities*
- *Safe off-street parking*
- *Farm visits available*
- *Complimentary tea/coffee*

$	
Double	$130-140
Single	$80-90
Child	neg

Homestay
Bed & Breakfast

Bedrooms	Qty
Double	1
Twin	1
Single	
Bed Size	**Qty**
King	
Queen	1
Double	
Single	2
Bathrooms	**Qty**
Ensuite	1
Private	1
Guest Share	

Once settled in our roomy ground floor bedroom and lounge, our guests remark on the beauty of the lake and mountain views and how they change throughout the day. It was this aspect that drew us to this peaceful ½-acre section, when we left farming near Wanaka six years ago. Our architecturally designed house has two spacious bedrooms and 360° views of lake and mountains. By chance we became involved in homestay activities and have greatly enjoyed the experience. We realised we had a great wealth of information about the area that we could pass on to our guests. Through our membership of "Lake Wanaka Tourism" we are kept informed of all tourist activities in the area. Whatever you want to do, we are happy to organise it. We look forward to enjoying your company in our beautiful area.

DIRECTIONS: From town take Lakeside Road to Beacon Point Road, right to Manuka Crescent. We are opposite Manuka Crescent Motels.

Oak Tree Bed & Breakfast

4 Little Oak Common, Meadowstone, Wanaka
Ph (03) 443 9106, Fax (03) 443 9109
email: *r.s.mulqueen@xtra.co.nz*
www.oaktreewanaka.com

@home NEW ZEALAND

Tariff : N.Z. Dollars	
Double	$130-150
Single	
Child	

Bedrooms	Qty
Double	2
Twin	1
Single	
Bed Size	**Qty**
Super King	1
King	
Queen	1
Double	
Single	2
Bathrooms	**Qty**
Ensuite	1
Private	1
Guest Share	

Bed & Breakfast
Homestay

Features & Attractions

- *Warm & friendly hospitality*
- *Spectacular mountain views*
- *Modern spacious home*
- *Email & internet facilities*
- *Short walk to lake*
- *Peaceful setting*
- *Off-street parking*
- *Delicious breakfast*

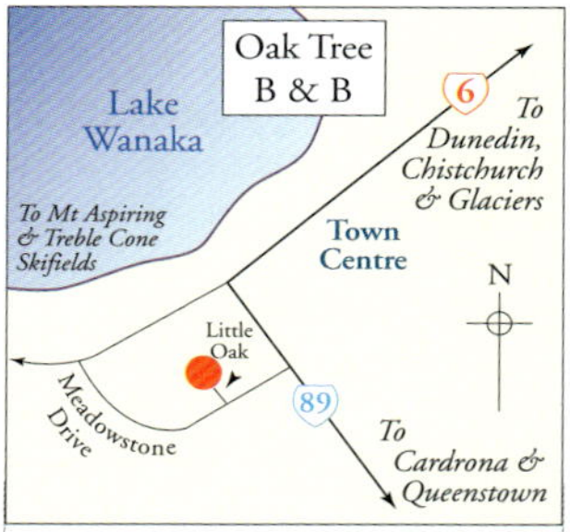

DIRECTIONS: From town travel left along lakefront. Turn left into Meadowstone Drive. Little Oak Common is 3rd left

Oak Tree Bed & Breakfast ~ accommodation with friendly hospitality and stunning views of surrounding mountains and the magnificent Southern Alps. Within easy walking distance to lakefront and town centre, you will find a great range of restaurants, from casual to fine dining, cafés, bars, shops and the famous Cinema Paradiso. Our home is modern and spacious with comfortable beds, quality linen and electric blankets. A delicious continental breakfast is served in the dining area, at a time of your choice, whilst taking in the same superb views. Free laundry and email facilities available. Your hosts, Sharlene and Ray, invite you to take time to discover and experience the splendour of our alpine area in the heart of Mt Aspiring National Park. Ray works at the local 'Warbird Aircraft Collection' and for the renowned 'Warbirds over Wanaka' international air show. We are happy to advise or help you with either your plans in Wanaka or ongoing travel arrangements.

PEAK - SPORTCHALET

36 Hunter Crescent, Wanaka
Ph (03) 443 6990, Fax (03) 443 4969
email: *stay@peak-sportchalet.co.nz*
www.peak-sportchalet.co.nz

Features & Attractions

- *High quality standard*
- *Fully equipped kitchen*
- *Sun decks*
- *Cosy log fire*
- *Close to lake & walking tracks*
- *Drying room*

$	
Double	$105-140
Single	$85
Child	neg

Experience our Hospitality and Ambience

Bedrooms	Qty
Double	2
Twin	1
Single	1
Bed Size	**Qty**
Super King	1
Queen	1
Double	
King/Single	2
Bathrooms	**Qty**
Ensuite	2
Private	1
Guest Share	

Welcome to **Peak-Sportchalet**, your Qualmark 4 Star Accommodation in Wanaka. We would like to invite you to stay in our guest suites including our studio/double and self-contained Chalet. All are individually designed and appointed with fine furniture, ensuite or private bathrooms and also equipped with TV, DVD and sound system. Sliding doors open onto private sundecks. Awake refreshed after a relaxing night's sleep on our prime quality mattresses and duvets. Our luxury Chalet has 2 separate bedrooms, sleeping up to 5 guests, fully equipped kitchen and underfloor heating in the bathroom. The logfire provides an alpine ambience.

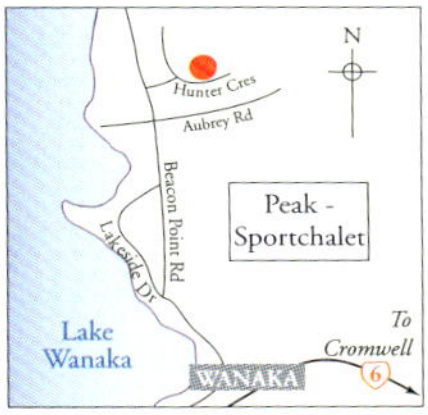

Start your day healthy with our memorable breakfast-buffet in front of an open fire. We also cater for special diets. Experience our hospitality and ambience.

STONEBROOK BED & BREAKFAST

18 Stonebrook Drive, Wanaka
Ph (03) 443 8150, Fax (03) 443 8154
Mobile 021- 341 460
email: *d.a.stretch@xtra.co.nz*

Features & Attractions

- *Friendly hospitality*
- *Mountain & lake views*
- *Off-street parking*
- *Internet & laundry facilities*
- *Ten minute walk to town*
- *Special diets by arrangement*

$	
Double	$125-135
Single	$95
Child	neg

Homestay Bed & Breakfast

Bedrooms	Qty
Double	1
Twin	1
Single	
Bed Size	**Qty**
King	
Queen	1
Double	
Single	2
Bathrooms	**Qty**
Ensuite	1
Private	1
Guest Share	

Friendly hospitality awaits you on arrival at our new home, close to the lake. Drink-in the splendour of the mountains from your bedroom or the guests lounge. Walk to town in 10 minutes; longer if you study the history tiles along the millennium walkway. Our aim is to ensure your comfort, give friendly and helpful service and quality food, to make your stay a memorable experience. Food is our speciality, from home-baking, tea or coffee on arrival to delicious continental and or cooked breakfasts. Special diets catered for by arrangement. We'd like to share with you our enthusiasm for our natural environment and can offer suggestions of places to see and exciting things to do – in this idyllic corner of the globe.

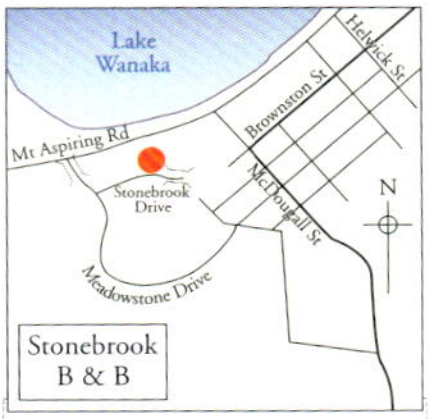

DIRECTIONS:
From Helwick St. travel along Mt Aspiring Rd. for 1.2km, turn left into Meadowstone Dr. 1st left into Stonebrook Dr.

Riverside Bed & Breakfast

11 Riverbank Rd, Wanaka
Ph (03) 443 1522, Fax (03) 443 1522
Mobile 027-464 0333
www.riversidewanaka.co.nz

@home NEW ZEALAND

Tariff : N.Z. Dollars	
Double	$125-165
Single	$85-95
Child	

Bedrooms	Qty
Double	2
Twin	1
Single	
Bed Size	**Qty**
Super King	
King	1
Queen	1
Double	
Single	2
Bathrooms	**Qty**
Ensuite	1
Private	1
Guest Share	

Bed & Breakfast
Homestay

VISA MasterCard

Features & Attractions

- *Quiet & private location*
- *Extensive garden & views*
- *Warm & friendly hospitality*
- *Generous breakfasts*
- *Many walking tracks*
- *Golf course nearby*
- *Ski fields*
- *Local vineyard*

We welcome guests to our quality built home. With sweeping mountain and rural views, extensive grounds and gardens, we offer privacy and a quiet location. Overlooking the Cardrona River we are 100m off SH8 and 5 minutes to Lake Wanaka and its excellent restaurants and cafés. Personal care is taken to provide a warm and peaceful atmosphere, where our guests can relax and enjoy tea or coffee with home-baked cakes and biscuits. Individually decorated and well appointed guest rooms with quality linen, hair dryers, electric blankets and central heating provide our guests a high level of comfort. We have 2 guest lounges, one with an open fire. In summer, wander the grounds, have a game of petanque or relax on the shady terraces. Enjoy a continental breakfast with home-made bread and muesli, muffins and fruit or start your day with a sumptuous cooked breakfast. A Guest's comment, ***"The Best Eggs Benedict"*** D.&D. Canada. ***Arrive as Guests, Leave as Friends.***

Renmore House

44 Upton St, Wanaka
Ph (03) 443 6566, Fax (03) 443 6567
Mobile 027-434 2075
email: *renmorehouse@xtra.co.nz*
www.renmore-house.co.nz

Tariff : N.Z. Dollars	
Double	$185-210
Single	$150-170
Child	

Bedrooms	Qty
Double	3
Twin	
Single	
Bed Size	**Qty**
Super King Twin	3
King	
Queen	
Double	
Single	
Bathrooms	**Qty**
Ensuite	3
Private	
Guest Share	

Bed & Breakfast
Homestay

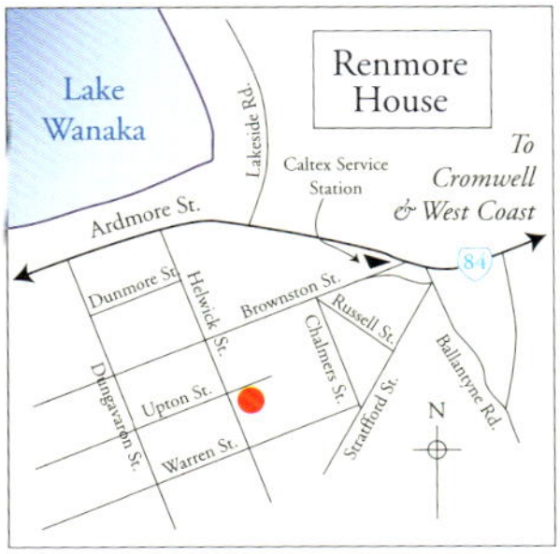

Features & Attractions

- *2 minutes walk to town*
- *Mountain bikes to explore*
- *Peaceful garden setting*
- *Spring-fed stream with trout*
- *Assistance with itinerary*
- *Laundry facilities*
- *Scrumptuous breakfast*
- *Close to 3 skifields*

Blair, Rosie and Sophie the cat, look forward to welcoming you to our home in Wanaka. **Renmore House** is situated in a quiet exclusive cul-de-sac 200 metres from Wanaka lakefront, cafés, restaurants, bars, shops and art galleries. Enjoy panoramic views from our decks or relax in our garden beside spring-fed Bullock Creek. The entire ground floor, including separate guest lounge and laundry, is devoted to guest use. A mini-bar fridge, tea and coffee making with home baking, guest library and a variety of games are available.

Having been born in Otago and travelled extensively, we are very proud of our beautiful environment. We'd both love to take time to ensure you are getting the best value for time available in our area and the rest of the South Island. An excellent golf course with superb views is within 5 minutes walk. There are fishing guides, kayaking, boating, canyoning, wonderful walking tracks, scenic flights, skiing and numerous other activities.

TIR NA NOG LODGE

23 Studholme Road South, RD 1, Wanaka
Ph (03) 443 7111, Fax (03) 443 7111
Mobile 027-438 1443
email: *tirnanog@lakewanaka.co.nz*
www.tirnanog-lodge.co.nz

Tariff : N.Z. Dollars	
Double	$100-120
Single	$90-100
Child	

Bedrooms	Qty
Double	3
Twin	1
Single	
Bed Size	**Qty**
Super King	
King	
Queen	3
Double	
Single	3
Bathrooms	**Qty**
Ensuite	2
Private	1
Guest Share	

BB **Bed & Breakfast and Self-contained Accommodation** SC

VISA MasterCard

Features & Attractions

- *Private country retreat*
- *Free-in-house movies*
- *Internet, laundry facilities*
- *Ski-storage, drying room*
- *Spa pool*
- *Barbeque & outdoor fire*
- *Ski fields & golf courses*
- *Friendly animals*

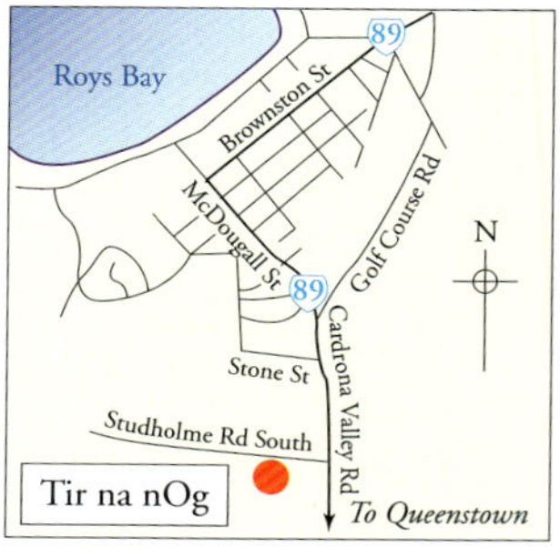

Tir na nOg Lodge is a friendly, relaxed countrystay Bed & Breakfast, set in four acres of farmland, only three minutes drive from Wanaka town. Guest accommodation ranges from a self-contained two or three bedroom cottage to studio units. All have ensuite or private bathrooms, tea and coffee making facilities, TV/ DVD, electric blankets and expansive views of mountains and the Cardrona Valley. Additionally, all guests have free access to the internet, in-house movies, laundry facilities, the BBQ and outdoor fire, ski storage and drying room and the spa pool. Breakfast can be provided by arrangement. Off-peak rates and multiple night discounts are also available. Our **Lodge** is handy to the lake, golf course, horse trekking, vineyards, skifields and tramping in the National Park. Your hosts, Diana and Lyal, warmly welcome you to our **Lodge** and the serenity of Lake Wanaka. Equally welcoming are our friendly dogs, Max and Millie, the highland calves, James and Hamish, and Angus, the cat.

DIRECTIONS: Studholme Rd South is a no-exit road, 3 min drive from centre of Wanaka, off the Cardrona Rd or Crown Range Rd to Queenstown. The Lodge is the 1st driveway where the seal ends on Studholme Rd South.

Townside Studios

65 Helwick Street, Lake Wanaka, Central Otago
Ph (03) 443 8640
Mobile 021-158 5838
e-mail: *townside@paradise.net.nz*
www.townside.co.nz

Features & Attractions

- *1 min. to shops & cafés*
- *3 min. walk to lake*
- *Private courtyard garden*
- *Very central location*
- *Separate entrance*
- *Cosy cottage charm*

Public jetty - Lake Wanaka

$	
Double	$95-140
Single	$95-110
Child	n/a

Self-contained Studios Available Nov. to June

Bedrooms	Qty
Double	1
Twin	
Single	
Bed Size	**Qty**
King	
Queen	1
Double	
Single	
Bathrooms	**Qty**
Ensuite	1
Private	
Guest Share	

Operating November to June each year.

Ideally located in the centre of town. Just a few minutes walk to lake, shops, cafés, galleries and local attractions. Only five minutes drive to golf course. Townside Studio has a cosy cottage charm and is private, spacious and sunny. Doors open out onto your very own deck and secluded court yard where you can enjoy breakfast, brunch or a drink at sundown. Private ensuite, tea & coffee making facilities, refrigerator, TV, DVD and CD. Queen bed and quality linens and furnishings throughout. Continental breakfast.

Good food, friends, wine and time in Wanaka – life doesn't get any better.

The Tin Shed

431 Riverbank Road, RD 2, Wanaka
Ph (03) 443 7449, Fax (03) 443 7049
Mobile 021-462 654

Features & Attractions

- *Beautiful mountain vistas*
- *Easy access to Lake Wanaka*
- *Boating, golf & climbing*
- *Close to restaurants & shops*
- *Peaceful countryside location*
- *'Downtown' Wanaka 3 min.*

$	
Double	$120
Single	$110
Child	Neg

Bed & Breakfast Homestay

Bedrooms	Qty
Double	2
Twin	
Single	1
Bed Size	**Qty**
King	
Queen	2
Double	
Single	2
Bathrooms	**Qty**
Ensuite	1
Private	
Guest Share	1

You are warmly invited to enjoy our home and our hospitality, plus our spa. We (sometimes) share our home with adult children and Samoyed (dog) Nikita who welcomes guests as much as we do.
Our home is very close to Wanaka, world renowned for its lake, the beautiful alpine vistas and marvellous restaurants and emerging vineyards. We have close proximity to the lake, fishing, mountains, golf, climbing, walking and other outdoor pursuits. This includes skiing, being only 20 minutes from the three skifields, the Snow Farm, Cardrona and Treble Cone and one hour to Queenstown to the Remarkables and Coronet Peak.

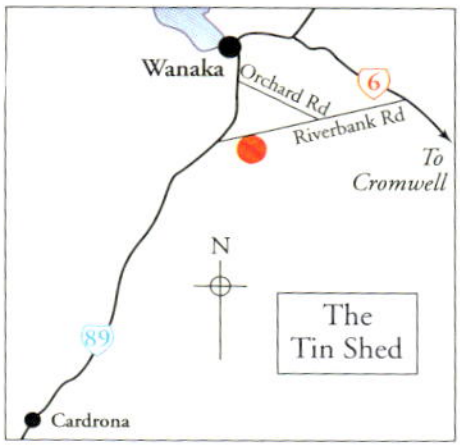

Wanaka Homestead Lodge & Cottages

Cnr Mt Aspiring Rd & Homestead Close, Wanaka
Ph (03) 443 5022, Fax (03) 443 5023
email: *stay@wanakahomestead.co.nz*
www.wanakahomestead.co.nz

Tariff : N.Z. Dollars	
Double	$195-299
Single	$195-245
Cottages	$225-480

Bedrooms	Qty
Double	4
Twin	1
Single	
Bed Size	**Qty**
Super King	5
King	
Queen	
Double	
Single	5
Bathrooms	**Qty**
Ensuite	5
Private	
Guest Share	

Bed & Breakfast Lodge & Self-contained Family Cottages

Features & Attractions

- *200m to lake shore*
- *Peaceful parkland outlook*
- *B&B, Room-Only or Cottages*
- *Walk to Rippon Vineyard*
- *Inclusive hot tub & laundry*
- *Huge, comfortable, new beds*
- *Complimentary wine, nibbles*
- *Inclusive Internet & bicycles*

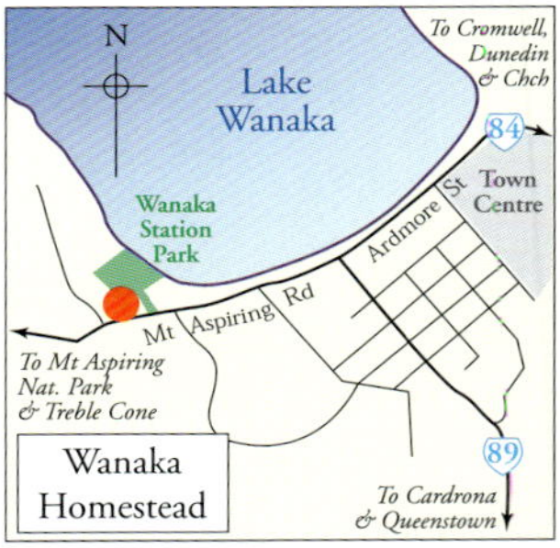

Friendly new luxury lodge and cottages, located just 200m from the shores of Lake Wanaka and walking distance to Wanaka's vibrant township. Overlooking parkland, **Wanaka Homestead** is well positioned for easy walking track, ski field, and National Park access. The purpose-built **Homestead Lodge** provides informal luxury in a 5 bedroom boutique B & B. Each guestroom has ensuite facilities and extremely comfortable new twin, super-king or huge California king beds.

Gourmet breakfast is inclusive, served by the log fire, exposed beams and sumptuous sofas in the guest lounge.

Complimentary facilities include under-the-stars hot tub, broadband and Internet, mountain bikes and laundry.

Alternatively our charming **cottages** offer self-contained and serviced "home from home" style accommodation with real warmth and character. Our website is well worth a visit too.

Villa Vista

161 Stone Street, Wanaka
Ph (03) 443 7094, Fax (03) 443 7094
Mobile 021-1012941
email: *s.a.anderson@xtra.co.nz*

Tariff : N.Z. Dollars	
Double	$140-170
Twin	$140-170
Child	

Bedrooms	Qty
Double	1
Twin	1
Single	
Bed Size	**Qty**
Super King	
King	
Queen	1
Double	
Single	2
Bathrooms	**Qty**
Ensuite	
Private	1
Guest Share	

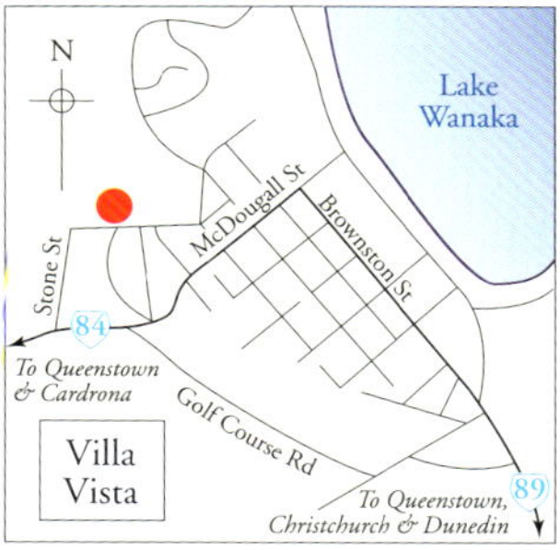

DIRECTIONS: Travel along the lakefront on Ardmore St. Turn left into McDougall St. (Queenstown, Cardrona - Highway 89) Travel 1.5km to turn right into Stone St. Travel 600m to 161 Stone St (on your left)

Bed & Breakfast
Homestay

Features & Attractions

- *Stunning lake & mountain views*
- *Warm, friendly hospitality*
- *Off-street parking*
- *Golf course 5 min drive*
- *Single party bookings only*
- *Free pick-up from coach, airport*
- *Private courtyard*
- *Laundry, internet facilities*

Margaret and Stewart welcome you to **Villa Vista.**

"There are no strangers here – just friends we haven't met yet"

Share with us our modern home and garden in this most beautiful corner of New Zealand. Relax in the lounge or courtyard while taking in the breathtaking panoramic views of Lake Wanaka and surrounding mountains. Breakfast in the summer can be served in the courtyard, cooked or continental, at a time to suit our guests. Stroll to the lake, restaurants, cafés, bars, shops and art galleries.

We offer one queen room and one twin room, all with wool underlays and electric blankets. Single party bookings only. Central heating and a log fire make for cosy winter evenings. A short drive takes you to three internationally known ski fields for family, experienced or cross country skiing. There are many pleasant scenic walking tracks for all ages and fitness levels. Our interests include family, hospitality, golf, and Stewart also enjoys fly fishing.

Wanaka Jewel

7 Foxglove Heights, Far Horizon Park, Wanaka
Ph (03) 443 5636, Fax (03) 443 5637
Mobile 027-285 6234
email: *wanakajewel@xtra.co.nz*

Tariff : N.Z. Dollars	
Double	$140-175
Single	$120-140
Child	

Bedrooms	Qty
Double	2
Twin	
Single	
Bed Size	**Qty**
Super King	
King	
Queen	2
Double	
Single	
Bathrooms	**Qty**
Ensuite	1
Private	1
Guest Share	

Bed & Breakfast
Homestay

Features & Attractions

- *Peaceful park like setting*
- *Warm & friendly hospitality*
- *Spa, gym, pool, BBQ complex*
- *Tennis court, putting green*
- *Stunning lake & mountain views*
- *3 ski fields within 30 minutes*
- *Off street parking*
- *Walking tracks*

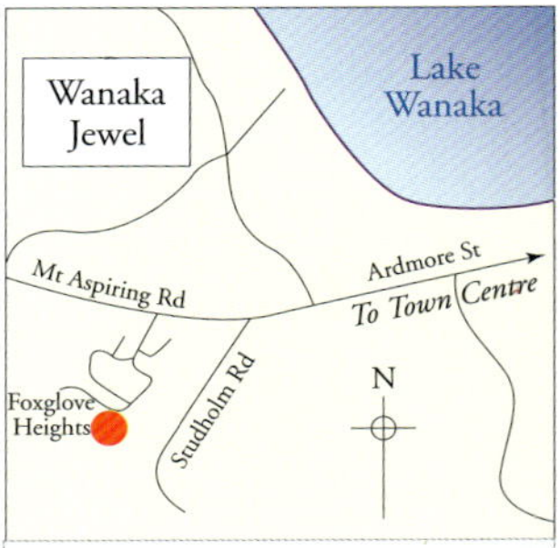

DIRECTIONS: 2.5 km west of Wanaka central, off Mt Aspiring Rd.

Welcome to Wanaka Jewel – a stay in paradise.

Wanaka Jewel is a newly built, luxury home with a purpose-built Bed & Breakfast suite – set on one acre, surrounded by beautiful majestic mountains and superb lake views close to town. Your separate suite has private entrance and parking. Our beautifully appointed guest rooms have ensuite, quality linen, woolrest underlay, electric blanket, hairdryer, double glazing, radiator heating and a lovely patio to enjoy the view. Other facilities are fridge, microwave and TV. Complimentary tea, coffee and sweet treats available any time. The use of spa, pool, gymnasium, tennis court, BBQ, pitch and putting green is complimentary. Close to the famous Rippon vineyard and a 30 minute easy walk to town. Enjoy a sumptuous breakfast in our dining room. You can be assured of a warm welcome and a memorable stay. We have a friendly border collie who will also give you a big welcome. (Outside dog). We look forward to meeting you and sharing our paradise.

Lake Dunstan Lodge

Rapid No 485, Northburn, No 3 RD, Cromwell
Ph (03) 445 1107, Fax (03) 445 3062
Mobile 027-431 1415
email: *william.t@xtra.co.nz*
www.lakedunstanlodge.co.nz

Features & Attractions

- *Private, peaceful setting*
- *Trout fishing & golf course*
- *Wanaka/Queenstown 45 min*
- *Situated on lake edge*
- *Spectacular scenery*
- *Spa & laundry facilities*

Lakeside Stay
Bed & Breakfast

Double	$110-130
Single	$80
Child	neg

Friendly hospitality awaits you at **Lake Dunstan Lodge.** Our spacious home is privately situated on the edge of Lake Dunstan, 6 km from Cromwell, 60 km from Queenstown. We previously farmed sheep and deer in Southland and have a cat "Ollie". Our interests include Lions, fishing, boating, gardening and crafts. The large sunny bedrooms have lake views and attached open balconies, refrigerator, tea and coffee-making facilities available at all times. Guests share our spacious living areas with television sets and make free use of our spa pool and laundry facilities. Local attractions include orchards, vineyards, gold diggings, golf course, fishing (local guide available), boating, walks, four ski fields nearby. We welcome you to have an evening meal with us, or just bed and continental/full breakfast. Come and fish or just relax in our peaceful surroundings.

DIRECTIONS:
5 km from Cromwell Bridge on Tarras/Omarama Highway 8.
Sign at gate.

Bedrooms	Qty
Double	2
Twin	1
Single	
Bed Size	**Qty**
King	
Queen	2
Double	
Single	3
Bathrooms	**Qty**
Ensuite	1
Private	
Guest Share	1

Stuarts Homestay

5 Mansor Court, Cromwell
Ph (03) 445 3636, Fax (03) 445 3617
Mobile 027-252 9823
email: *ian.elaine@xtra.co.nz*

@ home NEW ZEALAND

Features & Attractions

- *Dinner by arrangement*
- *Golf, fishing, walks, boating*
- *Wanaka & Queenstown 45 min*
- *Off-street parking*
- *Wine & gold trails*
- *Quiet garden setting*

Double	$100-120
Single	$70-80
Child	

Homestay
Bed & Breakfast

Bedrooms	Qty
Double	2
Twin	1
Single	
Bed Size	**Qty**
King	
Queen	2
Double	
Single	2
Bathrooms	**Qty**
Ensuite	1
Private	
Guest Share	1

Welcome to **Stuarts Homestay** which is situated within walking distance of most of Cromwell's amenities. We are semi-retired Southland farmers who have hosted for over ten years. We enjoy sharing our modern sunny home and garden with visitors and a friendly stay is assured. Have tea, coffee and homemade baking available at all times. Share dinner with us (prior booking please) or just Bed & Breakfast (full or continental). We are also happy to transport you to and from buses.

Cromwell is a quiet and relaxed town which is known for historic gold diggings, vineyards, orchards, trout fishing, boating, walks and is close to major ski fields (forty-five minutes away).

Dunes Homestay on the 9th

13 The Dunes, P O Box 219, Cromwell
Ph (03) 445 3184, Fax (03) 445 3184
Mobile 027-222 4284
email: *info@duneshomestay.co.nz*
www.duneshomestay.co.nz

Tariff : N.Z. Dollars	
Double	$120-135
Single	$110-125
Child	neg

Bedrooms	Qty
Double	2
Twin	
Single	
Bed Size	**Qty**
Super King	
King	
Queen	2
Double	
Single	1
Bathrooms	**Qty**
Ensuite	2
Private	
Guest Share	

Homestay - Bed & Breakfast on the Golf Course

Features & Attractions

- *Golf from our front lawn*
- *Private residential community*
- *Purpose-built brand new home*
- *Wineries & restaurants nearby*
- *Cromwell - a sporting paradise*
- *Computer & internet access*

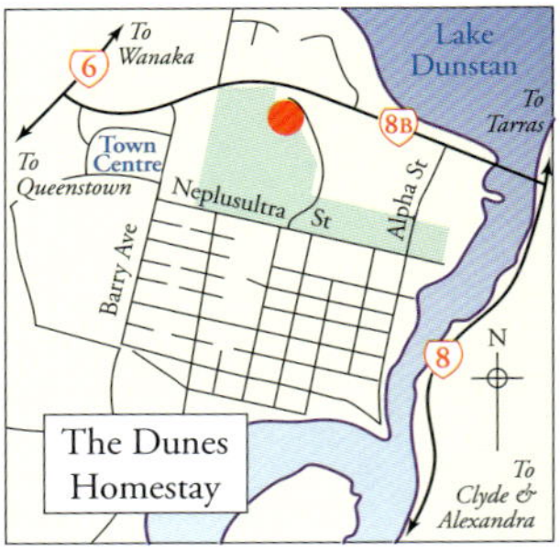

DIRECTIONS:
Please phone for easy directions.

Whether you desire privacy or our company, we will enjoy hosting you. Our new, sunny, purpose-built home is stylish, warm and quiet and is located in The Dunes, Cromwell's championship golf course.

Our home is ideally located for easy access to a large number of tourist attractions, including arts and crafts, orchards, vineyards, sporting facilities, heated indoor swimming pool, also great fishing (local guide available). Our comfortable non-smoking guest rooms have tea and coffee making facilities, fridge, Sky TV with teletext, free videos, clock/radio, electric blankets and hairdryers, private ensuites with showers.
Private entrances for your independence.
For further information see www.cromwell.org.nz

River Rock Estate

1 Shortcut Road, Cromwell
Mobile 021- 270 5518
Mobile 029- 270 5518
email: *info@riverrockestate.com*
www.riverrockestate.com

Tariff : N.Z. Dollars	
Double	$98-245
Single	$98-245
Child	n/a

Bedrooms	Qty
Double	3
Twin	2
Single	
Bed Size	**Qty**
Super King	
King	2
Queen	2
Double	
Single	2
Bathrooms	**Qty**
Ensuite	4
Private	
Guest Share	1

Bed & Breakfast Lodge
Boutique Vineyard

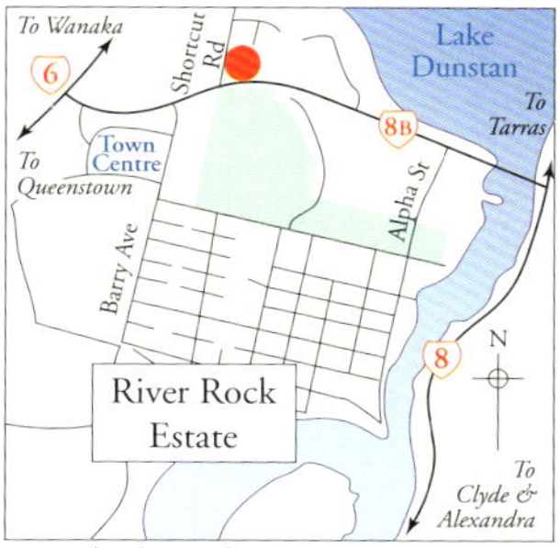

Features & Attractions

- *Luxury ensuite rooms*
- *Self-contained cottage*
- *Boutique vineyard*
- *SKY TV & Internet*
- *Restaurants & wineries nearby*
- *Adjacent to 18 hole golf course*
- *Central to five ski fields*
- *Queenstown/Wanaka 45 min.*

River Rock Estate is a three and half acre boutique vineyard growing Pinot Gris, Sauvignon Blanc, Pinot Noir and a variety of table grapes, also Argutas (Cocktail Kiwifruit). Accommodation is offered by way of two stand-alone luxury ensuite rooms, a self-contained two bedroom cottage, an American-style barn with a two bedroom loft and the soon to be built **River Rock Lodge.** The lodge will provide a conservatory dining room and house bar, snooker room and large entertainment area, outdoor spa pool and barbeque area and boat house, all with views over a small tussock-edged lake. The estate is located just a five minute stroll from the Cromwell township, where you will find an olympic sized swimming pool, mini golf, cafés and shopping. All located in and around the Cromwell Mall. Magnificent views of the Pisa, Carrick and Dunstan ranges, which surround this peaceful setting with the golf course just across the road. Queenstown, Wanaka and five ski fields are all within 45 minutes drive.
We look forward to your company.

VILLA AMO - *on Lake Dunstan*

9 Shine Lane, Pisa Moorings, No 3 RD, Cromwell
Ph (03) 445 0788, Fax (03) 445 0711
Mobile 027-286 8316
email: *VillaAmo@xtra.co.nz*
www.villaamo.co.nz

Tariff : N.Z. Dollars	
Double	$175
Single	$160
Child	n/a

Bedrooms	Qty
Double	2
Twin	
Single	
Bed Size	**Qty**
Super King	
King	
Queen	2
Double	
Single	
Bathrooms	**Qty**
Ensuite	
Private	1
Guest Share	

**Homestay
Bed & Breakfast**

Features & Attractions

- *Situated on Lake Dunstan*
- *Rugged mountain scenery*
- *Warm friendly hospitality*
- *5 skifields within an hour*
- *Peaceful, relaxing location*
- *Superb fishing summer/winter*
- *Vineyard and orchard tours*
- *7 minutes from Cromwell*

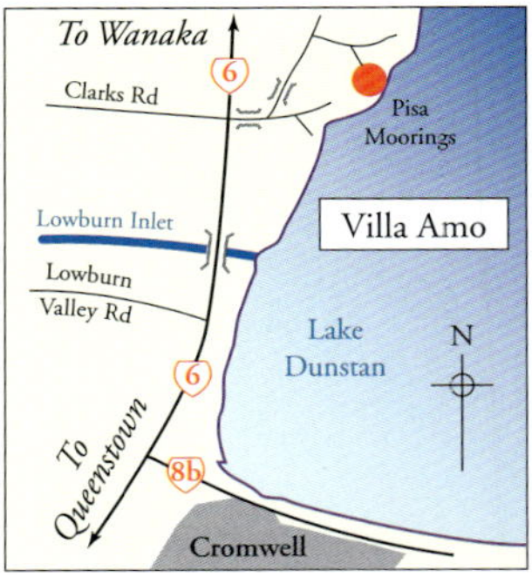

Welcome to **Villa Amo** in its tranquil lakeside setting on the shore of Lake Dunstan. Relax and enjoy warm hospitality while taking in the breathtaking lake and rugged mountain views. Built in 1996 **Villa Amo** is an ideal base from which to explore the many delights of Central Otago or visit Queenstown or Wanaka. Our spacious guest room has a comfortable queen size bed, quality cotton bed linen, tea/coffee making facilities with fridge, 20" television with teletext, is quiet and private as is the well appointed full bathroom. To start the day enjoy a substantial breakfast, cooked and/or continental, at a time convenient to you. We have superb fishing at our doorstep (summer and winter) and if required a professional fishing guide can be arranged. Cromwell has numerous attractions and historic walks or you may wish to visit our local wineries, orchards, craft shops, or Old Cromwell Historic Precinct. We are passionate about our region and would love to share with you our knowledge of this fascinating area, its history and its many attractions. A home away from home with that extra touch.

Walnut Grove

SH 6, Lowburn, RD 2, Cromwell
Ph (03) 445 1112, Fax (03) 445 1115
Mobile 027-477 4695
email: *walnut.grove@xtra.co.nz*
www.walnutgrove.co.nz

Tariff : N.Z. Dollars	
Double	$140-150
Single	$125-135
Child	

Bedrooms	Qty
Double	2
Twin	
Single	
Bed Size	**Qty**
Super King	1
King	
Queen	1
Double	
Single	
Bathrooms	**Qty**
Ensuite	2
Private	
Guest Share	

MasterCard VISA

Countrystay - Bed & Breakfast

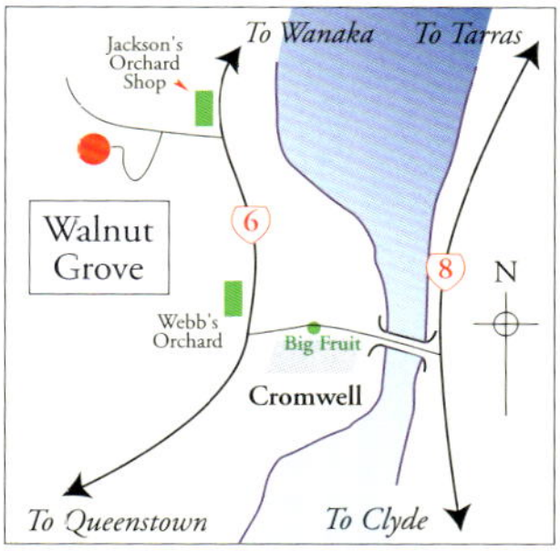

Features & Attractions

- *Spacious home and grounds*
- *Valley and mountain views*
- *Amidst working orchards*
- *Cromwell & restaurants nearby*
- *Historic goldmining area*
- *Vineyards and wineries*
- *Fishing, golf, walking*
- *Near Lake Dunstan*

Relax! Enjoy our world! A place for all seasons! With dry climate, wonderful scenery and a slower pace of life it is unforgettable. The adventure activities of nearby Queenstown and Wanaka or the Central Otago Rail Trail from Clyde (bicycles for hire from Clyde) are an easy drive! Spring flowers and autumn colours are magical. Taste fresh cherries, apricots, peaches, nectarines in season, savour the local fine wines year round!

Our smoke-free home is set in four acres with large garden and old shady walnut trees. It is a lovely setting. Comfortable guest bedrooms have television, clock/radio, coffee/tea making facilities and ensuite bathrooms. (The super-king is also available as two single beds). A laundry is available.

We have a Siamese cat and a friendly dog. We would be delighted to help plan your stay. We have travelled extensively, just love meeting people and would like you to make our home your home for your visit. Adrian is a member of Rotary. Reservations essential.

THE ORCHARD HOUSE

Rapid 90, Wanaka Rd, RD 2, Cromwell
Ph (03) 445 4484
email: *orchard.bb@xtra.co.nz*

Tariff : N.Z. Dollars	
Double	$200-250
Single	$180-230
Child	

Bedrooms	Qty
Double	2
Twin	
Single	
Bed Size	**Qty**
Super King	
King	2
Queen	
Double	
Single	
Bathrooms	**Qty**
Ensuite	2
Private	
Guest Share	

BA

Boutique Accommodation
Bed & Breakfast

LA

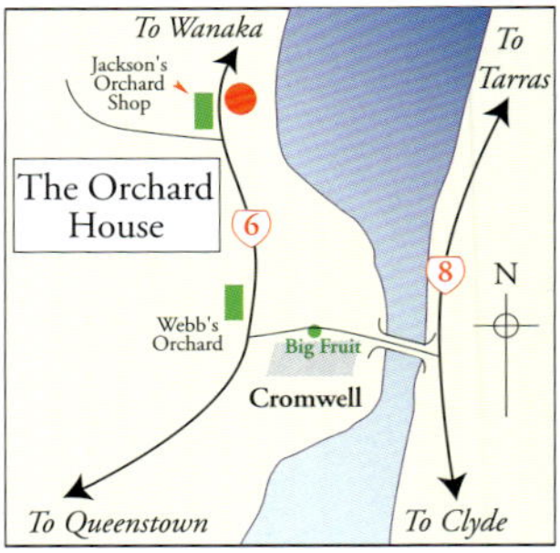

Features & Attractions

- *Luxury accommodation setting*
- *All season activities*
- *Hub of Central Otago wine district*
- *Complimentary local wine*
- *Set in a lovely orchard garden*
- *Short walk to Lake Dunstan*
- *Computer and internet access*
- *Complimentary fruit basket*

Trish, Fred and 'Bea' our friendly terrier, invite you to stay with us in our unique luxury executive accommodation. You will be surrounded by our beautiful garden in an orchard setting within a 10 minutes walk to Lake Dunstan. The Central Otago area is inviting throughout all seasons – fishing all year, fresh summer fruit, water sports, wonderful golf courses, vineyards, wine tasting, restaurants, heritage gold mining sites, spectacular autumn colours, skiing, snow boarding. In spring – wonderful orchard blossoms. Our location is on Main Highway 6, adjacent Jackson's Orchard, 2 min. from Cromwell and within an hour from Wanaka and Queenstown with all their wonderful attractions. Cooked and continental breakfast, served in your room or in the house dining room, includes local preserves and fruit. Our bedroom suites have private access including a balcony area for in-room breakfast, ensuite, king-size bed, tea making facilities, TV and internet access. Laundry facilities available and drying facilities for ski gear. We look forward to meeting you and ensuring that you have a happy, relaxing and enjoyable time with us at **The Orchard House**.

Old Villa Homestay Bed & Breakfast

13 Anglesea Street, PO Box 1, Arrowtown
Ph (03) 442 1682, Fax (03) 442 1682
Mobile 027-472 4543
email: *archie.june@xtra.co.nz*
www.arrowtownoldvilla.co.nz

Tariff : N.Z. Dollars	
Double	$130-150
Single	$110
Child	$20 u/13

Bedrooms	Qty
Double	2
Twin	1
Single	
Bed Size	**Qty**
Super King	
King	
Queen	2
Double	
Single	2
Bathrooms	**Qty**
Ensuite	2
Private	
Guest Share	

Homestay
Bed & Breakfast

Features & Attractions

- *Home baking jellies & jam*
- *Wine trails, cafes, restaurants*
- *Peaceful town setting*
- *Real southern hospitality*
- *Fifteen minutes to Queenstown*
- *Inviting log fire during winter*
- *Laundry available*
- *Hiking trails*

DIRECTIONS:
Just two streets from Arrowtown's main street. Please phone if you require further directions.

Just 15 minutes from Queenstown, Arrowtown is an historic goldmining town that has retained much of it's olde world charm and offers travellers a peaceful and stylish alternative to the hustle and bustle of Queenstown. Stroll along the Arrow River or through the many tree-lined streets with cafés, restaurants, arts, cinema and a selection of shops. For the more active, there are many walking tracks in the surrounding hills, two local golf courses, or 4-wheel drive tours through the Arrow Gorge with Macetown and its goldmining ruins. In keeping with the history of the area, your hosts June and Arch Flint have built this lovely restored timber villa in classic settler style on a fabulous elevated site overlooking the main settlement just two minutes walk away. You have the choice of the master bedroom with ensuite, breakfast bar and your own private verandah overlooking a fabulous garden setting or the second spacious double bedroom with mountain views and an adjoining bathroom with a claw foot bath. Enjoy a coffee and homemade muffins on arrival and relax in the warm and welcoming home of your hosts who will happily assist you with any travel or administrative arrangements.

Willowbrook

Malaghan Road, RD 1, Queenstown
(PO Box 118, Arrowtown) 9196
Ph (03) 442 1773, Fax (03) 442 1780
Mobile 027-451 6739
email: *info@willowbrook.net.nz*
www.willowbrook.net.nz

Tariff : N.Z. Dollars	
Double	$150-185
Single	$125-145
Child	

Bedrooms	Qty
Double	4
Twin	3
Single	
Bed Size	**Qty**
Super King	2
King	
Queen	2
Double	
Single	8
Bathrooms	**Qty**
Ensuite	5
Private	1
Guest Share	

Rural Bed & Breakfast and Self-contained accommodation

Features & Attractions

- *Peaceful rural location*
- *Guest lounge, two open fires*
- *Large garden with tennis court*
- *Door to ski lift - 15 min*
- *Millbrook Resort - 3 min*
- *Luxurious outdoor spa*

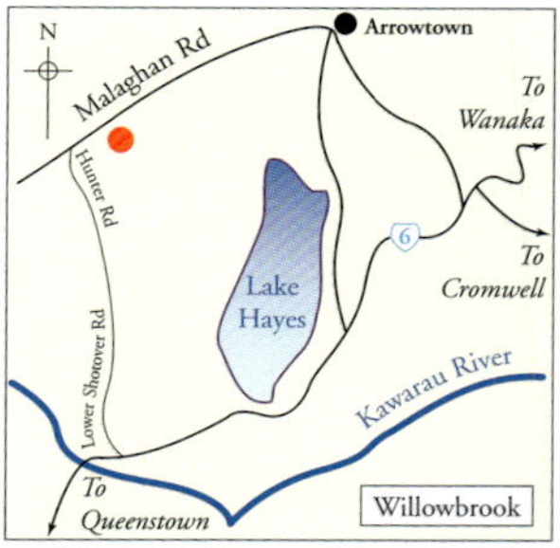

Willowbrook is a 1914 homestead at the foot of Coronet Peak in the beautiful Wakatipu Basin. The setting is rural, historical and distinctly peaceful, and with the attractions of Queenstown and Arrowtown only 15 and 5 minutes away respectively, Willowbrook can truly claim to offer the best of both worlds.

Four acres of mature garden contain a tennis court, a luxurious spa pool and several outhouses. The former "Shearers' Quarters" have been rebuilt and a hay barn renovated allowing Willowbrook to offer varied styles of accommodation:

Bed & Breakfast in the Main House - centrally heated double rooms, ensuite bathrooms, guest lounge with open fires and Sky TV.
The Barn – spacious accommodation with kitchenette, separate from the Main House. Super king bed, ensuite bathroom, lounge area with Sky TV and BBQ deck. Annex available for extra members of same party.
The Cottage – a delightfully cosy two bedroom cottage with full kitchen and laundry facilities. Ensuite bathrooms, underfloor heating throughout, Sky TV, spacious sundecks with BBQ and private lawn.
Willowbrook is within easy reach of four skifields and three very picturesque golf courses. Kate and Allan are your hosts. Expect a warm welcome, friendly advice and traditional South Island hospitality.

ARROWTOWN HEIGHTS

6 May Lane, Arrowtown, Central Otago
Ph (03) 442 1726, Fax (03) 442 1726
Mobile 027-279 1552
email: *info@arrowtownheights.com*
www.arrowtownheights.com

Features & Attractions

- *Close to 4 ski fields*
- *Courtesy car from airport*
- *Peaceful, private setting*
- *Award wineries/restaurants nearby*
- *Southern Hospitality*
- *Well travelled hosts*

$		
	Double	$130-150
	Single	$110
	Child	neg

Luxury Accommodation
Bed & Breakfast

Bedrooms	Qty
Double	1
Twin	1
Single	
Bed Size	**Qty**
King	
Queen	1
Double	
Single	2
Bathrooms	**Qty**
Ensuite	
Private	1
Guest Share	

You are always sure of a welcome at **Arrowtown Heights**. Your spacious and luxurious accommodation is in a separate wing ensuring complete privacy at all times.
Step out of your bedroom to sit and relax in the garden, enjoy the surrounding panoramic views or the luxury of the outdoor spa. Choose to have breakfast inside or outside on the patio. Join us for coffee and a chat, we are happy to assist and direct you to a wide range of sights and activities. Email, fax, laundry and a barbeque are all available.
We look forward to your visit, sure in the knowledge that you will enjoy this special part of New Zealand.

WILLOWBY DOWNS

792 Malaghans Road, RD 1, Queenstown
Ph (03) 442 1714, Fax (03) 442 1887
Mobile 027-222 0964
email: *willowbydowns@xtra.co.nz*
www.willowbydowns.co.nz

Features & Attractions

- *Pick up airport or coaches*
- *Real southern hospitality.*
- *Limousine tours arranged*
- *Close to ski fields*
- *Golf Courses nearby*
- *15 min to Queenstown*

$		
	Double	$130
	Single	$100
	Child	neg

Homestay
Bed & Breakfast

Bedrooms	Qty
Double	2
Twin	1
Single	
Bed Size	**Qty**
King	
Queen	2
Double	
Single	3
Bathrooms	**Qty**
Ensuite	
Private	1
Guest Share	1

With Pam and David you are assured of a genuinely warm and friendly welcome, ex hoteliers they are passionate and practiced in the art of southern hospitality. Our home is off Malaghans Road, 500 metres down a driveway and approximately 5 km from the historic goldmining town of Arrowtown passing Millbrook Resort on the way. This B&B Homestay has features that will make you feel at home. With a coffee or tea on your arrival, you can relax in this warm and sunny home environment. **Willowby Downs** has lovely, well appointed guest rooms, electric blankets, TV, laundry options available, with the guests welcome to use the email, fax and telephone facilities. You have the choice of two master bedrooms with elevated views of Coronet Peak and the surrounding area. Pam and David are able to arrange any extra tours or special events you may require.

GIBBSTON GABLES

Rapid 1802, SH 6, RD 1, Gibbston, Queenstown
Ph (03) 442 7159, Mobile 027-432 4160
email: *info@gibbstongables.com*
www.gibbstongables.com

Tariff : N.Z. Dollars	
Double	$250
Single	$200
Child	free

Bedrooms	Qty
Double	2
Twin	
Single	
Bed Size	**Qty**
Super King	
King	
Queen	1
Double	
King Singles	2
Bathrooms	**Qty**
Ensuite	
Private	1
Guest Share	

Luxury Bed & Breakfast
Top Class Facilities

Features & Attractions

- *Private cottage*
- *Swimming pool*
- *Wineries & wine cave*
- *Queenstown Airport 20 min.*
- *Free bottle of local wine*
- *Restaurants 10 min.*
- *Fabulous lunch 100m*
- *Email & laundry available*

DIRECTIONS: From Cromwell: 100m past Gibbston Valley Winery on left. From Queenstown: 1 km past Kawarau Bungy Bridge on right

Stroll through the vines and lunch at Gibbston Valley Wines' award winning restaurant. Maybe a tour of the only working wine cave in Central Otago. View the daring at AJ Hackett's original Kawarau Bungy Bridge or simply wander around the tranquil setting of mature trees, lawns and two hectares of garden. Alternatively, relax by the pool enjoying your complimentary bottle of local wine.

The Cottage, consisting of two bedrooms, a large bathroom and kitchenette is a smoke-free environment in the heart of the foremost wine growing area of Central Otago. It is only ten minutes away from the historic old mining village of Arrowtown and 25 minutes from picturesque Queenstown. Both offer a vast variety of quality cuisine. Tour the local wineries which are scattered throughout the valley and sample their wines. We live in an area where our work, growing grapes, is our passion. Your hosts, Helen and John Lane look forward to sharing their little piece of paradise with you.

Mt Rosa Lodge

Mt. Rosa Vineyard Estate, Gibbston Back Road,
RD 1, (PO Box 86), Arrowtown
Ph (03) 441 1484, Mobile 021-575 100
email: *info@mtrosalodge.co.nz*
www.mtrosalodge.co.nz

Tariff : N.Z. Dollars	
Double	$250-400
Single	
Child	

Bedrooms	Qty
Double	2
Twin	
Single	
Bed Size	**Qty**
Super King	1
King	
Queen	1
Double	
Single	
Bathrooms	**Qty**
Ensuite	2
Private	
Guest Share	

Luxury Lodge, Bed & Breakfast

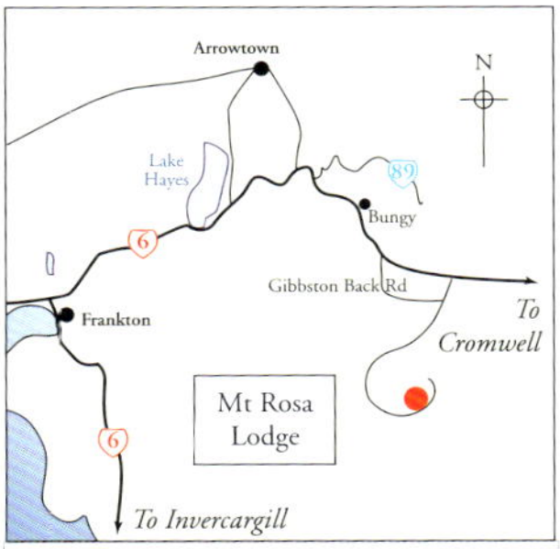

DIRECTIONS:
From SH6 turn into Gibbston back road, continue straight up (500m) into Mt Rosa Vineyard gates. Follow gravel road to lodge.

Features & Attractions

- *Mountain & vineyard views*
- *Wineries and cafés nearby*
- *Central to golf courses*
- *4 skiing mountains*
- *Vineyard walkways*
- *Open fire & outdoor fire*
- *Wine cellar dining*
- *Dinner by arrangement*

Mt Rosa Lodge is dramatically nestled high over the vineyards of Mt Rosa and Gibbston. The rooms are luxuriously appointed with private entrances and a guest fireplace is in one of the rooms for those cooler nights. Enjoy a glass of the region's Pinot Noir and local cheeses whilst sitting on your own private deck and view the sweeping vistas of vines and mountains. An array of wineries, cafés, golf courses, skiing mountains and walking tracks awaits your stay with us. Be spell-bound by the scenic wonders that Queenstown and the region has to offer you.

Relax in the evening in front of a huge open fire and as an option reserve your dining experience in our wine cellar. Brian has been in the wine industry for 30 years and Maureen is a Cordon Bleu graduate and is originally from Burma. An exciting blend of cuisines awaits you when dining at **Mt Rosa Lodge**.

RIVERBANK COTTAGE

Rapid 1350, SH 6, PO Box 1093, RD 1, Queenstown,
Ph (03) 442 1518, Fax (03) 442 1519
Mobile 021-347 804
email: *cottage@riverbank.co.nz*
www.riverbank.co.nz

Tariff : N.Z. Dollars	
Double	$215-265
Single	$195
Child	

Bedrooms	Qty
Double	3
Twin	
Single	
Bed Size	**Qty**
Super King	1
King	2
Queen	
Double	
Single	1
Bathrooms	**Qty**
Ensuite	3
Private	
Guest Share	

Boutique Accommodation
Bed & Breakfast

Features & Attractions

- *Four ski fields*
- *Golf courses nearby*
- *Fishing rods available*
- *Rafting and bungy jumping*
- *2 acre cottage garden*
- *Wineries*
- *Quilt gallery*
- *Restaurants 6 min.*

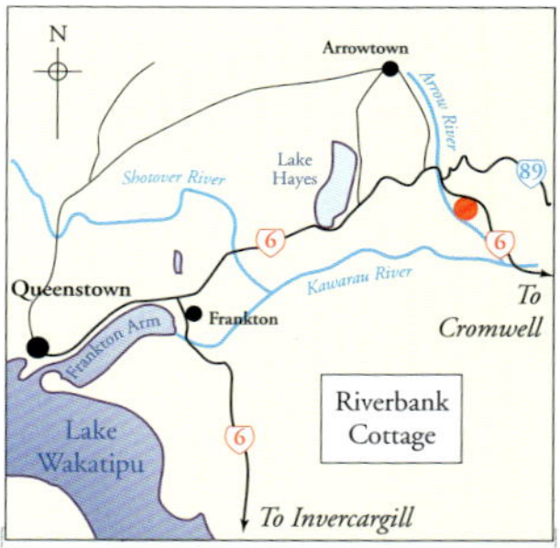

DIRECTIONS: From Cromwell drive 3½ km past Bungy sign, driveway on left. From Queenstown, 1½ km past 'Crown – Range' road sign, driveway on right.

Riverbank Cottage is situated above the banks of the Arrow River, and surrounded by deer farms, yet this beautiful secluded rural setting is only fifteen minutes from downtown Queenstown. The house is set in two acres of established cottage gardens with magnificent views of Coronet Peak, the Remarkables and surrounding mountains. **The Cottage**: Country style accommodation with full cooked breakfast included and each bedroom with ensuite. The guest lounge has beautiful views overlooking an extensive cottage garden, orchard and backdrop of mountains or relax in the shade of the courtyard in the height of summer.

If you are interested in quilting and patchwork, put a little time aside to look at the dozens of quilts on display in our gallery, or stroll out to the garages, where there is always an interesting car under restoration. If you require any help about what you should see or do during your visit, we would like to assist, as we have lived in the area for over 20 years. Our interests are quilting and patchwork, gardening, Ikebana, classic and antique cars.

Milestone

Ladies Mile, 1 RD, Queenstown
Ph (03) 441 4460, Fax (03) 441 4438
Mobile 027-541 4460
email: *jcturnbull@xtra.co.nz*
www.themilestone.co.nz

Tariff : N.Z. Dollars	
Double	$165-225
Single	$125-165
Child	Neg

Bedrooms	Qty
Double	4
Twin	
Single	
Bed Size	**Qty**
Super King	
King	1
Queen	3
Double	
Single	
Bathrooms	**Qty**
Ensuite	3
Private	
Guest Share	

Stylish Accommodation with Warm Hospitality

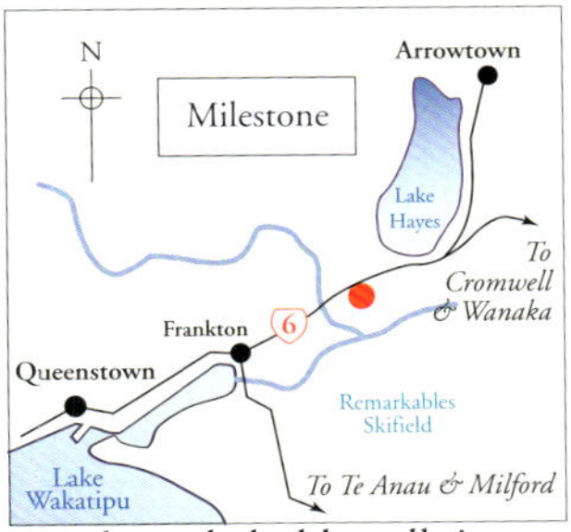

Features & Attractions

- *Rose-covered stone cottage*
- *3 acres of garden*
- *Gourmet full breakfast*
- *Queenstown 10 min*
- *Marriage celebrant*
- *Guaranteed southern hospitality*
- *Romantic, peaceful & private*
- *Children & extra guests welcome*

Milestone is a modern, comfortable home. A working water wheel and waterfall are part of the three acres of peaceful and tranquil gardens. The surrounding mountains are a wonder to behold at all times of the year. The rose-covered stone schist cottage is self-contained and an ideal honeymoon hideaway, and as a marriage celebrant Betty can arrange and perform the ceremony to accompany the honeymoon.

The cottage has a four poster queen bed and a custom made queen divan in the living room for an extra guest. In the main house is a romantic ensuite with antique furniture and a private deck. Upstairs the 'Remarkable Suite' has a king and single bed, dressing room, lounge and ensuite. Another queen bedroom is available for extra guests in the party. Each room is spacious with TV, tea/coffee making facilities and spectacular views. Children are welcome – a port-a-cot is available. At **Milestone** we offer luxury, romance, privacy and tranquility along with warm southern hospitality.

The Turret

Rapid No 712, SH 6, Lake Hayes, Queenstown
Ph (03) 442 1107, Fax (03) 442 1160
Mobile 021-027 43210
email: *theturret@xtra.co.nz*
www.theturret.co.nz

Tariff : N.Z. Dollars	
Double	$165-295
Single	$135-195
Child	

Bedrooms	Qty
Double	2
Twin	1
Single	
Bed Size	**Qty**
Super King	
King	
Queen	2
Double	1
Single	1
Bathrooms	**Qty**
Ensuite	2
Private	1
Guest Share	

Bed & Breakfast
Luxury Accommodation

Features & Attractions

- *Close to wineries & golf courses*
- *Close to four ski fields*
- *Opposite wildlife refuge & walkway*
- *Elegant cooked or continental breakfast*
- *Email & Internet access*
- *Award winning garden*
- *Stunning views*
- *Open log fire*

DIRECTIONS:
Overlooking Lake Hayes between Queenstown and Arrowtown on SH 6. Across the road from the Lake Hayes Pavillion.

According to the San Francisco Chronicle, "The Turret stands out in New Zealand". This distinctive lakeside retreat, ideally situated between Queenstown and historic Arrowtown, offers luxury accommodation with stunning garden, lake and mountain views.

Privacy, comfort and relaxation with warm Kiwi hospitality and a blend of French and Moroccan décor will make your stay a truly memorable one. Two of the guest rooms have french doors opening out onto the terrace, while the third (suite) has its own balcony. All rooms have fabulous views, tea and coffee making facilities and quality beds and linens. There is a separate dining and sitting room for guests' use.

Start your day with an elegant breakfast served at a time convenient to you, then go out and experience all that Queenstown has to offer.

Larch Hill House

16 Panners Way, Goldfields, Queenstown
Ph (03) 442 4811, Fax (03) 441 8882
email: *information@larchhill.com*
www.larchhill.com

Tariff : N.Z. Dollars	
Double	$120-160
Single	$100
Apartment	$190-260

Bedrooms	Qty
Double	2
Twin	1
Apartment	1
Bed Size	**Qty**
Super King	1
King	1
Queen	1
King/Single	2
Single	2
Bathrooms	**Qty**
Ensuite	2
Private	2
Guest Share	

Homestay/Bed & Breakfast
Superb Accommodation

DIRECTIONS: From Frankton drive 2½ km on SH6A towards Queenstown. At 'Sherwood Manor' turn right into Goldfields Heights. Panners Way is 2nd left, then 1st access on left.

Features & Attractions

- *Magnificent scenery*
- *Tranquil setting*
- *Generous breakfast*
- *All rooms - own bathroom*
- *10% discount for 4+ nights*
- *Golf courses & skiing nearby*
- *Adventure/itinerary planning*
- *Music, art and craft lovers*

Lesley and Chris offer you a warm welcome to **Larch Hill** in beautiful Queenstown. **Larch Hill House** is built on an elevated site overlooking the blue waters of Lake Wakatipu. It is surrounded by spectacular mountains which are snow-capped in winter. **Larch Hill** is only a 3 minute drive from the centre of Queenstown and within walking distance of the lake. Public transport passes the driveway. All rooms and sundeck overlook the lake and surrounding mountains. This home provides a feeling of relaxation. A restful theme flows through the bedrooms into the dining room with its library, opening onto a sunny courtyard surrounded by cottage gardens. On arrival you are welcomed with refreshments. In winter a roaring log fire awaits your return from a day's skiing or sightseeing. Our self-contained apartment is ideal for families or groups of 4. Breakfast is generous – home-made bread, yoghurt, fresh fruit salad and real coffee. We have pleasure in organising any Queenstown experience. Fax and email facilities.

Lake Hayes YOUR HOSTS: **Ian and Margaret Chamberlain** Ph (03) 442 1280

The Peony Gardens

231 Lake Hayes - Arrowtown Road, Lake Hayes
Ph (03) 442 1280, Fax (03) 442 1210
Mobile 027-436 1661
email: *ijchamberlain@xtra.co.nz*

Features & Attractions

- *Self-contained flat*
- *Close to 4 ski fields*
- *Restaurants 5 min.*
- *Peaceful rural location*
- *Golf courses nearby*
- *2 ha lovely garden setting*

Homestay Bed & Breakfast

Double	$130
Single	$100
Child	$20

Ian and Margaret welcome you to **The Peony Gardens**, situated at Lake Hayes. Our garden was the original 'Peony Gardens' and during November and December our gardens are a delight to see. The self-contained flat has two bedrooms, full kitchen facilities, heat pump and opens onto a balcony which looks over to the Lake and our 4 acres of garden and woodlands. A short walk will take you to the edge of Lake Hayes with wonderful views of the local mountains. We are situated between Queenstown and historic Arrowtown. There is easy access to four of New Zealand's best ski fields and four very scenic golf courses. We enjoy meeting people and we will do all we can to make your time here memorable, including helping to plan your trips if you wish.

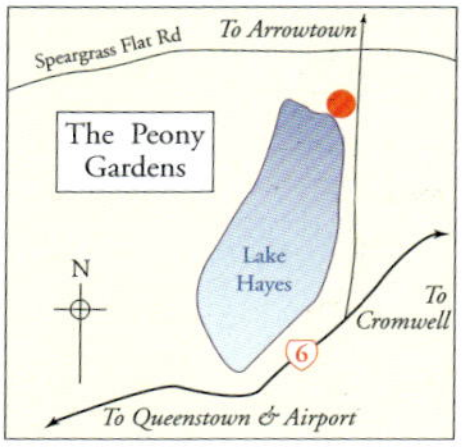

Bedrooms	Qty
Double	2
Twin	
Single	1
Bed Size	**Qty**
King	
Queen	1
Double	1
Single	2
Bathrooms	**Qty**
Ensuite	
Private	1
Guest Share	

Queenstown YOUR HOSTS: **Merlin and Raymond Sansom** Ph: (03) 441 8118

5 Star Lane

5 Star Lane, Queenstown, Otago
Ph (03) 441 8118, Fax (03) 441 8116
email: *stay@5starlane.com*
www.5starlane.com

Features & Attractions

- *Lake and mountain views*
- *Guest lounge and sauna*
- *Covered guest parking*
- *Delicious breakfast menu*
- *Air conditioning*
- *Laundry & Internet access*

Luxury Bed & Breakfast

Double	$165-245
Single	$125-225
Child	

"All the comforts of home in a four season paradise"

Enjoy the magnificent view from the guest lounge and your bedroom. Our newly built home has two guest bedrooms, each with a spacious ensuite bathroom, individually controlled heating/cooling, and a private patio.

We welcome you with tea, coffee and home baking. You can also make tea and coffee for yourself any time. The guest lounge/ dining room has a cosy fire in the winter, and air-conditioning in the summer. Television, a selection of books, games and videos are provided. Take time to relax and unwind after a day enjoying the many activities Queenstown has to offer. You can order breakfast for the time of your choice. Make the most of our personal attention and advice.

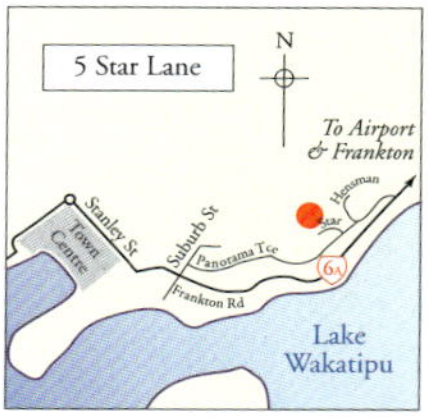

DIRECTIONS:
Take Highway 6a, Frankton Rd, turn up the hill into Hensman Rd, then 1st left into Panorama Terrace, 1st right into Star Lane.

Bedrooms	Qty
Double	2
Twin	
Single	
Bed Size	**Qty**
King	2
Queen	
Double	
King/Single	4
Bathrooms	**Qty**
Ensuite	2
Private	
Guest Share	

"Ferry Hotel" B&B Guesthouse (circa 1872)

Spence Road, Lower Shotover, Queenstown
Ph (03) 442 2194, Fax (03) 442 2190
email: *info@ferry.co.nz*
www.ferry.co.nz

@ home NEW ZEALAND

Tariff : N.Z. Dollars	
Double	$185-235
Single	
Child	Free u/12

Bedrooms	Qty
Double	2
Twin	1
Single	
Bed Size	**Qty**
Super King	
King	1
Queen	
Double	1
Single	2
Bathrooms	**Qty**
Ensuite	1
Private	1
Guest Share	

VISA MasterCard

Unique Historic B&B Guest House

Features & Attractions

- *Ideal for families & small groups*
- *10 min. to Queenstown/Arrowtown*
- *Fishing advice & guide*
- *Central to ski fields/local attractions*
- *Genuine historic building*
- *Peaceful & relaxing location*
- *Photo display of Hotel's history*
- *Huge wood-burning fire*

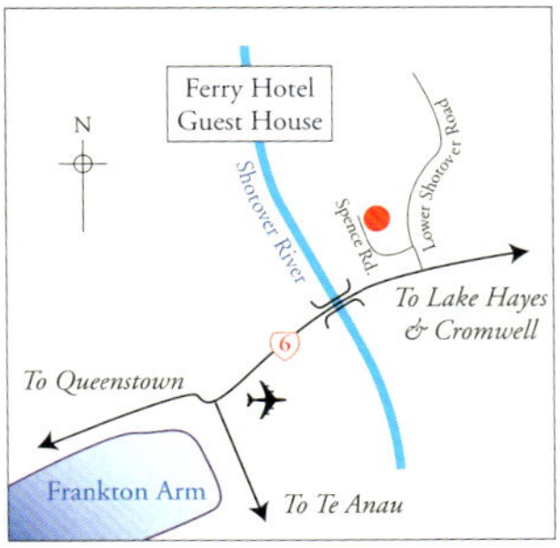

DIRECTIONS:
From State Highway 6 turn into Lower Shotover Road – Blue B & B Sign, follow left turn into Spence Road.

Old World Elegance aptly describes this delightful Guest House – not just a place to stay, but a feature of your holiday. Formerly a popular hotel for over 100 years, the **Guest House** is a local landmark. Your hosts Kevin and Glenys have traced the hotel's history back to 1868 and in the process ascertained that they are the 25th owners of the Hotel. Hosts accommodation is separate but adjoining the Guest House. Glenys enjoys helping you to make the most of your stay in Queenstown offering advice and information and making bookings for local attractions. Kevin will advise, guide or teach Fly Fishing, Buckley our friendly English Springer likes to walk you along our beautiful track by the river. **'Ferry Hotel' Guest House** has 3 bedrooms, one of them with an antique brass bed and character ensuite bathroom. There is a kitchen that Granny would have been proud of and a charming lounge-dining room decked with historic photos, paintings and memorabilia, and kept warm by a roaring log wood-burner. Laundry facilities and a gas BBQ are available. Alfresco eating areas are situated in the English cottage garden.

Queenstown YOUR HOSTS: **Angela and Bill Dolan** Free Ph: 0800 436 111

Kahu Rise

455 Littles Road, RD 1, Queenstown
Ph (03) 441 2077, Fax (03) 441 2078
Mobile 021-104 0009
email: *info@kahurise.co.nz*
www.kahurise.co.nz

@home NEW ZEALAND

Tariff : N.Z. Dollars	
Double	$190-220
Single	$140-170
Child	—

Bedrooms	Qty
Double	2
Twin	
Single	
Bed Size	**Qty**
Super King	
King	
Queen	1
Double	
Single	2
Bathrooms	**Qty**
Ensuite	
Private	1
Guest Share	

Bed & Breakfast
Self-contained Accommodation

Features & Attractions

- *Quiet rural location*
- *Beautiful mountain views*
- *Dinner by arrangement*
- *Skifields nearby*
- *Close to Queenstown*
- *Architecturally designed home*
- *Separate guest wing*
- *Delicious home baking*

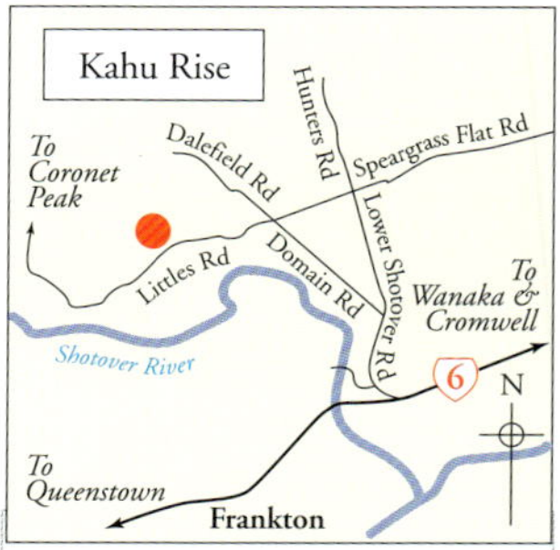

DIRECTIONS: From Queenstown, turn left off SH 6 onto Lower Shotover Road, just after crossing Shotover River bridge. Turn left onto Domain Road and left onto Littles Road. We are 1 km along on the right.

We warmly invite you to come and stay with us in our architecturally-designed home, set in 2½ acres of rolling countryside. From here you can easily access the nearby attractions of Queenstown, two skifields, golf courses, wineries, and historic Arrowtown. Your party will have exclusive use of our bed & breakfast accommodation wing. This comprises two double bedrooms, each with mountain views and opening directly onto the lawn and garden, plus your own full bathroom. There is an additional separate toilet and adjacent laundry. There is also a separate teenage sleepout. Tea and coffee making facilities, electric blankets, refrigerator and hair dryer are provided in the guest area. The house is centrally heated, covered parking is available. Each morning we serve freshly brewed tea and coffee and a delicious home-cooked breakfast at a time to suit. Dinner with complimentary wine by arrangement. Angela and Bill are well travelled, and together with their friendly family dog Tess, look forward to welcoming you at **Kahu Rise**.

Crown View B&B

457 Littles Road, Dalefield, Queenstown
Ph (03) 442 9411, Fax (03) 442 9411
Mobile 025-495 156
email: *info@crownview.co.nz*
www.crownview.co.nz

Tariff : N.Z. Dollars	
Double	$165-185
Single	$130-150
Child	

Bedrooms	Qty
Double	2
Twin	
Single	
Bed Size	**Qty**
Super King	2
King	
Queen	
Double	
Single	
Bathrooms	**Qty**
Ensuite	1
Private	
Guest Share	

VISA Maestro

Bed & Breakfast
Farmstay

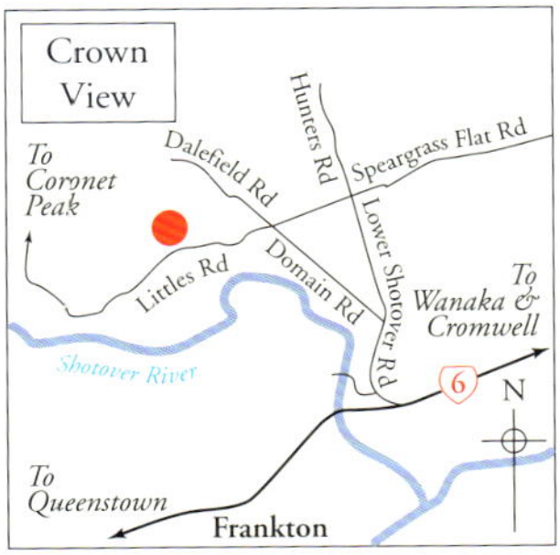

DIRECTIONS:
From Queenstown/Frankton Airport cross over Shotover Bridge, turn left into Lower Shotover Road, left into Domain Road, left into Littles Road. 600m on the right.

Features & Attractions

- *Quiet, peaceful rural location*
- *10 minutes to Queenstown and Arrowtown*
- *Separate guest lounge/open fire*
- *Four golf courses nearby*
- *Stunning mountain views*
- *Central to ski fields*
- *Warm hospitality*

Crown View is situated on eight rolling acres, with views of the Crown Range and the Remarkables. Share with us the peace and tranquility of country life, only 15 minutes from Queenstown/Arrowtown. Coronet Peak is only 10 minutes away. There is easy access to wineries, art studios, four golf courses, bush and track walks. We have two large bedrooms with king-size beds (alternatively 2 king-singles). One bedroom has an ensuite, the other has a private bathroom with spa bath. Both rooms have television, tea and coffee making facilities. Breakfast can be served on the upstairs balcony, in the garden or in the guest lounge/dining room, where you can enjoy our open fire. Efficient radiators in every room of the house will ensure you are kept warm and cosy. Reg,Caroll, our West Highland White Terriers (Archie and Dougall), sheep and chickens (fresh eggs for breakfast) look forward to welcoming you to **Crown View**. Come as a guest – leave as a friend.

Tussock Lodge

293B Lower Shotover Road, RD 1, Queenstown
Ph (03) 442 0752, Fax (03) 442 0751
Mobile 021-808 018
email: *relax@tussocklodge.co.nz*
www.tussocklodge.co.nz

Tariff : N.Z. Dollars	
Double	$130-240
Single	–
Child	–

Bedrooms	Qty
Double	3
Twin	1
Single	
Bed Size	**Qty**
Super King	
King	1
Queen	2
Double	
Single	2
Bathrooms	**Qty**
Ensuite	
Private	2
Guest Share	

Stylish Accommodation with Great Hospitality

Features & Attractions

- *Peaceful private rural location*
- *Stunning 360° mountain views*
- *Physiotherapy aromatherapy massage*
- *Email, internet & laundry facilities*
- *All day sun, central heating*
- *Skiing, walking, golf*
- *Guided fishing trips*
- *Art galleries, wineries, restaurants*

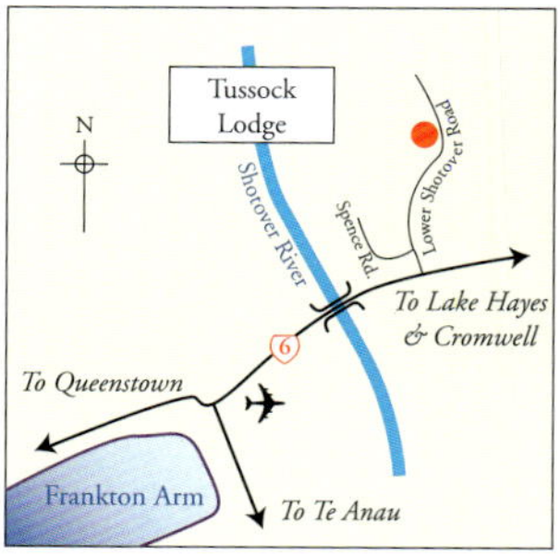

Relax in the peace and tranquility of our home set on 30 acres of parkland in the beautiful Wakatipu Basin. Enjoy 360° views of the mountains and surrounding countryside. Courtesy vehicle for pick-up/drop off at the airport. 10 minutes to Coronet Peak, 20 minutes to Remarkables. Enjoy local restaurants in Queenstown or quaint, historic Arrowtown. Child minding available in the evenings. Superb inhouse dining by arrangement featuring local produce and wines. Tennis court, mountain bikes, pétanque or take a quiet stroll in the grounds. Swimming and gym facilities at Milbrook just ten minutes away. Ease away those aches and pains with inhouse physiotherapy or aromatherapy massage. Luxury king size bedroom with private bathroom. Family suite of two bedrooms with private bathroom. One king, one queen and two bunks. Queen bedroom with private bathroom. Separate dining room and lounge with Sky television. Tea and coffee making facilities. Jill and Trev offer you a warm welcome and pleasant stay. –Qualmark™ applied for.

PENCARROW

678 Frankton Road, Queenstown
Ph (03) 442 8938, Fax (03) 442 8974
Mobile 027-413 1567
email: *info@pencarrow.net*
www.pencarrow.net

Tariff : N.Z. Dollars	
Double	$495
Single	
Child	

Bedrooms	Qty
Double	4
Twin	
Single	
Bed Size	**Qty**
Super King	3
King	1
Queen	2
Double	
Single	
Bathrooms	**Qty**
Ensuite	4
Private	
Guest Share	

Luxury Accommodation
Bed & Breakfast

DIRECTIONS: From Cromwell, Invercargill and Queenstown Airport take SH 6 (Frankton Rd) towards Queenstown. 1 km past Shell Service Station turn right at Greenstone Terrace Apartments (two tone brown) and take the middle drive up to **Pencarrow** on the hill.

Features & Attractions

- *All rooms are suites*
- *Four skifields nearby*
- *Four acres of gardens*
- *Snooker, darts, horseshoes*
- *Four golf courses nearby*
- *Stunning lake & mountain views*
- *Tourist room, table tennis*
- *Wineries, fishing, jetboat*

Every attention to detail has been undertaken by Bill and Kari to ensure your pleasure whilst in Queenstown! Enjoy breakfast on your time, activities co-ordinated and vouchers waiting for you in your suite, the afternoon "sweet in the suite", and an evening turn down service – *every detail: all that is Pencarrow!* Four acres of gardens to find a quiet corner for two or to join fellow friends around an outdoor fireplace. Reflect on the day at "Pondering Point" or unwind in the spa pool. Suites offer sitting rooms, writing desk, mini bar, coffee facilities, fresh flowers, Sky television, VCR/Stereo/CD systems and direct-dial phones. Ensuites with oversized spa bath, separate shower, double vanity, heated towel rail and undertile heating. Snooker room features a full sized historic snooker table and dartboard. "New River Lounge and Bar" with open fireplace and majestic views of the Remarkables and Lake Wakatipu. Dining room with antique fireplace. Wine cellar offering a selection of fine wines. "Kiwi Room" provides brochures, restaurant menus, videos, books, and games. Facsimile, laundry and bar services for an additional charge.

ANNA'S COTTAGE

67 Thompson Street, Queenstown
Ph (03) 442 8994, Fax (03) 441 8994
Mobile 025-693 3025
email: *annas.rose@xtra.co.nz*

Features & Attractions

- *Quality accommodation*
- *Very quiet location*
- *Tranquil garden setting*
- *Car parking at cottage*
- *Short walk to town centre*
- *Laundry facilities*

$		
	Double	$120-145
	Single	$90
	Child	

eftpos, MasterCard, VISA

Self-contained Suites
Breakfast Available – extra

Bedrooms	Qty
Double	3
Twin	
Single	
Bed Size	**Qty**
Super King	1
Queen	1
Double	
King/Single	1
Bathrooms	**Qty**
Ensuite	2
Private	
Guest Share	

DIRECTIONS: Take SH 6A into Queenstown, left at 2nd roundabout into Shotover Street, through 2 more roundabouts. Turn at Waterfront Apartments into Brunswick Street, which goes into Thompson Street. **Anna's Cottage** is signposted.

A warm welcome to **Anna's Cottage**. Myrna is a keen gardener and golfer and Ken has a love of fishing. Enjoy the peaceful garden setting and mountain views. **The Cottage** has ensuite, washing machine, kitchen and living room – dryer available. It is tastefully decorated throughout. The bedroom features Sheridan linen. Only a few minutes from the centre of Queenstown, with private drive and parking at the cottage. Attached to the end of our home is the self-contained **Rose Suite** with one queen bed with ensuite, small kitchen, television and featuring Sheridan linen. Washing mashine dryer available. Both guest ensuites have been newly refurbished. We will help and offer advice on all Queenstown activities.

THE STABLE

17 Brisbane Street, Queenstown
Ph (03) 442 9251, Fax (03) 442 8293
email: *gimac@queenstown.co.nz*
www.thestablebb.com

NZ HISTORIC PLACES TRUST · POUHERE TAONGA

Features & Attractions

- *5 min. stroll to town*
- *100 metres to beach*
- *Historic building*
- *Quiet cul-de-sac*
- *Trees, gardens & birds*
- *No need for a car*

VISA, MasterCard

Historic Building
Bed & Breakfast

$		
	Double	$160-180
	Single	$120
	Child	

DIRECTIONS: Follow SH 6A, veer right at the Millenium Hotel. Continue straight ahead. Brisbane St. (no exit) is 2nd on left. Phone if necessary.

A 130 year-old stone **stable**, converted for guest accommodation and listed by the New Zealand Historic Places Trust, shares a private courtyard with our home. The **Garden Room** is in the house. Both rooms are well heated with views of garden, lake or mountains. Tea / coffee making facilities are available at all times. Our home is in a quiet cul-de-sac and set in a garden abundant with rhododendrons and native birds. Less than 100 m from the beach. A small boat and canoe are available for guests' use. All tourist facilities are within easy walking distance. A courtesy car is available. Guests share our spacious living areas and make free use of our library and laundry. We can advise about and are booking agents for all sightseeing tours.

Bedrooms	Qty
Double	1
Twin	1
Single	
Bed Size	**Qty**
Super King	1
Queen	
Double	1
Single	2
Bathrooms	**Qty**
Ensuite	1
Private	1
Guest Share	

Coronet View Deluxe B&B and Apartments

Deluxe B & B and Appartments

30 Huff Street, Queenstown
Ph (03) 442 6766, Fax (03) 442 6767
Mobile 027-432 0895
email: *stay@coronetview.com*
www.coronetview.com

Tariff : N.Z. Dollars	
Double	$150-250
Single	$140-220
Child	$30

Bedrooms	Qty
Double	7
Twin	3
Single	
Bed Size	**Qty**
Super King	6
King	
Queen	1
Double	
King/Single	3
Bathrooms	**Qty**
Ensuite	9
Private	1
Guest Share	

Deluxe Bed & Breakfast

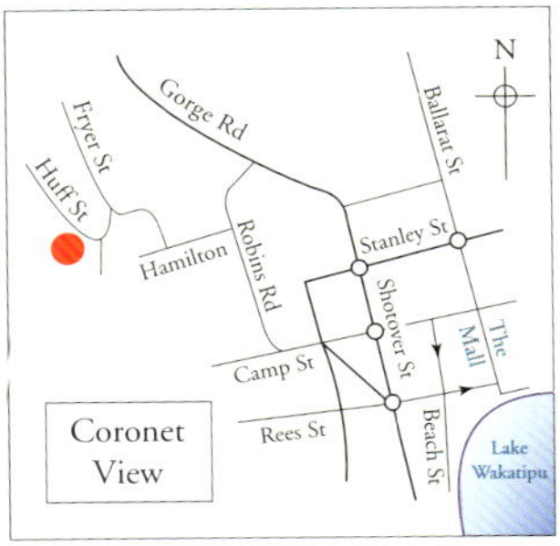

Features & Attractions

- *Wireless internet facilities*
- *Full laundry facilities*
- *Barbeque and spa area*
- *Full meal service*
- *Self-catering apartments*
- *Close to town centre*
- *Web booking service*
- *Guiding service & tours*

Centrally located just ten minutes walk from town, Coronet View enjoys superb views of Coronet Peak, The Remarkables and Lake Wakatipu. Beautifully appointed rooms offer every comfort in either hosted accommodation or private apartments. Coronet View offers ten luxurious guest rooms plus three fully self-contained private apartments. Guest common areas occasionally shared with gorgeous persian cats include elevated and spacious dining and living areas, outdoor decks, a sunny conservatory, outdoor barbeque, pool and jacuzzi area and computers with internet access. **Bed & Breakfast** - A home away from home with true kiwi hospitality. Most rooms feature super king beds with hand crafted fabric art quilts and all have sheepskin electric blankets. Your hosts are knowledgeable local people who can recommend and book your activities at no extra cost. **Apartments** - three apartments on site and also management of holiday apartments in other areas of Queenstown. 1-6 bedroomed apartments. Most configurations feature ensuites, super king beds, generous living areas, fully equipped kitchens and laundries.

BALMORAL LODGE

24 York Street, PO Box 1463, Queenstown
Ph (03) 442 7209, Fax (03) 442 6499
email: *balmoral.lodge@xtra.co.nz*
www.zqnbalmoral.co.nz

Tariff : N.Z. Dollars	
Double	$250-350
Single	$195-250
H. Suite	$325

Bedrooms	Qty
Double	4
Twin	
Single	
Bed Size	**Qty**
Super King	
King	3
Queen	1
Double	
Single	
Bathrooms	**Qty**
Ensuite	4
Private	
Guest Share	

Boutique Hotel
Bed & Breakfast

Features & Attractions

- *Superb location*
- *Spacious ensuites*
- *Stunning panoramic views*
- *Ambience of a luxury lodge*
- *Fabulous breakfasts*
- *Outdoor sundecks*
- *Landscape gardens*
- *800m to town centre*

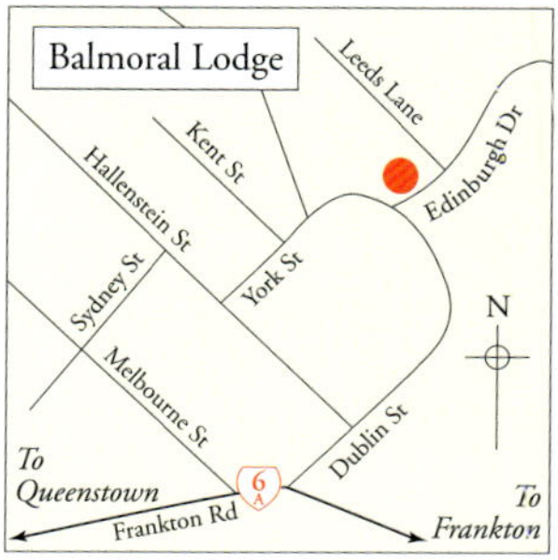

Balmoral Lodge is situated on Queenstown Hill, just 800 metres from the town centre, offering spectacular views of the lake and township from every room. Each room has king/twin or queen beds and is furnished with fine linens, plenty of pillows and large comfortable arm chairs, coffee and tea making facilities, TV and fridge. Internet access available. Ensuite bathrooms are spacious with shower over bath. Some rooms have spa baths. The Lodge is decorated in elegant furnishings, antiques and a display of fine art adorns the walls. A healthy, hearty breakfast is served in the dining room. Fresh fruits, homemade muesli cereals, fresh orange juice and yoghurt; also a full cooked breakfast of bacon, eggs and tomatoes. The Family Suite opens onto a private lawn and rose gardens. Our very spacious luxury Honeymoon Suite($325 per night), with king bedroom and all the trimmings for that very special time, has a double spa bath in the ensuite with commanding views from the room and the ensuite.
We have 24 years experience in Queenstown and can assist in planning your daily activities for you.

Fine Accommodation

5 Vancouver Drive, PO Box 1777, Queenstown
Ph (03) 441 8866, Fax (03) 442 9463
Mobile 027- 434 7209
email: *info@fineaccommodation.co.nz*
www.fineaccommodation.co.nz

Tariff : N.Z. Dollars	
Double	$185-220
Single	$185
Child	

Bedrooms	Qty
Double	3
Twin	
Single	
Bed Size	**Qty**
Super King	1
King	2
Queen	
Double	
Single	
Bathrooms	**Qty**
Ensuite	3
Private	
Guest Share	

Quality Home Bed & Breakfast

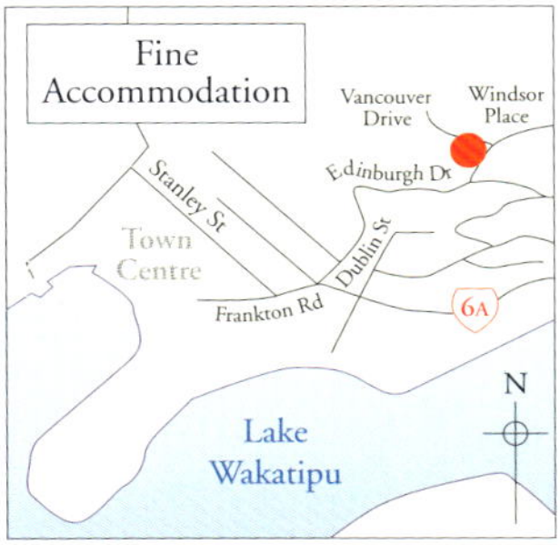

Features & Attractions

- *Adventure capital of the world*
- *1km to downtown Queenstown*
- *Licensed tour operators*
- *Quality ensuites*
- *Quiet and private location*
- *Hosts been in tourism 22 years*
- *'Walter' marriage celebrant*
- *Views of lake & golf course*

You are assured of a warm welcome at **Fine Accommodation.** Your hosts Dale and Walter are semi retired after being in the tourism industry for over 22 years and are opening their home for Bed & Breakfast. We have three good-sized bedrooms with ensuite, one with a spa bath. We supply a continental breakfast of fresh fruits, cereals, yoghurt, toast, fruit juices, coffee and teas. On request dinners can also be provided. We are experienced in advising about the many activities and dining experiences around the Queenstown area. Walter is a Justice of the Peace and a very popular wedding celebrant. We are less than 5 minutes from downtown Queenstown. Recent guest's comments: *"Wonderful accommodation and what views, thank you for looking after us so well."* David & Pat U.K. *"Gracious hosts who have warmly welcomed Chris and I to their beautiful home with magnificent view from every aspect."* Chris & Sandra, Australia. *"Stunning spot, great room & delicious breakfast."* Nancy Viner, Toronto USA.

 ▶ YOUR HOSTS: **Nery Howard and Michael Clark** Ph: (0800) 429 160

Trelawn Place

Watties Track, off Gorge Rd, Arthurs Point,
PO Box 117, Queenstown
Ph (03) 442 9160 Fax (03) 442 9667
Mobile 021-101 5805
email: *trelawn@ihug.co.nz*
www.trelawnb-b.co.nz

Tariff : N.Z. Dollars	
Double	$250-350
Single	$250
Child	$55

Bedrooms	Qty
Double	5
Twin	3
Single	1
Bed Size	**Qty**
Super King	1
King	1
Queen	1
King/Single	1
Single	4
Bathrooms	**Qty**
Ensuite	3
Private	2
Guest Share	

Luxury Bed & Breakfast
Self-contained Cottage

Features & Attractions

- *Unique location beside the Shotover River*
- *Fantastic mountain views*
- *Computer desk, internet access*
- *5 min from town centre*
- *Large private garden*
- *Walkway to river*
- *Outdoor jacuzzi spa, guest laundry*

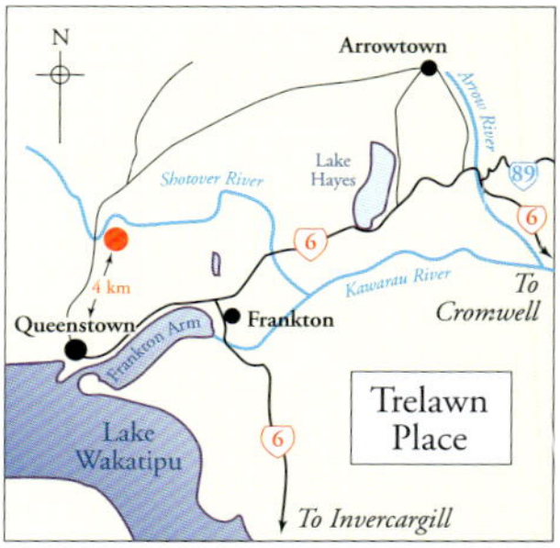

Sited dramatically above the Shotover River with gardens and lawns sweeping to the cliff edge, **Trelawn Place** is a superior country lodge only four kilometres from busy Queenstown. We have five comfortably appointed ensuite rooms, furnished with country chintz and antique style furniture. Our guest sitting room has an open fire and a well stocked library. Outdoors you will find quiet sitting areas and shady vine-covered verandahs. Generous cooked breakfast features home-made and grown produce. If you are missing your pets, a cat and friendly corgis will make you feel at home. A forty-eight hour cancellation policy applies. Helpful information and bookings for all activities.

Two self-contained cottages, a honeymoon hideaway, with Juliet balconies, cosy fireside, roses framing the door.

Windsor Heights

5 Windsor Place, Queenstown
Ph (03) 442 5862, Fax (03) 442 5865
Mobile 027-626 2353
email: *book@queenstown-holiday.co.nz*
www.queenstown-holiday.co.nz

Tariff : N.Z. Dollars	
Double	$160
Single	$120
Child	neg

Bedrooms	Qty
Double	1
Twin	1
Single	
Bed Size	**Qty**
Super King	
King	
Queen	1
Double	
Single	1/1
Bathrooms	**Qty**
Ensuite	1
Private	1
Guest Share	

Queenstown
Homestay Bed and Breakfast

DIRECTIONS:
Entering Queenstown on SH 6A,
pass Kingsgate Hotel on right,
then take 2nd street on right (Dublin Street).
Continue uphill into Edinburgh Drive,
then left up into Windsor Place -
we are No. 5 on the left.

Features & Attractions

- *Fantastic views*
- *Very quiet location*
- *Walking track close by*
- *Secluded courtyard with hot tub*
- *Laundry facilities*
- *4th generation local knowledge*
- *Email facilities*
- *10% discount for 3+ nights*

Our modern home sits high above Queenstown, offering breathtaking views of mountains and lake. We invite you to enjoy our sheltered courtyard and garden, complete with gas barbecue and large spa/hot tub or relax in our guest lounge with a view (pictured). A generous continental breakfast is also served in this room plus tea and coffee making facilities are available all day.

We are within walking distance of downtown Queenstown and its superb selection of restaurants and shops - about fifteen minutes but please be aware the walk back is a little longer and might require frequent stops to admire the views! A taxi costs approximately $6. As authorised booking agents we will gladly offer advice and help you plan your Queenstown activities. We share our home with a delightful, very friendly British Blue cat named Kristy.

CHARTLEA PARK

1 Chartlea Park Road, RD 1, Balfour
Ph/Fax (03) 201 6442, Mobile 027-285 5121
email: *ken.trish.mack@xtra.co.nz*
www.chartleaparkfarmstay.co.nz

Tariff : N.Z. Dollars	
Double	$130
Single	$85
Child u/12	$40

Bedrooms	Qty
Double	1
Twin	2
Single	
Bed Size	**Qty**
Super King	
King	
Queen	1
Double	
King/Single	4
Bathrooms	**Qty**
Private	2
Guest Share	1
Family Share	

Historic Farm Homestead
Unique Farmstay Experience

Features & Attractions

- *Farm experience*
- *Trout fishing rivers*
- *Vintage car/antique enthusiasts*
- *Beautiful garden setting*
- *Peaceful, rural retreat*
- *Relaxation at its best*
- *Home cooking a specialty*
- *Warm, friendly hospitality*

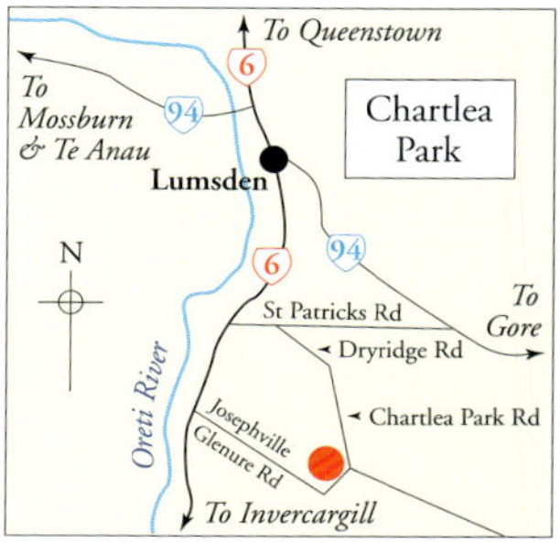

Chartlea Park Farmstay and the MacKenzie family welcomes you to a delightful corner of Northern Southland. Come and share a memorable experience on their 550 acre sheep, deer and beef farm.

Chartlea Park, the original Balfour Homestead, dating back to 1896 and once the hub of an 8559 acre estate, is perfectly positioned amidst some of the most beautiful New Zealand countryside. Our central position provides easy access to the delights of Invercargill, Te Anau and Queenstown (1 hour). Delight in wonderful home cooking, relax in our extensive garden setting, join us for a farm tour or assist with some farm activities. Or just enjoy the ambience of our home with its inviting range of antique treasures, reading material and music. We are committed to ensuring your time with us is **the** highlight of your holiday, from the welcoming refreshments on your arrival, through to your chance to meet and feed our pet animals to the tasty delights of your meals. For the keen fisherman we are minutes from some of the best fishing rivers around. Dinner on request at an extra charge.

Antler Lodge Bed & Breakfast

44 Matai Street, Te Anau
Ph (03) 249 8188, Fax (03) 249 8188
Mobile 025-684 1385
email: *antler.lodge@xtra.co.nz*
www.antlerlodgeteanau.co.nz

Tariff : N.Z. Dollars	
Double	$120-155
Single	
Child	

Bedrooms	Qty
Double	3
Twin	
Single	
Bed Size	**Qty**
Super King	
King	1
Queen	2
Double	
Single	
Bathrooms	**Qty**
Ensuite	3
Private	
Guest Share	

Bed & Breakfast
Self-contained

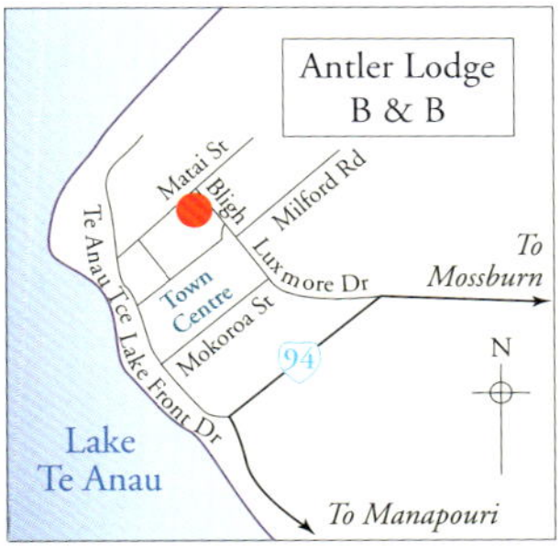

Features & Attractions

- *Quality accommodation*
- *Close to restaurants & shops*
- *Trip bookings & pick-ups*
- *Barbeque available*
- *2 fully self-contained units*
- *Continental breakfast*
- *Laundry facilities*
- *Off-street parking*

Helen and Chris warmly welcome you to Te Anau. We offer the privacy, independence and relaxation of self-contained units along with friendly helpful service. Our ground floor cottages have queen-size beds, full kitchen facilities and ensuite. While our upstairs unit has its own entrance to an attractive dining area that includes a refrigerator and microwave, the spacious bedroom, featuring warm timber and mountain views, has a king-size bed, a walk-in wardrobe and elegant ensuite. All our rooms have relaxing, comfortable furnishings with efficient heating and electric blankets and of course complimentary tea and coffee. Your choice from the delicious continental breakfast menu will be delivered to your room. Chris has a deer farm on the outskirts of Te Anau, he has a keen interest in golf and enjoys showing guests around Te Anau's lovely golf course.

Manapouri - Te Anau YOUR HOSTS: **Florence and John Pine** Ph: (03) 249 8598

CROWN LEA FARMSTAY

310 Gillespie Road, RD 1, Te Anau
Ph (03) 249 8598, Fax (03) 249 8598
Mobile 025-227 8366
email: *crownlea@xtra.co.nz*
www.crown-lea.com

Features & Attractions

- *Working sheep, cattle & deer farm*
- *Farmstyle dinners by arrangement*
- *Doubtful & Milford Sound day trips*
- *Farm tour available*
- *Local walking tracks*
- *Fishing rivers*

DIRECTIONS: Please phone for simple directions.

Farmstay

Double	$140-160
Single	$130-150
Child	

We warmly welcome you to **Crown Lea**, our 900 acre sheep, cattle and deer working farm, offering an informative farm tour and sheep dogs working, after 6pm, with spectacular views of Lake Manapouri, the Fiordland Mountains and Te Anau Basin. Following the farm tour, a traditional farmstyle dinner (NZ $35 per person) of home grown produce is served. Our large, modern family home has three bedrooms for guests, electric blankets on all beds, heaters in each room, ensuite and private bathrooms. **Crown Lea** is within easy access of Doubtful and Milford Sounds, the glow worm caves, Milford and Kepler tracks or the superb fishing rivers in our area. We recommend at least two nights to enable relaxing days enjoying the Sounds, caves, tracks, sightseeing or fishing. Having travelled ourselves, we enjoy meeting guests from all parts of the world and we and Harriet, our cat, look forward to meeting you.

Bedrooms	Qty
Double	2
Twin	1
Single	
Bed Size	**Qty**
Super King	1
Queen	1
Double	
Single	3
Bathrooms	**Qty**
Ensuite	1
Private	2
Guest Share	

Te Anau YOUR HOSTS: **Lyn and Lex Lawrence** Ph: (03) 249 7582

ROSE'N'REEL

89 Ben Loch Lane, RD 2, Te Anau, Fiordland
Ph/Fax (03) 249 7582, Mobile 025-545 723
email: *rosenreel@xtra.co.nz*
www.rosenreel.co.nz

Features & Attractions

- *Lake & mountain views*
- *Extensive garden*
- *Peaceful farm location*
- *Guided fishing available*
- *Feed tame deer*
- *Warm country hospitality*

DIRECTIONS: Please phone or email for bookings and easy directions

Deer Farm Bed & Breakfast
Self-contained Cabin

Double	$90-110
Single	$65-80
Child	neg

Genuine Kiwi hospitality in a magic setting five minutes from Te Anau. Hand-feed tame fallow deer and meet our two friendly cats and farm dog Jess. Relax on the verandah of our fully self-contained cabin and enjoy watching deer with a magnificent lake and mountain backdrop. The two-room cabin has cooking facilities, refrigerator, microwave, television, one queen and one double bed plus bathroom. Our modern smoke-free home is set in an extensive garden and has two downstairs guest bedrooms. Lex is a keen fly fisherman and guide and is available for guiding on our beautiful local rivers. Lyn loves to garden and enjoys sharing her garden with guests. Fiordland is a special place and we will do all we can to make your time here memorable, including helping to plan and book your trips if you so wish.

Bedrooms	Qty
Double	2
Twin	
Single	1
Bed Size	**Qty**
King	
Queen	2
Double	1
King/Single	1
Bathrooms	**Qty**
Ensuite	
Private	1
Guest Share	1

Cosy Kiwi Bed & Breakfast

186 Milford Road, PO Box 186, Te Anau
Ph (03) 249 7475, Fax (03) 249 8471
email: *info@cosykiwi.com*
www.cosykiwi.com

Features & Attractions

- *Sumptuous breakfast buffet*
- *3 minute walk to centre*
- *Immaculately clean*
- *Trip booking and pick-up*
- *Email and fax facilities*
- *Off street parking*

$	
Double	$140-160
Single	$130
Child	neg

Bed & Breakfast Guest House

Bedrooms	Qty
Double	7
Twin	4
Single	7
Bed Size	**Qty**
Super King	1
King	3
Queen	3
Single	7
Bathrooms	**Qty**
Ensuite	7
Private	
Guest Share	

Cosy truly describes how you will feel within our warm, architecturally designed, modern Bed & Breakfast home. We provide privacy with comfort. Our quiet bedrooms are spacious, ensuited with top quality beds, television, individual heating and double glazed windows. Enjoy a sumptuous buffet breakfast of homemade breads, topped with homemade jams, marmalade, fresh fruit salad, yoghurt, brewed coffee, special teas and our legendary pancakes sweet or savoury. We have a modern laundry, good off-street parking and luggage storage for track walkers. Our warm guest lounge provides excellent space to relax, chat and a computer to access emails.
Relax outside on our sun-terrace overlooking the ever-changing moods of the Murchison Mountains or stroll into the town centre to highly recommended restaurants (three minutes). We can recommend and book any sightseeing trips around Fiordland.

Rob And Nancys Place

13 Fergus Square, Te Anau, Fiordland
Ph (03) 249 8241, Fax (03) 249 7397
email: *rob.nancy@xtra.co.nz*

Features & Attractions

- *Warm, friendly atmosphere*
- *Quiet and peaceful*
- *Scrumptious breakfasts*
- *5 min. walk to town centre*
- *Off-street car parking*
- *Tour transfers to the door*

$	
Double	$130-150
Single	$130
Child	n/a

Bed & Breakfast Homestay

Bedrooms	Qty
Double	2
Twin	
Single	
Bed Size	**Qty**
King	2
Queen	
Double	
Single	
Bathrooms	**Qty**
Ensuite	1
Private	1
Guest Share	

Rob, Nancy and Chardonnay, our Burmese cat, welcome you to our quiet and tranquil home facing a park with mountain views. It's just five minutes walk to the lake and town centre. We are a couple, retired from farming and enjoy meeting people and cooking generous breakfasts with homemade preserves and bread. Our modern home includes a courtyard barbeque and gardens. Te Anau is a special place to visit, with the magnificent scenery of the Fiordland National Park, including Milford and Doubtful Sounds and walking tracks. All tours include pick-up and delivery to the door. Off-street parking and storage is available.

DIRECTIONS: Continue on around the lakefront to Matai Street, turn right, cross over Mokonui Street, first left into Fergus Square.

Blue Ridge Boutique Bed&Breakfast

15 Melland Place, Te Anau, Fiordland
Ph (03) 249 7740, Fax (03) 249 7340
Mobile 027-258 9877
email: *info@blueridge.net.nz*
www.blueridge.net.nz

Tariff : N.Z. Dollars	
Double	$175-225
Single	$165-215
Child	neg.

Bedrooms	Qty
Double	4
Twin	2
Single	2
Bed Size	**Qty**
Super King	
King/Single	2
Queen	2
Double	
Single	2
Bathrooms	**Qty**
Ensuite	4
Private	
Guest Share	

Bed & Breakfast
Superior Accommodation

Features & Attractions

- *Warm "kiwi" hospitality*
- *5 min. walk to restaurants & shops*
- *Delicious breakfasts*
- *Mountain views*
- *High speed internet & fax*
- *Guest BBQ*
- *Beautifully appointed rooms*
- *Spa pool*

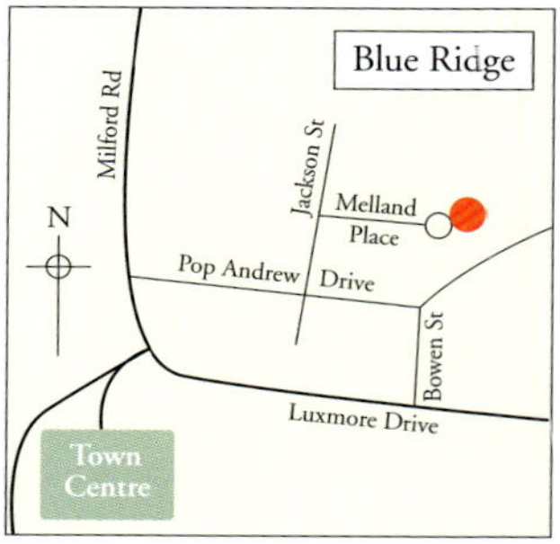

Two types of accommodation are available at **Blue Ridge.** *The Kea Room:* A comfortable queen room with TV, fridge, T&C making and a ensuite bathroom with bathrobes and a hairdryer. A heater and electric blanket are provided. This room has its own entrance which opens onto our patio. Luxury Studio Units: *The Kaka, Bellbird, & Tui Rooms* – Each has a comfortable king/twin or queen bed. The décor is tasteful and modern in neutral tones with rich, warm accents. Beds have luxurious bed linen with sumptuous drapes and throws and there is strong use of hand-crafted native wood and wrought iron in the furniture. There is a sofa, dining table, chairs and a TV. All rooms have kitchenettes with microwave, fridge, kettle and toaster. The ensuite bathrooms are beautifully tiled with underfloor heating, heated towel rail, heater, hairdryer and bathrobes. All rooms are double glazed and have electric heating. We are happy to make bookings for local attractions and excursions. Meet Latté and Meg, our very friendly Birman cats.

House of Wood

44 Moana Crescent, Te Anau
Ph (03) 249 8404, Fax (03) 249 7676
Mobile 021-250 0802
email: *houseofwood@xtra.co.nz*
www.houseofwood.co.nz

@home NEW ZEALAND

Tariff : N.Z. Dollars	
Double	$115-135
Single	$95-120
Child	

Bedrooms	Qty
Double	3
Twin	1
Single	
Bed Size	**Qty**
Super King	
King	
Queen	3
Double	
Single	2
Bathrooms	**Qty**
Ensuite	3
Private	1
Guest Share	

VISA MasterCard

Homestay
Bed & Breakfast

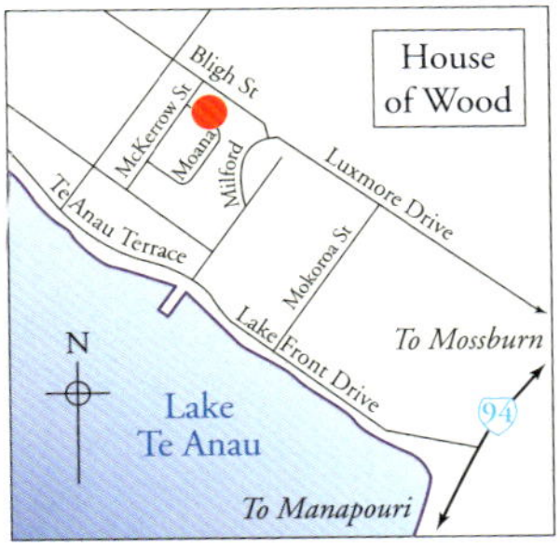

Features & Attractions

- *Fishing, golf and tramping*
- *Friendly hosts*
- *Fiordland National Park*
- *Town centre 2 min. walk*
- *Hearty cooked breakfast*
- *Dinner by arrangement*
- *Views of the mountains*
- *Mountain bikes available*

We welcome you to our home, built of exotic timbers, right in the heart of Fiordland. You will be able to appreciate the beautiful scenery when you view the landscape from the balconies. **House of Wood** is conveniently located within a two minute walk of the town centre with shops, restaurants, post office, and just a short walk to the lake. Cooking and baking has been a part of our business life in the past and we would like to share this with you, through our delicious home-cooked breakfasts and mouth-watering dinners. Our varied interests include golf, fishing and boating and we can help you share these by arrangement.
We can offer advice on a number of tours available and can book them for you. Tourist trips will pick up from our gate. We have two mountain bikes available for your use, for those who feel the need for some exercise. We look forward to meeting you and to sharing our beautiful slice of paradise. Laundromats nearby. Off season rates.

DUNLUCE BED & BREAKFAST

Aparima Drive, Te Anau, Fiordland
Ph (03) 249 7715, Fax (03)249 7703
Mobile 027-330 2779
e-mail: *info@dunluce-fiordland.co.nz.*
www.dunluce-fiordland.co.nz.

Tariff : N.Z. Dollars	
Double	$185-225
Single	$155-195
Child	

Bedrooms	Qty
Double	4
Twin	
Single	
Bed Size	**Qty**
Super King	
King	4
Queen	
Double	
Single	
Bathrooms	**Qty**
Ensuite	4
Private	
Guest Share	

Bed & Breakfast
Boutique Accommodation

Features & Attractions

- *Gateway to Fiordland*
- *Lake & Mountain views*
- *Private guest wing*
- *Delicious full breakfast*
- *High standard guaranteed*
- *Warm & friendly hospitality*
- *Luxurious ensuite rooms*
- *Walking distance to town*

DIRECTIONS:
From Milford Rd turn left into Howden Street and right into Aparima Drive. We are 300 metres along Aparima Drive.

We welcome you to **Dunluce Bed & Breakfast** – a brand new architecturally designed home, purpose-built with a guest wing offering guests comfort, warmth, privacy and panoramic lake/ mountain views. We are within walking distance of the town centre and a 2 minute drive. All rooms have full-length glass doors opening to private view facing decks. The rooms are modern and uncluttered with luxurious king-size beds, quality bedding, electric blankets, heating, TV and internet.

Tiled ensuites have glass wall showers, under-floor heating, mirror demisters, pure lavender toiletries, hair dryers and luxurious towels. Our deluxe room has a deep double soaking/spa bath. Guests have a private entrance and a lounge/dining room, where an extensive home-made continental and cooked breakfast is served. We have tea and coffee making facilities, home-baking, a guest fridge and a good selection of books, games and magazines. The lounge has air-conditioning, heating and a gas fire. We have ample parking space and offer locked storage and laundry facilities. We are able to give informed advice on local attractions and make bookings.

Blue Thistle Cottages

Rapid 168, Milford-Te Anau Highway, Te Anau
Ph (03) 249 8338, Fax (03) 249 8338
email: *info@bluethistlecottages.com*
www.bluethistlecottages.com

Tariff : N.Z. Dollars	
Double	$195-275
Single	
Child	

Bedrooms	Qty
Double	4
Twin	
Single	
Bed Size	**Qty**
Super King	
King	
Queen	4
Double	
Single	2
Bathrooms	**Qty**
Ensuite	4
Private	
Guest Share	

Luxury Cottages
Self-contained

DIRECTIONS:
Follow Milford-Te Anau Highway 94 1½ km from town.

Features & Attractions

- *Magnificent views*
- *On road to Milford Sound*
- *Complimentary fastnet connection*
- *Large ensuite bedrooms*
- *Sky/cable television*
- *Friendly hosts*
- *Peaceful & quiet*
- *Smoke free*

Welcome to **Blue Thistle**. Our luxury self-contained cottages were opened for guests in January 2004. We are situated on ten acres of land just 1½ km from Te Anau on the road to Milford Sound. Each cottage is individually decorated and all have superb views. The bedroom has a queen slat bed with quality linen and electric blanket. The large ensuite bathroom has heated towel rails, heat lamps, hair dryer, fluffy robes and toiletries. The lounge has cable/Sky television, telephone, fastnet internet connection and CD/ radio. The kitchen has a refrigerator, microwave and selection of teas and coffees.

We have been involved with tourism for the past twelve years, previously in Franz Josef and also in Picton. You are likely to be met by Paris, a very friendly German shorthaired pointer. We also have three cats and several friendly Dexter cows. Allow yourself a couple of days to relax and enjoy all that Te Anau and **Blue Thistle** has to offer. Discount for two or more nights. Now available large two bedroom cottage – minimum two night stay. No meals included.

TE ANAU LODGE

52 Howden Street, Te Anau, Fiordland
Ph (03) 249 7477, Fax (03) 249 7487
Mobile 021-064 9354
email: *info@teanaulodge.co.nz*
www.teanaulodge.com

Tariff : N.Z. Dollars	
Double	$200-300
Single	$170-270
Child	

Bedrooms	Qty
Double	8
Twin	3
Single	8
Bed Size	**Qty**
Super King	3
King/Single	3
Queen	5
Double	
Single	4
Bathrooms	**Qty**
Ensuite	7
Private	1
Guest Share	

Luxury Bed & Breakfast
Historic Convent

Features & Attractions

- *Historic 'Sisters of Mercy Convent' – in paradise!*
- *Holiday in a holiday at best little B&B in world*
- *Mo and Tchai, the DogueDeBordeaux welcoming party*
- *Let us arrange for you the area's 'best' activities*

DIRECTIONS:
Leaving the town towards Milford, Howden St is the 2nd left off Milford Rd.

Advance booking recommended.

Experience for yourself the genuine warmth of traditional ***Kiwi*** hospitality in our relaxed, peaceful haven, which simply 'feels like home'! A 1936 relocated convent, set on 2.7 hectares with breathtaking lake and mountain views. **Te Anau Lodge** is lovingly restored, maintaining its original charm with modern facilities, including central heating, modern bathrooms and spa baths. ***The*** most comfortable beds ensure you a blissful sleep. For your convenience, complimentary laundry facilities, wireless internet and luggage storage are provided. In true Kiwi style, enjoy our famous leisurely breakfasts in the 'Chapel', a feast for the eyes as well as the taste buds! After your day's adventures relax in the library or courtyard with complimentary drinks. We'd be delighted to share your company and our local knowledge with you. You may prefer wandering through the gardens, watching the sunset, then gazing at the sheer brilliance of southern stars. Proudly New Zealand owned and operated; we pay attention to every detail, having the highest standards, where nothing is too much effort. If you desire the best accommodation and service, we invite you to come and stay with us!

Lochvista

454 State Highway 94, RD 1, Te Anau
Ph (03) 249 7273, Fax (03) 249 7278
Mobile 027-455 9949
email: *lochvista@xtra.co.nz*

Tariff : N.Z. Dollars	
Double	$140-170
Single	$140-150
Child	

Bedrooms	Qty
Double	2
Twin	
Single	
Bed Size	**Qty**
Super King	
King	1
Queen	1
Double	
Single	
Bathrooms	**Qty**
Ensuite	2
Private	
Guest Share	

Lakeside Bed & Breakfast

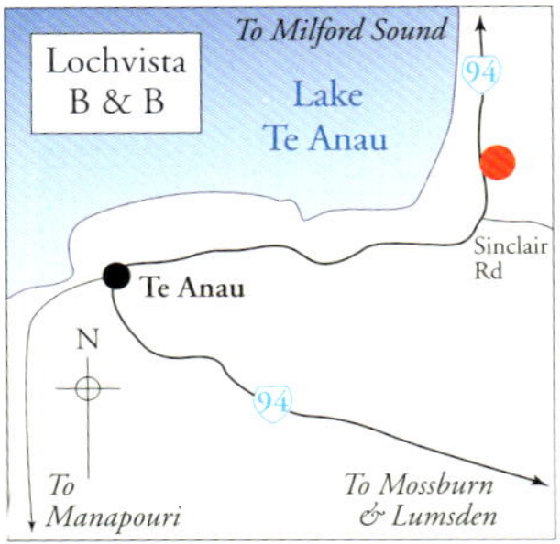

DIRECTIONS:
Travel along Milford Rd 4.6 km from the 80 km sign. Turn 1st right after Sinclair Rd and blue Lodge sign. Go 300m up road, turn right at the three letter boxes, following driveway down to house.

Features & Attractions

- *Stunning mountain views*
- *Shops, cafés, bars - short drive*
- *Fishing & golfing*
- *Tramping & hiking*
- *On road to Milford Sound*
- *Overlooking Lake Te Anau*
- *Spectacular lake views*
- *Glowworm cave excursions*

Welcome to magical Fiordland. **Lochvista** is situated on the Te Anau Milford highway just five kilometres from the town centre. **Lochvista** is ideally positioned, overlooking Lake Te Anau and the stunning Murchison Mountains. I have two rooms, one with king/twin bed and one with queen bed, both with ensuite, tea and coffee making facilities, refrigerator, television and hairdryer. French doors open onto the patio where you can sit and enjoy the spectacular views. Meet Mischief (my pet cat). Full cooked breakfast on request at $15 per person.

Fiordland has a great deal to offer and I am more than happy to help my guests with any bookings to make their stay more relaxing.

The Croft

Rapid 153, Milford Sound Road, RD 1, Te Anau
Ph (03) 249 7393, Fax (03) 249 7393
Mobile 027-682 0061
email: *jane@thecroft.co.nz*
www.thecroft.co.nz

Tariff : N.Z. Dollars	
Double	$130-155
Single	
Child	

Bedrooms	Qty
Double	2
Twin	
Single	
Bed Size	**Qty**
Super King	
King	
Queen	2
Double	
Single	1
Bathrooms	**Qty**
Ensuite	2
Private	
Guest Share	

Bed & Breakfast
Self-contained Accommodation

Features & Attractions

- *Magnificent views*
- *Tranquil surroundings*
- *Large ensuite bathrooms*
- *Warm & friendly Kiwi hosts*
- *On the road to Milford Sound*
- *Small farm with pet sheep*
- *Recently built private cottages*
- *Large private gardens*

DIRECTIONS:
Follow the Te Anau-Milford Highway 94 for 3 km from Te Anau town centre. **"The Croft"** and "Bed & Breakfast" signs are at the gate.
We are Rapid No. 153.

Warm hospitality and quality accommodation are guaranteed at The Croft, a lifestyle farm, just two minutes from Te Anau on the Milford Sound Road. Our two recently built self-contained cottages enjoy magnificent lake and mountain views, are set in large tranquil gardens.

Timber ceilings, window seats, large ensuite bathrooms, elegant furnishings are some of the highlights of our two spacious cottages.

Both have microwaves, refrigerators, CD/mini systems and televisions. Enjoy a generous continental breakfast with Ross and Jane or have it served in your cottage at your leisure.

Pets include Dolly the pet sheep, Mac the Jack Russell, and Kitty the cat. We have a small flock of sheep. Ross is a builder and Jane a past teacher. The Croft is an ideal base for all the many activities available in Fiordland. Sign at gate.

Shakespeare House

10 Dusky Street, PO Box 32, Te Anau
Ph (03) 249 7349, Fax (03) 249 7629
Mobile 027-559 7349
email: *marg.shakespeare.house@xtra.co.nz*
www.shakespearehouse.co.nz

Features & Attractions

- *All ground floor units*
- *10 min walk to town centre*
- *Courtesy car*
- *Trip bookings & pick-up*
- *Continental & cooked breakfast*
- *Internet & payphone on site*

$	
Double	$110-120
Single	$90-100
Child	$1-15

Guest House & Self-contained Accommodation

Bedrooms	Qty
Double	4
Twin/Triple	3
Quad	1
Bed Size	**Qty**
Super King	2
Queen	4
Double	
King/Single	2
Bathrooms	**Qty**
Ensuite	8
Private	
Guest Share	

Fiordland – the "Walking Capital" of the world – is right on your doorstep when you stay at **Shakespeare House**. Marg and Jeff extend a warm welcome to you and offer personal attention in a homely atmosphere. We are situated in a quiet residential area, yet are within walking distance of shops, lake, restaurants and attractions. Our units have their own private facilities, are warm and comfortable with tea/coffee, television and have the choice of king, double or twin beds. They open onto a sunny, relaxing conservatory where you may share your holiday experiences with other guests. We also have a two bedroom self-contained unit, which is popular with families or two couples travelling together. Our dining room catches the morning sun and has a lovely view of the mountains. Enjoy a substantial breakfast – either cooked from the menu or buffet-style continental. Good off-street parking, washing machine and dryers are available. We invite you to experience our hospitality.

DIRECTIONS: Drive north on Lake Front Drive, carry on along Te Anau Terrace. Dusky Street is the last right turn before the boat harbour.

The Cottage Homestay Bed & Breakfast

Waiau Street, Manapouri, Fiordland
Ph (03) 249 6838, Fax (03) 249 6839
Mobile 021-138 6110
email: *macduff@thecottagefiordland.co.nz*
www.thecottagefiordland.co.nz

Features & Attractions

- *Doubtful Sound boat, 2min walk*
- *Bush, mountain & water views*
- *Native bush walks and birdlife*
- *Genuine 'Kiwi' hospitality*
- *Yummy homemade breakfasts*
- *Peace and tranquility*

$	
Double	$120-140
Single	$100-120
Child	

Tranquil Cottage Homestay, Bed & Breakfast

Bedrooms	Qty
Double	2
Twin	1
Single	
Bed Size	**Qty**
King	
Queen	2
Double	
Single	2
Bathrooms	**Qty**
Ensuite	3
Private	
Guest Share	

Gateway to Doubtful Sound, an ideal base to explore the wonders of majestic Fiordland. Our spacious Homestay Bed & Breakfast in a tranquil country setting, offers old-world charm with loads of warm Kiwi hospitality. Enjoy a glass of wine or Southern Man beer before a pleasant evening stroll to one of our local cafés. Our cottage décor home has comfortable ensuite rooms and doors to cottage gardens where you may relax listening to the bird song, with bush, mountain and water views. A yummy homemade continental breakfast, which includes a boiled egg from Hamish's girls, is a good start to the day. May we, Don, Joy and Millie (our bearded collie), wish you a wonderful Fiordland holiday and safe travelling!

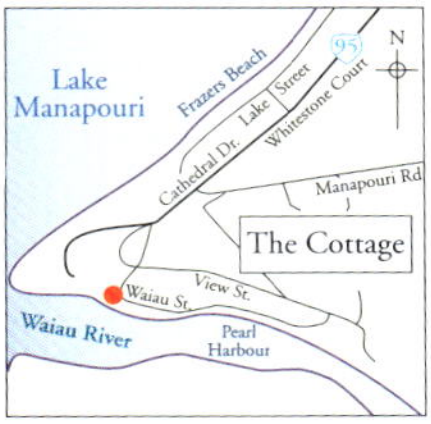

DIRECTIONS: Pass old churches, shop, garage on left, continue down hill towards Pearl Harbour. We are on the right.

About Time Bed & Breakfast

2 Whitestone Court, PO Box 18, Manapouri, Fiordland
Ph (03) 249 6962, Fax (03) 249 6954
Mobile 021-678 472
email: *stay@abouttimemanapouri.co.nz*
www.abouttimemanapouri.co.nz

Tariff : N.Z. Dollars	
Double	$210
Single	$210
Child	

Bedrooms	Qty
Double	2
Twin	1
Single	
Bed Size	**Qty**
Super King	1
King	1
Queen	
Double	
Single	
Bathrooms	**Qty**
Ensuite	3
Private	
Guest Share	

Bed & Breakfast
Homestay

Features & Attractions

- *10 minute walk to Doubtful Sound departure*
- *Double glazing & radiators*
- *Genuine "Kiwi" hospitality*
- *On edge of Fiordland*
- *Stunning views, spa pool*
- *Modern architectural home*
- *Dinner by arrangement*

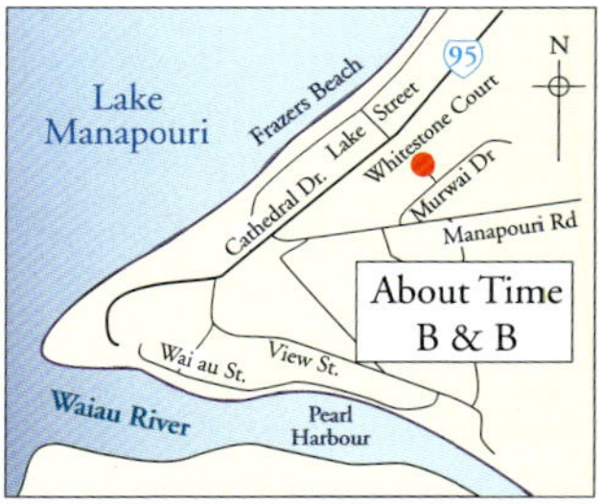

We welcome you to come and relax and take in the magnificent views from our modern architectural home, located on a rise overlooking Lake Manapouri, arguably the most beautiful lake in New Zealand and gateway to the wonders of Doubtful and Milford Sounds.

Our aim is to offer superior accommodation whether as a base to discover Fiordland or as a quiet retreat in which to sit back and relax. The house has been designed to afford views from every window, even from the bath in the ensuite. With double glazing and radiator central heating it offers winter warmth while the terrace and rear courtyard are great for indoor/outdoor living in the summer.
We are Liz and Steve Futter, and together with our Scottish terrier Angus we have found a most beautiful part of the world that we would love to share with travellers from near and far.
Local activities abound and we are here to help with bookings and advice. We would be happy too for you to join us for an evening meal.

CATHEDRAL PEAKS B&B

44 Cathedral Drive, Manapouri, Fiordland
Ph (03) 249 6640, Fax (03) 2496648
email: *cathedralpeaks@ihug.co.nz*
www.cathedralpeaks.com

Tariff : N.Z. Dollars	
Double	$150-250
Single	$130-200
Child	

Bedrooms	Qty
Double	3
Twin	
Single	
Bed Size	**Qty**
Super King/Twin	1
King	
Queen	1
Double	1
Single	
Bathrooms	**Qty**
Ensuite	3
Private	
Guest Share	

Beautiful Lake Manapouri's Boutique Accommodation

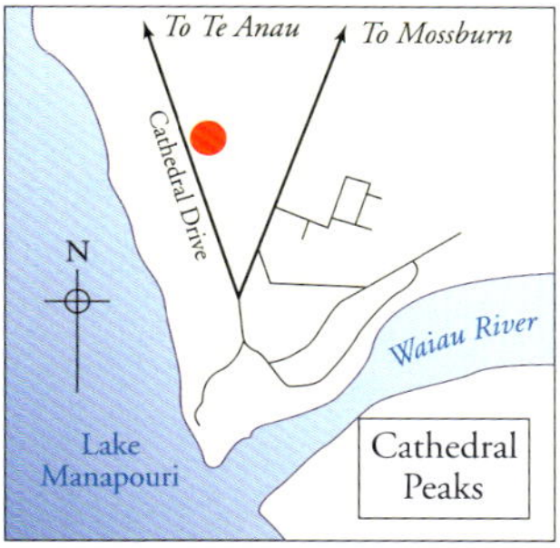

Features & Attractions

- *Smoke free*
- *Restaurant 3min. walk*
- *Spacious ensuite rooms*
- *Off-street parking*
- *Lake & mountain views*
- *Guest lounge/dining room*
- *Doubtful & Milford Sounds daytrips*
- *Fax, phone, email available*

Janice and Neal, your friendly hosts, warmly welcome you to share their new and tastefully appointed home. Take advantage of our lakefront location to relax and enjoy the majestic and stunning scenery from the comfort of your bedroom. Enjoy a continental or cooked breakfast in our exclusive self-contained guest lounge/dining room overlooking the lake. Rooms have tea/coffee making facilities, TV, heater, electric blanket, refrigerator and hairdryer. Looking towards the setting sun your view is rimmed with mountain peaks. Snow-capped in winter, unmarked by man's hand, their forested flanks lead your eyes to Lake Manapouri's edge. Forested islands blend into a silvered surface, which reflects mountain images, clouds, colours, stars, rainbows, the moon. Marvelous Manawapouri, even the name is shrouded in myth, mystery and mistakes. The mood ever changing, enchants – you may wish to never leave. 15 minutes drive to Lake Te Anau. 2 hours drive to Milford Sound. 15 minutes walk to the Doubtful Sound departure point.

Central Oamaru ▶ YOUR HOSTS: Yumi and Shige Koyama Ph (03) 434 9824

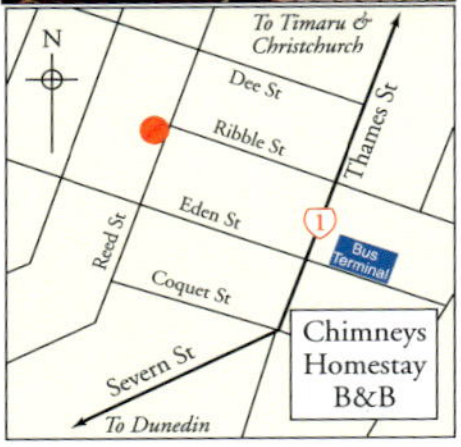

Chimneys Homestay Bed & Breakfast

46 Reed Street, Oamaru, North Otago
Ph (03) 434 9824 Fax (03) 434 9824
Mobile 027-308 6369
email: *chimneys@xtra.co.nz*
www.chimneys-bnb.co.nz

Features & Attractions

- *Central city*
- *Clean, comfortable beds & rooms*
- *Dinner by arrangement*
- *Full cooked breakfast*
- *Historical Oamaru*
- *Blue & Yellow Penguins*

Early 1900's Character House
Oamaru Stone & Native Timber

Double	$105-145
Single	$85-135
Extra pp	$5-30

Bedrooms	Qty
Double	2
Twin	1
Single	1
Bed Size	**Qty**
King	
Queen	2
Double	
Single	5
Bathrooms	**Qty**
Ensuite	1
Private	1
Guest Share	1

Welcome to the 'Capital of Penguins'

Chimneys Homestay Bed & Breakfast was built in 1910 as a doctor's residence using Oamaru stone and native timber. Its unusual design is full of character – we love this house, and we hope you will too!! Since purchasing the house in March 2005 we have invested a great deal of time and effort carefully refurbishing our home to its former glory. This is an ongoing process which is not finished yet! While staying at **Chimneys Homestay Bed & Breakfast**, you will re-discover the prosperity of the city of Oamaru about 100 years ago. We are located in the central city, handy to shops, bus terminal, Oamaru historical precinct and penguin colonies.

We are looking forward to seeing you here!!!

Oamaru ▶ YOUR HOST: Ian Murton Ph (03) 434 6524

Eden Lodge

39 Eden St, Oamaru
Ph (03) 434 6524
e-mail: *ian@edenlodgeoamaru.co.nz*
www.edenlodgeoamaru.co.nz

Features & Attractions

- *Historic Oamaru stone house*
- *Off-street parking*
- *Walking tracks & gardens*
- *Historic precinct*
- *Penguin colony*
- *Restaurants*

Historic Homestay
Bed & Breakfast

Double	$100
Single	$65
Child	

Bedrooms	Qty
Double	3
Twin	
Single	1
Bed Size	**Qty**
King	
Queen	1
Double	2
King/Single	1
Bathrooms	**Qty**
Ensuite	
Private	1
Guest Share	2

Eden Lodge is a historic Oamaru stone house built in the 1860's with extensions in 1906. Located in the centre of town, yet very private.

Relax within the house or wander around the developing gardens. Dine out at one of Oamaru's many fine restaurants. Walking distance to shops, public gardens, walking tracks, penguin colony and historic precinct. Galleries, museum, Whitestone Cheese Factory and Janet Frame House nearby. Local activities include fishing, tramping, Totara Estate, Moeraki Boulders plus many more!

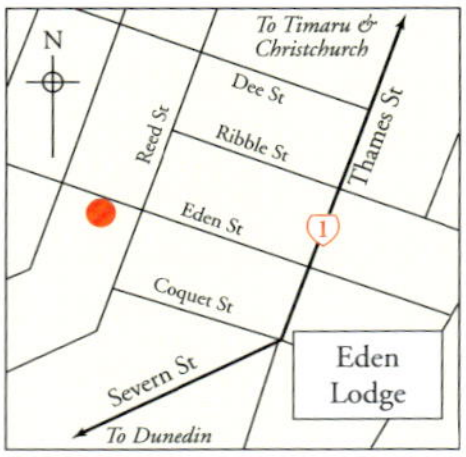

Do come and stay. I'm sure you will enjoy your visit.

Coral Sea Cottage & Ocean View Apartments

34 Harlech Street, Oamaru
Ph (03) 437 1422, Fax (03) 437 1427
Mobile 021-659 757 or 021-042 6997
email: *nmountain@xtra.co.nz*

Tariff : N.Z. Dollars	
Double	$90-140
Single	$39-85
Child	$0-25

Bedrooms	Qty
Double	2
Twin/Super King	3
Single	1
Bed Size	**Qty**
Super King/Twin	3
King	
Queen	2
Double	2
Single	2
Bathrooms	**Qty**
Ensuite	1
Private	2
Guest Share	

DIRECTIONS: From North: Take 3rd road on right (Harlech St) after New World (on right). From South: Drive through the town centre and head north. Approx 2km from town centre, take 2nd left (Harlech St) after shops. At end of Harlech St, go over cattle grid and turn left to Coral Sea Cottage and go straight ahead and up hill to Ocean View.

BA

Magnificant Views
Rural Setting

SC

Features & Attractions

- *Secluded cosy cottage*
- *Bright & newly equipped*
- *Panoramic ocean views*
- *Quiet & peaceful*
- *Rural ten acre location*
- *5 mins from town centre*
- *Famous blue penguins*
- *Historic stone buildings*

Come and relax at **Coral Sea Cottage** or **Ocean View** on a rural hillside with wonderful views of the ocean, town, harbour and surrounding countryside. Enjoy feeding our pet farm animals and visiting our son's art gallery. **Coral Sea Cottage** is a charming three-bedroom holiday home, colourfully decorated with a fishy theme in its own grounds. **Ocean View**, our home at the top of the hill, with magnificent panoramic views, has two bright new self-contained apartments - The Harbour Suite and The Penguin Suite. Sky TV, toys, cot and breakfast basket are available. We are near local shops and restaurants and five minutes drive to the historic town centre, art galleries and famous little blue penguin colony. Other attractions include yellow-eyed penguins, historic farm, surfing, golf and fishing. We look forward to welcoming you and are happy to offer help with planning your visit to our area.

"A touch of heaven in a busy world" (NZ guests).
"An absolute delight, the hosts, cottage and Oamaru" (UK guests).
"Great Beds", "Very friendly and informative" (Australian guests).
"Best stay we had" (German guests).

TOTARA PARK COUNTRY STAY

135 Maudes Road, PO Box 17, Oamaru
Ph (03) 434 8949
Mobile 027-228 5750
email: *totarapark@netspeed.net.nz*

Tariff : N.Z. Dollars	
Double	$120-160
Single	$80-110
Child	

Bedrooms	Qty
Double	1
Twin	
Single	
Bed Size	**Qty**
Super King	
King	
Queen	1
Double	
Single	
Bathrooms	**Qty**
Ensuite	1
Private	
Guest Share	

Countrystay
Bed & Breakfast

Features & Attractions

- *Country tranquility*
- *Separate, peaceful, private room*
- *Numerous animals*
- *3km to Oamaru*
- *Close to historic area*
- *Penguins*
- *Trout & salmon fishing*
- *Spa available*

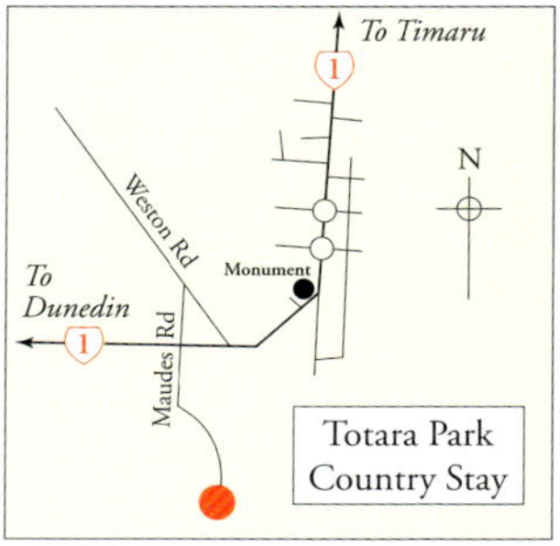

Just three kilometres from the centre of Oamaru, **Totara Park** is set amongst many beautiful trees, is very quiet and private. Bellbirds are frequent visitors. Domestic animals include Pogo, our pet rainbow lorikeet, who is most entertaining. Our guest room is large, separate and private with ensuite, refrigerator, television, stereo and snack facilities. The very comfy queen bed has quality linen and an electric blanket. Continental breakfast is substantial and includes homemade bread. A cooked breakfast is available and includes home grown and cured bacon. A spa and laundry facilities are also available.

Oamaru is close to the Waitaki River and within 2½ hours of Mt Cook. There are great climbing, tramping, boating and fishing opportunities this area.

The historic area and blue penguin viewing are just minutes away, as are the many restaurants and cafés in the town.

Highway House

43 Lynn Street, Oamaru
Ph/Fax (03) 437 1066
Mobile 027-200 2976
email: *cns@ihug.co.nz*
www.highwayhouse.co.nz

Features & Attractions

- *Historic Oamaru (stone)*
- *Harbour and blue penguins*
- *Idyllic rural scenery*
- *Free internet/email access*
- *English home/courtesy car*
- *French also spoken*

$		
	Double	$120-140
	Single	$100-120
	Child	neg

Boutique Bed & Breakfast

Bedrooms	Qty
Double	2
Twin	1
Single	
Bed Size	**Qty**
King	2
Queen	
Double	
Single	2
Bathrooms	**Qty**
Ensuite	
Guest Share	1
Family Share	1

Highway House offers a very convenient location for the many attractions and dining facilities in Oamaru. It is easy to find from both the north and south (see map). This 1935 Arts and crafts character house and garden have been redeveloped with professional interior design and horticultural expertise for the tourists' pleasure, comfort and convenience. Attention has been given to top-quality beds, large showers, internet access, garden seating and off-street parking, together with tasteful extras. We provide a cooked and/or a light Kiwi breakfast using appetizing and sustaining wholesome ingredients. Stephanie and Norman wish you to make the most of your stay in Oamaru and can assist with your travel plans.

A recent comment: *"Great hospitality and breakfast. A credit to tourism in NZ, Thanks"* Auckland.

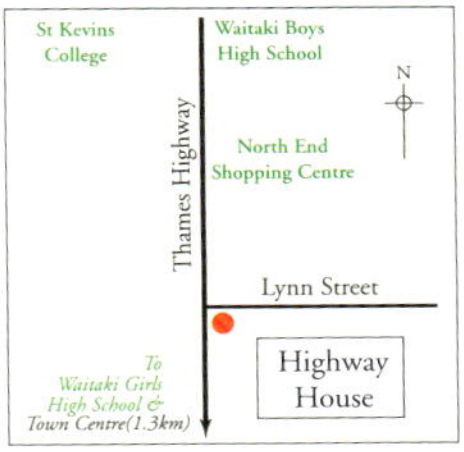

Homestead 271

271 Homestead Road, Oamaru
Ph (03) 434 2610, Fax (03) 434 2610
email: *office@globalife.co.nz*
www.globalife.co.nz

Features & Attractions

- *Countrystay on 15 acres*
- *Healthy Japanese cuisine*
- *Fantastic views*
- *Organic vegetable garden*
- *Spacious living room*
- *6 min. from town*

$		
	Double	$160-170
	Single	$120
	Child	

Countrystay Bed & Breakfast

Bedrooms	Qty
Double	1
Twin	1
Single	1
Bed Size	**Qty**
King	
Queen	1
King/Single	1
Single	1
Bathrooms	**Qty**
Ensuite	
Guest Share	1
Family Share	1

Japanese hosts, Kazuyo and Seiji operated Japanese food bars in Christchurch. Kazuyo is not only a Japanese chef but also takes cooking classes in Oamaru with the emphasis on health and diet. **Homestead 271** is situated on 15 acres of land with sheep, cattle and an organic vegetable garden. It has fantastic panoramic views of the mountains. You will enjoy a relaxing countrystay with healthy Japanese cuisine – different. It's great! The hosts speak English. In the morning you are served a full breakfast, Western style. By request we can also provide a Japanese-style, full course dinner for $50pp. Most vegetables are from our organic home garden. Booking by the previous day is essential. No credit cards accepted.

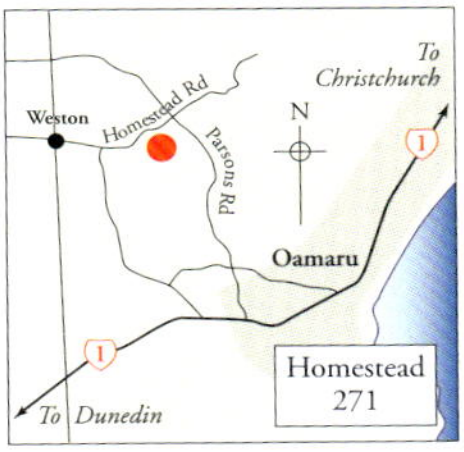

RANUI RETREAT

27 Woolshed Road, 8D RD, Totara, Oamaru
Ph (03) 439 5241
email: *happy1@actrix.gen.nz*
www.ranui-retreat.co.nz

Tariff : N.Z. Dollars	
Double	$125-160
Single	$100
Child	neg

Bedrooms	Qty
Double	2
Twin	
Single	
Bed Size	**Qty**
Super King	
King	
Queen	2
Double	
Single	
Bathrooms	**Qty**
Ensuite	1
Private	1
Guest Share	1

Bed & Breakfast
Homestay

Features & Attractions

- *Quiet surroundings*
- *Friendly hospitality*
- *Comfortable, warm rooms*
- *1½ hours to skifield*
- *Arts & craft pursuits*
- *Dinner by arrangement*
- *Local & organic food*
- *Close to golf courses*

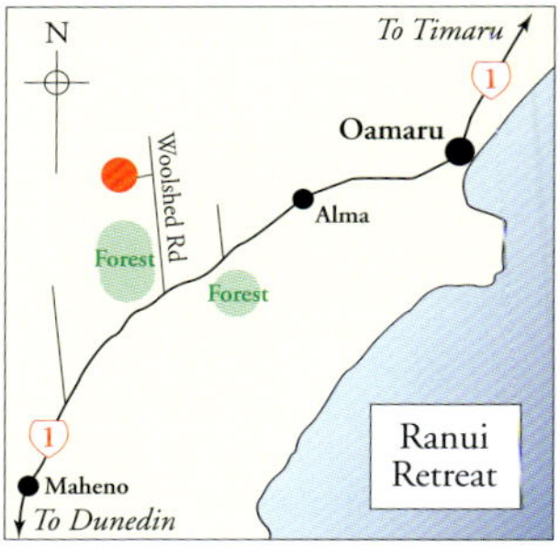

DIRECTIONS: Woolshed Road is off SH 1, second driveway on left.

Welcome to **Ranui Retreat**. We are eight minutes south of historic Oamaru and 200m off the main highway to Dunedin. Views of Otago rural landscape stretching to the Kakanui Mountains enhance the rural sense of this five acre property of mature oak, elm and ash trees.

The land was originally part of the nearby Totara Estate. The garden is planted out in native and exotic trees, shrubs and a newly established olive grove. There is birdsong aplenty. Character bedrooms include rich, handmade patchwork quilts and throws of unique design, which add to the relaxed ambience. You are welcome to join the family for the evening or you may like to retire to other spaces with music and a good book from our library selection.

CREEK FARM COTTAGE

387 Whartons Road, Maheno, Oamaru, North Otago
Ph (03) 439 5170, Mobile 021-1341 767
email: *marcusanddawn@xtra.co.nz*
www.creekfarmcottage.co.nz

Features & Attractions

- *Rural tranquility on 13 acres*
- *Local and organic food*
- *Trout fishing on the Waitaki*
- *Home baking*
- *Historic area and penguins*
- *Families welcome*

$	
Double	$86
Single	$86
Child	$20

Rural Bed & Breakfast

Bedrooms	Qty
Double	1
Twin	
Single	
Bed Size	**Qty**
King	
Queen	1
Double	
Single	2
Bathrooms	**Qty**
Ensuite	1
Private	
Guest Share	

DIRECTIONS: At Maheno turn into Kakanui Valley Road, follow this road until Whartons Road, turn left and Creek Farm is at the bottom of a steep hill on the left, about 8 km from Maheno.

Creek Farm a small holding of 5.41 hectares, with beef stock, 'chooks', lambs, and other pets, situated in North Otago, south of Oamaru. The **Cottage** offers a private, relaxing atmosphere, in a rural setting, yet not too far from Oamaru with its Victorian history, good restaurants and cafés, plus the blue and yellow-eyed penguins. Guests are invited to share our large garden with its lovely views and tranquility. Have a tour around the farm and see the animals. Homemade baking greets you on arrival. The **Cottage** is self-contained with a lounge/dining area, private shower room and small kitchen. Cooked breakfast is served in the farmhouse kitchen overlooking the garden. Continental breakfast can be served in the **Cottage** or in the main house. Stay a while and enjoy the wonderful sites within the Waitaki District and surrounding areas. Families most welcome and reduced rates are offered for children and longer stays.

GLEN DENDRON FARMSTAY

284 Breakneck Rd, Waianakarua, RD Oamaru
Ph (03) 439 5288, Fax (03) 439 5288
Mobile 021-615 227
email: *anne.john.mackay@xtra.co.nz*
www.glenhomestays.co.nz

Features & Attractions

- *5 acres garden & views*
- *Feed sheep & alpacas*
- *Private golf course*
- *Bush walks, birds, waterfalls*
- *Penguin & seal colonies*
- *Moeraki Boulders nearby*

$	
Double	$130-160
Single	$90-110
Child	$45

Award-winning Farmstay With Spectacular Views

Bedrooms	Qty
Double	4
Twin	
Single	
Bed Size	**Qty**
SuperKing/Twin	2
Queen	2
Double	
Single	
Bathrooms	**Qty**
Ensuite	2
Private	
Guest Share	1

DIRECTIONS: Please phone for directions.

Our modern, award-winning homestay is spectacularly sited on a hilltop with panoramic river valley and ocean views. Enjoy tranquility and beauty when you stay in tastefully furnished bedrooms, two with ensuites. Explore the 5-acre garden and small farm. Feed sheep and alpacas, stroll through the forest or along the river, or play a round on our private 9-hole golf course. After a day of exploring the delights of the area, join us for a three-course dinner with wine. We are very keen gardeners.

After a lifetime in large-scale farming and forestry, before retiring to this 100 acre property, we now relish the opportunity to share our lifestyle with guests. Our adult family all live overseas so we travel frequently and have a great interest in other countries and cultures. An overnight stay is not enough to do justice to this area, so plan to stay a while! We don't mind short notice!

Waikouaiti - Dunedin

YOUR HOSTS: **Barbara and John Morgan** Ph (03) 465 7239

BOUTIQUE BED & BREAKFAST

107 Jefferis Road, Waikouaiti, East Otago
Ph (03) 465 7239, Fax (03) 465 7239
Mobile 027-224 8212
email: *info@boutiquebedandbreakfast.co.nz*
www.boutiquebedandbreakfast.co.nz

Features & Attractions

- *Ideal setting to relax*
- *Situated on deer farm*
- *30 min. north of Dunedin*
- *4 hrs. to Christchurch*
- *Close to 2 golf courses*
- *NZ's oldest farm buildings*

Farmstay
Self-contained

	Price
Double	$130-180
Single	$100-120
Child	

The uniqueness of **Boutique Bed & Breakfast** is its tranquil ambience, situated amongst picturesque Otago countryside where the beauty of nature blends with exceptional hospitality to offer you a truly memorable experience. This charming historic cottage with its completely rebuilt interior, contains 3 luxury units. Each room has private entrance, bathroom and kitchen facilities, quality furnishings, linen, fresh baking and coffee on arrival, fruit bowl, tennis court and BBQ. Enjoy a freshly baked breakfast, either in your room, on the verandah while watching deer graze, or in John and Barbara's homestead. Afterwards enjoy John's complimentary farm tour before strolling on the beautiful Waikouaiti Beach, or observe yellow eyed penguins, seals and birds at Tavora Reserve. Visit historic buildings, local shops, cafés or the Moeraki Boulders.

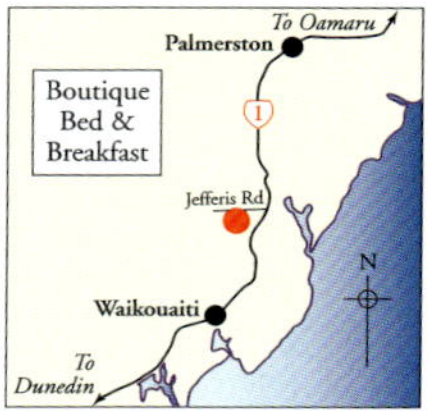

Bedrooms	Qty
Double	3
Twin	
Single	
Bed Size	**Qty**
King	
Queen	3
Double	
Single	
Bathrooms	**Qty**
Ensuite	3
Private	
Guest Share	

St Leonards - Dunedin

YOUR HOSTS: **Shirley and Don Parsons** Ph: (03) 471 0690

HARBOURSIDE BED & BREAKFAST

6 Kiwi Street, St Leonards, Dunedin
Ph (03) 471 0690, Fax (03) 471 0063
email: *harboursidebb@xtra.co.nz*

Features & Attractions

- *7 minutes to city centre*
- *Overlooking harbour*
- *Children welcome*
- *Complimentary tea on arrival*
- *Home baking*
- *Dinner by arrangement*

	Price
Double	$80-95
Single	$60-95
Child	$20

Bed & Breakfast Homestay
Spectacular Harbour Views

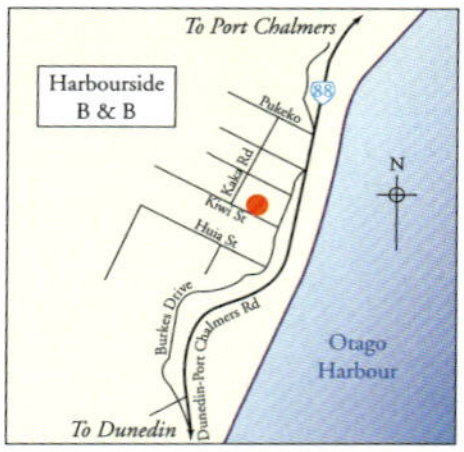

We are situated in a quiet suburb overlooking Otago Harbour and surrounding hills. Handy to all local attractions - Larnach Castle, Olveston, Royal Albatross and Yellow Eyed Penguin colonies, harbour cruises, Taieri Gorge Excursion train. Bookings can be arranged. There are many lovely bush walks close to the city. Children are very welcome (lots of preloved toys). We have a generous amount of living space for you to relax in after a busy day. Cooked breakfast is included and with a little notice, we can arrange a three course meal. Courtesy pick-up from bus or train.

Bedrooms	Qty
Double	3
Twin	1
Single	
Bed Size	**Qty**
King	1
Queen	2
Double	
Single	3
Bathrooms	**Qty**
Ensuite	1
Private	
Guest Share	1

DIRECTIONS: On Northern Motorway turn left towards Port Chalmers (SH 88) from Anzac Avenue onto Ravensbourne Road. After 5km at St Leonards turn left into Moa Street, left into Kaka Rpad, straight ahead to Kiwi Street, turn left to No 6

ATANUI

378 Heywards Point, No 1 RD,
Port Chalmers, Dunedin
Ph (03) 482 1107, Fax (03) 482 1107
email: *atanui@actrix.gen.nz*

Tariff : N.Z. Dollars	
Double	$100-120
Single	$80-100
Child	$40

Bedrooms	Qty
Double	1
Twin	1
Single	
Bed Size	**Qty**
Super King Twin	1
King	
Queen	1
Double	
Single	
Bathrooms	**Qty**
Ensuite	1
Private	1
Guest Share	

Farmstay with a spectacular view

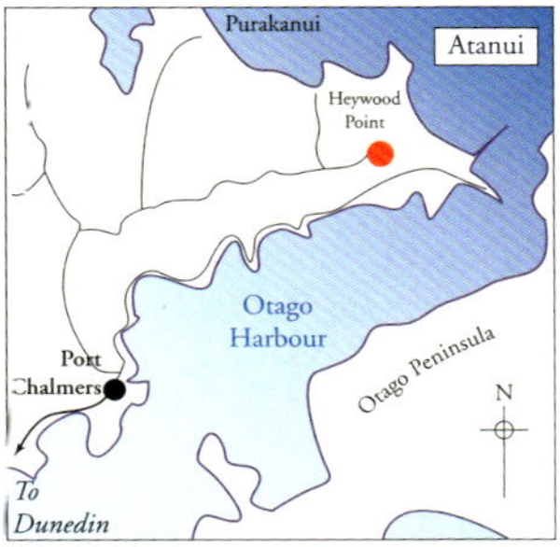

DIRECTIONS:
From north turn left at Waitati, follow sign to Port Chalmers till crossroads. Turn left (No Exit) on to next junction take Heywards Point Road (metal road) 4km on right. From south down to Port Chalmers Highway 88, follow sign up the hill to Long Beach till Heyward Point Road (metal road) 4km on right.

Features & Attractions

- *Walking tracks and beaches*
- *Pet animals and spa*
- *30 minutes from Dunedin*
- *Spa bath*
- *Spectacular views*
- *Quiet and relaxing*
- *Dinner by arrangement. $25 per person*

We welcome you to our spacious renovated stone house, in a peaceful rural setting only 30 minutes from Dunedin. From our home, which is heated throughout with radiators off the rayburn range, you can enjoy sweeping 220° views of the Otago Harbour, Otago Peninsula and the Pacific Ocean. Relax in the spa pool or feed our animals – emus, alpaccas, peacocks, pig and pet sheep.
Walking tracks and beaches are close by. Morning and afternoon teas with home baking are complimentary. Three course farm style meals are available by prior arrangement. We invite you to experience our hospitality and meet our cats Honey, Penny and Meg. You will love the unique awe inspiring setting of our farm and take back home lovely memories of this truly special place.

Leithview

234 Malvern Street, Leith Valley, Dunedin
Ph (03) 467 9944
Mobile 027-490 7117
email: *lvconstruction@xtra.co.nz*
www.leithview.com

Tariff : N.Z. Dollars	
Double	$150-180
Single	neg.
Child	neg.

Bedrooms	Qty
Double	3
Twin	
Single	1
Bed Size	**Qty**
Super King	
King	1
Queen	2
Double	
Single	1
Bathrooms	**Qty**
Ensuite	1
Private	
Guest Share	1

Country Living
Close to Town

Features & Attractions

- *Private native bush walk*
- *Large rambling gardens*
- *Five min. from town*
- *Home fed by spring water*
- *Peaceful location*
- *Prolific birdlife*
- *Glow-worm grotto nearby*
- *Spa pool under the stars*

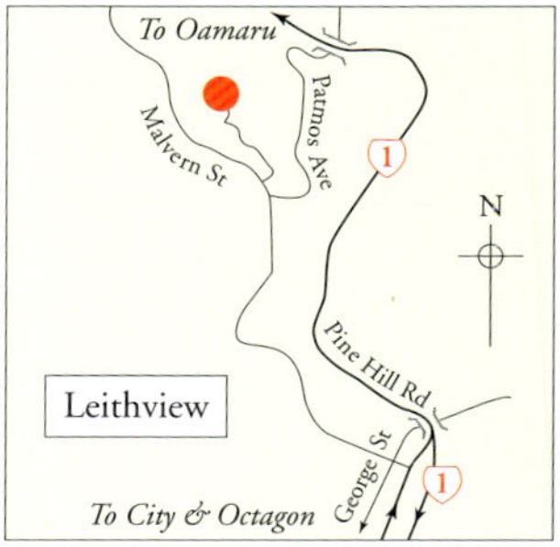

Marja and Peter would like to welcome you to **Leithview**, a 40 acre lifestyle property only four minutes from the centre of Dunedin. Our two-year-old home is nestled on the northern slopes of the Leith Valley.

All the bedrooms have a northerly aspect and their own private decks looking out over extensive gardens and native bush, including 200-year-old rimus and totaras. Stroll around the property amongst sheep and cattle, and then relax in our outdoor spa pool. The room rate includes a generous continental or cooked breakfast and evening meals are available on request.

Should you wish to renew contact with the hustle and bustle, we have the internet available and there is a bus stop at the bottom of our 500m driveway.

DIRECTIONS: Once you reach our letterbox, follow the gravel drive for 500m past the **Leithview** sign up the hill.

526 George Street

526 George Street, PO Box 112, Dunedin
Free Ph: 0800 779 779
Phone (03) 477 1261, Fax (03) 477 1268
email: info@hotel526.co.nz
www.hotel526.co.nz

Tariff : N.Z. Dollars	
Double	$100-150
Single	$100-150
Child	

Bedrooms	Qty
Double	7
Twin/Double	7
Single	
Bed Size	**Qty**
Super King	
King	
Queen	14
Double	
Single	2
Bathrooms	**Qty**
Ensuite	14
Private	
Guest Share	

Guest House

Features & Attractions

- *Downtown grand residence*
- *Adjacent university*
- *Adjacent museum*
- *Close to hospital*
- *Next to main shopping*
- *Disabled facilities*
- *Laundry, Internet access*
- *Full fire safety standard*

Welcome to **526 George Street**. This gracious residence was built in 1907 by Dunedin Hospital's surgeon Doctor Roberts as his grand family home. We are next to the City's retail shops and well over 50 restaurants and cafés on George Street. The property is on the flat, next to the National Archives Library, across the road from Otago Museum, across the Museum Reserve to the University of Otago and less than 400 metres from the hospital.

Our house is particularly suited for guests who have a link with any of the tertiary institutions and the hospital. The disabled access and facilities enable ease of use for a wheel chair around the spacious ground floor and lovely grounds. Suites range from doubles to large family rooms, enabling the house to cater for many accommodation needs. The house is a drop off/pick up point for sightseeing tours. Tours include wildlife - Albatross, Yellow Eyed Penguin, as well as Larnach's Castle and City Sights tours.

ALBATROSS INN

770 George Street, Dunedin
Ph (03) 477 2727, Fax (03) 477 2108
email: *albatross.inn@xtra.co.nz*
www.albatross.inn.co.nz

Tariff : N.Z. Dollars	
Double	$100-160
Single	$85-100
Child	

Bedrooms	Qty
Double	8
Twin	7
Single	8
Bed Size	**Qty**
Super King	
King	2
Queen	4
Double	2
Single	8
Bathrooms	**Qty**
Ensuite	8
Private	
Guest Share	

Quality Bed & Breakfast Guesthouse

Features & Attractions

- *Built early 1900's*
- *Main street of Dunedin*
- *All wildlife and city tours pick-up & drop-off here*
- *Open fire, off-street parking*
- *Free internet and email*
- *Close to restaurants, cafés, gardens, Olveston, Museum, University*

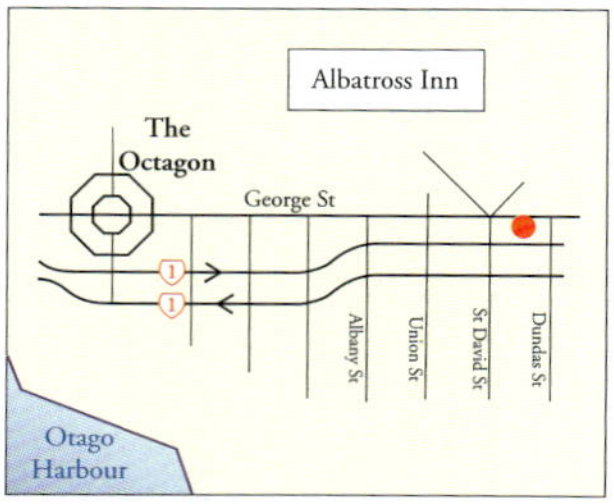

Welcome to Dunedin and Albatross Inn! Our beautiful late Victorian house is ideally located on the main street close to the university, gardens, museum, shops and restaurants.
Our attractive rooms have ensuite/private bathrooms, telephone, television, radio, tea/coffee, warm duvets and electric blankets on modern beds. Firm beds available upon request. Quiet rooms at the rear of the house. Several rooms have kitchenette and refrigerator. We serve freshly baked bread and muffins, fresh fruit salad, yoghurt, juices, cereals, teas, freshly brewed coffee.
We are happy to recommend and book tours for you. All wildlife tours pick-up and drop-off here. We can recommend many great places to eat, most just a short walk down George Street. Nearby laundry, non-smoking, cot and highchair. Some comments from our visitors book: *"The right balance of everything location, breakfast and lovely room. Delightfully different. Absolutely fantastic as always. Home away from home. A touch of class. Perfecto!"* Winter special $75 double - special conditions apply. Complimentary email and internet access.

Dalmore Lodge

9 Falkirk Street, Dalmore, Dunedin
Ph (03) 473 6513, Fax (03) 473 6512
Mobile 027-287 1517
email: *bookings@dalmorelodge.co.nz*
www.dalmorelodge.co.nz

Tariff : N.Z. Dollars	
Double	$110-150
Single	$85-110
Child	neg

Bedrooms	Qty
Double	2
Twin	1
Single	1
Bed Size	**Qty**
Super King	
King	
Queen	2
King/Single	2
Single	2
Bathrooms	**Qty**
Ensuite	
Private	1
Guest Share	1

Homestay
Bed & Breakfast

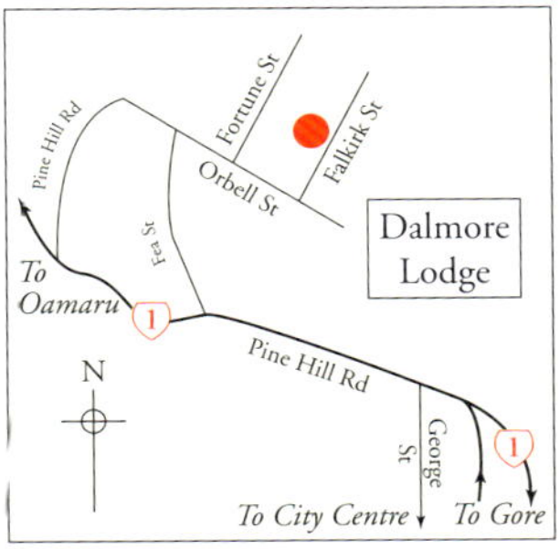

Features & Attractions

- *Peaceful atmosphere*
- *Magnificent views*
- *Yummy breakfast!!*
- *Fire safety standard*
- *Botanical Gardens nearby*
- *Close to shops & cafés*
- *Off-street parking*
- *Warm, friendly hospitality*

In its peaceful setting just two minutes off the Northern Motorway you'll find Dalmore Lodge. Our larchwood home offers spectacular views of harbour, Pacific Ocean, city lights, botanical gardens, hills, Otago Peninsula and rural areas. The balcony leads out onto a sheltered garden, where you can relax or just enjoy watching and listening to the native birds along with our (outside) cat Teagan.

The Queen/Family Room offers own access and private television and tea making facilities. Guests pantry downstairs - includes refrigerator and microwave. Also a separate guest television lounge upstairs - available to enjoy tea/coffee and cookies. Public transport at gate. We are only a short distance from university, museum, Community Hospice, Knox and Aquinas Colleges, hospital, shopping area, botanical gardens and restaurants. Dunedin City Council Building Code Compliant - allowing accommodation for up to eight guests. We look forward to welcoming you into our "home away from home" and to sharing knowledge of Dunedin and local attractions.

Belmont House

227 York Place, Dunedin
Ph (03) 477 3713, Fax (03) 477 3712
Mobile 027-477 0165
email: *enquiries@belmonthouse.co.nz*
www.belmonthouse.co.nz

Tariff : N.Z. Dollars	
Double	$225-280
Single	$160-250
Child	

Bedrooms	Qty
Double	3
Twin	
Single	

Bed Size	Qty
Super King	
King	1
Queen	2
Double	
Single	

Bathrooms	Qty
Ensuite	2
Private	1
Guest Share	

Luxury Accommodation
Heritage House

Belmont House

Features & Attractions

- *Centrally located*
- *Beautifully appointed rooms*
- *Full breakfast*
- *Quiet and peaceful*
- *Elegant guest lounge*
- *Great views & atmosphere*
- *Five minutes to Octagon*
- *Personalised service*

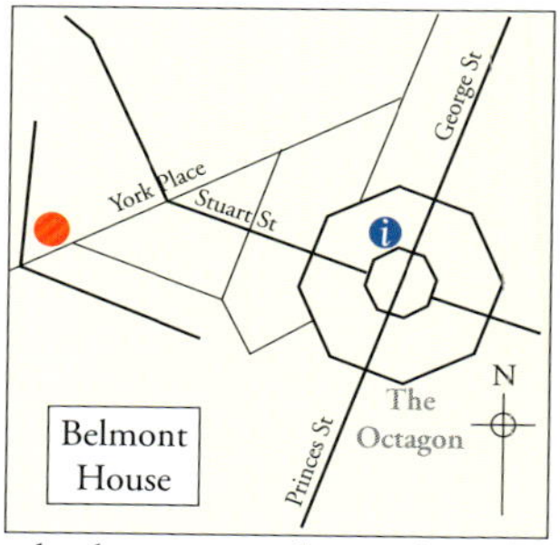

A short stroll from the city centre, **Belmont House** is situated on the city rise and affords grand views of the city, harbour and peninsula. Three spacious, well-appointed bedrooms, two ensuite and one private bathroom, are located on the upper floor. The rooms feature king or queen size beds, warm duvets, feather pillows, electric blankets, clock radios and heating. Fresh seasonal fruit, chocolates, magazines, books, fresh flowers, sparkling mineral water and bathrobes are also provided. Start the day with your choice of breakfast, served in the formal dining room. A selection of teas, fresh coffee and home-made biscuits are available anytime. The elegant guest lounge with city views is a relaxing and peaceful retreat at any time of the day. Curl up in a chair and relax with a selection of interesting books and magazines. A sound system, piano and television are at your disposal. **Belmont House** provides a quiet haven close to the vibrant city restaurants and attractions.

Advance booking recommended.

Barnett Lodge

34 Alva Street, Mornington, Dunedin
Ph (03) 477 9413,
Mobile 027-432 0350
email: *enquiries@barnett.co.nz*
www.barnett.co.nz

Tariff : N.Z. Dollars	
Double	$220-250
Single	$190-220
Child	$25

Bedrooms	Qty
Double	6
Twin	3
Single	4
Bed Size	**Qty**
Super King	3
King	
Queen	3
Double	
Single	6
Bathrooms	**Qty**
Ensuite	3
Private	1
Family Share	

Boutique Bed & Breakfast

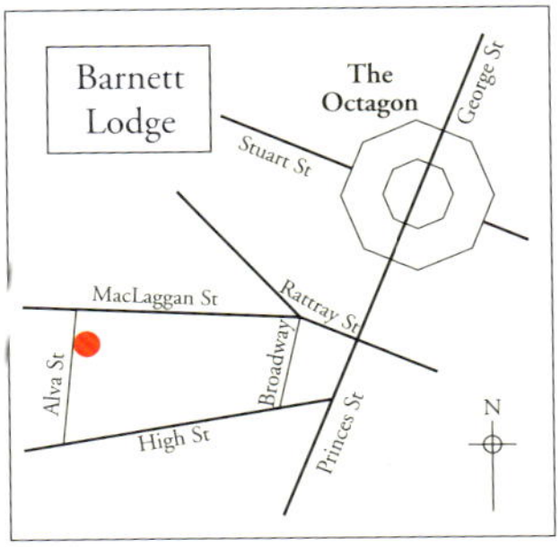

Features & Attractions

- *Warm and personable hosts*
- *Refreshments on arrival*
- *Local itinerary advice*
- *Excellent full breakfast*
- *Children welcome*
- *Complimentary laundry bag*
- *Easy walk to city centre*
- *Beside bush and parkland*

Barnett Lodge will appeal to travellers seeking accommodation at the quality upper end of the range.

The **Lodge** is a handsome Tudor residence built in 1938 for a wealthy businessman. It features original oak panelling, hand crafted beams and furniture in keeping with the Tudor style architecture in the reception area and lounge.

The dining room and 'den' make up the main floor. Upstairs, three suites - with excellent ensuites - are furnished with the highest quality beds and bedding, including luxury heated woolrest underlays. Each super-king bed can be split to twins if required.

The self-contained apartment below has two bedrooms - each accessing the ensuite directly - lounge and kitchen. Each lounge has a wonderful logburner.

We look forward to sharing your company.

Dunedin ▶ YOUR HOSTS: **Karen Jacquard and Paul Cardno** Ph (03) 474 5002

City Sanctuary Bed & Breakfast

165 Maitland Street, Dunedin
Ph 03-474 5002, Fax 03-474 5006
email:*charmingenquiry@citysanctuary.co.nz*
www.citysanctuary.co.nz

Features & Attractions

- *Inner city location*
- *Elegant, spacious rooms*
- *Quiet and peaceful*
- *Personalised service*
- *Special breakfast*
- *Free email & video library*

Inner City Oasis Bed & Breakfast

Double	$120-175
Single	$100-145
Child	neg

Welcome to our attractive, restored villa in an oasis of cottage gardens and large trees, yet only 1km to the city centre and all its attractions. Three lovely, spacious bedrooms each have: queen bed with fleecy electric blanket, fresh flowers, oil heater, phone, TV and internet connection. One ensuite with spa bath and shower, and two private bathrooms. Relax in the guest living room with home theatre (a small library of CD's, DVD's and videos) and free email, or quietly unwind on the deck amidst the organic potager garden. Enjoy a special continental breakfast that includes home-made bread, smoked salmon and cheese. Paul's funky art abounds and a professional massage is available from Karen by appointment. 4 cats in residence.

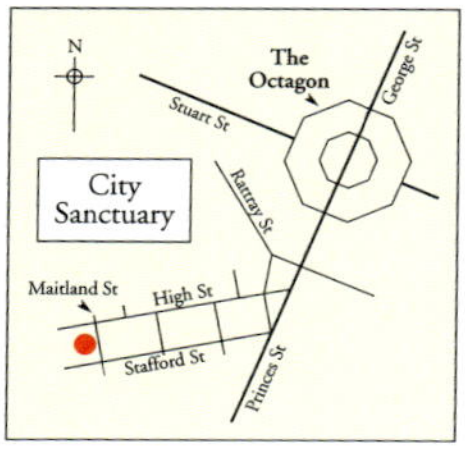

Bedrooms	Qty
Double	3
Twin	
Single	
Bed Size	**Qty**
King	
Queen	3
Double	
Single	
Bathrooms	**Qty**
Ensuite	1
Private	2
Guest Share	

Dunedin ▶ YOUR HOSTS: **Joanna Howie and Neil Sutherland** Free Ph: 0800 268 252

Deacons Court

342 High Street, Dunedin
Ph (03) 477 9053, Fax (03) 477 9058
email: *info@deaconscourt.com*
www.deaconscourt.com

Features & Attractions

- *Spacious bedrooms*
- *Private facilities*
- *Generous cooked breakfast*
- *Close to city centre*
- *Large rose garden*
- *Historical home*

Bed & Breakfast Guesthouse

Double	$100-150
Single	$80-120
Child	$20-30

Deacons Court is a charming, spacious Victorian villa 1km walking distance from the city centre and is on the city's heritage building register. We are only 500m from cafés, restaurants, bars and some of Dunedin's unique attractions and offer you friendly but unobtrusive hospitality in a quiet, secure haven. Guests can relax in our delightful rose garden and conservatory.

Our bedrooms are large and have ensuite or private bathrooms, heaters, TV and electric blankets. Complimentary 24 hour tea or coffee, free parking and laundry service available.

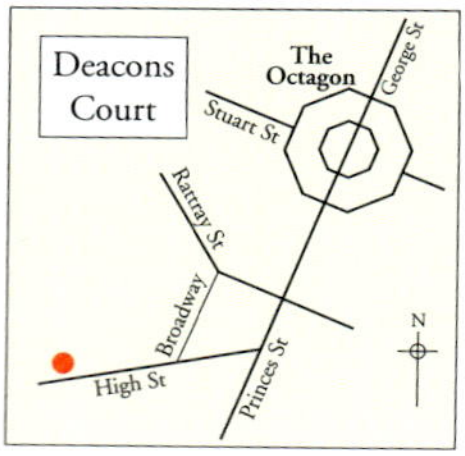

Bedrooms	Qty
Double/Twin	3
Twin	
Single	
Bed Size	**Qty**
King	1
Queen	2
Double	
Single	3
Bathrooms	**Qty**
Ensuite	2
Private	1
Guest Share	

Heriot House

26 Pitt Street, Dunedin
Ph (03) 477 7228,
Mobile 027-245 7719
email: *lcalvert@es.co.nz*

Tariff : N.Z. Dollars	
Double	$120-180
Single	
Child	neg

Bedrooms	Qty
Double	3
Twin	
Single	
Bed Size	**Qty**
Super King	
King	
Queen	3
Double	
Single	
Bathrooms	**Qty**
Ensuite	1
Private	1
Guest Share	1

Elegant Bed & Breakfast Accommodation

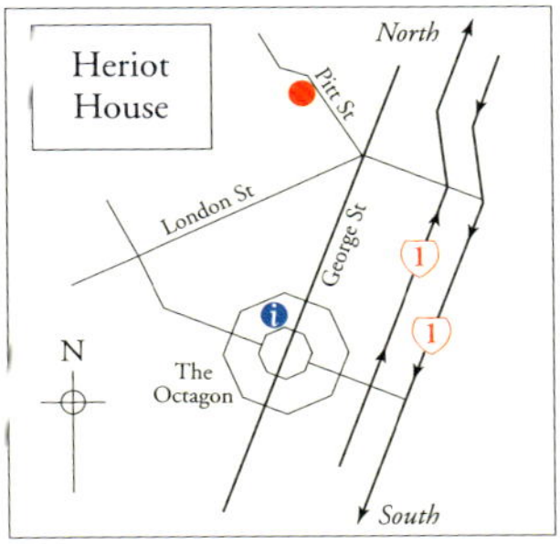

DIRECTIONS:
Travelling south on George Street turn sharp right at Knox Church into Pitt Street

Features & Attractions

- *Centrally located*
- *3 minutes stroll to cafés, bars and restaurants*
- *Off-street parking*
- *Quaint cottage garden*
- *Gracious Edwardian home*
- *Friendly, helpful hostess*
- *Sumptuous breakfast*

Louise welcomes you to stay in her gracious old home situated right in the heart of Dunedin.

Only a casual stroll to shops and the local restaurants, bars and cafés. The quaint cottage garden has a pleasant charm that will draw you out of doors to inspect the treasures hidden from view.

All guest rooms are on the second floor with an area set aside in each room for those who prefer to relax in private. There is also a separate television room and a sitting room available for those who want a coffee and to chat.

You are sure of a warm, friendly and comfortable stay at **Heriot House**.

Dunedin ▶ YOUR HOSTS: **Steve and Ann** Free Ph: 0800 749 472

GRANDVIEW

360 High Street, Dunedin
Ph (03) 474 9472, Fax (03) 474 9473
Mobile 021-101 9857
email: *nzgrandview@msn.com*
www.grandview.co.nz

Features & Attractions

- *City & casino a short stroll!*
- *Free internet & video library*
- *Complimentary laundry use!*
- *Huge deck/viewing platform*
- *Hot spa tub - great view!*
- *Sky television*

Bed & Breakfast
Guest House

$		
	Double	$90-185
	Single	$70-125
	Child	$20 u/15

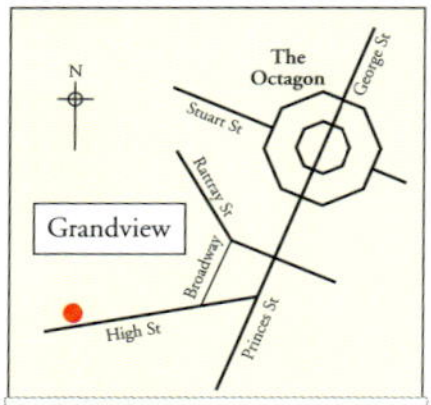

DIRECTIONS: Corner of High & Grant Sts - 400 mtrs up High St from the Casino on the right

Grandview is centrally located yet offers some of Dunedin's grandest views! The casino, restaurants, shops, cafés and bars are only a short srtoll away! Relax in luxury in this charming 1901 heritage listed "Edwardian mansion". Featuring magnificent panoramic views from our viewing platforms and hot spa! Tourist information and holiday planning, **Big** screen movie lounge, videos, SKY TV, **Fast** Internet, laundry facilities and scrumptious continental breakfasts are all a complementary part of the **Grandview** experience. Rooms to suit all budgets! From $70(Basic)to our luxury trendy spa suites for that "special escape" it's all here at **Grandview**. We strive to make your stay with us a time to remember and look forward to sharing our home with you!

Bedrooms	Qty
Double	7
Twin	3
Single	7
Bed Size	**Qty**
King	1
Queen	6
Double	
Single	4
Bathrooms	**Qty**
Ensuite	2
Private	1
Guest Share	2

Dunedin ▶ YOUR HOST: **Amy Ritchie** Ph (03) 487 7812

TIGGAS RETREAT

36 Sidey St, Calton Hill, Dunedin
Ph (03) 487 7812
Mobile 021-376 399
e-mail: *tiggersretreat@ihug.co.nz*
www.tiggasretreat.co.nz

Features & Attractions

- *Panoramic views city & harbour*
- *Close to all attractions*
- *Continental breakfast included*
- *Quiet, affordable comfort*
- *In-room tea/coffee, TV*
- *4 guests maximum*

Bed & Breakfast
Homestay

$		
	Double	$80-90
	Single	$70-90
	Child	neg

Affordable, warm, friendly southern hospitality awaits you at **Tiggas Retreat**, a 1920's-style arts and crafts home, nestled in a lovely garden on sunny Calton Hill. **Tiggas Retreat** enjoys glorious panoramic views from sunny, upstairs porch of Otago Harbour and Dunedin City.
Rebuilt in 2004, tastefully decorated **Retreat Suite** offers spacious guest lounge and separate bedroom tea/coffee lunch making facilities and microwave. Upstairs, enjoy your own private shower and separate toilet with soft bathrobes and towels supplied. Guest room beds, adorned in quality linen/electric blanket, offer a restful night's sleep, or snuggle up and watch TV! **Tiggas Room** captures morning sun, gorgeous views and lovely décor, with shared bathroom. Sumptuous continental breakfast (included in the tariff) is served in host dining room. Fabulous restaurants, city shopping, museums and art galleries, beautiful beaches and walkways all a few minutes drive. Beautiful Otago Peninsula –wildlife tours, harbour cruises. Airport 20 minutes drive.

Bedrooms	Qty
Double	2
Twin	
Single	
Bed Size	**Qty**
King	
Queen	2
Double	
Single	
Bathrooms	**Qty**
Ensuite	
Private	1
Guest Share	1

HULMES COURT BED & BREAKFAST

52 Tennyson Street, Dunedin, Otago
Ph (03) 477 5319, Fax (03) 477 5310
Mobile 027-435 1075
email: *reservations@hulmes.co.nz*
www.hulmes.co.nz

Tariff : N.Z. Dollars	
Double	$100-165
Single	$70-100
Child	enquire

Bedrooms	Qty
Double	8
Twin	4
Single	1
Bed Size	**Qty**
Super King	
King	3
Queen	10
Double	
Single	4
Bathrooms	**Qty**
Ensuite	8
Private	
Guest Share	3

Bed & Breakfast

Features & Attractions

- *Historic: built early 1860's*
- *Right in centre of Dunedin*
- *Off-street parking*
- *Complimentary laundry*
- *Young, friendly, intelligent staff*
- *Soltice, the cool cat*
- *Complimentary mountain bikes and Internet access*

Hulmes Court Bed & Breakfast is two beautiful homes only a few minutes walk from the heart of town and the Visitor Centre. Tennyson Street is quiet and we have private gardens, trees, decks and sitting areas. The **Victorian Hulmes Court** is one of the most historic homes in Dunedin. It was built in the 1860s by the first provincial surgeon Edward Hulme who helped found the Medical School. **Hulmes Too** is a large Edwardian home built next to **Hulmes Court** on the grounds of the original estate. **Hulmes Court** has a variety of rooms which cater for all tastes from the economical cute single Rose Room at $70 per night to our grand ensuite rooms in **Hulmes Too** at $165 per night. Your host Norman owns a variety of businesses and is interested in history, philosophy, geography and has stood for parliament twice. At the same time Norman at 40 and his staff are youthful, full of energy and travel widely. We provide complimentary laundry, internet and email, barbeque, mountain bikes and off-street parking.

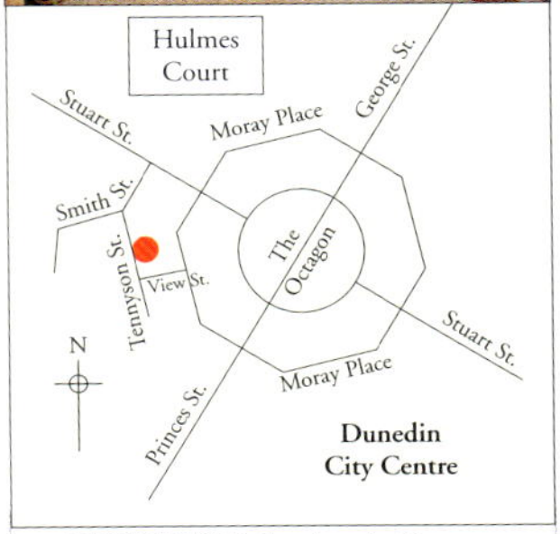

DIRECTIONS: Leaving the Octagon by Upper Stuart Street, take the 2nd turning on the left into Smith Street, then just 50m left again into Tennyson Street.

The Tower House

9 City Road, Roslyn, Dunedin
Ph (03) 477 5678, Mobile 021-347 287
email: *bnb@thetowerhouse.co.nz*
www.thetowerhouse.co.nz

Tariff : N.Z. Dollars	
Double	$110-140
Single	$80
Child	

Bedrooms	Qty
Double	2
Twin	1
Single	1
Bed Size	**Qty**
Super King	
King	
Queen	2
King/Single	1
Single	2
Bathrooms	**Qty**
Ensuite	2
Private	
Guest Share	1

Bed & Breakfast Guesthouse

Features & Attractions

- *Centrally located*
- *Restaurants nearby*
- *Smoke free inside*
- *Swimming pool nearby*
- *Wonderful views*
- *Friendly hospitality*
- *Delicious full breakfast*
- *Guest lounge & open fire*

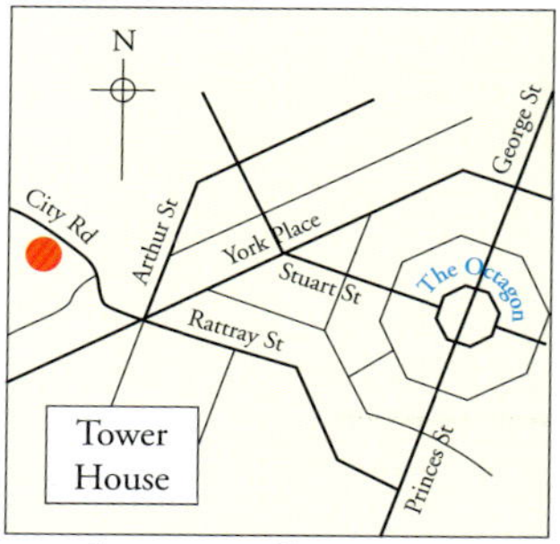

The Tower House offers visitors a magnificent panorama of Dunedin City and its beautiful natural harbour. It is ideally located, being close to the city and within walking distance of Roslyn Village and its pleasant restaurants. A ten minute down hill walk takes you to the city centre with its wide range of bars, cafés and restaurants. **The Tower House** has been designed for our guests to completely relax. Bedrooms are warm and comfortable with restful décor. The two double rooms have french doors opening onto a balcony where you can enjoy panoramic city views over a leisurely cup of tea or coffee. The morning newspaper is complimentary. All rooms have tea and coffee making facilities and televisions. Two rooms have ensuites and the others have a shared bathroom with an original claw footed bath. There is a guests' lounge with television and an interesting range of books and magazines. The lounge leads into a pleasant dining room where the full cooked breakfast, included in the tariff, is served.

Alloway

65 Every Street, Dunedin
Ph (03) 454 5384, Fax (03) 454 5364
email: *alloway@xtra.co.nz*
www.alloway.co.nz

Tariff : N.Z. Dollars	
Double	$180-200
Single	$175-195
Child	neg

Bedrooms	Qty
Double	1
Twin	
Single	
Bed Size	**Qty**
Super King	
King	
Queen	1
Double	
Single	1
Bathrooms	**Qty**
Ensuite	
Private	1
Guest Share	

Homestay - Bed & Breakfast

DIRECTIONS:
From Highcliff Road (the Peninsula high road to Larnach Castle) turn left into Every Street.

Features & Attractions

- *Wildlife, Walking Tracks*
- *Taiaroa Head, Albatross Colony*
- *Disappearing Gun, Seal Colonies*
- *Rhododendrons*
- *Yellow-eyed Penguins*
- *Glenfalloch Gardens*
- *7 min. to Dunedin City*
- *Great Architecture*

We are situated on the gateway to the Otago Peninsula, which features wildlife, walking tracks, Taiaroa Head, Albatross Colony, Disappearing Gun, Seal Colonies, Yellow-eyed Penguins, Glenfalloch Gardens and much more. We are seven minutes from the town centre. Our home is a modern interpretation of a traditional Scottish house and set in one acre of gardens and lawns, with indoor/outdoor living. Awaken to the sound of abundant bird-life in a quiet and secure neighbourhood. We serve delicious, healthy breakfasts. One luxury bedroom complete with one queen and one single bed, plus one luxury bedroom with one queen and one single bed. All rooms have tea making facilities, television, heaters, electric blankets. Separate facilities with modern guest bathroom. Relax far from the madding crowd. Businesspeople welcome. All non smoking, no pets and not suitable for young children.

THE OLD MANSE

76 Every Street, Andersons Bay, Dunedin
Ph (03) 454 6212, Fax (03) 473 9553
Mobile 027-434 4788
email: *bill.jill@paradise.net.nz*
visit-dunedin.co.nz/OldManse.html

Tariff : N.Z. Dollars	
Double	$90-130
Single	$90-110
Child	neg

Bedrooms	Qty
Double	2
Twin	
Single	
Bed Size	**Qty**
Super King	
King	
Queen	2
Double	
King/Single	1
Bathrooms	**Qty**
Ensuite	
Private	2
Guest Share	

Bed & Breakfast in Historic Home
Panoramic Views

VISA MasterCard

Features & Attractions

- *7 min. to Dunedin City*
- *Restaurants nearby*
- *Spectacular views*
- *Warm, friendly environment*
- *Off-street parking*
- *Gateway to Otago Peninsula*
- *Close to city beaches*
- *Children welcome*

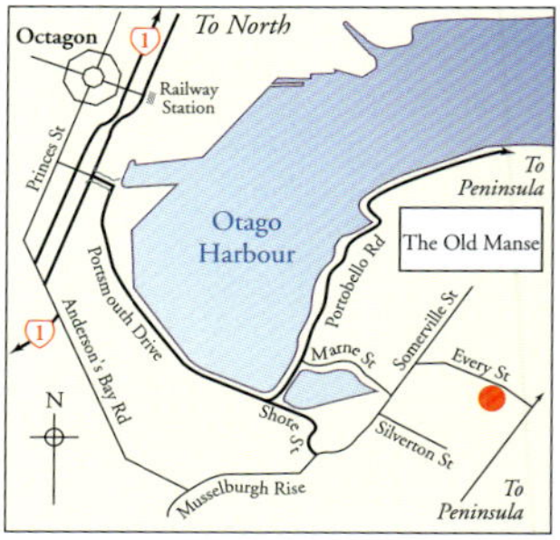

The Old Manse, name of the original homestead, was built in 1865 from kauri timber for the Andersons Bay Presbyterian church and sold into private ownership in 1901. The home was modernised in the 1980's, still maintaining its old-world grandeur, some kauri doors and the veranda posts.

Our convenient situation at the gateway to the Otago Peninsula enables guests to travel in a 'loop' to visit the wildlife attractions, yellow eyed penguins, seal and albatross colonies and the many walking tracks to pristine beaches.

Guest rooms and sitting room with TV, internet and a range of New Zealand literature, are private and comfortable with spectacular city, harbour and sea views.

Hosts have lived 20 years on the Otago Peninsula, enjoyed several overseas trips and will be happy sharing information to make the stay a memorable one.

Brynymor House

6, St Ronans Rd, The Cove, Dunedin
Ph (03) 476 1110
email: *brynymor@xtra.co.nz*
www.brynymorhouse.com

Tariff : N.Z. Dollars	
Double	$160-180
Single	$150-160
Child	

Bedrooms	Qty
Double	1
Twin	1
Single	
Bed Size	**Qty**
Super King	
King	
Queen	
Double	1
Single	2
Bathrooms	**Qty**
Ensuite	
Private	2
Guest Share	

**Bed & Breakfast
Luxury Accommodation**

Features & Attractions

- *Glorious 2.5 acre garden*
- *Panoramic harbour views*
- *Bellbirds and tuis*
- *Tranquil setting*
- *Private guest wing*
- *Sky TV and video library*
- *9 minutes to city centre*
- *Peninsula wildlife*

Brynymor House sits in a delightful 2½ acre garden in an idyllic harbourside setting. Whether on business or on holiday, treat yourself to a touch of luxury. You will enjoy relaxing on the verandah of our north facing colonial-style home overlooking the sea and mountains, or in the guest lounge or bedrooms, each of which enjoy panoramic marine views.

SKY TV, including all the sports channels, is available. The private bathrooms have heated floors and the bedrooms have electric blankets and individual heating. Coffee and tea making facilities, fresh fruit and snacks are provided and a choice of breakfast. The garden in our microclimate is yours to enjoy in all seasons of the year.

The Otago Peninsula attractions surround you and the city centre is only 9 minutes away. Take the sharp right turn before Glenfalloch Gardens into our pretty road, proceed to the top of the drive at the end where you will find our corner of paradise.

Pattons Hill

Rapid No 974, Highcliff Rd, RD 2, Dunedin
Ph (03) 476 1007, Fax (03) 476 1007
Mobile 027-436 3663
email: *rbhall@es.co.nz*

Features & Attractions

- *Tranquil & relaxed surroundings*
- *Magnificent harbour & ocean views*
- *Walking tracks & stunning beaches*
- *Close to cafés & restaurants*
- *Close to Dunedin City*
- *Vintage car enthusiasts*

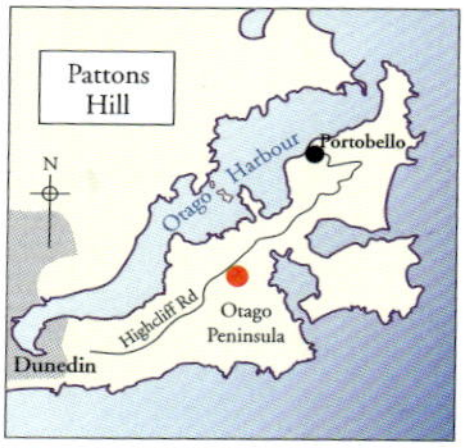

Bed & Breakfast Homestay

Double	$100
Single	$70
Child	neg

We welcome you to come and stay with us in our modern family home situated on a 30 acre farm block originally settled in the 1800s, and share with us country living on the beautiful Otago Peninsula. Handy to all Peninsula attractions including Larnach Castle, albatross, penguin and seal colonies and Taiaroa Head and Marine Aquarium. Enjoy magnificent views of Otago Harbour and Pacific Ocean and the ever-changing panoramic views from around the property. Guest rooms are located upstairs, all equipped with heating and electric blankets. Join us in the evening or if you prefer a quiet time, relax upstairs where there is a TV in the double bedroom. We serve continental or cooked breakfast. Children are very welcome. We have a strong family link with the Otago Peninsula and are most happy to share our knowledge and advise on local attractions.

Bedrooms	Qty
Double	1
Twin	1
Single	

Bed Size	Qty
King	
Queen	1
Double	
Single	2

Bathrooms	Qty
Ensuite	
Private	
Guest Share	1

Harbour Lights Homestay B&B

1 Wharfdale Street, Macandrew Bay, Dunedin
Ph (03) 476 1019, Fax (03) 476 1019
email: *harbourlights@actrix.co.nz*

Tariff : N.Z. Dollars	
Double	$100-125
Single	$75
Child	neg.

Bedrooms	Qty
Double	2
Twin	1
Single	1
Bed Size	**Qty**
Super King	
King	
Queen	2
Double	
Single	2
Bathrooms	**Qty**
Ensuite	1
Private	1
Guest Share	1

Homestay Bed & Breakfast

Features & Attractions

- *On beautiful Otago Peninsula*
- *Superb day & night harbour views*
- *Close to Dunedin City – 11km*
- *Taiaroa Head & Albatross Colony*
- *Yellow-eyed penguins & seals*
- *Armstrong Disappearing Gun*
- *Close to Glenfalloch Gardens*
- *Evening meals on request*

"What a view!" This is often the first remark of our guests upon arrival at **Harbour Lights Homestay**, but many have had a few pangs of regret at having to leave us. Many of our guests who have stayed here, now consider us as friends. We know how visitors feel upon arrival in unfamiliar surroundings, as our travels have taken us to many parts of the world. So please accept a warm Scottish welcome. The guest rooms are on the upper level to maintain our guests' privacy. All rooms are equipped with heating and electric blankets and include tea and coffee facilities. In the morning choose either continental or full cooked breakfast. Libby and Alex are looking forward to welcoming you to **Harbour Lights Homestay.**

CHY-AN-DOWR

687 Portobello Road, Broad Bay, Dunedin
Ph (03) 478 0306
Mobile 021-156 0715
email: *hermanvv@xtra.co.nz*
www.chy-an-dowr.co.nz

Tariff : N.Z. Dollars	
Double	$150-195
Single	
Child	

Bedrooms	Qty
Double	2
Twin	1
Single	
Bed Size	**Qty**
Super King	
King	1
Queen	1
King/Twin	1
Single	
Bathrooms	**Qty**
Ensuite	1
Private	1
Guest Share	

Boutique Accommodation
Bed & Breakfast

Features & Attractions

- *Panoramic harbour views*
- *Harbourside location*
- *Edwardian character home*
- *Dunedin - 20 minutes*
- *Albatross & penguins*
- *Great breakfast*
- *Dutch spoken*
- *Larnach Castle*

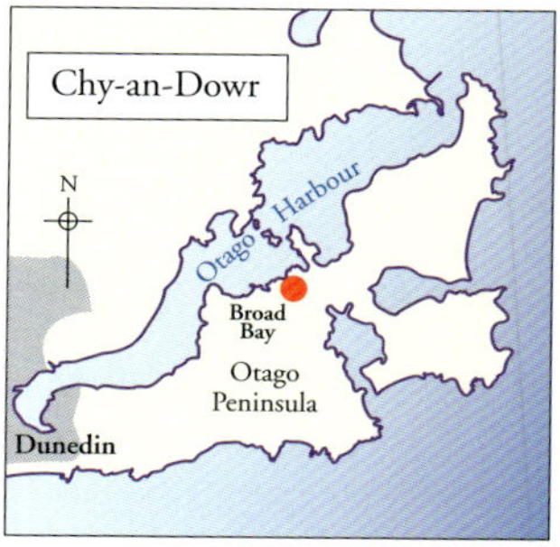

Chy-an-Dowr (House by the Water) is a quality B&B located on the scenic Otago Peninsula, halfway between Dunedin and the albatross & penguin colonies.

Our character 1920s home has panoramic harbour views and is situated opposite a small sandy beach. The upstairs guest area is spacious and private with comfortable rooms, bathrobes, tea/coffee, television, refrigerator, ensuite/private facilities and a sunroom with fabulous views. Enjoy a cooked/continental breakfast at your leisure.

Explore the Otago Peninsula with its many walkways and local arts and crafts. Originally from Holland, we enjoy welcoming people into our home and sharing our wonderful location with them.

DIRECTIONS:
Follow signs to Peninsula. We are a 20 min drive along Portobello Road from Dunedin. We are on the corner of Portobello Road & Clearwater Street in Broad Bay.

BROAD BAY WHITE HOUSE

11 Clearwater Street, Broad Bay, Dunedin
Ph (03) 478 1160, Fax (03) 478 1159
email: *broadbaywhitehouse@paradise.net.nz*
www.broadbaywhitehouse.co.nz

Tariff : N.Z. Dollars	
Double	$150-175
Single	$130
Child	

Bedrooms	Qty
Double	2
Twin	1
Single	
Bed Size	**Qty**
Super King	
King	
Queen	3
Double	
Single	1
Bathrooms	**Qty**
Ensuite	2
Private	1
Guest Share	

Luxury Accommodation
Spectacular Harbour Views

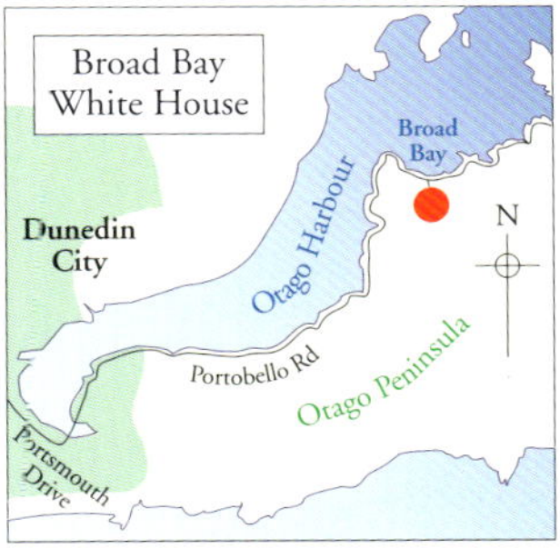

DIRECTIONS:
Follow the Peninsula signs from town along the south side of the harbour to Broad Bay. Take 1st turn right after the Broad Bay Boating Club. We are at the top of the street. Blue sign **'Broad Bay Whitehouse.'**

Features & Attractions

- *Tranquillity*
- *Spectacular harbour views*
- *'Superb food'*
- *Silver service*
- *Wildlife*
- *Penguins, seals, albatross*
- *Extensive gardens*
- *Friendly, knowledgeable*

Give yourself a taste of luxury with "superb food and hospitality", peace and quiet, privacy and panoramic views over the harbour. You can relax after a busy day sightseeing, take time to wander through our extensive gardens and enjoy the abundant bird life. Have a fun game of petanque (botchee), no experience of physical fitness required. Your bedroom will be spacious and has its own centrally heated bathroom. We use quality linen and bedding and also provide electric blankets. Waken to the morning song of native birds. All rooms have direct access to spacious decks with plenty of outside furniture for you to unwind with a glass of wine and complimentary cheese board or tea and coffee with cakes and biscuit.

Our semi-rural hideaway is located on the Otago Peninsula handy to the albatross, penguin and seal colonies, Larnach's Castle and other Peninsula attractions.

FANTAIL LODGE

682 Portobello Road, Broad Bay, Dunedin
Ph (03) 478 0110, Mobile 027-415 6222
email: *fantail.lodge@xtra.co.nz*
www.travelwise.co.nz

Tariff : N.Z. Dollars	
Double	$120-150
Single	
Extra pp	$25

Bedrooms	Qty
Double	2
Twin	
Single	
Bed Size	**Qty**
Super King	
King	
Queen	1
Double	1
Single	2
Bathrooms	**Qty**
Ensuite	2
Private	
Guest Share	

Harbourside Self-contained Cottages

Features & Attractions

- *Harbourside cottages*
- *Exclusive spa pool*
- *Albatross, seals, penguins*
- *Larnach Castle*
- *Romantic hideaway*
- *Lush garden setting*
- *Free use of kayaks*
- *Breakfast opt. extra*

DIRECTIONS:

From Dunedin take Portobello Rd along harbour towards Taiaroa Head. After 15 km (20 min) you will see Broad Bay Boating Club and jetty. Turn next right into Clearwater St and turn again hard right in front of two storey B&B house on corner. Straight on to #682.

Fantail Lodge offers self-contained cottage accommodation set in a lush harbourside garden. We are situated centrally on the Otago Peninsula, within easy reach of unspoiled beaches, albatross, seals and penguins. Relax on the verandah and enjoy the company of native birds. Walk to the local castle or paddle a kayak on the harbour. With so much to explore we recommend you stay for at least two nights and we offer a discount for longer stays. We are five minutes drive to the local store and restaurants and twenty minutes from Dunedin. The cottages are equipped for self-catering with an optional continental breakfast hamper for busy travellers. There are two unique cottages for you to choose from:

'Fantail Cottage' offers double bed accommodation with two singles on a mezzanine floor. Ideal for two, but comfortably sleeps four people.

'Bellbird Cottage' offers queen bed accommodation. Relax and enjoy the exclusive use of a spa pool under the stars. Perfect for a couple.

The Cottage

Broad Bay, Otago Peninsula, Dunedin
Ph (03) 476 1877, Fax (03) 476 1873
Mobile 027-228 3380
email: *thecottage@xtra.co.nz*

Tariff : N.Z. Dollars	
Double	$140-175
Single	
Child	

Bedrooms	Qty
Double	1
Twin	
Single	
Bed Size	**Qty**
Super King	
King	
Queen	1
Double	
Single	
Bathrooms	**Qty**
Ensuite	1
Private	
Guest Share	

Coastal Cottage
Bed & Breakfast

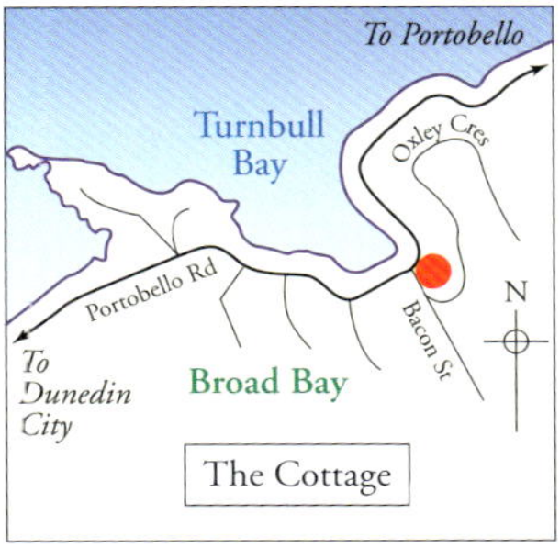

Features & Attractions

- *Olde-world charm*
- *Self-contained and private*
- *Optional hamper breakfast*
- *Sea views from verandah*
- *Close to wildlife*
- *Penguins, albatross & seals*
- *20 minutes from Dunedin*
- *Situated right by the water*

Whether you want to explore the wildlife of the Otago Peninsula with its great beaches and walkways, penguin, royal albatross and Seal colonies, harbour cruises and Larnach Castle or frequent the café scene, the galleries, the restaurants and city life of Dunedin, our **Cottage** is the ideal base for your adventures. Situated right by the water, this turn of the century fisherman's retreat is tucked among bush and trees with wonderful views of the harbour from the privacy of the verandah. **The Cottage** is full of old-world charm. It reflects the nostalgia of a bygone era whilst modern conveniences ensure a comfortable stay. The décor features the odd piece of original New Zealand art and numerous curiosities from yesteryear. Your hosts live nearby on the Peninsula. They are responsible for the scrumptious basket of ingredients for breakfast which is delivered to your cottage during the afternoon for the next morning. "If you spend only one night... you'll be sorry... A few days is best."(Grace Magazine).

THE LODGE - BROAD BAY

Broad Bay, Otago Peninsula, Dunedin
Ph (03) 476 1877, Fax (03) 476 1873
Mobile 027-228 3380
email: *julzandlutz@xtra.co.nz*

Tariff : N.Z. Dollars	
Double	$160-195
Single	
Child	

Bedrooms	Qty
Double	1
Twin	1
Single	
Bed Size	**Qty**
Super King	
King	
Queen	1
Double	
King/Single	2
Bathrooms	**Qty**
Ensuite	
Private	1
Guest Share	

Coastal Cottage
Bed & Breakfast

VISA MasterCard

Features & Attractions

- *Modern with warm ambience*
- *Self-contained and private*
- *Optional hamper breakfast*
- *Magnificent sea views*
- *Close to wildlife*
- *Penguins, albatross and seals*
- *20 mins from Dunedin*
- *Situated right by the water*

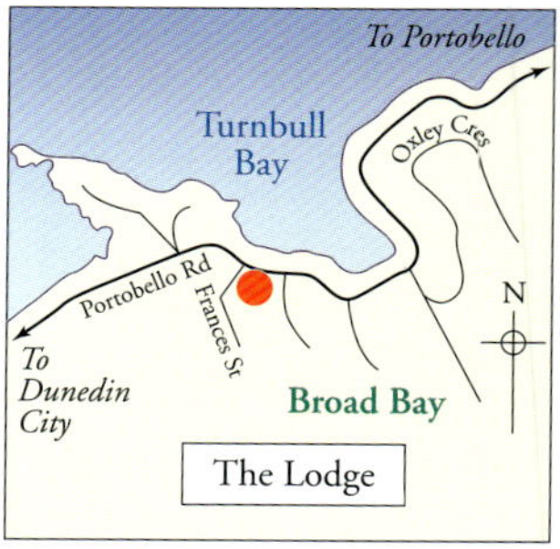

Explore the Otago Peninsula - royal albatross, penguin and seal colonies, great walkways and beaches, galleries and hidden gems, and a castle! Enjoy the city life of Dunedin with its cafés and galleries, shops and museums, its theatres and entertainment.
Then come home to this fully self-contained and private haven, relax and enjoy the breathtaking views of Otago Harbour.
The modern kitchen invites you to "cook up a storm", or you might choose to dine out at the nearby restaurants.
A scrumptious basket of ingredients for breakfast (optional) can be delivered by your hosts who live nearby on the Peninsula.

Arts Content Bed & Breakfast

1 Castlewood Road, Otago Peninsula
Ph (03) 476 0076, Fax (03) 476 0076
Mobile 021-152 3341
email: *artscontent@hotmail.com*
www.artscontentbnb.com

Features & Attractions

- *Absolute waterfront*
- *Panoramic harbour views*
- *Art Gallery on site*
- *Laundry facilities*
- *Secret garden with 80+ roses*
- *Larnach Castle 5min. drive*

$		
	Double	$125-150
	Single	$120-135
	Child	

B&B Self-contained
Absolute Waterfront

Bedrooms	Qty
Double	1
Twin	
Single	
Bed Size	**Qty**
King	
Queen	1
Double	
Single	
Bathrooms	**Qty**
Ensuite	1
Private	
Guest Share	

DIRECTIONS: From Dunedin follow signs to Peninsula. We are 15min. drive along Portobello Rd on the corner of Portobello Rd & Castlewood Rd in Company Bay. Look for **Arts Content** sign.

Arts Content is absolute waterfront, self-contained, cottage-style accommodation, ideal for a couple. Decorated in country style, it exudes charm and character. It adjoins our home and has private entrances and off-street parking. Enjoy sweeping, panoramic harbour views from the private deck. Leading off the spacious bedroom is your own ensuite. Upstairs is a lounge, dining, kitchen with comfortable seating including a sofa-bed. Heating is provided by a heatpump. Share our pleasure in our beautiful, 'secret' garden and take the time to stop and smell our 80+ roses. A continental, hamper breakfast is provided. Within easy reach of the city, we are ideally located to access all the attractions of the Peninsula. We also offer conducted Peninsula tours.

Crabapple Cottage

346 Harington Point Rd, RD 2,
Lower Portobello, Dunedin
Ph (03) 4780103
email: *kay@crabapple.co.nz*
www.crabapplecottage.co.nz

Features & Attractions

- *Close to wildlife attractions*
- *Pleasant, rural setting*
- *Private garden outlook*
- *5min. to restaurants & cafés*
- *25min. from Dunedin*
- *Restored settlers cottage*

$		
	Double	$130-140
	Single	
	Child	

Self-contained Cottage
Bed & Breakfast

Bedrooms	Qty
Double	1
Twin	
Single	
Bed Size	**Qty**
King	
Queen	1
Double	
Single	
Bathrooms	**Qty**
Ensuite	1
Private	
Guest Share	

Crabapple Cottage is a lovingly restored 1860s settlers cottage 25 minutes from Dunedin, on the beautiful Otago Peninsula. We are 10 minutes from the albatross colony, penguin beaches, Monarch Wildlife Cruises, off-road tours, the Portobello Aquarium, craft shops and beautiful beaches. Larnarch's Castle is a 20 minutes scenic drive away. Our character cottage has a very comfortable queen-size bed, modern bathroom with all facilities, and a kitchen/lounge area equipped for basic self-catering. Enjoy a generous breakfast tray which includes eggs from our own hens and relax in an armchair or in the private herb garden with views of the hills and full afternoon sun. We are 5 minutes from restaurants, cafés and a general store with post facilities. We look forward to sharing our cosy cottage with you.

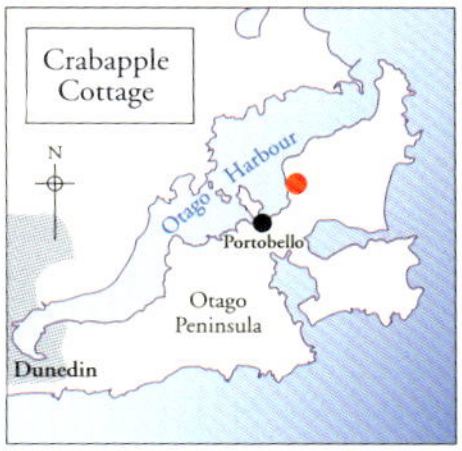

CONEHENGE HOMESTEAD

Rapid 1589 Highcliff Road, PO Box 50,
Portobello, Dunedin
Ph (03) 478 0911, Fax (03) 478 0914
Mobile 027-202 0464
email: *kolig@ihug.co.nz*

Tariff : N.Z. Dollars	
Double	$135-145
Single	$135
Child	

Bedrooms	Qty
Double	1
Twin	
Single	
Bed Size	**Qty**
Super King	
King	1
Queen	
Double	
Single	
Bathrooms	**Qty**
Ensuite	1
Private	
Guest Share	

Tranquil Rural Retreat
Boutique Bed & Breakfast

Features & Attractions

- *Magnificent harbour & sea views*
- *City & wildlife colonies 25 min*
- *Central & close to all attractions*
- *Single party accommodation*
- *Private native bush walk*
- *Meet donkeys & farm animals*
- *Ceramic artist*
- *German spoken*

DIRECTIONS:
1.2 km up the hill from Portobello Village, on Highcliff Road.
Advance booking recommended.

Conehenge Homestead is an oasis for the discerning traveller who seeks tranquillity and privacy. Nestling on the slope of Harbour Cone the Homestead offers magnificent views over the open sea, the Otago Harbour, the bays and rolling hills of the Otago Peninsula. Equidistant to all wildlife attractions of the Peninsula and the city's cultural and architectural heritage makes **Conehenge** an ideal base for a longer stay. Enjoy a walk on our farm and in our private native bush reserve. Your room and patio have a fantastic view over harbour and sea. The double room has its own private entrance, king-size bed, electric blanket, ensuite, television. The studio facilities include a bar fridge, microwave, toaster, complimentary teas/coffee. Tiled low allergen room, no house pets. Room service breakfast (or on your patio) features home-made continental specialty breads and other delectables. I am well travelled and am an established ceramic artist. Ich spreche deutsch. I invite you to view my unique art work and meet my favourites, Sootie, Sheeba and Limpy the sheep, and Dolly and Henry, our utterly spoilt donkeys.

Captain Eady's Lookout

2 Moss Street, Portobello, Dunedin
Ph (03) 478 0537
Mobile 021- 478 785
email: *capteady@earthlight.co.nz*
www.capteady.co.nz

Tariff : N.Z. Dollars	
Double	$130-155
Single	$120-145
Child	neg

Bedrooms	Qty
Double	2
Twin	1
Single	
Bed Size	**Qty**
Super King	
King	
Queen	2
Double	
Single	
Bathrooms	**Qty**
Ensuite	2
Private	
Family Share	1

Bed & Breakfast
Homestay

Features & Attractions

- *Harbourside location*
- *Close to Albatross Colony*
- *Stunning Peninsula beaches*
- *Secluded garden*
- *Penguins, seals & native birdlife*
- *Special breakfasts, dinner available upon request*
- *Large character home, warm in winter*
- *Antiques, paintings by local artists*

Captain Eady's Lookout is a delightful Bed & Breakfast situated on the water's edge at Portobello on the Otago Peninsula, just twenty kilometres from Dunedin. This character house is set on a small bluff overlooking the Otago Harbour. It was built early last century by Captain Eady, a ferry master. The upstairs bedroom, with its own balcony, overlooks the water. The bedroom below opens onto a secluded garden.

You may have a special breakfast in the conservatory whilst taking in the splendid views of the harbour. The house has many antiques and on the walls are paintings by local artists. Feel free to enjoy our large jazz collection. **Captain Eady's Lookout** is an ideal base from which to explore the Royal Albatross Colony, Larnach's Castle, and ocean beaches deserted, save for penguins and seals.

McAuley Glen

13 McAuley Road, Portobello
Ph (03) 478 0724, Fax (03) 478 0724
Mobile 021-237 1919
email: *maryandpat@clear.net.nz*

Tariff : N.Z. Dollars	
Double	$125-155
Single	$95-130
Child	

Bedrooms	Qty
Double	1
Twin	1
Single	
Bed Size	**Qty**
Super King	
King	
Queen	1
Double	
Single	2
Bathrooms	**Qty**
Ensuite	1
Private	1
Guest Share	

Bed & Breakfast
Homestay

Features & Attractions

- *Special breakfast/home baking*
- *Bike & kayak tours & hire*
- *Outdoor jacuzzi spa & sauna room*
- *Drive 20min to wild life attractions*
- *Internet/email/fax phone*
- *Walk 5min to café/bar/restaurant*
- *Laundry service/ off road parking*
- *Close to beaches and walkways*

Located in the heart of the magnificent Otago Peninsula is **McAuley Glen**, private, tranquil, ½ acre of beautifully landscaped gardens. Your hosts, Mary and Pat, invite you to sample their generous Kiwi hospitality in their lovely comfortable home. Enjoy our scrumptious breakfasts, a home-cooked meal or BBQ. Relax in the spa pool or the sauna, join us for refreshments and a chat. We are happy to help arrange your local excursions. Our guest accommodation floor, tastefully decorated, includes 2 bedrooms, separated by a lounge room. The luxury queen room has ensuite and a private patio garden entrance. The twin room has a separate entrance and private bathroom. Bathrooms are spacious with heated tile floors. Bedrooms have TV, heater, electric blankets, hairdryer, quality linens, chocolates and fresh flowers. The guest lounge accommodates a comfortable modern sofa bed that sleeps 2, has TV, CD, piano, tea/coffee facilities, microwave, fridge. **McAuley Glen** is also the home of Peninsula Bike & Kayak. Pat and Mary offer personal, fun-filled, informative guided tours, or hires. Experience amazing wildlife and fantastic scenery. Visit our site at www.bike-kayak.com

Peninsula B&B and Treetop Lodge B&B

4 Allans Beach Road, Portobello, Dunedin
Ph (03) 478 0909, Fax (03) 478 0909
Mobile 027-634 3661
email: *toni@peninsula.co.nz*
www.peninsula.co.nz

Tariff : N.Z. Dollars	
Double	$105-185
Single	$105-130
Child	

Bedrooms	Qty
Double	7
Twin	2
Single	
Bed Size	**Qty**
King	1
Queen	4
Double	1
King/Single	3
Single	1
Bathrooms	**Qty**
Ensuite	4
Private	1
Guest Share	2

Bed & Breakfast
Self-contained Accommodation

DIRECTIONS:
Follow signs to Peninsula.
We are in the centre of Portobello opposite the '1908 Restaurant' about 25min. drive from Dunedin.

Features & Attractions

- *Peaceful, scenic location*
- *Delicious home-baking*
- *Comfortable ensuite rooms*
- *Walk to great restaurants*
- *Fabulous harbour views*
- *Free email/internet/laundry*
- *Separate to hosts' dwelling*
- *Peninsula wildlife attractions*

Would you prefer to relax in the elegant and romantic Victorian ambience of **Peninsula B&B** – our beautiful 1880s villa – or enjoy the tranquillity of **Treetop Lodge** – a more rustic B&B with a separate self-catering cottage, nestled in a manuka forest? **Peninsula B&B** is situated in peaceful gardens, with views of the harbour from your room. Charlie, our friendly cat, will greet you when you arrive. Relish your delicious cooked breakfast in the morning, with home baking.

Alternatively, enjoy the tranquillity of **Treetop Lodge**, perched above the village of Portobello. Relax in the quaint wood-and-stained-glass rooms and take in the fabulous views of the Otago Harbour. Start your day with a delicious continental breakfast with home baking.

If you are travelling in a group, choose the cosy self-catering cottage, which sleeps four. All rooms have electric blankets and hair dryer. We can burn digital camera images to CD for a small charge. Stephen parle français. Ask about winter discounts.

Peninsula B&B: $NZ105-$NZ185/room/night (@home only)
Treetop Lodge B&B: $NZ105-$NZ140/room/night
Treetop Lodge SC cottage: $NZ120-$NZ140/night

Rugosa Cottage & Seafarers Cottage

1 Beaconsfield Rd, Portobello, Otago Peninsula, Dunedin
Ph (03) 478 1076
Mobile 021-234 4621
email: *rugosacottage@ihug.co.nz*
www.rugosacottage.co.nz

@home NEW ZEALAND

Tariff : N.Z. Dollars	
Double	$145-185
Single	$100-145
Child	

Bedrooms	Qty
Double	2
Twin/Double	1
Single	
Bed Size	**Qty**
Super King	
King	
Queen	1
Double	1
Single	2
Bathrooms	**Qty**
Ensuite	2
Private	1
Guest Share	

Bed & Breakfast Homestay and Self-contained

Features & Attractions

- *Relaxing, tranquil garden setting*
- *Harbourside location, seaviews*
- *Albatross, penguins, Larnach Castle*
- *Tours, excursions arranged*
- *Romantic hideaway*
- *Warm NZ hospitality*
- *Art and crafts*
- *Spa pool*

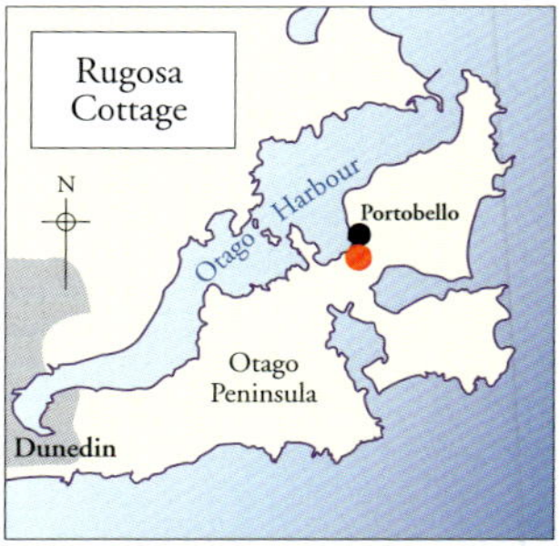

Welcome to **Rugosa Cottage and Seafarers Cottage.** Situated on the Otago Peninsula, our Bed & Breakfast overlooks the sea and is surrounded by beautiful gardens. Garden, book art lovers retreat. The cottages are decorated with panache, charm and a romantic ambience. Choose your accommodation, either our Rose Room with 4-poster queen-size bed, ensuite bathroom and French doors to rose gardens. Our **Seafarers Cottage** is self-contained with colonial bed, ensuite bathroom, small kitchenette – ideal for a couple who require a place of their own. French doors lead out to cottage-style gardens. A breakfast hamper is available. Alternatively you are welcome to join us for breakfast at **Rugosa Cottage.** Guests' comment: "*Charming would definitely be the best way to describe this oasis you have created. A pure feast for the eye and senses. No detail left untouched and the most amazing hostess we have ever experienced. It has been a true pleasure being spoilt by you, Anne.*" The Guillot Family.

HIGHLAND PEAKS

333 Chain Hills Road, RD 1, Dunedin
Ph (03) 489 6936, Fax (03) 489 6924
Mobile 027-351 0646
email: *info@highlandpeaks.com*
www.highlandpeaks.com

Tariff : N.Z. Dollars	
Double	$195-395
Single	$175-350
Child	

Bedrooms	Qty
Double	3
Twin	
Single	
Bed Size	**Qty**
Super King	2
King	1
Queen	
Double	
King/Single	4
Bathrooms	**Qty**
Ensuite	2
Private	1
Guest Share	

Town & Country Luxury Accommodation

DIRECTIONS: From SH 1 take Mosgiel exit, then turn towards Kinmont. Travel along Quarry Road continue left along Morris Road towards Fairfield over motorway. Turn 1st left into Chain Hills Road and take left fork to **Highland Peaks** on left at road end.

Features & Attractions

- *Dunedin & Airport 15 min*
- *Panoramic vistas*
- *Quality facilities*
- *Hydrotherapy spa*
- *Delightfully peaceful*
- *Albatross, penguins, seals*
- *Personalised, guided eco tours*
- *Feed our friendly animals*

"We built our house for guests to enjoy."

Newly completed, **Highland Peaks** specialises in warm hospitality, limited guest numbers and eco-tours. Located on a ridge top between Dunedin and the airport, with panoramic mountain and sea views and twenty one acres of country grounds, where you can enjoy privacy, tranquility, native birdsong and forest walks.
Highland Peaks is purpose-built from natural stone in an eco-friendly, modern design. You'll stay in a private guest wing with two very comfortable suites. You can unwind in spacious guest lounges, in front of a large fire in winter, or on sundecks in summer. Alternatively enjoy the views while relaxing in our hydrotherapy spa pool. Dinner is served by arrangement, with quality home cuisine complemented by fine NZ wines. Peter, an ecologist and former director of New Zealand's National Trust, is happy to share his knowledge on New Zealand's natural heritage. He also guides personal tours to see albatross, penguins, other wildlife and natural flora. We have a cat Jasper, dog Bud and friendly farm animals that you can hand-feed.

Braeside Villa

792 Maungatua Road, Berwick, Dunedin
Ph/Fax (03) 486 1232
Mobile 027-486 2789
email: *stay@braesidevilla.com*
www.braesidevilla.com

Tariff : N.Z. Dollars	
Double	$110
Single	$85
Child	neg

Bedrooms	Qty
Double	2
Twin	
Single	
Bed Size	**Qty**
Super King	
King	
Queen	2
Double	
Single	
Bathrooms	**Qty**
Ensuite	
Private	1
Guest Share	

Peaceful Countrystay
Original Homestead

Features & Attractions

- *Tranquil rural setting*
- *Guest lounge with open fire*
- *Cozy library with internet*
- *Native bush & wetlands*
- *Handy to Airport & City*
- *Rivers and lakes; fishing*
- *Well travelled, friendly hosts*
- *Dutch and American spoken*

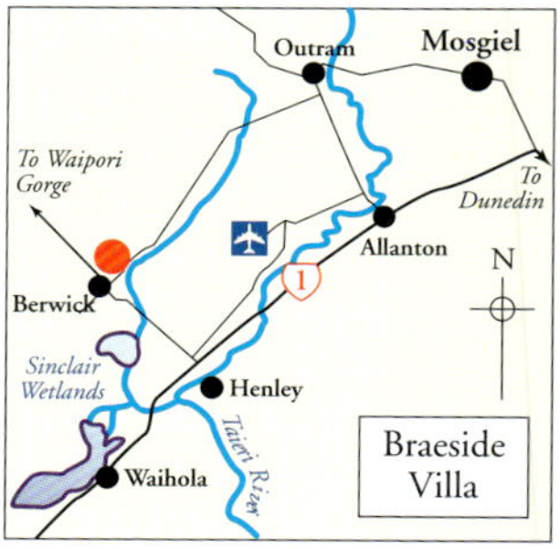

We warmly invite you to stay at our home, **Braeside Villa**, a century old farmhouse full of character and charm nestled in the foothills of Te Maungatua on a 25 acre farmlet. We offer you a quiet and peaceful country retreat where you can unwind in the garden, read a book or use the internet and relax in the guest lounge in front of the open fire. Stay in the original master bedroom with Tempur-Pedic mattress and a lovely garden view, or have a room with french doors opening onto the sunny veranda with a mountain view. We will indulge you with a cooked or continental breakfast to your taste including espresso coffee, freshly made juices and bread, served on the veranda or in the formal dining room.

Close by, you can explore the local mountains, rivers, native bush reserves and wetlands where opportunities for walking, bird watching, cycling, skiing, fishing and canoeing abound. We are passionate and knowledgeable about our area and can help you plan your holiday or be your guides for adventure! Braeside Villa is 30 minutes from Dunedin and 10 minutes from the Airport – come and stay, we'd love to meet you!

ARGYLL FARMSTAY

Rapid No 246, Clutha River Rd, Clydevale, RD 4, Balclutha
Ph (03) 415 9268, Fax (03) 415 9268
Mobile 027-431 8241
email: *argyllfm@ihug.co.nz*
www.argyllfarmstay.co.nz

@ home NEW ZEALAND

Tariff : N.Z. Dollars	
Double	$120-150
Single	$60-100
Child	neg

Bedrooms	Qty
Double	1
Twin	1
Single	1
Bed Size	**Qty**
Super King	
King	
Queen	1
Double	
Single	3
Bathrooms	**Qty**
Ensuite	1
Private	1
Guest Share	

MasterCard VISA

Farmstay
Bed & Breakfast

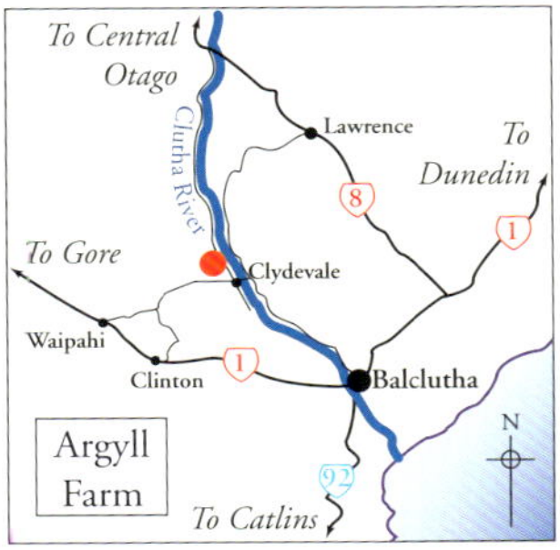

DIRECTIONS:
Please phone for easy directions.

Features & Attractions

- *Superior accommodation*
- *Garden room has conservatory*
- *Tea/coffee making facilities*
- *Farm tour included in tariff*
- *Homestyle cuisine available*
- *Tranquil rural views*
- *Fisherman's paradise*
- *Tuapeka Mouth ferry*

From the moment you step onto **Argyll Farm** you will experience the warmth, tranquillity and hospitality extended to you by Alan and Trish – third generation, sheep, deer and cattle farmers. **Argyll Farm** is situated on the banks of the Clutha River that provides guests with a unique opportunity to enjoy several recreational pastimes. We would like you to relax in our comfortable country home with a large garden, and beautiful views of green pasture and river flats. You can enjoy our day to day farm activities or enjoy quiet times. Go for walks, fish in the Clutha River bordering our property or explore. We will make your stay a memorable one, pampering you with exquisite accommodation and cuisine.

Our home is yours. Experience '**Argyll Farm**' for a magical stay.

Benhar - Balcutha

YOUR HOSTS: **Kate and Noel O'Malley** Free Ph 0800 301 224

LESMAHAGOW

Benhar Main Road, Benhar, Balclutha
Ph (03) 418 2507
Mobile 027- 457 8465
e-mail: *lesmahagow@xtra.co.nz*
www.lesmahagow.co.nz

Features & Attractions

- *Historic home & gardens*
- *Catlins scenic area*
- *Quality & comfort assured*
- *Evening dining*
- *Centrally heated*
- *Spacious bedrooms*

Boutique Bed & Breakfast

Double	$100-150
Single	
Child	

Lesmahagow offers excellent accommodation in an historic homestead and garden setting. Centrally situated, discerning travellers can make Lesmahagow their base to explore the Catlins region, Dunedin and the Otago Peninsula or the historic goldfields of Lawrence. Centrally heated, with delightfully furnished bedrooms and gorgeous bathrooms, you can be sure of wonderful hospitality, and a truly memorable stay. Feel free to explore and relax in our gardens or take time out to enjoy the guest lounge with an extensive range of books magazines and music. We offer evening dining utilising fresh produce from the garden and locally grown meats. Our special breakfasts, at a time to suit you, with freshly squeezed fruit juices, fresh fruits, home made breads, muesli and home baking will satisfy all taste buds! We love to help plan your day's activities and can arrange a variety of local trips for you. Come as strangers, leave as friends.

Bedrooms	Qty
Double	2
Twin	1
Single	
Bed Size	**Qty**
King	
Queen	2
Double	1
Single	1
Bathrooms	**Qty**
Ensuite	
Private	3
Guest Share	

Kaka Point - The Catlins

YOUR HOSTS: **Lyn and Selwyn Cardno** Ph: (03) 412 8181

CARDNO'S ACCOMMODATION

8 Marine Terrace, Kaka Point, The Catlins
Ph (03) 412 8181, Fax (03) 412 8101
email: *cardnos@xtra.co.nz*
www.cardnosaccommodation.co.nz

Features & Attractions

- *Great sunrises*
- *Native bush walks*
- *Yellow-eyed penguins*
- *Magnificent sea views*
- *Nugget Point Lighthouse*
- *Sea lions, seals, native birds*

Double	$90-150
Single	
Child	n/a

Modern Contemporary Accommodation

Bedrooms	Qty
Double	3
Twin	
Single	
Bed Size	**Qty**
King	
Queen	3
Double	
Single	2
Bathrooms	**Qty**
Ensuite	3
Private	
Guest Share	

45 minutes drive from Dunedin Airport, following the Southern Scenic Route, Kaka Point, a seaside destination with patrolled beaches in summer, is ideal to base yourself while exploring the spectacular Catlins - one of the last frontiers of tourist destinations in NZ, consisting of unique wildlife to spectacular outcrops. Or, simply relax, enjoying the spacious modern surrounding of your contemporary furnished accommodation. Each unit with its own entrance, is ensuited, has quality linen, wool rest electric blanket, woollen blankets, feather duvéts. TV, CD stereo, hairdryer, filtered water, BBQ area, and a 1 minute walk to the beach, restaurant/bar/shop. From your double glazed ranch sliders, enjoy amazing sunrises, wonderful views of the ocean and Nugget Point Lighthouse. An optional continental breakfast tray can be requested on arrival. These features and our hospitality will ensure your stay is comfortable and memorable.

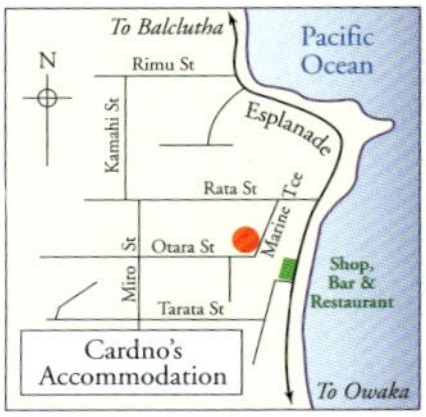

YOUR HOSTS: **Ester and Jack Johnson** Free Ph: 0800 105 134 **Owaka - The Catlins**

Kepplestone-by-the-Sea

9 Surat Bay Road, Owaka, Newhaven, The Catlins
Ph (03) 415 8134, Fax (03) 415 8137
Mobile 027-242 4235
email: *kepplestone@xtra.co.nz*
www.travelwise.co.nz

Features & Attractions

- *Sandy beach & Hooker sealions*
- *Close to penguins and falls*
- *Southern scenic route*
- *Separate guest house*
- *Royal Spoonbills*
- *Native birdsong*

$	
Double	$120
Single	$85
Child	$20

Beachstay Bed & Breakfast

Bedrooms	Qty
Double	2
Twin	1
Single	
Bed Size	**Qty**
King	
Queen	1
King/Single	1
Single	2
Bathrooms	**Qty**
Ensuite	2
Private	
Family Share	1

There are no strangers here, only friends we have not met.

Kepplestone-by-the Sea is situated 100 metres from the beach, where Hooker sealions bask. We are close to all Catlins scenery, waterfalls, walks, Royal Spoonbills. Enjoy private viewing of Yellow Eyed penguins. Spend a relaxing night in our separate guest house and watch tuis and bellbirds while having breakfast with our delicious homemade goodies.
Golf course nearby, clubs available.

DIRECTIONS:
Follow signs towards Pounawea, at golf course go across bridge and turn right to Newhaven and Surat Bay Road (3 km metal) first house on left

YOUR HOSTS: **Jeanette and Ian Ruddenklau** Ph: (03) 246 9557 **Fortrose - South Catlins**

Fortrose Retreat

Southern Scenic Route, midway Fortrose and Tokanui
Ph (03) 246 9557, Fax (03) 246 9557
Free Ph: 0800 305 020
email: *info@fortroseretreat.co.nz*
www.fortroseretreat.co.nz

Features & Attractions

- *Secluded & private*
- *Outside double spa bath*
- *Native bush walk*
- *Farm & garden tour available*
- *Beach, fishing & golf nearby*
- *Continental breakfast*

$	
Double	$165-200
Single	neg
Child	neg

Farmstay Cottage with Spectacular Views

Bedrooms	Qty
Double	1
Twin	1
Single	
Bed Size	**Qty**
King	1
Queen	
Double	
King/Single	2
Bathrooms	**Qty**
Ensuite	
Private	1
Guest Share	

We offer you a warm welcome to this five star, fully self-contained cottage on the Southern Scenic Route. A private road through native bush will lead you to your own secluded "retreat" accommodation, which is set on a hillside of our 850 acre sheep farm. Be as busy as you like exploring the rugged Catlins coastline, join us on a tour around our farm and garden or just unwind in this tranquil setting.
Sliding glass doors from the living room and master bedroom open onto your covered deck, where you can enjoy the panoramic views over rolling farmland to the sea with views of Stewart Island and Bluff in the background.
When you are ready, relax in your outside double spa bath, soak in the ambience of the peaceful country atmosphere and watch the stunning sunsets.

GREENBUSH B&B AND FARMSTAY

298 Fortrose-Otara Road, No 5 RD, Invercargill
Ph (03) 246 9506, Fax (03) 246 9505
Mobile 021-395 196
email: *info@greenbush.co.nz*
www.greenbush.co.nz

@ home NEW ZEALAND

Tariff : N.Z. Dollars	
Double	$150
Single	$120
Child	neg

Bedrooms	Qty
Double	2
Twin	1
Single	
Bed Size	**Qty**
Super King	1
King	
Queen	1
Double	
King/Single	2
Bathrooms	**Qty**
Ensuite	1
Private	1
Guest Share	

F **Bed & Breakfast Farmstay** BB

VISA MasterCard

Features & Attractions

- *Stroll a wild beach*
- *Dinner by arrangement*
- *Enjoy the wildlife*
- *Comfortable guest lounge*
- *Enjoy golf by the sea*
- *Relax in the garden*
- *Delve into history*
- *Centrally heated home*

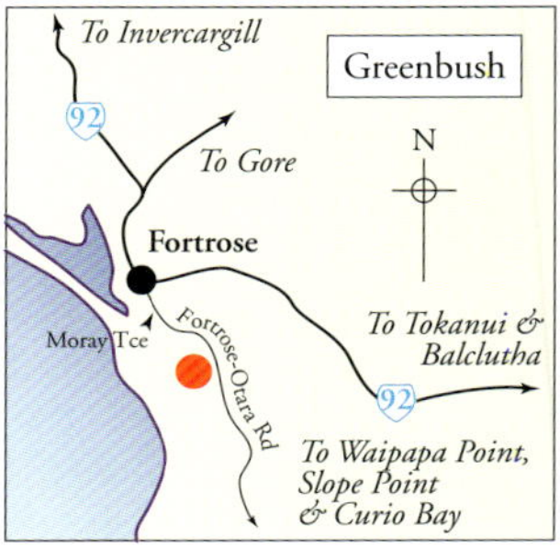

DIRECTIONS: At Fortrose on Southern Scenic Route turn into Moray Terrace, the Coastal Route. We are 4 km from that turn-off on the right hand side of Fortrose-Otara Road, Rapid No 298.

Ann and Donald McKenzie at **Greenbush Bed & Breakfast** are known for their wonderful southern hospitality. Greenbush is a 1000 acre family estate that dates back to 1865. A working sheep and cattle farm, guests at Greenbush have the opportunity to enjoy private beach access, the farm's lake and a farm tour. Nestled in two acres of garden, **Greenbush** is ideally situated five minutes from Fortrose off the Soutern Scenic Route. Within thirty minutes drive you can enjoy Curio Bay, Waipapa Point, Waipohatu and Slope Point, the southern most point in the South Island. **Greenbush** is forty minutes from Invercargill, an ideal stop-off either before or after visiting Stewart Island and Fiordland.

Curio Bay Boutique Accommodation

501 Curio Bay Road, RD 1, Tokanui, Southland
Ph (03) 246 8797, Fax (03) 246 8797
email: *accommodation@curiobay.com*

Tariff : N.Z. Dollars	
Double	$160-220
Single	$160
Child	

Bedrooms	Qty
Double	2
Twin	
Single	
Bed Size	**Qty**
Super King	2
King	
Queen	
Double	
Single	
Bathrooms	**Qty**
Ensuite	2
Private	
Guest Share	

Absolute Beachfront Accommodation
Spectacular Seascape & Wildlife

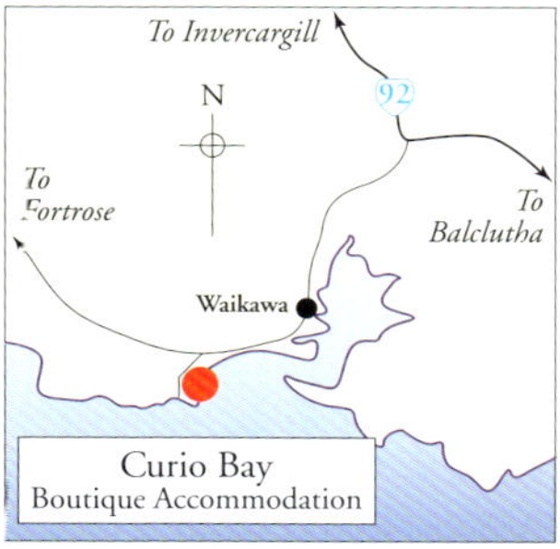

Features & Attractions

- *Absolute beachfront*
- *Fossil forest*
- *Hectors dolphins*
- *Stunning sea views*
- *Yellow-eyed penguins*
- *Wildlife at your door*
- *Breakfast not included, but can be supplied on request*

Looking for something a little different? – Then try one of our two new beachfront self-contained studios. Enjoy the spectacular seascapes from your super king bed. Hectors dolphins may be viewed swimming past your room between November and April. The 160 million year old fossil forest is only a ten minute walk along the beach. Yellow-eyed penguins also live at the fossil forest and may be viewed from the platform.

We offer a variety of music, freshly ground coffee and a place to put your feet up and relax. Our cell phone and television-free studios have solar heated water and floors, spacious bathrooms and sleep two to three people. Complimentary laundry facilities available on site. Continental breakfast supplied on request. Local restaurant, café, art gallery and museum are only five minutes drive away.

Come and escape to Curio Bay!

 YOUR HOSTS: **Alex and Nola Affleck** Free Ph: 0800 301 317

Affleck Homestay

13 William Street, Gore, Southland
Ph/Fax (03) 208 9437,
Mobile 027-472 1996
email: *nolalex@ispnz.co.nz*

Features & Attractions

- *Warm quiet home*
- *Great fishing and golf close by*
- *Close to town centre*
- *Use of laundry*
- *Dinner by arrangement*
- *Email, internet, fax*

Charming Homestay Bed & Breakfast

$	
Double	$90
Single	$50
Child	

Bedrooms	Qty
Double	1
Twin	1
Single	
Bed Size	**Qty**
King Twin	
Queen	
Double	1
Single	2
Bathrooms	**Qty**
Ensuite	
Private	1
Guest Share	

We were involved in farming sheep, deer and cattle on the family farm. Our home is close to the town centre, quiet, and on a large private section. Our interests include farming, family, gardening, travel, cards, and various community-based interests. We enjoy meeting people and are both of a friendly disposition.

Gore is ideally situated two hours from Queenstown and Dunedin, ninety minutes from Te Anau and Bluff. The rivers close by are world renowned for great trout fishing. Golf courses are not far away. Enjoy a visit to the unique Hokonui Moonshine Museum and the John Money Wing in the town.

We have email, fax and internet facilities available, if required. Advance bookings recommended. We invite you to experience our hospitality.

Smith's Farmstay

365 Wyndham-Mokoreta Rd, No 2 RD, Wyndham, Southland
Ph (03) 206 4840, Fax (03) 206 4847
Mobile 025-286 6920
email: *beverly@smithsfarmstay.co.nz*
www.smithsfarmstay.co.nz

Tariff : N.Z. Dollars	
Double	$110-140
Single	$100
Child	neg

Bedrooms	Qty
Double	2
Twin	2
Single	
Bed Size	**Qty**
Super King	1
King	
Queen	1
Double	
King Single	2
Bathrooms	**Qty**
Ensuite	1
Private	1
Guest Share	1

Fisherman's Retreat - Farmstay

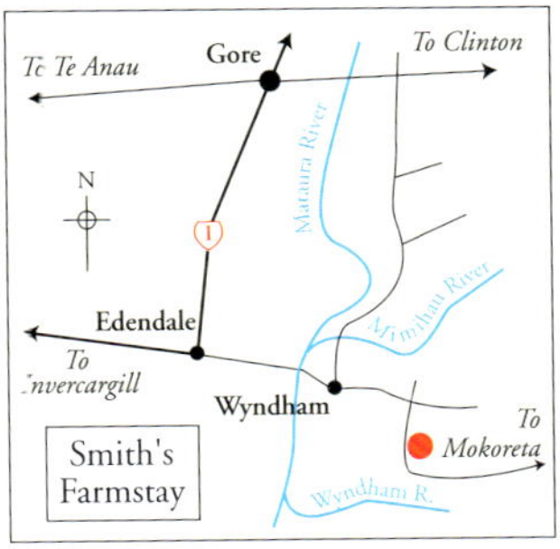

DIRECTIONS:
Drive to Wyndham:
only 4 km from Wyndham
on the Wyndham Mokoreta Road.
Smith's Farmstay sign at gate.

Features & Attractions

- *Genuine sheep farm experience*
- *Close to 'Maple Glen' garden*
- *Hand knitted jerseys - pure NZ wool*
- *Beautiful 'Catlins' area close by*
- *Trout fishing 5 km,*
- *Comfortable, quality beds*
- *Quiet, peaceful surroundings*
- *Dinner by prior arrangement*

Beverly and Doug assure you of a warm welcome to their modern farm house and 260-hectare sheep farm. We are situated on the hills above **Wyndham, only 3.65 km,** set in quiet and peaceful surroundings. The **Mataura, Mimihau and Wyndham Rivers, renowned for Brown Trout** are only a short 5 km away. Doug, a keen experienced fisherman, is only too happy to share his knowledge of these rivers with you. Beverly, a qualified nurse, enjoys cooking, floral art, gardening and hand knitting. Each bedroom has a view and is tastefully furnished to meet your needs. Genuine home cooking. Special diets available on request. You are most welcome to join us for the evening meal which is $40 per person. Children's rates negotiable. **Farm tour** and feeding of the animals when in season. We enjoy meeting people and both are of a friendly disposition with a sense of humor. Packed lunches, laundry facilities, fax and email also available.

84 on King

84 King Street, Invercargill
Ph (03) 217 3919, Fax (03) 217 3919
email: *84onking@xtra.co.nz*

Features & Attractions

- *Friendly hospitality*
- *Dinner by arrangement*
- *Email & fax available*
- *Close to city centre*
- *Walking distance to park*
- *Gateway to Fiordland/Queenstown*

Homestay Bed & Breakfast

$	
Double	$100-115
Single	$65-75
Child	

A warm welcome awaits you in our new home situated in the popular Windsor Shopping Centre adjacent to shops, restaurants and cafés and just a few minutes from the centre of Invercargill City. Our home is warm and inviting with underfloor heating and a sunny outlook. We are semi-retired farmers with interests in farming, golf, gardening, cooking, Lions and voluntary work in the community. Invercargill is a great place to spend a few days enjoying the green Southland farmland, bush walks, parks, golf courses and seashores on your way to Stewart Island, Fiordland or Queenstown. We have ample off-street parking or alternatively we will be happy to collect you from the airport or bus terminals.

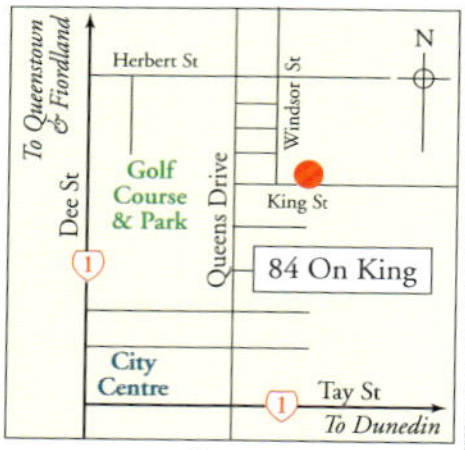

Bedrooms	Qty
Double	1
Twin	1
Single	
Bed Size	**Qty**
King	1
Queen	
Double	
King/Single	2
Bathrooms	**Qty**
Ensuite	
Private	
Guest Share	1

Glenroy Park Homestay

23 Glenroy Park Drive, Invercargill
Ph (03) 215 8464, Fax (03) 215 8464
email: *home_hosp@actrix.co.nz*

Features & Attractions

- *Warm hospitality*
- *Home cooking*
- *Quiet retreat*
- *Gateway to Fiordland & Catlins*
- *Excellent golf courses*
- *Invercargill – a garden city*

Homestay Bed & Breakfast

$	
Double	$110-120
Twin	$100
Single	$75

Exclusively yours in a quiet retreat, with parks, restaurants and shops only a short distance away. We enjoy meeting people and love to cook. We both garden, are enthusiastic golfers, with many courses nearby. Be our special guest and share an evening of relaxation and friendship. Dinner available. Invercargill, our garden city, has many historic buildings, lovely parks and gardens, and a unique museum with live tuatara lizards. Gateway to the pleasures of Fiordland, Queenstown, Catlins and Stewart Island.

Bedrooms	Qty
Double	1
Twin	1
Single	1
Bed Size	**Qty**
King	
Queen	1
Twin single	1
Single	1
Bathrooms	**Qty**
Ensuite	
Private	1
Guest Share	1

DIRECTIONS: **From Queenstown:** Turn left at 2nd set of lights, Bainfield Road, travel 500m – we are 1st on left, Glenroy Park Drive, 3rd house on left.
From Dunedin: Along main street (Tay Street) turn right at War Memorial towards Queenstown, travel approx 5km, turn right at traffic lights into Bainfield Road, then as above.

THE MANOR

9 Drysdale Road, Myross Bush, Invercargill
Ph (03) 230 4788, Fax (03) 230 4788
Mobile 027-667 0904
email: *the.manor@xtra.co.nz*
www.manorbb.co.nz

Tariff : N.Z. Dollars	
Double	$90-130
Single	$70-85
Child	neg

Bedrooms	Qty
Double	3
Twin	
Single	
Bed Size	**Qty**
Super King	
King	
Queen	3
Double	
Single	2
Bathrooms	**Qty**
Ensuite	1
Private	1
Guest Share	1

Homestay
Bed & Breakfast

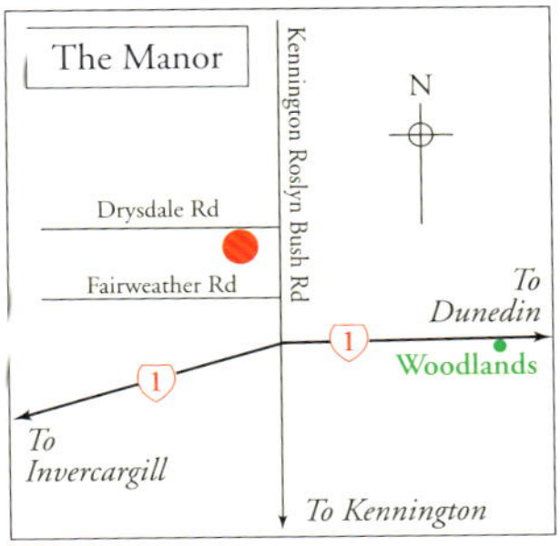

DIRECTIONS:
Signs on Highway One
at Kennington Corner.

Features & Attractions

- *Quiet & peaceful*
- *Warm home*
- *City 5 minutes*
- *Email & fax facilities*
- *Golf courses close by*
- *Dinner by arrangement*
- *Near Southern Scenic Route*
- *2.5hrs to Te Anau/Queenstown*

Relax and enjoy our warm, comfortable home with under floor heating, situated in a sheltered garden setting on our ten acre farmlet.

There's a private guest area with television, refrigerator, tea/coffee making facilities. Alternatively you are welcome to join us in our lounge. We are retired farmers, keen golfers, enjoy gardening, harness racing, travel and meeting people.

We invite you to dine on meals of fresh homegrown produce and continental or cooked breakfasts.

Courtesy pickup from terminals. A stop on your way to Stewart Island, Southern Scenic Route, Queenstown or Te Anau.

We would enjoy having you stay with us.

Fernlea Farmstay

Mokotua, No 1 RD, Invercargill
Ph (03) 239 5432, Fax (03) 239 5432
Mobile 025-313 432
e-mail: *fernlea@southnet.co.nz*
www.fernlea.co.nz

@ home NEW ZEALAND

Tariff : N.Z. Dollars	
Double	$130-140
Single	$100
Child	neg

Bedrooms	Qty
Double	1
Twin	
Single	

Bed Size	Qty
Super King	
King	
Queen	
Double	1
Single	

Bathrooms	Qty
Ensuite	
Private	1
Guest Share	

BA **Farmstay - Tourism Award Winning Self-contained Cottage** F

VISA MasterCard

Features & Attractions

- *Gateway to Catlins & Fiordland*
- *Dinner by prior arrangement*
- *Large in-built swimming pool*
- *On the 'Southern Scenic' route*
- *Peaceful farm setting*
- *Farm tour available*
- *5km to Mataura for fishing*
- *Golf course close by*

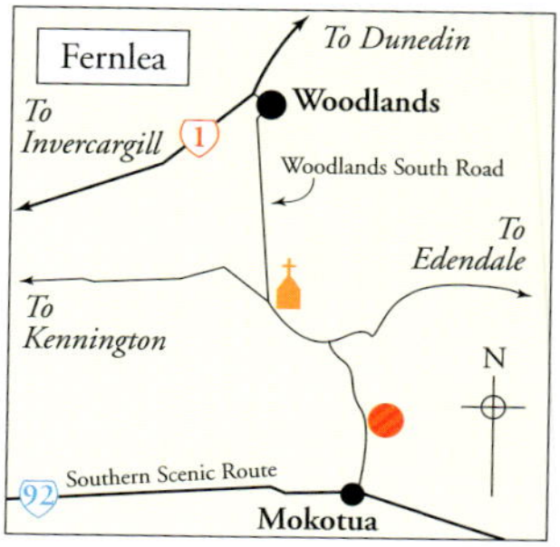

INVERCARGILL LICENSING TRUST Southland TOURISM AWARDS

Fernlea Bed & Breakfast was the winner of both the **'Hosted Accomodation'** section and overall winner of the **'Southland Supreme Tourism Award'**. Anne's cottage is nestled in its own private cottage garden – it is completely self-contained and can sleep four people. **Fernlea** is a working dairy farm of 500 acres and home to 400 Holstein Friesian cows, a small flock of sheep, free range hens and two doves. An entertaining farm tour is available.

Located on the Southern Scenic Route 20km from Invercargill it is an ideal location for visitors to relax and enjoy a taste of New Zealand farm life on their journey to discover the Catlins, or a stopover en route to Stewart Island, Te Anau or Queenstown. With prior notice we are happy to provide a delicious three-course dinner. We will make every effort to make your stay with us enjoyable and memorable.

Burtonwood Bed & Breakfast

177 Gala Street, Avenal, Invercargill
Ph (03) 218 8884, Fax (03) 218 9148
Mobile 021-314 024
email: *burtonwoodbnb@woosh.co.nz*
www.burtonwood.co.nz

Tariff : N.Z. Dollars	
Double	$125-225
Single	$100-180
Child	neg

Bedrooms	Qty
Double	4
Twin	
Single	1
Bed Size	**Qty**
Super King	
King	
Queen	4
Double	
King Single	3
Bathrooms	**Qty**
Ensuite	2
Private	
Guest Share	1

Quality Bed & Breakfast Accommodation

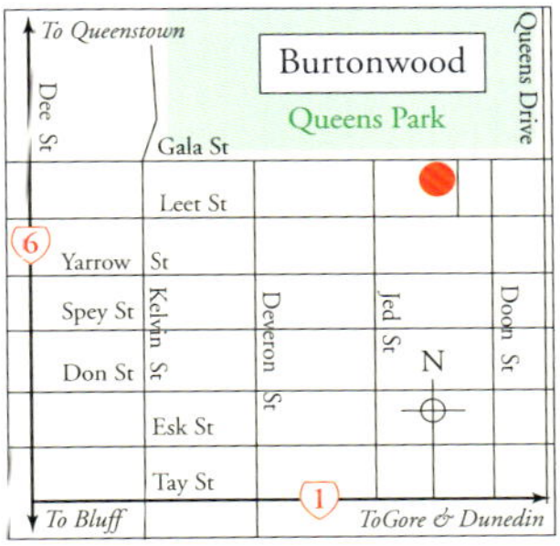

DIRECTIONS:
Please phone for easy directions
Free pick up/drop off to bus and airport

Features & Attractions

- *Adjacent to Queens Park/ Gardens*
- *Warm, sunny, secure rooms*
- *Wireless Broadband Internet*
- *Stadium Southland & Velodrome 2km*
- *Easy walk to shops, cafés*
- *10 min. from airport*
- *Off-street, private parking*
- *Beautiful gardens*

Beautifully situated opposite glorious Queens Park, this delightful Edwardian home has been beautifully refurbished with your every comfort in mind.

On the Southern Scenic Route, moments from the Visitor Centre, Southland Museum, Art Gallery and golf course. Great restaurants, cafés and sporting facilities, fishing and beaches, all within a short distance. Ideally situated for exploring the Southland Region. Dinner available by arrangement. Delicious, generous breakfast served in the guest dining room. Your 'home-away-from-home' with spacious guest lounge for your relaxation. An ideal place to take a break on your vacation. Have a gorgeous stay in Invercargill's iconic *"House-with-the-Cat-on-the-Roof"*!

Victoria Railway Hotel

3 Leven Street, PO Box 44, Invercargill
Ph (03) 218 1281, Fax (03) 218 1283
email: *vrhotel@xtra.co.nz*
www.vrhotel.info

Features & Attractions

- *Boutique Hotel in city centre*
- *Historic Places Category I*
- *Opp. Stewart Isl. Ferry Bus*
- *Old-world charm*
- *Architect. upgrade 2004*
- *Breakfast optional extra*

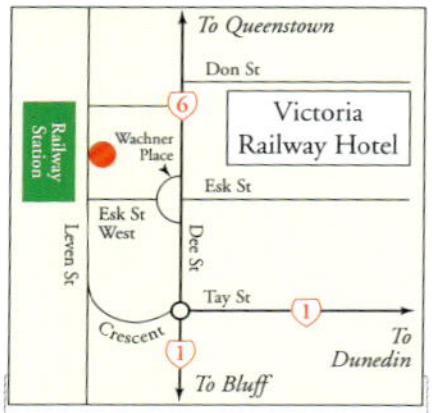

Boutique Accommodation

Double	$115-140
Single	$105-115
Child	$15

Come and enjoy old world charm and southern hospitality in a boutique hotel in the heart of the city. Built in 1896 we are a Class 1 Historic Places Heritage (Victorian style) building and we completed our architecturally designed upgrade in May 2004. We offer our guests a variety of accommodation options, including Executive, VIP and two ground floor accessible units. Guests can relax in our lounge bar before dining and then enjoy traditional home-cooked meals and a selection of fine NZ wines. The Stewart Is. Ferry Bus and the Atomic Shuttle depart from across the road. "Our stay with you has been so pleasant and we will have no hesitation to recommend you. Your friendly family atmosphere is excellent." Ray and Betty Johnson.

Bedrooms	Qty
Double	10
Twin	1
Single	6
Bed Size	**Qty**
King	
Queen	8
Double	2
Single	8
Bathrooms	**Qty**
Ensuite	11
Private	
Guest Share	2

Organic Acres

71 Avondale Road, RD 3, Winton
Ph (03) 236 9071, Fax (03) 236 9071
Mobile 027-496 8910
email: *organicacres@xtra.co.nz*
www.organicacres.co.nz

Tariff : N.Z. Dollars	
Double	$120-180
Single	$80-100
Child	$20

Bedrooms	Qty
Double	1
Twin	
Single	1
Bed Size	**Qty**
Super King	
King	
Queen	1
Double	1
Single	3
Bathrooms	**Qty**
Ensuite	
Private	1
Guest Share	

Self-contained Cottage with Views on Organic Dairy Farm

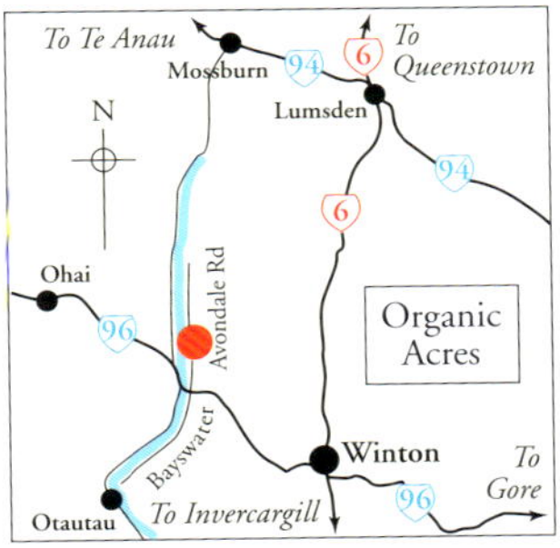

Features & Attractions

- *Self contained cottage with views*
- *Heat pump, TV, laundry etc*
- *Fishing on farm boundary*
- *Invercargill/Gore 45 min*
- *Bio Gro Certified Organic properties*
- *Te Anau 1 hr, Queenstown 1½ hr*
- *Cafés, banks, supermarkets 15 min*
- *Organic/vegetarian/meat meals*

Organic Acres is a unique farm experience that you will never forget. Southern hospitality is legendary and so is the scenery. Enjoy a leisurely drink on the veranda as you peruse the mountains and glorious spacious outlook. Then indulge in the best quality organic food at the homestead, which is grown right where you are!
The farm-stay cottage has all the comforts you will need, and if you feel energetic you can explore the workings of the farm and visit the animals on a guided tour with Peter or Glenys.
Scenic drives take you to busier places if that is what you are after. Queenstown - the world famous resort for summer and winter activities is a one and half hour drive and Te Anau is only an hour away. Te Anau is the gateway to Fiordland and Milford Sound, where there are many tramping tracks for all levels of fitness. Coastal scenic drive to sea-view dining takes just half an hour. Great fishing spots abound all over Southland and on the farm boundary.
You won't want to leave this award winning farm!

River Lodge Bed & Breakfast

93 Towack Street, Riverton
Southland
Ph (03) 234 8732, Fax (03) 234 8732
email: *rbjmdore@actrix.co.nz*

Tariff : N.Z. Dollars	
Double	$95-140
Single	$75
Child	

Bedrooms	Qty
Double	3
Twin	
Single	
Bed Size	**Qty**
Super King	
King	1
Queen	2
Double	
King/Single	
Bathrooms	**Qty**
Ensuite	2
Private	1
Guest Share	

Homestay
Bed & Breakfast

VISA MasterCard

Features & Attractions

- *Peaceful private garden setting*
- *Studio unit with spa bath*
- *Golf course & walking tracks*
- *Walking distance to beach*
- *River, harbour & mountain views*
- *Five minute walk to restaurants and shops*
- *Courtesy car to dining*

DIRECTIONS:
Only 30 minutesdrive from Invercargill on the Southern Scenic Route. Drive over the bridge,turn left and look for the yellow **River Lodge** sign.

We would like to welcome you to Riverton, a seaside retreat. Relax and enjoy our peaceful private garden setting with excellent views of the river, harbour and mountains.

We are within walking distance of the beach, bush walks, shops, cafés and wharfs where fishing and pleasure boats berth. We also offer a courtesy car to and from the cafés for evening dining, and if you are into fitness, we have two mountain bikes for your use. The house has two spacious downstairs bedrooms with private bathrooms. Upstairs is a private studio unit with a spa bath and superb views. If you are looking for a relaxing homestyle stay at the quiet seaside town of Riverton, River Lodge Bed & Breakfast is the place for you to stay.

We look forward to meeting you.

Sails Ashore & Kowhai Lane

11 View Street, PO Box 66, Stewart Island
Ph (03) 219 1151, Fax (03) 219 1151
email: *tait@sailsashore.co.nz*
www.sailsashore.co.nz

Tariff : N.Z. Dollars	
Double	$140-360
Single	
Child	

Bedrooms	Qty
Double/Twin	4
Twin	
Single	
Bed Size	**Qty**
Super King	
King/Single	3
Queen	1
Double	
Single	2
Bathrooms	**Qty**
Ensuite	4
Private	1
Guest Share	

Luxury Boutique Accommodation or Self-catering House and SC Flat

Features & Attractions

- *Rakiura National Park*
- *Private central locations*
- *All centrally heated*
- *Courtesy transfers*
- *Activities planning*
- *Professional guides*
- *Ulva Island tours*
- *Scenic Road tours*

Iris, Anne and Peter welcome you to Stewart Island, **Sails Ashore Boutique Luxury Homestay** and **Kowhai Lane Holiday Home.** Both overlook Halfmoon Bay and are about four minutes stroll from the waterfront. As well as delightful sea views both have private gardens for you to enjoy. Each house has a large sitting or sunroom, where you can enjoy our extensive library of books, photos and local interest DVD's. Telephone and internet is available, as is a guest laundry. For evening meals you have the option of eating out at one of the excellent local restaurants or alternatively have one delivered to you from their menu. An absolute 'must do' is a guided walk with us on Ulva Island, open sanctuary and conservation showpiece. You may choose to extend this to include a leisurely exploration of Paterson Inlet aboard Talisker, or enjoy a scenic road tour with us. At **Sails Ashore** our border terriers will be absolutely delighted to take you for a walk. Guests may come as strangers, we hope they leave as friends.

Sails Ashore is $360 per room per night (2 king, king singles)
Kowhai Lane Holiday Home is $150 per room per night (2 king/king single, 1 queen)
Kowhai Lane Self-contained flat is $140 per night (2 single or extra double).

Enjoy unique 'Charming' places to stay.

The

Translated Travellers' Pages

Herzlich Willkommen!

ようこそ！

歡迎！

"Lernen Sie das wahre Neuseeland kennen - die Neuseeländer selbst"

Bed & Breakfast in Neuseeland heißt Sie herzlich willkommen!

Eine überaus große Auswahl an Übernachtungsmöglichkeiten erwartet Sie in der Welt von "Bed & Breakfast" (private Übernachtung inclusive Frühstück) - vom einfachen Landhaus bis zum stattlichen Familiensitz. Überall werden Sie auf freundliche, aufgeschlossene Neuseeländer treffen. Manche von ihnen haben die Tradition des Gastgebens im Lauf der Jahre zu einer regelrechten Kunst entwickelt, auf die sie besonders stolz sind. Sogenannte "Homestays", "Farmstays", Gastehäuser oder "Boutique"-Unterkünfte - sie alle fallen unter den Begriff "Bed & Breakfast". Hier lernen Sie das wahre Neuseeland kennen: die Neuseeländer selbst.

- Ob Lehrer, Farmer oder ein pensionierter Angestellter, ob Künstler, Obstbauer, Heilpraktiker oder Schriftsteller, die Palette ist reichhaltig. Zum angenehmen Abenteuer kann die Übernachtung beispielsweise in einer Fischerlodge oder auf einer Schafsfarm im Hochland werden. Warum lernen Sie nicht nebenbei ein wenig reiten oder weben oder fühlen Sie sich einfach wie zu Hause in einem "Homestay" oder "Countrystay" in der Stadt oder auf dem Land. Die Neuseeländer sind bekannt als warmherzige Gastgeber, Sie werden sich überall willkommen fühlen und unvergeßliche Reiseerinnerungen mit nach Hause bringen.

Was Sie erwarten können

Bed & Breakfast in Neuseeland ist bekannt für guten Service. Die Unterkünfte sind sauber, verfügen über bequeme Betten und bieten ein gutes, reichliches Frühstück an. Natürlich steht Ihr Wohlbefinden an erster Stelle. Ihre Gastgeber werden Ihnen gerne bei der Planung Ihrer weiteren Reise behilflich sein. Die Gastgeber wissen am besten darüber Bescheid, was die jeweilige Region zu bieten hat. Nutzen Sie diese unbezahlbaren Informationen aus erster Hand.

Was man von Ihnen erwartet

Ihre Gastgeber werden alles versuchen, Ihnen den Aufenthalt so angenehm wie möglich zu machen. Vergessen Sie jedoch bitte nicht, daß Sie in den meisten Fällen in Privathäusern zu Gast sein werden. Bedenken Sie auch die scheinbar unwichtigen Dinge. Es empfiehlt sich beispielsweise, um einen Hausschlüssel zu bitten, bevor Sie abends länger ausbleiben. Falls Sie ein Ferngespräch führen wollen, ist es besser, zuerst den Tarif abzuklären. Sagen Sie bitte auch so bald wie möglich Bescheid, wenn sich Ihre Ankunft verspäten sollte. Ein wenig Rücksichtnahme Ihrerseits wird so dazu beitragen, daß alle Beteiligten die Zeit auf eine angenehme Weise verbringen.

Praktische Hinweise

Besonders während der Sommersaison können Sie unnötige Enttäuschungen vermeiden, wenn Sie Ihre Unterkunft im voraus buchen. Es empfiehlt sich auch, die Gastgeber einen Tag vor Ihrer Ankunft anzurufen, um die Buchung zu bestätigen und die ungefähre Ankunftszeit mitzuteilen. Einige Bed & Breakfast Häuser bieten einen Abholdienst von Bus, Bahn oder Flughafen an - dieser Service ist oft im Preis mit eingeschlossen. Sagen Sie auch bitte rechtzeitig Bescheid, wenn Sie bei Ihren Gastgebern zusätzlich zur Übernachtung gerne ein warmes Abendessen hätten.

Bed & Breakfast

Bed & Breakfast ist der Oberbegriff für alle Unterkunftsarten, die ein bequemes Bett, ein reichliches Frühstück und persönlichen Service im Preis einschließen. Während Ihres Aufenthalts werden Sie aufs Freundlichste von Ihren Gastgebern betreut.

Homestay

"Homestay" ist eine sehr beliebte Bed & Breakfast Variante. Sie wohnen in Privathäusern, die Gastgeber sind aufgeschlossen und freundlich und werden alles ihnen Mögliche tun, damit Sie sich "ganz wie zu Hause" fühlen nach dem Motto: "Sie kommen als Fremde und gehen als Freunde."

Countrystay

"Countrystays" sind Bed & Breakfast-Unterkünfte in ländlicher Umgebung. Sie wohnen meist in nächster Nähe von dem, was Sie am typischen Landleben so schätzen. Ob Sie wandern gehen wollen, angeln oder einfach nur die unbeschreibliche Natur pur genießen wollen, hier können Sie sich abseits vom Großstadtstreß in aller Ruhe erholen.

Farmstay

Wenn Sie echtes neuseeländisches Farmerleben hautnah genießen wollen, dann sind Sie im "Farmstay" gut aufgehoben. Üblicherweise können Sie bei der Farmtour mit auf die Weiden gehen und beim Füttern der Farmtiere mit dabei sein. Das Frühstück wird meistens mit der Familie zusammen eingenommen. Viele Farmstays bieten Vollverpflegung an.

G

Guesthouse/Inn

"Guest Houses" sind meistens Häuser, die eine größere Zahl von Gästen beherbergen, aber trotzdem eine persönliche Note aufweisen. Manche haben mehrere Aufenthaltsräume und einen speziellen Frühstücksraum. "Guest Houses" bieten im allgemeinen kein warmes Abendessen an.

BA

Boutique Accommodation

Der Begriff "Boutique" soll Ihnen sagen, daß es sich hier um ganz besonders schöne Bed & Breakfast-Übernachtungsmöglichkeiten handelt: eine geschmackvolle Inneneinrichtung, stilvolle Architektur oder ein romantisches Ambiente. Die Gastgeber dieser Häuser legen größten Wert auf gepflegte Gastfreundschaft.

LA

Luxury Accommodation

Die Luxusunterkünfte bieten eine hervorragende Ausstattung, exzellentes Essen und ganz besonderen Service. Oft sind diese Häuser architektonische Glanzstücke oder sie liegen in einzigartiger Umgebung. "Luxus" steht für außergewöhnliche Unterkunft und Gastfreundschaft.

SC

Self-contained Accommodation

Unterkünfte für Selbstversorger sind oft komplette Einliegerwohnungen oder einzeln stehende Häuschen mit eigenem Badezimmer und eigener Toilette und meistens mit Küche, Waschmaschine und Wäschetrockner. In manchen Fällen nehmen Sie das Frühstück zusammen mit der Gastfamilie ein. Es wird aber auch oftmals an die Haustür gebracht, oder Sie finden die Zutaten bereits in der Küche.

"Auf einen Blick"

Kontaktaufnahme

Wer sind die Gastgeber und wo wohnen sie? Wie kommen Sie schnell mit ihnen in Kontakt?

"Auf einen Blick"

Übernachtungspreis

*Alle Preise gelten für eine Übernachtung. **Double** ist der Preis für zwei Personen in einem Zimmer, **Single** der Preis für eine Person in einem Zimmer. In einigen Fällen ist zusammen mit der Buchung eine Anzahlung erforderlich. Frühstück ist im Preis mit inbegriffen (falls nicht ausdrücklich anders erwähnt). **Alle Preise gelten in $ NZ.** Bitte lassen Sie sich die Preise von den Gastgebern bestätigen.*

"Auf einen Blick"

Symbole für Kategorien

Mit diesen einprägsamen Symbolen können Sie Ihre bevorzugte Unterkunftsmöglichkeit schnell ausfindig machen. Dieses System ist besonders hilfreich für Reisende, die die englische Sprache nicht fließend beherrschen.

"Auf einen Blick"

Kategoriestreifen

Die Gastgeber beschreiben ihre Kategorie in ihren eigenen Worten.

"Auf einen Blick"

Besondere Details

In Stichworten die attraktivsten Details der Unterkunft und der Sehenswürdikeiten in der Umgebung.

"Auf einen Blick"

Kleine Straßenkarte

Im weißen Kästchen finden Sie den Namen des Hauses; der rote Punkt zeigt Ihnen die genaue Position. Im grünen Kästchen finden Sie die Wegbeschreibung.

Klar und übersichtlich

Schnell zu finden: Adresse, Telefon- und Faxnummer, E-Mail und Internetadresse.

YOUR HOSTS: Kristin and Stuart Campbell Smith Free Ph: (0800) 232 789 Rotorua Central

EAST WEST-BOUTIQUE B&B AND APARTMENTS
6 Toko Street, Rotorua
Ph (07) 348 5720, Fax (07) 348 5729
Mobile 027-278 5332
email: *eastwesthomestay@xtra.co.nz*
www.eastwesthomestay.co.nz

Tariff : N.Z. Dollars	
Double	$110-150
Single	$75-110
Child	$25

Bedrooms	Qty
Double	8
Twin	5
Single	
Bed Size	**Qty**
Super King	
King	
Queen	6
Double	1
Single	14
Bathrooms	**Qty**
Ensuite	2
Private	3
Guest Share	

Boutique Bed & Breakfast & Self-catering Apartments

Features & Attractions

- *Central to tourism & leisure*
- *Unique geothermal pool/spa*
- *Geothermal central heating*
- *Quiet, spacious units*
- *Self-catering apartments*
- *Tour bookings*

Your hosts, Stuart, Kristin and Rusty, warmly welcome you to their unique Boutique Bed & Breakfast and Self-catering apartments. Located in Rotorua's thriving central tourism district, their designer home and freshly decorated, fully furnished holiday apartments are minutes from all attractions. You are offered a choice of a spacious studio or one bedroom unit both featuring private ensuite bathrooms, fridge/minibar, tea and coffee facilities, TV/DVD and robes toiletries. Continental breakfast offers fresh fruit, home-made muesli, cereals, yoghurt, conserves, coffee and teas (included in rate). Cooked breakfast available. Also separately located on the property are three sunny, cosy, fully furnished self-catering two and three bedroom apartments, kitchen, laundry facilities, off-street parking, private entrances. Private hot spa, robes/toiletries.

"Ein persönliches Willkommen"

Dieser Text, von den Gastgebern persönlich verfaßt, beschreibt deren Lebensstil und Interessen, die Art der Unterkunft und was Sie als Gast erwarten können.

Nichtraucher

Abkürzungen

SH – State Highway
h.p. – halber Preis
N.A. – nicht zutreffend
neg. – nach Vereinbarung
Qty – Anzahl
Tce – Terrace

Direkt buchen - Extrakosten vermeiden

Wenn Sie die Buchung selbst vornehmen, haben Sie von Anfang an persönlichen Kontakt mit Ihren Bed & Breakfast-Gastgebern in Neuseeland und vermeiden unnötige Kosten.

Wie wird dieser Reiseführer benützt – Zimmerdetails

Gästezimmer

Double = Zimmer mit Bett für 2 Personen
Twin = Zimmer mit 2 Betten für 2 Personen
Single = Zimmer mit Bett für eine Person

Bad/WC

Ensuite = Bad/WC mit Zimmer verbunden
Private = Eigenes Bad/WC, aber separat
Guest/Family Share =Bad/WC wird von Gästen oder der Gastfamilie mitbenutzt.

Bedrooms	Qty
Double	
Twin	
Single	
Bed Size	**Qty**
King	
Queen	
Double	
King/Single	
Bathrooms	**Qty**
Ensuite	
Private	
Guest Share	

Bettgrößen
Super King *180 x 200cm*
King *165 x 200cm*
Queen *150 x 200cm*
Double *135 x 190cm*
Single *90 x 190cm*
King Single *90 x 200cm*

Kategorie Symbole

BB Bed & Breakfast
BA Boutique Accommodation
C Countrystay
F Farmstay
G Guest House / Inn
H Homestay
LA Luxury Accommodation
SC Self-contained Accom. & Cottages

Gängige Kreditkarten

Amex – American Express
Japanese Credit Card
VISA
Diners
Bankcard
MasterCard
Maestro
Eftpos

Mitgliedschaft in folgenden Verbänden und Gesellschaften

Kiwihost
Qualmark NZ
@home New Zealand.
Historic Places Trust

The @home New Zealand logo represents the leading organisation of Hosted Accommodation providers in New Zealand. It assures you of a warm welcome from friendly, helpful hosts. Accommodations displaying this logo have been assessed and meet the quality standards laid down by the association.

ニュージーランドの家庭生活を実体験！

～ニュージーランド・Ｂ＆Ｂへのお誘い～

ニュージーランド人は、旅行者に対する心暖まる、フレンドリーなもてなしを誇りとする国民として知られています。この「ニュージーランド風のもてなし」をじかに体験できるのが、Bed & Breakfast（ベッド・アンド・ブレックファースト、B&B）です。これは一般のホテルとは一味ちがった、アット・ホームなサービスを身上とする宿泊施設の総称で、その具体的な中身はいろいろです。宿泊の場所でいうと、町中の一軒家・コッテージ・釣り場のロッジ・高原の牧場・乗馬や機織りの学校・お城（！）といった具合に多岐にわたっています。実際の名称としては、 Guest House (ゲスト・ハウス)、 Inn（イン）、Boutique Accommodation （ブティック・アコモデーション）、 Countrystay （カントリーステイ）などがあります。また、安いものから高くて豪華なものまでありますので、予算に合わせて選ぶことが可能です。B&B のホスト（host, オーナー）は現役の教員・農家・芸術家・信仰療法家・作家、さらにはもと医師や弁護士など、実に多彩です。ホストの中には、単に話好き、という人から、専門的なサービスを提供する人まで、さまざまです。B&B は、「本物の」ニュージーランドを体験するのに恰好の機会といえます。ホストと、趣味や仕事の話などで盛り上がるのも楽しみのひとつではないでしょうか。

皆様の旅行が楽しく、思い出深いものとなりますように……

WHAT TO EXPECT

きれいな部屋、寝心地のよいベッド、おいしくて量もたっぷりの朝食、真心のこもったもてなし…ニュージーランドの Bed & Breakfast は、サービスの水準が高いことで知られています。さらに、ホストからは、その地域や周辺の見どころに関する詳しい「生の情報」を得ることができます。お客様の興味・関心をホストにお伝えください。ホストは皆様の旅行がすばらしいものとなる手助けができることを願っています。

— 宿泊者の心得

WHAT IS EXPECTED OF YOU

ホストは、お客様が楽しく思い出深いひとときを過ごすことができるよう、最大限の努力をしていますが、お客様の側にも配慮いただきたい点があります。それは、B＆Bは、基本的には「一般家庭」に泊まる、という形式をとっているという点です。ですから、ホストやその家族にたいする「ちょとした」気配りが大切です。たとえば、夜、帰りが遅くなる場合には、余裕をもって事前にその旨を伝えておき、「合鍵」を受け取っておくとか、電話を使用する際には、あらかじめ料金の確認をしておく、などです。こうした心遣いが、B＆Bでの滞在を成功させるカギなのです。

WHAT TO DO – HINTS

B&B 宿泊の貴重なチャンスを逃さないためには、予約するのが一番です。（特に真夏は込み合います。）予約されましたら、到着の前日にホストに予約の確認をし、到着予定時刻を伝えておくことをおすすめします。ホストの中には、coach (コーチ、長距離バス)・飛行機・列車の発着場からの無料送迎サービスを行っている人もいます。また、到着日の夕食を希望される場合には、前日または前前日に、その旨をホストに伝えておきましょう。

ベッド・アンド・ブレックファースト

一泊・朝食付きの宿の総称です。快適なベッドと、たっぷりの朝食、それにホストの暖かいおもてなしを存分にお楽しみください。

ホームステイ

ごく一般の家庭で、ホストによる身近なもてなしを受けながら宿泊するものです。ホストは人と出会うのが好きで、宿泊客をまるで自分の家にいるような、和やかな雰囲気にしてくれます。宿泊客の皆様が、初めて会った時には「見知らぬ他人」でも、別れるときには「親しい友人」となることを、ホストは心得ているのです。

カントリーステイ

Homestay と同様、一般の家庭に滞在するものです。Countrystay の特徴は、場所が「いなか」にある点です。都会とはちがった、ニュージーランドの一面をじかに体験できます。

ファームステイ

ニュージーランドの農業について理解を深めたい、という人には理想的な機会です。動物たちと身近に接しながら、農場での生活を経験していきます。牧場内のツアーを行っているところもあります。通常、朝食はホストの家族とともにとります。場所柄、近所にレストランなどがないため、多くのFarmstay では昼食や夕食も出されます。

G ゲスト・ハウス

通常、規模が比較的大きく、他のB&B の施設に比べ、より多くの宿泊客を泊めることができる施設ですが、B&B ならではの、フレンドリーなもてなしは変わりません。複数のラウンジや、朝食室が用意されているところもあります。夕食は出されないのが普通です。

BA ブティック・アコモデーション

特色ある家屋を用いたB&B です。長い年月が醸し出す気品、優雅さ、ロマンス ― Boutique Accommodation は、宿泊客の皆様をそうした雰囲気の中に包んでくれます。この雰囲気をいかに盛り上げるかが、ホストの腕のみせどころです。

LA ラクシャリー・アコモデーション

最高の立地条件のなかにある宿泊施設で、施設内外はさまざまな魅力でいっぱいです。豪華極まる設備や食事、それに群をぬいたハイ・クオリティーのサービスが特徴です。

SC セルフコンテインド・アコモデーション

宿泊者のための独立した入口・バスルーム・ラウンジを含むのが普通です。独立した台所や洗濯質室が用意されているところもあります。宿泊施設は、一軒家のなかの一区画として存在する場合と、別棟の建物として存在する場合とがあります。朝食はホストの家族とともにとる場合、宿泊施設まで届けられる場合、朝食の材料が宿泊所に用意されており、宿泊者が自分で用意する場合とさまざまです。

"at a glance"
イージー・コントロール・パネル
ホストの氏名・所在地・連絡先など。

"at a glance"
ここに表示されているのは、一泊あたりの料金です。**Double**（ダブル）は、一部屋を２名で使用した場合の料金です。**Single**（シングル）は、一部屋を１名で使用した場合の料金です。予約の際に deposit（ディポジット、料金の一部前払い）が必要なところもあります。特に明記のない場合、料金には朝食代が含まれています。**料金の表記は、すべて「NZ ドル」です。**料金に関する詳しい内容は、直接ホストまでおたずねください。

"at a glance"
カテゴリー・シンボル
おさがしの B&B のタイプがすぐに見つかるよう工夫されたマークです。お役立てください。

"at a glance"
カテゴリー・パネル
該当する B&B のカテゴリーの、ホスト自身による定義・説明。

"at a glance"
フィーチャーズ&アトラクションズ
宿泊施設およびその周辺のみどころのご紹介。

"at a glance"
ロケーション・マップ
宿泊施設の位置が赤丸で示されています。白のかこみの中に施設の名称が記されています。行き方の説明が追加で示されている場合もあります。

クリアー・アドレス・ディーテールズ
宿泊施設の所在地・電話番号・Fax 番号・e-mail アドレス・インターネット・ホームページのアドレスといった、大切な情報はこちらをご覧ください。

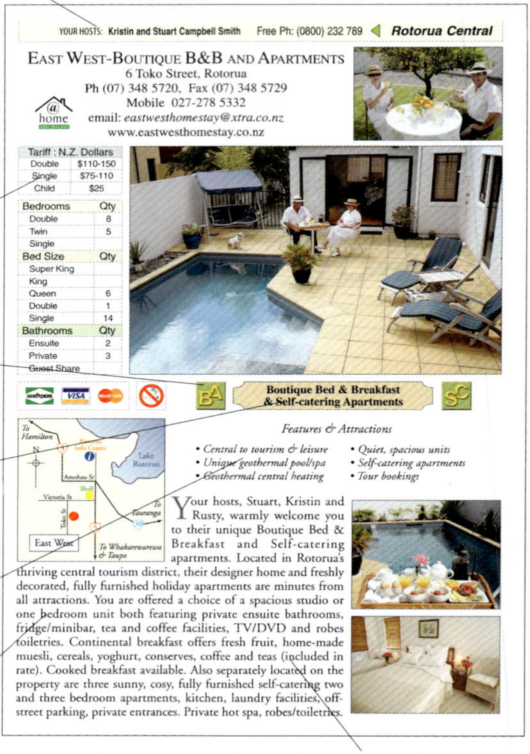

YOUR HOSTS: Kristin and Stuart Campbell Smith Free Ph: (0800) 232 789 Rotorua Central

EAST WEST-BOUTIQUE B&B AND APARTMENTS
6 Toko Street, Rotorua
Ph (07) 348 5720, Fax (07) 348 5729
Mobile 027-278 5332
email: *eastwesthomestay@xtra.co.nz*
www.eastwesthomestay.co.nz

Tariff : N.Z. Dollars	
Double	$110-150
Single	$75-110
Child	$25

Bedrooms	Qty
Double	8
Twin	5
Single	
Bed Size	**Qty**
Super King	
King	
Queen	6
Double	1
Single	14
Bathrooms	**Qty**
Ensuite	2
Private	3
Guest Share	

Boutique Bed & Breakfast & Self-catering Apartments

Features & Attractions

- *Central to tourism & leisure*
- *Unique geothermal pool/spa*
- *Geothermal central heating*
- *Quiet, spacious units*
- *Self-catering apartments*
- *Tour bookings*

Your hosts, Stuart, Kristin and Rusty, warmly welcome you to their unique Boutique Bed & Breakfast and Self-catering apartments. Located in Rotorua's thriving central tourism district, their designer home and freshly decorated, fully furnished holiday apartments are minutes from all attractions. You are offered a choice of a spacious studio or one bedroom unit both featuring private ensuite bathrooms, fridge/minibar, tea and coffee facilities, TV/DVD and robes toiletries. Continental breakfast offers fresh fruit, home-made muesli, cereals, yoghurt, conserves, coffee and teas (included in rate). Cooked breakfast available. Also separately located on the property are three sunny, cosy, fully furnished self-catering two and three bedroom apartments, kitchen, laundry facilities, off-street parking, private entrances. Private hot spa, robes/toiletries.

パーソナル・ウォーム・ウェルカム
ホストから読者へのひとことです。宿泊施設の特徴や、ホストの人柄・ライフ・スタイルといったものを垣間見ることができます。

No Smoking

Cnr – Corner: コーナー「角」
h.p. – half price: ハーフ・プライス「半額」
N.A. – not applicable: ノット・アプリカブル「該当項目なし」
neg. – negotiable: ニゴーシャブル「交渉可」
Qty – Quantity: クウォンティティ「数量」
Tce – Terrace: テラス

宿泊予約申し込みは、B&B のホストに直接なさいますと、ホストとそれだけ早くから知り合うことができ、また中間業者を通した場合にかかる、さまざまな手数料を省くことができるので有利です。

ガイドのてびき　―　客室・設備に関する記 述 について

Bedrooms

Double　=　二人用ベッドがある部屋

Twin　=　一人用ベッドが２つある部屋

Single　=　一人用ベッドが１つある部屋

Bathrooms

Ensuite　=　寝室に隣接

Private　=　各宿泊客専用

Guest Share/Family Share　=　他の宿泊客またはホストの家族と共用

Bedrooms	Qty
Double	
Twin	
Single	
Bed Size	**Qty**
King	
Queen	
Double	
King/Single	
Bathrooms	**Qty**
Ensuite	
Private	
Guest Share	

Bed Size
Super King *180 x 200cm*
King *165 x 200cm*
Queen *150 x 200cm*
Double *135 x 190cm*
Single *90 x 190cm*
King Single *90 x 200cm*

ガイドのてびき　―　カテゴリー・シンボル

BB　Bed & Breakfast

BA　Boutique Accommodation

C　Countrystay

F　Farmstay

G　Guest House / Inn

H　Homestay

LA　Luxury Accommodation

SC　Self-contained Accom. & Cottages

ガイドのてびき　―　お支払可能なクレジット・カード について

Amex – American Express

Japanese Credit Card

VISA

Diners

Bankcard

MasterCard

Maestro

Eftpos

ガイドのてびき　―　B&B が提携している協会・団体について

Kiwihost

Qualmark NZ

@home New Zealand.

Historic Places Trust

このマークは、ニュージランド流の暖かく、フレンドリーで、質の高いサービスを保証するものです。Kiwi Host (キウ イ・ホ ス ト) は、我が国をリードする顧客サービス・トレーニング・プログラムです。

介 紹

“體驗真正的紐西蘭—它的民族”

歡迎來到紐西蘭多樣化的旅店住宿簡介

紐西蘭的住宿，由小屋到別墅，從經濟單位到豪華大宅，您都會享受到在一個親切友善且好客的環境中居住。有多種不同的住宿方式：家庭住宿、農莊住宿、旅客之家、小客店、豪華旅店、鄉村住宿等等，他們一律提供給您一張溫暖的床以及香噴噴的西式早餐。這些都能讓您親身感受到紐西蘭的生活，認識居住在這裡的居民。您更可選擇嗜好與自己相似的家庭住宿，例如：老師、農夫、退休的專業人士、園藝專家、畫家、作家等等，住宿在他們的家，彼此交換心得，同時可享受獨特眞誠的招待，體驗在漁村、郊外綿羊、海外之家的生活。不管是旅館或多樣化的家庭住宿，除了種類多之外，還充滿了紐西蘭獨特的友善及好客，不論您選擇那一種住宿，您將都是一位貴賓，盡情享受生活，讓日後有個難忘的回憶。

介紹

期望什麼？

在紐西蘭床鋪及早餐享有標準服務的聲譽，住客會有最清潔、舒適的床，多種選擇熱烘烘早餐，及主人樂意友善的招待。除此之外，主人也會給於您居住地區的詳細資料。他們樂意幫您安排您在本地的旅遊計劃。他們豐富的經驗能增添您居住的樂趣。

對您的期望？

主人家會爲您做任何的事，讓您享受一個難忘的停留。可是，請記得無論如何您只是一個客人。所以，請您注意一些事，例如，如果您晚歸的話，要向主人索取大門鎖匙，或當您要打長途、國內、本地電話時，應先詢問主人才可使用電話。請讓主人家知道您將夜歸。您處身置地的設想，會使您及主人都感到滿意。

給予您的建議

事先訂好一間房間，以避免屆時沒房間的失望，尤其在夏天時。除外，在您出發的前一天致電到主人家確定您訂好的房間及讓他們曉得您幾時會抵達。有些主人提供接送服務，如果您有需要的話。如果您需要他爲您準備午餐的話，也請您早一、兩天前通知主人。

床鋪及早餐系列

床 鋪 及 早 餐 BB

床鋪及早餐是所有不同種類住所的代稱，供您選擇。除外，在您居住時間，主人更會給予您親切友善的招待，讓您有賓至如歸之感。

古 典 大 屋 H

在床鋪及早餐系列中，古典大屋的建築物具有古典氣息、整齊美觀、寧靜浪漫，是適合喜歡這類型的您來居住，主人將這些建築物的特質保持得非常好，確保您最佳的享受。

鄉 村 居 住 C

鄉村居住類似家庭住宿。您將居住於私人家庭中，慢慢地認識及接觸鄉村迷人的風景。許多鄉村住宿都靠近著名的旅遊風景區，能讓您最方便認識這些地方。

農 場 住 宿 F

如果您選擇在農場居住，通常會由農場主人一家人接待您。如有需要，可爲您安排參觀農場的行程，好讓您更加了解農場，您將跟農場主人一家人共同享用早餐；晚餐必須在事先通知，農場也將會爲您準備，因爲農場附近沒有餐館。

床鋪及早餐系列

G 旅客之家

旅客之家通常能容納較多的旅客。雖然如此，主人仍會給您友善親切的招待。旅客之家可能會有數間的客廳及餐廳。旅客之家不常提供晚餐給住客。

BA 家庭住宿

家庭住宿是最普遍的住宿方式，居住在溫暖、友善、好客的家庭中。主人喜歡認識不同的人，且樂意讓您有“家”的感覺，讓您曉得，您剛來的時候雖是一個陌生人，當您要離開時卻是以朋友的身份離開。

LA 豪華大宅

豪華大宅代表了一流的設備，上等的餐飲和超水準的服務，許多此類住宿都有各自的特色，給予您額外一流的享受，它們代表了優越的住宿。

SC 私人住宿

此居住方式，通常包括了，私人的走道、浴室及客廳。它可以是一個家庭中隔出來的一部份或是一整間小屋。早餐可在主人家享用，也可送到您的門口或餐室。

容易聯絡的範圍

您的旅店老闆；無論是何人，身在何處，都能迅速與他們取得聯絡。

明確的地址

明確的地址，應包括住宿的地址，電話和傳眞號碼，電子郵件地址與網址。

價目表

價目表上的金額，表示住宿一晚的住宿費。雙人（ Double ）表示兩人合用一間房間的價錢。當您預定房間時，您可能要預付訂金。價目表上的價錢通常包括早餐，除非有特別註明不提供早餐。全部價錢都以紐幣計算。請與旅店老闆確定住宿明細資料。

YOUR HOSTS: Kristin and Stuart Campbell Smith Free Ph: (0800) 232 789 Rotorua Central

EAST WEST-BOUTIQUE B&B AND APARTMENTS
6 Toko Street, Rotorua
Ph (07) 348 5720, Fax (07) 348 5729
Mobile 027-278 5332
email: *eastwesthomestay@xtra.co.nz*
www.eastwesthomestay.co.nz

Tariff : N.Z. Dollars	
Double	$110-150
Single	$75-110
Child	$25

Bedrooms	Qty
Double	8
Twin	5
Single	
Bed Size	**Qty**
Super King	
King	
Queen	6
Double	1
Single	14
Bathrooms	**Qty**
Ensuite	2
Private	3
Guest Share	

Boutique Bed & Breakfast & Self-catering Apartments

Features & Attractions

- *Central to tourism & leisure*
- *Unique geothermal pool/spa*
- *Geothermal central heating*
- *Quiet, spacious units*
- *Self-catering apartments*
- *Tour bookings*

Your hosts, Stuart, Kristin and Rusty, warmly welcome you to their unique Boutique Bed & Breakfast and Self-catering apartments. Located in Rotorua's thriving central tourism district, their designer home and freshly decorated, fully furnished holiday apartments are minutes from all attractions. You are offered a choice of a spacious studio or one bedroom unit both featuring private ensuite bathrooms, fridge/minibar, tea and coffee facilities, TV/DVD and robes toiletries. Continental breakfast offers fresh fruit, home-made muesli, cereals, yoghurt, conserves, coffee and teas (included in rate). Cooked breakfast available. Also separately located on the property are three sunny, cosy, fully furnished self-catering two and three bedroom apartments, kitchen, laundry facilities, off-street parking, private entrances. Private hot spa, robes/toiletries.

各種住宿的代表符號

設計這些容易辨認的符號，是爲了方便您預約訂房，對於不太熟悉英文的遊客們，這是絕對有幫助的。

住宿種類

旅店老闆會爲您詳細介紹住宿種類。

地區特色及焦點

您住宿的四周環境以及您住宿區域的特色與焦點，都會爲您列出。

區域地圖

您所住宿的地點，在地圖上將以紅點標示。旅店的店名，也會在地圖上刊出。通常爲配合找尋，也都有方向圖來確認正確方向。

“一項特別及溫暖的歡迎”

通常歡迎詞是由旅店老闆親自設計。有關店內設備以及獨特的住宿方式，都會有清楚的説明。

No Smoking

縮寫

Cnr—角落
h.p.—半價
N.A. —無此設備
Qty—可磋商
Tce—陽台

直接預約—省錢

與紐西蘭“床與早餐”
旅店系列的老闆直接預約住宿，
您從一開始就會省了許多
不必要的附加費用。

如何使用這本指南 — 客房資料

房　間

Double = 一或二張床提供兩人住宿的房間
Twin = 提供二張床給兩人住宿的雙人房
Single = 提供一張床給單人住宿的單人房

浴　室

Ensuite =浴室在您的房間內
Private = 提供您個人專用的浴室
Guest Share/Family Share =公共浴室，必須與其他家庭或住客共同使用。

Bedrooms	Qty
Double	
Twin	
Single	
Bed Size	**Qty**
King	
Queen	
Double	
King/Single	
Bathrooms	**Qty**
Ensuite	
Private	
Guest Share	

床的尺寸

Super King
180 x 200cm

King
165 x 200cm

Queen
150 x 200cm

Double
135 x 190cm

Single
90 x 190cm

King Single
90 x 200cm

如何使用這本指南 — 代號種類

- BB Bed & Breakfast
- BA Boutique Accommodation
- C Countrystay
- F Farmstay
- G Guest House / Inn
- H Homestay
- LA Luxury Accommodation
- SC Self-contained Accom. & Cottages

如何使用這本指南 — 旅店老闆接受信用卡付款

- Amex – American Express
- Japanese Credit Card
- VISA
- Diners
- Bankcard
- MasterCard
- Maestro
- Eftpos

如何使用這本指南 — 協會

- Kiwihost
- Qualmark NZ
- @home New Zealand.
- Historic Places Trust

這個商標就是保證您是受本地人所歡迎的，以及獲得親切友善的服務。Kiwi Host 是紐西蘭顧客服務訓練計畫的得獎者，我們確信我們對於您的重視，與您對於我們的肯定。

Special thanks to all of these friends who gave help and reassurance when deadlines loomed and spirits were low:

Tim Cornelius, famous Dunedin map designer.
Marion Wassenaar, brilliant graphic artist.
Joshua, Jamie, and Matthew Newman, photographers.
Karen Costello, proof reader extraordinaire.

Translations

German translation by *Uli Newman.*
Japanese translation by *Yoshi Isoyama at Transla NZ, PO Box 8069 Dunedin, New Zealand. isoyama@xtra.co.nz*
Mandarin (Chinese) translation by *Stephen Liu at Asian Communication Company Ltd Dunedin, New Zealand.*

Photographs:

Destination Northland. *Pgs 4, 21, 24; E-Mail: northland@xtra.co.nz*
New Zealand Post. *Pg 17 (envelopes), E-Mail: cschelp@nzpost.co.nz*
"Parua House". *Pg 9*
Tourism Rotorua. *Fly Leaf, E-Mail: marketing@tourism.rdc.govt.nz*
Tourism Wairarapa. *Pg 19; E-Mail: tourwai@xtra.co.nz*
West Coast Tourism. *Pg 21, E-Mail: tourismwc@minidata.co.nz*
Tourism Nelson. *Pg 312, E-mail: info@tourism-nelson.co.nz*

AUCKLAND REGION

COROMANDEL PENINSULA

HAMILTON REGION – TE KUITI

BAY OF PLENTY

ROTORUA

TAUPO –TURANGI–GISBORNE

WELLINGTON REGION

GOLDEN BAY–NELSON

MARLBOROUGH

WEST COAST

CANTERBURY–CHRISTCHURCH

SOUTHERN LAKES DISTRICT

SOUTHERN SOUTH ISLAND

Travel Notes

TRAVEL
NOTES AND QUOTES

TRAVEL
NOTES AND QUOTES

TRAVEL
NOTES AND QUOTES